Work Organisations
A Critical Introduction

Work Organisations
A Critical Introduction

Second Edition

Paul Thompson
and
David McHugh

No GUL bookplates etc
(AS)

MACMILLAN
Business

First published 1995 by
MACMILLAN PRESS LTD
Houndmills, Basingstoke, Hampshire RG21 6XS
and London
Companies and representatives
throughout the world

ISBN 0–333–64160–4 hardcover
ISBN 0–333–64161–2 paperback

A catalogue record for this book is available
from the British Library.

10   9   8   7   6   5   4   3   2   1
04   03   02   01   00   99   98   97   96   95

Copy-edited and typeset by Povey–Edmondson
Okehampton and Rochdale, England

Printed in Great Britain by
Mackays of Chatham PLC
Chatham, Kent

Contents

v

List of tables and figures

Tables

Figures

Acknowledgements

Re-doing a book should not be as much of a burden as creating it in the first place. But as usual, the project seems to have been around for an interminable time and once again we have to thank our families for their support through long nights and missed deadlines.

Our colleagues old and new, at the University of Central Lancashire and University of Edinburgh, have given sterling support. Chris Warhurst and Carol Jones, in particular have read chapters and offered invariably sound advice. Paul Thompson would particularly like to thank his fellow researchers – Terry Wallace, Jörg Flecker and Denis Nickson – whose work is drawn on in some of the chapters. We also owe particular gratitude to the many users of the book, some of whom have been kind enough to give us feedback along the way and about the plans for a new edition. Chris Smith, Steve Ackroyd, Alan Tuckman, Les Prince, Martin Corbett have been particularly helpful.

At Macmillan, Steve Rutt, who nursed us through the first edition, has done an even more sterling job on this one. Jane Powell has also provided useful support.

PAUL THOMPSON
DAVID McHUGH

The authors and publishers are grateful to the following for permission to use copyright material: Butterworth–Heinemann Ltd for a diagram from Terence Jackson, *Organisational Behaviour in International Management* (1993). Every effort has been made to contact all the copyright-holders, but if any have been inadvertently omitted the publishers will be pleased to make the necessary arrangement at the earliest opportunity.

Introduction

Our aim in writing the first edition of *Work Organisations* was to provide a critical alternative to the standard, often American, texts that still predominated in the 1980s, and to some of the derivative British versions. That 'standard' tended to combine a narrow and prescriptive orientation to issues of management, structure and organisational design; with a behavioural agenda dealing with issues such as personality and perception, where a focus on the individual appeared to have little relationship to the more 'structural' material.

'Critical' meant that we aimed to balance exposition and evaluation of mainstream writing and research, with an attempt to bring together the large, but often fragmented, body of writings from organisation and management theory, labour process analysis, feminism, industrial sociology and social psychology, where they were radical and relevant to the study of work organisations. Any orientation of this sort by definition had to be interdisciplinary, pluralistic and pragmatic in the sources it draws from for inspiration. The biggest problem was how to link the broadly sociological and more behavioural material. We did not pretend that any form of grand integration was possible. Our aim was to ensure that the discussion in the two main parts of the book were complementary in the kind of analysis used and issues discussed. We felt strongly that organisations are places in which attempts to shape the subjectivity and identity of employees are central to the purposes of management, and that this provided an important bridge and common focus between debates in the different chapters.

We have not shifted any of these aims for the second edition. But we have thought carefully about how successful we have been in achieving them. A second edition also gives an opportunity to reflect on the feedback through reviews, as well as responses from users. These have generally been kind, but we have tried to respond to some of the issues raised. One persistent theme has been that the book was not 'introductory' enough. This is a difficult one, because a satisfying book to write is one that engages with peers as well as students. Anyway, we have tried to make this edition more accessible in a number of ways, the most significant of which is to shift the discussion of general theory from the beginning to the end. In its new location, we can be more comprehensive about theory without getting in the way of a more straightforward and less burdensome entry into the issues.

A fresh start also gives an opportunity to be more comprehensive and to introduce materials that were previously neglected. So we have added new sections such as those on communication and leadership. Organisation theory and research, like organisation itself, is very diverse, and textbook writers have to be careful about simply reproducing partial accounts and experiences. We have, therefore, tried to introduce more comparative material that reflects that diversity. The rise of more internationally-orientated debates, such as those on globalisation, is but one example of the remarkably rapid changes in the organisation studies literature that has taken place in the five years since the first edition. The book seeks to reflect those changes and debates. There is now a substantial literature on gender and organisations that simply did not exist in the late 1980s. Most of that focuses on power rather than the conventional division of labour framework. We have, therefore, made issues of power into a separate chapter, reflecting this and the other significant debates arising from the work of Foucault and post-structuralism. Not every area of debate has undergone decisive shift. In chapters dealing with issues such as management and control, and organisation design we have simply tried to update debates and research. Though in the latter case we have substantially re-focused and extended the chapter to enable a more thorough discussion of the question of whether the end of the century is seeing the rise of the 'post-bureaucratic organisation'.

Structure of the book

Part 1 focuses on the areas traditionally dealt with by organisation theory and more sociological and structural writings. Chapter 1 seeks to explore three main questions: why are we interested in studying organisations? how should they be studied? and what are the general concepts and principles available to do so? These objects are achieved by contrasting the 'domain assumptions' of mainstream and critical approaches. By this we mean some of the basic ways that rival perspectives have looked at organisations and society. At this stage the idea is to keep it fairly simple. We do not look at theory or theories in depth, but at some of the underlying and underpinning assumptions. The more adventurous reader could go to Part 3 and immediately follow that through. But it is not *necessary* to do that in order to follow the substantive discussions in the chapters in between, where we develop an understanding of theory and research in a more incremental way.

A great weakness of much organisational writing is the failure to locate analysis in its historical context. Chapter 2 seeks to show how the major characteristics of large-scale organisations in the twentieth century – control, hierarchy and bureaucracy – came into being. We particularly try to identify the origins and developments of the best known, 'classical' theories of organisation, notably Taylorism, Weber and the human relations movement. The focus is firmly on the attendant practices and use by management, both in the periods when the ideas emerged and the legacies left for later eras. Such practices, however, were never universal. At the end of the chapter we introduce a recurrent theme of the book, that different organising logics are embedded in contrasting national and other institutional frameworks. For example, what is defined as management in Britain and North America is not necessarily the model elsewhere.

This point highlights the importance of the environment of work organisations. Yet such environments are often dealt with in a limited way, certainly once markets and technologies have been discussed. Chapter 3 outlines and evaluates the mainstream literature, including contingency theory and population ecology. But we open out the discussion in two ways. First by examining the political environment through the role of the state in labour markets and processes, including current attempts to restructure the public sector. Second, by focusing on the new international environment, which gives us an opportunity to look both at accounts of globalisation and its effects, and more recent institutional theories of organisation.

The study of management rightly occupies a central place in the study of work organisations. But much of the writing has a narrow and technical conception of its nature and activities. Chapter 4 contrasts the extensive body of knowledge on management in mainstream literatures with radical perspectives and research that begins with analysis of management as control and as a labour process. A discussion of the extent to which management operates strategically is an essential part of this section. Traditionally, because organisations were conceived of as cohesive and unitary, the related theme of power was much neglected in mainstream writing. At best it was projected as a series of micro struggles, analogous to 'office politics'. Chapter 5 examines this literature and contrasts it to models of power drawn from radical theories. Of the latter, concepts drawn from Foucault and his emphasis on disciplinary power have become particularly influential in recent years, and such theorising is explained and criticised. Foucauldian perspectives have made their mark in analysis of gender and sexuality, but the issues go far wider than that. Organisations are gendered in many of their most everyday ways of operating. Though this is a theme that runs throughout the book, this chapter enables a closer look to be taken at this process of gendering organisational analysis.

Those who own and run organisations are continually looking for ways to design them more effectively, whether in terms of jobs, structures, communications systems or values. In the past, that mainstream debate has taken place within the framework of how to design bureaucracies differently. The emphasis now, from managerial and many radical theorists, is on post-bureaucratic organisation, influenced by new environmental challenges and the Japanese model. Chapter 6 examines this supposed paradigm shift and looks in detail at research evidence in the key areas: firms and markets, the labour process, and corporate structures. In conclusion, a qualified defence of bureaucracy is made.

In the 1980s, corporate culture was perhaps the main talking point in managerial literature and was put forward as the key factor for business success. Chapter 7 looks critically at the merchandising of corporate cultures and examines whether it is an attempt to constitute a new form of 'organisation man'. Linking the debate to other contemporary issues such as the rise of Human Resource Management, the chapter examines the extent to which the management of culture can be successful in generating commitment and internalising values.

Part 2 begins by considering and defining the elements of what we term the 'subjective factor' in the study of organisations, which we see as manifested in the experiences of organisational participants and in the identities through which they transact with others in organisational environments. Our examination of these issues of subjectivity in Part 2 is initially viewed through psychological approaches which tend to focus mainly on behaviour as opposed to experience. The intention here is not to ignore the sociological and structural accounts of subjectivity available in the areas covered in Part 2. Rather, we begin in Chapter 8 by examining the deficiencies of behavioural approaches, along with some of the instruments and techniques, using the topics of perception, learning, attitudes, personality and motivation, in order to indicate how a closer articulation of structural and behavioural explanations can benefit the understanding of organisational subjectivity. In Chapter 9 we extend the theme taken in this chapter, examining how major theoretical areas within Organisational Behaviour have been incorporated into the agenda of regulation and control and the divisions of roles and practices within the discipline itself.

The study of what has come to be termed 'Organisational Behaviour' (OB) does in fact incorporate elements of the full range of academic disciplines and subject specialisms which might reasonably be expected to have something to say about people's lives in organisations and the influences on their activities. The major foundations of OB and the major inputs to the content of texts in the area are however informed mainly from the perspective of 'organisational psychology', which is in turn founded upon the subject divisions within social psychology. The treatment of subjectivity in organisational psychology does not typically develop upon the humanistic foundations of such issues within social psychology. It is generally subordinated to OB's agency in legitimating, developing and refining the social practices within which subjective identities are continuously recreated in images appropriate to the relations of social production. This theme is followed up in detail in Chapter 9 before moving on to examine explanation in the areas of groups, stress, communication and leadership. The aim again is to assess the nature and adequacy of the traditional agenda of mainstream study for an understanding of our experience of organisational life and how this shapes the construction of the identities through which we face it.

Chapter 10 attempts to integrate the themes of Chapters 8 and 9, first using an emphasis on motivation theories in order to investigate the mobilisation of commitment in modern work organisations. The focus on motivation and commitment is then used to explore the internalisation of self-controls and providing linkages to developments in technology and the field of Human Resource Management. In doing so, the later sections of this chapter tend to revisit many of the areas covered in Chapter 7, but viewing them from an OB perspective. Readers will note some repetition of assertions of the relation of psychological knowledge to managerial ideology and practice. This overlap in the issues we investigate in Parts 1 and 2 is to some extent a recognition that since many readers will only dip into the book and not read the 'whole story' as intended, these points must perforce be made often. To those brave souls who traverse the whole text, we apologise in advance.

In Chapter 11 we return to consider in more detail the nature of identity and the contrasting approaches and resources a redefined agenda would need to focus on better to address issues of subjectivity. In particular, we address social relations such as those of domination, gender and ethnicity which are central features of work organisation. The issue of how subjectivity is experienced, structured and transformed within organisations is explored through the medium of the *'identity work'* performed by organisational participants as a response to pressures on the identities they secure for themselves. These are viewed first from the context of the individual, then through a re-examination of groups, and lastly through the manner in which managerial identity work acts to structure the experience of everyone in organisations, regardless of hierarchical position.

Part 3 returns to the territory of the broader theorising of organisations, drawing on and linking to some of the substantive issues in previous chapters, as well as new themes such as agency and structure. Chapter 12 examines in detail the theoretical resources drawn on in mainstream and critical writing. The question of rationality is a central one in both traditions and through an examination of new, post-modern analyses of organisations, we explore the issues at stake and conclude that rationalisation remains a fundamental principle of organisational life and that rational enquiry, in a modified form, is an indispensable part of the theorising process. The chapter and book end with a wider discussion on the nature and uses of organisational knowledge. How do theorists using different paradigms speak to each other? How do managers use theory in practice? How can participants at work learn from past and present to create more democratic, as well as more efficient, organisations?

PART 1

CHAPTER 1

Studying organisations: an introduction

As citizens of an industrial society, we tend to have a love-hate relationship with large-scale organisations. We frequently berate them for being bureaucratic, wasteful and placing us under the shadow of 'Big Brother'. Yet we take them for granted as providers of employment, public welfare, private services, and even charity or other voluntary activities. In the not-so-distant past, information, leisure, economic needs and other basic life processes were more likely to be directly and locally produced or consumed. Now, complex economic, social and political organisations provide a network of individual and social relationships through which we participate in society at local, national and global levels (Gareth Morgan, 1990).

Such organisations have therefore become a focus for academic analysis. For the time being, let us define organisations as consciously created arrangements to achieve goals by collective means. The significance of this definition will become clear later, but the important point to note is that the same paradox that affects public attitudes is often reproduced intellectually. Those very 'efficiencies' which derive from the scale and structure of organisations create conditions of domination over human liberty and democratic institutions. But even as trenchant a critic as Perrow, who notes that organisations are tools that can mobilise immense ideological and practical resources for those who control them, argues: 'If we want our material civilisation to continue as it is . . . we will have to have large scale bureaucratic enterprises in the economic, social and governmental areas. The development of industrialisation has made this the most efficient way to get the routine work of a society done' (1979: 56). This view is not necessarily shared by all commentators today. Indeed, from popular management writers to post-modernists, organisation – at least in the sense of action to create order – has become something of a dirty word. The fashion instead is for decentralisation, disorganisation and even chaos (Peters, 1989): big and bureaucratic is bad. But we are running ahead of the story.

The theory and practice of organisation has developed around bureaucracies, deriving partly from the work of Max Weber, who, at the turn of the century, was most responsible for drawing our attention to the significance of large-scale organisations. As the division of labour in society and at work became more complex and difficult to manage, the responsibility and means of co-ordination of core activities became focused on specialised units. The essence of organisation is the creation of regular, standardised behaviour and orderly structure. For Weber the characteristic features of society would be complex and highly developed administrative structures governed by rules, hierarchy and experts. Most people would work for or become clients of such bureaucracies. In current discourse, such developments are linked to the wider growth of *modernism*, in which planning, calculation and a hierarchy of authority spread to most areas of social and cultural life.

Some modern writers came to believe that such an *organisation society* reached fruition in the post-1945 period (Kerr *et al.*, 1960; Bell, 1960; Prethus, 1962). The dominant themes were that private and public corporations had helped to usher in a new era where politics, ideology and conflict had been superseded by rational, scientific decision making, guided by a new, enlightened though powerful, administrative élite. Standardised mass production and consumption went hand-in-hand with central direction of the economy and state by professional managers and politicians. A special sort of person – *organisation man* – was even evoked who could be relied on to be one of the vehicles of such techniques, given that his personality and commitment was subordinated to the corporation (Whyte, 1956). As Biggart comments, Whyte was describing, ' a generation of organisational workers who had been moulded by the needs of the corporation . . . conservative, impassive little grey men. Their lives in the organisation were routine and largely unemotional' (1989: 4). The emphasis on 'man' is not accidental. An organisation society was predicated on the assumption of male corporate warrior, sustained by women at home providing the practical and emotional support.

It was pointless to desire significantly different arrangements, as all industrial societies were destined to converge into a single, similar type. The hierarchical and bureaucratic large-scale organisation, with its particular form of technology, was placed at the centre of mature industrial society. In retrospect this kind of perspective is more of an ideology masquerading as science than an accurate description of social trends. Organisation society and 'man' are part of an imagery where:

> all the major institutional landmarks of modern industrial society – the factory, the welfare state, the business corporation, representative democracy, an independent civil service, universal education and medical care – were firmly set in place and

equipped to manage any new problems which were likely to emerge in the foreseeable future. Institutional fine-tuning and technical adjustment were all that was necessary to maintain social stability and economic development. (Reed, 1985: 99–100)

Grouping developments under a catch-all label of organisation society or 'complex organisations' became a means, however unintended, of stopping asking questions about how such arrangements had come into being, how they were maintained, and whether they were necessary. In particular it obliterated real differences between organisational experiences, such as being a worker in and consumer of public or private services, or being an organisation in a capitalist or non-capitalist society; and in the origins and effects of different types of technology in varied cultural settings. In other words, such frameworks obscured the social contexts and social choices made about the nature of organisations – how they are structured, managed and experienced.

With this is mind, it is better to think in terms of a variety of *organising logics* that arise out of those contexts and preferences. These may not all resemble the conventional bureaucratic way of doing things. For example, direct selling organisations (DSOs) such as Amway or Avon have been among the fastest-growing commercial organisations.

> Compared with traditional firms, DSOs appear loose and out of control. They represent an apparent management nightmare that only a thick rule book and a platoon of managers could keep together. In fact, DSOs have almost no rules and, compared with most firms, few managers. Home Interiors and Gifts, for example, with 30 000 distributors, has only thirty-five managers . . . Direct selling has a logic too, but is radically different from the logic of bureaucratic organisations . . . a conscious alternative to firms as a way to organise economic activity to make a profit, as a technique for managing labour, and as a means of earning income. (Biggart, 1989; 5–7)

This example could be seen as part of the challenge to bureaucratic organisation which we shall examine fully in Chapter 6. However, that does not mean that there is nothing of value in the study of large-scale organisations. Whether existing organisational structures and practices are necessary and efficient, or whatever forms are dominant, it is demonstrably the case that greater power over our lives is exerted through such processes. Organisations mediate between the wider society and the individual, and joining an organisation as an employee exposes the individual to substantial direction and control. Despite the self-activity of their members, organisations as corporate bodies do have economic and political powers above and beyond those of the particular individuals that comprise them. In fact there is every indication of a concentration of those powers in a small number of organisations that is far from enlightened in its effects on us as workers or citizens.

This was a perspective raised decades ago by C. Wright Mills (1959), who dubbed those who commanded major organisations the 'power élite'. Today, takeovers and mergers continue unabated, whether the beneficiaries are tycoons such as Rupert Murdoch or faceless financial institutions. This is not one-sided. Work organisations remain crucial meeting places of contending social forces: owners, managers, professions, and workers; which generate and reflect contradiction and change. Note here that we are speaking of *work* organisations. This is not an accident. We agree with the approach taken by those such as Salaman (1979) that organisations are not a coherent category of objects capable of being studied in a distinctive way.

This is not the orthodox approach. By defining organisations as purposeful systems characterised by co-ordinated action towards an objective, Donaldson (1985: 7) can link together corporations, schools, families or neighbours fixing a fence. But though work may take place within a charity or a political party, its nature and purposes are different from those which operate under market discipline. Organisation may be necessary to ensure that co-ordinated action of any kind takes place, but actions vary enormously by the type of objective. Take Buford's account of his time among extremely well-organised football hooligans:

> Extensive preparations had gone into Manchester United's last meeting with West Ham – coaches had been hired, with complex routes into the city to evade the police, the arrival times staggered so that everyone did not appear *en masse* . . . Problems of leadership, organisation, 'big numbers', a hierarchical command structure: the technocrat phrasing did not obscure that what Steve was describing was a civil disturbance involving several thousand people. (1991: 119–20)

Only by operating at an excessive level of generality and abstraction is it possible to treat things as diverse as scout troops and transnational companies within the same analytical framework. Salaman makes a similar point:

> a genuine sociology of organisations is not assisted by the efforts of some organisation analysts to develop hypotheses about organisations in general, lumping together such diverse examples as voluntary organisations, charities and political organisations . . . It also obstructs the analysis of those structural elements which are dramatically revealed in employing organisations, but not necessarily in all forms of organisation. (1979: 33)

This is implicitly recognised in orthodox writing, which, most of the time, is not about organisations *per se*. Though comprehensive formal definitions may be retained, the overwhelming amount of writing and research is about business. Why then refer even to *work* organisations? It is certainly true that it is the profit-seeking nature of business organisations that creates their distinctive forms of management, control or other social relations. Such forms of organisation remain the structural core of advanced societies, even allowing for the decline in the proportion of those engaged in manufacturing activities. It is primarily for these two reasons that the bulk of this book is geared towards those events and experiences.

But in the end it is neither possible nor desirable to maintain a complete distinction between business and other forms of work organisation. Parts of the public sector have always operated in a market environment, and this tendency has rapidly increased in parts of the health service, local government and other public spheres in recent years. In addition, management methods or technologies may arise in a specific sector, but are frequently applied in modified forms in others. Finally, as Weber recognised, there are continuities of structure and practice deriving from the bureaucratic forms present within all large-scale organisations. For these reasons, though recognising the limitations, we prefer to retain work organisations as a broad framework. It does not mean that they are studied in isolation. Families and state structures are just two of the forces that interact with work organisations and whose links need to be examined.

Nevertheless to make a positive case for the distinctive study of work organisations does not settle who should undertake organisational analysis and how. The former question is not as bizarre as it sounds: analysis in this area has traditionally been contested by a variety of disciplines and sub-disciplines, including industrial sociology, management theory, organisational sociology and psychology, and industrial relations. This is not the place to provide detailed descriptions or historical explanations of such disciplines (see M. Rose, 1975; Hyman, 1981).

Indeed a case could be made for increasing overlaps in subject matter and conceptual frameworks. There is an increasing number of courses under the heading of organisation studies or related titles, whose primary focus is on work organisations. Though different strands will have their own more specific interests, such as motivation or skill and work satisfaction, there is a growing number of areas of overlap. If we take management strategy, it is clear that a considerable amount of research has been done from a labour process perspective, within an industrial relations framework and by management studies itself. Similar points could be made with respect to job design, labour markets and a range of other issues. We welcome this interdisciplinary framework and its effect on organisation studies, and hope that this book reflects and encourages it.

But organisation studies cannot be said to be the sum of these and other parts. Since the 1950s a particular approach, normally labelled 'Organisation Behaviour' (OB), or sometimes 'Organisation Theory' has become dominant. It is drawn mainly from management writings and organisational psychology, but enthusiastically borrows from sociology, economics, anthropology and other areas; thus laying claim to be genuinely interdisciplinary. Although the borrowing of concepts may be eclectic, it is not random; rather it is structured by specific problematics (a network of concepts orientated towards a core idea). OB focuses on social behaviour in the enterprise, directed chiefly towards problems of motivation and the performance of individuals and groups in relation to different structures and practices. Organisation Theory is, according to Donaldson, concerned with the trivariate relationship between structure, contingency and performance; or, put another way, it is 'mainly about the analysis of different designs, and their contingencies and their outcomes' (1985: 121). When both are taken into account, the result is that: 'These writers have attempted to draw together and distil theories of how organisations function and how they should be managed. Their writings have been theoretical in the sense that they have tried to discover generalisations applicable to all organisations' (Pugh, 1971: 9). This approach is found in most American and some British textbooks and business schools. Therefore, though organisation studies has always been – by its very nature – interdisciplinary, it has often been on a narrow, management plus psychology basis. Even this 'combination' is unsatisfactory, because there is frequently little connection between the 'structural' and behavioural material. The latter is dealt with under a 'topics' approach, with separate chapters on perception or personality; often with few links with each other, with organisational life, and to the chapters on organisational design, environment or management theories that follow. A dualistic analysis is implicitly or explicitly the underpinning, which separates an analysis of the individual from that of the structural in the form of groups, society and the like.

One of the limiting factors has been the gradual split from sociology. Organisational sociology has had a less than peaceful co-existence with orthodox approaches. In the last twenty-five years there has been a shift in the study of organisations from sociology departments to business and management schools (Hinings, 1988). The orientations of OB and Organisation Theory are far narrower and more prescriptive. Donaldson (1985: 71–2, 119–20) defends this by reference to different levels of analysis. Issues of class and power, ideology and social stratification, and economic contradictions are the province of sociology. Organisation Theory concentrates on the problems of people working inside organisations. Advocates of this approach thus seek to deflect criticism of neglect of wider concerns by moving the analytical goalposts. It is impossible to study satisfactorily something like the division of labour or hierarchy of groups in a business, without an understanding of the broader social division of labour and power structure.

Some sociologists have also accepted that the split means that they are studying different objects in distinct ways. For example, Albrow argues that, 'The organisation theorist is concerned to help managers and administrators. By contrast, the sociologist is "impractical". His search is for understanding untrammelled by the needs of men of affairs' (Albrow, 1973: 412). Such a view may be in part descriptively accurate, but it has dangerous consequences. It tends to legitimise the separation between a narrow perspective which is only interdisciplinary to meet the needs of management problem-solving, and a broader analysis that neglects the dynamics of day-to-day practices in organisations. The view taken in this book is that there is a basis for a reformulated organisation studies which has a specific competence in the sphere of work organisations, retains the capacity to cross discipline boundaries, and which combines theoretical and practical emphases.

Most of the discussion so far has focused on questions concerning the parameters and scope of the study of organisations. This is not the only or main problem with the 'Organisation Theory' that Donaldson (1985) attributes to North American business and management schools. Indeed, it was dissatisfaction with the texts written from within or influenced by this tradition that led us to embark on the process of writing our own in the first place. Despite Donaldson's spirited defence, this literature continues to reproduce a taken-for-granted view of organisations with respect to their structures and processes, and notions of effectiveness and rationality. The rest of this chapter seeks to open up this discussion by examining what we have called the 'domain assumptions' of orthodox or mainstream approaches, before going on to outline some alternatives that inform the way we have attempted to understand work organisations in this book. So as to avoid the discussion getting too complex at this stage, we have not dealt with the theoretical resources that mainstream or critical approaches draw from. They are outlined in Part 3.

Domain assumptions of mainstream approaches

This section seeks to spell out the underlying or 'domain' assumptions in mainstream organisation theory. Though there are varieties and differences, a number of dominant ways of thinking can be identified.

Organisations as goal-seekers

If organisations are consciously created instruments, then their purpose can be defined in terms of goal-seeking. This is unexceptional and, in fact, provides a means of distinguishing organisations from social institutions (for example, families) or movements (for example, feminism), which do not manifest systematic structures and processes for controlling relations between means and ends. But further definition is more controversial. Goals are seen as preferred states which organisations and their members attempt to achieve through collective and co-ordinated action: 'the planned co-ordination of the activities of a number of people for the achievement of some common, explicit purpose or goal' (Schein quoted in Mullins, 1985: 2). In this 'goal model', action and values are seen in terms of consensual collectivities. Goals are formulated, policies and objectives flow from them, and inputs in the form of activities are created, which, in turn produce outputs that allow for realisation of goals and organisational success.

Though there may be vague reference to 'environmental influences', the starting point tends to be located within, rather than outside the organisation: 'there is an assumption that the organisation has some capacity to resist environmental constraints and set its own pattern' (Benson, 1977: 5). It is true to say that obstacles and variations in these processes *are* acknowledged. Members of organisations may have goals which are contradictory to senior management; creating gaps between formal and informal, official and operative, goals and actual policies (Perrow, 1979). For example, scientific and technical workers tend to be much more committed to their job than to their company, and tensions arise between employees' desire to pursue research projects for their intrinsic value and pressure on employers to monitor and even close down those projects (Randle and Rainnie, 1994). Furthermore, sub-units of the organisation develop a life of their own, partial devolution of responsibility resulting in goal displacement (Selznick, 1949). It is management's job to ensure the best possible fit between the goals of different 'stakeholders'. Emphasis on goals does not enable distinctions between different forms of organisational activity. Various classification schemas exist based on types of goal-seeking which are beyond the scope of our argument. For a more detailed look at the issues, see Eldridge and Crombie (1974), and Clegg and Dunkerley (1980).

In search of the rational-efficient organisation

The emphasis on collective goal-seeking can only be sustained by a vision of organisations as *rational* instruments or tools; indeed this was a prime theme of Classical Management Theory, which formed the basis of modern organisational analysis. When we talk of rationality, we normally refer to the logical nature of beliefs or actions. This is an aspect of mainstream perspectives, but the basic feature concerns the development of suitable means to reach specific ends. It therefore becomes inseparable from a notion of *efficiency*. The emphasis is on rationally designed structures and practices resting on processes of calculated planning which will maximise organisational effectiveness. Some traditional theorists have described this in terms of the 'one best way' to run organisations. A more acceptable version of the rational model recognises the contingent nature of the process: 'Organisational arrangements are viewed as the outcomes of means–end decisions to bring situational circumstances and structures into alignment in order to enhance efficiency' (Bryman, 1984: 392).

Most mainstream texts continue to deny that there is one formula to fit every situation, but any serious examination of popular management writing and the associated business fads shows that the search for blueprints and formulas has not been forgotten (Pascale, 1990; Huczynski, 1993). This can be seen by the rash of books imitating the American bestseller *In Search of Excellence* (Peters and Waterman, 1982). All examine the activities of companies to find the winning formula. At the level of the individual, the equivalent is the endless exhortation to become the 'successful manager', the 'one-minute manager' and so on. Interestingly Peters and Waterman attack the 'rational model' embodied in the classical theorists such as Weber and F.W. Taylor. But their objection is actually to a particular type of rational action that is based on following rules, techniques and structural devices. They quote Selznick approvingly: 'It [the organisation] refers to an expendable tool, a rational instrument engineered to do a job . . . the transformation of an engineered, technical arrangement of building blocks into a social organism' (1982: 98). For them the key role is played by the distinctive values or culture of an organisation, for this has the effect of binding the various participants together. This is what has apparently made Eastman Kodak, MacDonalds, Texas Instruments and other companies successful (see Chapter 7 for a full discussion). The magic formula may differ, but the framework of rational action = efficiency remains the same.

Order and hierarchy

Mainstream theory is strongly influenced by ideas of organisations as co-operative social systems; self-regulating bodies, tending towards a state of equilibrium and order. This, in turn, rests partly on a notion that organisations are or should be *unitary* bodies combining the activities, values and interests of all their participants. Each part of the system plays a positive, functional role in this process, for example by generating binding social values. Thus the organisation is a system of interrelated parts or sub-units, for example departments, groups and individuals; each functioning to mobilise resources towards meeting wider goals. These parts are at the same time differentiated and interdependent, aiding processes of integration and co-ordination.

The managerial requirement to integrate potentially diverse goals and activities, could, of course, take place in a number of ways. But mainstream theory has tended to emphasise the advantages of a particular pattern of roles and responsibilities. Earlier we quoted Schein on the need for co-ordination to achieve goals. The extension of that sentence reads, 'through division of labour and function, and through a hierarchy of authority and responsibility'.

Such an interpretation of the division of labour has always played a leading role in ideas of how to sustain the social solidarity necessary for the survival of the 'organism' of society or enterprise. Current managerial rhetoric is awash with terms such as 'empowering' the workforce and self-managed teams, which suggest a different way of doing things. We shall examine such claims in Chapter 6.

Managerialism

Part of management's social engineering role is to maintain the maximum degree of harmony and generate feelings of belonging in the workforce, reflecting literally the definition of organisation as 'form into an orderly whole'. Common to all versions of rational efficiency is that the logical basis of action is held to reside with the manager. In contrast, employees who restrict or oppose such action are frequently held to be acting irrationally, governed by a 'logic of sentiment', rather than one of efficiency. The more overtly managerial writers are understandably full of references to what management *should* do, and in this sense are clearly *prescriptive* in nature. For some, the role of organisational analysis is to 'help managers in organisations understand how far their behaviour can positively influence their subordinate's productivity' (W. Clay Hamner, quoted in Karmel, 1980).

Effectiveness becomes synonymous with management effectiveness, and options in debates are situated within that framework. Donaldson (1985: 86) disputes this by arguing that though both are concerned with systems effectiveness, their viewpoints are distinguishable. After all, if they were the same, there would be no point in supplying prescriptions. This is true, but the parameters are strictly circumscribed, as in the example supplied – that an organisational analyst might advise greater or less socialisation into company beliefs, with no question of the legitimacy of the beliefs themselves.

Not all mainstream writing is openly managerialist. But the underlying assumptions seldom stray too far. In the preface to a recent popular textbook (Buchanan and Huczynski, 1985), Lupton remarks that social scientists should not attach themselves to any one organisational group or its problems. But he then gives two examples of key 'puzzles'. Why and in what conditions do workgroups restrict output? What are the origins and costs of impeding technical innovation? Similarly Karmel (1980) identifies key questions. Why do people sabotage equipment? Why does the introduction of a computer make many people unhappy? Why do subordinates not obey? Alternative 'puzzles', such as why are alienating technologies designed in the first place, are conspicuous by their absence. In addition the way such problems are defined, and the recurrent use of the term *practitioners* can only refer to management practices.

A science of organisations

In terms of methodology, many mainstream writers take what Benson (1977) refers to as a 'simple positivist view'. That is, they tend towards the use of methods and a view of reality borrowed from the natural sciences. There are two particularly important features involved. First, there is great emphasis on *measurement* of organisational phenomena for example, types of structures, technologies, leadership styles, and even the fit between them. Secondly, there is an attempt to discover clear cause and effect relationships, Donaldson (1985: 84) stating the need to, 'reaffirm the commitment to valid general causal laws as the goal'. He asserts the superiority of science over lay accounts, which is hardly the point. It is a question of the nature of the scientific approach, particularly the mistaken emphasis on laws. The fact that no one can actually identify any does not seem to worry Donaldson, as this is no proof that they may not yet be discovered in the future! Inevitably under the mantle of science – whether administrative, organisational or behavioural – these general-isations are intended to apply to *all* organisations. On this basis, analysis and intervention can be used to predict and control events, and make prescriptive recommendations. Stress on technique rather than values matches the idea of organisations as technical instruments. When combined, these attitudes towards scientific intervention into the organisation itself tend to be taken for granted, rather than treated as problematic. Some criticisms have been raised alongside the exposition, but the next section opens this out more comprehensively.

An evaluation of mainstream perspectives

Mainstream perspectives are not homogeneous and there are tensions, as will be explained in Chapter 12, between concepts derived from Weber, Durkheim and other key figures. There is also much of value in the body of ideas, both in terms of the issues raised and empirical work generated. Nevertheless, we can identify the outline of a number of interrelated criticisms, many of which are followed up in other chapters. *Rationality* and *efficiency* have been important themes, and no one should deny that they are legitimate aspects of organisational analysis. But in mainstream theory they are presented largely in neutral terms, as if rationality was a simple determinant of organisational structures, processes and goals. Processes are reduced to a matter of technique; devising the appropriate kind of structure, or best fit with a particular environment. A cosy picture is developed of a functional relation-ship between rational organisations and a rational society. This perspective removes issues of politics, power and control from organisational choices, and critical questions concerning means and ends. Donaldson (1985: 101) tries to get round this by separating the latter; 'The concern of with rational means rather than values is part of what makes such studies apolitical'. But there are as many contestable choices to be made about how to design jobs or authority structures as there are about the ends to which they are put.

A rational *model* emphasising features such as calculability is further confused with rationality or reasonableness *as such*. As Fischer and Sirriani put it: 'For the critical theorist, mainstream writers have confused the rational model of efficient administrative behaviour with organisational rationality itself . . . organisations must be conceptualised as tools for the pursuit of personal, group or class interests' (1984: 10–11). Furthermore, traditional notions underestimate the role of rationality and efficiency as ideological constructs which help to legitimise the positions, rewards and activities of dominant groups (Salaman, 1979: 177–82). For example, when changes such as mergers or closures take place, they are often described in terms of *rationalisation*, as if the decision of managers or boards of directors are inevitable and the only way of doing things. It is important to acknowledge the contested nature of rationality, underpinned by the struggle for scarce organisational and social resources; and indeed, this is the direction taken by an increased range of organisational theorists (Bryman, 1984).

This is insufficiently recognised in mainstream perspectives because they are underlaid by an assumption of harmony of interests. This is reproduced in another crucial sphere, that of the division of labour. The way that tasks, functions and jobs are divided, with the consequent specialisation and hierarchies, is all too often regarded as an unproblematic, technical or functional necessity. The origins and workings of the division of labour is neglected as an issue, influenced by analyses which emphasise differentiation and interdependence. As a consequence, many deep-rooted features of organisational life – inequality, conflict, domination and subordination, manipulation – are written out of the script in favour of behavioural questions associated with efficiency or motivation. Some of these features may be seen as pathological or temporary phenomena arising from breakdowns in organisational systems, rather than a fundamental product of the structuring of the division of labour.

Notions of social harmony have also distorted an understanding of *goals*. As we saw earlier, mainstream writings have made some progress towards acknowledging goal diversity and uncertainty. This is welcome, but there are still weaknesses. Oppositional goals cannot be confined to the 'personal'. As Clegg and Dunkerley observe: 'There is no notion of rational structural sources of opposition being generated in the normal processes of organisation' (1980: 317). A sense of reification is still present, in which the organisation is treated as a thing, and the only legitimate goal-seeking collectivity. Problems cannot be avoided by the use of the 'stakeholder' model (Donaldson, 1985: 24), which postulates a spurious pluralism in which goals are held to be the result of a relatively equal trade-off between the preferences of competing, but co-operative groups (employees, managers, owners, customers). Nor is it enough for Donaldson to assert that the higher levels of management simply 'edit and select' from competing claims.

The notion that formal organisations, made up of different members, are constituted to co-ordinate wider goals as if they are a form of social contract (Albrow, 1973: 408), underestimates the extent to which dominant power groupings have set those goals and shaped the appropriate structures. In practice, co-ordination or co-operation may reflect pressure, constraint or acquiescence to power as much as shared goals. Let us take an example to illustrate the problem – the Wapping dispute. In the mid-1980s, Rupert Murdoch announced plans to move production of his press titles from Fleet Street to a new site. This was planned in secret and sprung on the workforce. The subsequent strike was used as an excuse to dismiss over 5000 workers, most of whom never got their jobs back. there is not much sign of a trade-off among stakeholders here. The power accruing from ownership gave Murdoch and his associates the means to enforce their objectives. Even those, notably journalists, who voted to accept the move, did so in a context of bribes (£2000 and BUPA membership, or threats (the sack). As one *Sunday Times* journalist wrote at the time, 'In a property-owning democracy, the price of the average citizen's soul is a little less than the cost of his or her mortgage.' But in one sense there is a pluralism in work organisations, though different from 'stakeholding'. The array of interests and interest groups that exists goes beyond a conventional management and labour dichotomy. One of the reasons that Murdoch won is that he was able to exploit divisions between journalists, mainly male printers and largely female semi-skilled workers, and white collar employees – all of whom had a history of sectional antagonism over wages, jobs and working conditions.

So, there *is* a sense in which we can refer to 'organisations' having policies or goals, but they have to be clearly recognised as frequently the property of particular individuals or groups. For example, in the late 1970s, the then Chairman of British Leyland produced the Company Plan. The extent to which it was not the product and property of the employees as a whole can be seen from subsequent events. It was put to the workforce in a ballot and rejected. Edwardes then implemented it anyway. A final broader point on this issue is important. As we saw earlier, to define or classify organisations in terms of goal-seeking distorts the differences between them. We need to differentiate between different types of goals and the wider economic and political influences upon them; and to consider how they are constructed and in whose benefit they operate. The example used earlier of direct selling companies is illustrative of alternative *organising logics* that can operate between and even within organisations. Different logics lead to the choice of particular managerial mechanisms. The scientific workers referred to earlier are subject to normative controls which attempt to mobilise commitment to the work combined with a large degree of operational autonomy. Many other white collar workers in conventional bureaucratic hierarchies are being managed through much more economistic methods, such as performance-related pay.

The failure to analyse these processes adequately underlines the extent to which organisational analysis remains consciously or implicitly management-orientated. Texts remain a curious and confusing mixture of analysis and prescription. Emphasis on a stream of advice and solutions to managers consistently undermines the generation of valid and realistic knowledge of organisational processes. Two qualifying points to this criticism need to be made: first, there *is* a need to study management as an activity; second, an openly 'management science' servicing the needs of such groups inevitably reflects existing socio-economic relations. But such an orientation is particularly dangerous to a broader organisational analysis. As Watson (T. Watson, 1980) points out, management requirements are likely to focus on short-term pragmatic relevance related to task achievement, or towards the ideological expedience of unitary and consensual views of organisational life. Theorists can become, in Baritz's (1960) words, 'servants of power', enmeshed in restrictive client relationships within the business firm. The problem is less that of the corruption arising from lucrative contracts (though it is worrying when yesterday's advocates of participation become today's advisers on union-busting) than that of knowledge and problem-solving on management terms. Thus Organisational Theory is helping to constitute a particular reality without critically analysing it, and runs the risk of reducing theory and practice to a technology of social control.

Not only does this limit the ability of analysis to be a resource for a wider range of participants, it has the negative consequence of ignoring lower-level employees except as objects or in their defined 'roles' (Salaman, 1979: 47). Limitations arise from the service role itself. Reed observes, 'organisation theory has presented management with a stock of "moral fictions" (such as "managerial effectiveness") that disguise the social reality of contemporary management practice' (1985: 95). Despite or perhaps because of that role, there are frequent complaints that official theory propagated to business students and managers is out of touch with the 'real world'.

In conclusion, we would argue that mainstream perspectives have often functioned as theories of regulation and are bound up in the purposes and practices of organisational control. This has prevented the development of 'any coherent or consensual theoretical object of the organisation' (Clegg and Dunkerley, 1980: 213). Instead organisational and societal reality has tended to be taken for granted, with emphasis on that which is prescriptive and short term. Viewing organisations as natural systems and as largely autonomous bodies has produced a limited capacity to explain historical changes and the political and economic contexts in which organisations operate. The overall objections of critical theory are summed up by Fischer and Sirriani: 'Common to all of the approaches is a concern over the conservative/elitist bias of organisational theory, a general absence of social class analysis, a failure to connect the organisation to the political economy of the larger social and historical context, a general neglect of political and bureaucratic power, and the ideological uses of scientific organisational analysis' (1984: 5).

Domain assumptions of a critical approach

Like their mainstream counterpart, critical perspectives are based on a variety of ideas and theoretical sources. The starting point is obviously critique itself: the identification of the weaknesses, limitations and ideological functions of orthodoxy. The two traditions are not always different on every point, and there are some partly overlapping objectives for some of the strands of thought, including humanisation of work processes and non-bureaucratic forms of organisation. Nevertheless through the critique an outline of a different agenda begins to emerge, with a concern for issues of power, control, domination, conflict, exploitation and legitimation. What of the more positive alternative? What do we mean by critical? Any alternative perspectives necessarily start from different guidelines and assumptions about organisations and society. Though the issues overlap, we have followed the convention of the equivalent mainstream section and divide it into parts.

Reflexivity

Critical perspectives must first of all be *reflexive*. That is they must have the capacity to reflect upon themselves, so that values, practices and knowledge are not taken for granted. Nor can we take our own experiences for granted. A useful example is provided in the novel *Nice Work*. Robyn Penrose, a university lecturer in English, is sent to shadow the managing director of a local engineering factory. She finds the noise, dirt and disorder of the foundry hard to comprehend:

> What *had* she expected? Nothing, certainly, so like the satanic mills of the early Industrial Revolution. Robyn's mental image of a modern factory had derived mainly from TV commercials and documentaries; deftly edited footage of brightly coloured machines and smoothly moving assembly lines, manned by brisk operators in clean overalls . . . The situation was bizarre, so unlike her usual environment, that there was a kind of exhilaration to be found in it, in its very discomfort and danger, such as explorers must feel, she supposed, in a remote and barbarous country. (Lodge, 1990: 121 and 130)

Despite or perhaps because of the lack of understanding, she blunders into actions that spiral out of control. In fact, our inability to experience large organisations directly in the same way – as individuals or small groups, subordinates or power holders – creates special problems for studying organisation, problems which are often resolved through the use of unsatisfactory substitutes such as metaphors – organisation are 'like' machines, garbage cans or prisons (Sandelands and Srivatsan, 1993).

We have referred previously to unproblematic conceptions of phenomena such as goals and productivity. But a key example of a problematic conception would be that of gender. Existing analyses have largely treated gender divisions as irrelevant, or in practice invisible, despite: 'the persistent fact that women's position in any organisation differs from men in the same organisations' (Woolf, 1977: 7). In this sense, orthodoxy has been as much 'male-stream' as mainstream (Mills and Tancred, 1992).

Instead of reflecting the concerns of established power-groups, organisational theory should reflect critically on and challenge existing attitudes and practices. It can draw on the distinction between practical and technical rationality identified by Habermas (1971) and subsequently espoused by many other radical writers. Technical rationality is based on the instrumental pursuit of taken-for-granted goals such as 'efficiency'. In contrast, practical rationality emphasises conscious and enlightened reflection which would clarify alternative goals and action based on the widest communication and political dialogue. These concepts are, in themselves, rooted in Weber's differentiation between a formal rationality concerned with calculable techniques and procedures, and substantive rationality which emphasises the values and the desired ends of action.

The embeddedness of organisations

A further guiding principle is the necessity to be *historical* and *contextual*. Organisational theory and practice can only be understood as something in process, otherwise the search for general propositions and instant prescriptions becomes disconnected from reality, as it has done in conventional ahistorical approaches (Littler, 1980: 157). It is also necessary to counter the tendency to see organisations as free-floating and autonomous; and the concentration on the micro-level of analysis, or single enterprise. This means locating organisational processes within their structural setting, examining the interaction with economic forces, political cultures and communities. To return to the gender example, it is impossible to understand the emergence and development of the sexual division of labour in organisations only from within. We have to go outside, to the family and patriarchal structures in society as a whole, in order to reflect back.

This approach means more than diffuse references to the environment. In theoretical terms, organisational issues cannot be comprehended outside of the totality constituted by capitalist society in general and the mode of production in particular (Burrell, 1980). Donaldson objects to this on the grounds that locating explanations within the wider social system denies that organisational phenomena are topics of enquiry in their own right. But no convincing argument is put forward to justify the desirability or possibility of such analytical autonomy, to say nothing of seemingly denying the validity of the work of Weber, Marx and Durkheim. Donaldson raises a more pertinent point when he argues that, 'the notion of totality is a reference to everything – nothing is left out' (1985: 124). It is indeed important to avoid reducing totality to a meaningless level of generality: we do not always learn very much from general references to the effects of capitalism and patriarchy. There may not be a smooth fit between organisations and each part of the 'totality', but it is possible and necessary to show the concrete ways in which organisations are embedded in specific social, political and economic structures.

Multi-dimensionality

Explanations must not only be multi-layered, but multi-dimensional. Different modes of analysis are needed to deal with the complexities and levels of human behaviour in organisations. As we have seen, mainstream theories separate the behavioural dimension from employees' roles within the division of labour. Clearly people are constituted as individuals at the level of their identities and emotions, but that process is informed by the same 'structural' and collective phenomena that shape management strategies and job design, the broader social relations of production between capital and labour, or between the sexes.

Radical writers have long been critical of the psychological component used by mainstream theory as part of the explanation of organisational behaviour. Objections have been made to the treatment of people in organisations as 'psychologically determined entities' with abstractly and individually defined needs – for example, for self-actualisation or belongingness. This has led some critical writers firmly to reject *any* psychological orientation. Clegg and Dunkerley argue that people should be considered, 'not as subjectivities, as unique individuals or social psyches, but as the bearers of an objective structure or relations of production and reproduction which are conditioned not by psychology but by history' (1980: 400). Although sharing this critique of psychological orthodoxy, we reject the view that people can be considered only as bearers of objective structures. The fact that managers and workers find themselves caught up in structural processes does not mean that they are merely passive agencies or operate solely at a group level. Any circumstances are experienced inter-subjectively, reconstructed and modified.

A purely structural analysis, even where it allows for human action and resistance, fails to get sufficiently inside those routine everyday experiences in which people react, adapt, modify, and consent to work relations. As concepts of motivation, perception and the like inadequately address the problem, some account of subjectivity and identity is necessary. Nor is the question of subjectivity significant solely at the level of the individual. A critical psychology should also identify the ways in which organisations act as 'people processors', whether through informal cultural practices or formal managerial strategies to mobilise consent.

That is not to say that it is easy to integrate the different dimensions. Our aim in this book at this stage is to establish complementarity and points of connection rather than synthesis and the solving of underlying theoretical questions. As subjectivity and psychological theories are the province of later chapters, we shall say no more at this stage.

Dialectics and contradiction

Many critical theorists (for example, Benson, 1977; Storey, 1983) utilise the notion of dialectical perspectives as a crucial means of explaining the dynamic of organisational change. In abstract terms a dialectical process refers to a movement from thesis to antithesis and synthesis and derives from Hegel and Marx. More frequently it is used to denote a reciprocal interaction, between structure and human agency or between conflicting groups. It is not always usefully employed. Gareth Morgan (1986: 266) produces a list which places 'oppositions' as varied as capital and labour, young and old and even sales and production on the same level. But a more focused emphasis on the interaction and structured antagonisms between key economic actors is valuable. We refer to 'structured' because group conflicts are shaped by contradictions – forces pulling in opposite directions – for example, between private ownership and collective social needs. These contradictions help reproduce antagonistic relations which are built into work organisation and society, and which in turn generate conflict and change.

The most direct application of dialectical pespectives to work organisations is expressed in the idea of a reciprocal relation between managerial control and worker resistance. Management control strategies are fundamentally a means of dealing with contradictions, uncertainties and crises in their socio-economic environment. New methods of control inevitably provoke and shape forms of employee resistance and sometimes counter-'strategies'. Over a period of time, management responses are likely to develop into alternative control methods, blending with and going beyond the old. For example, piecework was introduced as means for management to set targets and control through monetary incentives. But the shop floor frequently devised ways of asserting their own controls over output and earnings. In the 1970s employers in the motor industry responded by establishing new payment systems based on 'measured day rates', but still using control techniques based on work study and measurement. Over a period of time workers developed their own methods of adaptation and resistance, so the cycle continues.

This kind of perspective puts more substance into the traditional idea of an interaction between formal and informal dimensions of organisational life. However it is formulated, we can view organisations as continually having to respond to and counter *disorganisation*: a process which is underpinned by the divergent goals and interests discussed earlier in this chapter. Those who command organisations are required to mobilise a variety of resources to counter disorganisation. Although the actors themselves may not see it in these terms, we can pull together a variety of practices under the conceptual umbrellas of power, control and persuasion or consent. The factors underlying such choices and the different forms managerial and employee action take will be key and recurrent themes of this book.

Social transformation

The fact that we have argued against prescription does not mean a lack of interest in the 'practical' or the applied. We have tried to approach this in a number of ways. First, by giving an account and evaluation of up-to-date empirical research into work organisations, rather than the make-believe simulations that accompany many conventional texts. This involves critically examining as an issue in its own right the interventions made by social scientists as researchers or consultants. Second, by always analysing theories and practices together and as part of specific economic and political contexts. Showing how theories are used by managerial and other groups may sound unexceptional. But the dominant tradition has been to treat the major theories of organisation and management primarily as ideas systems and historically sequenced. The result is that most students do not get a realistic and informed view of the practicality of theory. In addition the impression is often given that theories developed in the past are outdated and 'wrong' compared to the latest favoured perspective. When these are inevitably replaced, cynicism about theory and organisational analysis is the likely result.

But alternative 'practicalities' have to go further than this and provide resources for social transformation. In this context, Benson adds a further aspect of a dialectical perspective, that of *praxis*, drawing on the previously discussed notion of practical rationality. Praxis involves developing analytical resources which go beyond reflexivity and can help members of organisations constrained by existing relations of ownership and power to reflect critically on and reconstruct their circumstances. Though some critical theorists advocate the prioritisation of 'philosophically informed armchair theorising' (Burrell, 1980: 102), we would agree with Benson's emphasis on theory as an emancipatory guide and as a means for *empowering* a wider range of organisational participants. When empowerment is used by management theorists and practioners to describe 'enabling' employees to chase more customers or do three more jobs, the term joins a long list whose rhetoric is not matched by reality.

A critical use implies no particular form of politics or intervention, but rather empowering employees to make more choices and to act more effectively to transform workplace relations. It may be argued that this reproduces a one-sided partiality that is the reverse of the management orientation of mainstream theories. There is always that danger. But the existing realities and power relations in organisations will, for the foreseeable future, enable critical theory to maintain a certain distance and intellectual independence. Furthermore, any critical theory not testing its ideas through empirical investigation or practical intervention is ultimately arid.

Finally, we should make clear that our project does not involve a rejection of the idea of organisation theory, merely a particular conception of it. It is necessary to treat mainstream theory as a series of overlapping perspectives sharing certain ideas and methods, while differing on others. Some concepts and research are useful and compatible with a critical approach, others are not. None can be considered simply as 'tools of management', or as embodying the values and interests of the dominant class. Such a view wrongly assumes that there is such a clear set of interests that can be reflected at a theoretical level. The tortuous history of organisational theory and practice in fact reveals a consistent tension between different approaches to regulation, which, in turn reflects the conflicting pressures to control *and* engage the workforce. All but the most unreflexive perspectives require some distancing from existing practices in order to act upon them in a way that will be a resource for management. We return to theories as a resource in Part 3. Meanwhile, subsequent chapters in Part 1 aim to examine critically the complexities of those relations between organisational theories and practices, beginning with the historical development of large-scale organisations.

CHAPTER 2

The emergence of large-scale organisations

Organising the new work forms

The aim of this chapter is to locate and explain the formation of the large-scale industrial bureaucracies that have been the primary object of analysis of the subject of organisation studies. Our time frame focuses on the crucial period at the beginning of the twentieth century, but moves backwards and forwards in order to understand the process of emergence of such organisations as the foundation of business development.

By the beginning of the twentieth century business organisations were beginning to be, 'transformed from chaotic and ad-hoc factories to rationalised, well-ordered manufacturing settings' (Goldman and Van Houten, 1980: 108). This was not just a product of growth, merger and technological innovation. It was also a question of *management*. Though the trend was in its infancy, firms were beginning to move away from particularist and uneven practices, towards the beginnings of an industrial bureaucracy. Indeed the two were intimately connected, given that the increasing scale of work organisation meant that it was no longer possible to rely on personal or unspecified forms of direction. Changes involved systematising and stabilising both the practices of management and the organisation of the labour process. Job hierarchies; new patterns of work supervision, measurement and reward; as well as greater specialisation and detailed division of labour, became more characteristic of organisational life. It is important to trace the genesis and development of this industrial bureaucracy, reflecting on the theoretical issues through the work of Weber, Taylor and others. As we argued in Chapter 1, mainstream writings largely lack this kind of historical and comparative character. Moreover, they tend to treat managerial and organisational theories as ideologies with universal effects.

Theories of management are not 'invented' and applied. Rather they form a resource through which both academics and practitioners try to understand and act. How that happens will depend on different social contexts and the histories that have shaped them. Of course, we do not have the space to provide a detailed business history that captures all events, variations and issues across societies. The aim is to give a broad picture that locates ideas in context and that focuses particularly on employment and labour process questions. In this chapter that picture is predominantly of USA and British circumstances. Nevertheless, in the final section we shall discuss how specific that experience is and compare it briefly to the formation of large-scale organisation in some other national contexts.

The rise of the factory system

Work processes prior to the factory system were not characterised by an extensive division of labour, nor by directly imposed coercive authority. In handicraft and domestic production, small producers were typically involved in independent commodity production, often based on the family structure. They owned their own means of production, worked according to their own patterns, and sold the goods at markets. Some trades or crafts were organised through the guild system. This combined employer and employee, normally within the framework and traditional authority of apprentice, journeyman and master. Neither system was flexible enough to be an adequate basis for responding to the needs of an emergent market economy. Industrialisation and the new capitalist production relations developed from a variety of organisational structures, including artisan production, co-operatives, centralised manufacture and the putting-out system (Berg, 1985). We want to focus mainly on the last.

Though the site of the work remained the 'cottage', workers continued to retain their own tools and capacity to organise their own work, and there was little division of labour. A relationship of wage labour was established, merchants supplied the raw materials and owned the finished product. Some historians see the putting-out system as a phase of *proto-industrialisation*. Rural workers were the ideal labour force, as they were worked for less than their urban equivalents and were too isolated to organise against the merchant's pricing. New markets, sources of capital accumulation and training grounds for entrepreneurial skills also constituted important features. Berg rightly notes that this 'phase' was not universal, took different regional and other forms and had varied outcomes. But the point of transition from cottage to workshop and then factory raises crucial *organisational* issues.

Mainstream theory commonly asserts that the new and more complex forms of organisation, with the associated detailed division of labour and hierarchies, developed largely because they were *technically* required by the scale of production, technology and related factors. A number of writers, notably Marglin (1974) and Clawson (1980) have used specific historical evidence on the factory system to challenge this general explanation. It is directed at helping to explain why workers were deprived of control of process and product through the centralised organisation of the factory system. A common response is to argue that the impetus was the necessity to shift from hand production to power-driven machinery located in a central source. In addition, there was the benefits of division of labour, pointed to in Adam Smith's famous pin factory example.

Both Marglin and Clawson show that bringing workers together in workshops and later in the factory – for example in the weaving and spinning trades – did not necessarily involve power-driven machinery or any other technical innovation. In fact, contrary to technological determinist arguments, 'organisational change precedes, both historically and analytically, the technological revolution which is the foundation of modern industry' (Clawson, 1980: 57). The issue of the division of labour is more complicated. Marglin does not argue that it, or hierarchy, were brought into being by capitalist organisation of work. But a distinction is made between the specialisation of occupation and function that is present in any social division of labour, and the particular forms of specialisation involved in the putting-out system and then in the factory. The minute division of work was not necessarily more efficient; rather it provided a role for the capitalist to play in organising production and to take a greater portion of the rewards: 'The social function of hierarchical work organisation is not technical efficiency, but accumulation' (Marglin, 1974: 62).

Given the time lapse, the evidence on this question is inevitably patchy. What, however, is beyond doubt is that though the new framework provided an impetus for technical innovation, efficiency and technical superiority were not the only, or even primary, reasons for the rise of factory organisation. The putting-out system allowed workers a great deal of control over their hours, rhythm, intensity and quality of work. Furthermore, there was a high level of embezzlement of raw materials, as workers sought to secure a fairer return for their labour. Historians have provided a large body of evidence that the workshop and the factory were utilised as a means of discipline and control in order to facilitate capital accumulation (Pollard, 1965; E. P. Thompson, 1967; Landes, 1969). Coercive authority could be more easily applied, including systems of fines, supervision (for instance the overlooker system in textiles), the paraphernalia of bells and clocks, and incentive payments. The employer could dictate the *general* terms of work, time and space; including the division of labour, overall organisational layout and design, rules governing movement, shouting, singing and other forms of disobedience. Doray gives numerous examples of French factory regulations, including fines for faulty work, writing on walls or entering the factory through the wrong door. He does, however, point out that when applied to the labour process, regulations were not particularly detailed: 'They asserted, in repetitive fashion, the principle of the employer's authority over an unspecified range of activities' (1988: 27–8). It is not surprising that many workers bitterly resisted entry to the factory and the associated forms of discipline. In those early periods, employers were frequently forced to resort to groups such as convicts, paupers and child labour.

To break such resistance, new work habits had to be created appropriate to the discipline of labour time and cash nexus at the heart of the wage relation. Employers' concern with the moral issues of sexuality, drink, bad language and theft was directed less by fidelity to religious doctrine than to the *behavioural* characteristics – obedience, punctuality, responsibility and performance – linked to capitalist rationality and its new forms of organisational culture. As Clegg and Dunkerley observe, the triumph of the formal factory organisation was strongly determined by its 'moral machinery' (1980: 62). This term was used by the economist Andrew Ure, noted for his pertinent advice to employers. He and other such advisers, were, however, clear that neither the division of labour nor work values were sufficient for the purpose of achieving the goal of creating 'factory hands'. *Mechanisation* was necessary to destroy old work habits and to tie the worker to the 'unvarying regularity of the machine'.

Marx showed how workers were able to use the employer's continuing dependence on their handicraft skills and knowledge as a weapon of resistance. In turn, Ure recognised that the unity of capital and science was necessary to try to reduce skills to dexterities, to create a technical framework independent of the producers, and to reduce labour costs by *intensifying* work rather than the limited option of raising hours. Marglin's notion of the factory as a social control device independent of technology is therefore incomplete (Clawson, 1980: 54). Without these kinds of development, the formal control developed in the factory could not have been adequately realised. It is always necessary to resist the temptation to describe these processes of organisational change in finished rather than relative terms. Employer control remained at a very general level and still had to be accommodated to high levels of worker skill, knowledge and self-organisation. Work was still often labour intensive and there was little or no bureaucratic or management structures. To explain the further development of large-scale organisation we need to focus more closely on the evolution of forms of control.

Modes of control in the transition to bureaucratic organisation

There were a number of obstacles to the development of a more bureaucratic work organisation during the nineteenth century. Even a more mature factory system rested on control structures that were inimical to moves in that direction. As Littler (1982: 69) argues, British industry presented a spectrum of modes of control that, despite differences, were fundamentally non-bureaucratic in nature. Using a range of evidence, three basic modes can be distinguished.

Entrepreneurial or simple control   In early factories at the beginning of the nineteenth century, owners could exercise a large degree of power and control personally. Referring to the famous foundry owner, Bendix observes, 'Boulton maintained a personal relationship with his workers, knew their names and their families, and relied upon this relationship to ensure the discipline and work performance needed in his enterprise' (1956: 57). Exercise of authority under entrepreneurial control was therefore simple and direct, and sustained frequently by legal coercion and harsh market conditions. Even at this stage, however, it was not always possible to exert control personally. Foremen could be utilised, but also, 'an important preliminary solution to the control dilemmas of divided authority was to rely on family ties' (Rueschemeyer, 1986: 57). At the required minimal level of co-ordination, the family or close friends of the entrepreneur proved sufficient. Middle managers were virtually absent; in fact, many employers were hostile and suspicious about the idea of a separate 'class' of managers.

Of course this situation could not survive a growth in the size and complexity of operations. Littler (1982) notes that the familial framework was rapidly discarded under such conditions, particularly in the USA. Nevertheless, some writers argue that direct and often despotic entrepreneurial authority remained at the centre of what Richard Edwards (1979) describes as *simple control*. There are important qualifications to be made to the model of entrepreneurial or simple control, particularly Edward's version. It is extremely doubtful whether it was representative of the economy until the end of the nineteenth century as he claims, rather than confined to a minority of firms (Littler, 1982: 64). In addition, though despotic authority was certainly a pervasive influence, it often had to accommodate to the power of other figures in the enterprise, such as craft workers. Hence the image of the all-seeing, all-knowing employer underestimates the struggles at the frontier of control in the workplace. There is also considerable evidence that a more significant mode of control involved contracting arrangements.

Contracting   One of the main reasons why management was so slow to develop was the tendency of employers to delegate responsibility for work organisation to sub-contractors, around whom the employment relationship was constructed. We are concerned here with the internal contractor rather than the independent sub-contractor who was involved, for example, in outwork trades such as clothing and boots and shoes. Evidence from historians such as Pollard (1965) on the UK, and more recently Clawson

(1980) on the USA, shows that internal contracting was in extensive use in a range of industries, including textiles, iron and steel, mining and transport. What did the organisation of work consist of?

> The inside contractor made an agreement with the general superintendent or owners of a company to make a part of their product and receive a certain price for each completed unit. . . .Inside contractors had complete charge of production in their area, hiring their own employees and supervising the work process . . . were employees of the company, and in most cases they received a day wage from the company as well. (Clawson, 1980: 71)

They accumulated considerable status and power, both in the community through patronage, and in the workplace through their high income. In some cases this meant a social position and standard of living higher than company officials, and a capacity actually to pass on much of the detailed work delegated to them by the employer to assistants!

Nevertheless the intended advantages to employers were clear. Responsibility, risks and costs could be partly shifted on to contractors, thus creating greater flexibility in circumstances where managerial skills and knowledge of work operations were limited. In effect contracting functioned as a means of transition through a period of growing enterprise complexity and scale. It was certainly hierarchical, but not bureaucratic in the sense of centralised authority, rules and record-keeping. Yet it proved capable of handling expanded output and technical innovation (Clawson, 1980). It did not encompass all industries or all labour within the firm. Newer industries such as service and process industries and railways were based on direct employment relations (Littler, 1982: 68).

Craft control Contracting is often seen as overlapping with the 'helper system', in which skilled workers were assisted by a small number of less-skilled operatives. In some cases craft workers hired and paid them, thus reproducing contractual relations. However, the scale of operations was small, with often just one helper; the practices were exercised by craft workers normally within a trade union framework; and the system operated often in conjunction with foremen. In fact the helper system is the basis for a model of craft control utilised by writers such as Stone (1973) and Montgomery (1976), in which skilled workers had the power to plan and direct immediate work processes. It is important not to exaggerate this 'partnership in production', for we are talking about a system of worker-directed job controls. But though not the equivalent of employer systems, such controls had a significant capacity to resist and constrain employer authority. This was put succinctly by F. W. Taylor in 1911 about his experience in the steel industry:

> As was usual then, and in fact is still usual in most shops in this country, the shop was really run by the workmen, and not the bosses. The workmen together had

carefully planned just how fast each job should be done, and they had set a pace for each machine throughout the shop, which was limited to about one-third of a good day's work [that is, the maximum possible]. Every new workman who came into the shop was told at once by the other men exactly how much of each kind of work he was to do, and unless he obeyed these instructions he was sure before long to be driven out of the place by the men. (1947: 128)

This was somewhat exaggerated in order to prove the need for Taylor's scientific management system, and particularly neglected the role and powers of the foremen. Though this varied from industry to industry, there was a far more extensive range of powers and functions than foremen hold today. The foreman's empire included substantial influence over both the manner and timing of production and the cost and quality of work, and responsibility for employees – often including hiring and firing. They operated under similar delegated authority to inside contractors, and enjoyed parallel status within and outside work. But that role must be seen within the framework of craft controls. The foreman would sometimes be a master of his trade or chief skilled worker, and would have to share or at least accommodate to the powers of craft workers and contractors.

Decay and decline of traditional controls

Despite the variety of control relationships, each in its own way functioned as a constraint to management and bureaucracy. The shift further in this direction in the last quarter of the nineteenth century must again be seen not merely in terms of gradual evolution and advance of technique. There were social contradictions as well as inefficiencies in traditional methods. Simple control is a clear case. During the period in question, the size and complexity of industrial firms increased considerably. During the last third of the century the average plant in the USA more than doubled in size and by 1900 there were 443 with more than 1000 wage earners (Nelson, 1975: 4). The impetus for change included mergers, concentration of resources, technical innovation, and shifts away from local and regional markets. This leap was particularly marked in the USA, given its late entry onto the industrial stage, and the relative freedom of business from social reform traditions and strong union organisation.

˙ Such processes inevitably affected existing social relations, being characterised by an increasing separation of entrepreneurs and top managers from the daily activities of the workforce. Organisationally the crucial issue was a growing gap between the structures and expertise of management, and a more extensive division of labour, with its requirements for new forms of control and co-ordination. For capital, the solution had to go beyond the employment of more managers, towards transforming the structures of managerial activity itself.

Problems associated with internal contract had more to do with contradictions than straightforward inefficiencies. According to Clawson, these were in two major areas. The very fact that the company had entered into subcontract arrangements meant that it was difficult to evaluate such activities. Contractors therefore used that power to keep employers as much in the dark as possible, aided by the fact that companies seldom kept many formal records. In addition to the income, the consequent social position of contractors was a problem, in that it was difficult for employers to motivate their own officials, who often felt inferior in power, status and rewards to the larger contractors. Craft job controls were also a serious obstacle to employers taking full advantage of mechanisation and expanded but more competitive markets. As Stone notes of the steel industry:

> At the same time that their labour costs as a percentage were rising, the labour system also prevented employers from increasing their productivity through reorganising or mechanising their operations. The workers controlled the plants and decided how the work was to be done. Employers had no way to speed up the workers, nor could they introduce new machinery that eliminated or redefined jobs. (1973: 26)

This again may be a somewhat exaggerated description, but it helps to explain why both contracting and craft arrangements came under increasing attack. Employers began to abolish internal contracting in order to shift income to the company and to create a hierarchy under their own control and acceptable to their own officials (Clawson, 1980: 119). Companies often tried to convert some of the contractors into foremen, but many preferred to quit. The power of craft workers was also increasingly challenged in the 1880s. A minority of firms tried to formulate a system of co-partnership, in the UK and France based largely on profit-sharing schemes geared explicitly to ensuring loyalty to the company (Brannen, 1983; Doray, 1988). There were other head-on clashes in the 1890s, including those between the Amalgamated Society of Engineers and their employers in the UK, and major conflicts in the US steel industry, such as the Homestead strike of 1892 (Stone, 1973).

Employers began to assert their general right to run production as they saw fit. This took a particularly virulent form in the USA with its weaker unions, as manifested in the 'open shop' campaign run by some employers. The predominant measures used by capital there and elsewhere to challenge and change existing modes of control, were, however, less dramatic. An important area was to modify the role of *supervisory labour*. This often involved breaking up the foremen's empire, with a shift away from traditional functions such as hire and fire and work organisation, towards the narrower but vital sphere of task supervision and discipline. As Littler (1982) shows, this was accompanied by considerable sub-division of the foreman's role. Examples include supervisory labour carrying out quality control, rate fixers, and 'feed and speed' functions. A further interrelated change was in *payment systems*, which became more centrally determined; undermining the bargaining role played by foremen and contractors. In addition, piecework and bonus arrangements spread rapidly.

Significantly, the new systems required some formal standards of effort and labour management record keeping. Payment through the office indicated a move towards a more direct employment relationship. It should, however, be noted at this stage in the battle for control of output, that management techniques were generally not sophisticated enough to include time study or job analysis, and were constrained by workers' initiative and knowledge. Companies frequently had to rely on the cruder measures of rate cutting and employment of 'rate-busters' to prove to the workforce that quotas could be increased.

We have already noted that such changes required an increase in *record-keeping*, given the need to specify objectives and keep track of results. The administrative aspects of a management system thus began to be set in place, including that of simple cost accounting. In some companies simple organisation manuals began to appear, complete with management principles and charts (R. Edwards, 1979: 30). Technological changes accompanied administrative ones, further increases in the detailed division of labour and mechanisation were facilitated by the greater knowledge of productive processes that capital was gaining. Not only was greater output achieved, but the capacity of employers to dispense with skilled workers and exert greater controls over labour generally through standardised procedures was enhanced. As one employer remarked, 'I want machines so simple that any fool could run them' (quoted in Goldman and Van Houten, 1980: 116). Engineering principles orientated towards treating workers as simple costs of production were therefore becoming more important than personal and direct controls.

Of course these developments were part of a broader process of the creation of the modern business enterprise. Chandler (1962, 1977) stresses that viability was only achieved when the 'visible hand of management' rivalled or replaced the market as a means of co-ordinating the flow of materials through enterprise and economy. In other words, a managerial hierarchy was able to supervise a large number of operating units and to co-ordinate, monitor and plan their activities. The path to the new forms of enterprise began in the USA with the railroads and the need to manage their vast regional operations, but gradually spread to other sectors, as modern big business in the decades before 1917 was able to integrate mass distribution and mass production. In this context, some firms developed from the internal growth of small single-unit firms who developed national and global networks, others from mergers. The new consolidated, multi-departmental enterprises centralised the administration of production and research facilities, and established vertical integration, attempting to control supplies and markets. Though the convergence between the growth strategies of firms and their new structures was not to reach its climax until after the First World War, with the development of multi-divisional, multinational enterprises, a salaried managerial class was fast rising in numbers and power (Supple, 1991: 501–2).

Management as a conscious and specialist activity was enhanced by the spread of associations and journals dealing with management methods (Clawson, 1980: 167–8). Entrepreneurial ideologies were complemented or challenged by more professional concerns with the 'labour problem'; and direct recruitment from colleges grew, though specialist technical training was still relatively limited. In addition a growing army of clerical, technical and administrative employees was necessitated by new payment systems, record-keeping and mechanisation; as well as the other growth functions of purchasing, sales and finance. It was not just a case of management hierarchy: by the turn of the century the workforce was subject to structures of what Richard Edwards (1979) refers to as *hierarchical control*. As other writers put it, 'differential job statuses and wages for workers were an integral component of the hierarchical nature of the industrial pyramid' (Goldman and Van Houten, 1980: 122). Job ladders and individuated reward systems were also a means of compensating for the growing homogenisation of labour by artificially dividing the workforce (Stone, 1973).

It must be stressed that these measures were experimental and varied in nature. Different countries and even sectors had their own unique characteristics and influences which added to the incoherence of transition processes (Littler, 1982), a process we shall return to in the final section of the chapter. Finally, though there was a great advance in managerial organisation compared to the earlier period, even in the USA it was still very much in its infancy. There was still little systematic and long-term planning, and as for work organisation, management 'was unable to make the qualitative leap to a different system because it had no alternative conception of how production should be organised' (Clawson, 1980: 168). That situation was soon to change.

Classical theories and the bureaucratisation of production

Taylorism and systematic management

The major means of change was through the work of Frederick Taylor and his 'scientific management' system. Not that Taylorism was unique or totally new: only time and motion study could genuinely be put in that category. A trend towards *systematic management* was already identifiable, as we have seen with instances of more formal management methods, cost accounting, standardisation of work, and use of less-skilled workers. Nyland (1988: 56) comments that, 'The "systematisers" were a diverse group of engineers, accountants and works managers who argued that US firms had grown to a size where the internal functioning of the enterprise was becoming increasingly chaotic and wasteful'.

When Taylor proclaimed his new system as a 'science', some British engineers described it as common sense masquerading under a high-sounding title (Geoff Brown, 1977: 158). Understandable though the reaction was, it missed the point. Taylor was not just in the right place at the right time, he played a crucial role in *theorising* and *popularising* the new ideas. Furthermore, it was intimately connected to a body of practice, with Taylor 'Napoleon of the war against craft production' (Clawson, 1980: 202). Taylorism was therefore the most conscious part of the systematisation of management, and of the regulation and control of production.

Such developments met the needs of capital in that period (M. Rose, 1975: 58). This was particularly the case in the USA, where larger corporations were developing higher levels of product and labour specialisation to cope with rising demand (Littler, 1982). A shift away from skilled labour towards unskilled immigrant workers was taking place, but still within the context of a relatively high-wage economy. This required new forms of co-ordination, integration and control; and methods of keeping down labour costs. The orientation of larger firms towards professional managers, engineers and consultants additionally provided a supportive framework for the rise of Taylorism. Engineers were central figures and carried out wide-ranging activities, including extensive refinements in accounting procedure (Nelson, 1975: 50). In the 1890s Taylor began to publicise his ideas about time study and piece rates, mainly through the American Society of Mechanical Engineers, and gathered round him a group of enthusiastic adherents.

His own work was first carried out at the Midvale Steel Works (owned by a friend of the family), in a variety of 'detective' roles ranging from unskilled labourer, machinist, clerk, gang boss, foreman, master mechanic, chief draughtsman and chief engineer. Experiments were also carried out in a small number of other firms in old and new industries. It was not just in the USA that such initiatives took place: by the time of the First World War one per cent of French as well as US firms had introduced schemes, often in new sectors such as electrical manufacturing and automobiles (Fridenson, 1978) and there were similar initiatives on a smaller scale in other European countries. In Britain, a minority of firms experienced the arrival of works engineers, rate-fixers, progress men, operations inspectors, work hustlers and other representatives of the growing army of non-producers (G. Brown, 1977: 149–52).

Principles   Many discussions of Taylorism in organisational texts discuss its defining principles around the idea of the employee as 'economic man' and are thus able to treat it as a failed theory of motivation. This is a far cry from the real basis of Taylor's ideas, which were concerned with the control of the labour process. Taylor was adamant that his system was a total package – one best way of organising work. Though affecting the activities of management and workers, the ideas were developed directly out of his obsession with combating the kind of worker's control of output – labelled 'soldiering' – observed at the steel works. He distinguished between natural and systematic soldiering: the former referring to the tendency to want to take it easy, the latter to practices deliberately geared to maximising rewards and job security. To solve the 'labour problem' a number of basic management principles were advanced:

1   The development of a science for each element of work
2   Scientific selection and training of workers
3   Co-operation between management and workers to ensure that the work is done according to the science
4   Equal division of work and responsibility between management and workers, each side doing what they are best fitted for.

These sound rather bland, but their significance can only be understood when set against Taylor's description of inefficient practices. Included under this were 'rule of thumb' methods of deciding on the nature of work tasks; workers choosing their own methods of work and training; and worker's knowledge being the basis of productive technique. He was particularly critical of management by initiative and incentive, when workers were given inducements to use their skills and know-how in the most economical way, without strict managerial determination of tasks.

Scientific management started from the belief that management had to reverse existing power relations in production: 'The management assume, for instance, the burden of gathering together all of the traditional knowledge which in the past has been possessed by the workmen and then of classifying, tabulating, and reducing this knowledge to rules, laws and formulae' (Taylor, 1947: 36). The continual concern with rules and laws in Taylor's writings show why it can be located firmly within a process of bureaucratisation of production. As Braverman (1974: 119) makes clear, it can also be seen as a control system based on the monopolisation of knowledge by management and its use to specify each step of the labour process. This 'separation of conception and execution' is clearly echoed in Taylor's comments such as: 'all possible brain work should be removed from the shop floor and centred in the planning and lay-out department' (quoted in Braverman, 1974: 113).

Other aspects of the above principles are not so prominent. Take selection: Taylor's search for workers who would follow his instructions to the letter is legendary. His tutelage of Schmidt, picked for his strength and stupidity, was repeated elsewhere, such as the selection of Pinnell – 'the hardest working man' in a railway factory – by time and motion men on behalf of British management (G. Brown, 1977: 156–7). When even his time in the lavatory was recorded and only measured after breakfast when his energy was greatest, it was little wonder that Pinnell came to wish he was dead. But despite the interest of some of Taylor's followers, explicit techniques to place the right worker in the right job remained an underdeveloped part of scientific management.

What about the previously-mentioned emphasis placed by OB on Taylorism as the model of 'economic man'? This is largely misleading. Like most of his contemporaries interested in management reform, Taylor *did* believe that workers were motivated by the pursuit of rational self-interest and that incentive wages – in the form of a differential piece-rate system – were the solution to most labour problems. The tendency to restrict output, however, was seen as an unnecessary product of the absence of any scientific authority for work standards. Management could ensure co-operation on the basis of a consensus established by objective work measurement. Economic incentives could be used to overcome the hostility of workers to giving up traditional job controls. This exchange proved to be a limited and fragile basis for co-operation and certainly did not ever eliminate restriction of output. But an instrumental view of human labour was a far cry from a complex theory of motivation. Taylor was far more concerned with breaking the power of the work-group and removing the basis for collective bargaining through individualistic payment systems (Littler, 1982: 55).

Ideology and practice   The consequences of the operation of such principles were explicitly recognised by Taylor. There would be a need for: extensive work measurement to predetermine tasks; the employment of cheaper, deskilled and substitutable labour in more fragmented jobs; a large increase in the number of non-productive employees to enforce, monitor and record new work arrangements; and functional foremanship that subdivided traditional responsibilities and involved reporting to the all-powerful planning department. It would, of course, be foolish to believe that all of this came to pass smoothly. In fact, there are a number of writers who believe that Taylorism was a 'practical failure' and was not widely implemented due largely to worker resistance and employer suspicions (Palmer, 1975; R. Edwards, 1979; Goldman and Van Houten, 1980). This is often complemented by arguments that its significance is as a management *ideology* which was itself later discredited (M. Rose, 1975; Burawoy, 1979).

What is the balance of these two processes? We should certainly not underestimate the ideological purposes. Taylor himself emphasised the pressing need for a 'complete mental revolution' in the attitudes of the two parties. Whatever success was achieved can largely be attributed to the stress on the *scientific* character of the system, which trades on the predominantly uncritical attitudes to knowledge under such a mantle. Its technical orientation was of particular appeal and use to engineers in their struggle to establish themselves as the core management group in US industry (Armstrong, 1984). But there was a potential appeal to workers and unions from the same source; 'Under scientific management arbitrary power, arbitrary dictation, ceases; and every single subject, large and small, becomes the question for scientific investigation, for reduction to law' (Taylor, 1947: 211). The theoretical separation of authority from hierarchy was an attempt to construct some level of consent in the employment relation; and, with the increased productivity and wages from the system, was to be the basis for the co-operation promised in Taylor's principles.

In practice it never quite worked like this. As an ideology of science it strengthened management by providing, 'the technocratic rationale for authority in formal organisations' (Kouzmin, 1980: 68). It was also flawed and contradictory in nature. It is strange that a science of management had to be based on knowledge and skills appropriated from workers. Of course it never was a science, but rather a control system, and has tended to be seen as a set of techniques to be countered and contested by generations of shop stewards. In one of his weaker moments, Taylor even admitted the stopwatch had an element of 'guesswork'.

Most of the misunderstandings concerning the practical success of Taylorism stem from confusion about what *criteria* to employ. Many of those who see it as a failure are viewing Taylorism as a coherent and total package. This is understandable given that it coincides with Taylor's own views and his tendency to withdraw co-operation when companies refused to follow all the complexities of the schemes. But it is wrong. We need to redefine the criteria in two ways. First, as already indicated, we must consider it as part of a broader movement of systematic management that was implemented in a variety of forms. Second, it was also implemented in a selective manner: 'employers looked upon scientific management exactly as Taylor insisted that they should not: as an arsenal of devices designed to simplify and improve the management of labour' (Bendix, 1956: 286). All the elements were juggled about by companies according to their needs and prejudices. A close analysis of the early literature on 'Taylor firms' by Nelson (1975: 68–78) showed that none fully represented the principles set out in *Shop Management*. References to time study can be found in every firm, and planning departments were widespread. But incentive payment schemes were patchy and employers found that functional foremanship embodied too many layers of responsibility.

Once these factors have been acknowledged, we can recognise a widespread, if uneven, diffusion of key aspects of Taylorist practices in industrial societies in the 1920s and 1930s (G. Brown, 1977; Clawson, 1980; Littler, 1982; Nyland, 1988). Taylor's death in 1915 opened the door to a variety of consultants to introduce further versions of scientific management. Some were short-cut emulators, other were Taylor's disciples such as Gantt, and the Gilbreths with their extension of Taylor's early emphasis on the study of fatigue and their advances in the use of cameras to record and time movements. This factor and changes in the external environment guaranteed that scientific management did not spread in pure form.

In current managerial and sociological literature Taylorism always appears as a dynamic duo with *Fordism*. Links there certainly were. Henry Ford's innovations in technical control through the flow assembly line extended Taylorist principles such as job fragmentation and allowed for a greater level of intensity of labour through speed-up of the line and other measures (Littler, 1982: 56–7). In addition, the scale of Ford's operations and his willingness to introduce the 'five dollar day' as a means of combating labour turnover, enabled another of Taylor's principles – high wages for high productivity – to be realised. Ford's plants did not use the apparatus of Taylorite time and motion study, but the management nevertheless collected a considerable amount of information on tasks, so that, for example, they had enough information to produce 7800 individual job-profile sheets (Doray, 1988: 96). This reinforces a crucial point, that we must not fetishise Taylorism at the expense of the broader trend towards 'scientific' management. The managerial regime at Ford had its own innovations in labour utilisation, stretching the semi-skilled labour by a permanent process of de-manning and flexibility: a mode of operation that challenges the stereotype of rigid machinery, products and labour under mass production (Williams *et al.*, 1992b).

Meanwhile, in Europe, the most extensive implementation of neo-Taylorite schemes came through the *Bedeaux system*. Charles Bedeaux was a French full-time management consultant whose schemes were based on his 'discovery' of a universal measure for all work, given the name 'B unit'. He aggressively sold them as a cheap and quick method that did not need to have major consequences for existing management structures. Like the Gilbreths, he entered the unexplored territory of fatigue through basing the measurement on the proportions of work and rest required for completing a task. Though he had considerable international success, Bedeaux had his greatest impact in Britain, where employers used the circumstances of the 1930s depression to install the system and utilise it for the purposes of rate-cutting and speed-up (G. Brown, 1977; Littler, 1982). This example illustrates the way that scientific management varied in both form and timing between and within countries. Whereas Britain's late adoption differed from the US and French models, other economies such as Germany and Sweden followed distinctive paths; for example, combining rationalisation measures with greater use of psychological testing (Fridenson, 1978). Contrary to some recent studies, Taylorism did influence the organisation of work in Japan, but 'was used as a vehicle for job analysis and standardised procedures rather than as a comprehensive control system' (Littler, 1982: 156–7). Aspects of the latter, notably the separation of thinking and doing, as well as individual output norms, did not fit into pre-existing patterns of fluid job boundaries, work teams and the power of foremen over production planning.

Lack of uniformity was undoubtedly influenced by the pattern of resistance from a variety of groups. There has been well-documented resistance from craft and non-craft workers, using every method from strikes to informal disruption (Nadworny, 1955; Brown, 1977; Montgomery, 1976). Workers were particularly opposed to effects such as deskilling and speed-up, because, as one put it, he 'never knew a rate to be raised after a time study' (quoted in Baritz, 1960: 98). But the plain fact is that resistance did not succeed in stopping the long-term diffusion of scientific management, though it certainly delayed and mediated it. This is often put down to the gradual shift in union attitudes from opposition to reluctant accommodation and occasional enthusiastic co-operation. There is a great deal of truth in this assessment, though some unions had always had a conciliatory attitude, and the behaviour of official structures should not be confused with rank-and-file members who continued resistance. Indeed, the very institutionalisation of scientific management guarantees that it is accompanied by a low-intensity war at shopfloor level.

Changes of this kind were influenced by later progressive Taylorites who lacked his hostility to trade unions and were prepared to give them an institutionalised role in work study and bonus schemes. Scientific management could also be given an progressive aura by its association with planning, Nyland (1988) showing that some of its adherents advocated the extension of the system to the whole society constraining the role of markets. He also correctly points to the neglect of Taylorism's wider capacity to improve work efficiency in the spheres of scheduling, stores management and purchasing and plant lay-out. Though whether this is enough to commend Taylorism despite the control dimension is more arguable.

Supervisory and managerial resistance also continued to be a considerable constraint both in the USA and Britain (Nelson, 1975: 75–6; Littler, 1982: 181–2). New schemes tended not only to change traditional roles, but to erode decision-making powers. Employers and managers often found it hard wholly to embrace Taylorism. Taylor was often bitterly critical of their competence. It challenged their traditional judgement, discretion and powers, to say nothing of straining their patience through contract stipulations that the company must do as exactly as he told them. The high costs, disrupted routines and social antagonisms meant that failure was more often linked to managerial opposition than that of workers.

Given the evidence, the problem of Taylorism is not *whether* it was introduced, but *how*, and what its *limits* were as a control system. We shall return to the former later, but with respect to the latter, right from the start many employers realised that Taylor's neglect of 'the human factor' and of what Friedman (1977) calls 'the positive aspects of labour' such as know-how and goodwill, made it impossible to use on its own. We shall return to the combination with psychological methods later, but even as a means of bureaucratisation of production, Taylorism was insufficient.

Weber and administrative theories of management

For some writers, the concept of bureaucratisation of production is a problematic one. Braverman (1974: 120) objects that it endorses the mistaken view that such work arrangements are endemic to large-scale organisation rather than a product of capitalist social relations. We have already made our position clear in Chapter 1. Our argument in this book is that bureaucratisation *is* a universal tendency, but can only be understood through the specific forms it takes in different modes of production or more specific business systems. But there is a different point at stake. Braverman's influential theory of the labour process is constructed on the implicit assumption that what we have been describing as bureaucratisation could be fully represented by Taylorism. However, what Taylorism provided was a system of detailed control over work, aided by a set of bureaucratic rules, and Clawson (1980: 248) argues that this is in contrast to Weber's stress on the remote and impersonal qualities of bureaucracy.

We shall return to this question later. For now it is sufficient to observe that Taylorism had far less to say about the *employment relationship*: 'those structural conditions which surround the appointment, promotion and dismissal of individuals' (Littler, 1982: 37). Scientific management was meant to be able to be applied at any given level of task or technology, but it 'left management in the position of having a set of principles laying down how to make its workforce more productive, whilst possessing no body of knowledge that specifically applied from supervisory levels upward in the organisational hierarchy' (Clegg and Dunkerley, 1980: 99). This was particularly important in the context of the previously observed growth of middle management – middle managers were monitoring the performance of the operating units under their command, but were not subject to systematic evaluation themselves. It is Weber and other theorists of formal management and administration who can give us a greater understanding of developments of this nature. The emphasis here is on *understanding*: Weber was not a theorist-practitioner like Taylor, and the ideas discussed below were not immediately implemented in organisations.

In common with most other writers, we do not intend to list all the complex features of bureaucracy that Weber includes as defining characteristics, but instead to group them under two headings:

The employment relationship The office is a vocation and a full-time undertaking. Officials are selected on a basis of technical qualification, education and expertise. There is separation of office and office-holder: it is not his or her property and the employee does not possess the means of administration. Thorough and expert training is part of the conditions of employment.

A career structure is provided based on the organisational hierarchy. Tenure is for life, with fixed salary, pension rights and appropriate social status. Officials are appointed by higher authority, not externally elected, and promotions are similarly regulated, for example, through seniority.

Work structures and relations   There is a hierarchy of offices, with continuous and regulated activity within a fully ordered system of super and subordination. Within the chain of command, there is a division of labour based on defined responsibilities, rights and duties. Calculable rules and regulations, impersonal modes of conduct and a common control system govern the conduct of work. Written documentation are the basis of management of the office.

From these characteristics it is understandable that some may question their links to the *bureaucratisation of production*. After all, the impetus for Weber's analysis came primarily from the organisation of the state and the regulation of administrative employees. The historical context is also important for an understanding of the significance of measures such as full-time work as a vocation. In the period under consideration, it was still important to break away from patrimonial, charismatic and other relations, whereby people could be placed in position through inheritance and similar 'private' attributes. The emphasis on calculable rules and regulations may also seem a bit abstract. But both examples highlight that the ideal type of bureaucracy is linked to Weber's wider theory of *rationalisation*.

We discussed the problematic character of the idea of rationality in Chapter 1, but rationalisation is held to be the key modernising characteristic for the development of industrial societies. Authority in industrial societies was rational because it was formal and based on precise and predictable rules, calculation and accounting. For these reasons the bureaucratic organisation and administration best permitted the development of appropriate attitudes, structures and practices in public and private sectors. In this context, bureaucracies are a specific type of rational-legal authority: officials work within a framework in which command and task are based on authority derived from impersonal rules. But Weber's theories are not as separate from production as they may appear. He made it clear that they referred to bureaucratic *management* as well as administration. The Weberian 'causal chain' (Collins, 1986: 21–9) links the concept of rationality explicitly to the emergence of capitalist enterprise and markets. These were held to be rational because of their capacity for calculability, predictability and routinisation – through production, distribution, accounting and market pricing mechanisms. Preconditions for this 'rationalised' capitalism started from the complete private appropriation of the means of production, which Weber said must be unhampered by 'irrational obstacles' such as workers' rights to participate in management. In addition, there was the need for common management, free labour under the compulsion of the 'whip of hunger', mass markets, minimal trade restrictions and institutional, legal support from the bureaucratic state.

Weber also argued that large, capitalist enterprises were becoming 'unequalled modes of strict bureaucratic organisation' (Weber, 1984: 32). He was aware and approving of the role played by scientific management in this process. It was 'completely' the ideal vehicle for the necessary imposition of military discipline in the factory, given its capacity for dehumanisation and conditioning of work performance. Techniques such as Taylor's 'shop cards', which specified the daily routines of employees, were ideal vehicles of bureaucratisation. What is more, Taylor saw management by 'scientific' methods as a move away from traditional authority where owners and managers attempted to control by inefficient personal means. On reflection, it is therefore possible to see that Weber's schema is not only compatible with Taylorism, but also that the practices he describes can reinforce systems of work control. Formal structures of management enhance centralisation of power, and hierarchical organisation aids functional specialisation, task fragmentation and labour discipline, while emphasis on predictable performance minimises the discretion of employees.

But, as Littler (1982) argues, it is in the sphere of the employment relationship that Weber adds something new. The career structure linked to the bureaucratic hierarchy strengthens a commitment to the organisation absent from Taylorism. A specific form of bureaucratic motivation is also sustained by the identification of job security, status, rewards and performance to organisational structure. Employees may react against the bureaucratisation of control embodied in rules prescribing the way a task is performed, but welcome rules governing selection, training and promotion within the employment relationship. Nor is it necessarily confined to office administration. Some modern radical theorists argue that employers are increasingly turning to strategies of bureaucratic control for the shop floor. Edward's research on companies such as Polaroid, IBM and General Electric points to two crucial features of the strategy. There is a finely graded stratification and division of the workforce; the hierarchical structures devised to divide and conquer, tending to 'break up the homogeneity of the firm's workforce, creating many seemingly separate strata, lines of work, and focuses for job identity' (R. Edwards, 1979: 133). In addition, impersonal rules form the basis of company policy. Detailed and specified criteria for job descriptions and performance are monitored by supervisors, rather than work tasks being directly enforced. The stress is on positive incentives in performance, not negative sanctions. Taken together with the job security and 'career' structure through job hierarchies, long-term identification with the company can be built.

Hence, contrary to Clawson's view, impersonality and 'remoteness' can be an effective control mechanism. This kind of use of Weberian categories as explanatory tools indicates their continuing relevance, but also their limitations. Clearly bureaucratic structures have no universal rationality. Rather they are in part consciously constructed by employers for specific purposes that cannot be reduced to 'efficiency'. A further qualification needs to be made in relation to the *legitimacy* arising from bureaucratic systems. Undoubtedly they can generate loyalty and commitment. But the position of shop floor workers is not comparable to the higher officials of a public organisation such as the civil service, which provides long-term security and stable career structures with a minimum conflict of interests. Private companies are seldom able to match those kind of conditions, and the centrality of the wage-effort bargain will always tend to introduce uncertainty and conflict into the employment relationship.

Insights derived from Weberian theory have been applied in Britain and the USA from the late 1940s. But companies were able to draw on parallel developments in classical management theory in the inter-war period. Other theorists of formal organisation, were, like Weber, concerned to tackle the administration of the whole enterprise. By far the most significant was Fayol, a Frenchman who shared the engineering and management background of Taylor. 'Fayolism' inspired, amongst other things, the reorganisation of railway and engineering companies, and department stores in France (Fridenson, 1978); and translation of his short text enabled wider influence. His main concern was to establish the validity of studying and training management itself, not just the management of others. Emphasis was put on formulating general features of management, first in the form of five elements; planning, organising, commanding, co-ordination and control – then through fourteen principles. The themes contained in the latter echo and extend Taylor and Weber; including division of work, stability of tenure, authority of command and subordination of the individual interest to the general (for the full list see Pugh, 1963: 66). One principle, that of unity of command, differed sharply from Taylor's belief in functional authority.

The basis of the approach in Fayol and other similar theorists such as Gullick and Urwick was orientated to rationalising management structures, often through centralisation and specified spans of control; emphasis on the managerial role in setting and securing goals; and planning for the optimal use of resources. Modern management came to take many of these things for granted. which led some to invest Fayol's theorising with a high status and lasting effect. In fact his work was more of a practical guide with simple 'plan-ahead proverbs' (Perrow, 1979: 70) akin to today's numerous management handbooks. Later writers are more likely to prefer the judgement of Clegg and Dunkerley that 'the "principles" are neither universally empirically applicable, nor theoretically coherent' (1980: 103).

What matters more than flawed, hand-me-down principles is that classical theories were engaging with real changes in economy and enterprise. When Chandler began to use the railroad as his blueprint for large-scale organisation, his emphasis was on the emergence of organisational charts, hierarchies of office and functional authority. This can be linked to a wider and related argument from Williamson (1975: 1981) that organisations emerge in the form of hierarchies when markets fail. Or to be more precise, when it is more efficient to internalise transactions – for labour, components, services and so on – within multi-divisional or vertically-integrated firms, than to have them mediated by and through the market. Because markets become increasingly complex, prices and other indicators cannot give complete information which allows individuals to cost transactions accurately. This uncertainty and complexity can often be better handled through organisations constituted as bureaucratic hierarchies, because they can monitor behaviour, establish rules and procedures and provide better information and control.

So, to return to Chandler (1977): by 1918, the 'visible hand' that had brought the vertically integrated bureaucracies into existence was extended to defining the role and specific tasks of top management within general offices. The context was a further centralisation of administration, often within new multi-divisional structures such as those at General Motors. This process included uniform accounting and statistical controls that allowed senior administrators to evaluate managerial performance and exercise long-range planning. In Chandler's later work (1990), he emphasises that investment in production and distribution that facilitated economies of scale is combined with further investment in managerial skills that lead to economies of scope and enhanced organisational capabilities. Supple comments,

From these viewpoints, the modern industrial firm is crucially characterised by expansion overseas, by product diversification, and (most significantly) by administrative complexity – that is, by the growth in the number of its operating units, each carrying out a different economic function and all co-ordinated by a management hierarchy. (1991: 504–5)

This focus on organisational design, strategy and structure, is valuable, but partial. The neglect of the informal dimensions of organisational life by classical theories left gaps that had to be filled.

Social science and industry: a courtship

'Increasingly the men who manage and direct industry, find themselves incapable of effectively controlling their organisations'. This is how Baritz

(1960: 3) begins his brilliant account of the historical uses of social science in US industry. Managers had, by the early part of the twentieth century, already drawn on the expertise of people such as Taylor and other consultants. But there had been little sign of embracing the emergent social sciences. This began to change in the period after the First World War when some major US corporations began financing industrial psychology and endowing business schools as part of a process of research and experimentation. Moves towards co-operation with social scientists arose from the same process as links with Taylorism; the vulnerability of management to the appeal of planning and science.

Enter the human factor

The instrumental attitudes of employers to any theories perceived to be of immediate use can be seen in the favourable attitude adopted towards the battery of tests and measurements offered to fit people to jobs (see Chapter 8 for more detail). This kind of intervention represented a version of Taylor's 'scientific selection of the worker' by other means. In fact the *Bulletin of the Taylor Society* carried articles discussing issues of human personality and arguing that newly recruited workers should be tested for personality, character and temperament. In 1915, an article about one factory noted that:

> A system of cards was used, one side of each card contained information about the worker's identity, parents, ethnic origins and previous employment; the other contained a certain amount of medico-psychological information ('anaemic, 'non-chalant') and notes on the individual's degree of motivation and way of life ('father out of work', 'mother agreed to take care of child', etc.). This was followed by his medical record (doctor, optician, dentist) and by basic health advice on the need for rest and fresh air. (Doray, 1988: 188)

Far from being different academic species, it is arguable that the human relations current partly derived from a form of Taylorist revisionism. Nevertheless the battle cry of 'neglect of the human factor' was directed against the costs of scientific management in terms of resistance and disenchantment. The simple appeal and apparent applicability of the variety of tests convinced a growing minority of employers. Problems arose when naive enthusiasm and unrealistic expectations quickly ran up against the crude nature and limited results arising from the techniques. By the mid-1920s, and in changed economic circumstances, the tests had been abandoned by most companies (Baritz, 1960: 71).

Accounts of the development of British industrial psychology (M. Rose, 1975: 65–87; G. Brown, 1977: 213–28) show it to be more sober, centralised, less consultancy-based and affecting even fewer firms. It took a particular interest – derived from experiences of the Industrial Fatigue Research Board during the war – in monotony. Fatigue was, as we have seen, an issue which also concerned the scientific management movement, linked as it was to the need for the successful measurement of work. Common interests and client relations again meant, as in the USA, 'a large proportion of their problems had to be taken over from the scientific managers' (M. Rose, 1975: 86). But despite sharing some common assumptions about efficiency, productivity and work organisation, British researchers established a distance from Taylorism.

Myers perceptively noted the hostility generated among workers by scientific management through its attack on skills, and the effects of speed-up and time and motion study. He made attacks on the notion of 'one best way', rightly pointing to the greater complexity of behaviour and industrial conditions. This critique was linked to a more sympathetic consideration of the need to convince the trade unions of the validity of social science interventions, and to win more generally the consent of the workforce. The relatively progressive stance of British industrial psychologists is further illustrated by their alliance with a small group of employers centred on the Quaker families such as Rowntree, who shared their enthusiasm for 'scientific planning' and dislike for the harsher aspects of Taylorism. When those companies began to utilise psychologists, however, there was still considerable suspicion and resistance from employees; particularly when they were introduced at the same time as scientific management methods (G. Brown, 1977: 216). The Quaker tapestry firm, Lee's, divided the managerial responsibility for 'psychology' and Taylorist 'mechanics' between the owner's two sons (Johnson and Moore, 1986). Most British employers, however, still preferred to cut costs simply by squeezing wages and exploiting favourable market circumstances.

But industrial psychology was not as isolated a phenomenon as it appeared. In the USA particularly it was part of a wider period of experimentation involving human relations and Taylorist management, as employers chose within and between the new techniques. Richard Edwards (1979: 102) gives an interesting example of the Bancroft textile company employing a consultant to introduce welfare work in 1902, and Taylor's follower Gantt to reorganise production in 1905! *Welfarism* was a significant part of that context. A paternalistic concern for the well-being of employees in return for loyalty and hard work, had a long pedigree in some companies. Company towns were one manifestation, as employers provided houses, schools, stores, sanitation and lighting in order to attract an adequate labour force. But the rhetoric had shifted from older themes of community and improving the working man to themes of entitlements and better working conditions (Barley and Kunda, 1992: 372).

Welfare work was also present in conventional circumstances. An increasing number of firms began to employ welfare secretaries whose role ranged from encouraging a 'proper moral atmosphere' to the provision of social and medical facilities. This interest was not philanthropic – 'Capital will not invest in sentiment', as one leading employer put it (quoted in Nelson, 1975: 104). It arose from attempts to grapple with the recruitment and motivation problems deriving from the increasing size of the labour force and a new industrial relations situation shaped by declining loyalty and rising unrest. There was a parallel development in the growth of employment or personnel departments as a means of dealing 'scientifically' with such issues – again showing an overlap with Taylorism. In the USA and Britain professional personnel bodies grew from the seeds of welfare work.

But in the latter country, welfarism was strongly connected to the study of fatigue in the laboratory of wartime factories. As in the USA, British welfarism was described by one of its leading members as combining 'pity and profit' (quoted in G. Brown, 1977: 185). Lee's issued 'partnership certificates' to employees who had shown a genuine interest in the company. Many workers, particularly the women who were its prime object, saw its motivation as directed primarily towards profit, given the emphasis on improving conditions for the sole purpose of maximising output. After the war, changing economic circumstances saw the decline of welfare initiatives. But in the USA, to a greater extent than Britain, there was a broader framework of 'welfare capitalism'. Companies such as General Electric, International Harvester and US Steel continued policies of off-the-job benefits in the form of insurance, health, pensions, social clubs, profit-sharing schemes and other measures (R. Edwards, 1979: 91–7).

But the process took many different forms. Take Ford, for example. The company had only limited social provision, but it had social control potential. The 'Sociological Department' had investigators who were empowered to visit homes to check on absentees and monitor an employee's family, values and habits. But this social control mechanism did not exist in the abstract. To act as a counterweight to the assembly line and associated problems of labour turnover and unionisation, Ford had profit-sharing schemes and the famed five dollar day. The department could therefore ascertain the 'fitness' of workers for these generous rewards!

In a period in which space was opened up for employers by defeated industrial militancy and repression of socialist organising, welfarism in the USA also had close ties to the development of company unions. This was different from the kind of enterprise unions initiated more recently by Japanese employers. The former arose primarily from wartime attempts to institute limited forms of worker representation, such as works councils. After the war many large companies, often utilising their new personnel departments, were quick to consolidate this trend by initiating company unions as a focus for formal grievance procedures, thus alleviating the need for independent union representation (Edwards, 1979: 106). There was some success in delaying or undermining unionism, and employers learnt some important lessons on the importance of controlled employee involvement and formal procedures. But, as in Britain, little survived the economic changes associated with the growing depression and sharpening social polarisation. Company unionism and welfarism did not provide an adequate means of pursuing the collective interests of workers, while at the same time they became a financial burden for employers without solving any of their fundamental control problems inside the factory.

Hawthorne and beyond

The Hawthorne studies occupy a pivotal place in organisational theory. Begun in the mid-1920s, the research was carried out in the large Hawthorne plant employing 29 000 workers making electrical appliances for Bell as a subsidiary of American Telegraph and Telephone (AT&T). Management regarded themselves as progressive, but this was with regard to a willingness to experiment rather than their general attitudes, for they were strongly anti-union. The significance of Hawthorne is not because of the results of the research as such, for both its findings and methods are widely regarded as highly questionable (Carey, 1967; Silver, 1987). Rather, it reflects two factors: first, the sustained nature of the intervention itself, combining psychologists, sociologists and anthropologists. In this way the courtship between social science and industry became something of a formal engagement; second, the interpretation of the results became the core of *human relations* theory and subsequent managerial practices. This was partly due to the propagandising work of Elton Mayo (1946), despite the fact that he did not join the team properly until 1928 and was much more peripheral than those who actually wrote up the detailed research, such as Roethlisberger and Dickson (1964) and, to a lesser extent, Whitehead (1938).

Let us retrace these steps briefly. Early experiments centred on varying the lighting for two small test groups of women workers. The purpose was to identify conditions affecting worker performance. Unfortunately no firm conclusions could be drawn, as productivity increased under every level of illumination and even for the control group that was not being subjected to any changes at all! At the time this caused great puzzlement, but it was later theorised that the real change had been the segregation of a small group, which blossomed under special attention and treatment. Thus the 'Hawthorne Effect' was born, through which it was recognised that the research intervention itself is an independent variable in its effects on human behaviour. Initially the puzzlement led to a further stage of experiments on groups of women selected for their degree of friendship with one another. Again the emphasis was on manipulation of environmental variables, this time of a greater variety: rest pauses, length of working day, group bonus schemes and so on. Observers, initially placed in a test room, were gradually encouraged to act like supervisors and become more friendly with the group. Until 1929, in almost all cases output rose, with the only consistent factor again being the effects of creating a special group with its identity strengthened by the replacement of two 'un-cooperative' members. However, worker interest in experiments declined and output fell with the onset of the depression. Furthermore, additional experiments with two other groups to test further the effects of incentives and rest pauses had inconclusive results, both experiments being discontinued amidst some discord.

All this confusion might appear to be grounds for giving up. But a more positive line was taken that a constant factor was the significance of employee attitudes and the influence of supervisory techniques upon them. The successful experiments were those that allowed the individuals to coalesce into a group, though it is difficult to imagine how the special conditions could be transferred.

> Right now I couldn't ask for anything better than I have. I just can't explain what it is but I sure like it in the test room . . . I think we work for the most wonderful man in the Western Electric Company. We have no boss. Mr.__ simply waits on us . . . We have privileges that a lot of the other girls don't have. We are allowed to go down and lie on the couch when we are tired or don't feel good, and the matron was told not to say anything to us. Of course, none of us have done that yet because we always feel pretty good and we have rest periods and can do anything we want to in those ten minutes. (Roethlisberger and Dickson, 1964: 144)

Attitudes are not simply created by interaction with management. Employee preoccupations arise from a variety of sources, so further means were found of identifying them. Even while the above experiments were going on, the company and researchers had initiated an interviewing programme to explore the relations between employee morale and supervision. 'Counsellors' were trained by researchers to play the role of the observers in the illumination phase. Over a long period of time a variety of formal and more open-ended techniques of interviewing were used as a means of gaining information and of detecting, diverting and redirecting dissatisfactions. The counsellor was told by the company, 'to watch constantly for signs of unrest and to try to assuage the tension of the worker by discussion before the unrest became active' (quoted in Fischer and Sirriani, 1984: 182). Employee complaints were treated as unreliable due to their vagueness (hot, cold, damp, smoky or dusty were apparently inferior to 'the temperature in the room was 67°F'); or because they really revealed some personal, external disturbance. Even when told of grievances, management did not act on them. Aside from letting off steam, the process could also be used to adjust employees to the work situation and screen out effective counsellors as management material.

A final phase of research linked together the concern with employee attitudes and the earlier focus on the group. The famed 'bank wiring room' experiments were based on an existing work-group carrying out wiring, soldering and inspecting tasks with a supposedly unobtrusive observer present. What was 'discovered' on the face of it was no different from Taylor's observations in the steel industry: the work-group systematically controlled and restricted output on the basis of their own conception of a fair day's work and enforced group norms on any fellow workers who deviated by overproducing (rate-busters) or underworking (chisellers). The interpretation and reaction was, however, sharply different. Despite the restrictions, cliques and hostilities, a more accommodating picture of group identities was endorsed. Instead of suppressing the group and attempting to individualise its members, human relations is concerned to cultivate its sentiments and switch its loyalties to management. Roethlisberger and Dickson note, 'It is as well to recognise that informal organisation is not "bad", as they are sometimes assumed to be' (1964: 559). As it is fruitless to try to destroy it, management's task is to achieve a greater harmony between the informal and formal organisation. This can be done through controlled participation, effective communication and socially skilled, humane supervision. Referring to the experience of one of the Hawthorne experimental groups, Mayo commented that, 'Before every change of program, the group is consulted. Their comments are listened to and discussed; sometimes their objections are allowed to negative a suggestion. The group undoubtedly develops a sense of participation in the critical determination and becomes something of a social unit' (quoted in Baritz, 1960: 88–9).

As an alternative managerial *tactic* this makes a lot of sense, indeed a minority of British employers were reaching similar conclusions (G. Brown, 1977: 243). Today, it is applied in a new and more sophisticated way in current Japanese management techniques (see Chapter 6). The problem arises from how Mayo and the human relations tradition theorised their understanding of Hawthorne. They were determined to fashion a general theory of behaviour in organisations. Later management theorists have dubbed a key element of this approach 'social man' (Schein, 1965). For Mayo, this started from a critique of the so-called 'rabble hypothesis' he attributed to economists and management theorists such as Taylor; in which individuals act solely according to rational self-interest. In contrast, 'social man' proceeds from the assumption that the major human need is for social solidarity which can be satisfied through group association. Naturally, this plays down the role of economic incentives. Such associations are seen to create social routines which substitute for logical and individual self-interest. Mayo preferred the term 'non-logical' to 'irrational', but the essential message is clear: workers act according to sentiments and emotions.

Contrary to some accounts, he did not believe that management was by definition and contrast rational, for all individuals were held to be governed by the same abstract instincts and needs. Rather managers and administrators could *become* rational, precisely because they can free themselves from social routines and the accompanying emotional involvements. This is an extremely curious notion, as any analysis of management shows that it has *its own* routines and 'illogicalities'. But it indicates the uncritical attitude of human relation's writers towards the economic élites. Interestingly the new theorists of corporate culture (see Chapter 7) manage to maintain the emphasis on emotions, symbolism and 'irrationality' without separating management and workforce in the same way.

It must also be said that the empirical basis for Mayo's assertions in the Hawthorne experience is very shaky. Group solidarity was carefully engineered through the selection and treatment of those workers involved, even to the point of replacing 'un-cooperative' workers. Even this did not sustain co-operative activity. Mayo interpreted restriction of output as a combination of group sentiments and lack of trust in management. But there are alternative and simpler explanations: 'Restriction of output by voluntary norms was a rational response by primarily economically orientated agents to the increasingly likely prospect of unemployment' (Clegg and Dunkerley, 1980: 131). Environmental influences on employee attitudes were recognised, but it was held that the consequences could be dealt with and 'adjusted' inside the enterprise.

The denial of economic factors led to some absurd psychologisms. Mayo used the curious term 'pessimistic reveries' to account for industrial unrest of any kind. Put another way, strikes and other actions that restrict output are obsessive preoccupations and signs of maladjustment, even to the point of identifying industrial unrest with mental breakdown and casting trade union leaders as psychological deviants! Not surprisingly, unions very rarely get mentioned in Mayo's writings. That did not stop later followers. The psychologist McMurry argued that not only were unions unnecessary when management acted fairly, but that workers joined unions not to protect their jobs and improve pay, but because of unconscious cravings to improve the emotional situation at work (Baritz, 1960: 175).

It would, however, be misleading to view human relations theory through its excesses. To add to 'social man', a second highly influential level of theorisation emphasised the essentially co-operative nature of the enterprise. In fact, the two were linked, as Mayo continually referred to the supposed eager desire of workers for co-operative activity. It is easy to dismiss this kind of analysis, particularly given the capacity of human relations researchers systematically to ignore or re-interpret conflictual processes. But they *had* identified significant changes in the socio-economic sphere that brought the issue of co-operation to the fore. They pointed to the disparity between the attention paid to technical efficiency and economic functions, and the absence of 'the development of skills and techniques for securing co-operation' (Roethlisberger and Dickson, 1964: 552). The need to improve the latter was especially important because, as Mayo recognised, the balance between technical and social skills had been disrupted as workers' traditional forms of craft socialisation and identity had been undermined by mechanisation and the assembly line.

Emphasis is therefore put on the role of management to use the formal organisation to intervene in the *informal*, so as to create and sustain consent. Only in this context can we understand what appears to be the superficial solutions of human relations practices, with their prescriptions of 'democratic' supervision, good communications, teamwork and socially skilled leadership. Mayo's 'lifelong obsession with social harmony' (M. Rose, 1975: 115), was not based merely on his distorted empirical observations, but was underwritten by an organic model of society in which equilibrium and stability are the natural order of things, while structural divisions and conflicts are pathological. Mayo was worried about the 'extensive maladjustment of our times' as a period of rapid change undermined values and atomised individuals. The task was to recreate a sense of community inside the workplace, a call we are again hearing from advocates of corporate culture.

During the same period, Chester Barnard, the President of the New Jersey Bell Telephone Company, was developing an even heavier emphasis on the basis for human co-operation, that was to have a major impact on later mainstream theorists (Perrow, 1979). Co-operation necessary to the survival of society could be most clearly observed in organisations. Unequal power and resources were irrelevant against the 'fact' that individuals voluntarily entered and submitted themselves to a common goal unachievable without collective effort. Organisations were rational and individuals were not. But, like Mayo, his virtual deification of the formal organisation still reserved the key role for management. The rationality of the 'non-personal' organisation was in practice again located with the executive élite, who, as decision-makers, had responsibility for what Peters and Waterman, in praising Barnard, describe as 'managing the values of the organisation' (1982: 26). For co-ordination was still required to *make* a system, particularly as a sense of common purpose was not always present amongst the 'lower participants'. Barnard therefore reinforced the emphasis, not just on co-operation, but on the balance of formal and informal. As Perrow points out, this is the most extreme identification with the formal organisation, devoid of any concern for the negative effects of power and domination, or even the stress in human relations theory on sympathetic supervision and controlled participation.

Consolidating human relations

Recognising the significance of co-operative activity was an advance, but it was wrong to transfer the analysis from the work-group to the organisation as a whole. The fundamental contradiction at the heart of human relations theory and of Barnard is that co-operation, even of the 'spontaneous' kind, has to be created. Reed refers to an intellectual schizophrenia whereby, 'a theoretical framework is forced to reconcile the contradictions generated by a metaphysic that assumes collective moral consensus as a social given and at the same time advocates the adoption of techniques whereby this may be engineered' (1985: 6). There is therefore a wide consensus among the critics we have discussed that the significance of the tradition is to be located in its *ideological appeal*. M. Rose (1975: 124) puts this most succinctly in his memorable comment that Mayoism is the twentieth century's most seductive managerial ideology in which social scientists and managers fashioned each other in their own image.

There is a great deal of accuracy in the view that one of its major functions was to legitimate the power and authority of both emergent professional 'classes' of managers and industrial consultants. The problem is that such an analysis can slip into giving the impression that human relations was a gigantic, if dangerous, con-trick with no purchase on reality. In part the reverse is true, for it only makes sense as a reaction to and means of shaping new realities. The depth of economic and political crisis meant that, 'by the 1930s corporate America felt under siege' (Neimark and Tinker, 1986: 25). Congress had passed corporatist legislation allowing companies greater control over markets and pricing in return for acceptance of codes governing minimum wages and maximum hours, plus guarantees of union membership and collective bargaining rights. In addition, the country was experiencing a huge strike wave of sit-down strikes and factory occupations. Large corporations bitterly resisted the 'New Deal' institutions and the union organising drive. But the more perceptive of them, also realised that, 'the crisis generated critical problems of social control and legitimation for management' (Boreham, 1980: 25). A second front was opened, drawing extensively on the human relations package of better communication, democratic leadership, co-operation and social integration. This went hand-in-hand with early versions of the managerial revolution thesis, General Motors claiming that the organisation was a community of stakeholders for which management was a trustee.

The success of strikes and union organising drives only consolidated a recognition of the importance of consent and attention to employee attitudes in the more general writings of human relations theorists, such as T. N. Whitehead in his *Leadership in a Free Society* (1936). Despite the weakness of the tradition in Britain, Whitehead's book was well received in progressive management circles worried about the changing position of business in a more democratic community. Human relations was able to provide greater legitimation of management authority than Taylor, because it went beyond the narrow confines of 'science' and formal organisation to address issues more in tune with the times. But it would not have made the same impact merely as a body of ideas. It had to help generate new *practices*.

Though it was still confined to a minority of even the largest employers throughout the 1930s, Bendix, Baritz and other researchers show that an increasing number of firms such as General Electric, General Motors and Proctor and Gamble, developed programmes influenced by human relations theory. The Hawthorne researchers had put considerable emphasis on 'personnel work' in its broadest sense of 'adequate diagnosis and under-standing of the actual human situations – both individual and group – within the factory' (Roethlisberger and Dickson, 1964: 591). With this background, greater consideration was given in many large companies to the training of managers and supervisors in the arts of intensive communication, social skills, and non-authoritarian leadership that would motivate as well as command. Personnel departments grew further, alongside more use of attitude surveys. General Motors managed to combine them neatly with spying on union activists, by employing Pinkerton detectives to carry out the tests! As previously, the war acted as a spur, large companies and the state finding the use of tests an invaluable means of dealing with the problems associated with the sudden employment of thousands of new workers. Despite a sustained attack by more critical academics, the diverse applications and effects of human relations theorus had established a bridgehead for the social sciences in industry, and, by the 1940s the movement had gained substantial institutional support (Barley and Kunda, 1992: 374).

Conclusion and evaluation

Back to the future?

This chapter is not intended as a history lesson. We have already referred to the danger of linear models which conceive of management theory and practice as self-contained models and eras swept away by over-hyped 'revolutions' in thinking and doing. Rather our concern has been to show how organisational theories draw from and allow us to explore the real emergence of complex, large-scale industrial organisations. Future chapters will discuss how this relationship has evolved, but in this final section, we want to provide some links between the two by briefly considering the practical and theoretical legacies left by the two major traditions of scientific management and human relations.

It is easier to start with what we have just left. The 1950s saw the relationship between social science and industry blossom still further, facilitated both by the development of OB and related disciplines in business schools specialising in the human side of the enterprise, and the training of middle and senior executives in leadership and management development (Barley and Kunda, 1992: 375). Rhetorical claims, however, foundered on a failure to demonstrate an exact and direct relationship between theory and practice. Perrow, for example, has written sceptically of the 'thirty year history of the effort to link morale and leadership to productivity' (1979: 97). Nor were the practices or solutions necessarily any less superficial than Hawthorne. Bendix (1956: 326–7) remarks that the National Association of Manufacturer's new-found attachment to 'two-way communication' was based on the assumption that employers relayed *facts* to the workforce to promote co-operation, whereas what workers say is *information* which management can use to 'eliminate misunderstandings'.

Despite the re-rise of harder managerial 'sciences' such as operations research and systems analysis, human relations approaches did not disappear. The body of research and to a lesser extent practical intervention moved on to new topics such as leadership styles and group dynamics. Whatever limits there may have been to its ideas and results, the human relations current continued to provide, in Bendix's words, a *vocabulary of motivation*. This term is particularly appropriate, given that the primary theoretical means of grappling with the 'human factor' moved onto the terrain associated with more sophisticated behavioural science techniques and issues centred on motivation and the school of psychology consolidated around figures such as Maslow, McGregor and Herzberg, who explored the full implications for management of responding to all members of organisations as a human resources (see Chapters 8 and 10 for further discussion). But the earlier human relations tradition, which had laid dormant and often abused for its naïvety suddenly became fashionable again in the 1980s. In particular, the influence of Japanese management techniques, with their emphasis on teamwork, work-groups and corporate cultures, brought human relations back into focus. That story is told in Chapters 6 and 7.

The legacy of Taylorism has been more disputed. Long reviled for its apparent barbarity and economism, scientific management was brought out of the broom cupboard by the radical theorist Braverman (1974). The argument that Taylorism constituted *the* means of managerial control in the twentieth century (see Chapter 4 for details) has been shown to be exaggerated, but there is plenty of evidence that key elements of the system have been updated and extended. Ossie Jone's (1994) entertaining account of life as a work study engineer in the 1970s and 1980s shows how the traditional techniques of method and time study were superseded by a system known as Simplified Pre-Determined Motion Time Study (SPMTS). This is merely one of a long line of innovations throughout the century. SPMTS was favoured by the engineers and would have delighted Taylor, in that it promised the illusion of the removal of the 'subjective' element of rating from work measurement. Such developments may not convince all the sceptics, given that they admittedly focus on a narrow, if well-known feature of scientific management. More convincing is the rise of the latest US management fix, business re-engineering or core process redesign, whose tools – activity value analysis, time compression management and so on – and ethos are clearly rooted in Taylorism and classical theories (Thackray, 1993). We shall pick up this story again in Chapter 6. But we should not get contemporary developments out of proportion. The lesson of *this* chapter remains. Taylorism and other management theories are not packages, and, given the separable nature of their elements, any practical legacy will be diverse and uneven. Furthermore, the history of large-scale organisations shows that managers combine elements of different approaches according to perceived need and fashion. The respective traditions embody a permanent tension between different approaches to the management of work organisation. Although this is frequently described in mainstream writing as technical and human organisation and the need to integrate the two, it may be thought of more accurately in terms of competing control systems. For example, in their historical survey of US managerial discourse, Barley and Kunda (1992) distinguish between rational (for example, scientific management, systems theories) and normative (for example, human relations, organisational culture) ideologies of control. Rather than one simply displacing another, there are successive and alternate waves paralleling broad cycles of economic expansion and contraction. Impressive as their schema is, like most organisational theory, it is derived from US experience. To round off this chapter, we want to make some brief qualifications to this tendency.

Beyond the American model

We have, during this chapter, pointed to a number of sources of variation in the way that Taylorism and the human relations tradition developed across and within various units – sectors, countries, companies – shaped by the requirements of cultural and other forms of adaptation and pressures of resistance from key actors. However, this framework still tends to assume models that arise and are adapted to at given stages along a single line of development. Chandler's account of the rise of the 'modern' integrated business enterprise can be used to illustrate the general argument. He does give a historically-informed explanation of the emergence of the phenomena. In general terms the USA was a seed-bed for managerial capitalism primarily because of the size and the nature of the domestic market (Chandler, 1977: 498–500). It was not only faster growing than other nations, but more open and less class-divided. This encouraged the techniques and technologies of mass production and distribution. In contrast, domestic markets in Western Europe were smaller and with slower growth. This limited the same kind of developments and kept greater reliance on middlemen to handle goods. Even where integrated enterprises did appear, they often remained small enough to be dominated by owner-managers. This kind of reasoning allows Chandler to evaluate other national experiences against this standard. British entrepreneurs are said to have failed to invest in manufacturing, marketing and management in key capital-intensive industries. As a consequence this 'personal capitalism', dependent on atomistic economic organisation such as the single-plant family firms in industries such as cotton and steel, was a pale version of its US counterpart: 'neglecting investment in administrative capabilities and research, dogged by short-termism, preoccupied with family and personal management, prejudiced against salaried managers, determined to ensure a steady income stream rather than to maximise growth and profits in the long run' (Supple, 1991: 511).

This account of stunted organisational capabilities makes an attractive link to *institutionalist* explanations for Britain's declining economic performance. Such frameworks point to factors which shaped industrial development: entrenched employee job controls; the separation of the banking system from the finance of industry; and educational provision that failed to provide adequately trained managerial and technical staff. As a result, managerial structures and expertise were underdeveloped and 'the British only adapted patchwork improvements to their existing organisational and productive structure' (Elbaum and Lazonick, 1986: 7). Echoes of such explanations can be found today in critics of short-termism and institutional failure in Britain's political economy, such as Will Hutton's influential *Guardian* columns. But the remit is much broader than Chandler's 'internal history' of business enterprise. In emphasising the role of educational, state, legal and other institutions, such writers can demonstrate variations in industrial development.

It can also be argued that given the similarities between financial and industrial systems the UK and the USA, Chandler's model of management and enterprise is even less likely to apply to other European countries. Modern American, or perhaps Anglo–Saxon, conceptions of management are built on assumptions of the superiority of a *general science* of co-ordination and control, a profession of management above particular specialisms and functions (Fores *et al.*, 1992). In comparison, the Franco–German tradition draws on quite different sources. For example, Rueschemeyer (1986) notes the significance of public administration as a bureaucratic model for private enterprise in Germany, while the French state has developed vocationally-orientated higher education to produce generations of technocrats for the private and public sector. Germany and a number of other countries also have a tradition of engineering-based technical competence as the base for industrial progress.

If the form and content of large-scale organisations is socially constructed, Supple's comments on Chandler have more general application: 'What his assumptions make it difficult to do, however, is to generalise his results to a rounded and substantial exploration of the interrelationships and evolution of economic systems generally' (1991: 510). Beyond Europe, this lesson is even more pertinent. Japan has received considerable academic attention for its distinctive forms of ownership and management. For example, in the influential corporate form of *keiretsu*, units are part of vertically organised enterprise groups clustered around a dominant company or companies. Interlinked shareholdings involving subcontractors and banks establish stability and mutual interest in the long-term success of the group, the joint risk-taking and access to capital avoiding the short-termism associated with the Anglo–Saxon model (G. Henderson, 1993: 38–9). Crucially, this risk-taking is also shared with the *state*, as in the well-known example of co-ordination of economic development through the Ministry of International Trade and Industry (MITI).

Such involvement is frequently a characteristic feature of *late industrialisation*. In Japan the commercial class was marginal to early industrialisation and the state was the primary agent in mobilising capital and mediating market forces (Littler, 1982). But the primary example of state-sponsored development is in Korea. Conglomerate enterprise groups, known as *chaebol*, are both directed and disciplined by the state through financial controls, subsidies and incentives. For example, following the bankruptcy of the leading cement producer in the 1970s, the South Korean government transferred its production facilities to another chaebol (Amsden, 1992: 15). This pattern has been repeated continually in the immensely successful restructuring process that has made the country into one of the fastest growing in the world. But the state is not the only manager of the industrialisation process. As Amsden (1992: 9) shows, 'Salaried engineers are a key figure in late industrialisation because they are the gatekeepers of foreign technology transfers'. With Korean firms choosing specialised engineers over administrators, we have a further example of different forms of enterprise management within managerial capitalism. Family ownership is a key dimension of South Korea's corporate structures and familism has been a further characteristic of some East Asian economies, particularly Taiwan and Hong Kong. Family business, particularly among overseas Chinese, operates according to particular lineage and inheritance rules, which, in turn, shape how businesses grow, given that a wider sharing of trust is constrained by the familial form. More importantly for our purposes, the forms of co-ordination and direction of the enterprise are necessarily distinctive: 'there is strong patrimonial and personalistic direct control, rather than on the more impersonalised, formalised and standardised control of the rational-bureaucratic model which we are familiar with from the West' (Clegg, 1990: 164).

Despite the success of the East Asian economies, we are not suggesting that these factors are the only or even main path to success. After all, there are substantial differences between those economies, as well as common contrasts to 'Western' models, highlighting the need for a comparative analysis of management structures and practices (Whitley, 1992a). In other words, the example demonstrates our final theme, that socially constructed organisational diversities are the proper object of analysis for organisational theory.

This is not a minor point. Measuring organisations and change against a single, linear standard rears its misleading head again later, this time with Japanese management replacing the American model. One of the recurring weaknesses that underpin this kind of thinking is an absence of or inadequate means to conceptualise organisations in their environments. This is the theme of the next chapter.

CHAPTER 3

Organisations and environments

The previous chapter provided plenty of evidence that the contexts in which organisations operate, whether they be the rise of monopoly capitalism, the ups and downs of the trade cycle, or political circumstances such as the American New Deal in the 1930s, profoundly shape their nature and development. But does this figure prominently in conventional organisational theory? Salaman argues that it does not:

> The society in which these organisations occur, and its relation with these organisations, has been very little studied. To the extent that the outside world does impinge on the structure and functioning of organisations, it is conceptualised not in terms of interests, values, class loyalties, ideologies, market developments etc., but as the organisation's 'environment'. (1979: 32)

Given that 'environment' can be taken to mean external conditions which encompass all the above, there is nothing in principle distinctive or problematic with the concept. That, however, is the problem. The criticism being made by Salaman and others is that the dominant readings of 'environment' lack substance: they are diffuse and fail to specify the local, national and systemic contexts in which organisations are located. This chapter traces those readings and discusses the issues they raise. It then fills in the gaps left by orthodox accounts, notably the new transnational context and actors; as well as the changing nature of the state in capitalist societies. Finally, we pose the question of how organisational theory should think comparatively in a world in which the environment is increasingly shaped by a global political economy. More recent and promising developments in organisational theory will be examined as part of this process, notably neo-institutional perspectives that see the firm as embedded in networks of institutional relationships that have different configurations across societies (Hamilton and Biggart, 1988; Whitely, 1992a).

This is all a long way from early organisational theory. It is conventional wisdom to argue that classical and other perspectives took no account of the environment. Instead they were concerned with manipulating the internal variables of an organisation in the service of goal attainment. Specific emphasis tended to be put on the development of rules or principles maximising the rational and efficient application of resources embodied in work design and other aspects of formal structure. Because this treats organisations as self-sufficient entities, or systems in and of themselves, it has been retrospectively dubbed *closed systems theory* (see Clegg and Dunkerley, 1980: 191–6). Human relations theory, too, has been criticised for suspending the firm in a social vacuum and ignoring the degree to which its problems were results of outside pressures (Albrow, 1973: 406). This is somewhat unfair. Researchers such as Mayo, Roethlisberger and Dickson did recognise the effects on employees from membership of wider collectivities, such as communities. The problem was more that they and their less discriminating followers tended to believe that the *solutions* could be found through internal adjustment.

If anything, the supposedly more sophisticated neo-human relations perspectives of Maslow, Herzberg and others were more guilty of closed system thinking. Their emphasis on a model of universal psychological needs that, once identified by the intelligent manager, could be harnessed through new forms of organisational design, completely isolated the individual and the firm from social structures (see Chapters 5 and 7 for further discussion). Since the 1960s, closed system approaches have largely been frowned upon. However, that does not mean that they have gone away, for two reasons. First, the focus remains overwhelmingly on the *individual* organisation and there is a tendency for theorists to highlight internal and predictable goals–means relationships that can operate as a 'buffer' to the environment (R. H. Hall, 1977). Second, the popular management search for a magical ingredient for organisational success which can be internally controlled also increases the likelihood of a constant reworking or accommodation to a closed system approach. A prominent recent example is the fashionable concern for organisational culture expressed through the writings of Peters and Waterman (1982) and their many imitators on both sides of the Atlantic.

Peters and Waterman utilise a schema derived from W. R. Scott (1978) in which four stages of theory proceed through closed system/rational actor (Weber/Taylor); closed system/social actor (human relations of all kinds); rational actor/open system (for example, Lawrence and Lorsch, see later); to the favoured open system/social actor. We have already argued in Chapter 1 that the authors do not depart significantly from a rational model, and would make a similar point with reference to closed systems. The whole selling point of the excellence genre is that the strategy and structure themes discussed in this chapter are out, and culture, style, symbols and values are in (see Chapter 7 for a more detailed assessment). Successful companies are those that create and manage a distinctive culture that satisfies employees and customers alike. If we examine their four elements of new theory (Peters and Waterman, 1979: 102) – people's needs for meaning, elements of control, positive reinforcement, and behaviour determinant of belief – they are largely psychologistic in character. The cultural solution is secured *within* the organisation.

Now this is admittedly not the whole picture. The environment *is* recognised through the notion that successful companies emerge through purposeful, though unpredictable, evolution. Though the Darwinian imagery of experiment and evolution is invoked, the message is simple. Companies survive and stay fit and well, by adapting to their environment. It appears that the essence of that environment is the customer. The logic is that successful companies are those that have a large market share, long-term growth and high profits. They have adapted to the (customer) environment. Success is therefore simply read-off from a diffuse concept of the environment. But we are still returned to internal organisational processes, for what made them successful in the first place, 'was usually a culture that encouraged action, experiments, repeated tries' (1982: 114). This is what Peters and Waterman mean by 'intentionally seeded evolution within companies'.

One final point needs to be made about closed systems. The use of the term 'systems' is not accidental. Mainstream writing has been dominated by varieties of *systems theory*, though greatly extending and modifying early conceptions. Organisations are systems of interrelated parts or sub-units – for example departments, groups and individuals – each functioning to mobilise resources towards meeting wider goals. These parts are at the same time differentiated and interdependent, aiding processes of integration and co-ordination. Systems theory is therefore an explanation of the pattern of functioning of organisations in terms of inputs, outputs and transformations, encompassing the variety of social, psychological and technical variables.

A crucial development, however, has been the acceptance of the importance of interaction with the environment, for the survival of an organisation depends on its capacity to adapt to markets, technologies and other situations. Even the description 'closed system' is partly a label of convenience, true only to the extent that the organisation as a whole and the relation between its parts (technical and social, different departments and functions) could be seen as itself analogous to system–environment relations. True systems theory is open and adaptive in character and we need to spell this out in more detail.

Adaptation theories

There are a number of different approaches and types of research that treat organisations in terms of adaptation and as open systems. But before considering them in detail, we need briefly to examine basic assumptions concerning who is adapting and what are they adapting to? Systems theory is multi-layered. At its simplest, this can be expressed as society–organisation–sub-unit (for example, department). As D. Elliot (1980: 96) notes:

> This boundary can be drawn anywhere for the purpose of analysis. If the system one is studying is the whole organisation then the boundary is between the organisation and its environment; if the system being studied is the work group, then the boundary is between this group and the rest of the organisation, which in this case is its environment.

But most writers treat the organisation itself as the system, and although the wider environment determines the general goals such as economic survival in a stimulus-response manner, the environment still tends to be defined in terms of the single unit of organisation. As Hannan and Freeman note, 'In the adaptation perspective, subunits of the organisation, usually managers or dominant coalitions, scan the relevant environment for opportunities and threats, formulate strategic responses, and adjust organisational structure appropriately' (1977: 929–30).

Although organisations are frequently seen as adapting to *the* environment, this is qualified and filled out by many writers. Mullins (1985: 12) claims that organisations are viewed in their total environment. Unfortunately this does not mean that they are situated within a coherent totality, but rather that lists of multiple influences are provided. John Child (1969) in examining a variety of classification schemes, notes that some use a narrow conception of *task* environment, based largely on economic factors such as customers, suppliers, competitors and self-regulating groups (for example, Dill, 1962). Child prefers a broader categorisation which takes in product markets, factor markets, technical knowledge and political and socio-cultural factors (for example, communities, social memberships and values). An even wider and influential set of factors is employed by R. H. Hall (1977): technological, legal, economic, political, demographic, cultural and ecological. A realistic analysis of the contexts of organisations take such factors into account. But in practice, as we shall see later, most research has tended to focus on the narrower frame, particularly on markets and technology.

Open systems

The most well-known adaptation perspective is the open system approach pioneered by J. D. Thompson (1967) and Katz and Kahn (1970). As indicated earlier, the starting point is the need for the organisation to transact with the environment – more specifically, to take inputs from the environment and convert them into outputs. The operation of the system in markets, and among other organisations, gives essential feedback about its performance measured by realisation of corporate goals. Attention is particularly given to achieving a proper balance of system parts. This would involve integration, co-ordination and differentiation of structures and processes, not just functions such as production or research, but activities of leadership, innovation and the like. It would be wrong to give the impression that these 'boundary exchanges' are characterised by smoothness. Though the organisation generally adapts and finds an equilibrium by responding to opportunities and risks in the environment, a central concept of open systems is that of *uncertainty* and related terms: stability, turbulence or indeterminacy. This uncertainty can arise in relations with the environment itself, through clashes with surrounding cultures, or rapidity of technological change; or internally in the organisation's members or sub-units. The interdependence of the system parts includes a measure of specialisation specifically to deal with this problem: 'we suggest that organisations cope with uncertainty by creating certain parts specifically to deal with it, specialising other parts in operating under conditions of certainty, or near certainty' (J. D. Thompson, 1967: 13).

An early conceptualisation of the conditions of uncertainty was the emphasis of Emery and Trist (1965) on the significance of the *causal texture* of environments. They developed ideal types ranging from a placid/randomised environment through to a turbulent one. The key differentiating feature is seen as the interrelationship of parts of the environment. Where they are causally interconnected in a complex and changing way, this increases turbulence and can inhibit or encourage different types of action by the organisation. For example, a government might suddenly introduce new rules under which a state industry has to open up a proportion of its tenders to foreign companies. This provokes considerable turbulence in the product markets affecting their traditional suppliers, which is also connected to major changes in the rate of technological advance. This is roughly what happened in the telecommunications industry in the early 1980s (Thompson and Bannon, 1985). The categories used by Emery and Trist are now regarded as rather outdated. More recent approaches are summarised by John Child (1984). From open systems research (which will be examined later under contingency theory), he identifies *variability* and *complexity* as key processes. 'Variability' refers to the difficulty of predicting changes and departures from previous conditions that will induce uncertainty. 'Complexity' is linked to the degree of diversity in organisational activities and the environments the organisation is operating in. This may mean difficulty in gathering and monitoring information necessary for effective performance. Each organisation needs to design the structures or processes in a manner which reduces uncertainty or adapts to the degree of environmental stability.

Aside from uncertainty, the other major factor shaping boundary exchanges is held to be *dependency*. Indeed, these factors may be linked: for example, when dependency takes an intra-organisational form, whereby the ability of sub-units to cope with uncertainty is shaped by the degree to which a sub-unit's activities are central, substitutable, or by when it relies on others (Hickson *et al.*, 1973). Outside the organisation, dependency is conditioned by the fact that the environment is a source of scarce resources which have to be competed for. Dependency is the reverse of power, 'As the resources increase or expand the organisation increases in power . . . since other organisations become more dependent on the resources' (Clegg and Dunkerley, 1980: 381). These issues have stimulated the development of the *resource dependency* model (Aldrich and Pfeffer, 1976) which draws on the broader *exchange theory* (Blau, 1964).

Organisations exchange with each other and negotiate the environment, seeking to exert power over the nature and rate of exchange. The goal of each actor in the exchange is to reduce its dependency on the other and to force the 'partner' to become more dependent on it. The concept of resource dependency becomes a way of understanding power relationships more generally, which we shall discuss in Chapter 4. But in terms of the environment, a classic case is the 'Just-in-Time' system used to control the flow of stocks and materials between large corporations and suppliers in Japan. It works on the basis that small sub-contractors are flexible on the terms of their larger 'partners'. Toyota, for example, relies on 35 000 small businesses, which are mostly in a totally dependent relationship. Or, organisations may minimise dependency by seeking alternative sources. This can be seen in the 'world car' strategy pursued by Ford and GM. By co-ordinating design, production and marketing across national boundaries, companies can ensure that components can be acquired from a considerably larger number of locations.

There is a danger of constantly talking as if organisations were 'things' adapting to the environment. However, in practice, open systems theory gives a central role to *management* to maximise a bounded rationality – in other words, to predict and design appropriate structures and responses and to manipulate resources and sub-units effectively. To some extent these processes depend on the access to and nature of information. Uncertainty affects the perceptions of managements and increases the likelihood of them maintaining flexible structures and methods. In a recent study, Newman and Newman go as far as claiming claim that, 'Information is that which destroys uncertainty' (1986: 503). Large organisations do not necessarily have stable control over their environments and the consequent management of diverse activities drives the growth of information work. To avoid information overload, top management requires assistance in using filtering mechanisms, for example 'technology' such as Decision Support Systems. The aim of such mechanisms is to make decisions about alternative courses of action take place under conditions of calculable risk rather than uncertainty.

This highlights the connection of environmental uncertainty and dependency to issues of *decision-making*, which has long been a significant aspect of research literature (March and Simon, 1958, Cyert and March, 1963). Because of unevenness in the informational, technological and other environmental conditions, and in internal power relations between sub-units, decision-makers frequently have to cope by forming *dominant coalitions* (J. D. Thompson, 1967). As a result, 'Organisational decision-making becomes much less a matter of unquestioned command or rational appraisal and much more a process of political bargaining and negotiation in which the exercise of power plays a key role' (Reed, 1985: 41–2). The positive aspect of this type of thinking is that it begins to see the organisation in a more pluralistic light, with some, albeit limited, recognition of power, bargaining and change processes. Given that dominant coalitions have to exert choice about alternative actions, it also qualifies the emphasis in systems theory on structures as functional imperatives arising from given environmental conditions (Child, 1972).

Open-systems theory has also been extended by the development of the concept of *socio-technical systems*, particularly associated with Trist and the work of the Tavistock Institute (Trist *et al.*, 1963). Primarily it is a way of identifying the key sub-systems and the relations between them in the 'conversion' process. Three sub-systems are identified: technical, formal role structure and sentient (individual feelings or sentiments). Working broadly within the human relations problematic of integrating the formal/technical and informal/social dimensions of organisation, an additional twist is given by putting greater emphasis on the technological environment. This environment of the work-group, in the form of equipment and lay-out, is seen as a basic constraint on the shape of work organisation. However, it does not simply reflect the technology, as the organisation has independent social and psychological properties. Management's task is to create a socio-technical system in which the two dimensions are jointly optimised and mutually supportive. There is some choice at the organisational level, but there are defined limits set by the need for 'economic validity'.

Research support has been particularly associated with Trist and Bamforth's (1951) study of the mining industry. Traditional methods of 'hand-getting' the coal had involved limited technology, short coalfaces, high work-group autonomy over the pace and distribution of work, and an egalitarian ethos. New 'longwall' methods bore similarities to mass production, with work fragmentation and more specific job roles. Not surprisingly this led to lower work commitments, higher absenteeism and a host of other standard problems. The researchers' solution was to accept the technology and lay-out, but to change the method of work to a 'composite' approach in which groups performed whole tasks, were paid collective bonuses and had a degree of self-regulation over job allocation. The results convinced them that management choice could be exercised in favour of methods which took greater care of socio-psychological needs, while accepting economic and technical constraints. Working within a similar framework, Miller and Rice (1967) were less optimistic about the capacity to match task and sentient systems, given that the latter can encourage attachment to routines which inhibit technological innovation and the 'primary task' of profit-making.

Like their human relations predecessors, the Tavistock writers adopt a unitary and socially harmonious view of the enterprise, taking for granted that the primary task is shared by all. This is also consistent with that tradition in taking technical and formal structures for granted, the difference lying in the language of management choice rather than worker adjustment. As Rose notes, once the above constraints have been accepted, even that choice is within strictly determined managerial limits, and 'the socio-technical systems concept may be seen as a device for helping production engineers to discover better "best ways"' (M. Rose, 1975: 216). For Trist and his associates, worker's choices are seen as non-existent in the face of a determinate environment. Resistance to management plans run up against 'uncontrollable forces in the external environment' (quoted in M. Rose, 1975: 216). In fact the mining study hardly utilised the wider environment in the analysis at all. Where the environment is mentioned, it is that of the 'seam society' immediately surrounding the work-group.

Contingency theory

The most noted application and extension of the open systems approach is grouped under the heading of 'contingency theory'. As Reed puts it; 'Eventually the theoretical developments taking place within the systems tradition culminated in a "contingency theory" of organisation which attempted to specify the appropriate "functional fit" between environmental settings and the internal organisational structures which they required' (1985: 100). In terms of the ideas discussed so far in this chapter, this does not sound very remarkable. Its appeal, however, is in part because of a powerful *normative* dimension, in which the emphasis is on practical applications (Legge, 1978). A situational approach requires a 'reading' of the firm's environment by managers and their academic helpers. Furthermore it appealed because the 'if-then' formula constituted an explicit break with the 'one best way' orientation of existing theories, while retaining powerful guidelines for what power-holders should actually do to sustain effective organisation. By the mid-1970s contingency theory was the dominant approach and had been applied to specifics such as payment systems as well as to general structures (Lupton and Gowler, 1969).

Curiously, as a theory it rested primarily on research that took place largely prior to its own development. The most noted was that of Burns and Stalker (1961), who studied twenty firms in Scotland and England drawn mainly from the textile, engineering and electronics industries. Management systems and structures were classified according to a range of environments differentiated by degree of predictability and stability. They found that firms operating in an environment with relatively stable and predictable markets, and to a lesser extent technologies, such as those in textiles, tended to have what they called *mechanistic* systems. This broadly resembled bureaucratic models where there is centralised knowledge, clear hierarchy, task specialisation, vertical communication, and a general emphasis on formal structures, decision-making, values and rules. By contrast, in environments where there is more rapid change, uncertain markets, and complex technologies with a requirement for constant innovation, such as in electronics, a more *organic* system predominated, that was less bound by traditional structures and roles. Instead, though structures remained within a general hierarchy, they utilised dispersed information centres; lateral communication; meritocratic and expert positioning, ethos and practices; and more flexible tasks and rules.

Rather than getting embroiled in arguments for and against bureaucracy or any structural arrangements, Burns and Stalker were able to argue that both systems were suitable and rational for specific market-led situations. Successful companies were precisely ones which had adapted their strengths to environmental requirements. They did recognise that they were discussing ideal types and that relationships were not rigid. Organisations facing changes in the environment may have to move along the spectrum or mix particular characteristics. Though this is normally less noted, Burns and Stalker also recognised constraints to changing structures away from mechanistic models, even where it was environmentally desirable. These arose particularly from entrenched interests and routines, consolidated through the operation of internal political systems (Wood, 1979: 353).

The American writers Lawrence and Lorsch (1967) extended this type of analysis by showing that it is wrong to treat firms as homogeneous structures. Sub-units are likely to have different environments and therefore require specific structures and management in order to be successful. As a result, a crucial problem for the organisation is finding a balance of differentiation and integration. Their research was based on a smaller number of firms in plastics, food and containers. So, for example, whereas the research departments of the plastic's companies operated in dynamic, innovative environments that were reflected in long-term orientations and the least bureaucratic arrangements, production had a stable, technical environment and was dominated by short-term concerns and more bureaucracy. Sales departments were somewhere in between. High performing firms were those that not only manifested a high degree of differentiation of structures and goals but had coped by developing adequate means of integration, such as specialist teams with responsibility for integrating diverse activities. Of course, those organisations where the sub-units do not have to vary significantly can be co-ordinated through conventional command structures. As with Burns and Stalker, the emphasis is not on which theoretical model is 'out-of-date' but on a continuum of models suited to alternative environments.

The final piece of notable contingency research by Woodward (1958, 1965) shifts the emphasis away from market environments to *technology*. She started the research as a means of testing traditional propositions popular in administrative theory, such as relation between formal structures or size and performance. But in studies of around 100 firms in South East Essex in the mid-1950s, no consistent correlations were found. Instead, a relationship between 'technological complexity' and organisational structure was claimed. Technologies were grouped developmentally according to supposed complexity under a variety of broad categories – eventually reduced to unit and small batch production, large batch and mass production, and process production. Woodward commented: 'While at first sight there seemed to be no link between organisation and success, and no one best way of organising a factory, it subsequently became apparent that there was a particular form of organisation most appropriate to each technical situation' (quoted in M. Rose, 1975: 203).

Among the aspects of formal organisation found to have a direct association with the technical production system were length of line of command, the extent of the span of control of chief executives and of supervisors, and the ratio of managers and clerical workers to production personnel. Problems of running organisations with different technologies varied. Unit and process technologies were both found to have little bureaucracy and simple organisational structures based on line specialisation of basic task functions. This is linked to the predominant problems of product development and marketing for such technologies, which put the emphasis on innovation. Woodward can be situated within a range of technological determinist writings popular in this period (Walker and Guest, 1952; Sayles, 1958; Blauner, 1964). As Michael Rose notes (1975: 202), such studies utilised fairly unsophisticated conceptions of technology as hardware and as the taken-for-granted physical aspect of production, with little or no recognition of social shaping or choice. In fact, there has been some disagreement over whether technology can be seen as part of an organisation's environment. As the dominant approaches have treated it as a factor 'out-there' determining the features of companies, it is perhaps justified to accept that it has to be discussed in that framework, without accepting its theoretical rationale.

One of the attractions of the theory generally is that any contingency can be posited as the key to structural variation and business performance. Hence *size* is seen as the major factor by some researchers such as the Aston Group (Pugh and Hickson, 1976) and Blau (1970). For the Aston researchers size was one of three primary contextual variables along with external dependency and technology. In turn, each predicts a series of structural variables: specialisation and standardisation, extent of concentration of authority, types of control over workflow. The Aston Group accepted the significance of technology in circumstances such as smaller companies or directly for production, but argued that increased size produced structural patterns based on impersonal control mechanisms, formal procedures, and higher numbers of administrative staff. Though there are associated problems, increased size also confers benefits through capacity to take advantage of specialisation. But the movement towards greater bureaucratisation is present in all three dimensions and it is a heavily deterministic logic where organisations, 'have to adapt to adapt in particular ways to the contextual or environmental constraints which face them' (Reed, 1992b: 137).

Donaldson (1985) mounts a strong defence of the research programme of which he was a part, while at the same time seeking to extend it. Design strategies are focused on the familiar territory of functional, divisional, area or mixed matrix structures. Strategy might appear to imply choice, but, 'The structure which is most appropriate for an organisation depends on the situational contingencies' (1985: 172). New formulas are developed, such as the adoption of functional or divisional arrangements depend on the extent to which product or area diversity establishes degrees of interdependency. For real choice to appear on the agenda, new conceptual frameworks are needed. We shall get there after examining the other major theorisation of organisation–environment relations.

Selection theories: the population ecology approach

The population ecology approach is a mainstream theory of organisation–environment relations that shifts the emphasis from adaptation to *selection* (Hannan and Freeman, 1977; Aldrich, 1979). In their seminal contribution, Hannan and Freeman do not deny that adaptation takes place, but argue that it is not primary and that there is limited evidence that 'the major features of the world of organisations arise through learning or adaptation' (1977: 957). In this sense, the perspective is more pessimistic about managerial capacity to rationally respond to external shifts. Change comes about largely through new organisations rather than internal transformation.

There are substantial constraints to organisations changing in order to adapt to the environment. For example, failing churches do not become retail stores and vice versa. Such constraints are based mainly on structural inertia, including non-transferable investments in resources and people; information blockages; the type of internal political systems identified by Burns and Stalker; conservative organisational ideologies and normative systems; plus external constraints such as legal, fiscal and political barriers. The stronger the process, the more the logic of environmental selection is likely to predominate over adaptation. A further criticism is of the emphasis on the single organisation as a focus of analysis. Instead the appropriate unit of analysis is taken to be populations of organisations; theoretical abstractions relating to classes of organisation that share some common features in terms of their relations with the environment.

What is this logic of environmental selection? Over a period of time, environments are held to select some organisations or classes of organisation for survival and others for extinction. Those that have survived are proof of a 'best fit'. As can be seen, the emphasis on natural selection involves borrowing, like systems theory, extensively from biology; transferring a Darwinian survival of the fittest to organisational life, with survival paths within each sector of competing firms. There is even a species analogue for organisations – blueprints which consist of rules and procedures inferred from formal structures, patterns of activity and normative orders, for transforming inputs into outputs (Hannan and Freeman, 1977: 934–5). One 'law' is that of requisite variety: organisations need to be as complex as their environment. If they are less complex, they are not likely to be adaptable enough. But over-complexity would probably mean that too much slack is being carried: 'populations of organisational forms will be selected for or against depending on the amount of excess capacity they maintain and how they allocate it' (Hannan and Freeman, 1977: 949). Furthermore the environment is an ecological system populated by sufficient organisations to allow for selection. The full process involves three stages: first, planned or unplanned *variations* from which appropriate structures or behaviours are drawn; second, natural *selection* eliminates undesirable variations; and third a *retention* mechanism which ensures the reproduction of those variations that have been positively selected.

The borrowings do not stop at biology, but draw from neo-classical or free-market economics. Perfect market competition tends to underlie the 'rationality' of natural selection: 'Organisational rationality and environmental rationality may coincide in the instance of firms in competitive markets. In this case, the optimal behaviour of each firm is to maximise profit, and the rule used by the environment (market in this case) is to select out profit maximisers' (Hannan and Freeman, 1977: 940). These 'natural laws' are shaped by the kind of competitive struggle over limited resources identified by the resource dependency school. Competition also produces a crucial process for population ecology theory, that of *isomorphism*. When equilibrium conditions obtain, the structural features of organisations – for example, the appropriate degree of specialism or generalism – will correspond to the relevant features of the resource environment. Those organisations that fail will be selected against, though organisations can also purposefully adapt. Of course equilibrium models can be too simplistic. To help deal with this the concept of *niche* width is used. A niche consists of the combinations of resource levels at which the population of organisations can survive and reproduce themselves. It is difficult for new organisations to enter already-filled niches where they cannot compete with existing social and economic resources.

Despite the use of some sophisticated historical models to handle data, population ecology analysis frequently remains at a highly abstract level.

Hannan and Freeman admit to a frustration with the level of empirical information (1977: 959), a problem which arises partly from the choice *not* to focus on particular organisations, but on populations over long periods (Clegg and Dunkerley, 1977: 376). But the problems derive from the theory as well as the method. As Perrow (1979) argues, ecological perspectives are attractive to some theorists because behaviour and events can be interpreted as natural. Evolution through natural selection gives the impression that patterns of activity that serve society are maintained, while those that are dysfunctional fortuitously disappear. Though contingency theories generally allow more scope for individual actors to learn rationally from processes of adaptation, the remarkable thing is not the distinctiveness of population ecology but how much it has in common with adaptation approaches. We are still in the world of 'best fits', with organisations responding to environments. Hannan and Freeman (1977: 929) admit that processes involving selection can usually be recast at a higher level of analysis as adaptation processes.

Environments are not only given determinate power, as in all systems theory, but they are literally reified through the language of environments acting on passive organisations. Somehow managerial actions to change work rules, create dual internal labour markets or hire temporary workers instead of full-timers can be elevated to a principle of natural selection which rewards flexible organisational forms (Aldrich and Stabler, 1987). Perrow (1979: 243) notes that such reification makes it difficult to for workers to say 'I was fired by the environment', adding that:

> the new model of organisation–environment relations tends to be a mystifying one, removing much of the power, conflict, disruption, and social class variables from the analysis of social processes. It neglects the fact that our world is in large part made by particular men and women with particular interests, and instead searches for ecological laws which transcend the hubbub that sociology should attend to.

This neglect of choice is at the heart of the general critique that can be made of the approaches discussed so far, and it is to this that we now turn.

Critique and alternative

We have already made a variety of criticisms on our journey through mainstream perspectives. Of course it would be foolish not to recognise that such research on organisation–environment relations has generated some useful knowledge of structural differentiation within and between organisations. The best of it, drawing on perspectives such as resource dependency, has introduced issues of bargaining and power partially on to the agenda. The appeal to 'practitioners', particularly of contingency theory, can be located in the more realistic clarification and yet expansion of managerial role and of organisational success. Indeed at one level the general argument is correct. Clearly organisations do face environmental constraints and often need to adapt to new markets or technologies to survive. For some people, the 'if-then' formula became difficult if not impossible to criticise, precisely because it was based on a 'horses for courses' argument. Wood notes: 'Thus ironically an approach which began by dismissing previous work as "panaceas" became itself the new panacea, the "situational approach to management"' (1979: 336).

Contingency theory and wider adaptation and selection perspectives have, however, rightly been criticised for their *environmental determinism*. The starting point of such critiques has often been John Child's (1972) influential concept of *strategic choice*. Strategic choice can operate with reference to the context of the enterprise, performance standards or organisational design. Most emphasis is, however, given to restoring the significance of the internal environment and particularly the degree of discretion available to power-holders and decision-makers within the dominant coalitions identified earlier. Contingency and other mainstream perspectives neglect the role of policy formulation and intervention, or see it only in terms of adaptation to the environment. One of the crucial factors this ignores is the existence of multiple contingencies which affect the capacity to achieve internally consistent responses and any potential correlation between structure and performance. There is sufficient 'slack' in most organisations' position and resources to allow different strategies to be considered and pursued, without incurring performance penalties or diseconomies.

The conceptual schema used by John Child allows for important breaks with determinism compatible with a radical analysis. He explicitly distances himself (1972: 6) from technological determinism by stressing the role of decisions relating to control of work. The empirical evidence in this area has been provided in studies from a labour process perspective, including those by Noble (1979) and Barry Wilkinson (1983a). Noble's work allows us to focus on the neglected issue of choice of technology itself, in this case the development of numerical control in engineering which allowed management to replace the direct input of craft workers by tapes that were externally programmed. He shows that an alternative technology for automating machine tools existed in the form of a 'record playback' system that retained operator skills. This was passed over in part because management preferred a system which enabled them to transfer skill from shop floor to programming office and shift authority and control.

The latest forms of Computer Numerical Control include machinery which can utilise a manual data input, system through which programming can be carried out by the operator at the machine. One of Wilkinson's case studies shows how a machine tool company bought in one MDI machine and eight which had been conventionally designed with the intention that programming should take place away from the shop floor. No significant performance differences were found, but senior management indicated a preference for the latter on specifically *organisational* grounds. The other cases of automation in the West Midlands focused on the more usual issue of the design of work organisation around the technology. Two of the companies concerned with plating and rubber moulding followed the conventional path of attempting to eliminate worker discretion and intervention. However, an optical company preferred a strategy of compensating for deskilling effects by a comprehensive system of retraining, job rotation and enhanced responsibilities which gave management greater flexibility. In all cases, there was no determinate relationship between the technological environment and work organisation, nor technological 'impacts' independent of human choice and negotiation.

At a wider level, Child's analysis moves beyond the dominance of technical criteria in organisational practices', 'recognising the operation of an essentially political process in which constraints and opportunities are functions of the power exercised by decision-makers in the light of ideological values' (1972: 22). How far does Child's early work take us? Certainly too far for Donaldson, who criticises his work for accommodating to the 'critical camp' by emphasising the politics of organisational action. Strategic choice theory is thus counter-productive because, 'Study of effective structure requires concern for functional imperatives or systems needs' (1985: 147). Ambiguity is the enemy of design knowledge. For example, if contingencies are variables that specify appropriate structure for high performance, talk of multiple contingencies which can affect a variable makes it impossible to specify unambiguously the right structure for high performance (1985: 144).

Yet there is a good deal of ambiguity as to whether Child's work has sought to modify or supplement contingency and systems theory or significantly to depart from it. Wood notes, 'Put simply, he is arguing theoretically for the inclusion of managerial ideology as an intervening variable between the environment and organisational design' (1979: 350). This orientation had heavily influenced an action theory (Silverman, 1970) which contested the 'metaphysical pathos' of perspectives that produced pessimism and fatalism about structures and choices in organisations. It challenged models of goal consensus and social engineering based on neutral knowledge, shifting the emphasis to internal processes and the diverse behaviour of organisational members. In addition, action approaches stressed the wide variety of environments beyond the economic, particularly the orientations to work developed in community life.

However, at this stage Child tends only to consider strategic choice as a variable and within management terms. Options that involve contesting existing power relations are made largely redundant. As Whittington (1988: 532–3) argues, property rights and structures of class, gender and ethnicity endow a limited circle of actors with command over resources to make strategic choices. Furthermore we need to break from the idea that environments produce situational imperatives, or the population ecology equivalent that environments can only select out a specifically appropriate form. Child's recent work (Child and Smith, 1987) from a 'firm-in-sector' perspective recognises that changes are primarily triggered by markets, but choices still remain and new strategies require an intellectual or cognitive reframing among management.

To illustrate the general anti-determinist point, take the 1980s wave of privatisation in Britain. There is no evidence, even from conventional economic indicators, that an organisation such as British Telecom was inefficient or ill-adapted to markets as a public enterprise. The decision to privatise was a strategy shaped by the hostility of the Conservative Government to state ownership and the material interests of senior management who wished to substitute market disciplines for public accountability. Under privatisation new structures and practices could be followed, notably an orientation away from the householder to the business customer, the development of a market-driven corporate culture and the extension of decentralised profit-centres.

Changes in organisational forms, structures or practices may be legitimised by reference to the vocabulary of efficiency or fit with the market environment, but they remain social and political choices. Population ecologists take bankruptcy rates as a major indicator of 'natural' selection. Yet this can be a direct result of government monetary policies, as in Britain in the early years of the first Thatcher administration. The general point can be illustrated in more detail with reference to the British coal industry, drawing on the research of Hopper et al. (1986). Traditional structures, in what was then the National Coal Board (NCB) were based on 'loose coupling' between the financial, production, marketing and other parts of the organisation. This allowed management to localise and contain contradictions arising from the diverse demands of those parts, and to deal with short-term uncertainties. One of the most significant effects was to isolate the long-term plans and interests of the technical and productive core of the NCB from environmental change and financial pressure. Two further influences on structures and practices need to be recognised.

First, the degree of job regulation exerted by miners in conditions in which conventional managerial controls are difficult to establish (Kreiger, 1983). Second, the relative dominance of professional engineers among management which was production-led, interested in stable long-term planning and partly tied to mining communities and cultures. Strategies pursued by the NCB in the 1980s, particularly after the appointment of Ian McGregor as Chairman, were aimed at breaking these patterns. Decentralisation was a major theme, with specific emphasis on 'economic pits' and 'economic' instead of production centres, as part of a national rationalisation of resources. The Government and Treasury particularly encouraged the enhancement of financial controls as a link between state policies and enterprise practices.

This included the use of Financial Information Systems as a monitoring device, and the strengthening of the NCB's own financial department, which was wedded to an ideology of market fitness. Such controls were complemented by the development of strategies of technological control through the MINOS system, which gives management far greater capacity to monitor and direct the labour process underground.

This is an example of the kind of research within, or stimulated by, labour process theory that has deepened conceptions of strategic choice. We shall examine this perspective in Chapters 4 and 12. Earlier, better-known contributions on managerial control strategy (Friedman, 1977; R. Edwards, 1979; Burawoy, 1979) had established an analytical framework. In his later work (1984: 231) Child refers in detail to Friedman's ideas of strategies of direct control and responsible autonomy. Direct control corresponds broadly to the scientific management tradition of close supervision, minimal responsibility and treating workers as machines. In contrast, responsible autonomy is mindful of the negative effects of worker resistance and the potentially positive gains from worker co-operation and involvement. Hence the stress on enlarged responsibilities and status, lighter controls, greater security and sometimes enriched jobs. These are not abstract choices. Responsible autonomy is more applicable to well-organised workers with controls over external or internal labour markets, who therefore need to be treated as central or core. Workers who are poorly organised, less skilled, and working for companies in highly competitive product markets are more likely to be directly controlled and treated as peripheral. This distinction, however, is too crude and does not fit all sectors. We shall return to issues of core and periphery in Chapter 6.

For Child, Friedman's analysis appears to confirm the relevance of managerial choices within market environments. But this neglects the wider nature of radical explanations. No matter how strategies are described, and Friedman is only one variant, they are shaped not just by markets, but by the capital–labour relation itself. Management is caught in the contradiction of needing to exert control and authority over labour to secure profitability in competitive conditions, while requiring workers to be motivated and co-operative. These contradictions are also conditioned by the general dynamics of capitalist production, either in a particular sector or in the economy as a whole. The development of monopoly capitalism has enabled large firms with power over markets and access to 'scientific' planning and management to experiment without being under undue pressure for short-term profits. Friedman rightly argues that *any* strategy will generate its own contradictions and tensions as it provokes resistance, facilitates worker organisation and power, or becomes inflexible in new circumstances. For example, during the 1940s and early 1950s most motor industry workers were treated as core, reflecting powerful shop floor organisation, favourable markets and need for post-war co-operation. But management was put under pressure by intensified competition to challenge the resultant wage systems and rigidity of work-group practices and manning levels.

Following intense struggles in the late 1960s and early 1970s, management at Ford, Leyland, Chrysler and other companies has been able to take advantage of recession and restructuring to shift power relations, often involving a return to more direct controls. Similar variability in managerial strategies, conditioned by capital's contradictory labour requirements and changing economic and political contexts, can be observed with reference to other dimensions of organisational life, such as job design or worker participation schemes, issues we shall examine in Chapter 6.

A further form of choice open to management is over the nature and sources of *labour*. Labour markets are clearly part of the organisational environment, and decisions about who to recruit are important. Employers may not always have much discretion, but the basic criteria of controlled costs, stability and minimisation of risk has been well documented (R. Jenkins, 1982). Hence employers may look for workers with characteristics such as family men with commitments, as at Ford (Beynon, 1975), or draw on informal Protestant family networks in Northern Ireland telecommunications plants (Maguire, 1986). In the former case the company hopes that mortgage and other responsibilities will mean financial dependence and unwillingness to strike; while in the latter, employment of people from the same family can increase the sense of social obligation and act as a social control over behaviour such as absenteeism. But a more significant choice is over the *location* of a workplace. Radical labour market theorists (Garnsey *et al.*, 1985) rightly regard the firm as a social organisation acting collectively. In locating a plant to utilise a specific form of labour, it is segmenting the market, though such effects can also occur when employees seek to build 'shelters' round their own jobs (Freedman, 1984).

There is plenty of evidence to show that large companies have often made their location decisions with specific cheap or controllable labour sources or stable industrial relations in mind (Whitaker, 1986). Modern 'high tech' companies have consciously tended to select young, female labour in places such as Edinburgh's 'silicon glen', or the telecommunications industry on Merseyside (Thompson and Bannon, 1985). Locational decisions can additionally shape environments in a broader way. When GM finally chose Spring Hill, a small town outside Nashville, Tennessee, for its Saturn plant, it was the end of a process which began with a public specification of decision criteria. The subsequent beauty contest had 38 out of 50 states offering a total of 1000 sites which would be created to the requirements (Meyer, 1986: 78). Tennessee has laws outlawing union closed shops. Locating new plants in small towns has been an increasing policy of GM, with the effect that the company *becomes* the environment.

Recruitment and location policies are examples of the power of organisations to *enact* environments. Perrow makes a related and further criticism of population ecology theory. He argues that to begin with the question 'why are the so many kinds of organisations?' is to ignore reality. When we are dealing with the big corporations such as the auto giants, it is simply not the case that there is evidence of significant differences. Furthermore the large firms very seldom die and they dominate the environment of the host of small organisations around them, as we saw in the example of the Japanese 'just-in-time' system currently being copied in the West. Perrow (1979: 243) concludes, 'If there is little variation, and little negative selection, then, what is the value of the theory?'

This capacity to set limits to environments was a sub-theme of Child, who drew on Galbraith's (1967) analysis of the 'new industrial state' to argue that any significant countervailing powers to big business had broken down (J. Child, 1969: 54). This stands in sharp contrast to the complacency of conventional open systems theory (Thompson and McEwan, 1973: 158), which only conceives of organisations dominating their environment in extreme circumstances, which in turn will generate the countervailing powers dismissed by Galbraith.

Child also sees his own insights as indebted to the work of the business historian Chandler (1962, 1977) on strategy, previously discussed in Chapter 2. Chandler showed how a new multidivisional structure was created as a strategic response to short-term and long-term market trends, and technological innovations. The refashioned structures allowed for an improved internal division of labour and resource allocation based mainly on the separation of longer-term strategic planning from operational decisions and practices. A decentralist strategy established market-type conditions within firms. There are parallels between these strategies and more contemporary attempts to extend markets within firms by creating quasi-independent profit centres which have to compete with one another and treat everyone else as customers. In addition, Williamson's related transaction-cost analysis also shows that the thrust of emergent giant corporations was to intervene in and shape economic environments in circumstances where the growth of managerial power in large corporations coincided with the declining influence of the market.

However, there are limitations to how far these frameworks substantially rework conceptions of organisation–environment relations. For Chandler, though the focus is on strategy and the 'visible hand' of management the extent to which it can incorporate real choice is open to question. The emphasis on the superiority of the multi-divsional firm as a form of adaptation to new market and technological imperatives strongly resembles contingency theories. Nor does Williamson's 'transaction costs' theory allow for much diversity. The problem arises from treating the growth of firms through internalisation of the costs of transactions in an unproblematic way. As Granovetter observes, there is an implicit functionalism in the argument that, 'whatever organisational form is most efficient will be the one observed' (1985: 503). It is true that firms do seek to internalise costs and for some of the reasons mentioned – environmental uncertainty and bounded rationality. But efficiency may not be the driving force or outcome. For example, given the research on mergers and acquisitions (Thompson *et al.*, 1992), it would be foolish to believe that every organisation taken out of the market is less efficient or that the newly created combination is more so. Firms take over others often because their control over resources gives them the capacity to dominate their environment, including other firms.

This inability to analyse the power resources available to the various parties in transactions is something we shall return to in the next chapter. More realistic analyses do have that orientation. Teulings notes that, 'large corporations do not comply with the laws of every market, but rather the other way round' (1986: 146). An organisation with a monopoly or semi-monopoly position can, for instance, create a product market through its own sales policies, or displace parts of its costs onto the environment, as with unchecked industrial pollution. To return to the example of mergers, such processes increasingly create environments to which other organisations and sections of the community have to adapt. For example, there has been a tremendous concentration of media resources through mergers and takeovers such as those initiated in many countries by Rupert Murdoch. This not only creates a new business conglomerate, but gives enhanced power to shape cultural and political environments, and the ideological climate of a whole society.

A major theme to come out of this discussion is the need to take large firms seriously as economic actors in their own right (Whitely, 1987). Though there are a variety of competing options or rationalities within organisations, the subsequent actions frequently constitute market environments more than they are constituted by them. The most obvious case of the capacity to control and change environments is that of the *transnational company* (TNC). The size of such companies' activities usually leads to considerable impact on national economies (Dicken, 1992). The issue is less whether the TNCs are willing to adapt to the environment in the form of national conditions, than how they contribute to changes in those societal institutions.

Increasingly TNCs can call on resources and structures which are superior to those of many nation states. One of the crucial powers is mobility of capital across national and international boundaries, enabling an evasion of laws on taxes and profits in a particular country. Markets can be shaped and their ebbs and flows ridden by cross-subsidisation and transfer pricing of goods, services, technology and loans between related activities in their global structure. Domination of a product market can reduce dependence on external sources of finance. Clairmonte and Cavanagh (1981) illustrate the process with reference to textile transnationals, adding the point that those in oligopolistic positions can act as price-makers, thus subordinating markets through cartels and other mechanisms. In the case of the Third World, many countries such as Sri Lanka and Malaysia have actually created an environment in the form of 'Free Trade Zones' in order to attract foreign capital. They offer virtual freedom of operations, cheap labour, bans on unions and maximum repatriation of profits (Mitter, 1986). Such dependency, however, is not just a feature of those regions of the world. The capacity of governments in advanced nations to control TNCs is often limited. During the 1974–9 Labour Government a planning agreement was drawn up with Chrysler which the company later unilaterally broke, with the Government being able to impose any penalty or constraint. (Coventry Trades Council *et al.*, 1980).

Such powers are further enhanced by changing corporate forms, with a gradual shift from structures based on centre–periphery relations, to global firms which have, 'foreignbased units with groupwide functions in management, manufacturing, marketing and/or research and development' (Forsgren, 1990: 9). Firms can be effective 'social carriers of techniques' standardising the environments around them. The role of TNCs in spreading new technology and production organisation techniques across the globe is widely acknowledged, particularly with reference to Japanese firms (Edquist and Jacobsson, 1988). True, this is not a wholly new phenomenon. In the postwar period the giant US corporations transferred work organisation and managerial techniques across capitalist countries. But today there is more rapid diffusion of 'best practice'. Smith and Meiskens argue that the more extensive integration of corporate structures noted above, allied to factors such as the internationalisation of consultancy, business schools, and the market for management literature, is enabling more rapid learning processes. A global economic and political order, 'has resulted in a transformation of particular national patterns of work organisation, management and labour relations into universal standards of best practice' (1995: 20).

This is not to say that TNCs and other large firms have total power over national and local environments. For example, national government policies still often support 'their' TNCs in the race of globalisation, in particular, where political and military hegemony is at stake. Though states can no longer act as if national economies were insulated from international competition, they can still play key roles in promoting technological competence, subsidising capital accumulation or bargaining over production and investment decisions (Gordon, 1988; Jenkins, 1984; Jessop, 1992). As Whitley notes (1987: 140) the capacity of large firms to determine their own market 'niches' requires a level of analysis of the political economy of international and state agencies, yet this is seldom recognised in organisational analysis.

The state and the political environment

Given the importance of the state as a political and economic actor in the environment of work organisations, it is remarkable how little attention it has received in the mainstream literature. The political environment may occasionally be listed among the variables, but it is rare for it to be followed through. Radical texts such as Clegg and Dunkerley (1980) do discuss the issue in some detail, but much critical workplace research often simply takes the state as a shadowy background factor acting in the interests of capital, without specifying how or why it does so. With both sets of perspectives, these issues are often left in practice to other branches of social science, notably political theory. This section tries to redress that balance a little by raising some of the issues that any more detailed analysis would have to deal with.

Theorising the state

We take the 'state' to comprise a set of institutions based on the government and legislature; the executive and administrative branches; the coercive apparatus of military and police; the judiciary; and the arms of the local state and the advisory bodies known as quangos. The definition goes beyond the government, simply because processes of power and decision-making cannot be contained within a single focus. Though nor can they be contained within the state, as we shall see.

Two poles constitute the major theoretical alternatives. For a *pluralist* analysis (Dahl, 1958, 1978) groups in the political élite have to compete for electoral support among citizens and interest groups. The latter and pressure groups are the main ways through which participation in government and decision-making takes place. As a consequence, power is widely distributed and the state acts as a kind of referee or neutral arbiter between rival interests and claims. As Held (1984: 40–1) notes, more recent pluralist writings recognise uneven resources, access and treatment, but still within a Weberian belief in multi-dimensional sources of power (see Chapter 4). Though mainstream theory cannot be explicitly linked to such a conception, is compatible with it, as McCullough and Shannon identify (1977: 74):

> it may be noted that in so far as a view of the state is implied by organisation theorists, it is usually that the state is itself a characteristic organisation that operates regulatively in the interstices of other organisations and is checked both internally by the aims of its members and externally by those of other organisations whose interests it ultimately safeguards.

Most theoretical work on the state has been done within or in response to a *Marxist* tradition. An orthodox Marxist view takes its lead from Marx's statement that the state is but a committee for managing the affairs of the whole bourgeoisie. Hence the state is an instrument of the dominant class and the political environment is firmly subordinate to economic power. Such a straightforward 'instrumentalist' view is seldom expressed today, though Holloway's (1987) analysis of industrial trends, which claims that managerial strategies *lead* state policies, is an example. Contemporary Marxists are more likely to refer to the state having a *relative autonomy*, a concept originally developed by Poulantzas (1975). Paradoxically, this is required because the state must manage the affairs of the whole of the dominant class. Capital is divided by different and potentially conflicting factions and interest groups, such as finance and manufacturing. The state can in theory act as a collective capitalist: attending to long-term interests even against particular business demands; providing facilities such as a national transport network or housing that single capitals cannot; and regulating and incorporating demands from subordinate classes through concessions and institutional channels which do not threaten existing class power.

Why is there this emphasis on *must*? Although some writers (Miliband, 1969) put additional stress on the common class origins, experiences and values of political, economic, administrative and judicial élites, the basic argument is a *structural* one. The state's activities are constrained by having to operate within the existing market framework. Particularly in a world system of interlocking manufacture, trade and finance, no nation state can ignore the requirements of capital accumulation and reproduction. Capital can utilise its resource power to place unique pressure on the state's economic management processes.

But it is possible to recognise that the state has a high level of dependency on capital accumulation for its economic resources and success, without accepting that its form or activities can be derived solely from the class relation to capital. Writers such as Offe (1984) and Crouch (1979) recognise that though the prime function of the state is to create the conditions for successful *accumulation*, state institutions have to respond to popular pressures even where that might create conflict with business interests. Gains made by labour or other social movements may thus be genuine advances, rather than conspiratorial concessions to maintain class domination. In a more general sense, system stability, including state institutions, requires a level of loyalty, consent or even just acquiescence from subordinate classes and groups (Clegg *et al.*, 1987: 286). Taken together, the conditions are created for the state to have a *legitimation* function.

The problem is that the two functions may be antagonistic, particularly when the state is involved in its standard crisis-management practices. Offe (1984) uses the example of the growth of the welfare state, with such institutions developing in part because the state needed to compensate for the inability of the market to meet social needs. To the extent that welfare provision is a response to popular demands, it sustains public legitimacy. Yet at the same time the welfare state threatens the accumulation process by expanding the range of social activities met by non-commodity forms, or by generating fiscal crises with an expanding social wage and budgets. Though

Offe's options for the state and political solutions are beyond our scope, such contradictions can certainly be observed in the continuing conflicts about public expenditure in the UK and other advanced industrial societies. In examining other issues, we shall suggest that the accumulation/legitimation framework provides a useful analytical tool.

Dimensions of state economic activity

Five interrelated dimensions of state activity can be identified that affect the environment that work organisations operate in.

State as economic manager   The state's most crucial role has been to provide a macro-economic and micro-economic framework favourable to business operations, especially in the more interventionist post-war period. This can range from traditional forms of demand management, control of the money supply and interest rates, to wage regulation and tax structures. Take the example of *enterprise zones* in the UK, which were set up in two batches on inner city and urban conurbation sites by the Government in the early 1980s (Shutt, 1985). Using a model of economic regeneration influenced by Third World zones in which capital is allowed to operate without restriction, the British version includes rates and tax exemptions, 100 per cent tax allowances for capital expenditure, freedom from training levies, and simplified planning regimes. Though policy development has moved on, the example illustrates how state practices have been focused on managing the process of industrial rationalisation and reconstruction, a task beyond the market alone. Sometimes this has been through special interventionist bodies set up by Labour Governments such as the Industrial Reorganisation Corporation in the 1960s and the National Enterprise Board in the 1970s; or through straightforward government departments under the Conservatives. Considerable resources have been poured into sectoral planning, encouraging mergers and industrial concentration, and funding plant modernisation. If anything, state intervention in the UK has been underdeveloped compared to France, or MITI in Japan, which Clairmonte and Cavanagh describe as 'a superbly honed state instrument which, in conjunction with the corporate leadership, periodically rationalises Japan's chemical and textile industries' (1981: 20).

In certain conditions these processes have taken a *corporatist* form, where the state seeks to regulate both polity and economy, and reduce uncertainty by bringing in capital and labour as formal interest groups. Under the Heath and Wilson/Callaghan Governments of the 1970s, tripartism involving the CBI and TUC was a consistent feature until broken by the Thatcher administration (Grant, 1983). But economic management is not necessarily the result of rational planning. It frequently takes a reactive form, reflecting state dependence on the resources of capital. The most obvious manifestation is the continual subsidisation of investment, such as the £148 million in aid to Ford for its Bridgend plant and the estimated £100 million to Nissan in the North East. Subsidising capital appears to be the main feature of successive government's regional policies, with no guarantees that companies will not simply close down grant-aided plants, as Plessey did in the late 1970s without even informing the National Enterprise Board. The state also indirectly subsidises investment costs through social management and collective provision. With reference to new town policies, Cochrane and Dicker note that this was, 'part of the state's response to the needs of private industry for better facilities. As in so many other areas of the economy, the provision of new sites and an associated labour force could not be organised by individual firms and the state had to intervene' (1979: 9).

State as employer   With the spectacular growth of state services and public corporations such as the National Coal Board in the UK, the state became the key employer. Even in the US environment of low intervention, public employment grew by eight million between 1952 and 1980 (Cousins, 1987: 123). In theory this gives the state the possibility of creating distinctive organisational models. In practice public corporations in coal, steel and other sectors were firmly required to act according to market criteria, with no essential differences in management structures, though the nature of service work generates different employment relations. What the British state *has* done is to use its position as major employer to 'set standards' in its general regulation of incomes and industrial relations. Wages have been specifically kept down, leading to a rise in public sector unionism and militancy. During the late 1970s and the 1980s public corporations and others taken into state ownership, such as British Leyland, saw a government-directed management offensive led by appointees such as Michael Edwardes and Ian McGregor, which had a wider 'demonstration effect'. Under Thatcher the state was able and prepared to finance long set-piece confrontations with miners, teachers and civil servants in a way that private employers would find difficult (MacInnes, 1987: 93). More recently the objective has been to break the power of public sector unions by squeezing expenditure through cash limits, decentralising bargaining and by contracting-out services.

State as persuader   Though legitimation is a facet of all state activities, its communicative power and resources gives the state unique persuasive capacities. In the UK and US the state has frequently acted to 'sponsor' particular managerial and organisational initiatives, aimed at spreading them beyond the advanced sectors of capital. During the First World War, President Wilson used the War Labour Board to push arbitration mechanisms and works councils as an alternative to independent unionism (R. Edwards, 1979:

105), and in the Second War Stafford Cripps, the Labour Minister of Aircraft Production, used his powers to spread new work study techniques, human relations, welfare and personnel methods, and psychological testing (G. Brown, 1977: 272–4). Royal Commissions such as the Donovan Report (1968), are a favoured method which had an important influence on the institutionalisation of collective bargaining. In the early 1970s governments in many countries produced reports advocating work humanisation as an antidote to dissatisfaction and disruption. More recently the Conservatives have been exhorting companies to develop participation and involvement schemes as a response to the threat of EC legislation on industrial democracy, as well as using the Department of Trade and Industry, the Treasury and quangos to spread the word about the value of flexible working practices, TQM and other managerial techniques (Pollert, 1988a). On the other side of the political divide, the Australian Labour Government and its union allies have developed extensive initiatives, such as the Best Practice Demonstration Programme to promote new practices and indeed languages of workplace reform (Campbell, 1994). Such developments have been strongly influenced by the experience of the Swedish social democracy and state-directed innovations through the Work Environment Fund and other bodies.

In a democratic society, the state's persuasive role is normally subject to some constraint and certainly pales into insignificance compared to the massive social engineering programme undertaken by the state in Singapore. Barry Wilkinson (1986) reports that the government has gone beyond the normal use of state bodies and incentives to encourage training and skill development, by also directing its attention to desirable attitudes and behaviour. A Productivity Movement is charged with 'inculcating the productivity will' through every form of media, under the imprint of Teamy the Bee. In part this is an attempt to spread a paternalistic version of human relations techniques for managers whose companies get subsidies for sending them on courses. But the general campaign reaches its peak with the Social Development Unit's attempts to encourage graduates, and more recently 'O'- level and 'A'-level holders, to 'meet, marry and breed'. One year of exhortation, however, including all-expenses paid trips to exotic beach resorts, produced definite evidence of only two marriages!

The state as legislator   As with legitimation, legislation accompanies most forms of state activity, yet it has been a core function of the state to provide a legal framework governing industrial relations and employment practices. Hyman (1986) shows that the historical commitment of British employers and the state to a system of minimal labour law was conditional on the former's economic strength and the relative weakness of trade unions. When the material basis for voluntarism was eroded by economic decline, more assertive workers and crisis management by the state, we saw the beginnings of intervention through the abortive Industrial Relations Act of the Heath Government in 1971, revived in more favourable circumstances in the 1980s. Since then there have been successive waves of legislation which have severely restricted the rights to strike and picket, narrowed the definition of lawful industrial action, and undermined the enforcement of the closed shop. Though employers have seldom had to use the Acts outside of celebrated instances such as the Wapping dispute, a legal framework has been established supportive of managerial prerogatives and capable of easing problems of reorganisation of production. As Sir Jeffrey Stirling, Chairman of P&O Ferries, noted, when using that framework during the 1988 dispute: 'This Government has given companies like ours the right to manage' (*Guardian*, 29 April).

Of equal importance has been Conservative legislation in the wider employment field. In the 1980s we have seen: the abolition of the Fair Wages Resolution, dating back to 1891, which obliged governments and private contractors to pay the going rate; Wages Councils which set minimum wage rates disbanded or their coverage restricted to adult workers; and abolition of aspects of Labour's previous employment protection legislation with respect to union recognition, rights on unfair dismissal and maternity leave, and for part-timers (Standing, 1986; MacInnes, 1987). Such measures have been part of an explicit attempt to deregulate labour markets to ensure the freedom of employers to set wages and organise work as they see fit. Indeed government ministers regularly lecture their European and American counterparts on this essential ingredient of economic success compared to the bureaucratic regulation embodied in the Social Chapter of the Maastricht treaty.

Though it is not always connected to legislation as such, the other relevant state action with respect to labour markets has come through policies ostensibly directed towards training. The major arm of this intervention was at first the Manpower Services Commission (MSC). Begun in the mid-1 970s, a decade later the MSC had a budget of over £2000 million, a staff of over 20 000 and there were 670 000 people in Special Employment Measures (Standing, 1986). At first MSC schemes were little more than ad-hoc responses to youth unemployment. Though critics continued to charge that the object was to massage the unemployment figures and provide make-believe jobs with no permanent prospects, a longer-term strategy was beginning to develop. The Holland Report in 1977 had already revealed that employers valued behavioural qualities such as appearance, manners and adaptability to work more than qualifications that were of little relevance to the mass of semi-skilled jobs.

Evidence shows (P. Thompson, 1984; Finn, 1986) that through the various schemes, from the Youth Opportunities Programme to the Youth Training Scheme, trainees have been taught generic or transferable skills which were geared to performance and flexibility in low-skill jobs in the manufacturing and service sectors. This was backed up by behavioural and 'personal effectiveness' training in the form of social and life skills packages with the aim of providing a work ethic for this new reserve army of semi-skilled labour. At the same time direct intervention in youth labour markets was explicitly geared towards the lowering of wage rates. Central to this process was conditioning people to low training allowances, the destruction of expensive and union-influenced apprenticeship schemes and abolition of many of the Industrial Training Boards with traditional responsibilities in these areas. These were allied to a range of subsidies to employers – through the Young Worker Scheme, the New Worker Scheme and the Temporary Employment Subsidy – if they would take on young workers below wage rates specified by the state. The actual arm of intervention is no longer the MSC, but after a number of mutations, the Training and Enterprise Councils carry on at least some of those functions of state-directed training.

State as policeman   Weber defined the core function of the state in terms of its monopoly of violence and coercive power; indeed this was the basis of its autonomy. As the use of such powers to maintain industrial order is likely to undermine the legitimacy of the state and capital if used on its behalf, there are obvious constraints. This was felt less in the nineteenth and early twentieth century when the use of police and the military in disputes was a regular occurrence in the US and UK (R. Edwards, 1979; Hain, 1986). The notion of the police force as an arbiter and protector of the general interest is central to pluralist notions of the modern state. Yet coercive powers are still used in disputes, as we have seen during 1980s disputes in the UK at the Wapping print plant and during the miners' strike. In the latter there was every indication of a nationally co-ordinated police effort to undermine the effectiveness of the strike (Geary, 1985).

Geary uses historical comparisons to argue that there has been a shift to more repressive police tactics that are less subject to informal community controls. Yet compared to Reagan's repression of the strike by the Professional Air Traffic Controllers Organisation, in which the state dismissed the employees, scrapped PATCO and carted its leaders off in irons, this seems small beer! Constraints still remain in all complex societies. Degrees of tolerance and repression depend strongly on the perceived political consequences both for the police themselves and the wider state apparatus. Most police involvement in disputes is not marked by intent. Rather it is a reflection of the legal framework under which they are expected to guarantee property rights on picket lines or in other circumstances. We should also remember that the state's policing role has a social dimension. A notable example was the law on social security used in the miners' strike. This assumed that unions paid strike pay regardless of whether they did so in practice and even to non-members, with a resultant large reduction in benefits payable to dependants of strikers.

Restructuring the public sector

We have already spoken of the significance of the state as an employer, even allowing for governmental erosion of large parts of public provision in Britain and other countries. That part of the sector normally referred to as 'public corporations' – for example, as British Coal – operated largely under conditions comparable to other commercial operations. But to what extent does the public service sector constitute a distinct environment for organisations? The answer sheds some important light on a comparative analysis of work organisations and their contexts. We seek an explanation by focusing on trends in British Government policy towards public services, important because they have acted as a model for change in other countries. We can identify a number of key policies – cuts and tighter financial controls such as cash limits on the total budget of each service; recommodification through privatisation or contracting-out; a new managerialism based on the introduction of private sector practices; a shift of decision-making to the central state apparatus; and the creation of internal markets. The result has been a profound shift in the boundaries and character of state activity.

What did it shift from? Public services were bureaucratic hierarchies traditionally characterised by collaborative or collegiate styles of decision-making and administration which rested heavily on the power of professionals over resource allocation to services based on need and equity. Such arrangements were underwritten by a bargain between professionals and the state in which the latter set the general rules within which the privilege of professional authority operated and provided shelter from the market.

The subsequent transformation processes will be illustrated by looking primarily at heath and education. Cousins (1987) demonstrates that attempts to introduce tighter managerial controls are not new. A number of reports were vehicles for rationalisation processes which sought, among other things, to establish the dominance of management. The Griffiths Report played a particularly important role. It argued that the NHS required a central directing force which could allocate and monitor resources. Hence a dual strategy was to be pursued: general managers were to be appointed who could assert managerial prerogatives and make 'technocratic' decisions about the health service as equipment and manpower; and medical professionals such as consultants, would be drawn into managerial activity, mainly through involvement in clinical budgeting. A new Management Board was also established to strengthen central control over strategic resources. The Report was also important for its emphasis on private sector practices. Sir Roy Griffiths was previously managing director of Sainsbury's and considerable (though largely unsuccessful) attempts were made to recruit the general managers from private industry. In other parts of the public sector such practices took the form of financial scrutiny under the auspices of the Audit

Commission, the Raynor efficiency drive in the Civil Service, and the use of performance measurement and university departments as cost centres in the 1985–6 research evaluation exercise prompted by the Jarratt Report.

Until the late 1980s emphasis was largely on controlling public expenditure costs and inputs, but then it moved to 'the instrumental objectives of economy, efficiency and effectiveness' (Farnham and Horton, 1993: 241). Such instrumentiality was not simply a managerial rationality. The policies took on a more sharply political tone. A convergence could be noted between a longer-term shift from administration to management shaped by the fiscal crisis of the state, and the ideological thrust of 'new right' politics that are in principle hostile to public and collective provision. Privatisation is favoured by the latter, as it is the most direct means of introducing market mechanisms and profitability criteria, but it may not be politically feasible – competitive tendering has been a more frequent mechanism. Managers are given greater leverage to rationalise labour-intensive forms of work organisation. As Cousins (1987: 177) points out in relation to health 'If an in-house tender wins, however, the service has still been subjected to the discipline of competition and although labour is not conducted for the extraction of profit, the labour process is organised *as if it were*' [our emphasis]. In more recent times the health service has been subject to the creation of an internal market based on a split between purchasers (fund-holding doctors and heath authorities) and providers (self-governing trusts or private sector organisations). As hospitals and staff sell their services, this is intended to mirror conventional market competition for price and product.

In education the creation of such arrangements has not been as easy. League tables of published exam results and other performance indicators in secondary education are rather a pale imitation of even an 'internal' market, while parental (that is, 'consumer') choice is more ideology than reality, given the geographical and resource constraints. As for higher education, the end of the binary system has enabled, as one of our more cynical colleagues put it, the (old) universities to achieve (ex) polytechnic status. In other words, the experience of state-directed funding to achieve lower unit costs functions as a demonstration effect for the previously more autonomous and better resourced institutions. To add to increasing state-financial targets and penalties, the new, combined sector is subject to regular research assessment exercises and evaluations of teaching and other functions through the HEQC. Willmott sums up the results succinctly: 'A quasi-market for teaching and research resources is being constructed in which institutions and departments compete with each other to drive down unit costs and thereby formally increase their exchange value, measure in numbers of students taught and numbers of grants and publications achieved' (1993b: 18).

Although the state is the main force acting to restructure the public sector, it cannot always be the direct agent. The new regimes require a more powerful general management and administrative infrastructure as a disciplining force.

We have seen the well-documented rise in the proportion of administrators in the NHS or consultants turned into clinical budget-holders; while in schools and universities heads are expected to act and think as business managers or chief executives, with the rhetoric of line management and programme managers proliferating at lower levels. Also, accountants are developing a higher profile in enforcing cost consciousness and standardised procedures as the new managerialism is everywhere accompanied by the apparatus of performance measurement, quality audits and other techniques imported from the private sector.

But what are these guardians of the new managerialism actually 'disciplining'? The answer must largely be the remnants of professional autonomy. Cutler (1992: 4) argues that the Jarratt Report, 'saw the corporate interests of universities as subverted by the sectional ploys of professionals', whose producer interests were entrenched in their semi-autonomous departments. The establishment of internal markets and enhancement of central controls breaks what increasingly looks like a Faustian bargain between professionals and the state (Brazier *et al.*, 1993). In health, Dent (1993) characterises the change as one from professional autonomy to the system of responsible autonomy discussed earlier in this chapter. The latter is different in that its extent and nature is determined by managerial strategies. Indeed the overall process produces a shift from management by professionals to professionalisation of management.

Nevertheless considerable constraints on change remain. Public service organisations may adopt the language of markets, but objectives and practices are still distinctive. For example, no amount of renaming students as 'customers' can give them the power and choice of consumers in product markets. Operational criteria for performance measurement or other indicators of 'efficiency' also lack the clear parameters deriving from the capital–labour relation, and such criteria are still likely to be shaped by policy and budget decisions arising from the political apparatus. A comment from the then NHS Director of Personnel Len Peach, about the Griffiths Report remains true: 'We recognise that the politicians will make the strategic decisions. The management decisions are about how to implement them' (quoted in the *Guardian*, 9 June 1986). A similar point is made by Batstone *et al.* in their study of the Post Office. They argue that:

> The essence of the distinction between public and private lies in the fact that though they may be encouraged to act commercially, state enterprises pursue politically determined objectives which complicate the process of strategy formulation and implementation. (1984: 7)

State services are even more open to public discourse and interest group pressure, hence the constraints on Conservative administrations simply dismantling the NHS. We can see in such examples a version of the previously discussed tension between the state functions of accumulation and legitimation, as well as tensions between state managers and central government control. Public and private also continue to be distinguished by the role played by professional groups. The power of state service professionals is no longer unmediated, as they face pressure from government and general management for reorganisation of their work. Higher professions are beginning to experience the vulnerability to managerial control and domination by élites that has previously applied to female-dominated and semi-professions such as nursing (Cousins, 1987: 110). But their power resources are by no means exhausted. For example, doctors can utilise their socially-constructed expertise and power over employment conditions to 'claw-back' measures such as clinical budgeting, though internal markets are a more difficult obstacle than managerialism (Dent, 1993). However, it remains the case that processes such as medical audit and quality assurance in higher education are still run by professionals themselves.

Though privatisation in its varied forms continues to undermine the basis of public provision, the factors discussed above place significant difficulties in the way of the strategies of state managers to reorganise work processes and assert greater controls. Evidence collected by Cousins (1987) shows that managers have to balance the cost benefits from measures such as contracting-out against the ceding of control over staff to an external firm and the loss of commitment and cohesion from existing teams, to say nothing of potential declining standards for which they may be blamed. The new power-holders also have to be wary of the reported disillusionment of professional employees about the 'ascendancy of managerial values' (Farnham and Horton, 1993: 244). Employees, both manual and professional, can also use the ethic of service and welfare to challenge the legitimacy of managerial decisions purporting to be based solely on technocratic rationality. Employees' organisations themselves, of course, have to seek legitimacy for *their* actions in the political environment. It has taken the unions a considerable period of time to recover from the damage done by the 'winter of discontent' of 1979, in order to mount more effective public campaigns.

Glover *et al.* (1986: 19) point out that the Management Board set up in the wake of the Griffith Report was never given the formal space or authority to act in a manner independent of political interference which was necessary to implement the Report effectively. Hence the whole process of management is a complex bargaining and balancing act. Although this may be true of all management, the factors which shape it in public services are both distinctive and more wide-ranging. The problematic nature of management strategies of control form a major feature of the next chapter.

Retheorising the state: a reflection

It would be tempting to see the above trends in terms of a convergence in the nature of public and private sector organisations. In fact, if we take seriously Chandler and Williamson's strictures on large-scale organisations taking transactions out of the market, perhaps the move away from vertically-integrated hierarchical public organisations towards market-directed forms of resource allocation and exchange makes the public more like the private is supposed to be! State organisations *are*, as Marxist writers emphasise (Carchedi, 1977), intimately connected and often subordinate to capitalist political economy. It is also the case that the rationalisation and intensification of service work makes the experiences of workers increasingly comparable to those in private industry. But, as we argued in the previous section, such measures are primarily the result of specific political choices and practices, rather than any law of capitalist development. In addition, Cousins uses the work of Habermas (1987) and Offe (1984) to show that there are still different *modes of rationality*: 'state welfare organisations are not governed by the logic of maximising profits, although they are dependent on the revenues derived from profits and the prosperity of the private sector' (1987: 4–5).

What, however, of the conventional dimensions of state activity discussed in the previous section? The range of examples in each of these areas *appears* to support an instrumentalist view of relations between capital and state. They certainly indicate that the political environment shaped by state practices in a capitalist society is likely to be favourable to business organisations. It is a more unequal competition for access to the state and its resources than allowed for in most versions of pluralist theory. However, most of the examples are from the last fifteen years, when we have seen highly distinctive political and state frameworks. The *outcomes* of state interventions in the economic environment are conditioned by three main factors: the balance of power between classes and related interest groups; the prevailing ideological climate; and the dominant political project within the various state apparatuses. For example, to return to the relations between the state and professions, not every offensive against 'producer interests' was successful. Lawyers have been more effective in defending their autonomy against proposals to increase and police the market in legal services, in part at least because the judiciary were able to lobby effectively and utilise powerful protectors within the state machinery (Brazier *et al.*, 1993: 209–12).

Though such conditions can be localised in time and space, they are normally part of broader changes in relations between the main political and economic actors. In the UK, USA and some other industrial countries, there has been a sharp move away from corporatist and 'social democratic' practices that had formed the basis of what commentators call the post-war consensus. Such a state accomplished its tasks by putting a premium on ideological and

social cohesion, integrating and organising various interests through wage
and price controls, social compacts, arbitration and conciliation procedures,
regional employment premiums and the like (Lehman and Tinker, 1985). The
new direction has been towards 'neo-liberal', market-driven practices in
which;

> Political efforts at neo-corporatist institutional design have come to a standstill
> almost everywhere . . . many governments now seem to place little hope on
> negotiated adjustment and no longer see it as their responsibility to protect the
> principle of joint regulation from the disruptive effects of a severe power imbalance.
> (Streek, 1987: 286–7)

As an example, the kind of tripartism that existed between the state, CBI and
TUC has been cursorily jettisoned by the Conservative Government. Such
constellations of practices constitute different modes or ways in which
interests can be represented and organised by and through the state (see
Jessop, 1982: 228–41, for a detailed discussion).

The point of outlining these changes is to emphasis that they *are* changes.
There is no evidence to show that there is any permanent or essential relation
between capital, labour and the state, or between the political and economic
environments in which business organisations operate. After all, the recent
changes are not universal. Austria still has its corporatist 'Economic and Social
Partnership', with a high level of institutionalised co-operation between the
state, unions and employer's organisations; despite a change of government,
Sweden retains a state apparatus with high levels of control over the labour
market and high levels of welfare expenditure; and the co-determination
system of works councils in West Germany gives employees a level of
involvement in the management of industrial change markedly higher than in
the UK or USA.

Just as importantly, we cannot assume that the 'neo-liberal' state strategies
are necessarily and unambiguously of benefit to capital, even when acting in
its name. Let us return to some of the examples we used earlier. The first wave
of enterprise zones were a spectacular failure, with the main effect being to
transfer existing small businesses short distances from places where the state
gained revenue from their rates and taxes (Shutt, 1985). In many parts of the
country the opposition to the zones was led by business interests such as local
Chambers of Commerce. Yet the government's response was to create a new
set of zones! If we turn to industrial relations legislation, a number of
measures described earlier went too far for the CBI and influential groups
such as the Engineering Employer's Federation. They complained in written
evidence and through delegations about the dangers to stable industrial
relations from excessive restrictions on the closed shop and on the rights of
unions to discipline their own members, as well as the proposals to make a 70
per cent affirmative vote necessary for strike action. Finally, let us consider the

MSC and training policies. Despite the massive expenditure on training schemes, employers all over Britain are complaining of skill shortages. These schemes have a dubious record in relation to the provision of trained manpower. Given that Britain's best performance at the 1994 Skills Olympics was a bronze medal in hairdressing, there is obviously some way to go in the effectiveness of such schemes. This is not surprising when the major considerations of the state have been to manage the political crisis of mass unemployment; the emphasis being on placing sheer numbers on schemes and removing others from benefit in order to get official statistics down; on being seen to be doing something about unemployment; and on providing a work ethic, even when no regular work was available.

One of the things all three examples have in common is a tension between the accumulation and legitimation functions of state practices. The political project articulated by the Conservative Governments has to be seen as capable of maintaining ideological coherence and dynamism to its social bases of support, and indeed to itself. That is likely to undermine or at least mediate its practices geared to providing conditions for successful accumulation. Nor are these the only relevant examples of policies that had at least partially negative effects on business interests. In the early years of Thatcherism, the effects of monetarist measures such as high interest rates and low public capital spending led to a bitter clash with leaders of the CBI, with a feeling that the state was favouring finance rather than manufacturing capital. As MacInnes (1987: 94–5) points out, the business sector tolerated Thatcherism in this period because they associated themselves with the general project compared to any alternatives, and because they gained the benefits from the shift in power relations *vis à vis* labour.

Finally, in drawing out some theoretical conclusions, we would endorse a number of the factors Pierson (1984) identifies as characterising post-Marxist theories of the state. The concept of relative autonomy solves few problems. The state does not function unambiguously in the interests of a single class; it is a state *in* capitalist society rather than *the* capitalist state, and it is an arena of struggle constituted and divided by opposing interests rather than a centralised and unified political actor. National differences are an important factor in the specific evolution of state structures and practices. In trying to explain why the British state has traditionally failed to pursue effective policies for economic restructuring and growth, P. A. Hall (1986: 278) observes that, 'the precise form it [political response] takes is strongly influenced by the institutional setting within which the state finds itself'.

Skocpol (1979) uses a state-centred perspective to argue that states have their own distinctive structures, histories and interest groups developed from transactions with increasingly complex, transnational environments. There is a need for an organisational perspective which recognises that, 'all states are composed of complex and often internally contradictory and inconsistent organisational apparatuses' (Clegg *et al.*, 1987: 281). In Britain there are obvious tensions between the Treasury and other ministries, arising from the former's organisational dominance and there may be strains and contradictions within structures. So, for example, within quangos such as the Training and Enterprise Council empire are varied groups of functionaries carrying out state management tasks. In a complex bureaucracy, different groups inevitably develop their own resources, values, interests and funding practices, moderated by which client group (enterprise agencies, colleges) they transact with. Goals set by the core state apparatus have to be filtered through these layers.

The above analysis has tried to produce a multi-dimensional framework for understanding the state as an environment. It is the task of organisational theory to be able to locate firms and other organisations within an equally complex conception of the environment in a rapidly transformed world. Fortunately an increasing range of theories are facing that task.

The local and the global in new business environments

The main purpose of this chapter has been to examine how interactions with the environment shape different organisational forms and practices. We have argued that even when taking account of the outside world, much orthodox theory does so in an economically and technologically deterministic way. That is, they tend towards single-track notions of efficiency that can only be embodied in specific design configurations between environmental variables (product markets, technologies) and organisational structures. The environment either rules or has rules for successful adaptation and selection. Strategic choice and notions of enacted environments bend the stick back in the other direction, but it is worth discussing whether their are theoretical frameworks that allow us to move beyond narrow and impoverished conceptions of organisation–environment relations, while at the same time enabling us to see how large companies operate in an increasingly global context.

Institutional theories

A focus on culture is a traditional antidote to explanations which over-emphasise economic and technical convergence, given that the former has more scope for grasping 'local' variation and organisational distinctiveness. Institutional theories, which have been around in organisational analysis since the 1970s (Meyer and Rowan, 1977), have been the means for doing just that. Organisations still adapt to the environment, but to different features of it. The emphasis is on *normative* adaptation and the cultural rules to which organisations conform. This arises not from the requirements for efficiency, but from the need for legitimacy and resource support which is the reward for conforming. Indeed, in some cases rules may be ceremonial and transmitted through myths rather than being technical. Organisations not only conform to the environment, but to each other. This process whereby organisations increasingly come to resemble each other is described using the strange term 'institutional isomorphism' (Di Maggio and Powell, 1983). The main factors promoting convergence across companies are key agents who adhere to universalistic standards of best practice, notably professionals such as accountants, engineers and personnel officers, as well as the state itself.

We should not be misled by the term 'culture'. This is used to mean social rules embodied in institutional processes more than mental constructs carried about in people's heads. These institutional frameworks are essentially national – as Clegg puts it, 'A stress on culture as institutionally framed and nationally diverse' (1990: 151). An important feature of this approach is to affirm the possibility of successful organisational designs to promote industrialisation in different institutional environments. The emphasis on diverse organisational rationalities is usefully strengthened through the concept of *business systems*, associated particularly with the work of Whitley. G. Henderson (1992: 4) describes them as 'distinctive ways of co-ordinating economic activity which give rise to particular configurations of market–firm relations'. The advantage of this concept is that it attempts to tie together in a coherent way the historical, cultural and institutional processes which shape national or regional economies. It enables a focus on the way in which state, financial, industrial relations and other systems combine together to influence organisational practices. We have already discussed at the end of Chapter 2 the role of factors such as state direction and family ownership in East Asian economies and they figure prominently in institutionalist accounts (Hamilton and Biggart, 1988; Whitley, 1992; G. Henderson, 1993). Dominant social institutions generate distinctive business recipes, such as the state-dependent forms in South Korea, that are relatively similar within nation-states.

Such *organisational* theories have a great deal in common with broader institutional perspectives in sociology, particularly the *societal effects* approach (Maurice *et al.*, 1980). Their research showed that work organisation patterns differ markedly due to nationally specific institutional logics that produce stable organisational and employment patterns. Such logics are particularly located in education, training, labour market and industrial relations structures. This helps to explain why salary structures, career patterns, management and authority relations vary among closely matched French, German and British firms. Within a similar framework Lane (1991) has looked at relations between large, medium and small firms in Germany, France and Britain. She demonstrates that the distinctiveness of 'populations' of organisations arises from their transaction with specific industrial orders. As a consequence national patterns continue to reproduce divergence rather than the homogeneity predicted by old-style convergence theory (Kerr *et al.*, 1960).

Societal effect approaches have stressed the principle of functional equivalence, thus appearing to avoid determinist or 'one best way' fallacies. However comparison is accompanied, implicitly or explicitly, by evaluation. For example, the comparisons of France, Britain and Germany in the work of Lane consistently favour the last, particularly with reference to the organisational and technical competencies of firms and their underpinnings in educational training systems. Strong arguments promoting the positive lessons of East Asian business systems can also be seen in the work of G. Henderson (1993).

There are, however, problems within institutionalist frameworks. The earlier versions reproduce a view of 'the organisation as a passive reactor to the environment' (Bryman, 1993: 87) which is equally deterministic as population ecology or contingency, though shifting the focus to normative pressures. Even the more complex accounts run the risk of producing a mirror image of the convergence argument, focusing solely on difference. It is, of course, true that work organisation and other features of the industrial order will always differ from others on a local and national basis. Whether such explanations were ever viable in the past, it is very doubtful whether they are now. Societal institutions are increasingly subject to 'external' pressures for change. As Smith and Meiskens observe: 'Institutional analysis tended to focus on and reinforce national differences. The immediate problem with this perspective is to account for change and the dynamic nature of economies which are global, not nationally bounded systems' (1995: 3). It is inaccurate and unrealistic to go on treating organisations as 'societies in miniature' in the manner of Sorge *et al.* (1983: 54), who say that 'the differences between societies are so pervasive as to be immediately and consistently noticeable in every unit'. In reality, as we shall see in Chapter 7, large business organisations such as IBM are themselves carriers of distinctive financial, employment or technical practices.

Such perspectives are not necessarily conceptually tied to the state as an object of analysis. Neo-institutional approaches are becoming more sophisticated in their understanding of environments, particularly when being extended to cover sectors, regions, and systems. With a small number of giant TNCs increasingly dominating sectors, and with 'best practices' spreading rapidly within them, industry recipes consisting of conventions governing marketing, pricing, production methods and industrial relations can become influential (Whitley, 1987). Sectors can be conceived of as an 'organisational field' linking firms and the broader society (Di Maggio and Powell, 1983). Arias has demonstrated the value of this orientation in her analysis of the pharmaceutical industry in Ecuador. Multinationals operating in the area spread modern HRM practices from their headquarters to their subsidiaries. But local firms do not mimic the multinationals and 'seem to constitute a world of their own organised along family business lines' (1993: 24). Organisations in the two fields are responding to different normative environments and relational constraints, such as rules set by government favourable to the largest players. Despite the persuasiveness of the analysis, Arias goes on to argue that the relevance of national boundaries remains paramount. But does it?

Globalisation

With half the best-selling contemporary management books putting 'global' in their titles, we can be sure that a considerable amount of hype surrounds the idea. But globalisation has also become a focal point for an important debate about contemporary organisations and the economy (for example, Smith and Elger, 1994) and for a range of serious accounts of the refashioning of key sectors such as engineering (Edquist and Jacobsson, 1988) and high technology (Henderson, 1989). The process can be said to consist of a number of interrelated tendencies.

The internationalisation of production and services   Foreign direct investment and industrial location have obviously been long-term developments. What is newer is the organisation and co-ordination of activities by TNCs at a global level: 'Rivals compete against each other on a truly worldwide basis, drawing on competitive advantages that grow out of their entire network of worldwide activities' (Porter, 1990: 35).

Stateless corporations   Transnationals that utilise foreign direct investment (FDI) to establish 'globally' integrated production or service chains, are increasingly the key players. They are differentiated from multinationals that create branches in separate countries in order to penetrate domestic markets. Though genuinely 'stateless' corporations are rare, contemporary corporate structures articulate a complex network of parent–subsidiary relations, as well as direction and co-ordination of economic activities across national boundaries. Know-how which is gained centrally or in one particular subsidiary operating unit is capable of being transferred to the various subunits of the corporation.

World markets   This is not merely the growth, but the integration of world trade. Included within this framework are the development of relatively standardised global products such as the 'world car' announced by Ford in 1994, the erosion of protected national industries (for example, European telecommunications industries or previous state firms), and the acceleration of movement out of mainly domestic markets by particular national capitals.

Increased integration into the international division of labour   Within the ideal type of globalisation, 'distinct national economies are subsumed and rearticulated into the system by essentially international processes and transactions' (Hirst and Thompson, 1992: 360). This may include the development of international state apparatuses which interact with and shape the interntional division of labour (Pitelis, 1993). New countries (for example, China), regions or social formations, notably the new post-Communist economies of Eastern Europe, are gradually brought into the financial and corporate workings of the global economy and pressurised to specialise in the provision of certain goods or services, such as cheap labour.

The internationalisation of financial markets   Not only have markets for finance become truly global in the recent and more deregulated past; there has been a closer integration with production. Transnational banks offer new services to multinationals, such as the financing of acquisitions, management of liquid assets and leasing arrangements. At the same time increasing numbers of banks are subsidiaries of multinationals. It is therefore possible to speak of transnational finance capital in which the two actors, 'are organically linked in their internationalisation' (Andreff, 1984: 66).

Such trends are undoubtedly influential ones, with the result that the space for the national and local is squeezed as organisational forms and practices demonstrate convergent tendencies. This can be seen in Austria and Sweden, which are societies with traditionally distinctive national models embodied in social settlements and ways of regulating the political economy. But such arrangements are under considerable strain from the rapid internationalisation of their domestic economies. Sweden has had to cope with the dual pressures of an accelerated drift of capital abroad and competition at home from Japanese models and other variants on lean production. The closure of Volvo's Udevalla and Kalmar plants has had a particularly destructive effect on attempts to create a new 'Swedish model' based on innovative work organisation. Sandberg (1993: 8) comments that, 'The management of Volvo does not seem to be able to resist the pressure of comparisons and the possibilities of moving the production between units, that the alliance with Renault will bring.'

That convergence is aided by other processes. Supranational state systems such as the EC are not new, but 'What is significant today is the sheer increase in their number, the growth in their territorial scope, and their acquisition of important new functions' (Jessop, 1992: 10). The Social Chapter of the Treaty of Maastricht is just one example of the development of webs of rules involving the standardisation of qualifications, social rights, quality systems, and employment regulation (Cressey and Jones, 1991). The much-vaunted British opt-out is already looking hollow as European law overrides national decisions and TNCs apply the provisions of the Chapter anyway. There is more rapid diffusion of 'best practice'. True, this is not a wholly new phenomenon. In the postwar period the giant US corporations transferred work organisation and managerial techniques across capitalist countries. Smith and Meiskens (1995) argue that the more extensive integration of corporate structures, allied to factors such as the internationalisation of consultancy, business schools, and the market for management literature, is enabling more rapid learning processes. Finally, more advanced information technology, such as computer networks for co-ordination and control is facilitating standardisation and integration of corporate activities.

All these trends exist and are important, but we have to add some qualifications. There is a danger of simply reverting to the earlier determinism and unproblematic notions of efficiency. This danger can be illustrated by reference to *The Machine that Changed the World* (Womack *et al.*, 1990), which has had a substantial influence on governments and companies. Drawing on the experience of Japanese production systems and extensive research into the motor industry, the authors promote the principles of 'lean production', which they claim produces efficiently with half the human effort, with considerable zeal. Such principles 'can be applied equally in every industry across the globe' (p. 8), as long as automobile companies adopt the necessary structures and practices to promote diffusion. An example of the latter would be 'an integrated, global personnel system that promotes personnel from any country in the company as if nationality did not exist' (p. 4). We are not concerned here to evaluate the merits of lean production, but its status as a universal 'best practice'. The study has been heavily criticised for getting the statistics wrong and exaggerating Japanese advantage (Williams *et al.*, 1992a). For example, the authors do not explain how Toyota and other firms take labour out of production, ignoring the specific features of post-war Japanese labour relations, where defeated unions and malleable workforces allow high levels of work intensification. Berggren (1993) questions whether the record of Japanese manufacturers at home and in the US transplants on high work speed and employee surveillance, low health and safety standards and exclusion of union involvement in regulating production would be acceptable in the very different European context.

Though there is some evidence that aspects of production practices can be uncoupled from culture and transferred across national boundaries (Florida and Kenney, 1991), the claim of superior ways of organising *production* separates it from the supportive institutional context – the industrial relations system, the subordinate networks of suppliers, state and financial sector support. In other words, we are back to the social embeddedness of economic action discussed earlier. *The Machine the Changed the World* is an extreme case of ideas of globalisation or convergence following single paths. Just like the older convergence theory, discredited for its technological and other determinisms (Kerr *et al.*, 1964), all linear models, including the popular notions of moves from Fordism to post-Fordism or mass production to flexible specialisation (Aglietta, 1979; Lipietz, 1982; Piore and Sabel, 1984), need to be treated with suspicion because they work on stereotypical ideas of homogeneous, static systems and underestimate the pattern of adaptation and varied diffusion that 'best practices' go through. The pattern is still strongly shaped by the residual powers of nation-states to create distinctive contexts for economic activity which firms have positive reasons to adapt to (Hirst and Thompson, 1992; Whitley, 1994); and mainstream business analysis (Kitschfelt, 1991; Porter, 1991) provides useful insights into how there are still important variations by sector in processes of industrial innovation and competitive advantage.

Conclusion

In this discussion it has often seemed that it is impossible to develop models of organisation–environment relations that escape the dichotomies of determinism/choice, convergence/divergence. For TNCs this apparent paradox is reflected through the contradictory pressures to standardise their operations, products and services so as to maximise the scale and scope benefits of global integration, while at the same time attempting to serve the needs of specific markets. The current favourite for solving this problem is the prescription for such organisations to be *glocal* (Bartlett and Goshal, 1992). But it is easier to devise a slogan than to solve substantive theoretical and practical issues. To go any further we need to pull together what we know of the forces that shape organisational forms and practices.

A model developed by Smith and Meiskens (1995) is useful here, where they distinguish between three kinds of effects on work organisation.

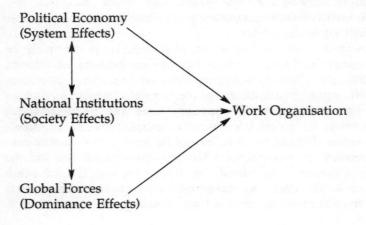

System effects are commonalities generated by social formations such as capitalism as a mode of production or patriarchy. All societies and the organisations within them have to operate within the parameters set by systems, for example competitive relations between enterprises, the conflicting interests of capital and labour. These processes create rules of the game which shape social relations in the workplace and constrain organisational choices.

Tsoukas (1994a) demonstrates how this operated with respect to firms in state socialist systems, utilising the previously-discussed concepts of institutional theory. He argues that socio-economic systems have a macro-logic that conditions and provides continuities in the organisational characteristics of firms irrespective of particular histories and societies. In the case of state socialism, collective ownership, command planning and a heavy emphasis on ideology leave little space for autonomous economic agents. Firms therefore increase their chances of survival by displaying conformity, often of a 'ceremonial' nature, to the party-state apparatus. The macro rules and institutions are isomorphically reproduced at micro level, overseen by the party structures in the workplace and a hierarchical and rule-bound style of management: 'The organisation becomes a political-cum-ideological miniature of the state' (1994a: 34). It is perfectly possible to explain the dependent relations between state and enterprise in such societies without the baggage of institutionalism and allowing for more variations (see Smith and Thompson, 1992), but the general point about system effects still stands, and indicates why naïve attempts to transfer managerial techniques from West to East may fail, given that the transition from command to market economy is still in its early stages.

Under capitalism, the relations between system and organisation are more loosely coupled and there is greater diversity of institutional configurations at both levels. This is where *societal effects* are most pertinent. As we have already discussed this point extensively, we need not dwell on it here, except for one observation. Some nation-states provide stronger and more distinctive institutional environments than others. Japan is always the example, but Sweden, Germany, or Austria would equally fit the bill. What they have in common is a strong social settlement between key actors – capital, labour, the state – which structures the relations between them and enhances the connections between social, economic and political institutions.

Societies with strong social settlements are more likely to generate *dominance effects*. This is because particular societies come to represent conceptions of success and progress, with models of 'best practice' concerning labour markets, labour processes and other factors exported from one society to another. You will have noticed that this term is always put in inverted commas so as to signal that it is not meant to be taken literally. 'Best practices' are socially constructed and not necessarily simply read off from actual success. They are read through ideological spectacles and mediated by a country's position and power in the international division of labour. Dominance does not indicate automatic or uncontested adaptation. There is always competition between such practices, aiding the process whereby key actors in and across societies 'search' for viable and legitimate models. This framework is useful, with one serious limitation. Work organisations are made to be the recipients of influences, embedded in contexts rather than an independent force. Given the immense power of contemporary TNCs this is unfortunate. To take one example, firms such as IBM, Toyota or McDonald's are also creators and purveyors of 'best practice'. The diagram would need to be redesigned to indicate reciprocal influences.

How the various influences of system, society, 'best practice' and organisation align themselves is not predictable or in a fixed hierarchy. Social scientists need to show how the levels are linked in concrete instances. So, when discussing how managerial and organisational knowledge is diffused, Arias (1993: 30) argues that 'Cross national research on transfers should be done within a neoinstitutional framework that allows a shifting of levels of analysis from the organisation, to the field, to the national, to the world-system level'. G. Henderson (1992) also fleshes out an institutional analysis by outlining *modes of articulation* between national and global economies. For example, most of the manufacturing economies of the EC articulate to the world economy as independent exporters, with firms distributing and marketing under their own name. In contrast some sectors of the East Asian economies and those of Central and Eastern Europe are more likely to be involved in commercial subcontracting where production is structured in commodity chains driven by the demands of distributors and retailers rather than manufacturers.

Global capitalism remains a dynamic system in which different strategies are available to establish competitive advantage for companies and countries. In that competitive struggle forces of divergence and convergence are in continual tension. Different facets of societal or corporate organisation will be subject to differential pressures. For example, the industrial relations systems of firms are the least likely to be internationally standardised, because they are most embedded in national institutional frameworks. Production and management systems, however, are subject much more directly to dominance effects from perceived 'best practices' and the need of TNCs to integrate their diverse activities and structures (Thompson *et al.*, 1995). The 'environment' therefore has to be conceived not as a given force within which dependent organisations adapt and transact, but as a global political economy whose levels provide a shifting dynamic within which organisations reciprocally *inter*act.

CHAPTER 4

Management and control

We saw in Chapter 2 that the first quarter of the twentieth century marked the emergence of professional management as social force, specialist occupational category and set of distinct work practices. This development was integral to changes in the organisation of capitalist production, with the modern bureaucratic enterprise increasingly based on the joint stock company, often in the new multi-divisional form, with its separation of ownership and management. In this type of structure, middle managers headed autonomous divisions which integrated production and distribution by co-ordinating flows from suppliers to consumers in the more clearly defined markets (Chandler, 1977). Such divisions administered their functional activities through specialist departments. All this encouraged the professionalisation of management and the rapid spread of administrative techniques. Management thought became intimately linked to the appearance of a distinct occupational grouping, organisational theory being used as a resource to understand the complexities of the large-scale organisation and management's role within it.

A key theme underlying the contradictory and partial organisational prescriptions, strategies and tactics was the belief in principles and even 'laws' concerning the nature of managerial activities and functions. As John Child observes:

> Management's claim to professionalism, for instance, was only plausible if it could be shown to possess some uniform and generalised body of knowledge upon which its practioners could draw. The so-called 'principles of management' could be presented as a theoretical base upon which the subject of 'management' rested. (1969: 225).

Much of this development was during the inter-war period of 'classical' writers such as Fayol, Taylor and Barnard, discussed in Chapter 2. As we saw, Fayol was the most concerned to elaborate common characteristics of management. These consisted of *planning* general lines of action and forecasting; *organising* human and material resources within appropriate structures; *commanding* the *activities* of personnel for optimum return; *co-ordination* of varied activities; and *control* to ensure consistency with rules and command. These were situated within a detailed set of principles reflecting the division of labour and hierarchy of the bureaucratic enterprise, tempered by equitable treatment and personal responsibility. One of the effects of this way of thinking was to define managerial functions by a process of abstraction from specific activities into a conception of *general* management (Armstrong, 1987a). Managerial work would differ not in kind but only in the proportion which is actually 'managerial'. This would have a profound influence on management thought, spreading the idea that knowledge, skills and experience are common and transferable.

Meanwhile, in Britain, Mary Parker Follett was producing prescriptions for a science of behaviour informed by the concerns of the human relations tradition. Management could learn this science because it was derived from situational laws governed by the needs of the system. As such, management could represent and integrate all interests through its capacity to apply optimal solutions through depersonalised authority. Classical writings have now been superseded in the post-war period by a body of more detailed studies of management. Indeed, the study of organisation has become synonymous with that of management. In the Anglo-American tradition of organisation theory, management studies has emerged as an 'intellectual field' sustained by an extensive network of educational and training institutions (Whitley, 1984). The more confident asserted the viability of a management or administrative science whose methods and knowledge could support rational activities and decision-making. A post-war generation of 'new systematisers' (Barley and Kunda, 1992: 377) ranged from those who developed techniques of Operations Research such as Critical Path Method and Program Evaluation and Review Technique, to contingency theorists with their attempts to specify causal relations between environmental and structure variables, and motivational schemas based on rational calculation. Employees were either absent or objects to be acted on through the new systems. The new ground rules drew on 'hard' knowledge that could be learnt by managers in general rather than functional specialists. Such an approach competed with the influence of human relations perspectives, with their notion of training managers to learn how to exercise social and leadership skills.

This chapter aims to examine such claims through an analysis of the nature of management. It will argue that though both traditional and recent research offer important insights, the perspectives are partial and flawed. In particular they neglect important dimensions such as power and control, confirming the diagnosis of mainstream perspectives in Chapter 1, as well as the divisions and contradictions embedded in the managerial labour process itself. Of course power and control are not just adjuncts to a discussion of management.

This and the following chapter set out the central debates about control and power in organisation in their own right.

The nature of management

The modern literature (for example, Drucker, 1955; Stewart, 1967; Mintzberg, 1973; Kotter, 1982) shares the central concern of the classical writers to identify common functions and criteria for effectiveness. There has been an even greater emphasis on the individual as a unit of analysis, a problematic of 'what do managers do?' (Hales, 1986). The answer given is a positive one. Drucker starts his well-known text by saying that 'The manager is the dynamic, life-giving element in every business . . . the only effective advantage an enterprise has in a competitive economy' (1955: 13). Texts continually invoke as examples captains of industry such as Lee Iaocca, the ex-Chrysler boss. In this elevated role, the manager is presented almost as a free-floating centre of power. Organisations are still frequently treated as closed systems, with the assumption that 'it was largely within management's own powers to fashion behaviour and relationships as might best suit their own purposes' (J. Child, 1969: 168). Paradoxically, by focusing on the individual, management can be analysed as if it was homogeneous, leading to the conception of the 'universal manager' carrying out a generalised set of functions standing above any specific context (Mintzberg, 1973).

Theorists could agonise about whether management was science, art, magic or politics (T. Watson, 1986: 29), but all options rest on the analytical and practical skills of 'successful managers'. The constant struggle for competency is further linked to the assumption that management *effectiveness* is tangible and identifiable (Hales, 1986: 88). To this end anything can be quantified and learned. The focus of course changes. It may, for instance, be the fashionable qualities of managerial excellence (see Hitt *et al.*, 1986: 1011).

These various assumptions underwrite the more fundamental view of management practices as a neutral resource, the central task of which is deciding what should be done and getting other people to do it. In this view, which we describe as *technicist*, managers can embody and carry out the central mission of the organisation and secure its desired objectives. This links back to the idea discussed in Chapter 1 of managers as the guardians of organisations being rational tools to secure goals. By conceiving of the ends as unitary and the means as objectively rational, the socially-constructed, political character of organisational arrangements is removed (Berkeley Thomas, 1993: 37).

Managers are also seen as functionally necessary in a deeper sense. The functions are 'indispensable' and are ones which 'no one but the manager can perform' (Drucker, 1977: 39). As Willmott observes (1984: 350), this view confuses the general process of management of resources with the role of managers empowered to command others within specific institutional frameworks. Put another way, it wrongly assumes that, 'the management function must, of necessity, reside with a particular category of agents who manage or administer other agents' (Hales, 1988: 5). In particular circumstances, work teams or worker co-operatives can equally be said to be carrying out managerial functions.

Organisational theories seldom acknowledge the wider context in which managerial work is undertaken. Whitely argues that it is better to attempt to, 'specify general features of managerial tasks in terms of their functions in the organisation and change of economic enterprises as interdependent units of resource co-ordination and control, rather than identifying the characteristics of all jobs by "managers"' (1984: 343). Elsewhere, the wider theory of a 'managerial revolution' was being articulated. Part of the idea of an 'organisation society', as discussed in Chapter 1, the theory rested on a particular interpretation of changes in the nature of the large corporation. As the dominant form, joint stock companies were held to be characterised by a separation of ownership and control, share dispersal and a corresponding rise in the importance of a professional managerial élite who run the new corporations. Although the growing significance of management is indisputable, many adherents of the theory (Berle and Means, 1935) took the new corporate system to be a 'purely neutral technocracy', with managers with different backgrounds and experiences exercising social responsibilities. Tougher versions (Burnham, 1945) envisaged a managerially planned and controlled society beyond the workplace, with management becoming the dominant class of all industrial societies.

The managerial revolution thesis had a wider significance for social theory, often influenced by systems thinking (Reed, 1984: 278). At its core was the view that capitalism as a system based on individual private ownership was being supplanted by a post-capitalist society in which old political disputes about ownership were irrelevant (Dahrendorf, 1959). But these theoretical developments enabled management writers such as Drucker to assert that 'we no longer talk of "capital" and "labour", we talk of "management" and "labour"' (1955: 13). Some scepticism was expressed by senior managers who referred to 'claptrap' about social responsibilities, reminding their colleagues that they remained the servant of their employers (J. Child, 1969: 152–3). Managerial capitalism had extended its tentacles. But we should remember the qualifications made in Chapter 2 about the culturally-loaded nature of such theory and practice. Organisational life in Germany and other countries was not dominated by the search for a profession of management: 'Continentals appreciate the specialist nature of most executive jobs: they do not see why specialists should be described as "managers", nor are they notable for having occupational groups which call themselves "professionals". European business does not seem to have suffered through the lack of either idea' (Fores and Glover, 1976: 104).

Managers as leaders and decision-makers

Having set out the basic assumptions of mainstream approaches, it is useful to highlight some of the further dimensions of research which shape the broader view of management activities. From the 1950s onwards considerable attention has been paid to the interrelations between management, leadership and decision-making. Textbooks are normally quick to point out that all leaders are not managers and not all managers have or even need leadership abilities. Indeed there is a modest sub-literature on leadership qualities as such; for example on whether successful leaders all have or need particular personality traits. We are concerned, however, with the way in which leadership studies frequently merge with those of management by virtue of a focus on effective management *styles*. In fact most texts not only use the terms 'management' and 'leadership styles' interchangeably, they refer to the same research.

A common starting point is often McGregor's (1960) famous theory of X and Y assumptions that management have about people. The former leans towards Taylorist notions of employees who dislike work and initiative, and therefore have to be directed and coerced; while the latter accepts that they have self-direction and self-control if they are committed to organisational goals and are involved in decision-making. People need whipping versus people are better at whipping themselves, as someone once mischievously put it. McGregor's theory is clearly part of the human relations tradition and follows through the perceived results of the Hawthorne studies in terms of the beneficial effects of participatory leadership and sympathetic supervision. A variety of subsequent studies developed categories based on a comparison between democratic and autocratic management or leadership styles. The dominant message is that democratic leadership is better, both for increasing morale and productivity, and for improving the quality of decisions. How democratic it is remains open to question. Most new styles have always left management command structures intact. Nichols and Beynon quote one manager at 'Chemco': 'Democratic leadership is the only way. But you'll know that won't you. Psychologists have proved it with children' (1977: 123). Those evaluating the results of such styles have also been sceptical, with Perrow noting that 'the history of research in this area is one of progressive disenchantment with the above theses' (1979: 98).

Some of the studies are careful to allow for combinations of styles or particular styles in appropriate circumstances. In addition, Fiedler's (1967) research offers a thoroughgoing contingency approach in which effectiveness is linked specifically to organisational context. By developing a 'least preferred co-worker scale', the suitability of a task or relationship orientated leader was shown to be dependent on the degree to which the task is structured, the leader's position power, and the relations between leaders and led. But even this has a relatively limited notion of the context of management practices, and rests on individualistic and small-scale scenarios. The literature on leadership and management styles has failed to integrate a deeper analysis of how management strategies develop and their interrelationship with the political economy of the firm and society. We shall return to this question later.

A crucial part of leadership is decision-making, Simon (1960) regarding the latter as synonymous with management. It is therefore not surprising that this has been another focus for researchers. For example, organisations have been analysed as decision-making systems, while Mintzberg (1973) has used 'decisional roles' as one category of classification of management activities and functions. Traditional approaches tend to start from a *rational choice* model which having assumed consistency of goals, requires the setting out of decision-making alternatives and assessment of likely outcomes. Once again the emphasis is on skills and techniques to aid the optimal or 'one best' decision. Assessments must take into account the technical and human requirements, one text recommending a balance of the skills of Captain Kirk and Mr Spock from Starship Enterprise!

Social scientists can help managers to design appropriate centralised or decentralised structures; identify stages in the process, such as generation, evaluation, choice, implementation and follow-through; and ensure an awareness of the behavioural dimensions of decision-making in groups. This may include specific techniques, the best known of which is brainstorming. Another important area is access to information and the design of management information systems. One of the purposes is to separate routine, 'programmed' decisions and enhance the ability of management to concentrate on strategic decisions (Stewart, 1970). The above emphasis reinforces a technicist view of management processes and activities. It further neglects the inequalities in access to information which structure decision processes, which are frequently legitimated by reference to technical expertise (J. Child, 1973). The *politics* of decision-making is also highlighted by Pettigrew (1973), who points to the hierarchy of powers shaped by the control of resources.

Researchers are aware, however, of limits to rationality. March and Simon (1958) introduce the concept of 'intended rationality', recognising that there are considerable constraints to the capacity to access and evaluate a full range of options. The existing structures of specialisation and hierarchy in organisations, as well as the routine practices identified in a Weberian analysis, will limit the content and flow of information and set agendas for decision-making. As a result, organisational participants are boundedly rational, have to work with simplified models of reality and there is 'limited search' and 'satisficing' rather than optimal choices. Cyert and March (1963) point to similar processes such as 'uncertainty absorption', whereby in order to maintain stability of operations, rules and processes are geared to short-run decisions and frequent reviews. What emerges are policies and decisions by 'incremental comparison'; not a rational science, but a 'science' of muddling through (Lindblom, 1959).

Management practices: a new realism?

Demarcating the boundaries of rationality helped to extend the study of management. But discussion of the core issue of defining and classifying activities moved on to a more detailed 'realism'. Fores and Glover argue that, 'observation shows that [this] classical view is largely a convenient fiction. . . In reality, executive work is complex, confusing to the outsider, and rarely predictable (1976: 194). What 'observations' are they talking about? By getting a large and varied group of managers to fill in diaries, Stewart (1967) drew up classifications based on how they spent their *time*. This produced emissaries, writers, discussers, troubleshooters and committee men. A later study (1976) focused on patterns of contact – this time identifying hub, peer-dependent, man-management and solo. In contrast, Mintzberg (1973) confined himself to five chief executives and classified ten roles under three headings: under *interpersonal* come figurehead, leader and liaison; under *informational* – monitor, disseminator and spokesman; and under *decisional* come entrepreneurial, disturbance-handler, resource allocator and negotiator. We would agree with Hales' observation that many of the categories used in these and other studies are largely interchangeable, for example leader/figurehead/spokesman. New terms such as 'network building' and 'setting agendas' correspond in substance to old favourites such as 'planning'. He produces a composite list from six of the best-known studies, which 'exhibit striking parallels with the supposedly outdated "classical principles of management"' (1986: 95). In addition, some of the variations merely reflect managerial *ideologies*, with modern writers in a more democratic era preferring to describe command as motivation (Mullins, 1985: 121).

Nevertheless, it remains the case that the new empirical studies do partly break with traditional approaches and those found in popular management books. Once the complication of producing labels and lists is set aside, more realistic insights are available. We have already referred to Cyert and March's findings on the short-term incrementalism in the sphere of decision-making. But the significant breakthroughs are aided by a willingness to use a greater variety of research methods than those used in broad-brush analyses of managerial functions. Structured or unstructured observation methods, time-

TABLE 4.1   Managerial functions

(1) Acting as a figurehead and leader of an organisational unit
(2) Liaison: the formation and maintenance of contacts
(3) Monitoring, filtering and disseminating information
(4) Allocating resources
(5) Handling disturbances and maintaining work flows
(6) Negotiating
(7) Innovating
(8) Planning
(9) Controlling and directing subordinates.

Source: Colin P. Hales, 'What Do Managers Do?: A Critical Review', *Journal of Management Studies*, 23: 95.

budget studies and self-report questionnaires can capture a greater sense of fluidity and processual factors (Horne and Lupton, 1965; Stewart, 1967, 1976; Mintzberg, 1973; Kotter, 1982; Burns, 1982).

Such studies reveal that the image of the reflective strategist, thinker and planner is a myth. An alternative picture is indicated through the language of realism. Though there are variations between the studies, management practices are said to be opportunistic, habitual, tactical, reactive, frenetic, ad-hoc, brief, fragmented, and concerned with fixing. This arises primarily because the manager has to adapt to continued uncertainties, limited information and contradictory pressures, not least on time and energy. As a result, routines are shaped by short-time spans, the domination of face-to-face interaction and lateral communication in gathering and using information. For Mintzberg, this actually corresponds to managerial preferences for use of informal structures, gossip and speculation.

Nor are such activities necessarily bad for effectiveness and efficiency. Though energy can be dissipated in conflict and power struggles between cliques, Kotter (1982) points out that patterns do emerge based on establishing and maintaining *networks* vital for co-operation and a flow of information. Finally, though the focus is on the internal world of the organisation, the new realism is not incompatible with an analysis of environmental pressures. Loveridge's (1982) study of manufacturing companies in the Midlands showed that marketing and financial pressures, plus the need to accommodate to the power of workforce job controls, led in the direction of federal structures and short-term reactive policies and a concern with implementation rather than planning.

The realist challenge to the idea of the scientific and rational character of management is useful and widely accepted. It has not, however, established unchallenged intellectual domination. Not only do textbooks remain influenced by prescriptions from Fayol, but preoccupations with *new* lists of functions can still be described as variations on a classical theme. Indeed, the actual choice of new lists is extensive. Many pop management writers recycle a limited number of activities under new and more exotic titles, including that of jungle fighter and gamesman. Lists are merely the outward form of a belief in a transferable and common *essence* of management. Partly in response to the excesses of claims about new forms of organisation and management, influential voices are calling for a return to that 'essence', though it is redefined as the pursuit of rhetoric, identity and robust action (Eccles and Nohria, 1992). Nor is this impetus purely theoretical. Recent years have seen the rise of a competence movement, primarily in the USA and the UK, which aims to specify a common currency of occupational standards and to develop managers with the aid of behavioural and task measurements (Burgoyne, 1993).

There are also inherent limits and even drawbacks. It is, as Hales (1988) notes, an *internal* critique, and at the heart of the problem is the fact that it is at the *empirical* level only. Realism can show us that management is not what it is made out to be. Instead it portrays the activities of managers, 'as a quite arbitrary set of roles with little suggestion as to why they are as they are' (Armstrong, 1986: 19). The pervasive image of ad-hocery and muddling through seems to deny both purpose and coherence. Hales (1986) rightly observes that by focusing on individual jobs, rather than on management as a process, behaviour is unsituated and neglects the institutional context and functions. This is worsened by the tendency of behavioural analysis to concentrate on observable activities in a non-problematical way. For all its limitations, responsibilities and functions were the focus of classical theory, and many of the criticisms levelled at it have been attacks on a straw man (Berkeley Thomas, 1993: 51). In this sense, 'realism' marks a retreat from a broader framework of analysis. Understanding managerial work requires questions to be asked not just about what managers do, but about what they have to ensure others do. In other words, an emphasis on the *control* of particular organisational units in the labour process, though Hales later qualifies this by referring to control as one phase of the management process (1988: 5). The next part of this chapter will look in more detail at the relationships between management and control. Many of the issues raised by the realist critique are returned to when we assess perspectives on control strategy.

Control

There is not a great deal to say about the treatment of control in mainstream writing. Given the assumption of goal consensus, the issue is often simply ignored or trivialised. When it *is* discussed explicitly in standard textbooks, the chapters devoted to it are sometimes of a rather bizarre nature in almost omitting any reference to conflicts between groups. The talk is of technical inputs and outputs in a self-adjusting system, performance standards and feedback mechanisms. Control is reduced to a *monitoring* device, with management's role being to check progress, ensure that actions occur as planned and to correct any deviation. It is also seen in a unitary way: 'controlled performance' with an assumption of goal-consensus. Some writers (Lawlor, 1976) put an emphasis on people desiring control – for example, getting enjoyment from dependence on higher authority. Resistance is smuggled in occasionally when discussing the *behavioural* implications as people 'react' to control processes, requiring management to adjust strategies accordingly.

We do accept that not all control processes arise from or are structured by antagonistic interests. Stock inventories and financial budgeting are necessary and not always conflictual features of any system of work organisation. A written job description may under certain conditions actually allow employees to assert power or control. But most control processes remain difficult to separate from the social relations of work, even when they appear to be neutral. This was the important conclusion of Blau and Schoenherr (1971), who used the concept of *insidious* controls to highlight the way in which management can utilise impersonal and unobtrusive means. Examples include selective recruitment of staff whose sense of professionalism or expertise enable them to work without direct controls; use of resource allocation as a financial discipline; and controls embodied in technology. Thus even those staff who exercise considerable work autonomy, such as those in higher education, have a series of indirect constraints over their actions. This kind of research is one of the few bridgeheads into the much wider body of work on control from a radical perspective.

Radical perspectives

Radical writers on organisation and management frequently *begin* from an analysis of control relations. The first radical text to make a major impact on organisation theory began by defining the theoretical rationale of organisational analysis: 'For this volume we have proposed as such an object the concept of organisation as control of the labour process' (Clegg and Dunkerley, 1980: 1). This framework derived from Marx's analysis of the capitalist labour process, which was updated and revitalised by Braverman (1974) and a range of other 'labour process' theorists discussed below.

All societies have labour processes, but under capitalism the labour process has specific characteristics. The most significant is what Marx referred to as the transformation of labour power into labour. In other words, when capital purchases labour it has only a potential or capacity to work. To ensure profitable production capital must organise the conditions under which labour operates to its own advantage. But workers pursue their own interests for job security, higher rewards and satisfying work, developing their own counter-organisation through informal job controls, restriction of output and the like.

To resolve this problem, and because they are under competitive pressure from other firms to cut costs and raise productivity, employers seek to control the conditions under which work takes place. Control is not an end in itself, but a means to transform the capacity to work established by the wage relation, into profitable production. It is a term, summarising a set of mechanisms and practices that regulate the labour process (P. K. Edwards, 1990). Richard Edwards (1979: 18) distinguishes three elements in any system of control:

1   direction and specification of work tasks;
2   evaluation, monitoring and assessment of performance;
3   the apparatus of discipline and reward to elicit co-operation and compliance.

Such elements may, however, be best described as *detailed* control, in that they are normally connected to immediate work processes; whereas *general* control refers to management's capacity to subordinate labour to its direction of the production process as a whole. This distinction made by P. K. Edwards (1990) and other writers is of significance in that it allows for recognition of tremendous variations in how detailed control is exercised. Such a model can even allow for employers giving workers significant discretion over tasks, as in semi-autonomous work groups, *if* it maintains the employers' overall control. Control is also not absolute, but, at least at the immediate level, a contested relationship. Conflict is built into the wage-effort bargain, with even mainstream writers recognising that an employment contract outlining required performance runs up against employees with their own goals and wants.

What about the role of management in this process? Claims of independent actors carrying out a neutral role are disputed by evidence concerning the top strata of management (Zeitlin, 1974). By their motivation, social background and connections, rewards and share-holdings in corporations, most managers are part of the capitalist class. Although this is a useful corrective, this 'sociological' analysis is not the crucial point. For example, a number of entrepreneurs, such as Alan Sugar of Amstrad, are from a traditional working-class background. But what matters is the structural location and functions in the organisation. If anything, entrepreneurs from this background tend to identify even more closely with their new role.

Proceeding from an analysis of process and functions, radical theorists (Carchedi, 1977; R. Edwards, 1979) argue that management performs a *dual* function in the enterprise. Managerial practices are a necessary means of *Co-ordinating* diverse activities and services, particularly as production becomes a more collective process. However, they also bear the imprint of the antagonistic social relations within the capitalist labour process. These require management to carry out functions of *control* and surveillance, exercising hierarchical authority over workers separated from the means of production. Though it is not always clear that it is possible to distinguish between a 'neutral' co-ordination and an 'antagonistic' control, managers do act as agents carrying out the 'global functions' of capital, functions which, as we observed in Chapter 2, were delegated as part of the bureaucratisation of production. The idea of agency conjures up rather crude images of conspiracies and empty vessels: 'In the capitalist system, the principal function of management is to exploit labour power to the maximum in order to secure profits for the owners of capital' (Berkeley Thomas, 1993: 61). But the generality 'to the maximum' is meaningless. There are only specific and diverse means through which the requirements of capital are brought about, in which management takes an active rather than a predetermined role.

Radical analyses often get tangled up in attempts to designate managers to precise class positions. This theme does not concern us here (though see Johnston, 1986 for a critical account). What is important is that we have available a framework for understanding management practices which provides an alternative to the dominant combination of behavioural and managerial revolution theories. The fact, for example, that executives of a large corporation have the formal status of employees is, as Braverman observes, merely the form given to the domination of capital in modern society:

> Their formal attribute of being part of the same payroll as the production workers, clerks and porters of the corporation no more robs them of the powers of decision and command over the others in the enterprise than does the fact that the general, like the private, wears the military uniform, or the pope and the cardinal pronounce the same liturgy as the parish priest. (1974: 405)

Instead of the separation of ownership and control, radical writers distinguish between *real* or economic ownership and agents holding actual *possession* (De Vroey, 1975; Carchedi, 1977). Managerial agents are governed by the external constraints imposed by the dynamics of competition and capital accumulation, with profitability remaining the crucial criteria through which the successful management work is judged. If anything, this is enhanced by property ownership and related forms of control becoming increasingly depersonalised with the rise of finance, pension funds and other institutional shareholders. Individual enterprises become 'simply units in a structure of intercorporate relations' (J. Scott, 1985: 142), the division of ownership and possession resulting in greater vulnerability for managers who know they may be removed from office (Holland, 1975).

A structural analysis does not imply that the growth of new forms of managerial labour is irrelevant. The heterogeneity of management has increased with the sheer extent and diversity of delegated functions and the competing groups, such as accountants and engineers, who lay claim to them. Within an increasingly complex hierarchy, middle and lower-level managers occupy 'contradictory class locations' (E. O. Wright, 1976) carrying out functions as agents of capital *and* as salaried employees. They are likely to exercise 'partial' possession; operational rather than allocative control, to use the language of organisational analysis (Carter, 1985: 122). We shall return to the significance of these divisions later.

Management strategies

Radical perspectives have been conditioned by Braverman's (1974) argument that the twentieth century has seen the tightening of managerial control, primarily through the application of Taylorist and scientific management strategies. Detailed evidence is provided of the extension of such methods from simple to complex production and their use in the transformation of clerical labour. When allied to managerial shaping of science and technology through mechanisation and automation, work design and organisation continue to embody key Taylorist principles such as task fragmentation and the separation of conception and execution. Braverman provided an important corrective to the widespread view that Taylorism was a failed system, superseded by more sophisticated behavioural theories to be used for motivational and job design tools (see M. Rose, 1975).

But it is widely recognised that Braverman overestimated the dominance of Taylorist strategies and practices, and underestimated the varied and uneven implementation, influenced by worker hostility, management suspicion and appropriateness to given environments. In Chapter 2 we tried to reach a balanced assessment. If Taylorism is taken to be part of a broader movement towards 'scientific' management focused on fragmentation of tasks and their subjection to increasing job measurement and evaluation, as well as the structuring of work processes so that skills and planning activities are located off the factory and office floor, then particular elements remain a highly significant component of control strategies, though seldom on their own (see Chapter 6 for a more detailed discussion of issues of modern job design).

Precisely because Braverman confused a particular system of control with management control in general, the question of *strategy* was put firmly on the agenda because of the resulting debate on alternatives. This is not to say that issues of strategy had no place in the existing organisational literature. We have already seen in Chapter 3 how Chandler (1962) regarded strategy, defined as long-term planning and resource allocation to carry out goals, as the characteristic feature of the modern multi-divisional firm. But control over employees was not dealt with systematically. Strategy has also been increasingly part of the agenda of the business policy and corporate management literature (Steiner and Miner, 1978). Radical perspectives differ from both in avoiding the prescriptive search for the 'best way'; remaining free to analyse what management *does*, rather than what it *should* do.

What of the alternative strategies raised in the labour process debate? Some of the best-known contributions have already been discussed in previous chapters. Richard Edward's (1979) model is based on historically successive dominant modes of control which reflect worker resistance and changing socio-economic conditions. A nineteenth-century system of *simple* or *personal* control by employers exercising direct authority gave way to more complex *structural* forms with the transition from small business, competitive capitalism to corporate monopolies. The first of these forms was *technical* control typified by the use of the assembly line which can pace and direct the labour process. The contradiction for management is that it created a common work experience and basis for unified shop floor opposition. In contrast, a system of *bureaucratic* control (see Chapter 2) embedded in the social and organisational structure of the firm rather than in personal authority, offers management a means of re-dividing the workforce and tying it to impersonal rules and regulations. With his co-thinkers among radical economists (R. Edwards *et al.*, 1975; Gordon *et al.*, 1982), Edwards has also argued that employers consciously create *segmented* labour markets as a response to economic crises and as a divide and rule strategy, particularly using gender and race.

In contrast, Friedman (1977) rightly eschews the notion of stages, preferring to set out ideal types or strategic poles of responsible autonomy and direct control which run parallel throughout the history of capitalism (for a description see Chapter 3). Each strategy generates its own inflexibilities in areas such as hiring and firing and task specification. The choice of strategy is governed by variations in the stability of labour and product markets, mediated by the interplay of worker resistance and managerial pressure. There is, however, an element of common ground in the belief that there has been a gradual historical tendency towards more consensual, integrative strategies, internal markets, institutionalised rules and in some cases, work humanisation schemes. This is also the view of the other major control theorist, Burawoy (1979, 1985). He periodises the development of capitalist work organisation in terms of the transition from *despotic* to *hegemonic* regimes. The former involved relations of dependence and coercion that did not prove viable for capital or labour. Workers sought collective representation and social protection from the state. Capital also had an interest in state regulation of conflict and a minimal social wage that would boost purchasing power. The shift to hegemonic regimes was also based on an internal state in the workplace that provided an 'industrial citizenship', using grievance machinery and regulated bargaining that minimised possible resistance and class solidarity.

This kind of judgement of long-term trends has not looked quite so accurate in a period where many companies have used the recession to restructure the workplace. Whereas some writers (see MacInnes, 1987) doubt whether the basic features of industrial and employment relations have significantly changed, there is certainly considerable evidence that in Britain and the USA many employers are consciously reconstituting employment practices in a harsher and more authoritarian way. In the USA (Parker, 1985) there have been aggressive de-unionisation campaigns and 'concession-bargaining' which forces workers to renegotiate worse pay and conditions. Although Britain's deeply-rooted union tradition largely prevents extensive de-unionisation and concession-bargaining, there has been a strong emphasis, particularly in the newer industries, on single-union and 'no-strike' deals; reduced demarcation and increased flexibility; more direct management communication with the shop floor, by-passing shop stewards; as well as new human resource initiatives such as quality circles (Morgan and Sayer, 1984; and see Chapter 6 below).

Events of this nature have led Burawoy to define the new dominant factory regime as one of *hegemonic despotism*. This is not a return to arbitrary tyranny, but the apparently 'rational' power of a capital that is mobile across the globe, over the workforce. (1985: 150). But regardless of the pervasiveness of such trends, new conceptual categories of this nature merely illustrate the fundamental problem of the control theories we have been examining. Alternative strategies have been put on the map, but too often within what has been described as the 'panacea fallacy' (Littler and Salaman, 1982) or 'monism' (Storey, 1985). That is, the idea that capital always seeks and finds definitive and comprehensive modes of control as the solution to its problems. Admittedly, this is somewhat less true of Friedman, who in his own defence argues that responsible autonomy and direct control have in-built contradictions and are, 'two directions towards which managers can move, rather than two predefined states between which managers choose' (1987: 3). But there is still a sense of a search for all-embracing categories, which have their parallels in behavioural theory, such as Etzioni's (1961) structures of compliance, or Schein's (1965) linear models of economic, social and complex man.

Nevertheless, the control debate has sparked off an extensive and useful amount of empirical work within the parameters of labour process theory. Early case studies tended to focus on reaffirmation of theses of deskilling and tighter controls (Zimbalist, 1979), or critiques of them highlighting moderating factors such as markets and worker resistance (Wood, 1982). More recent efforts have been concerned to establish trends in their own right. Studies dealing with the introduction of new technology have stressed that deskilling and direct control represent only one aspect of a range of management strategies. We have already discussed the variations shown in Wilkinson's study (see Chapter 3). John Child's (1985) research shows even more clearly how ideas of strategy can be used, whilst recognising variations in goals and environments. He identified a variety of strategies, including elimination of direct labour, sub-contracting, polyvalence or multi-tasking and job degradation. These were connected to an even wider set of influences, including those of national economic cycles, government policy and the culture of organisations.

Some research has tried to apply models to specific industries, but without any claims for universality. A good example is the use by Murray and Wickham (1985) of Richard Edwards's theory of bureaucratic control. They studied two Irish electronics factories employing mainly female semi-skilled workers, showing that direction, discipline and evaluation are all carried out according to explicit rules rather than direct controls. Supervisors do not monitor production performance and enforce discipline. This is left to inspectors on the basis of statistical records that can identify the operators responsible. Supervisors, however, are central to processes of evaluating the social character of the 'good worker' in order to facilitate promotion through the internal labour market. The elaborate and artificial hierarchy created at the plants meant that one-third of workers had been promoted from the basic assembly grade, thus confirming Edward's view that employees are given positive material reasons for complying with bureaucratic rules.

Other studies have focused on specific strategies and processes of control such as recruitment policies (Fevre, 1986; Maguire, 1986; Winstanley, 1986) which are neglected in an exclusive focus on the labour process. The most extensive research has been carried out on *gender*. Socially-defined notions of femininity as a form of control have been observed in multi-nationals operating in the Third World (Pearson, 1986). Plant management consciously exploits cultures of passivity and subordination by combining an image of the company as a patriarchal family system with the manager as father figure, with Western-style beauty competitions and classes (Grossman, 1979). In the West, Grieco and Whipp's overview argues that 'managerial strategies of control make use of and enhance the sexual divisions in society' (1986: 136). Studies of office and factory workers (Glenn and Feldberg, 1979; Pollert, 1981; Westwood, 1984; Bradley, 1986) show that management use womens' marginality to work, arising from the family, to frame their labour control policies. Strategies of paternalism and restrictive controls on supervision and piece-rates are frequent, though not always successful or uncontested.

In reflecting on the above debates, a degree of common ground emerges. Product and labour markets, worker resistance and a range of other external and internal factors are recognised as moderating control strategies and shaping power relations in the frontier of control between capital and labour. The variations in strategy that result are not random, but reflect the fundamental tension we have talked of between managements' need to control and discipline, while engaging workers' commitment and co-operation. Strategies therefore contain inherent contradictions (Storey, 1985; Hyman, 1987). These are enhanced by the difficulty of harmonising the different managerial functions, sites of intervention and decision-making, that include technology, social organisation of labour and relations with the representative bodies of employees. Hyman notes that, 'there is no "one best way" of managing these contradictions, only different routes to partial failure' (1987: 30). Management of large organisations is therefore likely to try combinations of control strategies and practices, appropriate to particular environments or sections of the workforce. As one of us has remarked elsewhere:

> The most consistent weakness of existing theory has been to counterpoise one form of control to another . . . No one has convincingly demonstrated that a particular form of control is necessary or inevitable for capitalism to function successfully. (P. Thompson, 1989: 151)

Questioning the idea of control strategies

The above 'consensus' does not satisfy those within and outside the radical perspective who are critical of the explanatory power of concepts of management control strategy. For some, the problem with a Marxist-influenced agenda is that, like more orthodox accounts, it wrongly assumes high levels of rationality, this time applied to top management (Bryman, 1984: 401). Others go beyond the previously-noted criticism of 'panacea fallacies' to object to the treatment of management as omniscient, omnipotent and monolithic. Based on her study of chemical plants, Harris mocks the image of managers who have the attributes of deity and 'papal innerrancy' when dealing with workers, commenting that radical writers assume that senior management 'always know what is in capital's interests and unfailingly order things so that they work together for its greater good' (1987: 70). There are conflicts within management reflecting contending interests groups and the difficulty of carrying out integrative functions. Nor is it always possible to draw a neat dividing line between workers and managers, given that managers are also wage labourers subject to controls. The distortions in such analyses are held to derive from a wider determinism and functionalism in which 'managers are regarded as unproblematic agents of capital who dispatch their 'global functions' in a rationalistic manner' (Storey, 1985: 195).

Capital's interests are not given and management practices cannot be 'read-off' from them. Assumptions of a 'tight-coupling' underestimate the diversity and complexity of such practices, and the significance for decision-making processes within the enterprise. It is also the case that in addition to the responsibilities that managers have to the control apparatus of the enterprise, they need to control their own personal identities and make sense of their own work in the employing organisation. Managerial work therefore has a 'double control' aspect in which there is a strategic exchange between individuals and organisations (T. Watson, 1994). The consequence of the above critiques is the belief that too few insights are generated into what 'flesh and blood' managers actually do.

At a general level many of these criticisms would be accepted across a wide spectrum. But some would carry it much further: 'current uses of the terms "strategy" and "control" are somewhat misleading guides both to actual management conduct and to the causes of particular outcomes in work organisation and industrial relations' (Rose and Jones, 1985: 82). We can break this down into two issues: do identifiable management strategies exist? and are practices centred on controlling workers? Those who argue against the idea of coherent strategies with a fixity of purpose believe that management activities are more likely to be piecemeal, un-coordinated and fragmented, with at best a striving for logical incrementalism. Management is concerned primarily with 'keeping the show on the road' (Tomlinson, 1982: 128), corresponding with the 'realist' views discussed earlier.

Supportive research exists in areas such as work reorganisation schemes (Rose and Jones, 1985) and new technology and skills in engineering (Campbell and Currie, 1987). Any strategic capacity is held to be inevitably undermined by a plethora of sites of decision-making; varied objectives among different management specialists and interest groups; the need to smooth over diverse and contradictory practices; and the requirement of sustaining a consensual accommodation with employee organisations. The result is an unpredictable variety of managerial intentions characterised by a 'plant particularism' (Rose and Jones, 1985: 96), and control structures as merely 'temporary outcomes' (Storey, 1985). Campbell and Currie plump for the idea of 'negotiated preferences' and there is a general orientation towards explanations based on *practices* rather than strategy.

Some of these differences may reflect the sector being researched. For example, engineering is well known for its 'seat-of-the-pants' approach to management, whereas other sectors such as food or chemicals are noted for a more strategic approach. Nevertheless, this kind of approach is confirmed by some writers on industrial relations (Purcell and Sissons, 1983), who note the problems created by the absence of management strategies towards their own employees, particularly of strategies that are integrated into overall business objectives. Instead there is a continued dominance of reactive and opportunistic practices directed towards immediate problem-solving

(Thurley and Wood, 1983: 209). What *kind* of strategy is said to be absent is not always made explicit. But the basic model used is similar to that popularised by Chandler, which, like many other adaptations to the business sphere, is strongly influenced by military experience and terminology (Shaw, 1990). That is, detailed and co-ordinated plans of campaign in which conscious, long-term planning based on corporate goals is supported by appropriate courses of action and allocation of resources. This can be seen in the business policy debate (Steiner and Miner, 1978) in which the burgeoning number of MBA students are warned of the negative consequences of the absence of corporate strategy.

But conceptions of management strategy in the above frameworks are in themselves problematic. A stereotyped polarity is set up between a conception of objective rationality which implies perfect foresight, choice and follow-through, and a bounded rationality of constrained choice in complex realities. Complaining that discourses of strategy are primarily about shoring up the power of senior managers and consultants, Knights and Morgan reject the concept altogether: 'Nothing new is really added by talking the discourse of strategy; on the contrary, a limit is put on our understanding of the special phenomenon because we are forcing action into a particular rationalistic and individualistic framework' (1990: 480). But the mistake is actually made by the critics. It is they who force action into a conceptual strait-jacket. By adopting a straw man of 'strong' strategy, they have set criteria for strategy so stringently that it becomes impossible to meet them (J. Child, 1985).

Although it is wrong to attribute rational intent to management, it is equally mistaken to assume that strategy has to be seen as always consistent, systematic and without contradiction. Strategies may not always be effectively followed through at the implementation stage, as with the introduction of new technology. They may not constitute a coherent package for the whole operation of a company, perhaps manifesting a disjuncture between job design plans and employee relations. Coherence is an important variable, but it has to be set against the knowledge of inevitable contradictions and the likelihood of 'loose-coupling' between planning and practices. Strategies are likely to be accompanied by bargaining within management and with the workforce, so making the end result uncertain. As Friedman rightly notes, 'Irrationality, inconsistency, lack of system certainly exist and must be allowed for; however, a more useful concept to introduce is failure' (1987: 294). Even where changes are introduced without clear intent, they can establish the preconditions for subsequent strategy (Hyman, 1987: 47).

Managers frequently act on the world with poor information, but they can and do act strategically. It is only necessary for researchers to show a degree of intent or planning, and to infer a logic over a period of time from the frequency and pattern of action, or from 'emergent outcomes' (Hales, 1988: 12). The same criteria apply to the activities of workers. Groups such as printers or doctors do not always behave in a fully conscious or coherent manner. But observation reveals a clear pattern of operation of occupational and job controls, and strategies of closure aimed at excluding competitors, often women (Cockburn, 1983; Witz, 1986). The latter point reinforces research on households that shows that strategies emerge from 'bottom-up', day-to-day activities; a weaker, but still legitimate sense of strategy that relies on social scientists observing and analysing predictable patterns (Wallace, 1993).

Of course, the capacity for strategy is not random. Certain external conditions are likely to push management in that direction. Streek (1987) puts forward a persuasive case that economic crisis and rapidly changing market environments have created a 'general strategic problem' whose core element is the need for *flexibility*. However, the very nature of uncertainty and varied conditions in sectors and countries produces different strategic responses. For example, countries such as West Germany and Austria, with traditions of tripartite state, union and employer bargaining, have seen moves towards flexibility that retains a strong union role and corporatist regulation of wages and labour markets. Streek's analysis not only builds in an explanation of such variations, it provides a framework for understanding the general conditions under which strategies develop. At times of crisis and readjustment, 'the variety of strategies and structures within the collectivity of firms is bound to increase at least until a new standard of "best practice" has been established' (1987: 284). This is not the case at all times. More stable environments produce routinisation of decisions, with management practices governed by tactical accommodations rather than strategic thinking. Britain in the 1950s is a case in point. Economic expansion and new markets, combined with labour shortages, created conditions for the growth of powerful shop steward structures and localised bargaining. Industrial relations were characterised by short-term considerations and 'fire-fighting' which became a dangerous liability for employers as conditions changed in the next decade.

The second strand of critique questions whether the centrality given to control of labour is actually reflective of managerial behaviour. It is argued that we cannot view management strategies and tactics from the vantage point of the labour process, but must consider the role of product and labour markets, and technologies. Control proceeds in a complex cycle from planning to implementation, involving groups such as accountants and industrial engineers. Analysis should focus on the 'multiple constituents' of management expertise beyond the confrontation of capital and labour in the control of the labour process' (Miller and O'Leary, 1987: 10). Such a critique can be presented in a 'Marxist' form. Accumulation and costs of production are what matters to capital and its agents, not control. If anything, managers are dominated by problems of the *outcomes* of the labour process, including sales, marketing, supply and cash flow. Kelly uses the concept of the full circuit of capital to argue that we must be concerned not only with the *extraction* of surplus value through controlling the labour process, but its *realisation* through the sale of commodities, as well as the prior *purchase* of labour. On these grounds, 'there is no sound reason for privileging any moment in the circuit' (J. E. Kelly, 1985: 32).

Iin their research into the Imperial Tobacco Group in the 1970s Morgan and Hooper use a similar framework to distinguish between three circuits of capital: *industrial* capital refers to that used in the management and design of the production process itself; *commercial* refers to the sphere of buying and selling and therefore functions such as marketing, advertising; and *banking* refers to the process of capital used in lending and borrowing, governed by accountancy and financial controls. These distinctions are used to argue that radical theories of the labour process have often lost sight of the role of capital and ownership because of the emphasis on management control. The case study shows a series of strategies pursued simultaneously, representing the particular circuits. To break out of a static tobacco market, top management prioritised commercial and banking strategies, rather than developing existing labour processes. In particular, companies such as Imperial were drawn into investments in the share and gilts markets. These proved successful, but when the resultant money was invested in production they had disastrous results. Firms are thus conceptualised as 'sites of a complex integration of circuits of capital' (1987: 623), which management must integrate and control.

Other writers question whether control can be regarded as the factor which distinguishes between a dominant management and subordinate labour. Management has non-control functions and characteristics of employees, whereas workers exercise job controls and may be involved in the regulation of others (Melling, 1982: 249). At a more theoretical level, Cressey and MacInnes (1980) observe that workers have an interest in the viability of their own units of capital as well as in resisting subordination, matching capital's dual relationship with labour as a commodity and as a source of co-operation necessary for profitable production. Some mainstream writers use their own research into the chemical industry (Harris, 1987) and the chemicals, engineering and biscuit industries – for example, (Buchanan, 1986) – to argue that workers basically accept managerial authority, give commitment and effort willingly, and have convergent interests with management, thus negating any preoccupation with control. This is likely to be linked to a rejection of 'zero-sum' conceptions of power in which one side necessarily gains at the expense of the other (Harris, 1987: 77). Even some radical writers believe that capital and management are not necessarily dominant, with unions having considerably more power, even in a recession, than is usually acknowledged (J. E. Kelly, 1985: 49; M. Rose and Jones, 1985: 101).

It is certainly true that, as Hyman observes: 'If most orthodox literature on business strategy ignores or marginalises the conflict between capital and labour, most Marxist literature perceives nothing else' (1987: 34). This has a curious parallel with the virtual total emphasis in organisation behaviour on 'man-management'. So, the full circuit of capital is a very useful and necessary concept for understanding the capitalist enterprise. Furthermore, change and crisis often arise from disarticulation of the moments of the circuit (J. E. Kelly, 1985), as we saw in the Imperial example. Such concepts can be combined with more orthodox accounts of the changing pattern of *corporate control* that plot how large firms seek to solve their competitive problems by reshaping structures and forms of intervention in the market (Fligstein, 1990). Such 'modes of control' have included vertical and horizontal integration; the multi-divisional form; and more recently, financial means of integrating diverse portfolios built up through acquisition.

However, these perspectives do not invalidate a specific emphasis on relations of control between capital and labour. This is not just another process equivalent to marketing or financial accounting. The management of workers and work remains at the heart of the enterprise and indeed of economic reproduction as a whole. But such an orientation need have no marginalising effect on the analysis of other social relations. As P. K. Edwards (1987) observes, the problem of 'privileging' one part of the circuit arises only if the analysis assumes that this one part determines what happens in the others.

Nor are we saying that control is normally the *goal* of management; but rather that it is a *means* embodied in strategies and techniques. It is true that management strategies are not always developed with labour's role in mind. But it is ultimately difficult to separate a concern with 'outcomes' such as product quality or financial targets from acting on labour in some way. Strategies towards markets or technologies will often be constrained or moderated by labour policies and the practices of workers (Friedman, 1987). In addition, as John Child notes: 'strategies which are unspecific towards the labour process may still have relevance for it' (1985: 110). An example is the introduction of new technology, which much research shows is frequently used as a means of more general work reorganisation.

On the issue of the existence of co-operation and common interests, we would wholly concur. In fact, we would go further. As one of us has observed: 'Workers do not always need to be overtly controlled. They may effectively "control" themselves' (P. Thompson, 1989: 153). Participation in routine practices to create interest or increase rewards can generate *consent* to existing structures of control and power, as Burawoy's (1979) famous studies of production 'games' indicate. What is puzzling is why some writers insist on co-operative and consensual processes being counterpoised to those of control and conflict. It is increasingly recognised that all have to be theorised as different products of the contradictory relations within the enterprise. Not only do consent and control coexist, 'the mobilisation of consent' forms an increasingly central part of management–employee relations strategies in the newer sectors influenced by Japanese practices.

We also accept that workers exercise controls, but it would be a serious mistake to regard these controls as *equivalent* to those of management. This would fail to distinguish between *types* of control, particularly between the general and detailed dimensions referred to earlier in the chapter. At the general level of direction of production, managerial dominance is guaranteed by their stewardship of the crucial organisational resources. This is not 'zero-sum' because it cannot be 'added up'. Clearly, however, control of immediate work processes is largely zero-sum, in that if workers control a given item, then management cannot also do so (P. K. Edwards, 1990).

Bringing the threads together: management as a labour process

What is required is a structural analysis that can account for both the constraints on and complexities of managerial behaviour: a perspective that is neither deterministic or voluntaristic. *One* way forward begins from a remark made by Braverman, that 'Management has become administration, which is a labour process conducted for the purpose of control within the corporation, and conducted moreover as a labour process exactly analogous to the process of production' (1974: 267). An offshoot is that the alienating conditions attached to the purchase and sale of labour become part of the managerial apparatus itself. Though little more than an aside, it has been utilised by a number of writers, notably Teulings (1986), to produce an analysis of management's role in the administrative apparatus of industrial organisations. The very fact that management is a 'global agent' carrying out the delegated functions of capital, means that it is part of a collective labour process at corporate level. As we have previously indicated, this delegation in part reflects the transfer of functions such as co-ordination from the market to management and administration.

As that role has evolved, it has also become *differentiated*. So, for example, large administrative divisions are, in the case of accounting; 'producing nothing but elaborate mechanisms of control associated with the realisation of capital and its enlargement' (T. Johnson, 1980: 355). But it is not only a case of the emergence of specialised functions and departments.

Differentiation also takes place in terms of *levels*. Teulings puts forward a model based on the existence of four distinct management functions: ownership, administrative, innovative, and production (see Table 4.2). Two major consequences of the new division of labour follow. First, though the power of the administrative machinery of which management is a part has increased, the power of *individual* managers tends to diminish, due to the rationalisation and routinisation of their activities. With the development of more complex managerial structures, new techniques have been introduced to integrate, monitor and control middle and lower management (Carter, 1985: 98).

Years ago there might be five hundred fellas but you would only have one boss. Now everyone has a chief . . . You can't discuss the job with them, everything is

TABLE 4.2   **Institutionalisation of distinctive management functions at separate levels of management**

	Function	Levels
I	the ownership function — accumulation of capital	institutional management — creation and preservation of legitimations
II	the administrative function — Allocation of investments	strategic management — development of objectives
III	the innovative function — product market development	structuring management — new combinations of production factors
IV	the production function —control of the direct labour process	operational management — direction and co-ordination of direct labour

Source: W. M. Teulings, 'Managerial Labour Processes in Organised Capitalism', *Managing the Labour Process*, D. Knights and H. Willmott (eds), Gower, 1986.

ticked in little boxes now. The boss is scared because if they don't treat everyone in a standard way they are afraid the other bosses will report them. (Plessey engineer, quoted in Thompson and Bannon, 1985: 170)

Hale's analysis of management divisions of labour qualifies Teulings by showing that some management functions – those that the latter designates as operational – have their origins in the labour process rather than the market, and that there is not an exact correspondence between functions and levels. Those divisions are vertically fractionalised so that 'there is a differentiation within the performance of management work in terms of the extent to which agents are involved in the decision-making process' (Hales, 1988: 10). As Watson (1994) shows in his account of a major UK telecommunications firm, even senior plant-level managers will frequently find themselves frustrated by centralised control in companies that takes place at the cost their strategic inputs orientated towards long-term viability. from. Many will be subordinated to senior management through merely providing information from which decisions are made.

Managers managing other managers takes place in different forms in the modern corporation, whether it be multi-divisional structures, holding companies or conglomerates, where varying forms of decentralisation go hand-in-hand with increased accountability and monitoring. At a micro-level, techniques such as management by objectives are still important, though presented as a form of control and motivation arising from the *objective* demands of the task (Drucker, 1955), which reproduces an aspect of the relationship workers have with 'scientific management'. In other cases, managers become more literally victims of their own devices (Storey, 1983: 93), as shown in studies such as Nichols and Beynon (1977) on the chemical industry. The latter additionally note the flattening out of career structures and exposure to redundancy, characteristic of many managers. We know from other evidence (V. Smith, 1990) that middle managers in particular are becoming prime victims of organisational restructuring. Even the detailed studies of management functions discussed earlier in the chapter, have the purpose of restructuring and rationalisation. Both Mintzberg (1973) and Drucker (1979) favour using techniques to split-off routine activities from senior layers, introducing separation of conception and execution within management itself. This can now be further aided by computer technology and information systems.

The second consequence of changes in the managerial labour process is the growth of structural conflicts and imbalances between the different levels and functions. Teulings argues that each level of management tends to follow a rational logic of its own, enhancing the potential for defence of specific group interests – for example, between production-orientated operational management and the strata concerned with innovation in product markets. Such tendencies are worsened by the absence, or limits to, formal mechanisms to resolve or bargain conflicts. Instead they are likely to be dealt with at the operational level, leading to a disproportionate emphasis on changing the practices of shop floor workers.

One effect not discussed by Teulings is on managerial *ideologies*. The legitimatory content in management thought has traditionally been directed towards two objectives: convincing non-management groups who challenged managerial goals and activities; and sustaining common aspirations (J. Child, 1969: 228–9). This becomes more problematic with the development of competing claims to fashion management theories and practices. Such competition cannot be wholly understood within the kind of framework which talks of levels. It neglects the role of what Armstrong calls *inter-professional competition* (1984, 1986, 1987b). It has long been recognised that professional groups pursue market strategies based on claims to exclusivity of knowledge and monopolies over a set of practices (T. Johnson, 1972; H. Brown, 1980). But the examples and models have mostly come from the older and 'social' professions such as law and medicine, with professions active in business have seldom figuring as prominently.

One of the reasons for the neglect is that the sociology of the professions has emphasised the traditional 'role conflict' between professional autonomy and the bureaucratic principles of work organisation (Child, 1982; Rueschemeyer, 1986). Radical writers interpret these trends in terms of the conflict between acting for capital, and increasingly taking on the characteristics of employees. Some refer to the growth of a new professional-managerial class (Ehrenreich and Ehrenreich, 1979), with others preferring to talk of the proletarianisation of the 'middle layers' (Braverman, 1974). Though some insights can be gained from such perspectives, a primary focus on issues of class location is limited. Armstrong's model allows us to focus on the specific role of the professions in the managerial labour process.

However, Armstrong is critical of the latter concept. He agrees that lower management has been subject to greater controls and its own version of the separation of conception and execution, but he is concerned that attention is drawn away from the basic contradiction between labour and capital, legitimising the existence of any form of unproductive activity by referring to it as a labour process in its own right. But as long as the connections to the dominant capital–labour contradiction are maintained, we see no reason why the concept cannot be usefully employed. Armstrong prefers to talk of struggles for control within capital, reflecting the, 'tensions and contradictions within the agency relationship' (1989: 312). In other words, employers and senior managers are inescapably dependent on other agencies to secure corporate goals and policies.

So, in practice, management functions for capital are moderated by competition between occupational groups. Each profession has a core of specialist knowledge and activities which can form the basis of advancement through a 'collective mobility project'. But the core can only be effectively used if it is sufficiently indeterminate to prevent parts being detached, or routinised. Whereas the general point might apply to all professions, those active in *business* have to face rival claims over the carrying out of control functions. For example, drawing on the work of Layton (1969), Armstrong (1986: 26) argues that scientific management's techniques and justification for the control of labour through the 'planning department' was an expression of an ideology of engineering. Industrial engineering rests on the design of operating procedures which monitor and control labour costs (Storey, 1983: 275). But the attempt to place engineers at the apex of the firm through the diffusion of such techniques has clearly not been fully achieved, given that engineers do not predominate in the higher levels of management. At the heart of the 'failure' lies the difficulty of maintaining a monopoly over control practices which could be carried out by others.

To make matters worse, British development has taken place based on a definition of management hostile to engineering. This is because of a combination of finance and marketing as favoured specialisms, and the tendency to define management as a set of general functions and skills divorced from productive expertise (see earlier in this chapter). One commentator noted that a result has been, 'a whole generation of MBA students who will not go near a manufacturing strategy . . . They want to be in at the gin-and-tonic end with the financial strategy' (quoted in Armstrong, 1987b: 428). Other professions have gained because of the popular belief that the education of engineers does not equip them for dealing with people and money. As a potential agency they therefore experience difficulty in establishing the vital commodity of 'trust' with those in positions of power. It is therefore not surprising that many engineers seek a route out of production into senior management through courses such as MBAs. The consequent low status of engineering identified in the Finneston Report and by Child *et al.* (1983) is, however, as we have seen, a peculiarly Anglo–American phenomenon. In contrast, West German management is dominated by professional engineers, due in part to the historical relevance of engineering techniques and technical education to competition with British and other manufacturing goods, and to access to training in financial techniques.

In the case of accounting and other financial specialisms, there has been a dramatic rise from the days of poorly paid clerks and book-keeping tasks. Some of the factors involved include the development of *management* accounting as a cost control technique in the industrial restructuring during and after the depression of the mid-1920s. In the USA, the control function of management accounting can be clearly identified in the following definition from the National Association of Accountants:

> the process of identification, measurement, accumulation, analysis, preparation, interpretation, and communication of financial information used by management to plan, evaluate and control within an organisation and to ensure appropriate use and accountability for its resources. (quoted in Wardell, 1986: 28)

Other factors include, once again, the need for co-ordination and control over middle managers in multi-divisional companies; and the legal requirements for control through auditing. The cohesiveness of an accounting élite in business has been facilitated by the acceptance of an inevitable 'horizontal fissure' in the profession. This has allowed a range of routine tasks to be delegated to 'accounting technicians' (T. Johnson, 1980; Glover *et al.*, 1991), thus maintaining indeterminacy and monopoly over core practices. Accountants have also undertaken an aggressive campaign to encroach on the spheres of other professions through such measures as manpower audits and human resource accounting (Armstrong, 1986: 32). Though only a minority are closer to real power, the spread of a 'financial rationality' means that British boardrooms are increasingly dominated by those with a background in banking or accountancy, within a 'managerial culture which is often preoccupied with accounting measures and procedures' (Armstrong, 1988).

Such developments have begun to threaten the power of the *personnel* function, a segment of management which had also enjoyed a major long-term growth. From the days of its origins in company welfare workers, the Institute of Personnel Managers now has more than 20 000 members. Throughout that development personnel professionals have had a continual struggle to convince business power-holders that they could move from welfare to general management functions. They consolidated a hold over administrative functions such as interviewing and record-keeping, as well as expanding into the newer areas of staff development and determination of wage rates and incentives (Carter, 1985: 102). In a partnership of mutual convenience, the behavioural sciences have helped develop a mystique that, 'the personnel manager is probably the only specialist in the organisation whose role can be distinguished by the virtually exclusive concern with the management of human assets' (Mullins, 1985: 129). But the problematic of 'dealing with people' has inherent limits in establishing a monopoly of knowledge or practice, particularly when its 'behavioural nostrums' are routinely taught to the full range of business students (Fowler, 1985). It is therefore unsurprising that surveys (Daniel and Millward, 1983) have reported a lack of qualified and trained personnel staff in many companies. Fortunately for the profession other factors have been working in their favour, notably the spate of employee legislation and codes of practice in the 1960s and 1970s, and the recommendations of the Donovan Report (1968) that firms should centralise and formalise their bargaining procedures. Both measures allowed personnel to extend and monopolise spheres of expertise, as well exercise greater authority over lower line managers (Armstrong, 1986: 37).

But deregulation of labour markets, decentralisation of bargaining and scrapping of aspects of employment law, have given a further twist to the ratchet of interprofessional competition by eroding or redistributing established personnel functions. This is complicated by the rise of Human Resource Management (HRM). On the surface it seems positive – after all, personnel managers have long trumpeted the importance of treating human resources as an organisation's greatest asset rather than as a cost to be minimised. HRM can then be seen as an upmarket version of personnel with a tactical name change (Torrington, 1989). This is perhaps the 'soft' version of HRM, with the harder versions stressing the integration of the management of human resources into core business strategy and practice (Guest, 1989; Storey, 1989). The significance of the latter is that it enables, perhaps necessitates, other managerial groups, particularly line managers, to take HRM 'on-board'.

Whether it is *in fact* becoming more strategic or more effective is open to dispute (Guest, 1990), but the perception of greater centrality has sparked off a struggle by managers across a variety of functions to absorb the rhetoric and responsibilities of HRM (Poole and Mansfield, 1992). The efforts of traditional practioners to defend and carve out new territories was not helped by a widely reported study from a team at the London School of Economics that produced headlines of 'Personnel officers are a waste of time says new study' (*Independent on Sunday*, 15 May 1994). Perhaps, like other professional groups, personnel is heading for a split: 'a polarised profession consisting of a mass of "clerks of works", performing routine administrative work for a newly self-confident line management, whilst a few élite "architects" of strategic human resources policy continue to operate at the corporate headquarters level' (Armstrong, 1988: 25).

The kind of analysis in this section usefully adds to an understanding of the complex levels and functions within the managerial labour process. As Whitely (1984) argues, there is limited standardisation across managerial tasks and this helps to explain the lack of progress in establishing management *as such* as a profession. The growth of MBAs and other qualifications suggests attempts to develop certification of skills and knowledge, as well as a career route. But they can best be seen as a form of individual credentialism and filter into higher-paid jobs, and not necessarily a convincing one, with some employers showing considerable scepticism (Oliver, 1993). The jibe 'masters of bugger all' may be unfair, but it reflects historic tensions between generalism and specialism, as well as a feeling that the content of many courses is pitched above business requirements and the realities of middle management work. It may be that employers, at least in the UK, will turn towards a more practical competency-based certification through the Management Charter Initiative or other aspects of the National Council for Vocational Qualifications.

A focus on competing agencies and professions also emphasises the specific historical bases and differences in the development of management theories and practices; particularly between different national traditions, though we have little space to elaborate on them here. The discussion also embodies the general purpose of this chapter, that of developing a structural analysis of management that recognises the contradictory sources of influence over activity. Hence it becomes possible to utilise a conception of agency that accepts considerable variation in management practices, as well as enabling us to understand the rise of new groups competing for influence. For example, business consultants, research and development engineers and IT analysts are using their knowledge to challenge the existing expert division of labour (Reed, 1992a).

Of course, this is far from the last word on these issues. For example, Chapter 11 attempts to develop an understanding of the individual and subjective orientations of managers compatible with the framework outlined here. But for now, we move to the related theme of power.

CHAPTER 5

Power

'The natural place to look for an understanding of power in organizations is that extensive body of work known as "organization theory"' (Cockburn, 1990: 76). However, in contrast to control, most traditional organisational behaviour textbooks simply do not have chapters on power, or if they do, admit that it has been largely ignored or subsumed within other issues such as leadership (Luthans, 1981: 387). Cockburn's explanation is that such theory has been devised from the viewpoint of the owners and managers who control organisations. This may be less a case of reflecting the viewpoint of managers, than the conventional ways of viewing their activities which we examined in the previous section. Willmott (1984: 350) sums this up succinctly: 'the common sense, technical, images developed by managers to account for their activities get returned to them in the form of apolitical descriptions of the reality of their work'.

Power relations can be simply written out of the picture, for example by redefining 'subordinates' as 'non-managers' (Mullins, 1985: 238). They then have a shadowy existence, hidden within discussions of why management finds it 'difficult to delegate', and focusing on personal disposition rather than the structures of power that shape them. Debates on management style will contain occasional advice on *when* to use authoritarian methods – Hitt *et al.* writing that in today's large corporations 'fear must be used cautiously' (1986: 43). Furthermore, power is the hidden agenda when managerial prerogatives are stressed, though the ideological needs of management may blunt the directness of language. But what else is meant when the phrase 'management must manage' is used?

Some of the roots of the neglect can be traced to the historical association in organisation theory between rational, formal organisation and legitimate authority (Clegg and Dunkerley, 1980: 433–4). Reflecting a wider functionalist perspective that sees power as 'a legitimate regulation in a society based on common values' (Barker and Roberts, 1993: 195), theorists such as Parsons see authority as granting a consensual 'power to' structure the behaviour of others

132

(Storey, 1983: 54–5). 'Zero-sum' notions of power, in which there are clear and incompatible differences of resources and interests are explicitly ruled out. Alternatively, power is linked to the breakdown of authority and the growth of informal practices. This can be seen in a standard definition of organisational power quoted in Luthans, 'the management of influence to obtain ends not sanctioned by the organisation' (pp. 197, 389). As a result, any research that does exist on power concentrates on its *exercise*, taking, as we shall show later, the formal organisation and deeper power relations for granted.

Power in mainstream theory

How then is power conceptualised in mainstream theory? Within the small, but growing literature on power the dominant orientation is towards an analysis of the *micro* or *internal* politics of organisations, which Pfeffer defines as: 'Those activities within organisations to acquire, develop and use power and other resources to obtain one's preferred outcomes in a situation where there is dissension or uncertainty about choices' (1981: 10). To sustain this approach, Organisation Theory draws on a definition of power developed by Dahl (1957), which itself is based on Weber (1968). Power is seen as the ability of A to get B to do something B would not do otherwise, despite any resistance.

A narrow focus on power in a solely organisational setting was itself indicative of what Hinings (1988: 4) refers to as the continuing divorce of organisation theory from sociology. Within this framework one of the best-known contributions is from French and Raven (1959), who start from the concept of 'bases of power' located in organisational resources. They are available for use singly or jointly by the manager, but depend on the perceptions and responses of those 'targeted'.

Reward: The use of resources as rewards, where the target values the chosen method and believes it can be delivered. Can include not just money, but promotions, increased job satisfaction and social recognition.

Coercive: The capacity to enforce discipline. Rests ultimately on the fear of the likelihood of psychological or material punishment, whether loss of overtime bonuses or humiliation in front of the peer group for poor sales figures.

Referent: The personal characteristics of the manager are perceived as attractive by employees, generating feelings of identification. Similar to Weber's concept of charismatic power.

Legitimate: Power is made acceptable by subordinates acquiescing in the right of power holders to influence them. Linked strongly to the idea of authority.

Expert: The existence of power as knowledge or other forms of expertise attributed to individuals or groups, which others feel obliged to accept. It is in itself a type of legitimacy.

There is some evidence concerning the application and effectiveness of these sources of power (see Luthans, 1981: 395–401). Not surprisingly, it shows that non-formal sources such as expert power impact most favourably on organisational effectiveness. But given the questionnaire methods used, this may tell us more about cultural expectations than actual work practices.

That is not the only problem. The French and Raven categories are widely regarded as too individualistic, though the basic argument about individual bases of power is developed in more depth by Pfeffer (1992). Power is seen as a structural process linked to task specialisation. Given that some tasks are more central than others, the individuals involved have more chance to exert influence. However, in practice the relational structures of power are more likely to involve *networks* (Knoke, 1990) or *coalitions* (Cyert and March, 1963) which compete for resources and influence within organisations. Individuals seeking sources of power normally have to work within sectional interest groups, such as departments or specialist occupations. Pettigrew's (1973) research showed computer programmers locked into a power struggle with systems analysts. Their weapons were ideologies of expertise, exclusivity of technique by avoiding written records, and control of recruitment policies. Political *skills* are vital in these processes and may be seen in a positive light by some managerialist commentators: 'Anyone who loves accomplishing things must learn to love (yes, love) politics' (Tom Peters in the *Independent on Sunday*, 15 May 1994). Skills such as advocacy may be useful to the company in a competitive environment and the management of creative contention is central to the building of alliances and informal networks that are sometimes dubbed 'dominant coalitions' (Kotter, 1982).

This political view clearly starts from 'realist' assumptions which, 'see the manager not as a servant of the owners nor as a technocrat serving the system, but as a manipulator trying to compete and co-operate with others in order to pursue his own ends' (Lee, 1985: 206). Such a vision of sectional interests and firms as sites of struggles between different groups and coalitions is also of necessity *pluralist* in that it begins from a recognition of multiple and competing goals, as well as internal bargaining processes. Indeed, organisations can be conceptualised as politically negotiated orders which are neither the harmonious entities beloved of managerial theory or the arenas for class conflict associated with radical critics (Bachrach and Lawlor, 1980). A practical spin-off can be seen in current business practice which is currently awash with references to stake-holders. Admittedly this is a 'soft' version, where companies take an inclusive approach that treats shareholders as just another group alongside employers, customers, suppliers and the wider community (RSA Inquiry, 1994; Handy, 1994). Tougher varieties recognise owners as a more powerful player among the multiplicity of interests (T. Watson, 1994).

The resultant internal political systems do, however, tend to stabilise themselves through the stake in the survival of the whole system held by the competing parties and the extra power wielded by top management. What are the dynamics of the internal power structure? A coherent explanation synthesising a range of other studies is provided through the *strategic contingencies* model of Hickson *et al.* (1973). This starts from the observation that it is necessary to treat power as about the allocation of scarce resources and as the property of a social relationship – particularly the departmental division of labour between purchasing, marketing and so on – rather than individual action. These social relations are shaped by external and internal factors.

At the external level, we return to the open-systems model discussed in Chapter 3. Coping with uncertainty is a crucial feature in transactions between organisations and the environment. The internal institutions charged with this responsibility are the *sub-units* such as departments. Power enters the picture through the familiar frame of resource-dependency, because those sub-units which can cope with uncertainty will be able to exercise power in their competitive struggle for resources with their rivals. Hickson and McCullough (1980) use the example of purchasing agents who were trying to expand their limited power base by trying to move from merely placing orders and ensuring delivery, to the provision of information to management and planning new products. The tactics used involved building alliances with contacts in other departments and manipulation of rules. But power could only really be gained when the customer environment contained a variety of suppliers, thus increasing the dependency of other sections on purchasing.

Such examples indicate that structural contingencies constitute a number of variables which shape power. Ability to deal with uncertainty is complemented by the degree of *dependency* on other units, the extent to which activities are *substitutable*, and on the overall level of *centrality* to the organisation. Therefore power is gained through the process of exchange and control of strategic contingencies. Though the point is not often made, this kind of analysis can be extended to shop floor employees. 'Lower participants', as Mechanic (1962) describes them, can also utilise power derived from control over uncertainty. Amongst his examples were hospital orderlies who exploited their skills and access to information in order to control waiting lists for operations against more senior medical staff disinterested in administration. In a more industrial relations context, Marchington (1982) has explicitly used the strategic contingency framework to analyse the power of workgroups in the production cycle.

A critical evaluation

The literature on internal politics and power is very useful, particularly when set against the traditional conceptions of rational, a political management. But there are costs which arise from the limitations of pluralism (see Chapter 3 for a broader discussion). Talk of stake-holders and a multiplicity of interests is too often a comfortable rhetoric which is fundamentally unrealistic about the distribution of power inside organisations. Owners hold the key stakes in corporate resources and even employee's countervailing powers have diminished sharply in recent economic, political and legal climates. There is also an illusion about management. Of course, managers represent a sectional interest, or more precisely a series of sectional interests. But they are also an agency of ownership interests, not passive prisoners, but certainly constrained actors. Even Watson's (1994) informative and determinedly pluralistic account of managers trying to assert their desires to maintain manufacturing interests at ZTC, has to recognise that they are working within short-termist, cost-cutting rules set by the dominant corporate coalition.

There is also the issue of the relation between internal and external power relations. Limitations flow from the analysis being confined to a particular *level* of power relations. Power is analysed through its symptoms, by what is observable through behavioural exchange and by identifying who the players are. Such an approach tends to trivialise power by treating it as office politics. Even when dealt with in a more substantial way, as in strategic contingency theory, the focus is primarily on *horizontal* power relations: 'Conventional organisation theory seldom considers the power within organisations, the power exemplified by top management, as an expression of power relations external to the organisation' (Cockburn, 1990: 77).

Vertical power hierarchies are set aside by the interpretation of the division of labour as consisting of relations between sub-units. Such neglect is reinforced by the tendency to see managerial authority and goals as always accepted by workers, or at least subject to joint regulation and negotiated outcome through the interplay of power. Substantial power differences and sources of dissension are therefore underestimated. We need to deal with 'power over' as well as 'power to', and treat managerial authority as a form of organisational power. Though power is multi-faceted, zero-sum circumstances can and do exist, whether that be manifested in distribution of profits in dividends or wages, or the right to bargain collectively or not.

Clegg's (1977) early critique is pertinent to this debate. French and Raven and strategic contingency theory can show how managers use resources to exercise power. Neither explain the prior distribution of power – how some people come to have access to these resources while others do not. The exercise of power is premised on institutional frameworks and rules; 'the "power" of the sub-unit has to be grounded in the prior *capacity* to exercise power which managers possess' (Clegg, 1977: 27). Furthermore, managerial power has to be located within deeper structures of economic domination which underpin its use and legitimacy. A prime example is the concentration of ownership and control in the transnational company. The power to switch resources and relocate operations simply cannot be explained at the level of the single enterprise and its sub-units. Without such a structural framework, we are left with a micro-level analysis capable only of explaining the skills of 'politicking' rather than political power. We are also left with a view of managers solely as self-interested manipulators and power-seekers and with little understanding of the broader dynamics and constraints that dispose management to use power in the first place.

These differences in perspective can be clarified by reference to the wider debate on power, taking the three-dimensional model of Lukes (1982) as a framework. The behavioural literature is primarily one-dimensional, in that it focuses on the observable activities of particular 'subjects', seeking proof of power in processes such as decision-making. This formulation, which draws on Weber's definition outlined earlier, is specifically linked to intended effects and imposition of will: 'Power is only relevant to our understanding of behaviour and organisation, when there is conflict' (S. Dawson, 1986: 148). On this basis rests the behavioural assumption that power can always be observed and measured.

In the broader debate, the one-dimensional view has been criticised by writers such as Bachrach and Baratz (1962), utilising the concept of 'non-decision making'. This may sound odd, but refers to the capacity of power-holders to limit those issues which are contested or even discussed. The approach usefully distinguishes between the sources and bases of power. By controlling agendas and mobilising the bias inherent in greater access to institutional resources, values and even the language of legitimacy, they can keep to safe issues and exclude others that threaten their interests. Though the research deals with political actors, there is no doubt that management actions can be seen in this light. Crucial decisions regarding investment or the introduction of new technology very seldom reach normal bargaining, except perhaps to deal with the consequences. In industrial relations terminology they are 'non-negotiable', particularly when market trends favour employers. Even with worker-director schemes such as those at British Steel in the 1970s, management could manipulate the rules of the game and socialise workforce representatives to the extent that their interests were not seriously contested (Brannen, 1983).

Lukes (1974: 21) pays tribute to this 'two-dimensional' analysis, but argues that it remains too much on the terrain of observable behaviour. Elite power can prevent grievances, and therefore conflict, from ever arising by shaping the very wants and preferences of subordinate groups. This is not a question of brainwashing, but of the hidden structures of power. Market mechanisms and the distribution of wealth and property constitute power relations – such as ownership rights – which frequently come to be taken for granted. Nor should the formation of consent be conceptualised as a process distinct from the operation of power. Though there are concrete practices that arise from such relations, they are not always observable in the traditional sense. Power does not necessarily need a subject. As Clegg and Dunkerley observe, 'Much of the time the power of capital does not have to be exercised to be present . . . because this exercise is grounded in a structural "capacity" which frequently obviates the need for its exercise' (1980: 495). Put another way, is power the production of effects or the *capacity* to produce them?

Though the processes cannot always be measured, the outcomes can, in terms of structural inequalities between groups. For Lukes, this indicates that a latent conflict exists, 'which consists of a contradiction between the interests of those exercising power and the *real* interests of those they exclude" (1982: 284). His three-dimensional explanation of power in general, therefore coincides with radical perspectives on organisational power, which would draw on Weber and Marx's analysis of the deeper economic roots of domination. This involves a different understanding of 'dependency', in which there is a 'fundamental asymmetry of power between employers and workers' (Rueschemeyer, 1986: 76), based on workers' lack of control of the means of production. The propertyless have to, 'seek access to resources owned or controlled by the few' (Fox, 1974: 284). When Nissan opened their factory in the North East of England, they had 30 000 applications for 300 jobs. Not surprisingly, this enabled them to pick workers and a union wholly on their own terms.

Nevertheless, Luke's work has been subject to considerable criticism, even from other radical theorists (see Clegg, 1989). He wants to retain an emphasis on power that presupposes human agencies that make choices, but on the other hand recognises that those choices are not equally available in circumstances of differentially constraining structures. At the level of individuals it is fairly easy to attribute intentions, but this is much more difficult when the individual is given an 'interest' because of membership of a group – whether it be capital and labour, men and women, or professionals and skilled workers (Barker and Roberts, 1993: 210). When Lukes argues that A may shape B's preferences in a manner inimical to B, how do we know what the latter's 'real' interests are without attributing preferences to B or arguing that what B actually thinks or act is 'false'? How do we recognise the power to persuade without reproducing totalitarian images of agencies that control all our thoughts and desires?

Lukes never adequately resolves these dilemmas about structures and agencies. It may be possible to identify inequalities of power in terms of more and less successful struggles to deploy ideological and economic resources, rather than through the idea of interests (Hindess, 1982), but the debate on dimensions of power demonstrates that there have been intractable problems in defining what power is and where it is located. An increasing number of radical theorists have sought refuge in the work of the French writer, Foucault, to escape those limitations.

Foucault and disciplinary power

On the face of it, an analysis based on surveillance techniques and forms of knowledge originating in monastic and military orders in the sixteenth and seventeenth centuries (Foucault, 1972, 1977, 1984), might seem to have limited relevance to contemporary organisation theory. But the attraction is based on the approach to power and how it can be applied to modern (or post-modern) organisations: 'deeply embedded within his detailed analyses of concrete historical situations and events there is a rich and complex model of the mechanism of power which is of direct relevance to organisational analysis' (Marsden, 1993: 108).

That appeal derives partly from restoring an idea of power as productive rather than prohibitive or solely repressive, creative as well as limiting. But this is not a mere echo of Parson's emphasis on positive-sum rather than zero-sum relations. For power is held to be the central feature of social life from which there is no escape. Foucault uses the term 'capillary' to explain that power does not come from above, from a central source. Rather, it 'circulates through the entire social body' (Fraser, 1989: 24), down to the lowest rungs, reaches and localities. Power is embodied in heterogeneous micro-practices, in everyday life rather than in a special sphere. But as particular forms become generalised in a network of relations, Foucault allows himself to use the term 'strategy' to describe the results. Resistance may break out at different points in the chain and though that resistance recreates power, it promotes a ceaseless process of shifting alliances and tensions. Power, therefore, is discontinuous rather than stable.

Nor is power something which is possessed by an individual or group. This commits the sin of belief in a *sovereign* power held by agents making rational decisions or attached to and formally administered by states, corporations or other groupings. From a Foucauldian perspective, power is understood without reference to agency, its mechanisms impersonal and independent of conscious subjects. In one sense this seems to extend Luke's third, structural dimension of power in which the agency (such as capital) and its effects remain hidden. But Foucault's disciplinary power removes entirely a deliberately controlling relationship between subject and object, the imposition of A's will over B (Barker and Roberts, 1993: 216), even when conceived of as thought control and ideological hegemony (Clegg, 1989: 182). Power does have a focus, but operates not through agencies but *discourses*: practices of talk, text and argument which continuously forms that which it speaks.

Disciplinary practices produce knowledge which is inseparable from power. Language thus becomes a central feature in the discursive production of power, and power/knowledge discourses constitute norms of acceptable conduct, constructing social identities.

All this sounds very abstract, but Foucault underpins his concepts by a historical account of the emergence of a distinctively *modern* power. Pre-modern sovereign power had depended on personalised bonds of obligation. In contrast, the techniques of disciplinary power were developed and refined in religious institutions, prisons, asylums, hospitals and workhouses at a local level, rather than overseen by the state. Such micro-techniques were concerned with evaluating, recording and observing individuals in an exhaustive and detailed way. During the early nineteenth century, surveillance spread from the institutions that were first faced with the mass management of large groups of people, especially to the factory:

> The dark satanic mills of Yorkshire and Lancashire simply latched on the disciplinary apparatus already let loose from the monastery into the poor house, the work house, the orphanage, the barracks and so on. (Clegg, 1989: 173)

But the prison remained the purest exemplar and microcosm of disciplinary techniques and knowledge: power is fundamentally *carceral* in character.

In the range of modern institutions, power also becomes increasingly focused on the body as an object, distinguishing Foucault's analysis from a more conventional emphasis on ideology and moulding of the mind. Developing originally in the eighteenth century, *bio-power* was aimed at the control of wider populations, their movements, gestures and routines, such as the posture of pupils and marching steps of soldiers. These processes were also facilitated by the partitioning and regulation of time and space (Dandeker, 1990: 25). Penology, medicine and psychiatry become the focal points for the development of new power-knowledge discourses which punish deviation from normative standards.

The most potent imagery of Foucauldian theory is the *panopticon* – Bentham's design principle based on a circular building with central observation tower – which, from prisons to the new model housing estates, facilitated a unidirectional disciplinary gaze. In other words the observed can be seen but cannot see, while the observers see everything but cannot be seen. So effective are such practices that the individual began to discipline themselves to be, in Foucault's words, docile and useful bodies. The overall effect of disciplinary practices is summed up by O'Neill: 'in the bourgeois social order the prison, the factory and the school, like the army, are places where the system can project its conception of the disciplinary society in the reformed criminal, the good worker, student, loyal soldier and committed citizen' (1986: 51–2).

Applications to organisations

O'Neill is one of those theorists who have used Foucault to help *reconstruct the past*. The process of the emergence of the factory and large-scale organisation is overlaid with the conceptual apparatus of the disciplinary society. Indeed, much of the material discussed in Chapter 2 is represented in precisely this way. Many radical writers described the early factory in terms of the attempted subordination and surveillance of recalcitrant workers, using the work of historians to illustrate how employers used new systems of rules and control techniques to induce 'appropriate' morals and work habits. Similarly, industrial discipline was a central theme of the later rise of Scientific Management, which Weber praised for its military character. Equally, such systems also involved an immense expansion of managerial knowledge and calculation of worker's time and motion. Theorists working in the tradition of Marx and Weber see these developments as the necessary preconditions for sustaining the appropriation of profit and the removal of the obstacle of worker control over aspects of the labour process. But for followers of Foucault, 'The causality is all wrong. New forms of disciplinary power preceded the establishment of the factory by at least two centuries' (Clegg, 1989: 188).

Foucauldian perspectives are also proving a means of *reframing the present*. The work of Townley (1990, 1993), Burchell *et al.* (1985) and Marsden (1993) focuses on identifying the social technologies of contemporary specialists in human and organisational behaviour as power/knowledge discourses. These latter-day 'soft cops' in HRM, accounting and consultancy are concerned to, 'observe, examine and normalise performance and behaviour' (Marsden, 1993: 118–19), carrying on a tradition established by human relations and its efforts to habituate the employee to the changing conditions of work in the large corporation. All the elaborate emphasis in organisational theory on power expressed through the politics of decision-making, inter-group conflicts over resources, regulations and rights are held to be a sideshow diverting attention from the substance of power. At the heart of that process is the monopoly of knowledge by management and its agents, a form of discursive closure that marginalises other representations and identities (Deetz, 1992).

It is in Deetz's analysis of disciplinary power in the modern corporation that we see the most complete application of Foucault. Organisational processes act to produce corporate obedience, where, 'The disciplined member of the corporation wants on his or her own what the corporation wants' (1992: 42). How this is actually achieved is vague, given the need of such theory to avoid mentioning deliberate operations of directive power. But attention is drawn to an accumulation of local power/knowledge discourses that disperse into norms and standard practices of moral, medical, sexual and psychological regulation. Elsewhere in the same book of readings, reference is made to the capacity of knowledge products of personnel and organisation psychology (such as performance appraisal) to, 'gaze at, scrutinize, classify and count individual characteristics and behaviours. Collected data are analysed and stored, ensuring that an individual's legacy, good and bad, is not forgotten' (Steffy and Grimes, 1992: 192). New forms of surveillance, when specified, rest largely on illustrative examples drawn from the power of information systems and the behavioural technology arising from the expansion of culture change programmes. Willmott (1994) supports Deetz's critique of the colonising tendencies of the modern corporation, arguing that the creation of monocultures displays nascent totalitarianism. Employees are not only coercively socialised, but positively attracted to such cultures because they learn to tie their own identities to the associated norms and knowledge. Their subjectivity becomes 'self-disciplining' as individuals begin to feel secure within the corporate identities (Knights and Willmott, 1990: 550).

We shall look in more detail at issues of corporate culture in Chapter 7. But whatever the source of new processes, Deetz argues that the effects are greater than the prison exemplar, because the modern corporation goes home with its members and colonises competing institutions such as the media (1992: 38). Similarly, in supporting and explaining Foucault's view that all organisations resemble prisons, Burrell (1988: 232) argues that, 'Whilst we may not live in total institutions, the institutional organization of our lives is total'. Opposition is largely self-defeating, since those who play the game become addicts to the rules, and the pursuit of sovereign rights through bodies such as trade unions hides the disciplinary processes which produce the struggle in the first place (Deetz, 1992: 42). In addition, resistance does not threaten power, because 'It means that discipline can grow stronger knowing where its next efforts must be directed' (Burrell, 1988: 228). Clegg is similarly pessimistic in noting the organisational outflanking of resistance, due to subordinated agencies, 'Lacking the organizational resources to outmanoeuvre existing networks and alliances' (1989: 19). As Collinson (1994) observes, this analysis draws on Foucault in arguing that knowledge and information structure access to power. Subordinates either have too little of both or their knowledge of the probable outcome of action is so predictable that it is similarly inhibitive.

This imagery of all-powerful total institutions is reproduced in another Foucauldian-inspired literature, whose object of inquiry is new production techniques such as Just-in-Time (JIT) and Total Quality Management (TQM) (Sewell and Wilkinson, 1992; Delbridge *et al.*, 1992; Webster and Robbins, 1993). Marrying Foucault and Braverman, they argue that more effective surveillance techniques enhance managerial control of the labour process. Webster and Robin's alternative history of the information revolution traces a line of descent from Bentham's original conception of the panopticon, through Taylorism as a means of monopolising knowledge in management, to the contemporary flexible firm which has the capacity of IT to centralise information from an increased range of geographically dispersed units.

Shop floor techniques utilise more extensive information systems which can collect data on worker performance and behaviour. This is described as an electronic panopticon which brings the disciplinary gaze to every aspect of worker activity. Because stockpiles of labour and parts are eliminated through JIT, production arrangements are highly visible. The associated power/ knowledge discourse is effective because the information is generated from and fed back through teams of employees that appear to have autonomy, but in practice internalise production norms and discipline themselves through systems such as Nissan's 'Neighbour Watch' (Garrahan and Stewart, 1992). As a consequence of such discipline and the removal of any 'slack' from the production system, 'worker counter-control (in the sense described by Roy and many others) is effectively eliminated . . . the ultimate goal of management under a JIT/TQM regime must be recognised to be Total Management Control (Delbridge *et al.*, 1992: 105). Chapter 6 explores further current trends in the reorganisation of the labour process, but we cannot take the above description for granted, regardless of its current vogue status.

Critique

Whether Foucault's history is accurate or his methodology competent is beyond our scope (but see Giddens, 1982; Walzer, 1985; Habermas, 1987), and, we suspect, not pertinent to his appeal in and out of organisational analysis. New languages to describe old realities are always attractive to academics, in this case despite, or perhaps because of the obscure and opaque terminology. Dandeker (1990) re-caps the history of the growth of the modern business enterprise, rounding up all the usual suspects – Chandler, Edwards, Clawson, Williamson, Littler – without ever demonstrating that his over-arching concept of *surveillance* depicts anything new or distinctive. At a more micro level, Townley (1990) re-packages the personnel function as a power/ knowledge discourse with the Foucauldian terminology of dividing practices (enclosure, partitioning and ranking), with similarly unconvincing effect.

Townley's work is a good example of the over-privileging of language and discourse. She argues that personnel can be understood as the provision of language or knowledge to reduce the space between what the formal contract of employment promises and what the employee's practice delivers. Aside from the fact that all managerial agencies operate in this gap, such conceptions distort the power resources available to and drawn on by those involved in managing the employment relationship. Language is part of that resource, but it is not, of necessity, the defining feature. Employment laws and labour markets may be more significant in empowering personnel, and may have only peripheral connection to any new power/knowledge discourse. In the context of accounting controls, Armstrong (1991) argues that Foucauldian analyses present disciplinary powers without reference to material sanctions and rewards. For example, the new accounting regime at the American company ITT was adhered to, not because those involved had internalised its disciplinary discourse, but because they were paid 25 per cent over the going rate to do so:

> when confronted by resistance, the systematic surveillance and behavioural norms of disciplinary power can only work within a matrix of physical coercion, economic power, negotiated order, or some combination of these. In other words, Foucauldian representation of the manner in which accounting controls operate are incomplete because Foucault's 'microphysics' of power is itself incomplete. (Armstrong, 1991: 31)

In Chapter 1 we used the example of the Wapping dispute involving News International and print unions. A combination of bribes, threats, sackings and the use of new anti-union employment legislation were among the 'non-discursive strategies' that proved highly effective in Rupert Murdoch's victory.

When we examine capital and its managerial agencies, it is clear that power is *somewhere*. Power is both a relationship and controlled and administered by collectivities. It therefore remains legitimate to refer to 'power-holders', though never in an exclusive and uncontested sense. Nor is power necessarily invisible, 'low profile' (Fraser, 1989: 23), or used unilaterally only as a last resort (Deetz, 1992: 40). We do not need to refer to high-profile disputes to illustrate these points. As we have seen, employment relationships in this century have become progressively more bureaucratised. Yet Deetz (1992: 37) criticises Richard Edward's (1979) theory of bureaucratic control because it refers to identifiable rule and routine instead of a complex set of practices which become internalised as common sense and personal identity. This judgement is hopelessly inaccurate. Far from taking rules of payment, measurement and task allocation as given and natural, workers and their representatives have engaged in a persistent low-intensity war to use and manipulate them to their own advantage. Not only that, but there have been highly visible artefacts, such as Ford's 200 page 'Blue Book', for each side to draw on as a resource in the power struggle. Such examples confirm other evidence from shop floor life that specific forms of knowledge are a key resource through which resistance can be mobilised (Collinson, 1994).

A Foucauldian perspective removes the dimension of rationally intended behaviour. The contested rationality between capital and labour is reduced to a local site of struggle. It is claimed that having de-centred the loci of power, Foucault may be 'the last pluralist' (Clegg, 1989: 7). It is true that there is an emphasis on the dispersed and local character of power, with associated micro-technologies of discipline investigated in their own right. But the label of pluralism does not sit well with the theoretical substance of disciplinary power, which has prison and panopticon at its centre and determining force, and all organisations conceived of as total institutions, going way beyond Goffman's (1961) intentions. By treating the workplace as an extension of disciplinary practices and the factory, hospital and other organisations as paler versions of carceral institutions (Burrell, 1988), the specific character of employment relations in a capitalist society is lost. For example, control is treated merely as another version of discipline, and one functionally orientated towards the creation of obedient bodies rather than sustaining exploitation (Clegg, 1989: 176). Vague and extravagant references to control over body and soul can only be justified by extreme examples such as aids testing in the workplace (Deetz, 1992: 140–1).

A further problem, as Fraser observes, is that, 'Foucault calls too many different sorts of things power and simply leaves it at that' (1989: 32). For radical theorists in a labour process tradition, the situation is seen somewhat differently: 'Power is expressed in organisations through the control of the means and methods of production' (Clegg and Dunkerley, 1980: 476). Though power will be exercised in order to re-assert control by management, this should not mean that power is marginal or subsumed under control. The ability of employers to exert controls over labour is conditioned by a variety of different power relations. In particular companies or sectors, crucial factors will include those arising from product and labour markets; the state of employer and worker organisation; and factors identified by strategic contingency theorists such as management dependence on specific occupational and work groups. As we have seen, control structures are also shaped by broader non-industrial power relations, such as those embodied in employment laws which sustain the power of capital, or relations of social dependence in the community which are transferred into the workplace. Processes of control and power are both independent and interrelated inside and outside the workplace. More concrete discussion should reveal those complexities, not treat them as synonymous or analogous.

Finally, there is the problem that because power is everywhere and nowhere, the impression can be given that it is a force that there can never be any escape from. Resistance is part of the formal picture, but is under-theorised (Smart, 1985) and the dice loaded against it, because, 'only power is positive and productive, while resistance is simply a reaction to its production' (Dews, 1987: 99). Fragmented, insubstantial and counter-productive, resistance largely disappears from view, to be replaced by the language of docility and obedience (O'Neill, 1986: 55). In fact, the whole conceptual framework is saturated with the language of colonisation and conquest – images more appropriate to *Invasion of the Body Snatchers* than the complexities of organisational life. The problem is not so much with the Foucauldian description of new managerial techniques of power, but the assumption that they actually *work*. Having removed intent from action, perhaps the gap between talk, text and reality ceases to be a problem. Even within managerial options, no strategy can be preferable to another, Foucault arguing that liberal discourses may function as part of the deployment of power at capillary level, concealing relations of domination (Fraser, 1989: 26–7).

As with Lukes, Foucault's motives in trying to transcend the limitations of sovereign or one-dimensional power are admirable. But the result has been a conceptual and practical prison rather than a genuinely complex picture of power. Though Lukes' framework is flawed, the recognition of different levels or dimensions of power remains valuable. To unpack the notion of power further, we need to allow for the possibility that it may be a highly distinctive phenomenon inside different social relations. This can be seen more fully by focusing on gender and sexuality.

Read this section

Gender, sexuality and power

Though power has been taken as a given in explanations of gender inequality, the two processes have not been systematically defined and connected until recently. Because power was viewed as something possessed by men, the focus was on oppression. Feminists, like other academics, have been discovering the significance of power as a concept. The collection of papers collected in Davis *et al.* (1991) largely accept that power in gender relations operates in a broadly similar way to power in other social relations, and therefore they grapple with the familiar range of theories discussed earlier. Lukes' and other multi-dimensional models of power are attractive because they encourage attention to the 'hidden' structural and ideological faces of power. Foucauldian concepts are also influential (D. Cooper, 1994), as we shall see later.

However, such discussions are not necessarily linked to work organisations. There *is* a massive and important body of research and theory on gender and the workplace (see Dex, 1985; Walby, 1986; P. Thompson, 1989), but that debate on the sexual division of labour focused on occupational divisions, differential control in the labour process, segmented labour markets, or more broadly on patriarchy and capitalism. Organisations tended to be treated as passive recipients of wider social forces, with power only appearing indirectly – for example, through access to employment. It is essential to, 'see how organizational forms structure and are themselves structured by gender' (Witz and Savage, 1992: 8).

Such absences and disconnections are not surprising, as the visibility of gender in organisational analysis itself is low. Recent surveys (Acker and Van Houten, 1992; Hearn and Parkin, 1992; Collinson and Hearn, 1994) have trawled the major landmarks of theory and research from Taylorism to human relations and contingency theory, and have noted that though organisational processes are clearly influenced by gendered power relations, employees and managers appear to have no gender, and men and management are synonymous. Weber, however, is placed firmly in the centre of this 'malestream' organisational analysis. For him, the rise of bureaucracy brings with it an instrumental rationality in which impersonal rules, procedures and hierarchies are operated with technical efficiency. This is contrasted with traditional forms of authority reliant on individual privilege and personal allegiance. Issues of gender and sexuality are thus despatched to a private realm along with patrimonial and patriarchal relations, no longer to endanger rational-legal authority in the public sphere.

Gendering organisational analysis

Gender might be banished from the theory, but this was far from the actual practice of organisational life, as many critics have subsequently argued (Pringle, 1989; Cockburn, 1991; Wilson, 1995). The disparity between ideal type and reality was, in fact, picked up earlier by one of the few feminists working within conventional management theory. Kanter's (1977, republished 1993) *Men and Women of the Corporation* was a landmark work, setting out a serious critique of the male bias within internal power structures and an explanation for the widely-observed 'glass ceiling' restricting progress up the hierarchy (Rees, 1992: Davidson and Cooper, 1992). The emphasis on *internal* is important, because Kanter does not treat the corporation simply as a reflection of the outside world; 'to a very large degree, organizations make their workers into who they are' (1993: 263). Adopting what she describes as a structural model, Kanter identifies three central determinants of behaviour: the structure of opportunity, the structure of power and the proportional distribution of people or social composition of jobs. This approach is distinguished from a variety of largely individualistic explanations in which the cause of unequal access to opportunity and power is located in socialisation, sexuality, psychology or natural disposition. No research exists that proves any sex differences in power as manifested through leadership or management styles: 'a preference for men is a preference for power' (Kanter, 1993: 199).

But locked into the lower reaches of the hierarchy and sex-segregated jobs, women internalise relative notions of worth. Cycles of powerlessness are further reproduced through the perceptions and actions of men, who use power resources to reproduce structures in their own image. Dominant organisational cultures and ideas of rational decision-making are thus overlaid with notions of masculinity and the space for difference is closed down (K. Ramsay and M. Parker, 1992). One gender comes to be defined as temperamentally unfit for power: 'Women are not capable of authority. And they turn into nasty people when in authority' (Cockburn, 1991: 89).

As Pringle (1989) remarks, Kanter sees patrimony and other evidence of organisational sexuality as pre-bureaucratic relics. She works within a neo-Weberian tradition that reveals the informal and varied nature of bureaucracy. But that particular form is not fate. If women are not 'different', the acquisition of power by women could or should 'wipe out' sex in the workplace and it is organisations that have to be remade, not individuals. Kanter's desire to emphasise the social construction of gender rather then the burdens of sexuality is understandable, but leads to conceptual problems. First, that process of social construction is conceived far too narrowly. Though it is useful to locate specifically organisational dimensions, 'Curiously absent is any sense that men and women are locked, indeed formed, in an unequal gender order that spans not only work, but childhood, sexual intercourse, domesticity, street culture, and public life. There is no sense of how the organisation came to take the damaging form it did' (Cockburn, 1990: 86). As a consequence, neither individual nor systemic male power is adequately confronted. Secondly, in arguing that powerlessness, not sex, is the problem for women, Kanter fails to see the way that the two processes are interwoven, or how new forms of power and control appear around the construction of sexuality (Pringle, 1989: 88).

Part of the problem is that Kanter utilises the narrow Weberian conception of power as freedom of action and ability to get things done. Though it is structural rather than individualistic, as with French and Raven, her whole discussion covers the well-trodden territory of the first dimension of power as a relatively fixed resource operating through the panoply of peer alliances, sponsors and the like. Though insightful in its own terms, such a framework inevitably neglects the broader dimensions and relational character of corporate patriarchy (Witz and Savage, 1992: 16). Kanter's work represents the best of her tradition, but the limitations of orthodox organisation theory, particularly the tendency to separate the workplace from broader social and historical processes, is frequently reproduced. Though she opened the gate, other perspectives had to be present to establish gender as a fundamental structuring principle of power and organisations (Mills and Tancred, 1992; Witz and Savage, 1992).

To some extent the gendering of organisational analysis can be seen as bringing fresh insights to existing issues. Organisational culture is a case in point. It functions as a useful gateway to gender analyses because culture focuses on the way that individuals construct the understandings and subjectivities that underpin behaviour and structure (S. Acker, 1992). Culturally-defined norms and values therefore crucially contribute to maintaining and reproducing the dominant patriarchal ideologies and practices (Alvesson and Due Billing, 1992; Green and Cassell, 1994). The argument is that in bureaucracies, women are strangers in a male-defined world. This goes beyond the obvious cases of resistance to women attempting to establish a presence in largely male preserves such as the police and fire service (Salaman, 1986; Keith and Collinson, 1994). There is evidence of women managers being perceived as threats to male self-image (Sargent, 1983; Cockburn, 1991). The latter study quotes one female senior manager, 'They certainly saw me as a huge threat when I first came. They made me feel very, very uncomfortable for six months. The woman bit. Men don't like it. They don't feel comfortable with women as superiors' (Cockburn, 1991: 141–2). Such women, as Sheppard's (1989) study found, often feel compelled to devise strategies of how to 'blend in', by modifying appearance and behaviour.

Cultures, are, however, not homogeneous. Different types of masculinity may produce a range of managerial styles, from authoritarianism, paternalism, entrepreneurialism, careerism to informal relations where men form an in-group which simultaneously differentiates them from other groups of both sexes. The last group corresponds to the 'locker room culture' identified in a typology developed by Maddock and Parkin (1993): other gender cultures include the traditional 'gentleman's club', the 'barrack yard', and the more contemporary 'gender blind' and 'feminist pretender' arrangements where 'new men' affirm equal opportunities but nothing has really changed.

Such studies are a useful addition to more conventional accounts of bureaucracies as male career structures. Public and private bureaucracies developed along gendered lines, introducing large numbers of women into routine clerical jobs. The existence of practices such as marriage bars, where a female employee would be compelled to retire on marriage, facilitated the retention and promotion of male clerks. In this sense, the growth of large-scale organisations has seen the creation of mini-patriarchies where the expansion of the public sphere is shown to be, 'premised on men's power and dominance in the private domains' (Hearn, 1992: 81). Even when those practices finished, evidence from more recent studies (Crompton and Jones, 1984) shows that internal labour markets inside public and private bureaucracies provided alternative career routes for male clerical employees.

A different, if predictable, twist to the gendered analysis is given by those utilising Foucauldian and post-structuralist perspectives. Preferring to talk of symbolic rather than material resources, such writers emphasise the existence of a bureaucratic discourse which relies upon a male rationality that shatters the apparent neutrality of rules and goals (Ferguson, 1984; Pringle, 1989). Whereas Pringle stresses the requirement of masculine rationality and its associated identities in the workplace to do battle with the feminine 'other', Ferguson locates the problem in women's exclusion from the public realm. When they do emerge, not only are their jobs marginalised, but so too are the more expressive values and modes of action developed in the private sphere. Such an alternative rationality can provide a means for women and other people in subordinate positions to challenge bureaucratic, male power. Other contributors to the debate treat gender as a form of power/knowledge

(Fineman, 1993; Putnam and Mumby 1993). It is argued that instrumental rationality within bureaucracy is defined by its opposition to emotionality. Feelings expressed by employees are either denied, suppressed or appropriated by the company for its own, instrumental ends. Drawing on work such as Hochschild's (1983) study of US airline attendants, it is argued that gender rules signal what and when feelings are appropriate. Employees thus engage in emotional labour based on internalised, but publicly observable management of those feelings, estranging mind from body. Examples and arguments drawn from such perspectives, increasingly depend, however, on analysis of sexuality instead of, or in addition to, gender. It is to this which we now turn.

Enter sexuality

Sexuality had begun to creep out of the shadows of gender in the sociology of the workplace through well-known studies of female (Pollert, 1981; Westwood, 1984) and male (Willis, 1977) wage labour, and the use of sexuality and gender as a method of control (see Thompson, 1989: 196–7). Its entry into organisational theory has largely been contingent on two developments. First, the critique of the previously-mentioned Weberian model of *de-sexualised bureaucracies*. From an absence, sexuality is suddenly to be found everywhere – in language, practices, relationships, displays, design, hierarchies and managerial strategies – though there is a tension between seeing it as partially-submerged underlife in the wake of an all-conquering calculative rationality (Burrell, 1992), and a substantially-embedded set of practices much nearer the surface of everyday organisational life (Hearn and Parkin, 1987; Hearn *et al.*, 1989).

The second route to visibility is via the issue of *sexual harassment* at work (Gutek, 1985; Stanko, 1988; Di Tomaso, 1989; Collinson and Collinson, 1989). Whether at the office party or in promotion processes, it is a means through which individual men exert their power over women. The varieties of forms of harassment can be seen as power plays or controlling gestures arising mainly as responses to the threat to identity and material interests when women enter male occupational territories, or from the abuse of power in supervisory and other authority relationships. Unlike Kanter's analysis of gender, sexuality cannot be confined to the organisation. Barbara Gutek's detailed and authoritative study utilises the concept of sex-role spillover to emphasise the broader social connections: 'the carryover into the workplace of gender-based roles that are usually irrelevant to inappropriate to work'. These may range from conceptions of women's nurturing capacity or being a sex object, to the stereotype of men's natural leadership ability.

We can see that this issue pulls academic and practical attention back to the triangle of gender, sexuality and power. But the understanding of power is precisely the factor that divides contributors to the debate. Though sexual harassment is clearly *about* power, it does not necessarily involve a particular *theory* of power. Whereas Gutek does not see sexual coercion as the norm of male–female relations inside or outside work, the increasing number of radical feminists writing in this area are only too happy to. Admittedly much of this has nothing to do with the workplace as such. Sexuality is seen as the primary source of male power (McKinnon, 1978), and heterosexual desire as the eroticisation of conquest and subordination (Jeffreys. 1990). Harassment is the conduit to the organisation in recent studies focusing on academia (Ramazanogolu, 1987), social work (Wise and Stanley, 1990) or professional education (Carter and Jeffs, 1992). What these and other writers have in common is the view that harassment is not aberrant, unusual or different in kind from flirtation, banter or affairs: 'it is instructive to note that "sexual harassment" and "ordinary sexual encounters" follow more or less exactly the same levels of expression' (Wise and Stanley, 1990: 20). All this is a version of McKinnon's argument that organisations are the site of compulsory heterosexuality. One of the few specifically organisational versions of the perspective comes from Adkins. She uses case studies from service industries to argue that, 'women employees had as a condition of their employment the requirement to provide sexual services for male customers and employees' (1992: 214). This is not meant literally, but refers to controls over forms of dress, appearance, engagement in being chatted-up and other verbal sexual interactions. Women's work is therefore eroticised subordination.

As a theorisation of power, this takes us back to zero-sum notions, in this case men and women are erotically joined solely through mutual threat and share no common interest. Or as Carter and Jeffs (1992: 240–1) put it, 'Sexuality is always about power and is always about "us" as well as "them".' Feminists and others influenced by Foucauldian perspectives would agree that sexuality and power are intimately linked, but strongly question its characterisation. Foucault's writing sees sexuality and the body as central to power and its reproduction, and in Pringle's (1989) work on the boss–secretary relationship is its most imaginative application.

Such studies, 'explore how power disciplines and shapes women's bodies, movements and expressions' (D. Cooper, 1994: 437); though it works through internalisation and self-monitoring rather than being co-erced from the top or as the result of ideology. Recent emphasis has been put especially on the process of *embodiment*. Beyond the obvious examples of dress and display, consideration has been given to the routine degree of sexualised body work through interactions of doctors, nurses and other medical staff (Witz *et al.*, 1994), and the associations between skill and physicality in police work (Keith and Collinson, 1994). In the latter, bodily discourses provide not only a means of keeping women officers in their proper, feminine place, but are used to make further, regional distinctions: 'In the South the people are like the landed gentry, so the police are just big girls' blouses' (female police sergeant, quoted in Keith and Collinson, 1994: 17).

Seeing organisational sexuality in terms of discursive production necessarily requires an emphasis on social construction and fluidity rather than fixed and essential power relations:

> Subjectivity is constituted through the exercise of power within which conceptions of personal identity, gender and sexuality come to be generated. Thus, men and women actively exercise power in positioning themselves within, or finding their own location amongst, competing discourses, rather than merely being 'positioned by' them. (Brewis and Kerfoot, 1994: 8)

Research shows that some of these positioning processes are based on discourses of *difference*, which promote negative representations of women or men who do not play the masculinity game (Collinson and Collinson, 1989; Cockburn, 1991). But this will vary according to work situations and the available knowledge resources. Studies of local government and banking by Witz *et al.* identified the deployment of discourses of gender *complementarity*. Mixed-sex work-groups were endorsed by management as a means of countering the undesirable effects of all-male or all-female sociability. But employees positioned themselves too, finding fun in flirtation and romance. Contrary to the radical feminist argument, 'All the women drew an extremely clear boundary between 'flirtation' and 'sexual harassment' (1994: 20).

Greater space to see the interrelationships between power and pleasure arises from Foucault's theorisation of the former as productive, relational and capillary. Viewing events from the 'bottom-up' and through micro-practices is much less likely to result in behaviour being read-off from universal conceptions of position and behaviour. Even Pringle's secretaries were far from passive objects of the boss's banter, deriving pleasure from imitating, exaggerating or ridiculing existing stereotypes (1989: 103). These discursive practices in which women use sexuality and 'sexy chat' as a means of acting as subjects are found in other studies, best exemplified in Filby's (1992) account of daily life in betting shops. Though management tried and partly succeeded in using women's bodies and personalities to promote the product, female employees turned the tables by developing their own aggressive 'scolding' and 'joking' routines to keep customers and managers in *their* place.

Evaluation

Foucauldian theory and research on power and sexuality has proven a useful antidote to essentialist conceptions of men as automatic power-holders and women as eternal victims. It reinforces existing research which shows the workplace as a site for a variety of forms of sexual and romantic relationship (Thompson and Ackroyd, 1994a). Sexuality is the most complex of social relations and, 'we need a model of power relations which can also deal with power as it is exercised in friendly or intimate encounters' (Davis, 1991: 81). Of course, all sexual relations cannot be described in this way. But in even the most instrumental of sexual exchanges, prostitution, the dynamics of power and control cannot necessarily be described as men securing direct power, nor as motivated solely by the desire to affirm a masterful manhood (O'Connell Davidson, 1994a: 2).

But it is the very specificity of sexuality as a site of power that creates a problem. In different ways, both the radical feminist and Foucauldian perspectives fail to recognise this. For each theory sees sexuality as the standard template of how power works, and this has a number of negative consequences. Radical feminists cannot see sexuality without seeing power, 'both its intention and its end, its product, is power' (Wise and Stanley, 1990: 15), hence fail to grasp its varied construction and practice. Foucauldians, at least those writing in this area, cannot see power without seeing sexuality, and therefore tend to extend the latter's reach beyond its usefulness. Much of the rhetoric about the body falls into this trap. For example, Witz *et al.* comment on a woman manager who had worn a red suit in order to get noticed at a dinner:

> It really does serve to illustrate how embodied organizational participants can call up their embodiment through ways of presenting the body. The choice of a red dress is evoking a number of associations between red and the womanly body – the most obvious is the association with red and sexuality, the least obvious is that between red and bleeding . . . (1994: 23–4)

Ironically, these kinds of argument run the risk rightly identified by two of the same authors in another context, that the avalanche of writing on sexuality is beginning to squeeze out attention to those many aspects of the 'gender paradigm' that are distinguishable from issues of sexuality (Witz and Savage, 1992).

The very fluidity and complexity recognised in post-structuralist perspectives may not be as applicable in other sites of power, particularly when we remember that the object of analysis is *organisational* sexuality. Whereas power is zero-sum in only the most coercive sexual encounters, in many workplace situations, it is, as we argued earlier, often not as negotiable and is possessed and exercised by agents with a radically unequal access to power resources. Organisational sexuality is therefore influenced by the potential characteristics of both sites of power, with varied consequences for choice and constraint.

A further worry about Foucauldian theory is that it tends to overestimate the former at the expense of the latter, 'Power here is not the oppressive power implicit within liberal feminism as a zero-sum analysis where power is a possession. Rather, power for Foucault is productive, it allows us to think ourselves and our individuality as we find/fit ourselves in(to) various discourses' (Brewis and Kerfoot, 1994: 8). The problem is that organisational processes, gendered and otherwise, are not just discourses in relation to which we can position ourselves. The constraints to the success of equal opportunities policies, for example, are also linked to material sources of power, particularly those expressed through internal and external labour markets. Without this recognition of relatively durable structures and constraint, gender risks 'being swallowed up in the bottomless swamp of permanently shifting meanings and ambivalent discursive constructions' (Komter, 1991: 47).

In presenting bureaucracy as a discourse in general, and a discourse of male rationality in particular, current theories are in danger of throwing the practical and theoretical baby out with the bathwater. We shall return to the issue of rationality and make a qualified defence of the Weberian position in the final chapter. But in the following chapter the nature of contemporary bureaucracy organisation is our main theme.

CHAPTER 6

Organisational design: beyond bureaucracy?

Definitions and issues

There may be room, as we saw in Chapter 5, for legitimate debate over the extent to which coherent managerial strategies exist. But it has been an incontestable feature of all theorising that the various dimensions of organisational life are subject to some degree of conscious planning and patterning through *design* processes. The accompanying issues have been central to the discipline, Donaldson arguing that 'Organisation Theory seems to be distinguishable as a body of thought by a concern for internal characteristics such as differentiation, standardisation, specialisation, integration, coordination and the like' (1985: 118). Indeed, the notion of design is central to the whole idea of rational organisation. Structures, tasks or cultures are seen as manipulable by management, design being central to the achievement of corporate goals. It is also therefore the key to 'good' or 'effective' organisation (J. Child, 1984: 3): if you get it wrong, much of the investment in people or other resources will be likely to go to waste. For example, Cummings and Blumberg's case studies on the introduction of advanced manufacturing technology showed that ineffective use was primarily linked to a failure to redesign the work process and context when the technologies were implemented (1987: 54–5). Hence old task structures and functions were retained which undermined the potential for new interdependent relations and self-regulating groups.

Debate has moved on in a number of ways in recent years. Theorists have increasingly questioned the extent to which conventional notions of design, based around bureaucratic principles, are effective. As we shall illustrate in this chapter, this argument is not new. The additional element comes from the belief that there are powerful external and internal stimuli for companies to

155

make a fundamental break from bureaucracy, producing the post-bureaucratic organisation rather than modified forms of bureaucracy. An even more radical argument has challenged the idea of rational design itself and its appropriateness to a fast-changing, even 'chaotic' business environment. This debate will form a major part of this chapter. But for the moment, it would be jumping ahead of the story. During most of this century the science and politics of organisational design has remained on more conventional territory.

Discussion of design variables has proceeded from the assumption that correct *structure* is the key to good performance. An organisation's structure refers primarily to the patterns and regularities in its division of labour by task or function, its hierarchies of authority and control mechanisms. There are, as usual, a number of ways in which the elements of structure can be conceptualised. For example, John Child (1984: 3–4) makes a distinction between the *basic* structure which allocates and co-ordinates people and resources, often through job descriptions, organisation charts and formal bodies; and the *operating* structure which specifies more detailed activities and forms of behaviour, such as those embodied in performance reviews, work plans, and communication, financial or reward systems.

Emphasis has traditionally been put on design techniques and those concerned with planned change, in order to cope with and keep one step ahead of the environment. But the more significant design issues are *how* they should be operationalised. Again, the literature has identified a fairly consistent set of design dimensions (Pugh *et al.*, 1968), decisions (J. Child, 1984: 8–9) or parameters (Mintzberg, 1983: 27). These include the:

- degree of job specialisation and formalisation;
- criteria by which units and activities are grouped – for example by function or product;
  and the size of those groupings;
- nature of the general 'superstructure' – tall, flat or otherwise – spans of control, and levels of management.
- type of integrative mechanisms and lateral linkages; and the
- decision-making structures, including degrees of centralisation and delegation.

There are a number of possible design configurations within these parameters. Generally, there has been a shift away from singular 'one best way' solutions, often based on standardisation and rules. In their place 'The organisation designer has been expected to mix good doses of long-range planning, job enrichment and matrix structure, among many other things' (Mintzberg, 1983: 2). The mix or choice is, of course, not a 'free' one. Account has to be taken of significant contextual or environmental factors. Not surprisingly, therefore, the design debate has been strongly underwritten by the *contingency* approach discussed extensively in Chapter 3. If we take some of the traditional 'show me your environment or technology and I'll show you what your structure should be' material from Woodward or Lawrence and Lorsch, then the scope for alternatives is fairly restricted. No matter how qualified by references to adjusting to uncertainties and complexities in the environment, 'most of the literature on organisational design treats it as a purely technical matter' (J. Child, 1984: 9). Yet in practice, strategic choices by organisational power-holders are made with reference not only to efficiency and profits, but to the related requirements to uphold and express forms of discipline and command (Fox, 1980: 182).

It is, of course, possible to create more complex contingency models, such as Mintzberg's five configurations, which recognise a greater variety of design options in the context of multiple contingencies. We shall return to these later. Other approaches, such as the information-processing perspective of Galbraith (1984), remain informed by notions of contingency. The greater the uncertainty of task, the more that decision-makers have to process information before executing it. Therefore the variety of structures and forms are indications of the different strategies pursued by companies to act on uncertainty, by increasing flexibility or decreasing levels of performance in order to cope. Galbraith argues that although organisations can follow combinations of design strategies, the choice is likely to be that which has the least cost in its environment.

A further alternative and current favourite is to return to 'best way' models. Dawson notes: 'after twenty years of contingency and its limits as a basis for organisation design, a view is now gaining ascendancy that it is possible to identify principles of good management which will be universally applicable' (1986: 133). This is channelled primarily through the 'search for excellence' genre (Peters and Waterman, 1982; Goldsmith and Clutterbuck, 1985), the apostles of Japanese management techniques (Pascale and Athos, 1982), or a combination of both, such as Ouchi's (1981) 'theory Z' organisations. How much they depart from contingency models is debatable, but we shall return to the major contemporary design approaches in more detail later. It remains the case that design models have still largely taken bureaucratic work organisation as their reference point, so this is where we start from.

Bureaucratic work organisation reassessed

Chapter 2 traced the origin and consolidation of bureaucracy as the dominant form of work and organisational design through Taylorism, classical management and Weber. In 1983 an influential article in the magazine *Business Week* heralded 'A Work Revolution in US Industry'. This 'revolution' is apparently directed against the major pillars of bureaucratic work organisation: functional specialisation and the resultant narrowly-defined, low-skill and low-knowledge jobs, enforced by management and by contractual bargaining over work rules set up to govern the workplace. Before we examine the challenges to that dominance, it is worth briefly specifying how such systems developed and what their essential characteristics are.

One of the most consistent themes of organisational literature is minimising uncertainty and this acts as a fundamental motif of bureaucratisation. Variables may be focused on the relations between the components of structure and the environment; between the components themselves; in decision-making processes; or in the 'technical core' of the firm, for example that of routinised tasks or mass production (J. D. Thompson, 1967). A traditional response has been to construct 'buffers' against uncertainties. These may take the form of stockpiling supplies; maintaining a surplus labour pool in the factory; or vertical integration by taking over companies up or down line from the organisation's core activities (Goldman and Van Houten, 1977: 114–5). The degree to which labour has been seen as a significant variable differs, but bureaucratic regulation of work has also been a recurrent theme.

Specialised division of labour, hierarchical authority, abstract performance standards, job specifications, and rule-governed procedures, are of course the things that come to mind. But it is worth remembering the point established by Richard Edwards that bureaucratic controls are not necessarily synonymous with close, direct or coercive authority. They rely more on *standardisation* of work processes, outputs and skills. By reducing the amount of stimuli, information and premises for decisions, behaviour can be formalised and regulated (March and Simon, 1958). The resultant indirect or unobtrusive controls are effective enough to enable the workforce to be trusted to make more decisions within established parameters, without necessarily having to change their attitudes. Popular and expert opinion points to the costs of wasteful bureaucracy. But as Edwards observes: 'The core corporations survive and prosper on their ability to organise the routine, normal efforts of workers, not on their ability to elicit peak performances' (1979: 146).

We have been talking as if such bureaucratic work organisation only favours management. This is to miss part of the point. Many of its features benefit workers, or at least those who are long-term, core employees. Such benefits include mobility through internal labour markets, seniority rules governing pay and lay-offs, grievance procedures, job protection and demarcation. In well-organised union workplaces, these are enforced through plant-wide collective bargaining or informal shop floor power. As part of this process, there is a limited movement towards positive benefits for co-operation rather than negative sanctions: 'a system of mutually binding rules, material and symbolic incentives, and eventually the emergence of an ethos that is impersonally oriented towards performance' (Rueschemeyer, 1986: 94).

Bureaucracy: the internal critique

Critics are now saying that this system has broken down, but for a long period the emphasis was on modifications to and different forms of bureaucracy. Given that bureaucratic structures are strongly associated with Weber, it is not surprising that his work has borne the brunt of critique. But the famous 'Weber debate' was primarily an *internal* one. Taking place in the 1950s and 1960s, it was conducted largely by neo-Weberian writers within a sociology of organisations tradition. Though their case studies questioned whether the bureaucratic ideal-type was fully rational and efficient, many of the assumptions concerning the functional imperatives towards specialisation and hierarchy were left intact, with the emphasis on the need for bureaucratic adaptation to social action.

These case study critiques have been reworked many times in texts, so we shall simply highlight some key issues. A central feature has been the unintended consequences of bureaucratic modes of operation, for instance in relation to *efficiency*. Writers such as Merton (1949) pointed to the dangers of rule-following becoming an end in itself, leading to the excesses of 'red tape'. Standardisation and predictability could easily degenerate into rigidity and defensive behaviour, a kind of 'trained incapacity' resistant to innovation. This was therefore proof of the dysfunctional effects of bureaucratic practices, though few went as far as Bittner's comment that: 'the inventory of features of bureaucracy contain not one single item that is not arguable relative to its efficiency function' (1973: 269).

Rationality does not escape. There is a whole sub-literature stressing the rational propensity for employees to break, bend or modify rules in order to get things done more effectively. Hence the oft-quoted adage that a 'work to rule' is an extremely damaging form of industrial action. Blau (1955) exemplifies this kind of argument through his studies of a state employment agency and a federal law enforcement agency in the USA. In the former, employees in order to place unemployed people, bent centrally laid-down rules. This involved the setting aside competitive assessment norms in favour of co-operative practices and altering the subsequent statistical records. At the law enforcement agency, it was more functional to ignore rules such as those related to reporting attempted bribery, in order to be in a position of power over the perpetrators at a later date.

Nor is specialisation or hierarchy necessarily functional to the overall goals of the organisation. This is particularly because there is a potential association between bureaucratic structures and *power*, as shown in the studies of two French state organisations by Crozier (1964). Hierarchy and specialisation can encourage groups to extend their own influence and discretion, displacing formal goals and replacing them by sectional ones. For example, maintenance workers in the state tobacco factory used the remaining uncertainty linked to their role to develop informal powers over other workers. In the UK, the television programme 'Yes Minister' also shows how senior civil servants oppose or redirect policies which run counter to their established interests. Selznick's (1949) study of the Tennessee Valley Authority illustrates how the tendency of specialised groups of officials to form power cliques can frustrate attempts to create forms of citizen participation. In keeping with a Weberian framework, however, Selznick sees these events as evidence of the inevitable triumph of bureaucratic rationality over democratic values (Reed, 1986: 29–30).

Finally, the case studies indicate the existence of alternatives within bureaucratisation. The most famous derives from Gouldner's (1954) examination of gypsum mines in a closed, rural community. This showed how a form of bureaucracy based on shared knowledge and consent to rules – characterised as a 'mock bureaucracy' based on an 'indulgency pattern' reflecting the nature of the community – was challenged by a new manager acting on behalf of a cost-conscious parent company. Control was reasserted in a 'punishment-centred bureaucracy' through highly centralised authority, formalisation of rules and new technology. A theme of the above debates was the 'costs' of control, predictability and purely calculative exchange. In part, this echoed themes from the still-influential human relations movement, notably the tension between formal rules and informal practices, as well as the need for a human dimension in design.

Alternative designs in a bureaucratic framework

Whereas Bennis was prepared to write-off bureaucracy as a 'lifeless crutch that was no longer useful' (1966: 263); neo-Weberians were more likely to seek to analyse or promote alternative forms of design within bureaucratic organisation. This was taken up particularly by those within a managerialist tradition rather than organisational sociology. Blau built on the existence of alternatives to advocate greater decentralisation, discretion and participation. More usually, writers simply recognised that bureaucratic organisation should be treated as a *continuum* rather than as a unitary phenomenon (R. H. Hall, 1973). All the features of the ideal type do not have to be present, and in fact some can function as substitutes for each other. The main illustration used is the distinction between control through centralisation and hierarchy, normally exercised over workers with routine tasks; and controls over professionals, experts and managers. Direct controls over decision-making are not suitable to the work of the latter with its emphasis on autonomy. Though there is a tension between professionalisation and bureaucracy, Hall shows they are not incompatible. As we saw earlier, discretion and delegation can be allowed within a rule-governed framework.

A similar trajectory away from unitary conceptions was made in the Aston Studies, briefly discussed in Chapter 3. Their search (Pugh *et al.*, 1963, 1969) to identify causal relations between size, other variables and bureaucratisation, led them to develop a structural taxonomy. Seven types were identified, distinguished through dimensions centred on how control over work activities was exercised. There were three main types. *Full bureaucracies* – closest to Weber's ideal type – were based on a high level of standardisation of activities, concentration of authority and impersonal control, but were held not to exist in pure form outside central government. In contrast, *workflow bureaucracies* had highly structured activities such as production schedules, but more decentralised authority within the command framework. This type was found to be characteristic of large manufacturing concerns. Finally, smaller branch plants or parts of local government manifested bureaucratised employment relationships, but a low structuring of activities, and control exercised in a more personal way. These were dubbed *personnel bureaucracies*. Some of the applications in the shape of structural profiles can be seen in Pugh and Hickson (1973); while a detailed critique of the highly formalised nature of the Aston studies is found in Clegg and Dunkerley (1980: 218–62).

Debates continued, of course, around old favourites such as tall or flat structures and on which criteria to group positions in units. In the real world, structures were becoming increasingly mixed in some way – for example, combining functional and divisional systems. The most promoted design of the 1970s was a *matrix* arrangement, in which one mode of organising activities is overlaid by another. This involves a joint decision-making process which cuts across lines of authority, breaking with the 'unity of command' principle. Matrix structures are linked to the development of liaison roles, integrating units and project teams earlier identified by researchers such as Lawrence and Lorsch (1967). Such arrangements may exist for short-term tasks, or on a 'permanent' basis. In practice, it could mean someone reporting to both a project team and the functional department.

The advantages are held to be a capacity to balance different demands on and use of resources; a retention of the benefits of functional organisation while exposing specialists to a wider range of influences; and increasing the potential for innovation (J. Child, 1984: 102). Some major companies have in recent times certainly been convinced of the potential and have adopted it – for parts of their activities in the case of ICI, or for the whole operation in the case of the then British Aircraft Corporation in the 1970s. Though there may be contingent reasons for adopting matrix structures, such as having to cope with more than one major focus of activities, it has been widely seen as a useful way of responding to an increasingly volatile environment by having instability 'built-in'. As ever, instability has costs too. Co-ordination in dual authority structures is considerably more difficult; highly complex structures may lead to more unwieldiness; and senior management may have to accept a good deal more conflict and 'politicised' relationships between sectional interests. Such structures may also be more problematic when attempting to weld together diverse units resulting from mergers and acquisitions, a factor that influenced the abandonment of the matrix model in Volvo's bus and truck division in the 1990s. (Thompson *et al.*, 1992)

Matrix structures are linked to Mintzberg's 'structure of the future' – *adhocracy*. This is part of his structures in fives concept, and as Mintzberg is probably the most influential writer on design, it is worthwhile ending this section by looking at his arguments. The arguments cannot be understood without some reference to the wider analysis of the growth of the component parts of large-scale organisation. Some of those parts are common to most analyses: an operating core doing the basic work in relation to products and services; a strategic apex of decision-makers and senior managers; and a middle line management as a link between the two. Standardisation as a means of controlling work activities creates the need for various forms of analytical techniques for design, planning, training and the like. This forms the basis of a *technostructure* involving categories such as work study engineers, personnel and accountants. In addition, complex organisations require the provision of indirect services ranging from the printroom to public services, which are designated as *support staff*. Given this context, the five basic configurations are:

Simple structure – direct supervision based on the strategic apex
Machine bureaucracy – standardisation of work based on the technostructure
Professional bureaucracy – standardisation of skills based on the operating core
Divisional form – standardisation of outputs based on the middle line
Adhocracy – rests on mutual adjustment/informal communication, with support staff playing the key role.

These configurations embody forms that pull organisations in different directions. Naturally hybrid forms can result, or different structures in different parts of the firm; but 'the organisation is often drawn toward one of the configurations in its search for harmony of structure' (Mintzberg, 1983: 288). This ties in with the research of Khandwalla (1973) into US manufacturing firms that found that internal consistency had the most positive correlation with high performance. If the five configurations are examined, we can see that all but the adhocracy are indeed variations on bureaucracy. Borrowed from Toffler's *Future Shock* (1970), adhocracy's design parameters are based on organic structures, low levels of standardisation and formalisation of behaviour, decentralisation, and matrix-like use of specialists. Mintzberg argues that none of the previous forms are genuinely capable of innovative responses to new environments. Adhocracy is also the only form that combines more democracy with less bureaucracy, avoiding 'sharp divisions of labour, extensive unit differentiation, highly formalised behaviours, and an emphasis on planning and control systems' (1983: 254). He acknowledges that, like matrix arrangements, it carries with it a necessary increase in conflict, aggressiveness and politicisation.

In conclusion to this section, we would argue that the traditional design debate has largely been concerned with 'fine-tuning' bureaucratic models. Some of the variations are influenced by changing contingencies and some because 'not all managers agree on ways to overcome uncertainties' (Goldman and Van Houten, 1980: 67). Overall, the contributions work within what Peters and Waterman call the 'hard S's'. This is not just systems and structure, but *strategy* as a means of co-ordinating and directing the structural elements from the apex (Hitt *et al.*, 1986). Again, only adhocracy appears to depart from the bureaucratic framework. Even the formation of strategy is believed to develop implicitly from individual decisions, rather than being handed down from the top. Adhocracy is a structural configuration that appears in essence to be anti-structure. It therefore prefigures and is in tune with the more recent orientation towards flexibility and decentralisation in broader management theory. Before we get to that, a further stopping point in the anti-bureaucratic revolution has to be examined.

Well before the anti-bureaucratic appeal of adhocracy, 'people like Argyris, Bennis, Likert and McGregor built their careers on the analysis of the psychological dysfunctions of highly formalised structures' (Mintzberg, 1983: 37). A group of 'structure critics' had emerged to parallel the 'structure designers' (Hickson, 1973: 113). Their calls for new forms of participative organisation and job design drew on a psychology that assumes universalistic higher order needs that can only be met by the provision of intrinsically satisfying work. Such predictions appeared to be pertinent in the 'crisis of work' that peaked in the early 1970s, when various governments launched initiatives that focused on the need for some kind of *work humanisation*. Behind this show of official concern lay tight labour markets and high levels of employment which gave firms problems in recruiting and retaining workers; and an upsurge in industrial unrest through strike waves, and less formally through absenteeism, high labour turnover and sabotage.

When focusing on the experiences of work humanisation, we face the problem of accurate knowledge. Many managers and academics have heard only of Volvo, which distracted from the wider nature of job design initiatives in that period. This should not be taken out of proportion. It was certainly not a 'third industrial revolution', as Hofstede (1977) claimed. By no means all companies responded to the 'crisis of work' by thinking about job redesign. Many, such as Plessey on Merseyside, simply attempted to tighten-up controls and introduce new pay and productivity deals (Thompson and Bannon, 1985). But it did involve a significant minority of large companies, often leading firms with a tradition of 'progressive' management methods, such as ICI, Olivetti, Philips, IBM and Polaroid, as well as new players such as Ford, General Motors and Volkswagen.

But from what we *do* know, the record of work humanisation is 'inconclusive on both efficiency and humanitarian grounds' (S. Dawson, 1992: 23). Using the managerial criteria of increases in productivity and quality, and reductions in absenteeism and labour turnover, there were consistent reports of gains, albeit uneven, in companies such as ICI, Philips and AT&T (Daniel and McIntosh, 1972). Also on the positive side, some of the initiatives aided a further break with determinism concerning technology or structure. But it is difficult to identify any consistent success in terms of the original claims for a genuine transformation of work or move away from bureaucracy. Many of the initiatives were in white collar or craft jobs where it was easier to assign wider responsibilities and discretion without expensive technological change or other major restructuring. Though there was restructuring of assembly lines, for example around work stations (Coriat, 1980), applications of job enrichment to manual workers were generally to the more trivial facets of work such as job rotation (Nichols and Beynon, 1977). Ramsay's (1985) survey of the international evidence concluded that with the onset of the recession, work humanisation had largely faded from view or stagnated even in Scandinavia.

Radical critics argued that, for all its good intentions, neo-human relations lacked a realistic analysis of the constraints embodied in the capitalist labour process. In principle task-centred reforms were attractive because they 'appear to solve the problem of how to give workers more discretion in the performance of their work without weakening management control over the broad objectives of the enterprise' (Hawkins, 1978: 119). But that fails to recognise the threat any far-reaching changes could have on existing forms of hierarchy and control. One famous instance was Polaroid's worker participation project that was so successful that it had to be ended, because the training director felt that they were getting to a position were supervisors and managers would not be needed (D. Jenkins, 1973).

Linked to the above was actual resistance from those managers and supervisors in the intermediate hierarchy whose positions are most directly threatened by elimination or redesign of their jobs. Those who use power as a resource within bureaucratic control have a material interest in opposing initiatives that break such systems down (Drago and MacDonough, 1984). There may also be a perceived threat to legitimacy, producing the defensive responses quoted in Jones, where managers, 'pine for the days when "a managers' job was to manage" or see the new innovations as "just another confidence trick"' (G. Jones, 1978: 14). Some writers took the experience of work humanisation as a further illustration that managerial interest in job reform and participation is of a *cyclical* nature (Ramsay, 1983, 1985). This is not so much the result of 'fashion', but of periods which combine economic pressures and a challenge from below to the legitimacy of capital. Work humanisation rose in such a period and largely bit the dust in the recession.

The disappearance of articles on job enrichment from management literature at the end of the 1980s seemed to confirm its failure as a means of moving beyond bureaucracy in the labour process. But it proved somewhat misleading to write off job redesign as a source of organisational innovation (Marchington *et al.*, 1993). Although the solutions of work humanisation proved unacceptable or unnecessary to capital, the issues it addressed low commitment and the costs of routinised work – did not go away. It could be argued that this wave of change was premature, in that some of preconditions for success were absent. A wide range of managerial and organisational writers point to new environmental 'shocks' which form a more fertile framework for a real anti-bureaucratic revolution is the basis of discussion in the second half of this chapter.

Contemporary developments: the post-bureaucratic organisation?

A paradigm shift?

The world of management theory and practice always appears to be changing fast, but new buzzwords and themes have surfaced during the last few years with bewildering rapidity. Popular management texts have stressed the need for 'change masters' that can handle innovation at every level (Kanter, 1984); new forms of 'transformational' leadership (Tichy and Devanna, 1986); the need for intrapreneurs (Pinchot, 1985) who can act autonomously and creatively across federal organisations (Handy, 1984); for committed and empowered employees (Martin and Nicholls, 1987); horizontal networks to replace vertical hierarchies (Hirschorn and Gilmore, 1992); learning organisations where knowledge is the only effective resource (Webber, 1993); and for self-managing teams to be the basic organisational building block (Peters, 1989). The language is dominated by Fs: fast, flat and flexible organisations; and Ds: decentralisation, disaggregation, disorganisation and delayering. It adds up to a widely-held belief that the days of bureaucracy are over.

Furthermore, the post-bureaucratic organisation (Heckscher and Donnellon, 1994) is indicative of a paradigm shift, a decisive period of transformation, the first since Taylor, Fayol and Ford. This development is continually trumpeted by popular management writers such as Drucker (1992), Peters (1989, 1992) and Lessem (1985). The new form of organisation moves from the 'holding' to the 'enabling' company, to collaborative joint ventures, management buy-outs, contracting out parts of the organisations, personal network-ing, mini-factories and industrial boutiques. The cause of such a shift is supposed to be our old friend, 'the environment'. New 'strategic contingen-cies' in a global economy marked increasingly by turbulence and volatility, produce environmental shocks arising from slower economic growth, intensification of competition, a rising rate of product innovation new forms of knowledge and information technology. The consequent forms of uncertainty and discontinuous change cannot be handled adequately by the bureaucratic structures and decision-making processes of traditionally designed organisations (Pascale, 1990).

It will be tempting for some to dismiss all this as inflated fantasies and prescriptions from the evidence-free zones of pop-management texts. But we have been getting a similar message about a paradigm shift from other sources. Organisational theorists such as Clegg (1990) are also convinced that Weber's iron cage of bureaucracy – rule-driven, hierarchical and centralised organisation – is no longer a requirement for efficiency. The particular influence on such writers (see Hassard and Parker, 1993) is a theorisation of paradigm shift based on a move from modernity to post-modernity. Indeed, for Clegg (1990: 2) 'organisation theory is a creation of modernity'. The latter is linked to an increasing division of labour, in which jobs, tasks and roles are highly differentiated. In contrast, 'Postmodernism points to a more organic, less differentiated enclave of organisation than those dominated by the bureaucratic designs of modernity' (1990: 181). Flexibility is, once again, the watchword, with integrated tasks and collective workers becoming their own supervisors.

Nor most we be bound by the constraints of rationality itself, with its emphasis on calculation, direction and design. With environments ever-changing and unpredictable, organisations are more likely to succeed by being *reactive*. Managers will spend their time promoting the core corporate values and symbols rather than strategic planning. This emphasis on living with chaos and managing culture echoes themes in popular management. The general account of society and organisations also resembles and overlaps with a further influential account of discontinuity, the distinction between *Fordism* and *post-Fordism*. So, for example, Mulgen (1988) refers to the replacement of 'strong power' under the Fordist corporations – characterised by pyramidal structures, formal rules and close controls – by a post-Fordist order based on weak power controls and decentralised leadership, horizontal communication and self-regulating units. Though the language of environ-mental turbulence is replaced by more academic and radical sounding post labels and phases of capitalism, the message that major changes 'out there' are compelling an organisational response is common, as is an emphasis on key influences such as new forms of information technology. The diagram following attempts to pull together the overlapping organisational themes in the various literatures.

A post-bureaucratic organisation?

Old	New
stability	disorganisation/chaos
rationality	charisma, values
planning	spontaneity
control	empowerment
command	participation
centralisation	decentralisation/disaggregation
hierarchy	network
formal	informal/flexibility
large	downsized/delayered

Before we go on to explain and evaluate such claims, it is necessary to focus on a further significant influence on conceptions of societal and organisational transformation.

Japan as design model

We have been talking as if the perceived need to respond to new market conditions has been the only 'learning experience' motivating Western business organisations. Yet the 'Japanese threat' changed the terms of competition in the 1980s and in doing so has set in motion a major process of emulating or modifying the ingredients believed to be the basis of superior performance. Not everything to do with Japan as a design model can be explicitly related to the issue of post-bureaucratic organisation. The predominant emphasis in the management literature, sparked off by the OECD Report (1977), Ouchi (1981) and Pascale and Athos (1982), has been on *management* skills, style and values. The last set up a comparison between Matushita Electric and ITT, and specifically their two leaders. In terms of the hard S's of strategy, structure and systems, the result was a draw. However, on the soft S's of style, skills and staff, a spiritual knockout was attributed to the Japanese. This reading of the sources of competitive advantage has more connection to the debates on corporate culture that form the subject of our next chapter. But if flexibility has been a central theme of the revolution against bureaucracy, then the Japanese experience of intra-firm and inter-firm relations can be seen as an important resource for contemporary debate.

Attention has been largely directed at initiatives in intra-firm relations, such as quality circles (see George and Levie, 1984). But innovation in production systems has been more broadly orientated towards product design, quality, labour utilisation, scheduling and stock control. Take, for example, the just-in-time system (JIT), discussed briefly in Chapter 3. Originally developed by Toyota, it consists of a group of related practices aimed at ensuring the exact quantity and quality of raw materials, parts and sub-assemblies are delivered 'just-in-time' for the next stage of production. Compared to the normal 'just-in case' practices, this keeps inventories and buffer stocks to a minimum (Sayer, 1986; Tailby and Turnbull, 1987). JIT is not merely an inventory system. To work properly it requires flexible labour utilisation and harmonising of tacit skills, close managerial involvement in production, multi-purpose machinery and reductions in set-up times. It feeds into the overall process of *kaizen* or continuous improvement. Such a system also frequently depends on a set of relations between large corporations and suppliers, normally characterised by tightly controlled multiple sourcing through layers of subcontractors.

There are two basic means through which the influence of Japan operates as a design model. First the *demonstration effect* of 'best practice' (Turnbull, 1987: 2). For the UK, this can be illustrated through the Nissan example (Garrahan and Stewart, 1992). When Nissan set up in May 1986 in Washington, Tyne and Wear, Norman Tebbit stated that, 'We want them to demonstrate to our auto makers . . . these aspects of Japanese industrial management' (quoted in CAITS, 1986: 20). A 'Nissan effect' has already been widely noted, drawing primarily from the single-union, no-strike deal. In fact it is not a no-strike deal, because the Amalgamated Engineering Union is not a negotiating partner! All matters of wages, conditions and company business are dealt with at plant level by a company council with direct worker representation conditioned by company veto. However, an initial deal was struck specifying complete flexibility and managerial prerogative. Team working, temporary workers and an intense work pace are also prominent features – the last causing low morale and drop outs (*Daily Telegraph*, 6 May 1987). It is hardly surprising that union membership remains low. But of more long-term importance is that Nissan has established the first British and possibly European example of a spatially concentrated production process (Crowther and Garrahan, 1987). A large site will enable the company to maximise influence over the industrial environment and the supply of components, moving towards a full JIT system. Employment and production practices are being built-in, not grafted on.

The Nissan effect can also be identified in the second way in which Japanese influence operates, the desire of British and other companies to *emulate* Japanese practices. This has been seen most prominently in the case of Ford. An early 'After Japan' initiative based on quality circles, an 'employee involvement' programme and a new management culture and structure foundered on workforce opposition (Giles and Starkey, 1987). The second attempt to achieve a 'Japanese' restructuring of jobs and shop floor practices culminated in the 1988 dispute. Explicit reference was made to Ford's plethora of grades compared to Nissan's two – manufacturer and technician. But Ford is by no means the sole example. In a similar period, Jaguar and Lucas introduced extensive experiments featuring JIT and employee involvement (Turnbull, 1986); while among the joint ventures, the Rover–Honda link-up was notable for its use of 'zone circles' and 'zone briefing groups' (D. Smith, 1987).

Since that period, the spread of Japanese transplants into the USA and Europe has been extensive and their apparent success has led to further pressures that combine demonstration effect and emulation. The transferable ingredients of Japanese productive expertise have been repackaged as the system of *lean production* pioneered by Toyota, particularly in *The Machine that Changed the World* by Womack *et al.* (1990). We discussed the issue of transferability in Chapter 3, but as a design template, lean production conforms to the anti-bureaucracy menu by stressing that in this brave new world, firms will employ teams of multi-skilled workers whose jobs will be more challenging, more productive and carry more responsibilities.

Having looked at some of the overarching themes of organisational transformation and their connections to post-bureaucratic design, this chapter moves on to a more specific look at the theory and research in the main substantive areas said to be shaping change. We shall give expositions of the arguments used by those advocating new models before subjecting them to evaluation and critique. (see P. Thompson, 1993, for a more detailed critique of post-modernism.)

Firms, markets and hierarchies

Many of the themes identified in conceptions of lean production and some of the other ideas discussed above have been packaged in a more comprehensive way by advocates of the theory of flexible specialisation (Piore and Sabel, 1984). This is the term given to efforts 'to convert the traditional highly integrated, corporate structure into a more supple organisational form capable of responding quickly to shifting market conditions and product demand' (Piore, 1986: 146). In its earlier form, Sabel's (1982) analysis preferred to speak of corporate attempts to maintain continuity with mass production, deskilling and labour controls; while moving away from standardisation. This *neo-Fordism* was seen as co-existing with a new 'high-tech' cottage industry which

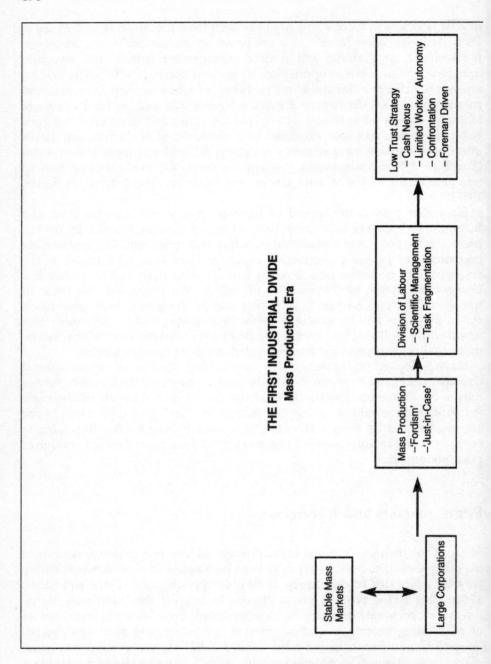

FIGURE 6.1 The flexible specialisation hypothesis

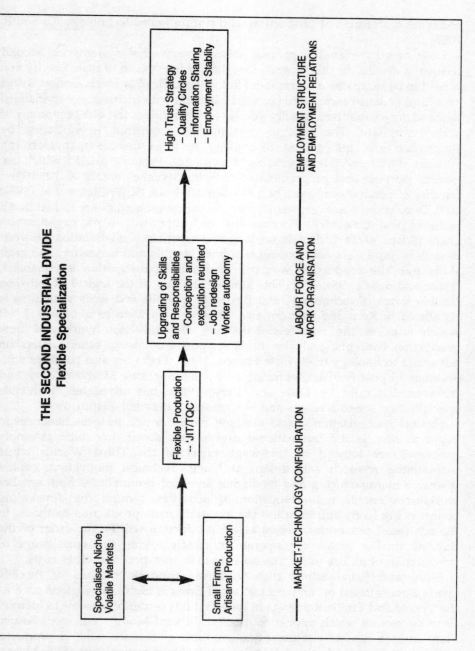

THE SECOND INDUSTRIAL DIVIDE
Flexible Specialization

Specialised Niche, Volatile Markets

Small Firms, Artisanal Production

Flexible Production -- 'JIT/TQC'

Upgrading of Skills and Responsibilities
– Conception and execution reunited
– Job redesign
Worker autonomy

High Trust Strategy
– Quality Circles
– Information Sharing
– Employment Stability

MARKET-TECHNOLOGY CONFIGURATION

LABOUR FORCE AND WORK ORGANISATION

EMPLOYMENT STRUCTURE AND EMPLOYMENT RELATIONS

Source: Thomas Bramble (1988) 'Industrial Relations and New Management Production Practices', *Labour and Society*, vol. 112, June.

combines craft forms of production with computerised technology (C. Smith, 1987: 1).

Later work declared a general crisis of industrial systems or 'second industrial divide'. In this formulation, the Fordist system of mass production is held to be incapable of permanent innovation. Flexible specialisation works on a kind of *design chain* (see Figure 6.1). It starts with increasingly specialised demand for customised quality goods, which renders the old economies of scale redundant. The shift to new market conditions is facilitated by production and information technology such as flexible manufacturing systems (FMS) and Manufacturing Automation Protocol (MAP) which are general purpose and programmable allowing switches within and between families of products on more of a small-batch basis (K. Williams *et al.*, 1987: 409). Once such choices are made, manufacturing economies are locked into a technological trajectory. Fragmented and repetitive work organisation characteristic of Taylorism is no longer compatible. Collaboration between designers, producers and managers is both feasible and necessary, and craft skills and 'the production worker's intellectual participation is enhanced' (Piore and Sabel, 1984: 278). This kind of analysis of the logical fit between flexible forms of technology, and flexibility in skills and work structures is paralleled in Kern and Schumman's *The End of the Division of Labour* (1984) which talks of the reprofessionalisation of production work and new production concepts; and also finds support from some other writers on advanced technology (Gill, 1985; Francis, 1986). There are also parallels with accounts of post-Fordism, popularised by the magazine *Marxism Today*, and more academically by Lash and Urry (1987); but advocates of flexible specialisation see differences and weaknesses (Hirst and Zeitlin, 1991).

Flexible specialisation is said to allow transnationals in some instances to begin to reverse the international division of labour, in which assembly processes are located in low-wage areas of the Third World, while maintaining research and design at home. Technical innovation, capital intensive manufacturing and far higher levels of productivity from smaller workforces enable redomestication of activities; though the developing countries are likely still to utilise the low-skill, mass production methods. In the advanced economies, decentralised production will be the order of the day, as smaller plants can operate efficiently within the same range of products and be close to the customer to save transport and other costs.

Piore and Sabel admit that working economic models of flexible specialisation based on networks of small firms is limited to regions such as the Veneto and Emilia Romanga in Italy. But it is certainly possible to identify firms or sectors which appear to qualify. General Motor's emergent Saturn Plant utilises flexible equipment to produce specifically tailored products, without retooling and with a high level of worker participation (P. B. Meyer, 1986: 74). Technology such as computer-aided design systems have enabled clothing firms both to create and then respond speedily to customer demands for a greater range of design and colour. Standardisation and long runs are said to become uneconomical. Computerisation also helps large firms such as Benneton to centralise marketing and skilled processes such as design and dyeing among its small core workforce of less than 2000 people, while decentralising its other production work to small subcontractors, and franchising its sales outlets (Murray, 1983; Mitter, 1986). The flexibility theme now moves downwards towards the firm and its boundaries.

Redrawing the firm and its boundaries

During periods of significant change in work organisation, attention is often directed towards a particular phenomenon, that is seen as an obstacle to efficiency. In the past it has been 'overmanning' or unofficial strikes. More recently, within the general reference to the defects of Taylorism and Fordism, it is *work rules*: regulatory mechanisms established by workers and managers to govern the workplace. The previously mentioned article in *Business Week* (1983) celebrated a revolution against rules that place constraints on management's right to allocate and organise labour. Under systems of bureaucratic organisation and control, employers had gained from rules by being able to specify job assignments closely and operate internal labour markets. Unions could restrict arbitrary power and enforce adherence to rules that benefited workers. In addition to such areas as task demarcation, seniority rules governing job protection, lay-offs and promotions were established. Because work rules were embodied in contractual relations rights and grievance procedures, they gave unions bargaining power. Employment protection in law also enhanced status rights which limited what employers could gain from contractual exchange (Streek, 1987: 241–2). The flexibility offensive is directed not just against the 'rigidities' of work rules, but also their high, often fixed, costs in terms of compensation and movement (Mangum and Mangum, 1986). When taken together with better pensions and other social and fringe benefits, senior management increasingly begin to see such arrangements; not just as an unnecessary burden, but as one American executive put it – as a form of 'corporate socialism'.

Flexibility therefore requires the firm's internal and external boundaries to be redrawn, bringing into question employment contracts and the location of work, as well as the previously-mentioned work rules (Guest, 1987). The most widely-used analytical framework for understanding the moves by employers to vary their workers and work is provided by the *flexible firm* model developed by Atkinson (1984) and the Institute for Manpower Studies (IMS). It is based on a break with existing unitary and hierarchical labour markets and organisation of internal means of allocating labour, in order to create a core workforce and a cluster of peripheral employment relations. Three types of flexibility are identified:

- *functional*: Core workers gain job security in return for managers' right to redeploy them between activities and tasks as products and production require.
- *numerical*: The capacity to vary the headcount according to changes in the level of demand so that there is an exact match between the numbers needed and employment.
- *financial*: Pay and other employment costs reflect the state of supply and demand in the external labour market; and support the objectives of functional and numerical flexibility.

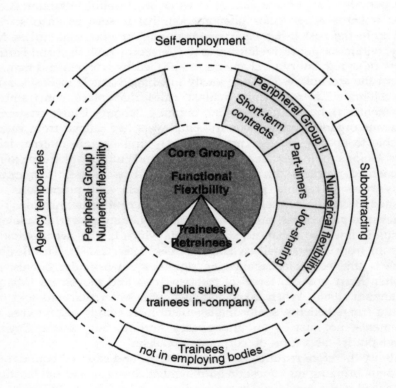

Source: G. C. Mangum, 'Temporary Work: The Flipside of Job Security', *International Journal of Manpower*, vol. 17, no. 1, 1986: 14.

FIGURE 6.2   Model of the flexible firm

IMS surveys showed that most larger firms contacted claim to have increased numerical flexibility, though sectoral variations indicated a predominance in service work (Atkinson and Gregory, 1986). Nor was it difficult to find high-profile examples of workplace agreements concerning functional flexibility. The most extreme, such as those at Nissan and at Sony, specify complete flexibility, even to the point of managers and clerical staff working on the production line if necessary (*IPM Digest*, 1986). Beyond general statements of manpower utilisation, agreements are mostly directed towards removing 'barriers' between grades and categories. This may be achieved by merging production grades or ensuring job rotation. But a crucial goal is 'multi-skilling' and the erosion of distinctions between production and other categories such as indirect, maintenance and even craft work. For example, production workers at Cadbury and Findus have to carry out maintenance work, while skilled engineering construction workers on oil and gas platforms must undertake semi-skilled or unskilled work if there is no craft work for them to do.

Emphasis has also been put on creating flexible craftworkers or 'crafticians', by focusing on the interfaces between crafts, and non-crafts, craft assistants, supervisors, and other trades (Cross, 1985). At Shell's Carrington site, management negotiated, under threat of closure, an amalgamation of the craft workforce into four trade groups with no demarcations. All non-management jobs were brought together under one technician heading and a single set of terms and conditions (CAITS, 1986). Even clerical groups have not been exempt. Lucas Electrical amalgamated many clerical tasks with manual tasks under a new grade of 'materials controller'. One of the characteristics of flexibility is a turn towards teamworking, such as the composite groups at British Shipbuilders, within which there is complete interchangeability. We shall return to such practices later.

There are a number of related changes worth noting. Modification and reductions in gradings have allowed the simplification of *pay structures* and bargaining. Many companies such as Shell have linked rewards and career progression more closely to individual appraisal and performance-related pay, thus undermining the traditional notion of a specific 'rate for the job'. Not surprisingly, this has often has the intention and effect of undermining trade union organisation, which has to adapt to a weaker, enterprise-based orientation based on single or reduced representation; local bargaining; and a shift from an industrial relations to a 'human resource management' framework (Streek, 1987: 299). Finally, there are alterations in the use of *time*. It does not normally involve an extension of flexi-time chosen by employees, or the 35-hour week beloved of trade unions, but rather consists of attempts by employers to vary attendance to meet fluctuations in workload and gain general control over time-scheduling. This includes buying-out overtime and breaks or ending them as rights, and introducing round-the-clock, round-the-shift systems, with the use of part-time and temporary labour to cover peak demand (Yates, 1986; CAITS, 1986; Wainwright, 1987).

What about compensating factors? Clearly any increased focus on a core workforce is likely to enhance the need for training and retraining, though this will be in-house and limited largely to firm-specific skills. The most touted carrot, however, is job security, which is linked to, 'the difficulty of implementing productivity programmes without the full co-operation of the employees' (Clutterbuck, 1985: 2). Prominent examples are drawn from the USA, notably the 'job banks' at Ford and GM, in which an equivalent number of jobs are created if production is outsourced. If workers are laid-off, they are promised retraining, relocation and income support (Mangum and Mangum, 1986: 12). It is accepted that whatever the limits, or any kind of security is considerably more than the growing army of peripheral workers is going to get. Indeed, the capacity to externalise uncertainty, costs and risks to a variety of holders of labour services, is the explicit rationale for numerical flexibility.

Early surveys for the International Labour Organisation (Standing, 1986), by the Confederation of British Industry (Yates, 1986) and ACAS (1988), indicated a substantial growth in numerical flexibility. More recent evidence (Casey, 1991; Marginson, 1991) also shows steady, if uneven increases in some of the categories discussed in more detail below.

Subcontracting This is argued to be the most significant development, facilitated by and helping to feed the decentralisation process. It can take the form of contracting out work or outsourcing the supply of components. Though not a new phenomenon, it is said to be breaking out of traditional fields such as cleaning, with half of all large firms in the UK having increased the use of subcontractors. In some instances, former employees are turned into suppliers of services, thus linking subcontracting to the categories below.

Self-employment This actually fell during the 1970s, but rose from 1.2m. in 1979 to 2.6m. in 1985 and has continued to increase rapidly (Casey, 1991), though this is difficult to disentangle from the effects of unemployment and the successive recessions. But many firms are transforming specialist and skilled work from waged employment to the supply of services, sometimes re-employing their previous workers. This is known as 'linked subcontracting' (Clutterbuck, 1985). The building industry has put enormous pressure on workers to move into the 731 self-employed category.

Temporary contracts Two-thirds of the ACAS respondents reported using temporary workers. The 5000 temporary help services make it the fastest growing industry in the USA. In the UK, some firms such as Control Data are using 'supplementals' on short-term contracts with poor conditions to act as buffer to their permanent staff (CAITS, 1986: 32). Nor is it confined to manual workers in manufacturing or to seasonal work. Universities and colleges are increasingly employing teachers on one-year, or renewable, rolling contracts. But these may be high-profile and unrepresentative examples, given that

Casey's (1991) examination of the survey evidence shows no significant growth.

Part-time Those working 16 hours or less have increased significantly in recent years, making the UK one of the highest users of part-time labour. Though part-time workers are usually female and in the service sector, the CBI and ACAS estimate that the trend is spreading to manufacturing and other sectors. Managerial proposals to increase the use of part-timers have been at the root of industrial trouble at a number of organisations, such as Ford and the Post Office.

Homeworking This trend has received a considerable amount of glamorous publicity through Rank Xerox's networkers, F International, ICL and other professional and white collar workers linked by computer in 'electronic cottages' (Control Data Corporation, 1985). But manufacturing homework, involving putting-out to women domestic outworkers, in sectors such as textiles, electrical components and toys is arguably more significant (Mitter, 1986; Allen and Wolkowtiz, 1987), though it remains a small number: one in twenty firms according to ACAS.

Franchising This also appears to be rapidly rising and spreading into service activity such as milk rounds (Labour Research Department, 1986b; O'Connell Davidson, 1994b). The latter example constitutes a classic example of transferring risk in an uncertain market and undermining trade unionism, while retaining control of supplies, prices and business style.

If these are trends in the labour market, what about work itself?

Control and commitment in the labour process

The labour process is a vital arena if the promises of the anti-bureaucratic revolution are to be fulfilled. Employees' attitudes have to be transformed from grudging compliance to high commitment and practices changed from narrow, demarcated tasks to fully flexible, interchangeable labour. We have already identified aspects of the proposed change through the idea of functional flexibility, but the influences and outcomes go deeper.

Employee involvement is a consistent theme. On the surface, the language and practices are a continuation of older quality of working life (QWL) initiatives. QWL has long been a generic or umbrella term subsuming anything from job enrichment to participation schemes. Though beginning prior to the main wave of Japanisation on the shop floor, it was been given force and coherence by mid-1980s initiatives such as GM's QWL and Ford's Employee Involvement programmes in the USA. Quality circles and related initiatives such as briefing groups were the most prominent practice during this period. Most did not last very long (Ramsay, 1991). Quality circles tended to experience a tension between their dual functions as *technique* and vehicle for localised *participation*. Many companies such as Reckitt Colman used quality circles as a catalyst for a period of organisational restructuring and dispensed with them once the goals had been achieved (Dunford and McGraw, 1987). Some companies tried to avoid a 'Japanese' tag by re-labelling initiatives. In the UK, Rover plant management prefer 'zone briefings' and 'zone circles'. The latter operate through management 'facilitators' who guide voluntary problem-solving groups. Techniques used included brainstorming and discussions based on 'thought starters', such as 'every member is responsible for the progress of a team', or 'strive to generate enthusiasm' (D. Smith, 1987: 23).

New forms of involvement derive in part from technology – such as flexible manufacturing systems and production processes, notably JIT. While it would be over-deterministic to ascribe 'needs', there is little doubt that both operate more effectively with higher levels of co-operation, knowledge and flexibility than previous configurations of technology and work organisation. Under JIT – workers are expected to do on-the-spot problem solving – indeed, they have little choice, given that reduced buffer stocks mean that subsequent activities would break down without such action (Tailby and Turnbull, 1987). In turn, this requires *multi-skilling* and the incorporation of inspection, maintenance and support activities into production operative's tasks, or vice versa. These processes also require increased *knowledge*, both of details of the work process such as quality control, and of a wider range of jobs. Pay for knowledge systems may be the form taken, in which learning of extra tasks is built in to the reward system.

Current labour process initiatives focus on teamworking and TQM. The managerial literature is full of exhortations to create self-managing teams so that, 'no boss is required' (Dumaine, 1990: 40). It is tempting to believe that these practices are extensions of previous goals and techniques which had a narrow and often short-term orientation. Mathews, however, argues that such elements of new production systems are not passing fads and differ sharply from QWL, which only grappled with the symptoms of workplace problems. Contemporary initiatives fundamentally reorganise the process of work: 'In place of command and control structures designed to enforce rigidity and compliance, the new production systems call for management that offers facilitation, guidance and co-ordination between self-managing groups of employees who are capable of looking after the details of production themselves' (1993: 7). This is a very ambitious and sweeping statement. But there is evidence that managements in an increasing number of companies are making a more concerted attempt to devolve responsibilities to the group, and to get the workers to think and act like managers, thus generating a genuine sense of shared values (Wickens, 1992; J. R. Barker, 1993; Mueller, 1994b). In this way the work-group can be used to redirect collective goals towards the company in a way that fulfils the old human relations dream. With such a team system in place, companies such as Saturn and NUMMI claimed that they would drop their formal worker participation programmes (Wood, 1986: 438).

TQM programmes also promise a broader, more holistic approach than localised quality circle techniques (Hill, 1991). In the pursuit of the goal of continuous improvement in the production of goods and services, TQM differs by starting from the top and cascading through the organisation. Flatter structures and reduced hierarchy develop as workers take increased responsibilities. Hierarchy is also reduced by a network of inter-dependencies arising from the necessity for employees to treat each other as internal 'customers'. Changes to job design are not the add-ons of old, but a genuine re-integration of conception and execution that is integral to the work process. Though TQM began by focusing on the 'hard' elements of capturing information about processes, it has gradually shifted towards a 'softer' orient-ation to employee commitment and appropriate cultures (A. Wilkinson, 1992).

Both teamworking and TQM require attention to what Wood (1986: 432) calls *attitudinal restructuring*. In other words, a much more explicit focus on shaping employee attitudes in spheres such as co-operativeness and self-discipline. As Andrew Sayer notes with reference to JIT, 'profitability can depend quite heavily on the performance of workers who are technically unskilled or semi-skilled but behaviourally highly skilled' (1986: 67). This helps explain the paradox that many companies are engaging in detailed and intensive selection and screening processes for relatively routine jobs, often recruiting young 'green' labour. We have already given examples from Japanese companies, but when the NUMMI plant was established all candidates for employment undertook three days of interviews, job simula-tions and discussion on the firm's philosophy and objectives (Wood, 1986: 434). Attention to attitudes is also reflected in an enhanced emphasis on communications. This was the purpose of Rover's zone briefing system, in which supervisors stopped the track to give information about output targets, sales performance and matters more specific to the 'zone'. Overall, the focus on behaviour, teamworking and personnel appraisal helps to explain the increased, though different role, for supervisors. Japan has the highest supervisory density among the advanced economies (Broad, 1987: 16). Attitudinal restructuring speaks to a range of issues more explicitly related to organisational cultures. We shall return to this question in the next chapter.

Restructuring the corporation

For mainstream organisation theory, challenging bureaucratic designs ultimately rests on change in the sphere of *structure*. In earlier times, organic structures or ad-hoceries were one way of adapting to the environment. Now it is frequently presented as the norm, a permanent condition of organisational life. To explain these arguments, it is useful to return to the four Ds with which we began this section.

Big is no longer merely not beautiful, it is positively dangerous and anachronistic. As part of a process of *decentralisation*, companies are said to be breaking up their bureaucracies and setting up smaller or independent units, or developing new corporate structures where divisions operate as autonomous profit centres with delegated decision-making powers. Integration will be provided by overall strategy, information technology and corporate cultures. After this organisational revolution, the more autonomous units will be 'guided by a coherent vision rather than by memorandum and managers-as-cops' (Peters, 1989: 31). Units will therefore be more loosely-coupled and decision-making more dispersed, as in matrix systems of multiple accountability. 'External' surveillance and control will be increasingly replaced by new forms of market disciplines between the autonomous units, or even work teams who are each others customers (Clegg, 1990: 180).

The break-up is linked to *disaggregation*, which goes beyond the internal redistribution of power by reducing the corporation to a relatively small core as central functions are dispersed to small firms, outsourced to specialist units and franchises, and sub-contracted to telecommuters in electronic cottages. Handy (1989) refers to this as a trend towards federalism, or beyond to the 'donut' organisation that has nothing in the middle. The centre has only to keep a broad watching brief on finance and longer-term policy. This deconcentration of capital (Perrow, 1992) puts into reverse the historic trend towards vertical integration: 'If the old model of organisation was the large hierarchical firm, the model of organisation that is considered characteristic of the New Competition is a network, of lateral and horizontal interlinkages within and among firms' (Nohria, 1992: 2). Such a characterisation of current trends connects to the vision promoted by flexible specialistion theorists, of industrial districts populated by small, entrepreneurial firms co-existing happily in a new division of labour with their scaled-down, larger sisters (Best, 1990).

Networks appear in another form, an alternative to internal hierarchy, as organisation go through a *delayering* process. While 'downsizing' is often a cynical euphemism for sacking people, claims are made for a trend towards flatter, less hierarchical forms where whole layers of middle management have been removed on the back of new, horizontal communication channels and devolution of responsibility to self-managing and project teams; a trend enhanced by single-status deals that remove barriers between categories of employees. Quinn Mills (1993: 8) even invents a new label – the post-hierarchical firm. He is also typical of many recent managerial writers in attributing to new forms of information technology a determinant role in facilitating many of the above changes. Fax machines and new computer link-ups are a key driving force of new ways of working: 'Today, technology is following its own dynamic direction toward distributed computing of greater and greater power and diffused, not centralised information' (1993: 15).

Finally we have *disorganisation*. Peters, for example, has travelled from 'thriving on chaos' to 'necessary disorganisation' in the ephemeral world of the 1990s. Bureaucratic structures and rationality are based on planning. In contemporary, unpredictable environments attempting to predict or control the future is pointless when there is no way of knowing what it is. As a result, 'The era of strategic planning (control) may be over; we are entering an era of tactical planning (response)' (Kanter, 1993, 2nd edn). Pop management writing is reinforced by post-modern perspectives that emphasise the reactive nature of organisational behaviour in circumstances where there is inherent uncertainty and disorder in a multiplicity of local situations (Cooper and Burrell, 1988); and new chaos theories of science in which nature appears as random as a throw of the dice (Freedman, 1992). Organisations are 'out of control' (K. Kelly, 1994) but that fine because that is part of the continual cycle of creation and destruction undertaken by 'mobius strip' organisations that have no identifiable top or bottom, beginning or end (Sabel, 1991).

Evaluating the changes

It can be seen that there are a number of overlapping organisational themes from the 'models' established through flexibility and other restructuring discourses. This sections returns to each set of issues and uses contemporary research to subject the associated theorisations to evaluation.

Firms and markets

Flexible specialisation rapidly became a new work organisation paradigm and therefore a target for extensive critique (C. Smith, 1987). A number of studies, notably that by Williams *et al.* (1987), have convincingly argued that the conceptual polarity between mass production and flexible specialisation is misleading.

If we return to contemporary trends, traditional mass production is still widespread, particularly where semi-skilled women workers doing labour intensive assembly and packing jobs remain a cheaper or more reliable option (Pollert, 1988a). In addition, mass production does not always use dedicated equipment to make standardised products; but can handle diversification within flow lines. Wood (1989b) has shown that the world car – the archetypal example of mass production within the international division of labour – remains prominent, albeit in modified form. Economies of scale have fallen, but the break-even point is still high. Japanese and other companies have established variety within mass production with the use of JIT and not always with advanced technology (A. Sayer, 1986). In fact, flexible specialisation and JIT may be in contradiction, as flexibility is undermined by a range of factors including single sourcing and the dependency between buyer and supplier (P. B. Meyer, 1986).

Nor on current trends are mass markets necessarily saturated. There are a huge range of industries still based on mass and large-batch production and the pattern with goods such as colour TVs and video recorders is for production to be based on families of interrelated models. Fragmentation of demand, or what companies call 'positioning strategies', is more often an attempt to create a market than to reflect new consumer tastes. Key industries, such as food, are actually destroying regional, craft production in the march towards global standardised products and marketing (C. Smith, 1991). Indeed, it is ironic that the most explosive global growth is in fast food, which is, 'dominated by homogeneous products. The big Mac, the Egg McMuffin, and Chicken McNuggets are identical from one time and place to another' (Ritzer, 1993: 155). Part of the obsession with the Fordist stereotype ignores the inconvenient fact that most plants in modern economies do not contain assembly lines (Williams et al., 1987: 421) Indeed, as we indicated in Chapter 2, the more recent research work of this team (Williams et al., 1992b) demonstrates that the operations of Ford's key Highland Park plant *never* corresponded to the description of inflexible Ford*ism*.

Even the identification of flexibility with manufacturing itself neglects the service sector as the major growth area of such practices (Hyman, 1988). The flexible specialisation thesis also overestimates the use of programmable technology. Advanced machinery such as FMS is very expensive, particularly for the small firms which should be in the forefront of customised production. Nor is all new technology inherently flexible or being *used* in a flexible way. The emphasis is more likely to be on control and co-ordination of the labour process, quality and routing, rather than product flexibility (Wood, 1989b: 9).

Overall, as the work of the Williams team demonstrates, the statistical and case study evidence used by Sabel and Piore is frequently poor or non-existent. Even on their 'home-ground' in Emilia–Romagna, the majority of production is still Fordist in nature, while quality craft work is the preserve of majority of middle-aged men: 'Semi-skilled assembly work, plastic-moulding, and wiring work is carried out by women, while heavy foundry and forging work is done by Southern Italian and North African workers' (F. Murray, 1987: 88). Small firms have been less technologically innovative than large ones, and their profitability rests primarily on long hours and low wages (Amin, 1991). One of the problems may be that flexible specialisation claims to be both an analysis of the causes of the crisis of the market system and a projected solution to it. It is therefore never sure whether it is talking about what *is* or what *should* be. Ironically, it is the radical writer Hyman (1988) who has to point out that the thesis represents a dangerous oversimplification of the strategic options open to employers, and that the practice is likely to be piecemeal application rather than an integrated package. Because the analysis treats the relations between markets, technology and work organisation in such an uncritical way, flexible specialisation is presented almost as a functional necessity (Wood, 1986: 416). In particular, by making technology subordinate to their demand-pull focus, choices remain limited and frozen, despite attempts to avoid a deterministic framework (C. Smith, 1987: 3–6).

What about the less theoretical cousin, the flexible firm model? Pollert (1988a, b) argues that both share vital commonalties, including a celebration of the market and consumer sovereignty; a legitimation of the view that the solution to organisational and economic problems lies in altering the behaviour of labour; the resurrection of a dual labour market analysis; and a futurological discourse underwritten by a post-industrial analysis in which flexibility marks the vital break from the past. Both flexibility arguments fuse 'description, prediction and prescription' (Pollert, 1988a: 43).

But the commonalties can be overstated. Precisely because one is a management policy model and the other a grand theory, the flexible firm can be utilised in some instances as an explanatory tool, without the burden of any wider conceptual and historical baggage. This argument has been forcefully extended more recently by Proctor *et al.* (1994), who note that almost all contributors to the flexibility debate carefully distinguish between their descriptions and critiques of flexible specialisation (or post-Fordism) and the flexible firm. It is perfectly possible to accept that employers may find the labour control potential of the latter more attractive and more feasible than ushering in the return of the craft worker.

Nevertheless, the empirical claims need to be scaled down before any effective use can be made of the model. Legge (1995) notes that there have been three types of problem raised by critics: empirical support, conceptual clarity and ideological agenda. With respect to the last, though the IMS did function indirectly as an intermediary between employers and government policy in the labour market, description was always more important than any prescriptive message. How accurate, then, was the description? We tried to summarise the evidence on extent of change earlier, but what of conceptual accuracy?

Aside from Pollert's 'deconstruction', the idea of a new *core* workforce has attracted a significant body of critical comment. A central point has been that the multi-skilling at the heart of functional flexibility represents a modest enlargement of the range of tasks required rather than any more fundamental change in the direction of skill enhancement (Elger, 1991) and that the pace of change has been slowed by worker resistance (Turnbull, 1986; Storey, 1992).

We shall return to this issue in the next section. A number of writers have also challenged the novelty of flexibility agreements by making explicit comparison to the productivity deals of the 1960s that also reduced demarcation and restrictive practices in exchange for greater rewards (Towers, 1987; MacInnes, 1987). Others have pointed out that the evidence collected by the IMS itself – for example, in the NEDO study (1986) – found that changes were widespread but uneven by sector; there was little evidence for any extensive flexibility; and that the changes themselves were mostly the result of short-term cost saving and threats of job loss, without sinking deeper roots or employment cultures at the 'core'. This coincided with scepticism in other commentaries (Elger, 1987; Hakim, 1990; Hunter and MacInnes, 1992); which raises the possibility that talk of flexibility may often be a post-hoc managerial rationalisation, rather than a product of the valued goal of strategic planning. The degree of strategic intent may, however, vary across countries, demonstrating the 'societal effects' we discussed in Chapter 3. O'Reilly's (1992) research on banking contrasts functional flexibility accompanied by training and upgrading in France, compared to its ad-hoc manner and orientation to work intensification in the UK – though moves towards extending employees' tasks are observable in different countries.

A highly critical examination of the evidence in relation to the *peripheral* category is made by Pollert (1988a, 1988b). She points out that evidence has tended to conflate long-term changes and standard practices to vary production with genuinely new employment patterns, an argument supported by Marginson's (1991) distinction between a high level of use and a change in use of non-standard employment. Pollert goes on to use a variety of sources to show that most of the figures for temporary, part-time, homeworking, self-employment and subcontracted work are greatly exaggerated. Again, where there have been increases it is often on the basis of already established practices, and on the basis of state sponsorship in the public sector rather than management strategy in the private. Finally, the use of 'peripheral' itself does not really do justice to the centrality of such forms of work, particularly that done by women, to a modern capitalist economy.

Nor is a precise differentiation between sectors always possible. Fast food chains such as McDonald's are one of the fastest growing parts of the economy. But this 'core' sector employing mainly young people, blacks and women on part-time and unsocial hours, has workers with decidedly peripheral employment conditions (Transnationals Information Centre, 1987). Alternatively, one can have regular, continuous employment such as contract cleaners, but still be insecure due to the particularistic choices available to clients and incoming management (Allen and Henry, 1994: 9); or be performing core functions such as research and development, but gradually be losing privileged status due to competitive, external contracting (Whittington, 1991a). Taken together with the problem of whether the model is a strategy to aspire to or a description of existing practices (Legge, 1995), this illustrates the conceptual ambiguities involved in identifying and operationalising the central categories.

On the basis of these criticisms of the flexible firm model, would it be right to concur with the judgement that this is a fad or fiction that will be forgotten in due course? Whereas full flexibility was always likely to remain a 'Holy Grail' that is desired but never quite attained (IPM Digest, 1986: 11), we would argue that dualism *is* a reflection of increasing reorganisation of manpower resources and control over the headcount. Proctor *et al.* (1994) rightly point out that it is too easy to adopt stringent criteria for strategic intent by employers that prevent a recognition of emergent strategy that shows consistency in patterns and decisions. This judgement reflects the broader argument about strategy and control made in Chapter 4.

One of the dangers of too sharp a dismissal of flexibility hype is that it diverts necessary attention away from the political character and casualties of the process. Though the rejection of the European Social Chapter, plus embrace of labour market deregulation and legal weakening of employee protection is particularly prevalent in the UK, a general growth in employment insecurity may be increasingly characteristic of a *risk society* (Beck, 1992). We have already indicated the limited progress towards any form of job security in large firms. It is often the reverse. For example, the British and US steel industries have both re-hired redundant workers under subcontractors with significant loss of pay, benefits and health and safety protection (Fevre, 1986; Mather, 1987). The most dramatic example is provided by the Burton Group in the UK, who announced in 1993 that they were turning most of their retail employees into part-timers who had to wait each day for a phone call to indicate whether they would be needed!

Most of the worst aspects are at the 'periphery'. Trends towards decentralisation in industries such as clothing are resulting in a modern 'burgeoning sweatshop economy' based on women and ethnic minority workers (Mitter, 1986). In an interrelated way the purpose of some policies is not flexibility *per se*, but the avoidance of remaining legislation which protects employee rights. This pushes hiring practices in the direction of part-time work below 16 hours, and temporary contracts, as the CBI admits (Yates, 1986: 34). Italian laws giving job security can also be avoided in firms with less than 15 on the payroll. The reality of homeworking is more likely to be super-exploitation and casualisation rather than the happy, autonomous employee in the electronic cottage (Allen and Wolkowtiz, 1987; Phizacklea, 1987). In fact, flexibility analyses largely set aside the issues of gender and ethnicity by recasting dual labour market as benign, progressive or inevitable (Pollert, 1988a).

Such concern for the casualties of flexibility echo experience from Japan, where the commonly referred to six 'pillars' of company practice are lifetime employment, company welfare, quality consciousness, enterprise unions, consensus management and seniority-based reward systems. Even taking this sympathetically as an ideal type, evidence suggests that it applies at best to the 20 per cent of core employees in large private and public corporations (Briggs, 1987; Dicken and Savage, 1987). The 80 per cent working in smaller firms and for subcontractors are largely excluded from fringe benefits, company welfare and job security; as (obviously) are the large number of those on temporary contracts, or casual and part-time workers within both sectors. Such secondary labour market characteristics are indeed found within the big companies themselves, as Kamata's (1982) graphic account of life as a temporary worker at Toyota illustrates.

The labour process

Scepticism concerning the promise of a move from command and control, low-trust relations, and fragmented tasks, towards creative, high commitment, participative work focuses on three areas.

Autonomy, control and surveillance   Evidence suggests that initiatives that go under generic headings such as 'Japanisation' are often used as a rationalisation device or organising principle for changes that companies may have initiated anyway. In this sense, any genuine degree of autonomy and involvement tends to be circumscribed by organisational 'short termism'. The case of Reckitt Colman in Australia (Dunford and McGraw, 1987) mentioned earlier, highlights this. After the QCs had achieved their initial aim as change catalysts, they were wound down, as management felt they were 'flogging a dead horse' – leaving behind a workforce cynical and hostile to any similar initiative in future. Similarly, the zone briefings at Rover engendered little enthusiasm from supervisors or workers, given the limited content and lack of genuine two-way communication. Researchers on Ford, Lucas and other plants make the point that programme failures partly reflect the difficulty of grafting high-trust practices on to low-trust cultures and environments, as well as 'an etiquette for managing power relations which has little cultural support' (D. Smith, 1987: 28–9). British companies have also shown little commitment to the compensations of job security.

Japanisation and flexible working may have allowed a re-appropriation of the *language* of participation, job redesign and even humanisation, but the claim that the programmes have ushered in a new era of worker participation is open to considerable doubt. Wood rightly notes that though QWL practices signal a move away from low-trust, low-knowledge systems, they do not signal a transition to any form of industrial democracy. This would be to demean the concept and to detach it from any conception of power relations. Whatever participation does exist is within a management decision-making process concerning issues of cost, efficiency and product quality (Giordano,

1985: 31). Though Meyer refers to real powers invested in work groups at Saturn, this is qualified by the comment that they 'represent actions which have already been routinised to the point at which machines could execute the functions' (P. B. Meyer, 1986: 84).

It could be objected that this research refers to an earlier stage of organisational change. What about the new forms of self-managed teamworking? A similar range of criticisms has been developed, that stresses the relatively limited nature of delegation of authority (Wood, 1989b; Boreham, 1992) Studies of the amount of decision-making autonomy in teams shows the empowerment rhetoric is often empty and managerial prerogative largely intact, with, for example, only a small minority of teams electing their team leader (Murakami, 1994). With respect to TQM, recent evidence shows that though workers do respond positively to attempts to draw on their expertise and reductions in close supervision, existing hierarchies still constrain attempts to delegate power and expand involvement for employees (Dawson and Webb, 1989; McArdle *et al.*, 1994; Kerfoot and Knights, 1994) and even managers (Munro, 1994).

In fact, a new emphasis on increased control has emerged from researchers, often influenced by the Foucauldian framework discussed in Chapter 5. It is argued that although TQM, teamworking and other aspects of new production systems devolve some responsibilities to teams and operators, tasks are – if anything – more closely monitored and strictly controlled, with the additional twist of extensive peer surveillance of attendance, productivity and the like (Delbridge *et al.*, 1992; Sewell and Wilkinson, 1992; Garrahan and Stewart, 1992). The last point is a new twist: self-management becomes self-policing, aided by electronic technologies (or panopticons, to use Foucauldian terminology) that allow management to have an omnipresent eye on the shop or office floor. For some researchers, the self-management imposed within the group though peer pressure is actually harsher than 'real' management in identifying and punishing deviation from the norm (J. R. Barker, 1993).

As part of this process, the increased emphasis on behavioural skills and appropriate attitudes also tightens control. This echoes earlier studies of workplace groups in Japan, which point to a strong element of compulsion. Itoh's (1984) account of Matsushita brings out a common theme that 'voluntary' activity in quality circles is founded on being forced to give suggestions: in this case, three a month ranked on a scale of one to nine. As Briggs notes, 'Japanese workers are explicitly rewarded for "desirable" behaviour, and ostracised should they display attitudes not in keeping with the company philosophy' (1987: 3). Loyalty is cemented not only through peer group pressures, but through cheap loans to buy houses and other financial inducements related to the process of creating 'company man'.

Labour intensification Critics challenge the 'working smarter rather than harder', argument, instead emphasising the costs for the workforce and rising rates of exploitation (Turnbull, 1987; Parker and Slaughter, 1988; Elger, 1991; Garrahan and Stewart, 1993): a view endorsed by Japanese, Canadian and German unions who have experienced varieties of lean production (Wickens, 1992). Intensification has been a major characteristic of advanced work arrangements such as JIT, which rely on continual and controlled pressure (Turnbull, 1987: 13) internalising disciplinary pressure within the group (A. Sayer, 1986: 66) and conforming to new behavioural rules. Slaughter gives a vivid account of 'management by stress' at NUMMI, where the goal is to stretch the system like a rubber band. Breakdowns and stoppages of the line are encouraged, as this can indicate where weak points are and how they can be corrected, fine-tuned and further stressed. Workers who fall behind may have video cameras trained on them to 'help' in this process. TQM is also partly geared towards eliminating slack and waste in the system and workers have reported that 'empowerment' involved considerably harder work (McArdle *et al.*, 1994). When *Business Week* (1983) discusses job flexibility, most of the examples are simply enlarging jobs by adding extra duties, cutting the size of work teams, or eliminating breaks. Beyond manufacturing, the introduction of internal markets, new forms of managerialism and funding cuts which increase the staff–'client' ratio in the public sector (discussed in detail in Chapter 3) is also leading to increased work loads. Previous models of self-regulation through professional autonomy are giving way to external regulation through assessment exercises, quality audits, and monitoring systems in health, education and other areas (Willmott, 1993b; Dent, 1993).

Tasks and rules   Though skill variety is necessary to exploit arrangements such as JIT and modular production, variations or new responsibilities such as self-maintenance may be small and it is more accurate to speak of an enlarged *number* of interchangeable tasks carried out by substitutable labour (Elger, 1990; Pollert, 1991; Delbridge *et al.*, 1992). This emphasis on continuity with the past is given partial endorsement by more realistic management writers such as Peter Wickens of Nissan. He admits that, 'lean production retains many Taylorist elements' (1992: 84), and notes that the work of line operators is still 95 per cent prescription and 5 per cent discretion. This indicates that though multi-skilling and multi-activity jobs are important, they may not quite be the end of Taylorism as we know it'! The study by Shaiken *et al.* (1986) explicitly refutes the flexible specialisation thesis by showing that in only one out of ten firms using numerical control machinery did management grant workers the central role in innovation and debugging. Similarly Kraft and Dubnoff (1986) indicate that computer programming work is characterised by increasing task hierarchies rather than more fluid work. Managerial ability to move across demarcation lines and combine tasks often reflects the reality of previously routinised and fragmented jobs. Putting these together, adding on further deskilled tasks (NEDO, 1986), or extra ancillary duties such as inspection, does not normally make a substantial difference to their content. As a worker at Lucas Electrical commented: 'The jobs are just the same, you just do more of 'em' (quoted in Turnbull, 1987: 17). Slaughter (1987) shows that teamworking at NUMMI involved specifying, measuring and timing every move in greater detail: describing this as 'superTaylorism'.

There has been a confusion in discussion that increased flexibility means fewer rules. In fact, it means the reduction of one *type* of rule, demarcation between tasks. Tasks themselves, at least in routine jobs, are still subject to high degrees of standardisation and workers in teams who are expected to learn each other's jobs can only do so because they are highly specified. What is more, the techniques for ensuring this – worksheets, performance codes and job evaluation – are classically Taylorist (Williams *et al.*, 1992a; P. Thompson *et al.*, 1994). Adler may call the system in operation at NUMMI and other advanced manufacturing plants a *learning* bureaucracy, but rules remains at the heart of the process: '[NUMMI] . . . is obsessive about standardised work procedures. It sees what one NUMMI manager has called "the intelligent interpretation of Taylor's time and motion studies" as the principal key to success' (1993: 103). Even the benchmarking systems underpinning TQM require a concern for standardised procedures and uniform, dependable practices (Wilkinson and Willmott, 1994; A. Tuckman, 1994).

If anything, bureaucratic rules have been spreading, certainly into the service sector. Evidence for the *bureaucratisation of service* is most recently associated with Ritzer's (1993) 'McDonaldisation of society' thesis, introduced earlier. He marshals a considerable array of evidence to argue persuasively that fast food chains are the tip of an iceberg that has extended Weber's principles of rationalisation in the form of calculable, predictable, quantified processes to an increased range of retail, leisure and media services. This echoes earlier research such as Gabriel's (1988) study of a variety of catering jobs. He demonstrates that the industry has shifted from reliance on the social and technical skills of the workforce to an industrial model which rests on standardised organisation of tasks and technologically-determined work pace. Service can also be bureaucratised by increased monitoring of employees, either through information technology such as the EPOS system in supermarkets or through 'control by customers' (Fuller and Smith, 1991). Many retail outlets believe that to maintain a competitive edge, a friendly, high-quality service encounter must be produced over and over again. Consistency of product is monitored through report cards and surveys on employee attitudes and behaviour through real and company-employed 'shoppers'.

The tendency identified by Fuller and Smith approximates to a further and more radical development in the bureaucratisation of service – *feelings rules.* This term draws on the work of Hochschild on flight attendants and other employees involved in emotional labour, briefly discussed in Chapter 6. As this will be discussed in more detail in later chapters, the pertinent point to note here is that service increasingly requires standardised displays of feelings

TABLE 6.1   Henry's table order of service

1. Customer greeted at reception.
2. Customer accompanied to table and given menu and special cards.
3. Waitress asks for drinks/wine order.
   Glasses for wine put on to table.
4. Drinks/wine dispensed.
5. Waitress takes food order (and wine) acknowledging specials.
6. Waitress offers:
   – choice of jacket potatoes or chips
   – degree of cooking for steaks.
7. Waitress reads order back to customer.
8. Waitress takes order for Pitta Bread.
9. Glasses for wine and wine to table.
10. Starter cutlery to table.
11. Starters taken.
12. Appropriate starter accompaniments.
13. All starters cleared.
14. Main course served.
15. Appropriate main course accompaniments.
16. During main course:
    – 'Is everything alright?'
    – 'Would you like more wine/drinks?'
17. Main course cleared.
18. Customer invited to go to sweet display/or given details.
19. Sweet and coffee orders taken.
20. Liqueurs offered with coffee.
21. Bill to customer – invite to pay at reception.
22. Customer pays.
23. Goodnight – acknowledge.

through smiles, forced niceness and other forms of verbal interplay and body posture. Putnam and Mumby note, 'When emotions are incorporated into organisations, they are treated as commodities' (1993: 43).

These trends are relatively new, at least for service, but paradoxically, manufacturing may be undergoing something different. We would argue that it is wrong to conceive of teamworking, TQM and related initiatives as a form of superTaylorism. A number of commentators have pointed to the fact that workers are controlling and monitoring themselves, whether they judge that negatively (A. Wilkinson et al., 1992) or positively (Adler, 1993). But this clearly matters. Though workers' knowledge continues to be appropriated by management, the move away from narrow specialisation and devolved responsibilities, however limited, marks a significant break from those parts of Taylorism based on a clear separation of conception and execution. More generally, the conception of skill needs rethinking in circumstances where the relation between a person and a machine is being replaced by the relation between a team and an integrated production system. Our own recent research (P. Thompson *et al.*, 1994) into changes in the commercial vehicle industry illustrates the point. Many of the *individual* tasks continue to be further deskilled under the impact of standardised procedures and uses of new technology. This is allowing management in the UK to dispense with expensive and 'inflexible' craft workers. But, the *collective* labour of the group involves expanded cognitive abilities and extra-functional skills, for example in the form of greater need for problem-solving and decision-making powers, or qualities such as communication and co-operation. This has the potential for enhancing job satisfaction, though it does have costs in terms of work intensification and control. With respect to the latter, though some controls are lightened, new ones are introduced whereby management asks for and rewards conformity to behavioural rules, particularly governing attitudes and action inside the team. An increased emphasis on selecting and training 'the appropriate worker' shows that a traditionally neglected part of Taylor's agenda is being renewed (Wood, 1989b: 11).

But these new control potentials are a far cry from the imagery conjured up by some radical theorists, particularly those influenced by Foucault, whereby the modern worker is placed inside a prison of all-powerful electronic and social surveillance. This confuses the formal characteristics of systems such as JIT and TQM, and the intent of some managements, with the real outcomes, which remain influenced by uneven and incompetent managerial delivery, plus continued resistance and informal controls operated by the workforce (Thompson and Ackroyd, 1995; McKinlay and Taylor, 1994; A. Tuckman, 1994). Differential outcomes are also shaped by the organisational and institutional context. In the previously mentioned study of commercial vehicles, skilled workers were still being used in Austria, in contrast to the UK, partly because the national training system provided an abundant supply at a cost that companies could afford due to the particular wage structures. Mueller's (1994b) comparison of the introduction of teamworking in Ford Europe and General Motors, shows that teamworking had been superimposed on Ford's tradition of controls over the shopfloor, which meant that they had developed more hierarchical arrangements which allowed for little autonomy. In other words, teamworking and other features of new production arrangements may not live up to the rhetoric of management and management theorists, but they have no essence: the form and content remain open to influence by the major organisational actors.

Corporate structures

The rhetoric of replacing the centralised bureaucracy by decentralised networks sounds attractive and a radical case can be made for its desirability, as Perrow (1992) does. But even he admits that the output of small firm networks on a global scale is 'probably trivial' (1992: 445). If it was simply a case of a new trend, then the charge could simply be one of exaggeration, or mistaking intent for outcome. In fact, a consistent theme of studies is the gap between the potential for decentralisation and skill enhancement, and the reality of subordination to traditional functional structures, narrowly defined cost efficiency and conservative cultures (Cummings and Blumberg, 1987; J. Child, 1987; R. Williams, 1988).

But the processes of change are also being misunderstood and misrepresented. Traditional bureaucracies are, in one sense, being broken up with the creation of a myriad of smaller units such as profit centres and internal markets within large firms. But we have to distinguish between the delegation of operational autonomy and strengthened financial and other controls by the central structures. Just as studies of the labour process such as Shaiken *et al.* (1986) show that the primary managerial concern remains that of centralising control and reducing unpredictability, so analysis of new corporate structures demonstrates that decentralisation of the form is accompanied by centralisation of the substance of power. At British Telecom, the system of profit centres relies on accounting structures and marketing forecasts to control and monitor costs: 'District managers, supposedly freer than ever in the age of devolution, complain of now being more tightly restricted by budgets imposed from above over which they have less influence' (Hallet, 1988: 35). Research into newly-privatised utilities in the UK report a large gap between the rhetoric of autonomous units transacting with each other and the reality that profit centres were mostly monopoly suppliers to each other and were closely controlled through corporate business plans, capital expenditure, employment and revenue allocations and targets (O'Connell Davidson, 1993). The sheer spatial and functional diversity of units at national and international level, particularly following complex patterns of merger and acquisition, has led to a considerable strengthening of financial control systems which give corporate headquarters much more sophisticated means of monitoring and regulating the management of subsidiaries (Thompson *et al.*, 1992). A recent survey of the largest companies operating in the UK revealed that in a substantial majority, 'headquarters exerts tight controls over business unit operations and profitability targets are not devolved' (Armstrong *et al.*, 1994: 13). The capacity of TNCs to establish standardised management systems and production organisation is facilitated by their ability to transfer know-how and 'best practice' within the organisation. The real networks are increasingly globally integrated production or service chains, with standardisation rather than local autonomy the main feature (Thompson *et al.*, 1995).

Disaggregation of functions and operations is another real trend, though some of its characteristic forms such as flexible specialisation are vastly exaggerated, studies finding little evidence for the operation of industrial districts (Amin, 1989). Some other processes have certainly increased, notably franchising. But case studies in this area (Felstead, 1994) demonstrate that business formats are imposed by the central company which dictate precise procedures and criteria governing operations, finance and transfer of 'know-how'. In the case of the shift from direct employment to franchised operations in milk delivery, the new philosophy of partnership between company and franchisee was contradicted by managers, who admitted that the system of supervising roundsmen was exactly the same as before, that their work was closely prescribed by the franchise contract, with the added 'bonus' that the franchisees had lost all previous employment rights and benefits. Like the self-employed workers studied by Rainbird (1991), any autonomy was largely lost in longer days, intensified labour and other signs of self-exploitation. The reality of dependency has also been established in Rainnie's (1988) authoritative study of small–large firm relationships. In industries such as clothing, the large firm is able to dictate methods and profit margins, and, as with supplier networks in JIT systems, transfer costs and uncertainties on to the smaller unit.

If we take the demonstration effect examples such as Benneton, we can observe a new extended hierarchy that takes in decentralised and deseg-regated units, but still has the powerful large firm at the centre. As Wood (1989a: 24) observes, 'the Benneton case does not match up to the image of a nexus of forms all flexibly specialised and employing highly committed, skilled workforces. It appears if anything more like a network dominated by the large firm along the lines of Atkinson's flexible firm'. What about the other sense of hierarchy – removing the middle layers? Again, this is undoubtedly a significant trend. But delayering is not synonymous with the destruction of hierarchy, at least not if it means any diminution of centralised power. Paradoxically, the thinning out of middle levels of command can actually lead to the power of strategic decision-makers increasing. In an organisational world constituted through line management, direct reporting and account-ability, the removal of intermediate levels, with their attendant committees and other structures, also removes the potential for coalitions of counter-vailing power. This is particularly the case in the public sector, where forms of control and co-ordination based on professional autonomy and self-regulation have been under attack from expanded corporate and state control. In higher education, universities have had to respond to research and course evaluation exercises from external funding agencies by greatly increasing the monitoring and control of performance at departmental and individual level: 'increased bureaucracy becomes necessary to cope with the proliferation of control, audit, monitoring, reporting and accounting functions that carry out the tasks previously undertaken by academics themselves' (Parker and Jary, 1994: 7). As we saw in Chapter 3, similar accounts could be given of the expansion of bureaucracy and central controls through general management in health and other sectors.

IT has a powerful role in all these processes – for example, when automated purchasing cuts out the need for specialised functions. But the idea that technology automatically redistributes power and democratises information flows is both naïve and deterministic. However, IT is flexible enough to allow for varied uses – as we have seen, the vast increase in information available on work activities can in itself reproduce managerial power to monitor, control and predict performance. Giordano accurately observes that this means, 'the development of an industrial organisation whose planning and financial decisions are centralised and whose operations are frequently decentralised and highly interdependent' (1985: 11). An example is given by the chairman of the international conglomerate, ABB. Its global information system helps control the 400 companies and 240 000 employees:

> We also have the glue of transparent, centralised reporting through a management information system called Abacus. Every month Abacus collects performance data on our 4500 profit centres and compares performance with budgets and forecasts You can aggregate and disaggregate results by business segments, countries and companies within countries. (quoted in W. Taylor, 1991: 100)

The practices described in this section are incompatible with images of disorganisation and firms being 'out of control'. Though complexity, incompetence and resistance will always constrain any managerial action, there can be little doubt that whether it be TQM or financial monitoring, standardised *planning systems* remain an essential feature of business practice.

Conclusion: in defence of bureaucracy?

We believe there is a convincing case that bureaucracy is far from dead. Yet we are under no illusions that the hype of the anti-bureaucratic revolution is going to go away. Bureaucracy has few friends and some of its enemies have a vested interest in permanent revolution. We are referring here to popular management discourse which, in order to sell the latest formula for firms, has continually proclaimed new forms of organisation in new turbulent environments, back at least to the 1950s (Eccles and Nohria, 1992).

It would be unfair to tar some of the academic critics with the same brush. Debates about flexibility and new production concepts are more serious and substantial. Nevertheless, the evidence concerning contemporary developments in organisational design does not justify a new paradigm or general theory of work organisation. Nor does change at firm level warrant the term 'post-bureaucratic'. This is not to deny that very important changes – for example, in the areas of decentralisation and disaggregation – are taking place, but their character is either misinterpreted or significance exaggerated. Too many contributors to the debate have taken bureaucracy to be a static ideal type, instead of a living, changing and diverse set of practices. Nevertheless, strong elements of continuity remain, both in capital–labour relations and the use of bureaucratic structures and processes. Where change is taking place, it is often in the direction of more bureaucracy. It is ironic that so many academics, who are in the firing line of the extension of rationalisation to the professions, should be so sanguine about the general condition of organisational and social life.

Our 'defence' in this chapter is, therefore, just an attempt to present evidence that it still exists. But we would like to make a partial defence of bureaucracy in another, more practical sense. In the 1960s and 1970s the view of management and rationality as neutral technique was replaced by an equally unhelpful hostility that failed to distinguish between particular forms of authority expressed through existing structures and systems, and the necessity for co-ordination and control of resources. Or, as Landry *et al.* (1985: 61) put it:

> There is a vital distinction to be made between 'management' and those people who hold managerial positions, and 'management' as an assortment of integrative functions which are necessary in any complex organization – planning, harmonising related processes, ensuring appropriate flows of information, matching resources to production needs, marketing, financial control, linking output to demand, etc.

This is part of an excellent dissection of the weaknesses of many community and other organisations in the radical movements in this period. Frequently they rejected any form of specialised division of labour and formal structures of decision-making, in favour of informal methods and rotation of all responsibilities. The result was seldom democratic or efficient. Sirriani (1984) also criticises such 'productive integrity', models in which all forms of involvement in the organisation must be total and holistic in character. Genuine criticisms of hierarchies and alienated work are thus lost in an attempt to put them into complete reverse. Desirable goals such as sharing and learning of skills to overcome fragmented labour are not given an adequate framework of expertise to sustain them. In fact, the political culture from which the organisations emerged, 'made it difficult to conceive of the genuine importance of skills such as financial planning . . . management and entrepeneurship. These skills were seen as capitalist and reactionary by their very nature' (Landry *et al.*, 1985: 30).

Some of the radical writers we discussed in Chapter 2, such as Clawson, have made useful analyses and criticisms of the development of industrial bureaucracy. Unfortunately, the associated work structures are then argued to have been developed and introduced for solely capitalist purposes. The difficulty is that in the desire to explain the social origins of organisational forms, bureaucracy and efficiency are simply reduced to specific class interests. This is reinforced by giving alternative socialist production relations a utopian capacity to avoid bureaucratisation altogether, in a model of 'total democracy' based on:

> the election of everyone above the level of ordinary worker, with no fixed hierarchy and no one having the right to give commands (except in so far as this right is temporarily delegated, with the commands always subject to the review of the group as a whole). Moreover, instead of a plethora of rules and an illusory focus on bureaucratically defined expertise . . . regulations are reduced to a minimum, freedom is maximised, and everyone becomes technically competent to do the work. (1980: 16–17)

This has echoes of the ideal type of collectivist-democratic organisation developed by Rothschild and Allen Whitt, though to be fair, this is part of a detailed and careful examination of the potential and dilemmas of real grassroots co-operatives. The problem is that it is of limited usefulness developing an alternative model of organisation based on a small number of small organisations, that as the authors admit, find it hard to survive in the surrounding sea of hierarchical organisations, market relationships and traditions of representative democracy' (1986: 73). Such practices may be possible in a small co-operative, though even this is extremely doubtful. In any large-scale and complex organization the efficiency and energy costs would soon make it impossible to operate.

Some of the same objections can be made to arguments that there is an alternative feminist mode of organising to an inherently male bureaucracy. most forcefully put in Ferguson's (1984) *The Feminist Case Against Bureaucracy*, but also by Bologh (1990). That alternative is based on caring, communal relationships developed in private realm, or friendship relations developed in small-scale womens' movement structures such as rape crisis centres and bookstores which run on the basis of personal relations, skill-sharing and egalitarianism, rather than formal rules and power games. Both attack liberal feminism (Kanter, 1993) for pursuing interests within existing organisations. A very effective critique of these views is developed by Due Billing (1994; see also Witz and Savage, 1992). Not only is it impossible to evade power, even in 'friendship organisations', but women have been changing bureaucracies and successfully challenging their gender bias and male cultures. As she notes, 'Rules could also be viewed as an asset for the people working in the organisation' (1994: 183). For, whatever the limits of formal equal opportunity policies or sexual harassment codes (Cockburn, 1991), it remains the case that they are an advance on the informal culture and rules of the game within which male power operates.

Rejecting utopianism does not mean accepting that the only option is to engage in power struggles within existing forms of organisation. There is a small but growing body of theoretical work (Sirriani, 1984; Rothschild and Allen Whitt, 1986; Clegg and Higgins, 1987; Ramsay and Parker, 1992) whose goal is to think through the problems of developing democratic work organisation that is also pluralist in nature, in that it recognises a variety of possible organisational forms of decision-making, ownership and involvement. Emphasis is put on feasible levels of task-sharing, egalitarian reward systems, democratic controls and participation, and co-operative cultures. This would result in what we call a *minimal bureaucracy*. Only by recognising certain necessary and distinct functions for bureaucracy can we begin to control and transform them. Clegg and Higgins comment that such arrangements:

> will neither eliminate rules nor the division of labour; in this sense it will not eliminate bureaucracy at all. To presume to do so would be chimerical. What we will achieve is a form of bureaucracy – administration by office and rules – which is not premised on hierarchy, but on collectivity; not on authoritarianism but on democracy; a new ideal type of a bureaucratic, democratic and collectivist organisation. (1987: 217)

Ramsay and Parker claim that what they call 'neo-bureaucracy', has similarities to the adhocracies and other forms of new organisation celebrated in the popular management literature. But the message of this chapter has been that there remains a massive gap between the rhetorical claims for the end of bureaucracy and the realities of organisation. We shall return in the final chapter to the issue of alternatives to bureaucracy and rationality.

CHAPTER 7

Re-inventing organisation man?

In 1956, William H. Whyte wrote the influential *The Organisation Man*, a vituperative attack on the 'social ethic' shaping the values of those in the middle ranks of private and public corporations. This oddly named ethic was a collectivist nightmare which morally legitimated the powers of society against the individual. Amongst those blamed was Mayo and his obsessive concern for belongingness and group adjustment. Whyte's solution was for the individual to fight a rearguard battle against the organisation, with the aid of some useful advice such as 'how to cheat at personality tests'. As Peters and Waterman note (1982: 105), the association with grey conformity made corporate culture a taboo topic. Culture only became acceptable as an issue when it was associated with the necessity for managers to be sensitive towards national diversities in the 'collective programming of the mind' (Hofstede, 1980).

But by the end of the 1980s, organisation man was back in fashion. Though some continue to doubt the idea of people 'belonging' to the company (Lessem, 1986), IBM's 'corporate fascists' with their historic emphasis on conformity and commitment could get their overdue kudos as well as smile politely on the way to the bank (Pascale and Athos, 1982: 186). Despite all the hymns of praise to corporations, the credit for reviving the issue largely goes to American academics and management consultants, notably the two mentioned above, plus Ouchi (1981) and Deal and Kennedy (1988) – all except Ouchi being connected to the McKinsey consultancy company. However, it was filtered, as we began to discuss in Chapter 6, through a reading of the Japanese experience that located their success in the existence of strong cultures and 'turned on workforces'.

Corporate culture, which can be defined as the way that management mobilises combinations of values, language, rituals and myths, is seen as the key factor in unlocking the commitment and enthusiasm of employees. To the extent that it can make people feel that they are working for something worthwhile, it is projected as part of the solution to the historic search for meaning or the holy grail of commitment in the study of organisations. For work humanisation theorists such as Herzberg and Maslow, that search was connected to the provision of intrinsically satisfying tasks through job redesign. The ground has now shifted to the psychosocial benefits from identification with the company and its superordinate goals. There may be characteristics which make companies successful, as in the famous lists of Peters and Waterman or Goldsmith and Clutterbuck – autonomy, zero-basing, productivity through people – but corporate culture is the core and the glue that binds the increasingly diverse activities together. When the project is defined as developing a non-deified, non-religious 'spiritualism', it is to be expected that advocacy often takes on a distinctly evangelical tone, with managers and workers exhorted to love the company. Such acts of will can break the 'attitudinal barriers' that hold firms back (Goldsmith and Clutterbuck, 1985: 5).

More conventionally, there is an emphasis on culture *strategies*, with senior management taking the process of value-shaping seriously. But perhaps 'strategy' is the wrong word. For, as we discussed in Chapter 6, corporate culture is part of a proclaimed shift from the hard S's of strategy, systems and their quantifiable objectives, to the soft S's of style and shared values. So, is this another fad of pop-management or a doomed attempt to transplant culture-specific Japanese systems? Certainly, corporate culture is less prominent now as other panaceas such as business process re-engineering and TQM take centre stage. But it has by no means been entirely displaced. The management of culture is recognised as one of the central features of HRM, given that (as we saw in Chapter 6) employment relationships are seen moving away from bureaucratic hierarchy and low-trust industrial relations towards securing real commitment (Guest, 1987; Legge, 1989). Similarly, the battle to introduce private sector styles and methods into public services and the widespread adoption of mission statements indicates that the identification and transmission of values remains on the organisational agenda.

Nor should we underestimate the shift in management theory, and to a lesser extent practices, that has been going on. Changing people's emotions or what they think has mostly been off-limits to the dominant strands in OB. It is summed up in Herzberg's answer to a question about the problems of employees at a seminar – 'don't worry about their attitudes or personality, you can't change them' (Carr Mill Consultants, 1973: 7). Similarly, when commenting on March and Simon's views, Perrow argued that, 'to change individual behaviour, you do not have to change individuals' (1972: 147). Under systems of bureaucratic or unobtrusive control, what had to be changed was the structure of communication, rules or selection, along with provision of the appropriate rewards and sanctions.

Managerial and professional employees *were* subject to moulding and socialisation processes, though how seriously or effectively is open to

B.A.

question. But for all the unitarist rhetoric about goals, routine manual and clerical workers were not really expected to identify with the company. It was more a case of 'if you've got them by the balls, their hearts and minds will follow'. *Normative regulation* changes this: 'it is only with the advent of the "excellence" literature that management is urged to become directly involved in determining what employees should think, believe or value' (Willmott, 1992: 72). How this is supposed to work can be seen in the statement from a manager at a famous high-tech US company: 'Power plays don't work. You

---

Organisation Development Manager
. . . to lead a major culture change
c.£23k+car

This is an outstanding opportunity to break new ground. Reporting to the main board Human Resources Director you will be a leader in planning and implementing a culture change strategy involving all aspects of this household name fmcg company's activities.

To achieve their high growth goals our clients, national leaders in an ethically attractive natural products market, are committed to evolving from the successful paternalism of the past to a people centred, quality, performance and market orientated culture.

A thoroughly rounded professional is required with exceptional conceptual and practical skills. 'Streetwise' and business motivated, your experience will include OD, assessment centres, psychometric testing, process counselling, sales marketing and performance management training, leadership of a training team. Applicants should be action orientated. Administrators and behavioural theorist need not apply.

The Company offers a salary package dependent on experience and potential contribution, backed with full, large company benefits including a company car. Located in an attractive semi-rural area in the South benefited by relatively low housing costs.

Please write with full details. These will be forwarded direct to our client. List separately any companies to whom your application should not be sent. John Woodger, ref.SB2464.

HAY-MSL Selection and Advertising Limited,
52 Grosvenor Gardens, London SW1W 0AW.

Offices in Europe, the Americas, Australasia and Asia Pacific.

HAY-MSL

Source: Advertisement from *The Guardian*.

FIGURE 7.1 'Sign of the times'

can't make 'em do anything. They have to want to. So you have to work through the culture. The idea is to educate people without knowing it. Have the religion and not know how they got it' (quoted in Kunda, 1992: 5).

∠ It is not the case that questions of attitudes were wholly by-passed in previous theory and practice. For example, the Neo-Human Relations tradition tried to develop ideas that could link individual aspirations to organisational goals through more open, participative and high-trust relationships (Legge, 1995). In turn this gave way to Organisational Development or OD, which was probably the most direct antecedent to the corporate culture movement. Bennis (1966) argued that the only way to change organisations was to change their cultures. Early OD was part of the same 'liberal' agenda as work humanisation. The prescriptions for a healthy organisation operated on similar assumptions about the capacity for human growth and the organisational blockages to it, as well as the same values of openness, trust and creativity (Argyris, 1967). OD complemented its productivity deals and job enrichment initiatives of the late 1960s and 1970s, unlocking the rigidities of attitudes and practice that are inevitably built into any organisation's management, its culture and history. But the emphasis was on planned change, process and technique such as sensitivity training and team building, rather than content issues (Roeber, 1975). It was also aimed at managers and a special category of change agents, rather than the whole organisation. By the late 1970s the OD movement had suffered 'a collapse of professional confidence in itself' (Harrison, 1984: 12), and a dismantling of some of the largest internal company units. Whatever the practical limitations, NHR and OD did not satisfactorily deal with values and commitment from a managerial standpoint. Meanwhile, companies still advertise for OD managers, but who can plan and implement culture strategies (see Figure 7.1). This is the new ball game: OD as specific techniques within a broader organisational culture and human resource context, and this time targeted at workers as well as managers.

Product and perspective

The corporate culture merchants

'In culture there is strength' is the ominous sounding new law of business life proclaimed by Deal and Kennedy (1988: 19). What such writers are actually talking about is a specific product: 'a culture devised by management and transmitted, marketed, sold or imposed on the rest of the organisation' (Linstead and Grafton Small, 1992: 332). But what is it that gives such strength? One of the most recurrent themes is *attention to employees*: ownership in a shared vision rather than changes in work or working conditions. The notion of 'pillars' occurs again, this time in creating a committed workforce. The British personnel writers Martin and Nicholls (1987) name three – a sense of belonging to the organisation, a sense of excitement in the job, and confidence in management. In general terms 'the notion of employee commitment is built on the internalisation of the norms and values of the organisation' (Kelly and Brannick, 1987: 19).

Interestingly there is explicit recognition of the benefits of *emotional* engagement: affectiveness more than effectiveness. As 'man is quite strikingly irrational' (Peters and Waterman, 1982: 86), employees can be appealed to through symbolism and the ceremonies and awards of 'hoopla'. In the new corporations it is the role of those at the top to act as symbolic rather than rational managers – as scriptwriters and directors of the daily drama of company life (Deal and Kennedy, 1988: 142). By symbolising the organisation internally and externally, heroes become a crucial component of the leadership process. For Deal and Kennedy, John Wayne in pinstripes is an appropriate role model. Leadership is invested with a large burden in cultural management, reflecting in part research which has identified the *founder's* influence in shaping values (Schein, 1985). A notable example is Anita Roddick's pivotal role in the Body Shop organisation. The publicity is that 'Work for the Body Shop and you're on a permanent high' and that high is sustained by training schools, roadshows and videos with the founder to the forefront. According to one trainer, 'Staff get desperate for the fix of Anita' (*The Times*, 28 September 1991).

In addition, the focus of such organisations is on disseminating values through stories, myths and legends about the company, its products and heroes, backed up by rites and rituals which reinforce cultural identification. The latter also helpfully facilitate the goal of a large dose of Skinnerian positive reinforcement, where *everyone* is made to feel a winner. Management in general is expected to use non-authoritarian styles to create a climate of trust. Some writers make a nod in the direction of feminism by referring to nurturing qualities and androgynous managers (Naisbitt and Aburdene, 1985: 207). Others are content to report the aim of shifting from an aggressive, confrontational and macho style at companies such as Ford and Rank Xerox (Giles and Starkey, 1987).

Though the package of corporate culture is new, some of the ideas are not. Pop management writers seldom discuss theoretical sources, but Peters and Waterman acknowledge that, 'The stream that today's researchers are tapping is an old one started in the late 1930s by Elton Mayo and Chester Barnard' (1982: 5). Human relations influences can most clearly be seen in the focus on managing the informal organisation; workers as irrational creatures of sentiment; and social needs to belong; whereas the shadow of Barnard looms over conceptions of the organisation as a co-operative social system and on the role of the executive in articulating and disseminating values and super-ordinate goals.

But there may also be deeper, less direct roots: 'it is in the various writings of Durkheim that a conceptual framework for discussions of corporate culture may be found' (Ray, 1986: 290). Ouchi is one of the few corporate culture writers to accept the need for a macro-sociological analysis that breaks from the interpersonal level so favoured by many organisational writers. His article with Johnson (1978) draws directly on a Durkheimean framework which sees a modern division of labour involving a loss of moral community and mutual obligation, with a decline in the role of the family, church and other institutions. Durkheim believed that the necessary function of social control and cohesion could be played by professions and occupational groups, a theme echoed later by Mayo. Ouchi and Johnson argue that Japanese work organisations have provided the necessary primary relations. Ray (1986) extends the analysis by pointing out that the corporation is expected to take on the functions embodied in Durkheim's realm of the sacred. Hence the emphasis both on faith in the firm and binding rites and rituals. Most corporate culture books draw on such assumptions. Deal and Kennedy do so explicitly: 'corporations may be the last institutions in America that can effectively take on the role of shaping values' (1988: 16).

What is the *evidence* for the dual claim that strong cultures exist and that they constitute the primary reason for better or even excellent performance? Many of the same companies tend to appear across the range of US books – IBM, Procter and Gamble, Hewlett Packard, McDonald's, Delta Airlines. So do some of the 'baddies', notably Harold Geneen and ITT, who seem to get in the neck consistently. In the UK the roll call includes Marks and Spencer, Plessey, Sainsbury, Burton and Schweppes. As for the information about the companies, the opening sentence of Deal and Kennedy begins, 'S. C. Allyn, a retired chairman of the board, likes to tell a story. . .' (1988: 3). With the partial exception of Ouchi, stories, vignettes and anecdotes about the dedication and commitment of corporate heroes and managers, or the devotion of ordinary employees, constitute a large proportion of the evidence presented.

Of course, they are not the only sources. Across the books, it is possible to find interviews with top management; testing the culture by conversing with the receptionist; profiles based on company documents; use of formal statements of objectives and philosophy and of biographies and speeches; and questionnaires filled in by chairmen asked to rank their firm according to 'excellence' criteria. Occasionally, as in Goldsmith and Clutterbuck, there is reference to interviewing people on the shop floor, but there is no sign of the results.

There is considerable positive reference to slogans such as Delta airlines 'the Delta family feeling'; IBM's 'IBM means service' and 'respect for the individual'; GE's 'Progress is our most important product'. Apparently *everyone* knows and believes in Tandem Computer's slogans such as 'It's so nice, it's so nice, we do it twice' (Deal and Kennedy, 1988: 9). McDonald's has an extraordinary quality assurance and level of care for its people (Peters and Waterman, 1982: xix–xx). The slogans of privatised utilities in the UK, such as BT's 'We answer to you', and the numerous statements of supermarkets and other companies about customer care could be put in a similar category (Legge, 1995). These kinds of statement about 'qualitative beliefs' are then linked to a second set of quantitative information detailing the superior financial and economic performance of the given companies over ten or twenty years. Strong cultures are the assumed link, but there is no direct evidence, or real discussion of other market or environmental variables. A rare statement of this kind comes from Deal and Kennedy, 'we estimate that a company can gain as much as one or two hours of productive work per employee per day' (1988: 15). No criteria or proofs are ever given.

Mini 'cases' are also developed in the popular literature – for example, of Hewlett Packard's 'HP Way'. Open-plan offices, open managerial styles, extensive formal and informal communication, and team and workforce meetings are just some of the mechanisms to generate the high commitment that is the key to quality and innovation. Stories about the heroic exploits of founders Bill and Dave reinforce a collective identity and organisational goals. Peters and Waterman found it impossible not to become fans. A more serious academic account of a similar organisation is given in Kunda's (1992) *Engineering Culture*. Most male engineers operate in what appears to be an informal, egalitarian, work and play hard environment, sustained by a commitment to job security and technical innovation. Slogans and metaphors permeate working life – 'do what's right', 'he who proposes does', 'having fun', 'tech is a bottom-up company', 'we are like a football team' – and there is a mini-industry of meetings, rituals and workshops that reproduce company culture.

Something like the 'HP Way' is a classic rhetorical device, a communicative symbol whose goal is primarily to mobilise organisational commitment and project community of interest. We are seeing this kind of corporate culture advocated as the solution to the problem of *global integration*. There are powerful globalisation tendencies in the international economy that are producing forces for standardisation within and between companies. Firms need to integrate an increasingly diverse number of activities and units, and, at the same time, there are pressures for them to adapt to the more rapid diffusion of 'best practice'. Many management theorists portray culture as the glue that binds those diverse units into cohesive and co-ordinated 'families' (Handy, 1984; Barham and Rassam, 1989; Rhinesmith, 1991). From this kind of perspective the TNC is primarily a 'management mentality' rather than a specific organisational form (Bartlett and Goshal, 1990).

From our own research into Swedish TNCs (Thompson *et al.*, 1993), elements of culture strategy can be identified. Senior management at Volvo (Bus and Truck) refer to 'family' and 'culture', though they are careful to talk of adapting it to the local situation, referring to the Dutch or Belgian 'Volvo family'. For the international hotel chain we have called 'Abba', the Abba Way is a concept which encompasses marketing, personnel management, accommodation and style of service. In addition, there is what is described as 'cultural training' which ensures that, 'our non-Nordic colleagues' have the correct training. Abba operate its own business school, which attempts to describe Sweden, 'Swedishness', Swedish service philosophy and service management (Abba Hotels, Annual Report 1990). This is backed up by a variety of training sessions on the Abba Way at unit level. Even with all these culture transfer processes going on, both companies feel the need to supply managers from the home base. At Volvo it is the custom to have a Swedish 'controller' in the companies abroad and interviews with corporate managers often include references to the need to have behaviour that is 'more Swedish'. In Abba, three out of the four hotels initially visited have Swedish or Danish general managers, and at a broader level there is evidence that the company has had successes in incorporating some staff into the 'Way'.

Much of the debate about culture at national and international level, particularly with reference to companies such as HP and 'Tech' is that the descriptions and debate frequently overlap with HRM. What is the link?

HRM and the management of culture

In Chapter 4 we discussed some of the changes in the personnel function. That debate is also relevant here. Though 'personnel' is seen as playing a more central role in cultural change processes, it is not the reactive and industrial relations orientation of old. The personnel function is being recast as *human resource management* (HRM), though it will not be the property of a narrow functional department (Tichy *et al.*, 1982: Beer *et al.*, 1985). Instead, the emphasis is on the integration of 'personnel' issues within the overall business strategy, with employees becoming a 'resource' equivalent to something like finance. 'Strategic' is a term continually invoked to refer to the management of employees at all levels directed towards the creating and sustaining of competitive advantage (Miller, 1989). As we indicated previously, the extent to which this harder-edged approach genuinely reflects substantial shifts of policy from the old personnel approach is open to dispute, but the intent to restructure the employment relationship away from low-trust, adversarial industrial relations systems is clear.

What does this have to do with culture? If employees are the strategic resource, then *commitment* is the key to unlocking the untapped human capital. In turn this requires conscious development of the value base of companies, such as mission statements, and new and expanded means of communicating them; as well as the battery of participative measures such as team working and team briefing to generate the high-trust culture associated with 'soft' versions of HRM (Storey, 1989; Guest, 1989). The imputed strategic character of HRM thus facilitates the development of strong cultures by integrating policies of recruitment, reward and retention. Culture becomes a shorthand for a new ideology and rules of the game accompanying a shift from collectivism to individualism in the management of the employment relationship (Sisson, 1990). Collective bargaining and unions are bad words in the new world of *unmediated* relations between the organisation and the individual. An example of the new practices is that of direct communication with the workforce. Winning companies have a culture that enables 'a passion for disclosure of information' (Goldsmith and Clutterbuck, 1985: 73). Hence the rash of briefings, videos, house magazines, open days and consultative forums. Trade unions are not given much of a part in strong culture companies. At best they are considered a recalcitrant junior member, and at worst an unnecessary obstacle. The HRM advocates Kelly and Brannick deliver a blunt warning: 'The ability to organise will be curtailed, if not openly challenged by management, and the role of the trade union as an element of the communication network will lose its significance' (1987: 20). In fact, such employment practices already constitute a significant part of strategies by a growing number of companies to make themselves union-free by removing or substituting for any employee desire for collective representation (Basset, 1989). Any independent, 'sub-cultural' source of alternative values, trade unions, profession or occupational groups, is therefore an obstacle to the development of a unitary, cohesive culture.

Certainly there are prominent companies that fit this picture, notably the major US computer firms. IBM (Dickson *et al.*, 1988) and Hewlett Packard carefully construct their employment practices to individualise employee's relations with the company. Prominent features of this approach are personal wage 'negotiation' and performance evaluation, immediate grievance accessibility to management, and an internal labour market which provides for mobility and job security. But is this typical? We know from case studies (for example, Martinez Lucio and Weston, 1992) and wider survey evidence such as the Workplace Industrial Relations Survey (Millward *et al.*, 1992) that HRM practices, in the UK at least, exist extensively in unionised workplaces.

Extending levels of identification between employee and organisation may be less distinctive than in the famous, often greenfield site examples, but research shows that many top companies have been engaging in widespread culture change programmes (Storey, 1992). More generally, especially for white collar and professional employees, measures designed to create a performance-conscious culture or environment have been spreading (Fowler, 1988, Hendry *et al.*, 1988). Within the overall process of managing a culture change, performance-related pay and new appraisal systems are often seen as a key element in transforming employee attitudes. Ratings in such areas as relationships and co-operation means that, 'subjectivity should not be scorned but rationalised' (performance management manual quoted in Fowler, 1988: 31).

Critics and questions

Questioning the novelty

The extent of strong culture companies is exaggerated. These are trends within some, but not all, organisations. Many companies, small and large, will carry on with 'weak cultures' and would not recognise a culture strategy if it landed on the managing director's desk. Indeed, the novelty of the phenomenon can also be overstated. Companies such as Cadbury and Marks and Spencer in the UK *do* have corporate cultures of a highly distinctive nature. Such companies have long used management styles based on 'sophisticated paternalism' which combine high levels of employment security and social benefits with careful screening of recruits, direct communication and in-house training, wrapped up in a 'philosophy' of respect for the individual (Miller, 1989). And all this before any thought of corporate cultures and human resource management!

Accounts by historians and sociologists show that we can trace paternalism back to older patterns. Joyce (1980) shows that from the mid-nineteenth century many Victorian firms, particularly those influenced by religious non-conformism, developed a social paternalism embedded in the interwoven fabric of work and community life. Though often associated with small firms, paternalism survived and changed form as size and scale increased, though family ownership still played a key role. At Lee's Tapestry Works on Merseyside between the wars, considerable efforts were made to develop 'a sense of belonging and a feeling of loyalty to the firm' (Johnson and Moore, 1986). There was an 'exceptional' family atmosphere, company saving schemes, a holiday camp, and partnership certificates issued to employees – or 'members' as they were called from 1931. Glucksman's study of factories in the inter-war period gives an account of the Peak Frean biscuit factory in South London. Though Peak Frean was not characteristic of the majority of firms, it prided itself on its welfare provision, had 'a large sports ground and games room, dances and social events were organised, and the house journal, *The Biscuit Box*, was distributed to all workers' (1990: 96). Both the companies were non-union. But this is not an inherent characteristic of such firms. Ackers and Black's (1991) overview and case studies in the development of paternalist capitalism demonstrates that major players – Pilkington, Rowntree, Cadbury –

came to accept a form of unionism and collective bargaining in their own paternalistic image.

Even after the war, many large workplaces generated employee identification based partly on stable employment, as well as being a focal point in and for local communities. A typical example is English Electric in Liverpool (P. Thompson, 1994). Worker identification with the firm was enhanced by almost all promotions coming from the shop floor, thus creating a strong internal labour market, though top management tended to be imported. The company owned houses and had its own hospital and dentist on site. There was an extensive company social life, including an annual sports day which catered for 10 000–12 000 children, a flower show, and a variety of clubs, dances and shows. These were all organised on a voluntary basis by a combination of management, staff and workers. The firm, though paternalistic, was not anti-union and officially recognised a number of appropriate trade unions. Though management did not always like it, they worked within an industrial settlement in which a system of bureaucratic controls over work and employment relationships empowered shop floor union organisation.

In the late 1960s, the company was taken over by GEC, their main competitor. They began to run down production and transfer products out of the place almost immediately. A new layer of senior management was brought in, with very different attitudes. Within a short time the whole social side of the factory apparatus was wound down. What happened at English Electric was indicative of the breakdown of the old culture paradigm under the impact of the first major wave of post-war restructuring of capital in the mid to late 1960s. Under the impact of this concentration of capital, firm mobility, mergers and acquisitions and the decline of company towns and occupational communities, old forms of identification tended to break down. British management responded in a variety of ways. There were many measures designed to tighten controls on the wage-effort bargain, for example the replacement of piecework by Measured Day Work. Others changed the pattern of accommodation and attempted to further the factory-level union organisation institutionalise. A smaller minority tried progressive work re-design schemes such as work humanisation, but, 'Anyone who talked about employee "loyalty" and "all pulling together for the good of the firm" was regarded as a nostalgic crank who did not understand modern industry' (Ackers and Black, 1991 , 30).

Paternalistic cultures became a minority phenomena, though they continued to exist in different forms, often in smaller firms. One such traditional paternalist company of 300 workers is described in a case study by Wray (1994). 'Ourfirm' built on local traditions of company welfare provision and a dependent, quiescent labour supply. Its management articulated a paternalist philosophy, high pay and profit-sharing, and links with the local community. Even here, steady growth led to difficulties in maintaining 'the personal touch' that underpinned paternalist relations. Middle management and demands for a union on the shop floor have grown in tandem. Despite the breakdown of old patterns, both case studies project continuities between paternalism and the rise of a new unitarism in the form of corporate culture and HRM, so that 'the future may look more like the past than the present' Ackers and Black, 1991: 55). But how reliable are the contemporary claims in the wider literature?

Questioning the evidence

Given the reliance of the product on stories, myths and other forms of 'organisation talk', what executives and managers say in words or on paper tends to be taken as proof for the existence of string and distinctive cultures. There is little critical reflection on this. Martin and Nicholls are at least honest in admitting that:

> we cannot be sure of the extent to which the companies we studied were *actually* successful in creating that commitment or whether that commitment contributed to their success. All we can say is that the managers in question *reported* that their efforts to create commitment met with a positive response and produced a significant improvement. (1987: ix [our emphasis])

In addition, they present some useful, if brief and largely propagandising cases. As for the most of the literature, much of the time even corporate slogans are taken as virtually incontrovertible evidence of culture and effects, because they are taken to be synonymous with superordinate goals.

With this kind of evidence, so much of it resting on bland management statements, unattributed quotes and plain assertion, it is tempting to dismiss the whole enterprise as a fairy tale. Drucker, the best-known management writer, pulled no punches in describing *In Search of Excellence* as 'a book for juveniles' and a fad that would not last a year (quoted in Silver, 1987: 106). The lack of rigour in research methodology has been a persistent theme of critics (Hammond and Barham, 1987: 8–14; Guest, 1992). Samples of companies – for example, those used by Peters and Waterman – were selected and treated in a cavalier and uncontrolled manner; dropping some from the original list and using evidence from others not in the sample at all (Silver, 1987: 113). The tenuous link between cultures, excellence and performance turned out to be highly fragile. Companies were included whose performance was far from excellent and a significant number subsequently ran into difficulties, as *Business Week* (1983) reported under a headline of 'oops!' An important book on IBM (Delamarter, 1988) – by a senior economist who had worked in the US Justice Department on the anti-trust case against IBM – pointed out that the company built up its dominance by undercutting its competitors in vulnerable market sectors and paying for it through excess profits from customers who had little choice. Commenting on *In Search of Excellence*, the author argues that

> According to the authors, IBM has benefited from a strong central philosophy that was originally laid down by its charismatic leaders, the Watsons. They present a simple, appealing model for IBM's success – excellence in management. But this view is dead wrong. IBM's success comes from the power of monopoly. (1988: xvii)

Follow-ups such as Peter's and Austin's *A Passion for Excellence* (1985) have failed to quell the doubts, particularly as the same author has apparently decided (Peters, 1987) that there are now no excellent companies in the USA. The treatment of theory and evidence is similarly suspect, with eclectic and uncritical use of parts that suit particular arguments, even if they are not compatible with the general perspective. The use of Skinner in *In Search of Excellence* is a case in point. A further remarkable aspect is the failure to learn from their main inspiration, the human relations tradition. There is no sign of recognition of the central flaw that arose from the Hawthorne Studies, that intervention based on 'attention to employees' produces independent effects on performance. At least some of the hoopla and contrived events could produce a stream of Hawthorne effects of a short-lived and superficial nature.

Of course, expectations of high-quality evidence from popular management texts would be somewhat naïve. Is there anything more conclusive from broader accounts of culture change programmes, particularly those associated with HRM? Legge (1995) attempts to evaluate that research and finds it inconclusive, due to a range of methodological and conceptual problems. There has been little research on the explicit links between culture and commitment, which would in many cases be premature anyway, given the need for an in-depth and longitudinal view of change. Even more importantly, both culture and HRM tend to have been treated as generic headings for a variety of interrelated changes, from which it is impossible to disentangle the key variable or variables. Although it is not surprising that, given the centrality of managers as focal points for the articulation and dissemination of values, many have absorbed the message, there is less evidence that this has worked its way fully through to the shop and office floor. Or, if it has, that the effects are on manifested behaviour rather than internalised values. This is a crucial distinction to which we will be returning to later.

Questioning the concepts

The previous discussion illustrates the need for a complex understanding of culture. Too often the corporate culture debate has working with impoverished conceptions of culture which mistake style for substance. A complex and realistic analysis would avoid treating culture as a catch-all for the soft aspects of management (Hammond and Barham, 1987: 10), or as a reified and monolithic phenomena. There is some recognition of *sub-cultures* on functional or gender lines, but not enough, and anyway these can be *managed* to produce a healthy tension within the corporate framework (Deal and Kennedy, 1988: 152–3). It is precisely this assumption that culture can be managed that is called into question by a range of critics that Willmott dubs 'culture purists'. Such critics take their cue from the influential paper by Smircich (1983) which argued that it is better to regard culture as something an organisation *is*, rather than something an organisation *has*. It is a process, not a checklist, and something continually being creatively remade by all participants, rather than fixed (Wright, 1994). As a result, in the context of a variety of often contradictory influences, cultural development is just not as amenable to direction or use as an integrative device as believed (Martin and Siehl, 1983: 53). Nor can it be simply fitted into overall strategic goals. As Ackroyd and Crowdy (1990) illustrate in their study of the highly distinctive informal interactions of slaughtermen, many of the meanings attached to work behaviour are embedded in particular class or regional culture. Their very externality adds to the lack of feasibility of managerial influence.

Whether it can be managed or not, it remains the case that the complexity of organisational cultures has been neglected and employees treated as an 'empty space' within which values can be inserted. There is, 'a tendency in the organisational culture literature to treat workplace culture as independent of the labour process' (Alvesson, 1988: 3). Without a recognition that the labour process is fractured by a variety of social cleavages, organisational analysis will continue to neglect the dimensions of conflict, power and even consent. For example, in Chapter 5 we looked at the way that workplace cultures were gendered and acted as barriers to the success of equal opportunity policies (Cockburn, 1991). Using such a framework, we can avoid nonsensical ideas that strong cultures produce conflict-free organisations (Kelly and Brannick, 1987: 1). After all, despite IBM's worldwide strategy for a union-free environment and sophisticated industrial relations system, it still has to contend with an international organisation of IBM workers opposed to its policies! (Howard, 1985). Even where IBM has been successful in securing employee identification with its individualistic culture, as in the west of Scotland, those same workers had *collectivist* attitudes towards general social issues and supported trade unionism, even if they felt a union was unnecessary in their particular circumstances (Dickson *et al.*, 1988). This illustrates a further important point, that any analysis should show what is unique about organisational as opposed to national, regional, family or other cultures. This is something that is largely absent from the management literature (Hofstede, 1986). On that basis it would be possible to examine how the societal and organisational cultures interact.

Given the numerous flaws, it is tempting to dismiss most writing on corporate cultures as simply describe the emperor's new clothes. In *Management Today*, Thackray (1986) argues that the American manager needs a language that goes beyond particular functions. Buzzwords therefore come and go and culture has entered on the scene as Western pride has been shaken by Japan, and old certainties have been eroded by economic and occupational shifts. New ideas are required to motivate the troops and a 'gaggle of culture consultants', as well as human resource and personnel teams and others whose empires expand with the literature, are feeding at the honey pot. It appeals to managers because it proclaims that their activity and skills can produce the results, as Mayo once did in relation to early human relations. Silver (1987: 123) also argues that corporate culture is the latest attempt by management consultants to 'wrap each new technique in packaging slightly different from that of its predecessors'. If it is a fad, and one that vastly overestimates its capacity as a change mechanism, then the whole trend is destined to go the same way as others: 'Culture appears to have been reduced to the status of yet another concept, which, like many before it, has reached the decline stage of its "life cycle"' (Ogbonna, 1992a: 6).

But all this is bending the stick back too far. Willmott (1993a) criticises the 'purist' position for moving from a judgement that the corporate culture literature is so deficient that it is unworthy of serious attention. Meek is an example, when she argues that if culture is embedded in social interaction, 'it can *only* be described and interpreted' (1988: 293, our emphasis). This may be underselling its potential as a control mechanism. There may not be a definitive authentic culture in organisations, but there clearly are 'official' ones that power-holders can at least attempt to impose on others.

Culture: commitment or control?

Corporate culture writers like to present their prescriptions as an *alternative* to control (Naisbitt and Aburdene, 1985: 53; Kelly and Brannick, 1987: 8). But the perspective is riddled with glaring contradictions. We are told that 'in institutions in which culture is so dominant, the highest levels of autonomy occur' (Peters and Waterman, 1982: 105); while Deal and Kennedy (1988) assure us that companies with strong cultures can tolerate differences (p. 153) and that outlaws and heretics are encouraged in companies such as IBM (pp. 50–1). At the same time the latter authors tell us that managers did not tolerate deviance from company values and standards (p. 14), and that middle managers as well as blue collar workers should be told exactly what to do (p. 78). The books are so anxious to convince us that these are anti-authoritarian, 'no-boss' set-ups, that we are expected to accept that calling workers 'cast members' (Disney) or 'crew members' (McDonald's) in itself banishes hierarchy and class divisions. In Silver's brilliant demolition of the excellence genre, he reminds us of the reality of McDonald's 'people-orientation': 'Behind the hoopla and razzle-dazzle of competitive games and prizes lies the dull monotony of speed-up, deskilled Taylorised work – at McFactory. And McFactory's fuel is cheap labour – part-time, teenage, minimum wage, non-union workers' (1987: 110).

Reconceptualising the process in terms of new forms of management control is not entirely foreign to the more academic of the culture literature, which openly describes the process as a form of organisational control (Ouchi and Johnson, 1978; Martin and Siehl, 1983). Nor is it inconsistent with many of the statements from the more popular works, such as, 'Strong culture companies go into the trouble of spelling out, often in copious detail, the routine behavioural rituals they expect from their employees' (Deal and Kennedy, 1988: 15). Cultural or *normative* control is essentially concerned with the development of an appropriate social order which provides the basis for desired behaviour (Kelly and Brannick, 1987: 8). Indeed, in order to let people loose to be 'autonomous' they have to be programmed centrally first, with a central role played by more intensive selection and training (Weick, 1987). Tandem Corporation's exhaustive selection process is likened to an 'inquisition' by Deal and Kennedy (1988: 12). One of the offshoots is that those who are chosen are likely to have a much more positive image of themselves and the company. It is not surprising, given such developments, that some management writers have begun to worry that corporate culture produces conformist thinking inimical to creative organisational development (Weick, 1987; Coopey and Hartley, 1991).

Cultural controls also operate through expanding the sphere of social activities in the organisation. Communicating company goals can take place outside the workplace. Part of GM's Hydra-matic Division's QWL program includes week-long 'Family Awareness Training' sessions at education centres (Parker, 1985: 17–19). This does not refer to the employee's nearest and dearest, but to the notion of company as family. Once outside the normal environment and in circumstances were everyone is individualised, psychological exercise and techniques are used to break down old identities. GM questionnaires rate those with limited scores on loyalty to the company as having a low quality of work life. Breaking down the boundaries between economic and social activities is something which is often characteristic of Japanese corporation's methods of using the peer group as a means of integrating both shop floor and managerial employees. Broad (1987: 11) refers to 'Social gatherings organised by team leaders and foremen are regularly held amongst all male employees'. The link to Japan is also made in Goldsmith and Clutterbuck's jolly account of management japes at Asda's social events: 'The schoolboy activities in these companies is strongly reminiscent of Japanese companies, whose evening carousals have traditionally been part of the cementing of the managerial team' (1985: 82). Many of the other books are similarly full of accounts of cultural extravaganzas that function to develop a sense of community through a form of *compulsory sociability*. There is also an increasing attempt to extend the culture of the corporation into other value-producing institutions. Naisbitt and Aburdene detail growing links between business, schools and universities in the USA. The offer of state financial inducements to higher education establishments in the UK if they will incorporate the teaching of entrepreneurial values and enterprise skills on their courses is a further example.

How should we understand the significance of this trend? Some radical theorists go further than simply analysing culture in terms of control by arguing that corporate culture represents an alternative and dominant mode. The key theoretical influence is the work of Ray (1986), who utilises the Durkheimean framework discussed earlier. She points out that bureaucratic controls, though an attempt to integrate employees positively through internal labour markets and the reward system, is still control by incentive. This may generate contradictions around the struggles of the workforce to establish work rules and job guarantees. In addition, 'while bureaucratic control may prompt individuals to act *as if* the company is a source of meaning and commitment, that is an entirely different matter from seriously believing it. In other words control remains externalised rather than internalised' (292–3). Even humanistic controls deriving from the various branches of the human relations tradition do not possess the real tools to generate sentiment or emotion. The difference is that *normative* control works less through formal structures and mechanisms than through informal processes, value systems and management of the emotions (some of which was discussed in Chapter 6).

Ray's analysis is complemented by like-minded empirical studies such as Alvesson's (1988: 1991) account of a medium-sized computer consultancy organisation in Sweden. The founders established an open and charismatic managerial style capable of generating strong emotional ties among the consultants employed. A particular problem for the management was that the work was by its very nature variable and flexible, and therefore could not be controlled by conventional means. It was also largely carried out at the client's workplace, potentially undermining the consultant's sense of identity with their own firm. This is compensated for by a large number of social and leisure-time activities with the emphasis on fun, body contact, informality and personnel support; which in turn build social and emotional ties and a sense of company as community. Some of these are consciously linked to presentations of corporate performance to enhance favourable perceptions.

Further support comes from research on the retailing sector. Employees have to be subjected to engineering the soul so that s/he can automatically deliver the quality service required by the new, more enterprising customer (du Gay, 1991a).Ogbonna and Wilkinson (1988) and Ogbonna (1992b) detail that engineering in a supermarket where management have initiated a substantially expanded staff training and development programme that ranges from the recruitment of 'like-minded' people to a 'smile campaign'. Supervisors claim that, 'We are able to detect when a check-out operator is not smiling or even when she is putting on a false smile . . . we call her into a room and have a chat with her' (Ogbonna, 1992b: 85).

Not only does this perspective counterpoise control through conventional rules and regulations to changing the way that employees think and feel, the latter is seen as 'considerably extending' the scope and penetration of managerial domination (Willmott, 1993a: 522). Willmott makes a forceful case that in combining normative rules with the erosion of alternative sources of identity:

> Corporate culturism extends the terrain of instrumentally rational action by developing monocultures in which conditions for the development of value-rational action, where individuals struggle to assess the meaning and worth of a range of competing value-standpoints, are systematically eroded. (1993a: 3)

Monocultures are designed to avoid contamination by rival ends or values and to the extent that they succeed, become the vehicle of nascent totalitarianism, accompanied by classic 1984-style doublethink of 'respect for the individual' in organisations where employees are seduced into giving up any autonomy. This analysis is wrapped up in the kind of Foucauldian terminology discussed in Chapter 6, where corporate culture programmes exert self-disciplining powers that trap people within the promise of secure identities and personal development.

The limits to culture

In criticising culture purists, Willmott persuasively argued that we should take corporate culture seriously. But perhaps he has taken its significance and effectiveness *too* seriously. In arguing that the 'governance of the employee's soul' (1993a: 517) is a key ideological element of a new global regime of flexible accumulation, he is in danger of over-extending the concept and maintaining a separation from traditional forms of control associated with Fordism, Taylorism and bureaucracy. Corporate culture should not be isolated as *the* defining feature of contemporary forms of control. Although Willmott rightly says that management is trying to extend the sphere of instrumental action to rules governing emotions and the affective sphere, traditional controls remain important in a number of ways.

Even within those organisations that do implement cultural controls, they are intended to complement, not eliminate, the need for bureaucratic, technical or other systems. In the supermarkets described earlier, employees are subject to surveillance by TV cameras in the managers' office looking for deviations from the desired behaviour, as well as controls through new technology that can record productivity – such as the EPOS (electronic point of sale) system. In Kunda's excellent ethnography of 'Tech' we are given examples of both normative and technical controls. With reference to the former, managers evaluate subordinates on personality criteria: 'Jim has a people problem. He is gruff and angry with people and says exactly what is on his mind . . . I want him to control himself. Next year he is going to be evaluated on that. I'm watching him. He knows it' (manager quoted in Kunda, 1992: 187). But employees are also aware that managers check up on commitment by looking at who is logged on the computer after hours. Though he sees a shift in focus from bureaucratic to normative controls at Tech, Kunda rightly acknowledges that systems of cultural control, 'build on, rather than replace one another' (p. 220).

This continuing reality can be ignored or misunderstood by making culture into an overarching concept. For example, Wright talks of the 'culture' of Fordism which, 'is converted from a mission statement into detailed practices, dividing each task into tiny details and specifying how each should be done' (1994: 2). In contrast, the culture of flexible organisations rely on empowered, self-disciplined workers. Culture in this sense, however, should not be seen as *everything*, but rather as managerial attempts to mobilise values and emotions to support corporate goals. An expanded array of often traditional rules and sanctions is then used to enforce the new moral order and extend levels of identification between employee and organisation. We only have to return to our previous examples of IBM and Hewlett Packard to see that their respective 'Ways' are sustained by careful structuring of the employment relationship around individualistic means and ends. Like the studies referred to earlier, Harrison and Marchington (1992) also examine the growth of customer care programmes in retailing, but argue that: 'The preoccupation with culture may blind us to the enduring importance of promotion structures, remuneration incentives, and working hours in shaping employees' acceptance of managerial initiatives' (1992: 18).

Nor is culture necessarily the glue which links the parts of a global organisation together. For example, the contemporary large firm is increasingly built through acquisition, merger and collaboration, thus bringing together component parts with very different histories. Though it is not impossible to extend cultural controls across the diverse units and activities, evidence shows that integration through financial controls is more likely (Thompson *et al.*, 1993). In fact, there are a variety of means of integration available, as persuasively demonstrated by Duenas (1993). Drawing on case studies of a number of companies operating in global markets, he argues that only IKEA, the Swedish-based furniture dealer, operates a cohesive corporate culture that consciously transcends national and other cultural differences.

Others included a common framework from a technical/professional culture in a company dominated by the engineering function (Elf Aquitaine); financial planning systems used to override cultural differences (Emerson Electric); and sophisticated management information systems co-existing with local autonomy (the Dutch multinational, Buhrmann-Tetterode).

Most companies will need or attempt some cultural dimension to the integration problem. In our research, most of the talk of culture and the need for 'Swedish behaviour' is, in our view, a kind of code for company-specific knowledge systems. Managers feel comfortable with talk of Swedishness, perhaps because it gives additional meaning and legitimacy. From this perspective, the prominence of Swedish managers in top positions in foreign subsidiaries is less to do with the superiority or distinctiveness of Swedishness than with the advantage such staff give in facilitating the smooth running of the 'global' management structure, with its attendant and often standardised knowledge system. For example, service TNCs need to transfer highly standardised knowledge and practice which supports a corporate brand (Child and Rodrigues, 1993: 11). We can therefore see that though cultural practices and strategies are part of a convergence process within TNCs aimed at enhancing integration – whether aimed at managers or workers – it is more accurate to speak of the value dimensions of *management systems* than the vaguer and looser term 'corporate cultures'. Furthermore, such systems are always subject to adaptation. Transnationals necessarily make 'compromises' with local situations and, implicitly, with competing values and ideas of competence.

What about the second element, the effectiveness of corporate culture as social engineering? Among radical critics there is a high degree of consensus on its limits, or at least to the extent to which commitment has been internalised. Take the British Airway's manager quoted in Höpfl (1992: 10): 'We know it's hype – they know its hype. It's okay. It's reassuring. It makes you feel good. But do I believe in it – well that's a totally different question'. Employees may be conceptualised as empty vessels in which to locate corporate values, but that is not how it works in practice. The research we have been discussing indicates that they may comply with demands for adherence to the language of mission statements, appearance and demeanour in the sales process, or participation in quality circles *without* internalising the values and therefore generating the 'real' commitment. Instead, employees may be aware that they are acting as a coping strategy (Ogbonna and Wilkinson, 1988), or go through the motions of cultural conformity while remaining sceptical that, for example, the 'Abba Way' was any different from the methods used by other international hotel chains (Thompson *et al.*, 1993). The dramaturgical theme is continued through employees developing a variety of means of disengagement or distancing from corporate values through cynicism, parody and irony. Advocates such as trainers for Body Shop may claim that cynicism cannot survive the participative culture, but that is belied by interviews with staff: 'They want you to feel part of a team, but you're not. They want you to feel important when you're just a shop assistant. If you want to stay there, you do better as a Roddick clone' (quoted in *The Times*, 28 September 1991). Considerable evidence of cynicism and distancing was also observed by Kunda. Many employees used an alternative language to describe the culture – 'the song and dance', 'pissing contests', 'Tech strokes', 'burnout', 'doing rah-rah-stuff'; or rival slogans – 'I'd rather be dead than excellent', 'There is unlimited opportunity at Tech, for inflicting and receiving pain'. Much of this ambivalence was directed towards maintaining a private self, or showing that they understood the real politics and status processes underneath the official surface.

Does the predominance of behavioural compliance without commitment matter? Supporters may point to a time lag whereby behavioural precedes attitudinal change (Schein, 1985). But in the light of serious research, this seems optimistic. Are we back full circle to Perrow's view that to change individual behaviour, you do not have to change individuals? Some critics would appear to agree. Drawing on their research into customer care programmes, Harrison and Marchington argue that, 'management does not actually have to achieve value change among the workforce to successfully implement customer care' (1992: 18). The conventional armoury of management control and remuneration measures may be sufficient. Perhaps this does underestimate the distinctiveness of 'hearts and minds' programmes. Our disagreement with theorists such as Willmott is not whether *some* firms try to develop monocultures, but with the extent to which they can ever be successful. Willmott (1993a: 538–40) argues that the very process of role-playing and cynical disengagement entraps employees in the insidious controls of the culture and confirms the appearance of tolerance and openness.

Such interpretations risk underestimating both the fragility of corporate culture and the creative appropriation, modification and resistance to such programmes. Corporate culture cannot eliminate the powerful informal group norms which are the bedrock of organisational life. Workgroups are just one of a number of sources of competing claims on commitment and loyalty. Attempts to prioritise an aggressive corporate identity may disrupt the delicate balance between these specific and superordinate allegiances. This is particularly the case in the public sector, where traditions of professional autonomy and an ethic of service are increasingly at odds with a new managerialism bent on central direction and enforcement of the bottom line (Anthony, 1990; Harrison and Marchington, 1992). Increasingly bitter conflict between general managers and staff in the NHS, universities and the BBC is indicative of the tensions arising from attempts by senior managers to impose a 'strong culture' and a web of rules to enforce it. Resistance may also be generated by the selective or partial nature of participation in the culture and its attendant reward systems. Such programmes are aimed often only at the 'core' workforce, as Kunda's case study demonstrates: Class 2 workers, mainly clerical and temporary, received inferior benefits and were treated as non-persons, 'just not techies' as one manager put it (1992: 209). Unsurprisingly, they only gave a minimal self back.

This example reinforces the point that culture is sustained by material, institutional supports. Senior management may be taking greater risks with such initiatives because employees are being asked to invest more of their public and private selves, thereby raising the possibility of enhanced resentment when the promises of large-scale culture change programmes prove difficult to deliver, as at *British Airways* (Höpfl *et al.*, 1992). This is but one of the trends in corporate development which are working against the stability of cultures of company loyalty. Contradictions are raised by the clash between concerns for individual development in organisations and the continuous pressure for rationalisation of resources and for more effort. In addition, what the management pundits are calling 'downsizing' – the cutting out of middle layers of the company discussed in Chapter 6 – is hurting most the, 'organisation men, conditioned to look to large corporations as the fountainhead of security' (Thackray, 1988: 80). Even some of the high priests of the free market are beginning to despair at the effects of merger mania and the acquisition and asset-stripping of companies. The consequent breakdown of co-operation in the organisation can be seen in examples such as the 1989 strike and dispute about the selling-off of Eastern Airlines in the USA.

Loyalty, obedience and goal identification are not easy to sustain when companies are scrutinising their policy manuals to remove implied promises of job security or even terminate benefits:

> How the hell can you preach this flexibility, this personal and business development at the same time as you are getting rid? As someone said to me yesterday, an operator, 'Why am I in here now doing the best I can getting this product out when tomorrow morning you are going to give me a brown envelope? I had no answer. (manager quoted in T. Watson, 1994: 209)

In essence this is no different from the tensions identified between 'hard' and 'soft' versions of HRM, where workers are expected to be both dependable and disposable (Legge, 1989). Ackers and Black raise the question of whether it is possible that new forms of corporate paternalism can ever reproduce the depth of social relationships fostered by firms embedded in local communities and stable markets: 'The impersonal, foot-loose multinational, with its mobile, diffuse, high turnover workforce, and even more transient management team, appears ill-equipped to fashion an emotional nexus with its workforce (1991: 56). This may be exaggerating the difficulty, but current trends at the very least expose the highly contingent nature of any culture–loyalty link.

Conclusion

In this chapter we have tried to set out both the significance of and the limits to attempts to re-invent organisation man. Given the theoretical faults and practical constraints, it is sometimes difficult to see why the product has been so influential, even outside the USA and UK. Undoubtedly, it fitted the mood of a certain period. Silver (1987) adds a wider ideological and political dimension to the explanation. He describes the excellence genre as 'Reaganism writ small', a glorification of entrepreneuralism and the capacity of the USA to stand tall again. It is certainly true that a clear sub-text of Peters and Waterman and Deal and Kennedy is that the discovery of excellent companies in the West means that all good things do not come from Japan. It is also true that the ideological content of most of the books often shows a sharp break with the old 'liberal' consensus. Deal and Kennedy say that the society suffers from too much uncertainty about values and that managers should have the conviction to set standards and not undermine them by being humane (1988: 22, 56, 76). In Britain, similar links existed between the rise of corporate culture and a broader ideology celebrating the market and the spirit of enterprise (du Gay, 1991b).

But it is not simply a sign of a particular times. For all the absurdities of content and presentation, the corporate culture literature has touched on genuine issues that, as we argued at the start of this chapter, were partly neglected in the past. These need looking at in a context free from the merchandising process. For the tragedy is that we have a lot to learn from studying organisational cultures (Frost *et al.*, 1985; Pheysey, 1993), particularly as culture mediates all change processes. Creating a culture resonant with overall goals is relevant to *any* organisation, whether it be a trade union, voluntary group or producer co-operative. Indeed, it is more important in such consensual groupings. Co-operatives, for example, can degenerate organisationally because they fail to develop adequate mechanisms for transmitting the original ideals from founders to new members and sustaining them through new shared experiences.

Such an emphasis by no means rules out studying specifically *corporate* cultures as management strategies. But this has to be within the plurality of cultures and interest groups in the workplace. Luckily there are rich sources to draw on, such as Salaman's (1987b) study of the occupational culture of the London Fire Brigade; accounts of making-out on the shop floor (Nichols and Beynon, 1977; Burawoy, 1979); and gender at work (Willis, 1977; Pollert, 1981; Westwood, 1984). Organisation 'man' may be back on the agenda, but the cultural agenda cannot only be set in the boardroom.

PART 2

CHAPTER 8

Issues in organisational behaviour

I have a reputation for getting people's backs up who work for me. I will help them if I consider they need it, but sometimes I give them the impression that I can't be bothered. I prefer them to learn by looking for themselves. So I'm fairly abrupt and indifferent. I'm not worried if they like me but I do want their respect . . . I don't like them to take advantage . . . .they often say, 'Oh we can't understand you, Allan, we try to be nice to you but you're not nice back.' I think there's only one I've not made cry . . . I don't think I have to do the job. My job is to keep them as busy as possible. I'd rather me be bored than them, otherwise if you do bring work for them again, it just leads to moaning and groaning. You can't keep all six happy at the same time. With some you can tell their monthly changes, even the other girls say so. Sometimes when they're having a good chunner about the inspectors I have to impress on them that if it was not for the men, there'd be no jobs for them, if the blokes don't go out and sell insurance. (Knights and Collinson, 1986: 158)

Defining the 'subjective factor'

Socially produced identities are a central factor delineating people's experience of work. As the authors of the Insco case study argue, Allan views his hierarchical position as a reflection of his own personal status and dignity. In his dealings with his female 'subordinates' he utilises a mixture of patronising humour, sarcasm and indifference in order to maintain a symbolic distance of authority, and 'motivate' them to work independently. His proud boasts also indicate the significance of gender to his work identity.

The case itself addresses the gendered aspects of job segregation and the social construction of skill in the insurance industry where 'Conventionally, the task is described in terms of an heroic drama in which intrepid and

males stride out into the financial world and against the odds
new business'. These 'almost mystical perceptions' of male skills
ed to the, 'internal staff of women clerks whose work is assumed
to be ... endant, supportive and secondary' (1986: 148).Far from the
aggressive instincts of the hunter, success in selling is seen to dependant on
the *gendered interpersonal skills* which are employed to maintain 'exclusively
male relationships' with insurance agents. At the same time, the devalued
work of the female clerks is essential in the maintenance of long-term client
support and after-sales service. Thus the success of the 'heroic' male is
paradoxically dependant on the 'stock of working knowledge' possessed by
the women which allows them to maintain their own personalised telephone
relations with clients. The unacknowledged and differentially rewarded *'tacit
skills'* employed in the administrative support role are 'further emphasised
when women also act as caring ego-masseurs or office wives for sales
inspectors who sometimes return to the office dejected after unsuccessful
appointments' (1986: 150).

> The continuation of such gendered job segregation is seen as being dependant on the
> continued acquiescence of the clerical staff to their subordination, even in conditions
> where Allan's highly coercive approach generates a level of anxiety or frustrated
> resentment which is expressed in internal conflict, poor standards of work, indif-
> ference, disenchantment or even resignation. (1986: 168–9).

These reactions from the women underwrite the prejudicial attitudes used by
the male managers to exclude the women from promotion to the sales force on
the basis that they are 'naturally' unfit to handle such macho work. But such
'reactions' are not in fact problems in themselves, they are in effect the range
of coping responses which the women see open to them, in that they
themselves have internalised the view that they are unfit to be sales 'reps'. By
accepting the gendered definition of themselves, the women are limited to
striving for personal material gain or 'symbolic security expressed either in
resignation, indifference or the search for future promotion within the clerical
ranks' (1986: 169). Such necessarily individualistic strategies are said to merely
reproduce the contradictions of job segregation and effectively to block any
moves towards collective action which would challenge their institutionalised
subordination.

Issues of identity raised in the Insco case are therefore central, but cannot be
dealt with without concepts deriving from the study of structural processes
such as organisational design, control strategies or the impact of wider social
formations. But they in turn will be incomplete without reference to the factors
surrounding the *construction* of the subjectivity and experience of those
involved. Organisational psychology should allow us to enter these areas
necessary for a fuller account of 'organisational behaviour' (OB). But, as the
discussions in Chapter 7 have begun to argue, the relation between

organisational psychology and the subjective factor in the study of work organisations is by no means clear. Though organisational psychology and its practitioners might be expected to have a natural concern with the identities and subjective experience of participants, the range of issues and topics traditionally presented in the area do not consistently address these concepts. Explaining Allan's relations to 'his staff' would thus be difficult using the theoretical models and concepts currently employed in introductory OB texts.

Our approach to the 'subjective factor' in organisations focuses on the experience of people in work organisations through the two common themes of subjectivity and identity. Both concepts present problems of interpretation and there is considerable overlap in their usage. Our use of 'subjectivity' follows Henriques *et al*'s. (1984: 2–3) twofold definition. First, the *'condition of being subject'* – the ways in which the individual is acted upon, and made subject to the structural and interpersonal processes at work in organisational life. Second, the *'condition of being a subject'* – possessing individuality and self-awareness. Thus the term encompasses the fundamentally contradictory experience of work and the subjective development and regulation of people's 'emotions, desires, fantasies, a sense of self' (Banton *et al.*, 1985: 44).

The concept of identity commonly involves the notion that there is an irreducible core of social and individual being that uniquely identifies each of us. Psychologically, identity variously incorporates concepts of self and self-esteem; structures of values, attitudes and beliefs; and personality and associated traits. Sociologically, it includes concepts of self and of roles and reference groups. Lasch (1985: 31–2), notes a shift of meaning that does not admit a fixed or continuous identity. What we do possess however, is a *'minimal self'*, which, because of our need for an 'emotional equilibrium', retreats to a 'defensive core, armed against adversity' (1984: 16).

Our usage then, incorporates the notion of *self-aware* and *participative* subjects, who maintain a valued part of their identity against the unpredictability of the external world, while at the same time being acted on and constrained by organisational ideologies and practices. These themes of subjectivity and identity are examined in the context of interrelated arguments which together provide a framework which is capable of addressing issues of structure, agency, individual action and experience. We are concerned to maintain a perspective rooted in a materialist conception of social production and existence. Capital – and management on its behalf – manipulate, direct and shape the identities of employees. This reflects the need to mobilise the consent and co-operation of workers in order that effective control may be maintained over the productive process. We also maintain a focus on the development of identity in individuals, and more especially the *reproduction* and *transformation* of those identities in the context of work organisations. Individuals are not the passive recipients or objects of structural processes but are constructively engaged in the securing of identities (Knights and Willmott, 1985), and the development of capacities

(Leonard, 1984). These, although influenced and shaped by organisational contexts and practices are at the same time the unique products of each person's history.

Organisational psychology: the mainstream agenda

In a review of the 'discipline' of organisational psychology as a professional practice, Blackler describes it as follows:

> The subject 'organisational psychology' can legitimately be understood to include all aspects of behaviour in organisations that may be studied from a psychological point of view. By common usage, however, the term is normally used to refer to applied social psychological studies of organisation. Important areas of practical and theoretical concern have included motivation, attitudes and job satisfaction, job and organisation design, interpersonal and group behaviour, leadership studies, approaches to participation and industrial democracy, conflict, decision-making, and the planning of change. (Blackler: 1982: 203)

This of course is by no means exhaustive of the work undertaken by organisational psychologists. Topics could be added from those more usually associated with occupational psychology – such as selection, placement and counselling. Historically the subject has a problem-centred approach and at present issues such as the psychological consequences of new technologies and unemployment have provoked much research.

The areas from social psychology which have been enlisted into organisational psychology's project of understanding human behaviour are often limited to those which have some functional utility. Texts tend to be presented under chapters or headings focusing on topics such as learning, perception and motivation, reflecting psychological explanations of individual personality; and topics such as leadership and group processes, which incorporate social-psychological explanations of interpersonal dynamics. However, the topics in the sphere of aggression, affiliation and prejudice, which within social psychology are assumed to deal with influential determinants of human behaviour, are not routinely assimilated into organisational psychology. This is an odd separation, given that such factors may be expected to have at least some bearing on practices within organisations. The difference is largely that the latter set reflects areas of subjective experience, which – although of importance to individuals and groups in organisations – is not of direct relevance to the production process, except insofar as it might interfere with it. Rather, the factors are treated as external to what is considered necessary and appropriate behaviour at work. Similarly, issues of discrimination, though a structural feature of organisational life, are marginalised and not constituted as significant objects of study. Aggression is addressed obliquely in OB through the issue of organisational conflict. But the perspective used examines conflict as a problem to be resolved or avoided rather than to be understood as a possible consequence of inequalities of power and resources.

We shall return to the general limitations of the mainstream agenda in the final section of this chapter. In terms of its content, that agenda can be thought of as a journey through the processes by which individuals become social participants who perceive, learn and are motivated beings with individual personalities. Our intention here is to treat the mechanisms and processes identified by competing approaches as inputs to, rather than exclusive accounts of, this developmental process. This is because the fragmented treatment of subjectivity in OB means that the implied journey through an individual's development into a social being never explicitly takes place.

The competing mainstream explanations of psychological and social processes are treated in OB texts almost as if they were discrete accounts of human development and activity. Taking an area such as learning (see below), which must be integral to any account of psychological development, the mechanisms and processes of apparently mutually exclusive perspectives such as the cognitive and behaviourist models are categorised through the assumptions about human nature which underly them. Thus we get the 'models of man' approach to OB, where theories are assessed through the assumptions they make and the implications of those assumptions for social behaviour. There is nothing intrinsically wrong with this as a method of analysis, but it does tend to reinforce the exclusivity of differing approaches which are in fact no more than varying conceptions of the basic processes by which we all develop and negotiate our changing identities.

The fact that these approaches often make incommensurate theoretical assumptions does not prevent their conceptions from being appropriate to the experiences of individuals at some time in their lives or in the various situations in which they find themselves. In this sense, it is entirely possible that both the cognitive and behaviourist notions of learning will hold some utility for the explanation of individual behaviour and subjective experience. Their applicability will of course vary according to both a person's unique history of socialisation and the strategies she chooses and develops both to cope with and possibly enhance her situation in life.

Our starting point here is not in the area of learning, even though development is essentially a process of learning. For our purposes it might be more appropriate to begin with perception, as the process of learning is itself dependant on the development of the perceptual processes which shape our view of the world. In fact, the processes of perception and learning are so thoroughly interdependent that they might best be treated as a single area – but we shall maintain the traditional conceptual division in order to engage with the existing forms of explanation in OB.

Perception: learning what to see

Perception is defined in terms of 'the active psychological process in which stimuli are selected and organised into meaningful patterns' (Buchanan and Huczynski, 1985: 33). This is usually explained within a perspective which emphasises information processing and seeks to explain how our perceptions of ourselves, others and our environment shape our attitudes and behaviour. The utility of understanding perceptual processes lies in the fact that people's perceptions of themselves and others can be manipulated to change attitudes to and behaviour in the situations and contexts within which work takes place. The practices associated with the 'japanisation' of British industry, such as single-status canteens and clothing provide an example of this, in that they are intended to alter perceptions of the divisions between management and labour, in order to create attitudes (see below) more compatible with organisational goals.

Perception, then, is the umbrella heading for the processes through which we organise and interpret the range of visual, aural, tactile and chemical stimuli which impinge on us. As these processes enable us to comprehend and order the world around us, they must also underly the manner in which we go about constructing identities.

The organisation, processing and interpretation of incoming stimuli are the basic subject matter of *cognitive* psychology. Much material in this area deals with the neurophysiology of perceptual systems. But as our focus is on organisational psychology we do not intend to deal with the detailed cognitive processing of information, as the ordering and organisation of these systems is not wholly determined by their structure. In social, interpersonal and self-perception, the determinants we are concerned with are the past and present influences and constraints on us and our actively directed interests. Perception, then, is not just the process of seeing, but involves our other senses and is intimately connected with the notion of intention. In other words, what we see and hear is transformed according to how our system of values, attitudes and beliefs informs our actions. The formative content of identity could, in this light, be viewed as produced by the filters through which our perceptions pass in order to select out what is of value to us.

Basically, to perceive something we have to be attending to it. This does not mean that we only take in those stimuli which we notice. Rather, we take in everything our particular range of senses *allows* us to. What it does mean is that we only actively process and act upon those parts of the incoming data which concern us. This concept of *perceptual selectivity* can be illustrated by a crowded and noisy office, where we cut out much of the background noise in order to concentrate on the people we are listening to. Yet we can still pick out and shift our attention to references to ourselves, or to other things that interest us coming from other parts of the room, temporarily or permanently cutting out the immediate conversation we had been intent on a moment before. Hence we appear to have some mechanism which can shift our attention and select the stimuli which we attend to, according to which appear of the greatest current relevance. Having to concentrate for long periods on a single type of stimulus – for example, components being inspected on a production line, requires effort in face of the distractions coming from other stimuli in our environment. Perceptions are often classified as primary or secondary on the basis of whether they come from actual or vicarious experience, though it may be more proper to view these classifications as related to forms of attention. Keltner (1973) claims that we primarily attend to strong or unique stimuli and secondarily to learned selection patterns, but we may also depend upon 'derived primary attention' where secondary perceptions become habitual and unconscious. The notion of perceptual selectivity underlines the *intentionality* of attention. We may not be consciously aware of directing our attention, because we are predisposed to notice some things rather than others. Our perceptual systems are structured to pay attention to things that change and things that stand out from their surroundings, and we might also perceive information as being more valid when it comes from what we consider to be an 'authoritative' source. Thus criticism of our work from a respected peer or a superior responsible for evaluating it will be taken more seriously than that from sources less close to our own interests. These filtering processes are summarised in Figure 8.1.

The outcomes of these processes are seen in the notion of the *perceptual set*, which refers to our individual and unique readiness to perceive what we expect to perceive. Our perceptual set reflects our own perceptions of ourselves and our social position and is, in effect, the outcome of our socialisation processes (see the next section). For instance, we often appear to be set to perceive people of lower status to ourselves as less competent, inferior and more generally inadequate. This type of set extends to social groups and to wider social divisions – men, for example, generally perceive women as less competent than themselves; reflecting the social value placed on gender rather than any reliable sex differences. Likewise men tend to attribute competence shown by women to luck rather than skill (Deaux and Emswiller, 1974), showing that their subjective adaptation of their perceptions will tend to reinforce the security of their male identity.

The consequence is that we actually put effort into interpreting the world around us, rather than simply taking it all in as a camera might. But a haphazard interpretation of the myriad stimuli coming to us would be worse than none at all. We need a system of interpretation, our perceptions need to be organised. Wertheimer and the 'Gestalt' school identified the classic principles of perceptual organisation up to the 1920s (see McKenna, 1994, or Mullins, 1993, for applications and examples). These principles show that we tend to place organisation on stimuli, by focusing on significant or moving rather than background factors, by associating stimuli that are close together, similar,

Environmental stimuli →	Sensations →	Attention →	Perception
Sources	Sensory filters	Attention filters	Perceptual organisation
Light	Range of sensitivity and threshold values of senses (e.g. not being able to see UV or IR light)	Stimulus characteristics (e.g. size, intensity, frequency, contrast, motion, rate of change, novelty)	Categorisation Figure-ground Proximity Similarity Closure (see below)
Air pressure			
Pressure			
Heat			
Chemicals			
Gravity			

Source: based on Cherrington 1989: 82–6.

FIGURE 8.1 The perceptual process

moving in the same direction or that appear to be a continuation of other stimuli. According to the principle of *closure*, we fill in gaps in perceptual input to give meaning to apparently disorganised information. The importance of the gestalt principles to providing insights into how we go about constructing our personal and social world is not generally given great emphasis in the organisational psychology literature, apart from the extent to which they can be utilised in the construction of the kind of test instruments used in recruitment and selection procedures. That our perceptions are ordered to extract and construct meaning out of our environment helps both to engender our individuality and makes us vulnerable to those who seek to limit or channel the kind of information we receive. By placing perceptual stimuli, people and events, into categories, we take shortcuts in our comprehension of the world: we enable ourselves to deal effectively with the numerous stimuli which impinge on our senses by reducing the necessity to analyse each new stimulus as a unique object. This does, however, mean that we treat the things and people that we interact with through their relation to the subjectively determined, but apparently objective, categories into which we place them. Thus, to some extent, we *reify* everything and everyone we come across. We produce them as mental representations which are our own creation, yet we treat them as if these images are in fact real. The images and slogans associated with corporate cultures and missions are precise examples of attempts to channel our perceptual organisation into acceptance of a dominant reality.

It is through this process of *categorisation* that the major perceptual processes dealt with in organisational behaviour texts can be understood. Categorising people on the basis of limited cues – such as gender, skin colour, bodily characteristics, social, regional and national identity – and then treating an individual as having the generalised traits associated with that category, is the pervasive phenomenon known as the *stereotype*, identified by Lippman (1922). This enables us to make quick assessments of others and of situations. You can, for example, have a stereotype of what a particular kind of person or meeting will be like and react accordingly, or you may need to assess quickly the intent of someone who enters your office or wants to come into your house. Although it has psychological uses to the individual, stereotyping can also have negative social consequences – for example, men in secretarial work might be seen as only seeking temporary employment, unambitious or gay (Callan Hunt, 1992). Stereotyping, then, is one of the mechanisms through which racism and sexism are socially enacted and given ideological justification. Thus a branch manager in a case study of the insurance industry comments on his perceptions of why women are unsuitable for sales work at 'Insco', 'Yes, it can be a soul destroying job, and women are either not hard bitten enough to ride off insults or those that can are pretty unpleasant people' (Knights and Collinson: 1986: 155). It would appear that in the face of an established stereotype, you just can't win! We shall use the Insco case as a way of linking some of the issues in this and the following chapters.

Another process given force by our categorisation of stimuli is the so-called *'halo effect'* identified by Solomon Asch in 1938, which is essentially another process of producing a stereotype. When we come across new persons or situations, we can only assess them in terms relevant to our own experience and the limited cues we have about them. This initial assessment, whether positive or negative, tends to be carried over into the attitudes we build up of that person or thing, because of the powerful categorisation effects of *first impressions*. Thus if we rate a new workmate in a positive fashion on the basis of our first impression, we would tend to continue to rate them positively in the future. Of course, the fact that we rate them positively will probably in itself improve our relations with them. This may produce a *self-fulfilling prophecy* (Merton, 1949) from our first impression and probably improve our opinion of our ability to judge others. The halo effect can work against stereotyping, in that meeting a member of a group we hold stereotyped views about who makes a good first impression on us may weaken a negative stereotype. On the other hand, we may simply view them as an exception and perceptual selectivity may bring us to focus on the aspects of their appearance or behaviour that fulfil the prophecies of our stereotypes. These processes might, for example, have powerful effects on new recruits, in organisations since stereotypical attitudes can be socially communicated. This is backed by evidence such as that of Salancik and Pfeffer (1978), whose *social information processing model* of job design implies that our reactions to our work are significantly influenced by cues picked up from our co-workers. In an organisation where the prevailing experience of power relations is unitarist and hierarchical, we might expect new managers or workers to hold stereotypes about each other that will heavily reflect categorising processes, in that their experiences will tend to be interpreted through the dominant attitudes of their peers.

We also have a tendency to categorise others in the same light in which we categorise ourselves. Suspicious or aggressive persons, according to this principle of *projection* – or, more properly, *assumed similarity* – will view others as being more suspicious or aggressive in nature than will people who tend to be more trusting or placid. We can apply this notion to the kind of attitudes and values currently espoused in the 'new realism' which supposedly permeates industrial relations these days. To someone who sees themselves as 'looking after number one', those who stand for the values of class solidarity and loyalty to the union might be seen as stupid, unrealistic or hiding a lust for personal power behind a facade of caring for others. Identity in this sense becomes the standard of social comparison by which we judge the world and those in it.

To project categorisations on to others, we must be categorising ourselves. We can produce stereotypes about ourselves, perhaps regarding our probable or favoured responses to certain people or things. We can also apply the halo effect to ourselves. If we perform well at a particular activity the first time we try it, we will tend to rate ourselves better in the future and vice versa. The major source of the categorisations we use are the various groups that we belong to, as the membership of these groups provides us with the basis of the identities which we take up in various situations. Thus the norms and standards of conduct of a group we belong to will inform both the kinds of stereotypes we use and the identity which recognises our right to make such judgements. If a group can be said to have an identity, then that identity is communicated to its members in their self-perceptions and becomes part of, possibly a major part of, their own identities. Given that the major groups that many of us belong to are related to work and work organisations, our identities will be constructed in terms of our perceptions of ourselves within work organisations. Even the identities of the unemployed might be defined to a great extent by their lack of attachment to work groups.

Organisation and categorisation of our perceptions enables us to comprehend and interpret our world, and on this basis we are able to make judgements which depend on how we interpret the intentions of others. This is a crucial task for any individual, as it is linked to the fashion in which we identify the links between cause and effect in events. *Attribution theory* (Heider, 1958), and developed by Kelley (1971), shows how we tend to be biased in our judgements of other's intentions. It is founded on the notion that we rationally calculate whether the reasons for actions are due to internal (or dispositional) factors or to external (or environmental) factors, based on our assessment of the distinctiveness and consistency of, and the amount of consensus about, any particular action. It appears that we have an inclination, termed the *fundamental attribution error*, to judge people's intentions in terms of dispositional factors (see Arnold *et al.*, 1991). We tend to attribute the causes of their actions to something based in their personality or nature. In the Insco case, women office workers are seen to require high levels of supervision and control. This is not attributed to their, 'experience of subordination and blocked mobility but to their gender'. The 'discontented and moody' behaviour they are seen to exhibit is thus attributed to their gender-based disposition and is further used to disqualify them from jobs in sales (Knights and Collinson, 1986: 151). Another form of perceptual error identified by attribution theory is that of *self-serving bias* which is the propensity to attribute our successes to internal factors and our failures to external ones, and vice versa for those of whom we disapprove. Heider also identified the *discounting principle*, which indicates that in social perception we may pay more attention to strong situational cues and ignore a person's disposition: for example, we may distrust the overtures of an insurance seller who asks about our heath, regardless of what we think of them as a person.

Attribution theory does imply, however, that the more information we have about the other person, the greater our capability of making accurate environmental attributions about their actions, and the better able we are to see things as not necessarily intended or inherent in their nature but due to their social and personal circumstances. The choice to initiate a strike may be attributed by employers or managers whose knowledge of their employees consists mainly of stereotypes, to bloody-mindedness or their militant nature. In Lane and Roberts (1971) account of the long strike at Pilkingtons in St Helens, the tradition of paternalism meant that management could only interpret the action in terms of intruders such as scousers, revolutionaries or both. One would hope, then, that attribution theory implies that a manager who knows something of what it is like to be at the lower end of an organisational hierarchy might be more likely to attribute their decision to factors relating to the workplace or its environment, making a more realistic assessment of the situation in the process!

To some extent we are, in making attributions, making assessments of the personality or identity of others. But our ability to make consistently valid attributions is questionable. We constantly have to make judgements on the basis of too little or inaccurate information. On this basis we are assumed to carry around our own *implicit personality theories* (Asch, 1938) about how people look and behave. These act as barriers to the kind of new information we shall take in about them. Also, according to Langer (1981), we often behave in a less rational manner than that assumed by attribution theory, using habituated scripts which we act out in appropriate situations. These factors, coupled with our tendency to make dispositional attributions, make both our perceptions of others and of ourselves highly subjective and prone to fallibility. We can add one last layer to the barriers to accurate perception, one which is receiving increased attention in these days of global markets and information exchange, namely *ethnocentrism*. This is the tendency to view the world through the values norms and roles of our own culture or even subculture and to devalue or show hostility to those of other cultures (see Jackson, 1994). Because our perceptual world view is learned, we can come to an understanding of other cultures by exposure and, in the case of modern export management and 'international management', by specific training. Our sensitivity to those in other cultures depends on monitoring our reactions to information filtered through our own ethnocentrism. Thus, in our construction of identities out of our perceptual world, we need to make constant reference to sources of knowledge and comparison which we have built up over time. We need to learn in order to check on the validity of the identity we have secured for ourselves and its appropriateness to our current context.

Learning and socialisation: seeing what to do

Learning is normally defined in such terms as 'a relatively persistent change in an individual's possible behaviour due to experience' (Fontana, 1981: 64).

Stimulus-response and/or cognitive models are usually given as the main explanations of this process, these attempting at various levels to account for how individuals come to gain the particular knowledge and abilities they possess. The use of learning theory is, on the other hand, tied to refining the processes by which individuals are socialised into the behaviour patterns required by organisations – for example, through prescriptions aimed at increasing the effectiveness of training programmes (see Arnold *et al.*, 1995, for a good account).

Our perceptual organisation enables us to comprehend our experience; but if we do not learn from it, then our experience is of little use. The concepts and mechanisms of individual learning are of fundamental importance to the understanding of how we build up both unique identities and common behavioural patterns out of perceptual experience. Accounts of learning might, then, be expected to focus on how and where we acquire the behaviours appropriate and necessary to our social functioning and survival. In the psychological literature this is usually presented in terms of models based variously on *behaviourist*, *cognitive* and *social learning theory*.

The behaviourist model focuses on *associative* and *instrumental* learning. In the former process, proposed by Pavlov and refined by J. B. Watson (1930), we learn to behave in a certain fashion because we identify and associate that behaviour with a particular stimulus. For example, a bell or buzzer signalling the end of a tea-break can cause us to stop what we are doing and go back to work even if there is no supervisor present to tell us to do so. We do this because we have identified the stimulus as signalling the danger of punishment for non-compliance and associate it with the behaviour of returning to work. We are thus *conditioned* to obey the buzzer. The process of instrumental learning or *operant* conditioning takes this a stage further, and provides more explanation of why we learn, in that it focuses not on the stimulus, but on the consequences which follow the behaviour. This process, pioneered by Thorndike and refined by Skinner (1971), focuses on the way in which the rewards and punishments which are the outcomes of a behaviour become associated with that behaviour. If we do not go back to work when the buzzer sounds and get away with it, then we are rewarded by extending our rest period and by avoiding the associated punishment. Thus the likelihood of our doing the same thing in a similar situation is *reinforced* by the positive consequences of the behaviour.

These two mechanisms have been used at one time or another to explain the learning of just about every type of behaviour by the process of *shaping*, being repeatedly conditioned to close approximations of the desired behaviour. They do not, however, tell us very much about the mental processes which allow us to associate stimuli and behaviour or to expect and assess consequences, given that behaviourism does not regard mental processes as open to examination. The positive (reward) and negative (punishment) aspects of reinforcement schedules do, however, fit neatly into what we term the 'technologies of regulation' which back up the processes of control in organisations. The incentives to work harder and the disincentives to social and collective interaction with other workers which a piecework system encourages present a good example of these strategies of control. McKenna (1987: 182-4) notes that the techniques of organisational behaviour modification which use conditioning and reinforcement principles to attempt to 'shape' the behaviour of workers (for example, in areas such as safety practices and absenteeism) are mainly confined to 'highly controllable situations', the basic flaw in such techniques being that they ignore the 'interaction between situational and personal factors', which are 'encapsulated in social learning theory' (1987: 184).

The theoretical base of behaviourism also does not really explain how we acquire a new behaviour. It does not explain how someone would ignore the warning buzzer the first time beyond doing it accidentally. Theorists such as Chomsky have constructed damning critiques of behaviourism in terms of the inability of conditioning, reinforcement and shaping to explain phenomena such as the acquisition and use of language. Social learning theory, on the other hand, explains novel behaviour on the basis of observing and imitating the behaviour of others. Thus we could become socialised into ignoring the buzzer and pushing the limits of how long we can take for a tea break as part of a social process whereby we both reinforce our own actions and are reinforced by the successful actions of others in our work-group.

To explain this we need some recourse to cognitive theory, which emphasises the role of insight and the building up of *schema*, mental maps which allow us to act on the basis of imperfect knowledge and expectation, rather than the trial and error approach of the behaviourists. For instance, we could learn to ignore the buzzer in the right circumstances on the basis of what are known as 'TOTE' units. These *Test–Operate–Test–Exit* units (Miller *et al.*, 1960) represent the pieces in which we learn a behaviour or a skill and process the information relating to it. The process involved is a simple feedback mechanism whereby we continuously monitor (test) the results of our actions (operations) until we successfully complete them (exit). TOTE units build up behaviours as part of subplans which feed into wider plans. Thus we might continually test out the limits of how far we can extend our tea break as part of trying to increase our time away from work we dislike, or as part of attempts to annoy a hated supervisor, or even as a formally constituted plan to resist management controls.

These behaviours can be built into scripts, so we use learned knowledge through applying categories of particular activities. This is the process involved in the notion of *action regulation* (Hacker *et al.*, 1982, cited in Resch *et al.*, 1984), whereby all action is hierarchically organised into sub-units representing sub-goals of the planned action. 'Actions are continually adjusted to changes in the environment' (Frese, 1982: 213), and are initially performed and learned at an *intellectual* level under conscious control. After time and practice they become more 'automatised' and are controlled at lower levels. *Flexible action patterns* are the middle level of control and represent standardised scripts which can be somewhat modified in the face of situational change. Whereas at the lowest or *sensorimotor* level, actions are stereotyped, automatic responses. When actions are learned to this level, the higher levels are made available for pursuing other goals and tasks. In highly routinised work, although actions may be made at the sensorimotor level there is no concomitant 'freedom' to pursue personal goals – at the intellectual level such work only frees us to be frustrated, or at best to daydream.

From the above perspectives, we can explain how we go about learning, but it is more difficult to explain how we know what we need to learn and what the appropriate behaviours are in any given situation. If we are to link learning to the construction of identity in organisational settings, we need to know how the demands of that setting are communicated to us and why we internalise them. When we join an organisation, there are demands on us to learn certain things (how to do our work, 'correct' attitudes and behaviour) and we need to learn how to survive in a new and possibly unfamiliar environment. This process can occur in a formal fashion, as in a training programme where we may learn about the work itself and the rules and procedures that surround it. But, more importantly, it can proceed in an informal fashion, stemming not from training but from our interaction with those we work with. Most people learn their work through observation and questioning of their workmates. One of the major industrial training methods has for a long time been the *'sitting with nellie'* approach, where the recruit works with a trained operative to learn the skills necessary to their task. The unlooked for consequence of this is that in this way the recruit may also learn how to cope with work, the short-cuts, or how to 'make-out' by manipulating the bonus system. A modern analogue of this approach is the practice of *mentoring*, where 'entrants' or candidates for promotion are guided and counselled through their career development. Kram (1983) identifies stages of *initiation, cultivation, separation and redefinition* in this type of relationship, the mentor effectively leading their charge to a stage where they can define their own relationship to the demands of their 'career cycle'.

The models and mechanisms of learning which it would be most appropriate to examine in this context are those which offer some account of the process of *socialisation*. Socialisation as a process fully reflects our focus in the next two chapters on the construction of subjective identity in both the sense of an individual becoming a subjective entity and that of the individual becoming subject to external influence. These two aspects of the socialisation process are not separate, although they are conceptualised differently in organisational literature and suffer the difficulty of being explained through psychosocial mechanisms rather than subjective experience. On the one hand, there are the aspects of socialisation which deal directly with the psychological process of learning, notably the 'social learning' model characterised by Eysenck (1947), which focuses on inherited differences in a person's ability to build up conditioned responses, and by Bandura and Walters' (1963) model which focuses on how conditioned responses to external stimuli are mediated by internal psychological processes. On the other hand, there are those aspects which deal with the ways in which a person is tied to the demands of the groups they belong to, though these too can be approached through the notion of social learning.

Social learning theories combine elements of cognitive and behaviourist theory to produce a model of learning which focuses on interaction. From this the basic process of learning is the observation of the behaviour of others: the *selection, organisation* and *transformation* of the stimuli provided through observation, and the subsequent identification with and imitation of selected parts of the observed behaviour. This process, known as *modelling*, goes further than mechanisms such as associative or instrumental learning, as it involves people generating their own rewards and reinforcements, and selecting behaviours in line with their own expectations and desired consequences. We do not slavishly imitate the behaviour of those about us or even of those who appear to act in the most appropriate fashion in the specific situation we are in. We select those aspects of the activity we observe which we can usefully incorporate into our own repertoire of appropriately scripted behaviours. By modelling our behaviour in this fashion we avoid both indulging in wasteful and possibly embarrassing attempts to fit ourselves to our surroundings by trial and error, while managing to exert some control and influence over our own activity.

The modelling process guides us to the appropriate behaviours demanded of us in our organisational *'role'* (see Biddle, 1979). The concept of 'role' has had too much interpretation for us give a full account; but, for our present purposes, roles can be seen as sets of self-categorised, stereotyped and scripted behaviours which enable us to act in a contextually consistent manner. Through modelling, our behaviour can be influenced by that of those we select as role models, those whom we perceive to be acting in a 'correct' or desirable fashion. By building our own behavioural repertoire out of selected actions of role models we can fit our actions to those required by the organisational culture. Close associations with role models can effectively form an informal 'mentoring' relationship. We also utilise negative role models to define for us the types of behaviour we do not wish to imitate, or those we perceive as acting in inappropriate or socially disapproved fashions. In other words, what an individual gains from the social learning process are guidelines and a framework for self-evaluation and action in the production of an identity which can cope with and blend into its surroundings. Examples of this might be found in the way that newcomers are socialised into sexually stereotyped occupations. In the Insco case for example the branch manager explains that, 'we try to keep people coming in at the bottom so that we can train them to our ways, get them used to the company' (Knights and Collinson, 1986: 161). The models the newcomer is most likely to emulate and compare themselves to are those who appear situationally competent, who fit the appropriate stereotypes and who hold the right attitudes, thus reproducing, for instance, the 'macho' image of the construction worker.

Socialisation through social learning does not, however, simply transform an individual into an image of what an organisation requires, notwithstanding Handy's definition of socialisation in OB terms as 'the process by which an organisation seeks to make the individual more amenable to the prevalent mode of influence' (1976: 134). We certainly do learn to produce in ourselves normative characteristics and produce identities with consistent social meaning, but at the same time we acquire and produce distinctive characteristics, those which define our identities. Even though social learning enables us to take on a normative role, our observations can just as easily lead us to enhance those things about ourselves which reinforce our personal rather than our social meaning.

The role models we use are not only those people with whom we are in immediate contact. In producing an identity we also use individuals and reference groups with whom we may have little or no interaction. We may base the image we present not only on those behaviours and models appropriate to our present context, but on those pertaining to roles and perceived identities to which we aspire. We may act in a way consistent with other shopfloor workers, but at the same time adopt some behaviours which link us with superiors if we desire promotion, or perhaps the representatives of a professional or trade union organisation, if we see the possibilities of enhanced meaning and identity as lying in that direction.

As intimated earlier, much of the work on learning theory has been linked to increasing the effectiveness of formal training programmes, the key concepts here being the *transfer of learning*, the *acquisition of skills* and adapting training programmes to the *'learning curve'* of the trainee (see McKenna, 1987, for detailed discussion of these). 'Learning transfer' relates to the conditions under and extent to which stimuli can be generalised to new situations. 'Skill acquisition' is generally approached through prescriptions about the nature of feedback (developed from Miller's TOTE model) to be given and how learning tasks should be broken down into assimilable chunks prior to practising the integration of the whole task. 'Learning curves' indicate that the rate of assimilation of learning tends to reach a plateau after a while and that careful setting of objectives is needed to get the trainee to the next stage of their learning. This last notion can be related to our earlier comment on action regulation, in that as action patterns are learned we need to go back to the intellectual level of learning to get to the next stage of integrating the total activity into sensorimotor action.

In recent years, there has been a much emphasis in management development circles on the notion of *'experiential learning'*, derived from

Kolb's (1976) work on the *'learning cycle'*. This suggests that learning takes place in four stages, related to our learning goals:

- seeking concrete experiences related to goals;
- reflective observation and interpretation of experience;
- forming abstract concepts and generalisations related to goals; and
- active experimentation on concepts, leading back to 1.

Kolb's notion that personal preferences will lead individuals to focus on particular stages of the cycle has led to the idea that people have specific *learning styles* which can be identified through use of the 'Learning Styles Inventory'. Kolb's learning styles relate to combinations of preferences for particular stages, as follows: *convergent* (3 and 4), *divergent* (1 and 2), *assimilation* (2 and 3) and *accommodation* (1 and 4). In much of the mainstream OB literature the styles are more usually linked directly to stages 1 to 4, as is the case with an application produced by Honey and Mumford (1982) who classify the stages as styles: *activist* (1), *reflector* (2), *theorist* (3) and *pragmatist* (4). Honey and Mumford's styles are used more as predictive personality traits (see below) and are claimed to explain why, 'given the same experience . . . some people learn while others do not' (promotional brochure for Honey and Mumford's 'Learning Styles Questionnaire'). The probability is, of course, that, given the same experience, what some people learn is that they do not want to assimilate the materiel their trainers are giving them.

The most recent outcome of this strand of work has been an emphasis on generating the 'right' *learning climate* in organisations and on the phenomena of the *'learning organisation'*. We shall return to this in the section 'Learning to change' in Chapter 10, but for the moment we only need to note that what we are often expected to learn in our working experience are the right *attitudes*.

The attitude problem

All that we see, learn, are and do are not just part of ourselves, but are part of the social world around us. Others can judge us on what we do and what we appear to be, and can attribute the reasons for our actions; but to predict how we are likely to react to situations, there are a limited number of possible avenues to be explored. In social and interpersonal terms, we depend a great deal on the verbal statements of others to estimate their likely responses to situations and events. Likewise we communicate our own position in regard to issues, objects, events and our social transactions and negotiations. Such statements of belief, evaluation and feeling are of necessity a major component of socio-psychological study and this study of attitudes has correspondingly been one of the main sources of data and practice in the development of OB.

When we consider the structured environment of the workplace, performance can be measured, though an employee could be a hard worker and a 'troublemaker'; personality can be assessed though this may often produce counter-intuitive results not trusted by the client (see next section); and behaviour itself can be regulated in attempts to ensure future compliance. However, such information as can be generated through such techniques does not necessarily provide the requisite depth of information for the planning and systematic control desired by modern organisations. Rothwell and Kazanas (1986: 15) argue that even 'sophisticated quantitative techniques' are, 'generally not superior to the kind of structured expert opinion that can be gleaned from survey results'. They further extend attitude surveys as fundamental to the process of Human Resource Strategic Planning in procuring 'a means of tapping employee creativity and knowledge about the organisation and of building genuine commitment to future success'.

In the 1870s Charles Darwin referred to attitude as the facial expression of emotion (Petty and Cacioppo 1981: 20) though these days attitudes are most commonly regarded as consisting of three main components: the conative (behaviourally-orientated), the cognitive (belief-orientated) and the affective (emotion-orientated). This is based on Rosenberg and Hovland's (see Ajzen, 1988) model, which more correctly identifies these 'components' as abstractions, based on verbal and non-verbal responses, from which the construct of attitude is inferred. The implication here is that the evaluations implicit in the components can differ while at the same time leading to a unified expression of 'attitude'. For example, an employee may dislike the kind of work undertaken in a new department he or she is being asked to move into (negative affect), but believe that the workers in that department are a cohesive and effective team to work with (positive cognition) and thus agree to make the move (positive conation) (based on Ajzen 1988: 20). It is important to note that in the example given the enquirer could infer a wholly 'positive' attitude from the conative component alone, unless the negative affect was actively expressed by the employee. More commonly it is mainly the cognitive component which is subjected to measure, for example Taber (1991: 598) claims that in one major area of attitudinal measurement, 'current job satisfaction assessments may be assessing what workers *think* about their job satisfaction, rather than how they *feel* about their jobs'.

Though discriminations between such components have been made in depth in the socio-psychological literature (see Ajzen 1988: 21–3) these distinctions are rarely carried through into the design or analysis of studies in the wider literature making use of attitudinal measures. In essence, attitudes are most often taken as indicative of an undifferentiated consistency of response which is in turn predictive of behaviour or intention. An implicit assumption of much research involving attitudes is that they are informed by and reflect value systems. The distinction between attitudes and values is generally that attitudes are directed toward specific objects and that values are evaluative standards. In effect this makes them an output of the filtering and ordering processes by which we perceive and learn. As such, attitudes have been considered as embodying psychological functions for individuals:

- Adjustment – utility of object in need satisfaction; maximising external rewards and minimising punishment
- Ego defence – protecting against internal conflicts and external dangers
- Value expression – maintaining self identity; enhancing favourable self-image; self-expression and self determination
- Knowledge – need for understanding, for meaningful cognitive organisation, for consistency and clarity (from Katz, 1960, in Kahle, 1984: 18).

There does not appear to be a great deal of confirmatory evidence for this model, and this may in some part be due to it being merely descriptive rather than prescriptive or diagnostic. It says little about the measurement of attitudes or the relation of attitudes to behaviour which has generated much of the research in the area.

According to Eiser (1986: 13), 'an attitude is a subjective experience involving an evaluation of something or somebody'. This active experience of perceiving, interpreting and evaluating experiences with a public reference to others should be contrasted with the more general usage of attitude as an object to be measured, correlated and tabulated. As subjective experiences, attitudes must have some consistent linkage to social behaviour or, as Eiser notes, 'it would be difficult to know what such verbal expression *meant*' (p. 13). The problem really arises when it is assumed that attitudes can predictably *cause* behaviour.

The failure of socio-psychological research to find strong correlative links between attitudes and behaviour led to a decline in attitude-based studies in the 1970s. However, work on the specificity of behaviour as related to attitude, notably by Ajzen and Fishbein, brought the subject back into focus. Ajzen and Fishbein argued (1980) that attitudinal measures have to correspond with the particular components of a behaviour in order for prediction to be possible. These component elements of behaviour are the specific *action* itself, the *target* of the action, the *context* in which the action is performed and the *time* the action is (to be) performed. The assumption is that the more of these components that can be measured accurately, the more likely it is that the attitudes will predict behaviour. The problem once more is that many attitude surveys only measure the cognitive target component, that is, the attitude to the thing itself – rather than the attitude to the use or doing of the thing or to the when, where and how in which the behaviour would be expected to take place. In other words, they ask 'what do you think of this?', without asking 'what about doing it under these specific conditions?'

Ajzen and Fishbein in their 'theory of reasoned action' link the prediction of behaviour to what we know of the person's *intention*, which is a function of both the attitude toward the behaviour and of their *subjective norm* regarding the behaviour. Thus we not only have to take into account their positive and negative feelings, but also the social pressures surrounding the particular behaviour. Attitude here has two subcomponents: beliefs about the consequences of the behaviour and affective evaluations of (that is, feelings about) the consequences (Perloff, 1993: 95). Likewise, subjective norms have two subcomponents, normative beliefs about whether significant groups or individuals approve or disapprove of the behaviour and the person's motivation to comply with such normative beliefs (p. 97). In addition to such qualifications and it should be noted that the Ajzen and Fishbein's model has been criticised for being too rational/cognitive in nature and that the effect of more 'mindless' behavioural associations, such as the accessibility of an attitude and the effects of past behaviour, selective perception/direct experience and habit (Triandis, 1980; see also Perloff, 1993) are also important determinations of the attitude – behaviour correlation.

Because of the presumed effects of attitudes on behaviour there is a concomitant concern with the possibility of changing attitudes (and hence behaviour). The possibilities of changing attitudes are often linked to the persuasive characteristics of persons as sources (attractiveness, trustworthiness and expertise); and as targets (high or low self-esteem); and of messages themselves (levels of threat). The routes to attitude change are generally explained in terms of Kelman's (1961) three sources of attitude change, compliance, identification and internalisation (discussed further in Chapter 10) and through the reduction of psychological tensions as conceived in balance theory (Heider, 1946) and cognitive dissonance theory (Festinger, 1957) (see McKenna 1994, ch. 6 for an extended discussion). Perhaps the most important aspect of attitude change in organisations is the gaining of public commitment (Deutsch and Gerard, 1955; Tedeschi *et al.*, 1971), where 'whenever one takes a stand that is visible to others, there arises a drive to maintain that stand in order to look like a consistent person' (Cialdini, 1988: 79 – perhaps the most readable source on influence processes). Public commitments are seen to produce more enduring effects in changing attitudes and behaviour than private commitments (see Eiser, 1986). Corbett (1994: 56) gives an example of this need for consistency in what he terms 'Internal Marketing': in competitions where tie-break questions are used to give a reason or slogan for buying a product, 'tens of thousands of people testify in writing to the product's appeal and they experience a powerful psychological pull to believe what they have written'. The discussions below on attitude surveys and personality tests and those in Chapter 10 on goal-setting and development profiling all represent attempts by organisations to gain public commitment to corporate objectives.

The paradoxical possibility that if attitudes are consistent and predictive because they reflect predispositions, then it will be very hard to change them, is seldom exercised to any great degree in the management literature which has made so much of the findings of attitudinal research. The likelihood is, however, that attitudes are much more variable than is often assumed, and that even if changing core values is difficult, the changing of more operational attitudes – and more particularly the generation of new attitudes – can be controlled by the use of agenda-setting devices, including attitude, morale and opinion surveys.

Hollway (1991: 90–1 and 146–50) cites various examples which indicate that the interpretation and use of such surveys has, since their inception in the 1930s, often been more of a public relations than a human relations exercise and that they 'could be used to produce a self-fulfilling prophecy effect' (p. 91). Rather than surveying and analysing individual and cultural diversity, they are largely tools of cultural conformity. Referring back to the earlier notion that norms and habits affect the translation of attitudes into behaviour, we might suppose that the best strategy for changing attitudes is to embed them in self-enacting scripts which people are forced to internalise as a necessary part of their social and organisational functioning.

The use of attitudinal measures in the workplace can be more readily understood with reference to the focus that Zimbardo *et al.* (1977: 52) note in looking at attitude change from the perspective of populations rather than individuals:

> Even though we cannot predict the behaviour of single individuals, we should be able to predict that people (in general) will *change* their behaviour if we can *change* their attitudes of greatest relevance to the behaviour in question. We cannot predict which people will change or how much they will change, but a change in the attitudes of the population should be accompanied by a change in the behaviour of the population.

In this light, the utility of assessing attitudes as a cultural technology of regulation can be demonstrated by Boddy and Buchanan's advice on managing 'change projects':

> **Assess attitudes.**   What evidence was there about the enthusiasm and commitment of those working on the project? Were there signs or hints of resistance, which might suggest a change of approach? Were staff becoming frustrated by delays, difficulties or changes to plan, which the manager needed to do something about? Or were they enthusiastic and positive about the activity, and going out of their way to make it work? (1992: 150)

This is presented as an element of 'Managing the control agenda', a major facet of the 'continuous monitoring process to keep variances acceptably small' (1992: 149). The important notion here is the status of attitudes as evidence: even if not the 'enduring entities' they are so often assumed to be, they reflect the psychic status of persons within evaluative hierarchies and the choices of individuals to show whether they intend to collaborate or not with managerial practices.

The values we internalise, the attitudes we exhibit, will all reflect the choices, however limited, we have made and the learned constraints within which we act. Our unique history of learning and socialisation enables us to produce a subjective identity which is malleable in both our own terms and those of the others and the organisations we encounter. We produce something which others see as our 'personality' but which in effect is simply an actively managed and continually rehearsed manipulation of our identity fitted to what we have to do and what we want to do.

Personality: masks for tasks

Personality is defined in terms of 'the physical, mental, moral and social qualities of the individual', (McKenna, 1987: 11) or whatever makes you different from other people. It is understood as a complex of characteristic features or traits which describe the particular types and/or dimensions through which personalities are categorised. This may be the ultimate contradiction in organisational psychology, in that the study of 'unique' personalities is placed almost wholly in the service of the production of standardised measures aimed at the categorisation and selection of individual so that they can be fitted into their appropriate niches in organisational cultures.

The psychological understanding of how an individual develops a distinctive personality depends, like that of perception, on the notion of categorisation. Because personality is generally understood within a series of categorisations, its relationship to the construction of identity cannot be separated from the activities of those who produce the categories. Hence the explanation of personality in an organisational setting is more directly connected to the use of personality theory by managers than is the case with perception.

Describing personality as that which makes an individual different from others essentially defines it as that which sets the boundaries of what you are and what you are not. However, the way the notion of personality is used in OB highlights this type of definition as an idealised, liberal conception which is in direct contradiction to operational concerns with the controlled performance of work. The study of personality from this angle centres around the identification and prediction of *consistent* and/or *distinctive modes of response* in individuals. Some of the more recent approaches, which attempt to account for the interaction of personality with situational factors, would term these modes of response as *dispositions*, which include emotions, cognitions, attitudes, expectancies and fantasies (Clark and Hoyle, 1988). Distinctive behaviours in this sense are not the same as uniquely individual behaviours. They would be typical ways of reacting to people or situations which would distinguish an individual as belonging to a category of persons. Thus a person who is seen to react in a consistently un-cooperative fashion may be placed into a stereotypical category whereby their future behaviour will be assumed to be typical of that sort of person who is 'difficult'. The important point is in the assumptions that this form of personality theory makes about the nature of individuals and their activities. Behaviour is assumed to be inherent in the individual's make-up, biologically or genetically fixed. Being fixed, it is possible to predict, and being possible to predict it becomes a useful tool in controlling behaviour. Personality theory becomes an exercise in discovering how these various modes of response vary over time and between situations in order to refine the levels of categorisation and prediction possible. For example, what kind of observed behaviour in a person is sufficient to label them as a troublemaker? Or what type of situation will influence a person to reveal different aspects of or levels of their 'undesirable' behaviour? Approaches such as those of Clark and Hoyle and of Aronoff and Wilson (1985; see Hosking and Morley, 1991: 9–13), which attempt to contextualise personality in the social process, do acknowledge that dispositions can be modified by situations and experience, but still focus on how these variables can be combined to predict behaviour.

For OB as a 'science' this process frequently results more in a battery of methodologies and techniques for selecting the 'right person for the job', than in an account of personality. These are used to select prospective employees or candidates for promotion into categories which will show how well they fit into the organisational culture, thus making it easier to take decisions about them. Personality tests and inventories effectively perform the same function for an organisation as stereotypes do for an individual or group. They help to sort out the bewildering variety of information available about organisational members into categories which can be easily comprehended and dealt with. The last thing which a science of personality of this sort is concerned with is that which makes us subjectively unique individuals. It might be interested in what makes a particular individual different from others, but only to the extent that it might be a pointer to a characteristic useful or damaging to the organisation.

In delineating categories of personality characteristics, psychologists tend to fall back on two main sets of concepts. The first of these, personality *types*, are predetermined categories which we 'fit' into and which represent broad generalisations of character such as 'moody' or 'lively'. The second, personality *traits*, are habitual behaviours or tendencies to behave in particular ways; for example, tendencies to react in an anxious, reserved or outgoing fashion. Types or personality factors are generally used these days to refer to patterns or clusters of traits or personality variables, which can be used to map the profiles of individuals using factor analysis of responses to self-report questionnaires. The Eysenck Personality Inventory (EPI: Eysenck and Wilson, 1975) groups clusters of variables – such as reserved, unsociable, quiet, passive, careful – into factors, in this case introversion. The factors used by Eysenck, introversion–extraversion and stability–neuroticism, are based on Jungian psychodynamic theory, as are those utilised by the Myers–Briggs Type Indicator and Cattell's 16PF. These days types are generally reduced to the 'Big Five' personality dimensions characterised by tendencies to extraversion, emotional stability, agreeableness, will to achieve and openness to experience.

Personality inventories are still used by organisations on tens of millions of people every year in selection procedures and to determine who will make good managers or will be eligible for promotion. Cattell's 16PF (Personality Factors) scale, which is based on the same basic types as the EPI, is widely criticised on both its content and generalisability and yet is still used because it appears to select people who will make good managers. Hollway (1984), notes that it does not really matter whether the 16PF tells us anything realistic about personality, as it actually works by fulfilling the expectations of existing managers about what makes a good manager. That is, people like themselves, who are in the main 'male, middle-class and middle-aged' and, in the West, most often white. Since it is possible to work out which are the appropriate types of answer to the questions, it does not really matter if the respondent does not actually belong to the same social groupings as the dominant organisational culture they are trying to enter. It will help if they do, as it makes 'correct' responses easier to identify, but the ability to lie correctly is just as good a sign that the candidate is capable of or willing to become the kind of person who will fit. The candidate who is unwilling to frame the right kind of responses, or is incapable of doing so, automatically selects himself or herself out, regardless of their actual managerial potential. For example, graduates going through the 'milk-round' career selection may sit similar tests up to five times in the course of their applications. The conclusion that such tests are used for 'people processing' rather than individual treatment of personal characteristics and differences is hard to escape, and produces the conclusion that they are more effectively 'gate-keeping' rather than selection methods. Indeed, such tests were originally used in the UK in the First World War, to screen out 'neurotic' soldiers – that is, those who did not want to fight! Current doubts on the use of tests have led to recommendations on using techniques such as structured interviews and role-playing in *assessment centres*, though the expense and effort involved makes it unlikely that these would be followed up extensively in smaller organisations.

Personality testing is currently undergoing something of a revival, as a new generation of computerised personality profiling systems are coming on to the market. Their ease and speed of use, combined with neat computer printouts detailing managerial potential, reinforce an air of spurious objectivity in their validity as managerial tools. Most of them are still of course based on systems such as the EPI, but do not impose the same levels of costs in licensing and in training for their administration and interpretation as the older paper-based systems. Their value is in their capacity to reduce complex factors to simple stereotypical categorisations. Thus they make the decision-making process for personnel departments simpler, more cost-effective and less dependant on skilled staff.

The underlying assumption behind techniques such as the 16PF that managerial ability is somehow related to personality factors would almost certainly ignore the kind of managerial ability it takes to say, hold down a job, run a household and bring up children. But of course the dominant cultures in most organisations and institutions are not composed of the working women who are generally the ones who have to display such abilities. The assumption is not about personality as such, but about having or aspiring to the right kind of personality. In contrast to managerial assessment, the assessment of shopfloor workers has traditionally focused on *psychometric* tests of *capacities* and *aptitudes* rather than personality. Psychometric tests examine factors such as verbal, logical and mathematical reasoning and are said to have high test-retest validity, in that they yield similar results over time for the same subjects, which is not necessarily the case with personality inventories. Both kinds of test are tests of the ability to do the job, the difference being that it is assumed that only in the higher levels of organisational hierarchies does personality become a relevant factor. The utility of psychometric tests is in essence their cost-saving ability to predict who is capable or willing to be trained. Hollway (1984: 50) also notes that where psychometric tests are used in assessment centres the more objective information they yield is still contaminated by the subjective preferences of decision-makers, possibly on the basis of photographs and biographical details attached to assessment forms. It is the pragmatic psychology of Taylorism which is at work here – as long as the person can do the job, who they are and what they are is of little importance. The personality of a manager is not important, as long as they have a 'managerial' personality.

Other personality factors and characteristics employed in assessment include *locus of control, self-monitoring, self-efficacy* and *positive/negative affect*. Locus of control (Rotter, 1972) refers to whether we believe that we control events (internal) or events control us (external); likewise self-monitoring (Snyder *et al.*, 1986) refers to how attentive we are to internal states (low) or to appropriate situational and interpersonal cues (high) in determining our behaviour. High self-efficacy (Bandura, 1977) is the extent to which we believe we can overcome obstacles and get things done, whereas positive and negative affect represent the extent to which we accentuate the positive and negative in ourselves. In managerial selection, assessment and development the preference is for the person who demonstrates an internal locus of control, low self-monitoring, high self-efficacy and positive affect. Thus supplicants for managerial status are measured against what is effectively a stereotype of an 'ideal' manager, who is mainly attentive to the demands of managerial identity and practice. In the areas of personality and attitude assessment, as with the notions of stereotyping, projection and attribution the assignment of categories on the basis of limited information can lead to damaging consequences. For example, the assigning to personality of a biologically fixed nature which can be assessed through the identification of types and traits can reinforce the notion that problems within an organisation are rooted within the pathological personality characteristics and behaviours of individuals. Thus the interpersonal, social and organisational problems that arise can be blamed on bad attitudes and in turn on bad personalities. The end result of this type of process is blaming the bad personalities on genetic inheritance and then we are one step from the attitude that says that to resolve the problems you need to remove the people who cause them (see Chorover 1979 and Henriques 1984, for extended discussions of biological and cognitive determinism in social theory and practice). At a less extreme level, the branch manager at Insco commenting on the traits appropriate to sales work in insurance delineates them in a sex-typed fashion which acts to render problematic the employment of women in this area:

> I'm looking for whether they've got drive, initiative and are basically a self-starter. So he must want to get on, and get on by his own efforts. (Knights and Collinson, 1986: 156)

The focus on traits and types in OB is a function of their utility in making personality amenable to classification and manipulation. Yet personality to a great extent is simply the observable manifestation of identity. It is essentially similar to the notion of social identity, which a person develops and constructs through negotiation and interaction with others. In this sense, personality cannot simply be a cluster of traits, it is a process. It is not something which can be measured in terms of the ways in which people tend to react. Personality is a proactive process in which people present to others the image which will most benefit themselves in the situation they are in. The process of acquiring a personality, a social identity, would itself be influenced by having to fill out an inventory such as the 16PF in applying for a post. It would necessitate giving an impression of your personality which was appropriate rather than accurate (see Chapter 10 for more on impression management).The personality exhibited in this situation would be a mask appropriate to the task at hand.

Though the mask we present might be appropriate to our own reading of how to cope with a situation, it might not fit other's expectations of how we should react. Argyris (1967) examined the extent to which the demands of managerial and organisational practices were inconsistent with the drive towards greater independence, self-control and complexity in the maturing personality. For employees, especially at the lower levels of organisational hierarchies, the imperatives of managerial control and decision-making may lead to frustration of their desire actively to pursue meaningful goals and to the employment of *defence mechanisms* to protect their personal identity. These defence mechanisms, which include regression to less mature behaviour, daydreaming, apathy and aggression, present a set of personality characteristics to managers which might lead to the kind of 'assumption trap' discussed in the next section, prompting managers to be even more directive and coercive. Likewise our assessment of the personality we need to exhibit might be inappropriate to guide our conduct in face of unfamiliar cultural contexts. Jackson (1994) proposes a '3Cs' (*context–content–conduct*) model of the factors which need to be accounted for in linking our individual differences to our behaviour in social processes (Figure 8.2).

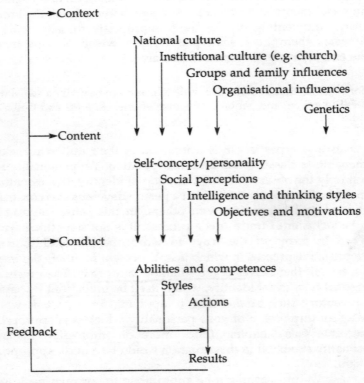

Source: Jackson (1993: 42).

FIGURE 8.2   The 3Cs model of context–content–conduct and individual differences

This model indicates that personality, like perception, is interdependent with our socialisation and intention. It is constructed in relation to the goals one is trying to achieve, to developing strategies to survive the circumstances one has to endure. It is a tool which allows individuals to manipulate their own environment, even as at the same time that it allows others to manipulate them in organisations. The personality component of our identities is the signal which indicates the types of influence to which we are open. In the end, the things which are the objects of the influences brought to bear on us, are arguably the major components of the developing identity which are dealt with in the mainstream agenda of OB – our motivations.

Motivation: the drive for satisfaction

William F. Whyte, writing in 1955 on economic incentives and human relations, spoke of the 'Five M's of factory life: men, money, machines, morale and motivation' (1957: 1) and it is the last of these, coupled with the aspects of satisfaction contained in the notion of morale that has to a great extent driven the primary interests of organisational management in psychological knowledge. Motivation, according to Sandra Dawson (1986: 7), 'refers to the mainspring of behaviour; it explains why individuals choose to expend a degree of effort towards achieving particular goals'. It is explained in terms of biologically based *needs* and *drives* and the selection of *goals* (content theories) and cognitively orientated notions of the *processing of information* on the rewards, costs and preferences for particular goal-related outcomes of action (process theories). The usage of knowledge of human motivation is linked to the service of organisational 'needs', in that motivation is understood in terms of the process of *social influence*. Even though Herzberg (1968) pointed out that in attempting to influence someone to work harder it is the manager who is motivated and not the worker, it is still the case that one of the principal concerns of organisational behaviour is to increase 'motivation' in the search for greater productivity.

Motivations are viewed as choices made about, or perceived predispositions to, certain behaviours and outcomes. They reflect the things we want and the strategies we choose to achieve or obtain them. Basically they can be explained in two ways. First in terms of instinctual drives which we are motivated to reduce – for example, when are thirsty we are driven to seek drink. Secondly, they can be described in the mechanistic terminology of stimulus–response, when we seek out those things which satisfy or reward us and avoid those which punish or cost us. However, since motivation also concerns choice and hence intention, it is necessary to explain how such

Motivational theories (a) content
(b) process (perception)

choices are made. This explanation is given within cognitively-orientated theoretical models which examine either the *content* of motivations, or the *process* through which they are expressed. The former examine what it is that motivates people through concepts such as goals, needs and 'motivators'; and is exemplified by the work of Maslow, Alderfer, McClelland and Herzberg. The latter examine how people are motivated through the processes by which behaviours are selected, directed, initiated and maintained. Included in this category is the work of Porter and Lawler, Adams and that of Vroom which is discussed in more detail in Chapter 9.

Both types of theory outlined above are concerned with the notion that humans direct their behaviour towards goals. In the case of content theories, the concern is with the source of the goals towards which behaviour is directed; and for process theories with the decision-making process by which goals are selected and pursued. There is another basic viewpoint on the importance of goals to motivation theory, which again reflects the managerial concern with satisfaction and performance. This is that motivation can also be viewed as the process of social influence by which agencies external to the individual can try to direct the selection and pursuit of desired goals by individuals. To a very great extent this aspect of motivation theory into which both content and process theories are incorporated is the practical focus of Organisational Behaviour as a whole. Thus practitioners in the area are concerned to understand the strengths and directions of human motivations in order to increase control over the performance of work-related behaviours.

An example of this is found in McGregor's (1960) conception of Theory X and Theory Y, which is often presented as a need or content theory of motivation. Students, and some texts, often represent theories X and Y as showing that there are two types of people, those who dislike work and responsibility, focus on economic security and need to be coerced into effort (Theory X) and those who like work, will accept responsibility for their own effort and are capable of innovation (Theory Y). However, these theories are more properly understood as a continuum of managerial attitudes to workers, whereby in Theory X views held by managers will produce an 'assumption trap' which leads to coercive behaviour on their part and thus a vicious circle leading to Theory X behaviour by employees. Likewise, theory Y assumptions should lead to theory Y behaviour, though of course there would probably be no 'virtuous circle', here as it would eventually lead to the complete abdication of managerial control. The practical parallel here is in the fate of Scientific Management and the Human Relations Movement. Both were assumed to increase motivation and performance and both could be said to fail on the basis of ignoring the effects of the assumption traps they produced, Scientific Management through assumptions of coercion through economic rationality and the managerial appropriation of control and expertise and Human Relations through the assumption that managers would give anything but lip-service to employee participation in decision-making.

The goals to which we direct our behaviour will constitute a formative influence in the identities we construct for ourselves. But this aspect of goal-related behaviour is not examined within Organisational Behaviour as a discipline, except to the extent that individual goals can be moulded or 'set' to fulfil organisational ends. Once again, the branch manager in the Insco case provides relevant commentary:

> I'm looking for someone who will work with me. So I look for some one who I think I can mould to my own ways, but they must already have the necessary spark and drive. (Knights and Collinson, 1986: 154)

Identity and related goals are treated as external to the position of workers in the productive process, in that goals are usually related not to intentions but to biologically derived drives, or more often needs such as those identified by Maslow (1954). Maslow's typology of human needs has been discredited to the extent that the 'prepotency' of 'lower order' physiological needs (that is, these needs must be fulfilled before 'higher order' social and psychological needs) is not supported, yet 'Maslow's Hierarchy' is still given prominence in most OB and management development texts. The probable reason for this, as we shall see in Chapter 9, is that theories which actually tell us something about motivation are too complex and dependant on contingent factors to have any simple predictive application in management practice. These 'needs' for food, shelter, affection, self-respect and individual growth are more accurately seen these days as operating on the basis of *intrinsic, social* or *extrinsic* stimuli. People are motivated and achieve satisfaction through factors which are internal or external to their work, from the work itself through the enhancement of skill, responsibility, status or authority; from their social relations in the workplace and from outside work through activities related to the family, leisure or other organisations to which they might belong. Intrinsically motivated persons are assumed to be influenced through their attachment to their work, and socially motivated persons through their peers, colleagues and group membership, whereas it is assumed that extrinsically motivated persons will only be influenced by aspects of their work that facilitate their 'outside' interests, such as pay levels, perks and increased leisure time. Though particular motivations may be more forceful for an individual at any one time, all three types of factor will have some bearing on how they direct their goal-related behaviour.

Organisational behaviour texts almost always refer to Maslow and his 'hierarchy of needs' but very seldom consider the satisfaction of needs within the organisational environment beyond the extent to which they can be manipulated to increase productivity. They are once again seen as external to the place of the worker in the productive process. Those in positions of control in work organisations do not see themselves as being in the business of comprehensively supplying the needs which Maslow hypothesises. They exchange financial and sometimes material benefits for the labour of employees, but beyond a minimal concern that workers should be satisfied with the conditions and rewards of work to improve performance, or at least to not disrupt production, little else is provided. Indeed, McClelland's (1961) typology of needs as affiliation, power and achievement does not take the lower order needs into account at all.

The hypothesised need for 'self-actualisation' and individual growth has repeatedly been incorporated into prescriptive packages, such as Herzberg's (1968) notion of 'job enrichment', which seek to improve the content of work to the point where workers will be self-motivated to improve their performance. However, as we saw in Chapter 6, such initiatives tend to fail on the basis that no real improvement is made in factors relating to the conditions of work and the job context or environment. For example, in Nichols and Beynon's (1977) study of job enrichment at Chemco, managers were motivated to pursue the 'New Working Agreement' on the basis that they were convinced that they would get at what makes workers 'tick' and thus be able to coax more work from them. For most of the workers involved, all that came out of this was an inadequate system of job rotation which was worse than the system they had evolved for themselves. Hence managers in this study were easier to 'motivate' because the context of their work was adequate.

Herzberg himself recognised this in saying that job rotation constituted 'job enlargement' rather than enrichment and this could result in no more than short-term improvements in productivity as it represented, 'adding nothing to nothing' (1968: 263–4). Such prescriptions are still offered by organisational consultants and still bought by organisational management, however, possibly because even short-term improvements in productivity offer some kind of competitive edge in the market. Motivation, in the above example, is reduced to the status of things or techniques which will motivate, a manipulative rather than an explanatory concept. The outgrowth of Herzberg's notions in Hackman and Oldham's (1980) *Job Characteristics Model*, links job redesign and enrichment to a diagnostic scheme which analyses work in terms of five variables (skill, variety, task identity, task significance and feedback) indicative of the extent to which a job could or should be redesigned. Although this scheme is widely cited in the literature, Hollway (1991: 107) reports that it was not popular with managers, in that its focus on the job rather than the individual did not fit the managerial ideology of the day.

The key concerns in these theories are to a great extent those which relate the concept of *job satisfaction* to that of task performance. However, the application of techniques based on the assumed relation between satisfaction and performance, which is difficult to define or measure in the first place, tends to ignore the operation of social, cultural, organisational and environmental factors which will all intervene to make a simple 'more satisfaction, more performance' relationship less likely. Argyle (1974) examined the relations between satisfaction and productivity, absenteeism and turnover, concluding that through absenteeism and turnover did have a direct relationship to levels of satisfaction, productivity only did so for highly skilled or intrinsically motivated workers and that even in these cases, individual differences were highly significant. It appeared that whereas, on average people did work harder when satisfied, some persons worked harder when less satisfied and some less hard when more satisfied. Working hard to make the time go faster in an unsatisfying job or just to forget about one's troubles is a familiar experience to many of us, and 'skiving' or systematic 'soldiering' is a classic response to fragmented or meaningless work where the only aspirational rewards available are those we can gain from controlling our own time and playing our own games (see Roy in Chapter 10).

Beyond these considerations, any meaningful view of the relation between job satisfaction and performance would have to recognise that alienated responses are rooted in the estrangement of workers from their creative capacities in the act of production, from ownership and control of the workplace, and from fellow workers. As the condition and responses derive, at least in part, from the basic structures of the capitalist labour process, changing them would require more than tinkering with peripheral aspects of work design. This does not mean that individuals will not report some sort of increased positive satisfactions. For example, Frese (1982) states that

> much of the work on job satisfaction has tapped an attitude which could be labelled resigned job satisfaction. Because of the unavailability of other jobs and ways to change the job situation, a worker has reduced his aspiration level over time and has become resigned to his job. (1982: 212)

Such feelings are directly related to powerlessness and lack of control over the job situation. Reduction of aspiration levels does not necessarily imply a lack of aspiration however – it could simply mean resignation to progression as defined by the rules and procedures of the organisation, an acceptance of bureaucratic methods of control and the ideologies which underly them. At Insco, for example, one of the female clerks who had been continually discouraged from applying for a position as a sales inspector decided not to risk the security of her position as senior clerk and redefined her aspirations in terms of, 'a woman's idea of going higher up within the company on the inside' (Knights and Collinson: 1986: 166). By considering the idea of progression into office management rather than sales she has started the process of redefining her goals in line with the gendered job segregation fostered by the company.

People experiencing passive satisfaction with their lot rather than active satisfaction with their work, may still be open to the types of influence exemplified by attempts at job enrichment or similar schemes. Herzberg's

(1968) two-factor theory of motivation suggests that the 'motivator' factors associated with job content and satisfaction are separate from the 'hygiene' factors associated with job context and dissatisfaction. The content factors, such as growth, responsibility, recognition, achievement and variety, are similar to those assumed to motivate people who value intrinsic rewards and the status and esteem components of social rewards. The context factors, such as salary, conditions, security, relationships and possibly policy and status, are similar in effect to extrinsic and social rewards, in that they make work either easier or more rewarding as they improve. Techniques such as job enrichment assume that if content and context factors are adequately met for individuals in organisations, then the motivation to work will be maintained. More importantly, they rely on the notion that people are passive recipients of organisational influences. If people do construct for themselves a passively resigned workplace identity, then the chances will increase that they will accept the redesign of their jobs on the basis that it will eventually improve their lot. The developments in flexible working practices and unitarist industrial relations in the 1980s may indicate that what has been identified as a 'new realism' is nothing more than the kind of coping engendered by having to adopt a passive workplace identity in response to environmental constraints such as high unemployment.

Job context and content factors are seldom if ever met adequately for everyone within the work environment, so attempts to influence motivation levels in individuals will always run foul of factors of which they do not take account. Thus, in addition to active attempts to 'motivate' individuals, organisations take advantage of the socialising pressures of work to create a climate where people are open to these kinds of influence. However, attempts to motivate or socialise individuals into accepting the managerial direction tends to ignore the decision-making aspect of the process of becoming motivated. If motivation is indeed the 'mainspring of behaviour', then it not only refers to the selection of goals but to the selection and development of the coping strategies and skills that individuals use to achieve those goals. Lee and Lawrence (1985) identify four factors which underpin all 'political' models of motivation that focus on decision-making:

- *Goals* – relating to values, interests and perceptions of individual opportunities and possibilities;
- *Strategies* – formulated to achieve goals or to react to threats to capacities to achieve them;
- *Coalitions* – exchanging commitment to group interests for support for goal strategies which cannot be achieved on an individual basis
- *Power* – assessing success of goal strategies and membership of coalitions, arriving at estimates of personal power to affect events and revising goals in line with this.

The first three factors are dependant on the fourth, in that 'An individual's perception of his power will affect the goals he sets, the strategies he chooses and the nature of the coalitions he joins' (1985: 78). Similarly in the construction of identities, perceptions of a persons' situational power will determine the sources of meaning which are appropriate to the maintenance of a secure identity.

Motivation may be influenced by either interfering with or facilitating the individual's capacity to perceive, formulate or implement one or more of these factors. Organisational strategies which simply restrict the employees' capacity to act in these areas will however probably lead to individual and group attempts to circumvent them, so techniques aimed at the 'motivation' of groups and individuals may not achieve their aims – they may exacerbate the situations they were designed to ameliorate by reproducing or reinforcing existing areas of conflict, by re-opening old issues or by introducing new topics of dispute.

Examples of strategies aimed at enhancing group motivation for managerial benefit have included programmes such as quality circles at the behavioural level and autonomous work-groups at the level of job design. Aimed at increasing production quality, overall productivity, workforce flexibility and job satisfaction, they depend on the production of work-group identities consonant with the collective goals of management. For them to work effectively through group identities remaining manipulable by management, there must be a continuing identification with organisational 'needs'. These in the end can only be sustained to the extent that the organisation enables group members to maintain comparative material benefits *and* secure identities. This however, has long-term implications for job security which are in direct contradiction to the aim of producing a flexible workforce responsive to the short-term demands for changes in product lines, working practices and manning levels. The threat of a reserve pool of unemployed labour is not sufficient to maintain the levels of commitment required by these programmes. Commitment based on the fear of losing one's job is only equivalent to the type of motivation achieved by holding a gun to someone's head. As soon as the threat is removed, so is the motivation. All that is achieved is an increase in the likelihood of retaliatory action.

In essence, then, the study of motivation in OB is the study of the processes of organisational influence and a study in the exercise of power and domination. No matter what the intent of consultants and practitioners in the area in terms of increasing job satisfaction and the elusive 'quality of working life', to management these techniques are effectively 'technologies of regulation' aimed at increasing control over behaviour and performance. Unfortunately, from a managerial point of view at least, in the long run such programmes cannot survive exposure to the contradictions inherent in trying to control subordinates who are actively attempting to control their own environment. We shall return to this theme in Chapter 10, where we shall re-examine motivation and consider some more recent developments in the area.

Conclusion: the limits of social and organisational psychology

We have used the topic-based approach in this chapter to illustrate some of the general problems of organisational psychology and the social psychology that partly underlies it, but these limitations need to be put in a broader context. Social psychology is concerned with individual behaviour as it exists in various contexts, but such behaviour is still what people do, not what they are. The discipline has tended to reduce its treatment of subjective experience to abstract and supposedly *quantifiable* traits and mechanisms which are compatible with practice-led assumptions as opposed to its dominant theoretical ideals. This is not to say that subjectivity is not an issue in social psychology, as there is an extensive literature on the subject of identity in itself, as is illustrated in the work of Lasch, Harre and so on. It is more the case that this literature has tended to be reduced to another specialist topic in the mainstream literature, often related more to developmental issues, rather than being seen as a fundamental aspect of the ability of socio-psychological theory to provide understanding of how we cope with everyday life.

This failure to adequately address the issue of subjectivity partly underlies one of the major problems which confronts social psychology. That is, the contradiction inherent in attempting to address both the individual and social determinants of human behaviour. Social psychology as a discipline purports to fill the divide between psychology and sociology, the tendency having been for the former to concentrate on the individual and the latter the social. But it does not escape the problem. Henriques *et al.* (1984) correctly identify the weakness as one of a dualism between individual and society. They argue that even when social psychology attempts to provide accounts of how the two sets of determinants interact in shaping behaviour, it tends to come down on the side of explanations which emphasise biology and/or individual rationality as causative agents. Social and structural factors are tacitly acknowledged as having some effects, but these are seldom treated in an explicit fashion. They are generally reduced to the status of intervening variables which complicate the action of the individually-based mechanisms and determinants of behaviour.

Social psychology and its development can therefore be seen as a product of the tensions and debates between competing explanations of behaviour. In utilising perspectives such as social learning theory, social psychology tacitly incorporates the essential portions of prior perspectives, notably psycho-analytic and behaviourist theory. These perspectives embody contradictory assumptions about the nature of human behaviour. Yet critiques and reformulations of these assumptions form the very basis of the development of the discipline itself. These are refined over time by the cycle of critique and reformulation to produce a discipline responsive to the needs of its individual, organisational and institutional clients. However, these tensions and debates serve in the end only to mask the fact that no wholly consistent body of theory of behaviour has been developed which can explain the social construction of identity. What social psychology actually does is continually to reproduce and repackage the tensions between the dominant competing assumptions about human behaviour. The end product of this process is generally to reinforce the understanding of social problems as residing in the deficiencies of individuals. Within the workplace, for instance, sabotage to machinery would be blamed on the deviant or even criminal tendencies of workers rather than on the working conditions or practices which they are often powerless to respond to in a more direct fashion. This kind of development and shaping of subjective experience in the workplace tends to be neglected or ignored.

Therefore the dependency of organisational psychology on social psychology for its theoretical resources is important in shaping its direction and application. The tensions may be partly avoided by maintaining a specific focus on individual and group behaviour within organisational contexts. An attempt is made to avoid confronting the main contradictions of the *individual–society dualism* which faces social psychology. Context is taken as a given or contingent factor which may be manipulated to alter behaviour. This conveniently leaves organisational psychology to deal with measurable and marketable packages of behaviour, which are easily incorporated into frameworks which of necessity theorise individuals as standardised social objects rather than specific social subjects with unique personal histories. The resulting treatment of individuals as subject matter rather than as subjective entities is commensurate with the dominant assumptions extant in social psychology as a whole.

Hence there is a double abstraction of behaviour, from its social and structural contexts, and from much of its subjective content. The humanistic critiques within social psychology in the 1960s and 1970s which were concerned with the lack of social context and individual meaning in existing theory and methodological practice have undoubtedly influenced organisational psychology. But the presentation of its traditional agenda has reproduced them as vague ideals rather than as core assumptions of the discipline. This remains a continuing contradiction between the way in which the major topic areas in organisational psychology are defined and the way they are used in the control and regulation of behaviour at work.

CHAPTER 9

Regulating organisational behaviour?

Industrial Psychology thus covers a wide field. It deals with the human, as contrasted with the mechanical and economic aspects of labour. Its chief aim is to reduce needless effort and irritation and to increase interest and attention throughout the workers in industry. (Charles S. Myers, 1926: 11)

In her excellent account of the development of the psychology of work, Wendy Hollway (1991: 4–5) cites Alec Roger as giving a neat definition of the paradigm for occupational/industrial psychology as 'Fitting the man to the job and the job to the man', (FMJ/FJM) in the 1950s. The issue here is one of the quality and integrity of the psychological practice and knowledge applied in the area and the FMJ/FJM paradigm gives us a client-centred definition which from the start has given a technical orientation to work in the area. Such a definition relies heavily on the notion of a value-neutral, objective science which is independent of the power relations in the organisations and societies within which it is practised. The truth is, of course, that both power and knowledge are not singular, unitary or completely objective. Even the person who fully believes they are a value-free carrier of fully objective scientific knowledge, has to utilise and exercise that knowledge in the real world and the one thing we do know is that power relations in organisations are seldom, if ever, completely equitable.

A further complicating factor here is the treatment of psychological knowledge in the literature and the texts which communicate this knowledge. Hosking and Morley (1991) give three types of theoretical orientation which they say have dominated OB texts. They cite Gordon Allport on the first two, which he terms the 'individualistic' and 'culturalistic' fallacies. This split parallels and illustrates what Henriques *et al.* (see Chapter 8) identify as the 'individual/society' dualism rife in social psychology. The third approach they identify is the 'more complicated without becoming more sophisticated'

(1984: 4) contingency approach, which is said to give weight to people and context, but is merely a 'statistical interaction' between 'inputs' from person and context. This argument allows that an attempt has been made to take account of variables affecting individual and group psychology and action in organisations, but that it does not have an adequate account of the social interactions through which people produce their contexts and are shaped by them.

This chapter starts out by examining the role of psychology and psychologists in the production of context and in reinforcing managerial power. From this basis we proceed to examine more of the mainstream agenda in OB as examples of how research has been incorporated not just into managerial practice, but into the very notion of management itself.

Organisational psychology and organisational behaviour: technologies of regulation?

The explanations, instruments and techniques developed from mainstream theories are active in sustaining and implementing a culture of domination in the workplace. Organisational psychology, though paradoxically informed by humanistic concerns, has both a role as an agent and a vested interest in mobilising the consent of organisational members. New practical and theoretical knowledges often become part of the repertoire of the science of organisational behaviour, functioning as *technologies of regulation* which are used to control and discipline employees.

Such practices were inherent in the origins and early development of the sub-discipline of *industrial psychology*. In the first two decades of the twentieth century employers drew on the variety of psychological theories on offer (Bendix, 1956: 200–1). *Behaviourism's* orientation towards 'human engineering' was a particularly useful source of advice for managers seeking to manipulate environmental stimuli in the form of penalties and incentives, in order to produce the appropriate worker response. At the same time, rival schools such as *instinct psychology* could suggest means of employers meeting 'innate' needs such as self-expression, which were being distorted by evil Bolsheviks and union organisers. Perhaps most practically, *vocational psychology* could provide a battery of tests and measurements for applications to selection and placement. It was in this last sphere that industrial psychology really took off in the USA, boosted by the extensive use of tests for intelligence and other factors during the First World War.

Psychology in industry had in fact begun in the area of advertising, but it soon shifted from manipulation of consumers to manipulation of workers. Most concepts and techniques were extremely primitive, but psychologists such as Munsterberg promoted the idea that they could be applied to the 'labour problem'. The accumulation of knowledge about individual differences provided the basis for a varied apparatus of testing and measurement techniques geared to vocational counselling, placement testing, and job analysis with suggested correlations between factors such as intelligence, personality and potential work performance. Munsterberg summed up the general aim as finding 'those personalities which by their mental qualities are especially fit for a particular kind of economic work' (quoted in Baritz, 1960: 3). There was a widespread tendency to claim bogus relationships between national or racial characteristics and suitability for jobs (Kamin, 1979). In Britain, organisational psychology was relatively isolated from its American cousin. The National Institute of Industrial Psychology, founded under the leadership of Charles Myers in 1921, took a painstaking and broader interest in the related issues of training, rest, monotony and fatigue at work (see Hollway 1991 for an analytical account of this process). But even here a considerable number of programmes of vocational guidance, selection and testing were dictated by consultancy pressures.

It was these kind of developments that led Baritz (1960) to develop his famous analysis of psychologists and other industrial social scientists as *servants of power*. The science of behaviour was seen as giving management 'a slick new approach to its problems of control' (p. 209). Included in the bag of schemes were attitude surveys, selection devices, motivation studies, counselling and role-playing. Events in the 1930s Hawthorne Studies, discussed in Chapter 2, were a particularly powerful confirmation of the social engineering role that could be played by social scientists, in this case under the framework of human relations theory. These kinds of superficial and manipulatory practices are still being recycled today. For example, the reaction to objective problems employees face in their work, recognised in the modern stress research literature, has led to the astonishingly innovative introduction of . . . employee counselling programmes! Baritz's great insight was to recognise that the service provided by social scientists to industry meant that 'control need no longer be imposed. It can be encouraged to come from within'. Workers could be manipulated to internalise the very ideologies and practices that ensured their domination.

A perfect modern example of this is the role played by industrial psychologists in some of the new human resource management techniques. The American writer, Grenier (1988) worked as part of a team hired by Johnson and Johnson, the medical products company, to create the required conditions for the setting-up of a new plant on a greenfield site in New Mexico. This involved many of the elements discussed in Chapters 5 and 6: quality circles and semi-autonomous work teams, status and symbolic harmonisation of conditions, and extensive socialisation into a corporate culture facilitated by psychological testing at the selection and hiring stage. None of this, of course, is necessarily negative or manipulative, even the secret tape recordings of work team meetings to help identify success in fostering group identity and dynamics. But the hidden agenda of the whole project was a 'union avoidance' campaign and this came to light when some of the workforce began an organising drive. The social psychologists became active and central participants in the struggle inside the heads of employees. All the supposedly innocent information collected became a means of screening workers and their attitudes. Team meetings in particular played an important role in identifying pro-union workers, Grenier being asked to develop an index through which to rank workers in their degree of support. Grenier later publicly revealed this process and himself became subject to surveillance and intimidation.

Not all social scientists, of course, have been concerned with such manipulatory practices and there has been a considerable amount of useful work done on employee satisfaction. The modern equivalents of Baritz's servants of power are not necessarily 'on the payroll', but still have a tendency to accept managerial norms as the parameters of their activities. In the same

Source: CAITS (1986), *Flexibility, Who Needs It?*, London, p. 34.

FIGURE 9.1 'Psychological warfare'

way as the newspaper owner does not have to threaten journalists to toe the editorial line, mainstream behavioural scientists generally internalise controls and largely unacknowledged self-censorship becomes the order of the day. In other words, the institutional relationship between the disciplines and their client groups remain a crucial problem.

Later, in developing out of industrial and human relations psychology in the 1950s and 1960s, organisational psychology brought to the study of work organisations an emphasis on descriptive and experimental research incorporated from social psychology. This was allied to the concern with applied work within organisations that had given impetus to industrial psychology in the early part of the century and the human relations tradition discussed in earlier chapters. Later inputs to organisational psychology from areas such as socio-technical systems theory and operations research have further cemented the relationship of the subject with the interests of power groups in organisations.

That the practitioners of organisational psychology and organisation theory are mainly located in such institutions as business schools rather than in industry or psychology departments, also reinforces the conception of the subject as a discipline in its own right, with its own client groups and professional concerns. At the same time, this distances organisational psychologists enough from their clients and subject matter to enable them to concentrate more on the theoretical understanding of organisations than was the case with the more strictly application-led industrial psychology. In turn, this enabled a retention of much of the humanistic theoretical orientation derived from social psychology. Theoretical ideals of this nature do not, however, often survive exposure to the needs of the main client group. As with industrial psychology before it, this results in the subject becoming chiefly directed towards the practical needs of management. A humanistic perspective fully cognisant of the effects of organisational work on the subjective identities of individual employees is unlikely to promote harmonious relations with clients whose major tasks include the deployment and control of an organisation's 'human resources'. Nor would an organisational psychology that grounded its theory and practice in an understanding of the politics of production be likely to be in a position fully to give itself over to the demands of these clients.

The roles of organisational psychologists

The relations between the practitioners of organisational psychology and their clients have thus formed a major influence on the development of the discipline and we can further our understanding through an examination of the complex and interrelated roles which they take up in these relationships. Blackler (1982: 204–6) provides a useful framework for the discussion, identifying four roles taken up by organisational psychologists:

- *Role as social critic* – evaluating organisational practices and predicting and studying the human consequences of organisational decision making;
- *Social policy adviser* – evaluating the criteria that govern organisation in general and exploring alternatives;
- *Change agent* – evaluating and exploring ways in which alternatives identified in the light of the above two roles may be practically implemented;
- *Management consultant* – assisting and facilitating the efficient and effective management of organisations and social resources in respect of both routine tasks and non-routine contingencies.

These roles are qualified by the identification of a number of shifts in the approaches taken by organisational psychologists. There has been a recognition that in serving various interest groups in organisations, a claim to 'scientific' impartiality is difficult to sustain. Their interests must to some extent follow those of their clients. A role of *'specialist helper'* has generally replaced that of expert adviser. In addition, there has been a move away from trying to implement widespread changes in organisations towards attempting more incremental changes which rely on 'securing structural supports for changes at the interpersonal level' (Blackler, 1982: 206). Lastly, they are beginning to recognise that they can make no claims to certain knowledge or laws of organisational behaviour, and that the concepts and models generated by them are mainly relevant in localised contexts. Overall, the effect of these qualifications would appear to be a shift to a far closer involvement and identification with the client.

Reflecting a general move towards what is now conceptualised as 'management research' Gummeson (1991, ch. 2; also see Easterby-Smith *et al.*, 1991; Gill and Johnson, 1991) examines consultant and researcher roles in terms of their implications for gaining access to organisations, giving (p. 34) a sevenfold characterisation of these roles as analyst, project participant, catalyst, OD consultant or interventionist, change agent, board director (catalyst and decision-maker) and lastly, 'management for hire'. The only real addition to Blackler's typology is the last, a role that is more indicative of the shakeout of middle levels of command that has been one of the main effects of the delayering of recent years (discussed in Chapter 6) than any active participation in either research or consultancy.

Although tending to serve particular client and/or interest groups, the products of organisational psychology, in the form of prescriptive packages or ad-hoc consultancy, are presented as being of potential general benefit to organisations, or specifically to some groups or individuals within them. Even if practitioners are aware of the contextual limitations of the knowledge they produce, such awareness is not necessarily reflected in the attitude of their clients to them and the discipline they represent. To the client, the impression is of a unitary discipline, supplying analysis, advice and practical techniques in support of their own goals and tasks. The function of the organisational psychologist is seen as a 'therapeutic' one, treating the pathological problems of the organisation in much the same way as psychoanalysts treat those of their patients. In turn, this can further reproduce and reinforce in the client a unitary, rational conception of organisations which is supportive of dominant ideological assumptions: for example, that organisations are entities with common internal processes and socially necessary functions, duties and rights. If organisational psychologists are becoming more closely involved with their clients, their problem is the risk of becoming locked into a self-fulfilling prophecy in which they are viewed and treated as the doctors or maintenance technicians of the organisational world and are forced to conform to this image in order to survive. This last shift is readily appreciated in the current pressure on academic institutions to become both more involved with and more dependant on industry in the scramble for funding.

How then should we evaluate the general relations between the four roles of social critic, policy adviser, change agent and consultant assigned by Blackler? The view of practitioners as belonging to a professional discipline responsive to the needs of client tends to subordinate the first three of the roles to the fourth. The critical role is to be distinguished from a genuinely critical theory. Although organisational psychology can present a humanistic critique of the consequences of particular organisational practices, it seldom produces a critique of the dominant social relations within the mode of production itself. Furthermore, the approach does not include a reflexive critique of its own role in producing and reproducing practices and techniques. The result is more an analysis of how subjective influences on production can be *controlled out*, than of how they can successfully be used to create democratic forms of work organisation and socially useful work. The role of social policy adviser is the arena in which the above is sold as a commodity of value to the client. Advice is supplied not on alternatives to existing practices, but on how reappraisals of them might be utilised and implemented in line with managerial goals.

Similarly, the role of change agent tends to avoid concern with alternatives in favour of technologies of regulation. This is not intended in a negative fashion, but the effects are frequently such for lower-level employees. Hollway (1984: 37–42) cites the techniques of job analysis and evaluation (for example, those developed by consultants such as Hay-MSL and Urwick, Orr and Partners) as examples of how systems designed to aid organisations in specifying critical requirements for adequate worker performance have their main consequences for the workers involved, 'in the direction of the increasing rigidity of work' (1984: 37). These three roles thus become indicators of the divisions of intellectual labour which are necessary to the work involved in the fourth role of management consultant. The true paradigm of the organisational psychologist is that of ensuring 'effective resource use': supplying advice, resources and training which are aimed at assisting organisations in efficiently managing the conflict and resistance which is a predictable consequence of hierarchically organised production.

The 'science' of organisational behaviour would appear, then, to embody a fundamental contradiction in the relation between the benign and humanistic assumptions which inform its 'critical' theory and its assimilation into and accommodation of managerial ideology and practice. It is employed in a project of fitting the lived experience of other organisational employees into marketable and manipulable categories. The irony is that in fulfilling this task, it manages to market itself in such a way that it becomes one more tool for the transformation into appropriate images of all those, including itself, that deal with work organisations. This leads almost inevitably to the situation where the very nature of the initiatives and interventions which practitioners put forward for the betterment of organisational life acts to block their possible success, in a 'Catch-22' fashion: the programmes are short-circuited by their own action. Value-free organisational psychology is not possible, but there is a difference between a grounded theory approach which takes full account of the practical reality in which it operates, and a functionary service which is subject to the demands of its client to the extent that it distorts analytical tools to no one's ultimate benefit. It is for this reason that in attempting to redefine the agenda of organisational psychology, it is not enough simply to provide an adequate explanation of subjectivity. The need is also for critical perspectives which can integrate an understanding of the social construction of subjectivity, with explanations of how organisational practices develop, and the role of social scientists in producing and refining them.

Importing critical theory and practice into the organisational psychology and behaviour? To say that the discipline cannot adequately account for subjective experience because it is subordinate to capital will mean little to people who have to earn their living within such regulatory structures. In such a context it appears reasonable that the rationale for the discipline is in making organisational processes both more effective and more tolerable. After all, its practitioners, like everyone else, can normally only work within the constraints of reality as it is, not as they might like it to be. Criticism may appear to be useful only to the extent that it aids the relationship between understanding and practical application. Ultimately this is true, and we discuss some of the possibilities for organisational change in our concluding chapter. However, we have to recognise that part of the limitations of the behavioural sciences derives from the very fact of a practical, problem-centred orientation. To change realities we have to start from developing further the available theoretical resources represented in the literature, in the recognition that they have their own role in the production of the practices which underwrite power relations in organisations.

To facilitate our own account of these relations we shall not attempt to survey industrial/organisational psychology as a whole (for a good historical account see Hollway, 1991), but we shall will take four more of the major topics which characterise the mainstream agenda as exemplars of how psychological knowledge is reproduced as technologies of regulation. The relation of these issues to individual psychology is not as clear as those explored in Chapter 9, but what they have have in common is their linkage to the reproduction of power relations in modern organisations, relations which are difficult to approach through the earlier topics. The first area we wish to consider in this chapter is possibly the most powerful behavioural technology for the structuring of power relations available to either individuals or organisations, the *group*.

The authority of the group

Groups in general are defined in terms which vary according to the aspects of the topic which are being studied. However, a composite definition could describe a group as 'a collection or coalition of people who interact meaningfully in the pursuit of common goals or objectives and who have at least a tacit sense of agreed standards, values and common identity' (based on Schein, 1965; and Drake and Smith, 1973). Groups are often referred to as the 'building blocks' of organisations and are studied in terms of the roles and associated norms generated within them, their role and communication structure, their interpersonal dynamics and their relations to other organisational coalitions and interest groups. Whether formally or informally constituted, cohesive or loosely associated, groups could be viewed in many situations as responses to pressures. Whether by individual design, accident or external determination, we live out much of our existence in the contexts of varying coalitions to which we are attached for a purpose. Groups in this sense are social and interpersonal tools, or even possibly technologies of action through which we achieve ends which are beyond our perceptions of personal power. At the same time, our activities are circumscribed by, and directed towards, whatever goals or ends the group exists to serve.

In organisations, groups tend to be formed around the divisions and stratifications inherent in structural and or social processes. Thus they can arise around and within sectional, divisional and hierarchical boundaries and also out of the interactions of groups of peers, workmates or social interests. Any individual is likely to have allegiances to any number of such groups at the same time, even though they might not actually consider themselves to be a member of any particular group. In the same way, our allegiances may change and shift without this registering in a conscious fashion. Numerous typologies of groups are in use, classifying them for example as *membership, affiliation* or *interest, formal* or *informal*. More useful classifications for the study of groups in the workplace examine them on the basis of levels of *skill* and *interaction,* closeness/type of *relationships* and the levels of *control* the group has over factors such as *methods and pace of work,* membership and *adherence to norms.* The various typologies of groups are often used very loosely in the organisational literature and even more so in the HRM literature, which often assumes global effects of group membership which are not always true of all types of group. For example, typologies which give groups as *task* (sometimes *project*), *team and command* (sometimes *technological*) can be interpreted as classifying groups according to the levels of control that the group itself has over the factors given above, task groups having high levels of control and latitude for decision-making, command groups having little or none.

Though the distinction between formal and informal groups is well-rehearsed in the literature, it is false in the sense that even the most rigidly constituted formal groups still have informal processes surrounding the interactions of members both within and without the group, and even loose informal coalitions have their behaviour formally constrained to some extent by the evaluative behavioural standards referred to as norms. In reality, this distinction should be restricted to whether the group has been formally or informally constituted and to who has control over the factors mentioned above. Hollway (1991: 70–1) for example, notes that the focus on the informal group in Mayo's Hawthorne Studies did not lead to practices based on the informal interactions of friendship or social affiliation, but rather to the genesis of the training group, 'temporarily constituted of strangers in isolation and permanently under the control of the trainer' (p. 71). Likewise distinctions based on the closeness and type of relationships in the group, normally given as primary or secondary groups, are again misleading in that the closer, mainly face-to-face interaction of primary groups – such as families, teams or groups of colleagues working on a task – are not of necessity of any more influence on the individual than is the more distant and impersonal secondary group such as a company, union, professional association or a public institution. There are certainly more opportunities for influence to be effective in the primary group, but since secondary groups very often act as reference groups (see McKenna 1994: 314–16), which we use as a source of personal or group standards or as a basis for comparison, they can be significant in determining the social and organisational roles to which we aspire or by which we are constrained. As such, they may have greater effects on our individual norms or values than the groups we presently belong to and may even be a source of conflict between our values and such groups.

Of particular importance within organisations are what Alderfer and Smith (1982) refer to as 'identity groups'. These are a special case of interest groups which can cut across sectional and hierarchical divisions and generally originate outside organisational boundaries, as they are often organisations themselves. Professional associations, pressure groups and most notably unions can come into this category. When they form a significant source of norms and values, they can exert considerable influence on workplace attitudes and behaviour, often in a fashion counter to organisational objectives. It is possible to see much of the culture/HRM movements of recent years as an attempt to undermine the influence of external identity groups and to shift the focus of reference back towards the employing organisation.

In terms of the definition given above, a given collection of people is not immediately a group and the process of group formation and maturation is seen as important in determining the eventual role relationships and the performance effectiveness of the group. The model of group formation most often cited is B. W. Tuckman's (1965), in which four stages of *forming, storming, norming* and *performing* lead to effective teamwork. A fifth stage, *adjourning* was later added to cover temporary groups (1977). This model has been adapted by Wanous *et al.* (see Cherrington, 1989: 390–2) to relate it to Feldman's notions on organisational socialisation as shown in Figure 9.2.

	New Group	→		Mature Group
Developmental Stage	Forming →	Storming →	Norming →	Performing
Group/Role Process	Orientation	Confrontation	Differentiation	Collaboration
Characteristics	Uncertainty Developing relationships	Conflict over power and influence	Shared expectations	Cohesiveness Commitment

Source: based on Robbins (1991: 276–8) and Cherrington (1989: 390–2).

FIGURE 9.2   Group developmernt process

Many groups would actually never reach the stage of the mature, collaborative group and many groups fall apart in the earlier stages. For example, if group cohesion does not develop, then the attractiveness of other social attachments might undermine the commitment of members to the purpose or task of the group. The command group described above has obvious barriers to ever being able to develop into the final stages owing to its formalised communication hierarchy. The way in which new members of organisations (for example, first-year students) form many group attachments before finally settling into a particular friendship group illustrates how competition for particular group roles may lead many prospective members to abandon the group rather than take up a role they are not prepared to play.

The reasons for individuals maintaining group membership are given by Schein (1985, 150–2) as rooted in their socio-psychological 'functions', in that they act to provide: a sense of belonging and identity; affiliation with others; and guidelines for behaviour and as a means for altering the formal structures of an organisation better to suit group members. An example of this is seen in Nichol's and Beynon's (1977) 'Chemco' study, where a formal job rotation system was introduced under a job enrichment programme which only allowed workers to move from one routine job to another. Yet the work-groups had already organised informal job rotation which allowed members to rest whilst others covered for them.

Groups can also be highly effective mechanisms for making out, and directly instrumental for their member's capacity to control the wage–effort bargain, as research such as Burawoy (1979) shows. On the other hand, however, groups also have formal, instrumental functions for organisations as a whole – and by implication for the dominant power groupings within them. In this sense, they are the basis for the distribution of work, the units of monitoring, control and data collection and an integral part of many organisational decision-making processes (Schein, 1985, 149–50). Groups and looser coalitions are also the arenas within which individuals secure identities and management attempts to regulate them. As identity groups, such as trade union, professional or employers' associations, they set the contexts within which individuals and smaller groups compete for power over the structures and processes of organisations and for access to the material and psychic rewards they can supply.

In terms of making out, groups can also be viewed as sites of socialisation and as a major venue of attitudinal change, as indicated by Lewin's (1947) experimental research showing the greater impetus to attitude change in group versus individual techniques. The identity constructs which are of great importance to individual meaning and social definition based on class, race, gender, or religion, are communicated to us through our participation in groups. This occurs through the behaviours and beliefs we internalise. The processes of socialisation through which the appropriate behaviours demanded by organisations are communicated to individuals depend on the operation of intra-group processes. Thus an individual entering an organisation becomes attached – or is assigned – to a particular group, wherein they 'learn the ropes' of how to survive and what is expected of them. As direct influence and hierarchical control is a possible source of threat to identity, it is possible that such moulding into appropriate images could be better pursued through the influence of peers. This can be seen clearly from the examples of use of peer group pressures as a form of social control in Japanese management techniques, discussed in Chapter 6. Similarly, when using the 'sitting with Nellie' approach to job training, companies would be foolish not to ensure that 'Nellie' is someone whose own workplace identity is at least roughly compatible with managerial objectives.

The extent to which we are influenced or affected by the particular groups we belong to is generally seen to be associated with the relative *cohesiveness* of different groups. Cohesiveness is both a function and consequence of the individual's attraction to a group. The motivation to remain a member stems from their subjective expectations concerning the personal, social or material rewards which are to be gained. It is not necessary, however, that we rationally calculate differential attractiveness and the rewards available. We might become members of various groups simply as a result of following appropriate scripts for making out in various social situations. Calculations of advantage and disadvantage may only actually apply when we become self-reflexive about our membership of a particular group. Most of the time we shall probably construct our own identity in line with the identity of the group on the basis that it is appropriate to the behaviours which the group carries out. When a group becomes something to cope with, rather than something that helps us to cope, we may reflect on the possibilities we have of rejecting one group membership for another, or of attempting to redirect the group and thus reconstruct its identity – or if these are not possible, of trying to redefine our own position in the group and thus our own identity within it.

Hosking and Morley (1991: 106–7) cite Janis (1972) on interpersonal versus task-based cohesiveness, which can respectively produce an 'illusion of unanimity' amongst group members and feelings of commitment to task-based norms. High interpersonal cohesiveness may lead to people suppressing personal doubts and bowing to group consensus through self-censorship, and high task-based cohesiveness may lead to selective perception and convergent thinking, especially in conditions where openness of expression is not encouraged. These are the kind of conditions under which Janis's (1972) notion of *Groupthink* occurs, where moral judgement and 'reality testing' are suspended, particularly in the face of high-risk decisions in high-status groups. A good recent example of this is the decision of the Thatcher government to prosecute in the 'Spycatcher' case, where concerns for secrecy and solidarity outweighed the opinion of the rest of the world that they could not win the case. Groupthink is said to be a special case of Moscovici and Zavalloni's (1969) notion of group polarisation, where social comparison processes and persuasive arguments can lead to groups shifting towards higher risk or more caution in decision-making discussions. The dangers of these effects to the efficacy of group decision-making has prompted a great deal of research on methods to avoid them and to make decision-making processes more effective. The techniques evolved include classics such as *brainstorming*, the *'Delphi'* technique, the use of *'devil's advocates'* and even *'dialectical inquiry'* (Sweiger *et al.*, 1986). It would appear that, from the point of view of organisational effectiveness, the interpersonal and political processes taking place in groups can become too powerful and that the decision-making capacities for which they are often employed must be restrained lest they lose sight of the 'common good' of the enterprise.

It seems possible, then, that it is the efforts we make to adapt to the groups we belong to which in the end make organisation and organisations possible, and the strength of group effects which produces the organisational 'need' for regulation and discipline. The consequences for the individual of not adapting to the authority of the group can be in physical or social sanctions, but are most often felt in the anxieties and tensions characteristic of *the* industrial disease of the late twentieth century, *stress*.

Stress: the force to adapt

There's a lot of tension now, and that makes people mean. We had more control before and less confusion. You could get things done. Every once in a while my head starts to throb. I can't take it. (Stock and Bond Transfer assistant cited in Zuboff, 1988: 143)

Managerial work was one of the first areas to be associated with the negative effects of stress, especially through personality traits linked with supposedly high rates of coronary heart disease (Rosenman *et al.*, 1964). These are associated with people with high levels of personal investment in their work, as is expected to be the case with those in managerial grades. Although it has since been established that stress-related illness is more likely to vary inversely rather than positively with organisational status, position and job-related skill (Cooper and Smith, 1985), there is still a great concern with managerial stress and its possible effects on organisational effectiveness.

Stress is an all-pervasive phenomenon the effects of which are detectable from the biological, through the psychological and the interpersonal levels, right up to sociocultural systems of values, knowledge and technology as recognised by C. D. Jenkins (1979). Jenkins' illustrative model identifies the capacities that can help us resist stress, the stimuli or stressors that can lead to a stress reaction the type and form of those reactions and the possible consequences of the stress continuing. It does focus however, as does most stress research, on the negative connotations of stress, such as heart disease and other illnesses. This is even though Selye, a pioneer of stress research, as early as the 1930s identified two main forms of stress, *distress* (often termed *strain*), which is the negative form found in conventional wisdom, and *eustress*; which is healthy, normal stress that leads to positive feelings and possibly to what have been termed 'peak experiences'. These forms of stress are possibly better thought of as positive and negative consequences of what is termed *arousal*, or the level of drive or motivation we put into a task. This notion arose from the work of Yerkes and Dodson (1908, see Fisher, 1986: 94–6) on the relation between drive level and learning ability, the idealised results of which are summarised in Figure 9.3. These results were mainly generated from exposing animals to deprivation or painful stimuli and went on to distinguish two functions of arousal, the *cue* function, which serves to guide behaviour and the *vigilance* function concerned with the amount of energy expended. The continuation of this line of research into the effects of various stimuli on performance has received both confirmatioh and qualification in work on

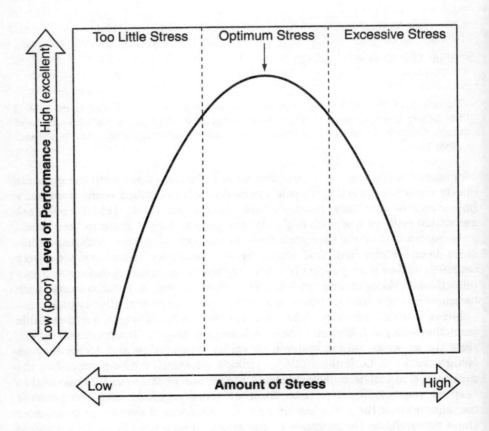

Note: the basic relationship indicated here, one of *diminishing returns*, could also be applied to the relationships between performance and inter-group and intra-group conflict, group cohesiveness and the effect of motivational interventions over time. It is also worth noting that low task performance could be viewed as high performance in task-avoidance!

FIGURE 9.3   Stress and performance

humans using incentives as well as negative stimuli. In general, three dimensions of arousal can be distinguished (Schonpflug, 1983, cited in Fisher, 1986: 109):

- *Arousal* – facilitating performance
- *Interference* – trying to ignore the stimulus
- *Compensatory effort* – putting in extra effort to the task

Thus, from the start, research into what we now term 'stress' has been focused on the facilitation and inhibition of performance, though the definition of stress has been problematic both in terms of whether stress causes illness directly (*aetiological*) or indirectly (*non-aetiological*) and because of the range of stimuli and other factors often cited under the catch-all definition of stress, for example, anxiety, fear, frustration and so on. In 1936 Cannon was the first to make the important link between behavioural changes and physiological responses to stimuli which upset the organism's homeostatic balance of energy provision. In order to avoid or defend against threats, the organism's circulatory, muscular and digestive systems react similarly to what is commonly termed a 'fight or flight response'. Heart and respiration rates increase, blood supplies to the skin and intestines are reduced while that to the muscles is increased, hormones such as adrenaline are released which both heighten arousal and promote the increased uptake of blood sugars to meet energy demands. However, it was Selye in 1956 who really promoted what we now know as stress-related illness in his identification of stress as 'the body's non-specific response to *any* demand that is placed on it, whether that demand is pleasant or not' (from an interview with Selye in Cherry, 1978: 60). Selye had been working since the 1930s on physiological stress in terms of his '*General Adaptation Syndrome*' which identified three phases in the body's response to stressors. The first phase, the *alarm response*, is where a stressor is perceived and the physiological responses given above take place. The *resistance phase* is where the organism adapts to the particular stressor, though at the same time becoming less resistant to other stressors. The final phase, exhaustion, is where the symptoms of stress-related illness (or the 'pathological end-state' in the Jenkins model above) develop when prolonged exposure or overload means that adaptation or resistance could not be maintained (see Selye in Clark *et al.*, 1994: 398). The problem for the organism here is that the stress response is both cumulative and additive, small stresses or prolonged low-level stress adding up to a larger effect and different stressors adding to the overall level of stress. The classic relation of stress to heart disease can now be understood in relation to long-term increases in heart rate and blood pressure and likewise the proneness when under stress to other illnesses such as bacteriological and viral infections by the long-term depression of the body's immune responses. Indeed, this model has been used to explain a multitude of phenomena from 'cold spots' in haunted houses (reduced bloodflow to the skin when something scares us) to 'butterflies in the stomach' when apprehensive or in love (reduced bloodflow to and contraction of the intestines).

Selye was attempting to distinguish the aetiological, causative factors in the stress reaction from the generalised responses, though Beech *et al.* (1982: 10) notes that this has not been followed up by most researchers, who refer to both causes and responses as stress, further adding to the confusion as to what stress actually is. Similarly, the distinction between eustress and distress is not followed up greatly in the modern stress literature, even though it provides the basis for the most important element of most contemporary models of stress and techniques for stress 'management'. This is that the outcome of the stress response in positive or negative terms is linked to the cognitive perception, interpretation and attribution of the stressors concerned. What one person perceives as stressful may be pleasurable to another we may change our interpretation of a stressor from something that causes us distress to something we might perhaps look upon as a challenge, or we might react differently to a stressor depending on our locus of control and on whether we attribute its cause internally or environmentally.

This cognitive aspect of stress is most commonly identified with the 'cognitive appraisal' approach of Lazarus (1966), who emphasised these aspects over the previous medical and physiological approach. However, Lazarus – like Cannon acknowledged that stress was a result of person–environment interactions and it was this factor which led to possibly the most popular modern approach to stress, promoted by the social psychologists Katz and Kahn (1966). This examines stress as a question of 'person–environment fit'. For Lazarus, individual differences in cognitive appraisal of what is stressful are accompanied by differing psychological strategies or approaches to how we cope with stress: *problem-focused coping* concerns trying to alleviate or manage the stressor, whereas *emotion-focused coping* concerns try to manage our internal responses to the stressor. These two categories of response describe almost the full range of modern approaches to managing stress, the question for most organisations being the cost-effectiveness of the approach. For Katz and Kahn psychological stress in social situations was linked to how well a person's skills and abilities matched the expectations of their social roles. Where the demands of a role or roles are unclear and norms and standards of social comparison are lacking, people may experience *role ambiguity*; and where competing role expectations for example, those that play a part in determining an individual's intra-organisational; and extra-organisational roles – cannot be fulfilled, we come into *role conflict*. Such pressures may also originate in *role overload* or *underload*, where the demands of a role are greater or lesser than expected. Role conflicts generally exist between differing expectations from the various parts of a person's *role-set* – those persons and groups who expect things of us – and are inevitable with the level of pressure that most of us are exposed to in or out of work since a person cannot always fulfil the demands of all their roles. In addition, we may experience role conflicts between external role demands and personal values and beliefs; or between a person's gender, ethnic or skilled identity and their treatment by other workers or by management.

The aforementioned links between stressors, attribution and locus of control can be illustrated by reference to the work of Winefield *et al.* (in Blau *et al.*, 1993) on unemployment in young adults, who, when compared to employed adolescents had lower self-esteem more likelihood of being depressed and having negative moods; and were more likely to have a high external locus of control. The attribution of the cause of their unemployment had a mediating effect, however – those who attributed it to environmental factors such as bad luck had higher self-esteem and fewer feelings of helplessness than those who gave internal attributions such as lack of ability (see Blau *et al.* 1993: 147). It would appear that where stressors are perceived as having internal causes this can bring about a form of self-fulfilling prophecy that can in itself add to the level of stress we feel, which is simply the other side of the coin to the situation where success and overcoming stressful situations can lead us to believe that we can achieve anything at all.

When specifically regarding stress in the work place, contemporary accounts of the stress 'process' often follow this notion of stress as 'resulting from a misfit between an individual and their particular environment' (Arnold *et al.*, 1991: 285) where internal or external factors push the individuals adaptive capacities beyond his or her limit. This view has been widely popularised by Cooper and his many co-workers who have found confirmation for their general model in studies covering a wide range of occupations and organisations. The model proposed by Cummings and Cooper (1979), a 'Cybernetic Framework for the Study of Occupational Stress', reprised many elements of the homeostatic medical model proposed by Cannon, as can be seen from the summary below.

- People attempt to keep their thoughts, emotions and relationships in a homeostatic balance or 'steady state'.
- For any individual the various elements of his or her physical and emotional make-up will have a balance, with which he or she is comfortable or a 'range of stability'.
- Stressors are forces which push physical or psychological factors beyond their range of stability, producing strain and provoking behaviour which attempts to restore the balance or feeling of comfort.
- The various behaviours individuals use to maintain their state of balance constitute their 'coping strategies' or 'adjustment process'.
- Knowing that a stress might occur constitutes a threat to the individual and threat can itself produce strain. (See Arnold *et al.*, 1991: ch. 16)

Derivations of this model, typologies of sources of stressors and the forms of pathological end-state to be encountered, as seen in the Jenkins model above, account for much of the modern stress literature. This tends to emphasise the amount of productivity lost due to stress, its inevitability and the benefits for the enterprise of managing stress. Costs are examined socially in terms of rates of heart disease, mental disorder and social dysfunction and in the workplace through effects on job satisfaction, performance and absenteeism rates; and more recently in the costs of compensation claims and health insurance (see Arnold *et al.* 1991: 287–91). Estimates vary on the cost of stress-related illness to industry, but figures in excess of 40 million lost working days (Lucas, 1986) have led to an increasing concern with organisational programmes to help individuals to cope with work-related stress, as well as conflicts between work and home life. Examples of these 'wellness' programmes include Pepsico's multi-million dollar 'fitness' centre, and the stress management programmes developed by the Trustee Savings Bank and Digital Equipment in the UK (C. L. Cooper, 1984). The 'Staywell' programme and Employee Advisory Resource of the Control Data Corporation in the USA, offered 24-hour advice on assessing health risks, medical screening and health education to help people to change life and work styles in healthy directions (Lucas, 1986; McKenna, 1994: 616). 'Companies have a major stake in promoting a healthier life style for employees, because of the potential benefits in reduced insurance costs, decreased absenteeism, improved productivity and better morale' (McKenna, 1987: 403).

In contrast to this view, the Labour Research Department (1988: 2) concluded that 'only a minority of organisations are tackling the problem directly' and that the main effort is towards management rather than prevention:

> Where they exist management 'stress control' programmes peddle individual victim-blaming approaches to stress problems that in reality can only be solved by changing workplace organisation and relations. (Labour Research Department, 1988: 2)

This individualisation of organisational problems as personal pathological reactions is effectively demonstrated by the use of stress inventories in the diagnosis and 'treatment' of stress. Such inventories commonly rely on identifying the extent to which the individual fits the 'Type A' behavioural pattern which Rosenman *et al.* (1964) labelled *coronary prone behaviour* due to the correlation with increased rates of coronary heart disease. The traits associated with Type A behaviour include achievement orientation, status insecurity, time urgency, competitiveness and aggression, traits which are often erroneously associated with managerial or leadership ability. The inventories themselves are problematic – as indicated by Selye, who claimed that 'all stress inventories in common use are somewhat flawed because they fail to give enough weight to individual differences' (Selye, in Cherry, 1978: 63). It is likely, however, that the mere use of a stress inventory does serve to educate and inform the respondent as to the nature of their problems. In the main, attempts to modify Type A behaviour tend not to concentrate on relieving the source of the strain but on modifying behaviour through goal-setting and time-management techniques, so that the stress is in effect being actively managed though personal self-control. The result of this is a reduction of the strain felt by the individual into a managerial control variable determining fitness to the required organisational role.

This is further demonstrated by the differential focus on coping in mainstream accounts. Again, the emphasis is not on dealing directly with the problem but with emotion-focused coping and what is termed *cross resistance*. This notion that increasing adaptive capacities in one area (for example, health and fitness) will increase resistance to other stressors, is the foundation of corporate wellness programmes. Emotion-focused coping is seen mainly in the popularity of relaxation training and indirectly in what is possibly the most common corporate response to stress, counselling. Relaxation training, and its derivatives including meditation and biofeedback techniques, are individual-centred techniques using exercises to reduce muscle tension and reduce stress through improved relaxation and identification of stress symptoms. Murphy and Sorenson (1988) in a quasi-experimental study of highway maintenance workers who were given either relaxation or biofeedback training, found that although the workers felt better both physiologically and mentally, the expected improvements in absenteeism and productivity were not manifested. What they did conclude, however, was that:

> Stress management may be most useful as an adjunct to organisational change interventions for example, increased participation in decision-making, improved worker autonomy, task identity and feedback and implementation of flexible work schedules. (Murphy and Sorenson, 1988: 181)

Counselling is an even less direct approach to stress, and at its best is effected by '*cognitive redefinition*' of the 'problem', much in the same way that psychoanalysis requires the patient to redefine their identity and world-view within a framework which makes their difficulties understandable. However, this kind of technique, like the 'talking cure' of psychoanalysis, would be expected to work best with long-term chronic problems and would not be cost effective on a large scale due to the intense, one-to-one relationship required. At its worst, employee counselling consists of a short interview, often with a hired-in consultant, and in response to episodic or acute problems which cannot be actually solved in this fashion beyond putting the problem into the context of 'organisational reality', as in, 'you need to pull your socks up or you'll be in trouble'. There is nothing new here, of course. Baritz' interpretation of the Hawthorne research points out that the outcomes of the research on employee counselling led some to the conclusion that, 'workers did not have compelling objective problems' (1960: 201). The rationale for this, according to a counsellor cited by Baritz, was that their grievances could be dealt with by allowing them to 'talk them out':

> It may not be even necessary to take any action on them. All that they require is a patient and courteous hearing, supplemented when necessary by an explanation of why nothing can be done. . . . It is not always necessary to yield to the worker's requests in order to satisfy them. (p. 201)

It is the ability of this form of counselling to address (albeit on a superficial level) individual differences and subjectivity which makes it highly cost effective in the stress management stakes, with the added benefit that it again persuades individuals that it is *their* problem. However, it is unlikely actually to remove the source of the strain experienced and does not necessarily increase adaptive capacities. The role of the organisation in producing unhealthy systems and conditions of work is in danger of being ignored. In its place we get systems reinforcing the self-attribution of stress and anxiety as personal problems to be coped with rather than structural issues to be contested.

To deal directly with stress requires problem-focused coping, where individuals or groups might actively design their own working environments and methods, negotiate their own roles or acquire new capacities. Such an approach, though highly effective in managing stress, would necessitate the vertical integration of control over work design and costs and is consequently not highly popular. Where external experts are brought in to initiate similar programmes – which may still have more wide-ranging effects than approaches based on emotion-focused coping – costs would still be as high as with job redesign, and the likelihood of being able to deal adequately with individual differences, such as with home/work conflicts, would be low. They would also work less well with situational stress factors such as role conflicts, as these are in general less directly identifiable as consequences of the organisation of work than are environmental stress factors (noise, chemicals or working with VDUs). This is precisely because they are attributed to an individual's incapacity to cope with the demands of work. The work of nurses and social workers provides a good example of organisations exploiting a person's ability to cope with untenable situations to the limit and only becoming concerned when the rate of turnover or lack of efficiency of skilled staff becomes difficult to manage.

In contrast to the stress management techniques outlined above, the Labour Research Department offered guidelines for dealing with stress on a collective basis, urging union members to research stress-related workplace issues that could be negotiated with management and to communicate results to all members and appropriate officers and institutions. The negotiation strategy itself gave the following advice:

- Concentrate on one, preferably winnable, stress issue to gain confidence. . .
- Do not be afraid to consider a long term strategy. . .
- Don't think of stress in isolation from other workplace hazards and issues. . .
  (Labour Research Department, 1988: 22)

Such collective attempts to alter conditions for the individual and the organisation are in direct contrast to the individual-centred methods that invoke the 'psychological fallacy' that 'since the organisation is made of individuals, we can change the organisation by changing its members' (Katz and Kahn, [2nd edn] 1978: 391). The LRD approach again highlights stress as an issue of workplace control – not only of job performance, but of personal lifestyle in support of this. Commentators such as Steele and also Handy support this view in relation to worker assistance and health programmes, while Orlans notes that counselling often only deals with problems at the individual level (see Wheeler and Lyon, 1992: 48–9). For models of stress which go beyond individual-level approaches and account for perceived levels of control, we need to go to work such as that of Karasek and Theorell (1990) or Fisher (1986). Karasek links job strain to dimensions of *demand* from the situation and the level of control, autonomy or *jurisdiction discretion* available to the individual in the workplace. High job demands and loads can be perceived positively in situations of high control, but where control is low, high demand is associated with strain and that in hierarchical, authoritarian conditions the best available coping response may be the reduction of effort (see Fisher, 1986: 157–7, 238). Karasek and Theorell (1990) also give evidence that low levels of social support may exacerbate the relationship between high demands and low control. Wheeler and Lyon (1992: 47) note that Karasek's approach, 'effectively recognises the relationship between the subjective experience of stress and the social conditions which may give rise to it'. Fisher takes this a step further in examining coping responses to stressful conditions as strategic responses, the range of which are constrained by life experiences and personal style. The implications of this trend in research are that not only are work and organisational designs significant sources of strain but they may also limit our adaptive capacities to cope with it.

In studying stress at work we must not however forget the person who feels the emotions and strain produced. Fineman claims that though organisations can be seen as 'emotional arenas', the persons within them are presented as 'emotionally anorexic', their emotions reduced to managerial control variables, 'the feelings of *being* organised, *doing* work and organising are hard to detect' (1993: 9). At the same time, he asserts that stress has 'come out' as an issue, in that counselling is at least provided by some and also to the extent that their is a tacit acknowledgement that 'being sick or off work for reasons of stress is acceptable – up to a point' (1993: 219).

If the negative consequences of stress are our body's way of telling us to slow down, then stress management is the organisation's way of telling us to keep up. Just as health and safety legislation recognises the concept of 'contributory negligence', stress management communicates the nature of power relations in the work place by bringing home to us our negligence in not being 'fit for work'. This represents the exercise of power through the medium of the very phenomenon which is often diagnosed as the source of many organisational problems, *communication*.

The power to communicate

Earlier we noted that perception and attribution processes can systematically determine or alter people's interpretation of events and others and the attitudes they develop. Our understanding of this in the social world and the workplace is based mainly on the concomitant effects on the communication process – effectively, the way we send and receive messages to each other. Such messages can be exchanged between individuals or groups and can convey information, ideas or feelings. The problems that can occur and the means of developing more effective communications have been a major element of the development of the techniques through which the knowledge-base of OB is applied in pursuit of organisational effectiveness. At its most basic this relationship can be seen in the effects of the amounts and complexity of information being transmitted or *communication load* (Gibson and Hodgetts, 1986). Both individuals and groups can be seen to undergo conditions of underload, overload or appropriate communication loading. These conditions are moderated by personal variables such as the ability and desire to communicate and organisational variables such as levels of co-ordination, physical proximity, routineness of tasks and constraints based on time and the number and quality of decisions to be made. Appropriate loading is seen to enhance motivation and productivity, underload to lead to alienation, apathy and demotivation and overload to increase stress, uncertainty and the tendency to make mistakes.

The study of communication in organisations traditionally examines the processes and flow of communications through channels and networks and the content, sources and nature of messages sent, these last being particularly relevant to the study of persuasive communications. The variables involved in the basic interpersonal communication process are given in Figure 9.4 and the level of variability possible at each stage makes it surprising that any successful communication happens at all. The characteristics of senders and receivers, coding, transmission and decoding systems are further complicated by the directions of flow and the levels of formality of the communications as well as the various kinds of 'noise' that can interfere with communications at any time.

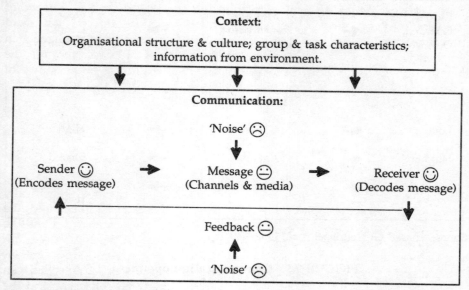

Source: based on Fisher, 1993: 6–21.

FIGURE 9.4   Context and the communication process

Such a model of communication has its drawbacks, in that it tends to view communication as a step-by-step rather than a simultaneous process and consequently tends to ignore the interpersonal dynamics of communication. This type of model needs to be augmented by sensitivity to the perceptions of the sender and recipient as well as the overall social and organisational contexts that give rise to the shared meanings that allow communication to take place. The perceived status, competence and intentions of the sender and, for the receiver, the various factors that we earlier identified as possibly distorting perceptions (for example, halo effects, projection and so on.) need to be accounted for. Notions of shared meaning relate precisely to Schein's (1985) model of organisational culture, in that shared assumptions, beliefs and rituals constrain the communication patterns of organisational members – especially where cultural beliefs are embedded in notions of openness or those of formality. Conditions of openness and informality may reinforce open debate, rapid and effective communication and loyalty, but at the same time may increase interpersonal conflict and reduce the ability to set and maintain goals and schedules. In conditions of formality and closed, hierarchical communication, debate and conflict may be lessened along with the ability to express new ideas, communications will be more precise and deliberate, and policies and standards easier to formulate and monitor.

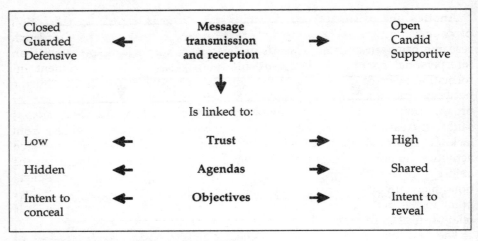

Source: based on Hellriegel et al., 1992: 440.

FIGURE 9.5   Communication openness

The assumptions and inferences made by senders and receivers in conditions of open versus closed communication have been analysed by Sussman (1991) in terms of the variables given in Figure 9.5. As the extremes of the closed condition are approached, the level of *meta-communication* would be said to increase so that all messages would be scrutinised for the hidden agendas and meanings they might convey. At such a level the interpersonal politics of linguistic gameplaying might become of greater importance than the overt content of the communications themselves. This in turn links the study of communication directly into debates on the dimensions of power in organisations, which can be seen in Kirkbride's discussion of power in the employment relationship (in Hartley and Stephenson, 1992: 77). In this, Kirkbride cites various sources to illustrate the point that the use of rhetoric and argument is part of the 'tactical dimension' of power by which meaning is manipulated both in the pursuit of legitimising control mechanisms and in underwriting political resistance. In particular, he cites Czarniawska-Joerges and Joerges, who examine 'organisational talk' as a form of 'unobtrusive control', in which linguistic devices in the form of labels, metaphors and platitudes can, 'enable [management] to manage meaning by explaining, colouring and familiarising, as opposed to the traditional methods of commanding, fighting and punishing' (1992: 77). The aspects of communication involved here are well summarised in Hosking and Morley (1991: 30, citing De Cindio *et al.*, 1988) as *pragmatic* (conversing on commitments to actions), *structuring* (conversing on commitments to roles and co-ordination) and *semantic* (conversing on meanings of words).

Another link between communication and power is in the oft-cited notion of communication as the 'energy' of an organisational system and much research has been directed towards understanding organisational rather than interpersonal communication, particularly in relation to Management Information Systems (MIS). Saunders (1981) has proposed a theoretical linkage between the use of MIS, communication and the relative power of organisational departments or groupings. The use of MIS in critical tasks is said to increase power by their ability to decrease *uncertainty* stemming from lack of information, to increase *non-substitutability* (the extent to which activities cannot be carried out by some other group) and to increase the ability to cope with higher levels of *pervasiveness* (the number of communication links with other departments). Though largely untested, this model does point to the importance of communications in maintaining power and role relationships in increasingly complex organisational structures.

The relation of managerial roles to communication has been seen as intimately associated with systems of shared and – more often than not – informal meanings. In her powerful study of computerisation in the workplace Zuboff (1988: 101–2) traces this relation back to Chester Barnard in the 1930s, who characterised organised communication in terms of the *means*, (that is, the people involved), and the *system* (that is, the positions they hold). From this Zuboff argues that managerial executives are responsible for communicating their 'action context' from their own particular facet of the organisation to other executives and 'so contributing to a shared sense of the whole' (p. 102). Such a 'sharing' demands a high degree of informal and face-to-face contact and for Barnard this requirement underwrote the notion that regardless of formal competencies the selection and promotion of executives was driven by the interpersonal politics of whether a candidate would 'fit' into the community with which they must perforce interact. Zuboff's analysis of the computerisation of managerial information/control systems appears to indicate that managers, in becoming dependant on these systems, may become insulated from 'organisational realities' outside their own networks and community of interest. Through this they might actually become less adept at the reciprocal communicative relationships they need to maintain up and down the organisation for effective control. She argues that not only do workers face new demands from new technologies, but that:

> Managers also are likely to face new communicative demands – for sharing interpretations, problem-solving, and making sense of complex and interdependent forms of data about people and events. (1988: 361)

Perhaps the most enduring view of research into, and managerial use of, communication comes once again from Whyte in 'The Organisation Man' (1957: 94). Whyte was so unconvinced by the state of knowledge on communication at the time that he argued that, 'it has no business whatsoever as a basic undergraduate discipline'. Notwithstanding the many subsequent advances in the area, his remarks on the 'technicians' who 'mentor' this process still ring true today:

> Many of these people don't even *like* the language. They torture it with charts, they twist it with equations and they have so little respect for the devices they recommend as the avenue to the masses that they never demean themselves with their use. Rarely has brevity been advocated so interminably.

Those most dependant on the power of communication are perhaps those who need to convince us that their construction of reality is somehow more powerful than our own. All managers need to do this to some extent and the most successful are those who appear to be able to achieve this through the exercise of the mysterious power known as *leadership*.

Leadership: might or myth

Leadership is defined by Buchanan and Huczynsci (1985: 389) as, 'a social process in which one individual influences the behaviour of others without the use or threat of violence'. Explanation in this area has focused on personality traits, styles of leadership and more recently on situation-contingent styles and the relations between leaders and group members. Although it is assumed that the threat of violence is not commonly relied upon nowadays to maintain positions of leadership, the continuing use of threats to, and sanctions on, financial and job security in organisations means that the 'social process' of leadership must be understood in its intimate relationship with the exercise of power (and possibly in the continued existence of bullying, sweatshops and slave labour). According to Fiedler (1976: 108), 'the acid test of leadership theory must be in its ability to improve organisational performance'. The study of leadership is then directly related to the improvement of management control strategies and to the refinement of the tactical options open to managers in the day-to-day practice of regulating workplace behaviour: for instance, the notion that various *'leadership styles'* can be adopted by managers in dealing with problems and subordinates in differing situations. In addition, leadership also serves as an almost perfect exemplar of how behavioural theory is incorporated into managerial discourse only up to the point where it becomes too complex for easy assimilation into ideology and practice, with the consequence that the managerial literature then tends to fall back on prescriptive generalities based on theory and research that has been long discredited or overtaken.

Katz and Kahn (1978 [2nd edn]) refer to leadership in terms of three sets of meanings which are often used simultaneously: first, there are the attributes of the occupancy of a position in a social structure, secondly the qualities or characteristics of a particular person; and lastly, the categories of behaviour associated with a particular person. Occupancy of position essentially refers to the position power of a person in an organisational hierarchy – regardless of their characteristics, soldiers are to obey officers, no matter who and what they are like. Characteristics and behaviours associate particular qualities with individuals in terms of their recognition as a leader by a particular group – thus an officer may have the power to lead but not be recognised as a leader.

The historical study of leadership tended to focus on the habits, sayings and characteristics of those recognised as great leaders, hence the 'Great Man' notion of leadership that is also referred to as the *Zeitgeist* (literally: 'Spirit of the Age') theory. According to this notion, leaders were born to lead and would rise to power and influence like the cream on the milk, or the scum on the pond, depending on whether you were a follower or a victim of their cause. People could 'rise from the ranks' if they had the necessary qualities, but of course this view did tend to favour those already in positions of social dominance in that they would be better fed, housed, educated and have access to resources and social networks unavailable to others. However, the search for what leaders had in common only managed to establish the range of variation possible in leaders, from the short balding French Emperor to the handsome, gay Macedonian one.

The failure of the search for common physical characteristics led to an effort to find common psychological factors in the 'trait approach'. The idea that particular traits can predict leadership ability and that leaders can be selected still holds fast in conventional wisdom, though in effect all this approach did was further to establish the wide range of possible characteristics that leaders can have. Stodgill's (1974) review of research on traits did not bring up any reliable correlations between leadership ability and particular traits and found that traits in general were ambiguous and ill-defined, a good contemporary example being the so-called 'helicopter ability' (Handy, 1980: 109) which is taken as the ability to 'rise above the situation and see the big picture'. Where we still see lists of leadership traits in the managerial literature their most abiding feature is that they are generally more representative of those traits thought to be stereotypically male, such as dominance, aggressiveness and rationality, rather than traits stereotypically associated with women such as passivity, nurturance and emotionality. Apart from this being largely unsurprising, it emphasises the point that leadership qualities can function as legitimising ideological support for the notion that it is the duty and obligation of the manager/leader to direct those not blessed by access to their particular sources of power. When viewed through the kind of assumptions made by managers in McGregor's 'Theory X' and the managerial control imperative of Scientific Management, the continuing popularity of this largely discredited approach is completely understandable. Indeed Selznick identi-fied leadership as partly founded on 'morally sustaining ideas' (1957) and 'socially integrating myths' (1957). The former mobilise support for the notions of compromise and restraint which underpin management's search for meaning and security. The latter are the superordinate goals which leaders appeal to in order to unite organisational members behind managerial strategies. Lately, fashionable 'Japanese' management styles (discussed in Chapter 6) can work to lock both managers and workers into appearing to make the organisation successful for the good of all. This is manifested in the single-status canteens and dress and the work-group discussion circles that channel perceptions of the organisation towards superordinate goals. In the end, possibly the most interesting evidence from the trait line of research were the somewhat disconfirmative findings on the acceptability of leaders to group members which appear to show that groups prefer high-status members as leaders and that the characteristics of followers determine the acceptability of leadership characteristics (Stodgill, 1974: 208–14). The most predictive factors in the characteristics of any given leader would then be their apparent status and the values, interests and personalities of their followers. What is indicated here is that leadership is a relationship with a group of followers or subordinates, a role and not a set of characteristics.

The work of Likert at Michigan, and more significantly Stodgill's work at Ohio State, opened up the possibility that rather than just selecting people with leadership traits, leaders could be trained and developed in the form and style of their behaviours and relationships with their group of followers or subordinates. The Michigan work followed on from the work of Lewin *et al.* (1939) which related three styles of leadership to the emotional climate and hence the assumed effectiveness of work groups. This followed in the trait tradition, in that the styles are assumed to be universal traits or at least enduring attributes. Of the first two of these styles, *autocratic* leadership continues the tradition of strong personal direction and control, and rule-bound relationships, while *democratic* leadership is less regulatory and emphasises collaboration and responsive relationships. This last style can be firmly linked to the Human Relations tradition in OB and begins to shift the view of leadership away from duty and direction towards responsibility and co-ordination, the managerial assumptions perhaps best exemplified in McGregor's Theory Y and Human Relations in general (though interestingly Stodgill, 1974: 365, relates Theory Y more closely to the permissive, *laissez-faire* style). This third style, *laissez-faire* leadership, did not provoke as much research effort as the first two – which can be easily understood, as it is often described as a style in which the leader fails to accept the responsibilities of the position.

The Ohio work stepped away from the trait approach in that it focused on describing leader behaviour which was open to modification and not an attribute of a person. Two specific forms of behaviour were identified, *initiating structure*, aimed at defining roles, patterns of communication, organisation and action; and *consideration*, aimed at developing working relationships, trust and respect. The only essential difference between these and the autocratic and democratic styles was that any given leader could rate high or low on either or both forms of behaviour. Overall, these bodies of work did lead to research and training programmes aimed at changing the leadership climates of organisations and the behaviour of leaders, climate being found to have more enduring effects on behaviour than training, and assumptions about managerial behaviour shifting for a time towards the notion that it was the duty of managers to co-ordinate rather than direct effort. Other work, such as that of Vroom and Mann (1960), found that style preferences depended more on the situation, autocratic styles being preferred where objectives centre around task accomplishment. Further developments in this direction appeared to show that autocratic styles were more acceptable in stressful or crisis situations, where the speed of decision-making may be more important than the quality of the decision. Stodgill's impressive 1974 review and summary of these approaches (pp. 403–7) concluded that 'In view of the complexity of leader behaviour and the variety of situations in which it functions, a conditional and multivariate hypothesis seems more reasonable than a simplistic, bipolar view of the leader–follower relationship' (p. 407), and that in general no one form of leadership could be guaranteed to produce increases in group productivity.

The notion that leadership is a role performed in a group context can be related to work such as that of Benne and Sheats (1948) on group roles, B. W. Tuckman (1965) on group formation, Bavelas (1950) and Leavitt (1951) on communication networks and Bales (1950) on the interaction analysis of group performance. Though these bodies of work tend to suffer criticisms stemming from the artificiality of their methods, a synthesis of their general principles rather than their detailed prescriptions can provide useful insights into the processes by which leaders may emerge from newly formed groups, especially when related to the often disregarded notion of leadership 'acts'. Leadership in this sense could be seen as a series of acts or behaviours which could be performed by any member of a group regardless of status and power. Acts would tend to fall into two major categories, as in Bales' group functions or Benne and Sheats group roles – task maintenance and group maintenance. The first of these relates to preventing irrelevant behaviour, overcoming goal barriers and rewarding performance; and the second to defusing tensions, offering support and encouraging and rewarding participation. The consistent and competent performance of acts in these categories would increase the likelihood of a particular individual emerging as a leader of a task or group-orientated nature as they internalise the success of their actions.

The performance of leadership acts within the arena of group formation could be seen as an input to Tuckman's process of role differentiation in the group (see above) and similarly as a mechanism by which members come to have differential access and control to communication networks. In this sense, an emerging leader would be the group member who most consistently performs leadership acts in the forming stage and influences the setting of interaction patterns in the group in the norming stage. From the development of Bales' work we also get the notion that a group may effectively have two leaders, as both task and group maintenance roles are necessary to group functioning, so that even where a formal leader is appointed to a group, an informal and subsidiary leadership role or 'second in command' may emerge, which would be occupied by the member who most consistently performs leadership acts of the opposite type to the formal leader (in this case most probably the group maintenance or socio-emotional role). Another strand of often ignored work which can add to this synthesis is Hollander's (1964; see also Katz, 1982) notion of *idiosyncrasy credit*, where a leader through consistent compliance with the norms and expectations of a group (and consistent performance of leadership acts?) gains 'credits' from the group which subsequently permits the leader to deviate from group norms. This is a simple concept with great explanatory power which again views leadership as a specifically group-orientated role, but a role which allows the leader to act outside of the normal social and task maintenance processes of the group in order to serve its interests. A leader may have to represent the group outside its own context or bring demands to the group which do not fit norms or expectations, and as such the ability to act idiosyncratically and innovatively may be of benefit to the group as a a whole. The implications of this concept could be extended to include the acceptability of leadership behaviours such as the selective reward and punishment of group members. So long as they have credit with the group, the leader can act in a manner which might not be acceptable from other members. When a leader is seen to act incompetently or deviates too far from group norms, 'credit' may pass to the member performing the subsidiary leadership role and shift the power relations in the group.

Many other elements could be added to a synthesis of the kind introduced above, which though grossly overgeneralised does highlight the notion that leadership is a process in which power, influence and role definitions are conferred on or competed for by group members in the mundane performance of tasks and getting on with others. A major fault of such a synthesis is that it cannot easily account for situational and contextual variables, and in considering these factors alongside leader behaviour, leadership theory moved towards *contingency models*, best exemplified in Fiedler's (1967) Theory of Leadership Effectiveness. This was based on his use of his Least-Preferred Co-worker Scale (LPC) with real-world groups of many kinds from bomber crews to basketball teams. Leaders were asked to rate their most and least preferred co-workers (MPC and LPC), those rating them similarly were designated 'high LPC' and found to be less controlling and more group orientated, those rating LPC's more negatively were designated 'low LPC' and tended to be more autocratic and task-centred (for a discussion of this see

McKenna, 1994; C. Smith, 1991). Leadership effectiveness was seen as dependant on *situational favourableness*, which was in turn contingent on levels of task structure(the more structured, defined and routine, the more favourable), leader–member relations (the more trust and liking for the leader the more favourable) and the leader's position power (the more power to coerce, reward and punish, the more favourable). Of these factors, leader–member relations were assumed to be the most significant and in situations of mixed favourableness the high LPC, employee-centred leader was found to be most effective. In very favourable or very unfavourable situations the low LPC, task-centred leader was more effective. Additionally, Fiedler also noted that groups might tend to have more than one leader and that in stable or mature groups structures the best combination might be a low LPC leader, with a high LPC second-in-command.

Though many studies have cast Fiedler's conclusions into doubt, the model does sit well with the notions that democratic leaders are preferred in most situations and that autocratic leaders will be more acceptable in crisis situations. What is less understandable in Fiedler's model is why the autocratic leader should be more effective in highly favourable situations. However, the notion that a leader's behaviour could be adjusted to fit the situation or that conditions could be adjusted to fit the leader remains a powerful influence in the field of study, offering as it does the idea that leadership is a variable that can be manipulated to achieve organisational objectives. Other models which extend the themes of situational and behavioural contingency are those of House and Mitchell (1974) and Vroom and Yetton (1973), which both bring in factors relating to the acceptability of leaders by subordinates. House's Path–Goal Model is termed a transactional theory as it considers the balance of exchange between leaders and followers, accounting for follower attitudes and expectations. It gives four dimensions of leadership behaviour which subdivide the traditional autocratic–democratic split into directive, achievement-orientated, supportive, and participative. Vroom and Yetton's model extends the notion of leader–member relations to consider the quality of leader decisions and the information and skill requirements of subordinates. They give four styles, similar to those of House: autocratic, delegative, group dominated and consultative. The achievement-orientated and delegative styles could offer a partial explanation of Fiedler's finding that autocratic leaders could be more effective in highly favourable situations, in that a mature, effective and cohesive group might prefer a leader who simply sets goals or delegates tasks and leaves them to get on with it. This form of leadership might represent the return of the *laissez-faire* leader to the extent that it is exemplified in the 'hands-off' approach often used with high-skill or status groups such as research and design teams.

The Vroom and Yetton model is known as a 'normative' or 'prescriptive' model in that it specifies leader behaviours further than the four basic styles and links these to decision-making approaches to be used in relation to a range of individual or group problems and situations. The decision-tree methodology used to decide which approach is the most appropriate is still in use as a heuristic to explain how decisions might be reached, but has less practical applicability in that it is complex to use because the variables are difficult to map on to real situations and produce few non-obvious results. The increasing complexity of leadership theory and research was recognised in Stodgill's conclusions to his 1974 review (411–29), where he noted that directions for future research would best be pursued under a conditional or contingency model, but warned that studies would have to account for interactions between more than thirty variables summarised below:

1. *Leader and follower characteristics*
   - Background (race, nationality and economic condition)
   - Identification (age, sex, physique and appearance)
   - Status (responsibility, authority and power)
   - Personality and behaviour
   - Expectations and values
   - Norm conformity and reference group identification
2. *Group characteristics*
   - Size and structure
   - Composition and homogeneity of membership
   - Task nature, difficulty, complexity and time constraints
3. *Outcome criteria*
   - Follower satisfaction and acceptance of leader
   - Group productivity, motivation and cohesiveness

If we add to the above intervening variables derived from context, structural factors and interaction processes, leadership becomes less of a unitary, predictable phenomenon and closer to Selznick's 'socially integrating myth', in that the multiplicity of variables involved has meant that numerous strands of research have been sidelined in mainstream OB in favour of more prescriptive models which link leadership to organisational development and change. Good examples of these are Adair's functional model of 'Action-Centred Leadership' (1979) and McGregor Burns 'Transformational Leadership'. Adair's model focuses on developing leader's awareness, understanding and skills in order effectively to perform and integrate the functions required by the task, team maintenance and individual needs of the group. Leadership here resides in the function and not in the person, and so is close to the notions of role-based leadership discussed earlier. However, the conception of group processes is not developmental and the model mainly deals with how formally appointed managers can be trained to be reflexive about how their behaviour affects group commitment and goals. Adair's model embodies some elements of transactional leadership and in its emphasis on achieving change can be linked to Burns' model, which highlights the leader's need to transform their followers through a focus on their intrinsic or higher-order needs rather than on a particular style. This is essentially a form of motivational 'consciousness raising' which attempts to highlight for the individual how they can satisfy their needs and desires through commitment to group (and of course managerial) goals. Though presented as being where 'leaders and followers raise each other to higher levels of morality and motivation' (1978: 20) it is effectively a group-based behavioural technology for turning self-gratification into a superordinate goal. It is unsurprising that this technique enjoyed great popularity in the 1980s, and indeed both this and Adair's model have served as the basis for numerous leadership initiatives in the area of organisational and managerial development.

The development of Burns' Transformational model by people such as Bass (1985) and Tichy and Devanna (1986) has brought back into the managerial literature on leadership a concept brought forward by Weber in the 1920s that had so far fallen out of favour that it rated only six lines and no index entry in Stodgill's opus:

> The *charismatic leader* operates with a staff of disciples, enthusiasts and possibly bodyguards. He tends to sponsor causes and revolutions and is supported by charismatic authority, resting on devotion to the sanctity, heroism or inspirational character of the leader and on the normative patterns revealed or ordained by him. (Stodgill, 1974: 26)

Stodgill does note that Weber's ideas on legitimate authority and leadership were becoming more influential in the USA at the time, but this more probably referred to the interest in the transition from patrimonial to bureaucratic forms of leadership and authority. The portrayal of the charismatic leader and its discourse of sanctity and disciples is a classic 'morally sustaining idea' that underwrote many of the sermons on visionary leadership from the corporate culture merchants of the 1980s. Causes and cultural change, heroic identification and the idea that everyone can turn themselves into a winner if they will only believe, were the stock-in-trade of Tom Peters and his numerous imitators – all that was missing was the bodyguards! Hollway's discussion of this phenomenon (1991: 140–4) notes that it attempted to reverse the trend of subsuming leadership into a management function or skill and to reintroduce 'soft' human relations ideas into the harder world of professional management training using the claim that such an approach was capable of capturing for management the 'intractable and intuitive side of the organisation' (p. 143). Hollway further suggests that in the end rationalistic management practice would find it 'hard to embrace' this cultist version of people management principles. All the same, the 'socially integrating myth' aspect was useful to many organisations to the extent that rationalisation could be easily disguised as revolution. In terms of changing attitudes through culture, whipping up some enthusiasm – even if it is mainly engendered by fear of being on the down side of downsizing – can beget the minimum public commitment necessary to get people on your side for long enough to achieve your desired changes.

Under the models discussed above, from House to Burns and beyond, the duties and obligations of management have moved from earlier directive and co-ordinating leadership to a model that is underwritten not so much by duties or obligations but rather by a desperate casting about for methods of controlling the motivation and commitment of workers through strategies which emphasise the manipulation of situations and the management of meaning. Leadership has come down to the management of other's self-control, a problem which Hollway claims has never been solved to the satisfaction of senior management (1991: 143). Johnson and Gill (1993) cite the work of Manz and Sims (1989) as a major contribution to leadership strategies aimed at producing self-regulation in pursuit of the 'Self-Controlling Organisation'. They suggest that 'extrinsic control mechanisms' (that is, traditional controls, external to the individual) should be judged effective to the extent that they, 'influence self-control mechanisms based on the internalisation of norms within individual organisational members' (Johnson and Gill, 1993: 121). The focus of leadership behaviour here is to encourage, 'self-reinforcement, self-observation, evaluation and control; self-expectation and goal-setting and rehearsal and self-criticism' (p. 131). This is not of course the 'abdication of responsibility' of the *laissez-faire* leader of old, but is more a recognition of the type of power that needs to be exercised to ensure the mobilisation of commitment necessary to labour processes embodying work intensification and reduced supervision. However, just as Hollway was dubious about the acceptability of such an approach to management, Johnson and Gill are also pessimistic about the advent of the self-controlling organisation, depending as it does on the 'democratisation of society in general and its institutions'. Of course, it is always possible that in an attempt to maintain their cultural acceptability workers could present themselves as intrinsically motivated and committed to self-control when the real source of their commitment is greed, guilt or fear – followers just cannot be trusted!

We now return full circle to the notion that leadership is about legitimating the exercise of power at both the strategic and interpersonal levels. It is not simply the wielding of power, but an inherent component of the armoury of tacit and open skills employed in the negotiation and brokerage of individual and group hegemony. This is exemplified in the approach taken by Hosking and Morley (1991: ch. 9) who see leadership as, '*a more or less skilful process of organising, achieved through negotiation, to achieve acceptable influence over the description and handling of issues within and between groups*' (p. 240). Their critique of leadership in HRM and OB centres around the entitative approach (based on Meyer *et al.*, 1985) they see as endemic in these literatures and exemplified by the treatment of person and organisation as separate entities, persons being theorised independently of their contexts, with the result that 'the concept of organisation is implicit and underdeveloped in the treatment of individuals and groups' (p. 40). Because of this, leadership processes are under-emphasised in favour of a focus on leaders and their manipulations of others in pursuit of 'organisational goals (p. 241). Rather than talking about leaders and followers, they speak of participants in relationships who perceive 'each other as achieving influence in different ways' with varying degrees of acceptability in a particular context and in line with our earlier comments on leadership acts, that all participants may 'and come to be expected to' make contributions' (p. 240). Hosking and Morley highlight the social construction of relational exchanges in terms of social, cognitive and political processes. They argue that cognitive processes need to be understood as 'sense making' rather than as instruments for diagnosing and selecting appropriate behaviours (p. 247). The political processes and power should not be viewed as mainly resident in structural factors and interpersonal influence but in the 'quality of relationships' and 'the context of interdependence' (p. 249). Finally, they examine the cognitive and political aspects of the organising process of skilful leadership through the 'vehicles' of *networking*, negotiation and enabling.

The political quality of networks lies in their influence on commitments to shared understandings, lines of action and the projection of shared valuations. 'Networking' is the process of relationship building by which persons build up 'organisational intelligence'. Leaders would be those who build enabling relations through negotiation with other participants (with networks of their own?) who can act as their 'eyes and ears' and on whom they can depend for specialised skills. Leaders' networks would probably be small and cohesive as more diffuse networks might jeopardise the quality of relationships (p. 252).

We should note that for all that Hosking and Morley's work is detailed, dense with examples and carefully constructed to avoid the failings of mainstream OB, what they conclude is most akin to a more rational and contextually grounded version of transformational leadership. Networking needs to take place in conditions of 'open-minded thinking' and participation, negotiation through 'acceptable influence' and enabling in respect of the valuations and projects of all participants and not just leader-derived goals (p. 258). They speak of a 'culture of productivity' where 'all participants take responsibility for the relational processes through which they may help and be helped', a laudable aspiration which is ignorant of the constraints of ideological structures and defensive identities. After all, in the end leadership is no more than what you do with it!

Conclusion

Of all the problem areas addressed by psychology in organisations, it is possibly the question of what constitutes leadership that has most acted on the construction of managerial identity. Groups are a tool, communication is a vital skill and stress is almost a badge of honour, but it is the status of the manager as leader which most acts to mobilise the commitment of managers to endure the role conflicts which are the inheritance of their position in organisational hierarchies. The commitment of managers, in that they of necessity must buy into ideologies of control, is more or less taken for granted. It is the ability of managers to infuse commitment in others that is the common measure of their fitness for leadership.

In the next chapter we shall return to examine motivation in more detail, using it as an extended exemplar of the kind utilised in this chapter. The project remains the same, but now we move on to assess to what extent psychological knowledge can deliver changes in employee behaviour in the direction of greater commitment to corporate objectives.

CHAPTER 10

Mobilising commitment

The problem arises when managements come to believe so firmly in their so-called motivation techniques and theories that they incorrectly attribute the behaviour they see with the attitude ('highly motivated') they impute with the source behind that behaviour. The very term 'motivation' in its shopfloor context, implies that workers are not intrinsically inclined to behave in the way their managers would want. (Hershey, 'A Practitioner's View of "Motivation" ', 1993: 10)

This chapter uses a re-examination of motivation theories as a lead into a more general discussion of the role of Organisational Behaviour and Organisational Psychology in control strategies. In particular, we wish to explore the extent to which theory and associated interventions are capable of delivering the levels of intrinsic job motivation and flexible commitment demanded by modern human resource management strategies. This parallels in many aspects the discussions of culture and control in Chapter 7. A linking theme for this chapter is provided by the model proposed by Myers and Myers (1982) of the relative degrees of managerial control available over factors ranging from the organisational to the psycho-biological.

This model is used by Jackson (1994: 73) as an introduction to a discussion of content theories within cross cultural comparisons. In a similar fashion, we wish first to consider Herzberg's (1968) pragmatic critique of the then current motivational practices before moving on to examine more recent developments in motivation theory.

The 'kick in the ass' life cycle

Herzberg in 'One More Time: How Do You Motivate Employees?' (1968) addressed the strategies available to the manager who answers the question, 'how do I get an employee to do what I want him to?', with the age-old

Factors	Examples	Degree of management control
Organisational	Nature of jobs Physical/technical environment Reward system Supervision Available information Organisational goals Organisational structure	High
Social	Reference groups Peer groups Work groups Role-set	Moderate
Psycho-social	Needs Perceived abilities Aspirations Personal objectives Perceptual set	Moderate to low
Psycho-biological	Genetics Nurture	Nil

Source: Myers and Myers (1982, in Jackson, 1993: 73)

FIGURE 10.1   Management control of motivating influences

response of 'Kick him!' (p. 256). Herzberg used his analysis to examine his notion (introduced in Chapter 8) that most attempts to 'motivate' workers produce nothing more than short-term movement towards a reward or away from a punishment, and through this to argue that to produce self-motivating workers, jobs must be enriched. More interesting for our present purposes though, is his analysis of the development of the techniques available to achieve the goal of at least short-term movement or influence, the so-called KITAs. Herzberg argued that the basic technique of the kick, or 'Negative Physical KITA', failed due to the problems of image and retaliation associated with a regime of punishment, and that psychologists had to come to the rescue by uncovering, 'infinite sources of psychological vulnerabilities and the appropriate methods to play tunes on them', that is, Negative Psychological KITA (p. 257). This form of KITA still being coercion and not motivation, Herzberg moved on to consider Positive KITA, noting that due once more to the failure of the traditional range of rewards employed by management (on the basis that they were subject to diminishing returns), they now had to listen to the 'behavioural scientists who, more out of a humanist tradition than scientific study, criticised management for not knowing how to deal with people' (p. 258). The self-replicating string of KITAs which resulted from this unlikely collaboration gave us, according to Herzberg, Human Relations and Sensitivity Training; Communications and Two-Way Communication; Job Participation and Employee Counselling. If we extend the roll-call of Positive KITAs to the present day, we can include everything from Herzberg's own critical output in Job Enrichment to Autonomous Working, Sociotechnical Systems, Management By Objectives and all the rest of the 'bag of schemes'.

The reason that all of these approaches and techniques are so easily incorporated into managerial practice despite their contradictory humanist assumptions is directly related to their reification (see below) of motivation and satisfaction. In order to provide support for their theoretical under-pinnings, the concretised abstractions they consist of are subjected to methods of experimental and statistical testing and measurement which directly facilitate their repackaging as prescriptive techniques and testing instruments. That they all offer no more than temporary influences towards greater commitment and goal consensus rather than avenues towards self-generated motivation to work is not important to management if, as we argued in Chapter 8, they give rise to even short-term productivity gains. This reinforces the status of the products of OB as an integral part of the labour process itself. It is almost as if the techniques and approaches coming out of behavioural science have their own version of the marketing concept of the *product life cycle*. As soon as one KITA is reaching its diminishing level of marginal utility, the research and development process of critique and hypothesis testing gives rise to a new one. That all that is new about them is often only the name is unimportant, as long as the 'improved product' is sufficiently distinctive enough to carry out its function as an ideological cover story for yet another technology of regulation. What is inevitable about them is that consultants will continue to charge ever larger fees for designing and implementing them, and that those they are aimed at will cease to be affected by them as soon as the instrumental or social rewards which they really offer become taken for granted.

The attractions of KITAs to managers parallel managers' attitudes to new technologies. KITAs have the intrinsic marketing advantage over their target audience in that if the competition has them, then managers feel that they have to have them too. The similarity goes further – in that – like new technologies – KITAs are often brought in by managements which do not fully understand them or their possibly deleterious effects on cultures based on established procedures and working practices. Worse still, they only ever work effectively so long as management remain committed to resourcing them properly and do not use them as levers for unilaterally increasing levels of control and productivity.

Motivation as a problematic concept

Motivation as presented in Chapter 8 lies at the heart of the explanatory project of organisational psychology and as such can be used to reflect generally on the limits and contradictions within mainstream theories and practices. At one level, motivation is a classic case of Adorno's concept of *'identity thinking'* (G. Rose, 1978), where a concept is used as if it denoted instances of something, when it does not. For example, individuals are not 'motivated' to perform well at a particular task or 'satisfied' with their job when the underlying reason for their performance is to maintain a reasonable level of subsistence and not to lose their job by falling behind. In this sense, organisational psychology assumes an identity between being motivated to do something and being constrained to do it by physical and social necessity. In Adorno's terms, one can only make proper use of a theoretical concept or construct in the context of the 'theory of society' through which it is itself constructed.

In taking the situational contexts in which behaviour in organisations takes place largely as given, the concepts used in mainstream analyses are often reified, involving 'the conversion of concrete social relations of production into abstracted, quantitative measures' (Wexler, 1983: 66). Reification can be viewed as a dual process. First, the products of human thought and activity are treated as things in themselves; and secondly socially produced concepts are treated as being intrinsic to individuals and organisations. Thus, in relation to the first part of this process, organisations are often treated as actual entities or organisms with their own needs, drives and characteristics analogous to those of people, rather than as the continuously recreated products of human labour and organisational ingenuity. Returning to the concept of motivation we can observe that it is often applied to organisations themselves, in that they are seen as having their own internally derived goals which can change to accommodate the environmental contingencies which the organisation is faced with – for instance, the current fashion for management and staff 'development' programmes designed ostensibly to meet the 'training needs' of organisations, but which serve mainly to locate organisational problems at the individual rather than the structural level (see Chapters 6 and 9).

The second part of the process can also be illustrated through the concept of motivation. Content theories such as that of Maslow (1954) utilised highly generalised typologies of needs which sought to explain the innate determinants of human behaviour in order that they might be better understood and directed by individuals. But they are developed in organisational psychology into measurement packages which seek to typify the range of needs applying to individuals in order to establish the minimum conditions for their compliance.

The content theories of motivation only ever really sought to explain motivation in terms of its directions, but lacked the sophistication to explain the strength of motivations. To be really useful in terms of selection or developmental training, it is the relative force of motivation which needs to be measured, this being seen in 'process theories' such as Equity theory (Adams, 1965) and expectancy theory (Vroom, 1964). Equity theory is based on notions of cognitive social comparison and exchange, expectancy on comparison of outcomes and preferences. These are reinforced by techniques which actively intervene in the selection and pursuit of goals such as Goal Setting (Locke and Latham, 1984) which is based on comparison and reinforcement of behavioural standards. All extend the basic notion of cognitive comparison to attempt greater levels of accuracy in prediction and control. Though in general empirical support for these theories is positive, expectancy theory in particular has been singled out for some criticism (see Arnold *et al.*, 1991: 178–9).

This effort to integrate 'human resources' more fully into the production process typical of the application of content theories is similarly present in the usage of process theories of motivation, as in the application of the expectancy theory of Vroom (1964). This seeks to quantify and predict the strength of an individual's tendency to behave in a particular way as an assigned probability which is given by the simplified expectancy equation: $F = \sum(E \times V)$, where F is the resulting motivation to behave in a particular way, E is the *subjective probability* or *expectation* that the behaviour will be followed by a particular outcome and V is the *valence* of the outcome or the *preference* that the individual has for that particular outcome. Since any particular behaviour has a number of possible outcomes, the calculation depends on the sums of all the measured values of $E \times V$, the sign $\sum$ indicating that we should add the resulting values obtained for each outcome. The E value, being a probability, can vary between 0 and 1:0 meaning that the individual estimates there is no chance of that particular outcome and 1 meaning that it is a complete certainty. The value of V is determined by asking the individual to rate the value they place on various outcomes along a dimension which would, for example, give those they preferred as +1, those they felt neutral towards as 0+ and those they did not prefer as −1.

If, then, the problem is to discover the motivation that an individual has towards working harder, we must first identify the possible outcomes which might result from their working harder – such as more pay, increased prospects for promotion, increased stress, a more positive attitude from the supervisor. Then the probability of and preference for (the E and V values) each of these outcomes occurring must be assessed; and the resulting values must be added to give us a value for F. The assumption is that the *higher* the value of F, the *stronger* the motivation to behave in that particular fashion. Of course, the value of F must be compared to some sort of baseline and therefore we might compare the scores for a particular individual over a number of different behaviours or the scores for a number of individuals on the same behaviour.

On the surface, this model appears to provide organisational psychologists with a simple and powerful *tool* for predicting behaviour. But the assumptions made in such a measurement present a number of problems. The first is in that expectancy theory provides a *rational-cognitive* explanation of individual behaviour. Can we assume that individuals make rational calculations based on their cognitive input in deciding whether to act in a particular way? Even assuming that this is the case, do these form the major determinant factor in their subsequent actions? These questions are often posed in organisational behaviour texts, but no adequate account is generally given of whether such assumptions are warranted. The question is simply stated prior to a discussion of what can be done with expectancy theory in terms of understanding motivational goals, in order to influence and alter people's behaviour.

An objection arises from those, including Langer (1981), who suggest that many of our behaviours are acted out in what they term a 'mindless' manner. Rather than behaving in an analytic, rational fashion, we in fact follow unconscious 'scripts' through which our actions are fitted to and determined as appropriate to the contexts in which they occur. Thus, in much the same way as we do not consciously think of the numerous and complex series of actions which we go through in performing even such an apparently simple task as making a cup of tea, we do not necessarily take an analytical and conscious part in performing many of the behaviours we must go through at work. Although we may consider and think about the options open to us and the best way of going about a particular task, the underlying motivation may simply be that we are following the script which we have come to learn as appropriate to that situation. The work of Roy (1973) provides examples of how both labour and social interaction in the workplace can take on the attributes of ritual. Roy's monotonous and fatiguing work of 'mincing plastic sheets into small ovals, fingers and trapezoids' (p. 208) was made 'relatively satisfying' in Baldamus' (1961) terms by turning the production process into a series of 'games' which varied the colour, shape and ordering of the components turned out. The self-induced scripting of the work itself was accompanied by the breaking-up of the working day into 'times', such as 'peach', 'banana' and 'pickup time'. 'Times' were constructed around the ritualised social interactions and verbal interplay in the brief interruptions to production which were repeated on a daily basis. Thus the behavioural scripts built up around eating, drinking and visits from outsiders reintroduced some level of meaning and interest for the machine operators into a deskilled labour process. Interest was further enhanced by the continuous repetition during work of 'serious' and 'kidding' verbal 'themes' centred around the characteristics and problems of the operators involved. In this sense, scripted behaviours become an effective, though not necessarily actively planned, mechanism for coping with the mundanity of working life.

A second and related problem for models of motivation are the narrow and over-deterministic accounts of experience which rational-cognitive theories of human behaviour produce. These place the responsibility for action on individuals rather than on the contexts in which they find themselves. This tends to reinforce the view that the pathology of organisations is based on the irrational actions of individuals. In this view the problems and uncertainties faced by organisations are caused by the self-serving behaviour of those who do not appreciate the 'big picture' of organisational life.

In the simplified example of expectancy calculations given above, it is fairly easy to see how the categories which define the possible outcomes of a particular behaviour are arrived at. What is also fairly easy to see is that there are almost an infinity of intervening variables or factors which would, for the calculation to be carried out, have to be taken into account. Even if the behaviour of individuals in organisations is largely carried out in the context of scripts which their socialisation into organisational life has taught them, they still bring to their working life an actively constructed identity which has been transformed within the organisation into an appropriate image. These behaviours and scripts do not exist in isolation. Even considering the possible outcomes of working harder on one particular task would involve an almost endless series of ramifications and secondary consequences. Thus to obtain a realistic prediction about how motivated a single individual would be to perform a particular behaviour would involve taking into account not only most of the behaviours applicable to their work and their life outside the organisation, but also those of similar individuals inside and outside the organisation, to provide a basis of comparison. The project of fully understanding how people are motivated from this perspective would involve identifying and explaining all of the subjective and structural influences on their lives and those of the others surrounding them.

In this light, the functional utility of such models would appear to be in establishing the minimum conditions under which workers can be mobilised to consent to the nature of work that is demanded of them. This is achieved through a narrow means of conceptualising motivation which supplies enough information about an individual to be useful in engaging their consent for working practices by actively manipulating their perceptions of expectations and preferences. Information about the social and material rewards available, or perhaps the danger of redundancy, can be manipulated to reinforce control practices by getting the worker to internalise the rationale for increasing productivity. What is effectively happening here is that extrinsic factors – those largely outside the control of the individual, such as pay and conditions – are being translated into intrinsic factors. These include those processes assumed to be under individual control, for instance satisfaction and motivation, thus making employees personally responsible for their own objective situation. Seivers (1986) goes further, by arguing that motivation is not an intrinsic factor of individual personality, but an artefact produced by the science of organisational behaviour; which acts as a surrogate for the meaning which people have lost from fragmented and dehumanised work.

> Motivation only became an issue – for management and organisation theories as well as for the organisation of work itself – when meaning was either lost or disappeared from work. In consequence, motivation theories have become surrogates for the search for meaning. (1986: 338–9)

That management has become such a great consumer of theories and techniques of motivation is in itself an indication that there is little in much work which can in itself act as a source of meaning and the basis for a secure identity. The attempts to introduce greater levels of participation, to 'humanise' work, to 'enrich' jobs, are in part a recognition that at least some level of commitment from workers is necessary efficiently to valorise capital. Attempts to 'motivate' are founded on the assumption that workers need to be led, but their theoretical bases do not examine the corollary that workers need to be influenced to co-operate because of their essential alienation from the productive process. The conventional view of the use of psychological knowledge in the area of motivation is generally that it is employed in order to produce greater harmony and integration in the workplace. However, the use of motivation as a manipulative concept implies not a lesser but a greater unitarism of outlook from management. The integration of individual and 'organisational' goals not only binds people ever closer to the productive process, but creates the climate where programmes such as the 'Total Quality Management' initiatives taken up by companies such as Philips and Jaguar make workers responsible for monitoring their own performance. The 'motivations' served are the managerial aims of greater 'unit' productivity – the drive for more work and less waste operating under the cover story of a *consensus-based* participation provided by motivational techniques.

Control and integration

The relative lack of success of process theories in managerial terms is due to the very complexity which makes them more powerful in explanatory terms than content theories. Most management development texts still present content theories in the main because they are simple, easier to demonstrate and they sound powerful; whereas cognitive/process theories suffer from the very fact that they are multifactorial and multivariate, with the implications that:

- there are too many factors which can affect the relations between effort, performance and outcomes;

- too many value associations have to be made in assessing outcomes;
- it is too difficult to place accurate values on variables;
- models require assumptions of complex mental calculations which are hard to reproduce and demonstrate.

This is probably best illustrated in what is probably the most powerful development in motivation theory to appear in the last ten years, Klein's *Integrated Control Theory of Work Motivation* (1989). What this theory manages to do is to integrate cognitive motivation theories, theories of scripted response, theories of causal perception and attribution and cybernetic theories. These last, combining information processing and the control of action, are based on Wiener's (1948) cybernetic hypothesis and the notion of feedback, and are similar to Miller's notion of TOTE units given in Chapter 8. The main elements of behavioural control theories are given below:

- cognitive   internal goals
                 information on current state
                 comparison of goals and state
- affective   perceived discrepancies
                 behavioural resolutions

Klein's model (see Figure 10.2) is essentially a metatheory which is aimed at accounting for the hypotheses generated by the various approaches it incorporates and according to Klein (1989) is consistent with the propositions of social learning, equity, expectancy and satisfaction theories. However, it is also claimed to focus more on individual's self-regulation in response to external influences – rather than on the effects of those influences – such as providing goals and incentives, as is the case with most motivation theories.

If we imagine that many of these processes – for example, the continuation of previous behaviour (7) – might themselves be organised into hierarchical systems of goal-directed action, the theory's potential explanatory power becomes enormous (see Arnold *et al.*, 1991: 185–7, and McKenna, 1994: 93–6, for more detailed expositions). Since the model does acknowledge the influence of individual and situational factors such as ability, past experience, social comparison processes, situational constraints and reward structures, this theory offers some hope of reconciling cognitive/rational theories with approaches emphasising subjectivity and its construction. The propositions which Klein derives from control theory are yet to be tested in any detail, but even so, as Klein demonstrates with his extended example of a salesperson trying to meet quotas, it does offer considerable insight into the dynamic processes of self-regulation in individual action and how, 'automatic and conscious processes operate simultaneously to initiate and direct behaviour' (1989: 168).

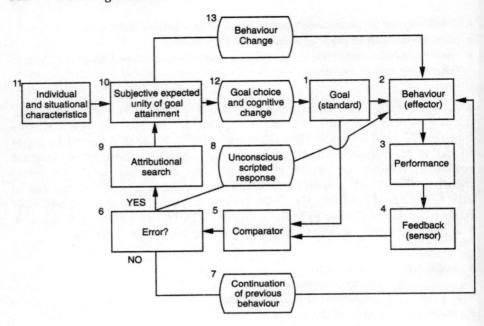

Source: Klein (1989: 1451)

FIGURE 10.2   An integrated control theory model of work motivation

On the basis that Klein's model represents an even more sophisticated and multivariate theory than previous accounts of motivation, the prediction would have to be that any practical applications are still a long way off. In line with earlier comments on process theories, we could also confidently predict that even with practical applications, it would not be capable of being utilised by managers until it could be reduced to a simplified procedure or technique, and the blunt instruments of Herzberg's KITAs will remain the dominant techniques employed in the process of mobilising commitment.

Control and self-concepts

Though Klein's model makes a comprehensive attempt to integrate content and process theories, it is still open to the kind of critique put forward by, for example, Shamir (1991) who claims that, 'current motivational theories are restricted in certain respects due to their over-reliance on individual-hedonistic assumptions and their over-emphasis on cognitive-calculative processes' (p. 405). The assertion of an individualistic, hedonistic bias, mainly in content theories, which Shamir takes from Steers and Porter (1987) and Etzioni (1988) is contrasted with more collective approaches to work motivation found in cross-cultural comparisons (Staw and Hofstede) and is illustrated in relation to the kind of influence strategies employed by 'Transformational Leaders' who try to, 'persuade their followers to transcend their own interests for the sake of the team' (Shamir, 1991: 407). According to Shamir, such an effect cannot be explained from the point of view of theories which highlight individual satisfaction. It is possible that the concept of subjective expected utility, as found in expectancy theory and incorporated by Klein, could account for such a phenomenon through the delayed gratification of situational rewards to be found in attachment to a superordinate goal. At the same time, the attempt to reconcile situational and cognitive factors brings in a second strand of Shamir's critique, in that such theories may have their greatest explanatory power in what Mischel (1973) characterised as 'strong' situations where there are clear goals and expectancies tied to performance incentives. The inability to explain 'weak' situations where there may be large variations in individual behaviour is tied to what Shamir argues is a tendency of motivation theories to, 'emphasise easily measurable and observable and relatively discrete behaviours' (1991: 408). This is illustrated with reference to the contrasting situations in notions of commitment, Shamir citing Marks (1977: 29) to the effect that they refer, 'a shifting number and range of rather ill-delineated performances rather than to ironclad and numerically consistent behaviours'. In that this, for Shamir, refers to the 'repetition or continuation' of acts, or 'broader patterns of behaviour containing many different acts' (1991: 409), it may be difficult for control theory to account for the number of variables involved, although the focus on unconscious scripted responses and hierarchical systems of goal-directed behaviour may offer up possible avenues of explanation.

Though control theory might potentially be able to answer some of Shamir's critique, albeit at the cost of a bewildering level of complexity, it would find it much more difficult to counter his further assertions that motivation theories tend to embody limited concepts of intrinsic motivation and to exclude values and moral obligations. Where control theory does embody assumptions about intrinsic motivation they come in through use of the 'subjective expected utility' employed by expectancy theory and Shamir argues that these focus on a task-based notion of individual motivation that emphasises the outcomes of acts and self-administered rewards. Such conceptions are said to ignore that fact that a task may have no intrinsically satisfying properties and yet might still be, 'motivating due to its meaning for the individual, for instance in terms of the affirmation of his or her identity and collective affiliations' (1991: 409). Even where motivation theories do make strong distinctions between intrinsic and extrinsic motivation, Shamir notes that the task-orientated focus tends to 'neglect the symbolic and expressive aspects of human beings' (1991: 409).

Shamir identifies the use of values in motivation theory as analogous to the concept of valence or preference in expectancy theory and contrasts this to notions of values as 'conceptions of the desirable' (from Kluchkhohn, 1962) rather what is than desired. Thus motivation theories are seen to focus on desires as exemplified in needs rather than motivation towards what is desirable, which may make external demands on the person. This more sociological approach to values is seen as necessary in order to explain 'individual sacrifices to collective concerns' (1991: 410) and the possibility of the existence a drive towards discharging one's moral obligations (from Scwartz, 1983: and Etzioni, 1988). This latter notion of 'denotic motivation' (Scwartz) is said to have been ignored by mainstream motivation theory (1991: 410), possibly because the correlation between values and specific behaviours is no better than the attitude–behaviour correlation (see Chapter 8), but it is the very variability of values across situations that makes them valuable in explaining motivation not apparently linked to particular intrinsic or extrinsic rewards.

The Self-Concept theory of motivation proposed by Shamir attempts to produce both a theory of general work motivation (investing effort in the work role) and general job motivation (investing effort in your current job). It does not attempt to explain the motivation to perform specific tasks and Shamir says that goal-setting and expectancy theory (to which we should add control theory) are more appropriate to such situations. Like Klein, Shamir integrates material from a number of sources, notably Bandura's (1986) social cognitive theory, 'structural symbolic interactionism' from Stryker (1980) and Gecas' (1986) self-concept theory. The assumptions driving the theory are given below:

1. 'Humans are not only goal orientated but also self expressive'. They, 'choose to spend time in situations that allow them to express their dispositions, attitudes and self-conceptions'.
2. 'People are motivated to maintain and enhance their self esteem and self-worth'. This is reflected in that, 'both competence standards and cultural values are internalised into the self concept in the form of evaluative standards'.
3. 'People are also motivated to retain and increase their sense of self-consistency'. 'In a sense, the self-concept is an ideology that people attempt to express and validate in their behaviour'.
4. 'Self-concepts are composed, in part, of identities'. 'People derive meaning from being linked to social collectives through their identities', and may operate on an 'authenticity motive' (Gecas) to reflect their 'true identity' in their actions.
5. 'Self-concept related behaviour is not always related to clear expectations or immediate and specific goals'. They may be motivated by faith and 'the imagined possibilities of the self'. (Shamir, 1991: 411–15)

Overall, general job motivation is seen here to be determined by the extent to which the person's self-concept is congruent with their current job and its situational context. Job-related identities are seen as central to the self-concept, though other identities (for example, national, ethnic and family) must be acknowledged (1991: 417). The theory is said to most powerful in 'weak' situations (see above) where goals and the means for achieving them are unclear and there is no explicit linkage between performance and external rewards (p. 416). However, Shamir does claim that the theory may be useful for explaining some 'strong' situations – for example, 'deviant, non-conforming behaviour such as whistle blowing' (p. 416), presumably on the basis that these activities have strong identity salience.

The implications of Self-Concept Theory are said to be in clearer explanations of organisational commitment, collective effort and the linkage between identities, values and intrinsic motivation. Further, it is claimed to make possible links between motivation and organisational culture and Pfeffer's (1981b) notion of management as symbolic interaction (Shamir, 1991: 419). Though self-concept theory does manage to step back from the rational-cognitive explanations of process theories and to broaden the concepts of intrinsic motivation found in need-satisfaction content theories, its emphasis on weak situations makes it difficult to align with attempts to explain the influence of managerial control strategies on motivation, which in many ways might be characterised by the attempt to move towards stronger situations where motivation may be somewhat easier to assess. Likewise, though Klein's control theory does emphasise control, this is more a theory of conscious and unconscious self-control – and though the promotion of self-monitoring is a major element of managerial strategy, control theory is not currently capable of explaining how restraints on acceptable goals and scripted behaviour are communicated to and internalised by the individual. However, it is possible that a linkage between the two theories and an explanation which can account for both strong and weak situation may be found in examining how socially produced identities operate in mediating the 'individual and situational characteristics' Klein identifies.

The need for such a synthesis can be demonstrated through Jackson's (1994: 83) summary of the influence of cultural factors on motivation. Jackson argues that in international comparisons, process theories are more portable due to their focus on 'universals' of motivation, but at the same time though 'static-content theories do not travel very well between cultures' (1993: 83) they might provide the most useful research. This is presumably because, by failing to be universal, content theories at least show that there is cultural variation in motivation. Self-concept theory might provide useful insights into how general work motivation is subject to cultural variation while control theory can provide explanation of the 'universal' processes by which persons choose specific courses of action.

If we can link both the content and processes of motivation to identity, we can focus on these as inputs to situationally determined strategies which people adopt to enhance the identities they have constructed. People would not be 'intrinsically' or 'extrinsically' motivated. Rather they would take meaning from whatever sources are available, inside or out of the work environment, and use them to enhance both the image they have of themselves and the images that others hold of them. In a work environment where possibilities for securing meaning are scarce, people might still be capable of taking meaning from the situation to the extent that they can gain some personal or collective control over their work. Strongly cohesive work-group cultures might in this sense actually identify with working practices to the extent of feeling that they, and not management, 'own' them. Attempting to redefine working practices in such situations might only detract from the sources of meaning available in the workplace and in essence attack whatever portion of identity resides there. If this is the case, then compensations, even assuming they are designed to satisfy both intrinsically and extrinsically derived motivations, would probably not overcome hostility to changes and they would be difficult to implement. The individuals and groups concerned would either attempt to revert to their old practices or would devise new strategies for regaining some control over and meaning from their work.

As far as the practical use of motivation theory at present is concerned, identity is essentially an *intervening variable* which acts to complicate applications. Taking account of individual identities would introduce subjective factors which would make motivations difficult to assess with standardised test inventories such as interest questionnaires. But it is already the case that social identity measures are being used almost as predictive personality traits – as, for example, in James *et al.* (1994) using measures such as self-esteem and collective esteem, value differences, expressiveness and perceived prejudice in assessing minority workers' health.

Engaging the intellect

Returning for a moment to the Myers model of motivating influences cited at the beginning of the chapter, it is evident that the processes described in control and self-concept theory operate mainly at the 'psycho-social' level where the possible degree of managerial control is said to be only moderate to low. As with Herzberg's commentary on motivational techniques and this chapter's opening statement from Hershey, the problem is an imperfect control of intrinsic motivational impulses which can only be partially corrected by the deployment of extrinsic rewards. To achieve systematic control, were this even possible, would require that psycho-social factors be regulated through social and organisational processes. However, these must be considered in relation to the effects of environmental variables (politico-legal, socio-cultural, market-economic and so on) which even in relation to

Leavitt's (1978) fairly basic model of the interaction between people, task, technology and structure, could be seen to produce a welter of mediating variables. Strategic responses to market pressures in turbulent environments have produced enormous internal pressures to change, and the main burden of such change in the end falls on people, as they are the factor over which management has the least reliable control. Thus changes in technologies, tasks and job design have produced pressures for structural changes which in recent years have been promoted through attempts to redefine cultural characteristics aimed at producing adaptive behaviours in employees.

Such structural and cultural pressures, driven by the ideologically legitimated need to change tasks and technologies and coupled with the long-term failure to control intrinsic motivation, have produced the whole panoply of modern-day KITAs, from the desperate attempts to reassert control over rewards in performance-related pay and share schemes, through group-based initiatives on autonomous working and quality circles, to the bludgeon-like tools of restructuring and corporate culture. What success these initiatives have is not in producing general job and work motivation, but in the production of short-term movement towards increased effort on specific tasks. If there are no long-term rewards for the increased performance in terms of self-expression, esteem, worth or consistency, then initiatives will suffer diminishing returns like any other KITA. The only routes which appear to be left for increasing general motivation are in the control of meaning and of group-based socialisation into work roles as the main psycho-social factors subject to external manipulation.

To achieve this form of change requires the transformation of behaviour and working practices and this requires that practices which have evolved into scripted behaviours be 'unfrozen' in Lewin's (1947) terms, so that re-socialisation can take place. As scripts are based on the kinds of flexible action patterns and sensorimotor learning discussed in Chapter 8, what would be sought here is the constant re-engagement of the intellectual level of learning so that behaviour is not directed by learned patterns of experience, desire or collective obligation, but by adaptive behaviour in response to constant uncertainty. This situation is reflected in Hopwood's (1974, cited in Johnson and Gill, 1993: 34–5) model linking social and administrative controls. Social controls, such as group norms, aimed at regulating output; and administrative controls, such as reward systems, aimed at increasing productivity, require enactment through their internalisation as self-controls. Johnson and Gill (1993: 34–6) extend this by reference to Kelman's (1961) work on conformity and Kanter's (1968) comments on organisational identity. In Kelman's eyes, internalisation is one form of conformity whereby the individual adopts the norms and value structures of 'significant others' in the development of their 'internal moral imperatives'. Compliance is conformity based on the motivation to gain rewards and avoid costs, which may be linked in organisational terms to Hopwood's administrative controls. Identification also involves 'significant others', but is conformity to the social influence they exert on the basis of our becoming emotionally attached to them, wishing to be like them or perhaps to be identified as one of the group or cultural community to which they belong. This last factor could be linked to Hopwood's notion of social controls, and the role of compliance and identification is finally linked to the idea of internalised self-controls through Kanter's concepts of 'mortification' and 'surrender' – the former involving the 'exchanging of a private identity for one provided by the organisation', and the latter the 'attachment of one's decision-making prerogative to a greater power' (Kanter, 1968, cited in Johnson and Gill, 1993: 35–6). The importance of this for Johnson and Gill (1993: 36) is that:

> it draws our attention to the processes that can disengage the individual from prior social and ideological attachments by redirecting his or her beliefs and norms towards those that predominate in any organisational context – whatever those might be.

This is linked to the development of organisational commitment through reference to Brown (1965) on the nature of conformity and moral development. Individuals are seen initially to obey external demands and sanctions and then to develop emotional attachments in 'everyday social interactions' which produce identification and eventual internalisation (Johnson and Gill, 1993: 36).

Though at first this would appear to offer a consistent account of how managerial control strategies can become internalised as part of our self-concept or identities, there are difficulties, most especially in the identification part of the process. The linkage between managerial controls and compliance is fairly straightforward, but internalisation here is unlikely, since compliance is dependant on continued reinforcement and would suffer from diminishing returns. Identification can lead to internalisation, but it is social control to which identification is linked and the values likely to be internalised are those of reference or membership groups rather than the managerial or corporate values expressed in control strategies. Kanter's notions seem to offer more possibilities for the internalisation of objectives and controls aligned with corporate strategy, but Kanter was talking about 'Utopian communities', which presumably have voluntaristic membership and thus a greater likelihood of members accepting appeals to superordinate goals.

The dilemma here is that the context within which internalisation takes place is as important to the outcomes as the process itself. As Hosking and Morley (1991: 5) note 'people are both products of their contexts and participants in the creation of those contexts'. The relation between person and context is one of 'assimilation' by changing the context and 'accommodation' by changing oneself. Relationships of this kind would make attempts to promote the internalisation of controls appear to be a one-sided process. Accommodation and compliance would be the normative valuation for those instituting control systems, whereas assimilation and identification would be the desired outcomes for those subject to control. Since the opportunities for assimilation of context are limited for most employees, it is likely that any accommodation that takes place is more a case of resigned acceptance than the result of a negotiated order and is more analogous to mortification than 'empowerment'.

However, J. R. Barker (1993) offers evidence that the values of control systems appear to be internalised by some groups of workers in specific circumstances. This is exemplified in the concept of 'concertive control' taken from Tompkins and Cheney (1985) which is an extension of Richard Edward's three control strategies (see Chapter 2). This fourth form of control:

> represents a key shift in the locus of control from management to the workers themselves, who collaborate to develop the means of their own control. Workers achieve concertive control by a negotiated consensus on how to shape their behaviour according to a set of core values, such as those of a corporate vision statement. (J. R. Barker, 1993: 411)

Here, though, it is both the organisation and its members which are seen to adopt a 'new substantive rationality' and a 'new set of consensual values'. It would appear that this represents the translation of administrative controls into social controls and thus achieving accommodation, assimilation, identification and finally internalisation. Barker's case study was of ISE Communications, a small US manufacturing company which adopted a structure based on self-managed treams in the late 1980s. the structural changes in the company are detailed in Table 10.1.

The process by which concertive control came into being was first through the development of a value consensus based on the vision statement, then the emergence of normative rules which were driven by the addition of new teams 'Members of the old teams responded to these changing conditions by discursively turning their value consensus into normative rules that the new workers could readily understand and to which they could subject themselves' (1993: 424). The final stage was the formalisation of these rules into a system which resembled in some ways the old bureaucratic structure. The formalisation of abstract values into specific behavioural guidelines was seen to provide a sense of stability and was not interpreted as the recreation of a bureaucracy, in that – though they represented a rational, rule-based system – the rules were formulated and enacted by the teams themselves. The teams were thus said to be 'their own masters and their own slaves' (1993: 433) and even though managing the 'concertive' system produced a great deal of strain in team members, they were reluctant to give up their control of their working practices, uncommitted workers not lasting very long. Barker's conclusion is that in the end even a self-managed rational apparatus only serves to bind

TABLE 10.1   Structure of ISE before and after the change of teams

Before the change	After the change
1. Three levels of managerial hierarchy between the vice president and the manufacturing workers.	1. Managerial hierarchy extends directly from the manufacturing teams to the vice president.
2. Manufacturing assembly line organises the plant. Workers manufacture boards according to their individual place on the line.	2. Team work areas organise the plant. Teams are responsible for complete fabrication, testing, and packaging of their assigned circuit boards.
3. Line and shift supervisors form the first managerial link.	3. Teams manage their own affairs, elect one person to co-ordinate information to them.
4. Workers have little input into work-related decisions. Managers make all decisions and give all directions.	4. Team members make their own decisions within guidelines set by management and the company vision statement. Teams have shared responsibility for their own productivity.
5. Management disciplines workers	5. Team members discipline themselves.
6. Management interview and hires all new workers	6. Team members interview, hire and fire their own members.

Source: Barker (1993: 417).

employees further to Weber's 'Iron Cage', resistance being at the cost of risking their human dignity by, 'being made to feel unworthy as a "team-mate"' (1993: 436).

This begins to resemble Kanter's notions of mortification and surrender, though based more on a form of responsible autonomy than on voluntarism. The self-managed responsibilities produced by the concertive system themselves begin to enact the construction of a rational apparatus, in that the formalisation of consensual values into rules could be seen as an adaptive mechanism to relieve the levels of stress induced by autonomous decision-making. Thus team members become, in Willmott's terms, 'responsible individuals' who seek the stability of a rational apparatus in that they 'are spared the anguish of choice because feelings of anxiety and guilt associated with this responsibility are contained within organisationally defined boundaries', (1994: 26). However, here it is the uncertainty produced by the move to self-management which unfreezes team members to the point where corporate ideals can be identified with, rather than the generalised uncertainty Willmott associates with, the 'indeterminacy and finititude of human existence' (1994: 26).

The Barker study demonstrates that re-engagement of the intellectual level of learning can be achieved through collective obligations which guide adaptive behaviour in response to manufactured uncertainty. But once again the identification here is not directly to administrative controls and managerial values – identification with the corporate mission is dependant on the continued abdication and transfer by management of responsibility and control to social consensus. Management has changed the context of control by changing the structures through which it is enacted, but the extent to which this represents simple compliance orientated on a new locus of control and not any real measure of internalisation must be questioned. Barker notes that team members are not aware of how their actions are controlled and still rely on normative pressures to discipline behaviour. What is achieved by this form of self-management is constant self-monitoring and environmental scanning by the team and learned changes in behaviour which are not necessarily accompanied by increases in either general or specific job motivation. As indicated earlier, what appears to be important here is not genuine motivation but the mobilisation of commitment. The commitment required is not to intrinsic values, but to the expenditure of effort in required directions. The mechanisms for accomplishing this may ride on appeals to values and the construction of meaning, but their aim is the attainment of strategically directed change.

Learning to change

The themes of strategic and self-managed change as a way of dealing with environmental uncertainty are currently characterised in the literature on what has come to be known as the 'learning organisation'. This notion, which can be traced back to the work of Argyris and Schön (1978) on 'theories of action' in organisational learning and to the work of Lewis (1984) and others on *open learning* and computer-based training, is said to be based on the recognition:

> that members of organisations must be equipped to create and sustain values, knowledge bases, processes, skills and systems which promote effective responses to change. This dictates the need for higher trust cultures, for responsive systems and knowledge workers who are capable of participating in making decisions and

solving problems at point of discovery and without reliance on complex command and control systems. (West, 1994: 15)

Numerous writers – including Senge, Lessem, Honey and Burgoyne – have been involved in promoting the idea of a learning organisation, a phenomenon which John van Maanen of MIT has described as 'what management in the 21st century will be about'. The learning organisation can be characterised by an emphasis on self-management, matrix-type structures, dedicated training and learning support and flexibility in working practices and environmental response (Sims *et al.*, 1993: 198). However, the use of practices under this banner can also be viewed as yet another vehicle for achieving organisational change or more accurately as Swieringa and Wierdsma (1992: 1) put it, for 'the changing of behaviour'. In this sense, there is little difference between learning organisation initiatives and the earlier notion of organisational learning – despite the distinctions between the two made by Jones and Hendry (1994). They associate organisational learning with HRM initiatives and traditional training regimes; and learning organisations with Pettigrew and Whipp's (1991) notion of 'organisational capability'. This latter is more in line with ideas on experiential learning discussed in Chapter 8 and can be linked with the discussion on informal socialisation which will follow in Chapter 11. The development of capabilities by organisational members will proceed in a tacit manner even where no formal training is given, as exemplified by the numbers of people in modern organisations who learn to approriate information technologies to their own use, learning much more than is required of them in their work. McHugh *et al.* (1994) note that in operational terms there appears to be little in initiatives towards learning organisations that moves beyond a form of goal-setting linked to HRM strategies:

> The linkage to strategy demands support for flexibility of organisation and open-ended intrinsic commitment, but for the learner the 'locus of control' is still external in that learning must be shown to achieve objectives related to their task and role. (McHugh *et al.*, 1994: 11).

Within earlier notions of open learning via computer assisted learning (CAL) Fuller and Saunders (1992: 32–3) note three basic rationales to open access learning; the *instrumental*, based on simple access to training opportunities; the *prescriptive*, based on empowerment of individuals and groups; and the *functional*, based on cost effectiveness. They argue that the prescriptive approach (that closest to the ideal of the learning organisation) is 'likely to be inconsistent with company objectives' and 'inevitably constrained by commercial and organisational factors'. The implication here is that even a sincere attempt to promote a learning organisation will face a tendency to slide back into Jones and Hendry's organisational learning approach, all that is left of the learning organisation being the legitimating rhetoric of employee empowerment.

In many ways, the idea of a learning organisation is similar to Selznick's 'morally sustaining ideas' and 'socially integrating myths' in relation to leadership as discussed in Chapter 9. This is to be expected, in that implementation of organisational learning can be firmly linked to 'New Wave Manufacturing'. Winfield and Kerrin (1994), in a survey of sixty Midlands manufactures and a case study of Toyota in Derbyshire, note that the 'continuous improvement programmes' associated with organisational learning are deployed directly alongside TQM and JIT programmes. The introduction of such programmes is criticised for a lack of attention to 'human resource issues' (1994: 8) and learning systems and techniques complete the 'whole package' necessary for the effective utilisation of 'new' production practices. Shrivastava (1983: 25) had earlier noted a link between organisational learning and the development and introduction of new management information and control systems, the failure of implementation of which was identified with lack of concern by designers for socio-cultural norms and existing learning practices within the organisation.

The learning organisation would appear to devolve 'into a simple goal-setting exercise underwritten by an appeal to the superordinate goal of organisational survival' (McHugh *et al.*, 1994: 14) and as such has little respect for current learning practices. Goal-setting as a technique is said not only to be effective with scientists, managers, and blue collar workers but is also thus assumed to extend earlier techniques such as Management by Objectives, in that it is claimed to work beyond supervisory and managerial grades. It is claimed by Locke and Latham (1984) to be a core motivational technique (p. 121) that can underpin job enrichment, behaviour modification or other processes. Human resources are fully utilised by directing attention and action, mobilising energy and effort, increasing persistence, and motivating the development of appropriate task strategies. It operates by breaking down goal-related behaviour into simpler sub-routines, in the way that scientific management does with physical operations, thus reducing the stress of dealing with complex goals. Locke and Latham portray it as a tool which 'gets results', but when used improperly can result in 'conflict, feelings of failure, increased stress, dishonesty' (1984: 171).

Goal-setting is an example of the extension of technologies of regulation into what has been termed a 'behaviour technology' which replaces 'impractical models and theories' with 'a technological approach to using human resources effectively for the creation of industrial wealth' (Wellin, 1984: 4). This attempts to integrate the body of knowledge in industrial and organisational psychology into contingent strategies for increasing effectiveness, or 'a practical bag of tools for solving human problems in organisations' (1984: 183). However, it is probable that such strategies will probably never work as intended. Even if individual subjectivity can act, as Knights and

Willmott (1985) argue, to separate people and blind them to their collective interests, it will still operate to motivate and enable them to circumvent such technologies of regulation for their own purposes. You can in no way guarantee that staff will develop the goals set for them, only that they will develop goals.

Systems of staff development provide an example of the extension of goal-setting techniques into attempts at the systematic regulation of workplace identities. Miller and Verduin (1979) place the theoretical base of staff development in perceptual psychology, assuming attitudinal and behavioural changes to be dependant on changing perceptions, as was argued in Chapter 8. The element of 'goal-setting' involved makes staff development the natural heir to MBO, but takes the notion one stage further. Instead of setting goals monitored by senior managers to ensure compatibility with organisational objectives, individuals are required to set goals compatible with their own aspirations and 'needs'. By emphasising the intra-organisational construction of individual identity, managerial strategies for transforming motivation and identity into influence and productivity are hopefully disguised.

In many ways the systems of profiling work utilised in staff development, and now as an integral part of organisational learning practices, act as self-administered and continuously assessed personality, attitude and aptitude inventories, providing both to management and staff feedback useful in the moulding of functional identities. Thus functional activities are integrated into social comparison processes and hierarchical relationships. Profiling can be reinforced by courses, trips and exchanges which act both as rewards and as reinforcers of group and organisational norms. Team-building exercises where members of the same group or organisation are required to dress similarly, and indulge in activities designed to increase group identification, can produce further facilitation effects. Employers such as Ford Motors also offer exchanges to production workers. They visit and work in plants employing new production processes and those which are said to have good productivity and industrial relations records. Return visits presumably imbue others with the values which have made particular plants 'successful'. It is also possible, of course, that such visits highlight worker's perceptions of their dispensability within the international division of labour.

Staff development works by encouraging self-attributions which reinforce organisational objectives and by focusing social comparison on functional activities. It can break down managerial, professional and supervisory work into operational units just as scientific management does with production work. Instead of appeals to ideologies of rationality, neutrality, objectivity and efficiency, it appeals to the subjective ideologies which support individual identities. The probability is that the success of staff development is like that of Organisational Development – dependent on the expectation effects that can be induced in participants (Evden, 1986), consultants (for example) needing to become 'evangelists' who can sell vision rather than working techniques. In this sense, both staff development and organisational learning are no different from attempts to change behaviour and working practices through cultural initiatives and more straightforward attitude change techniques. The use of devlopment profiling is the mechanism through which public commitment to change is acquired through individual's identification of their own 'training needs'. That this is seldom related to any real concern for individual development is evidenced by the argument that learning initiatives can be short-circuited by what Easterby-Smith characterises as an 'obsession with activity' (1992: 28) and Senge (1992: 38) as a concern with *performing rather than learning'*. This bias towards productivity over, and 'bottom-line' definitions of, growth once again confirms the paucity of claims to increase the motivational content of work and refocuses commitment as simple compliance (see Chapter 11).

The difficulties with and self-defeating nature of linking strategic demands to intrinsic factors and general work motivation must in the end question the extent to which systematic control of such factors is ever possible, and in the next section we shall examine the extent to which psychological discourses are claimed to construct systems of discipline and regulation in the workplace.

Committed to work?

Why is it that when a company wants people to direct their purchasing behaviour in a particular direction, they turn to advertising agencies for their expertise in *persuasion* but when they want to direct their own employees' behaviour in a particular direction they call it *motivation*? (Hershey, 1993: 10)

Hershey's concern in examining the practitioner's view of motivation essentially devolves to an appeal for line managers and HRM practitioners to employ the techniques of persuasive communication used by advertisers to compensate for the lack of success of motivation theory. This directly reflects the focus within the Myers model on the extent of managerial abilities to exert influence at the psycho-social level being limited to training and communication. Just as our treatment of subjectivity involves the notion of being a self-aware subject and of being subject to processes and structures, the notion of commitment implies both a condition of personal commitment to courses of action or belief and one of 'being committed' in the sense of being locked into a system which is somehow beyond our control. The first of these conditions is that aspired to in the mainstream literature on motivation, while the second is more representative of the critical literature on management. The latter view presents organisations as institutions to which we are committed against our will and where persuasive *therapeutic* techniques are utilised on us in order to produce a good 'organisation person'.

This view harks back to Goffman's notion of a total institution in his 1961 book *Asylums*. Such institutions – exemplified by prisons, mental hospitals and so on – were seen to have extensive, if not complete, control over their inmates' lives, backed by systems through which to enforce their formal rules. This does not imply that inmates are passive recipients of control and act to construct their own existence within the constraints of the situation. For example, both Goffman and later Becker *et al.* (1963) noted that these institutions also embody informal rule systems enacted by both inmates and staff which can work against the formal rules but which are necessary to the continued performance of their respective roles. The picture here is of total compliance to control but of resistance to, and lack of internalisation of, control systems – almost the opposite of Kanter's notions of mortification and surrender as outlined above.

The extent to which modern work organisations can be likened to total institutions is addressed by Kunda in his case study of control and commitment in 'Tech', a hi-tech US engineering company. On the surface, the resemblance to a total institution is slight, employment at Tech being economically rewarding and often desirable and members being continually involved in 'reflective discourses' which openly embody irony, cynicism and humour. But at the same time there is a pull towards an escalation of commitment to the corporation, and towards corporate definitions of reality, and continual pressure on the boundaries of personal privacy. The outcome according to Kunda, is that 'people over time are submerged in a community of meaning that is to some extent monopolised by management: a total institution of sorts' (1992: 224). The self is not surrendered or captured in Kanter's terms, but the foundations on which the self is built are continually undermined as the authenticity of experience is continually appropriated by corporate ideology.

The effect of such an appropriation of meaning is tantamount to overlaying rules of belief on to the systems of rules regulating behaviour, the imperfect articulation between the two giving rise at the same time to Kunda's reflective discourses and an amount of manufactured uncertainty and insecurity. The insecurity engendered is a classic precondition for the exercise of power through self-discipline, as exemplified in Grey's (1994) study of professional accountants. Within the particular firm studied, the uncertainty produced by exhortations of the superiority of accountants they employed, coupled with a secretive employment and promotion policy, led to constant self-surveillance. This was characterised by a search for 'signs of grace' signalled by formal indications such as salary and job ratings and allocations, and informal signs such as working and social relationships with superiors. Such social comparisons were not only made with peers but with the extent to which individuals fitted the 'types' provided by successful partners. Where 'grace' is found, this reinforces the self-confidence of the individual and engenders a self-fulfilling prophecy of success. Thus to gain, in Whyte's (1957: 404) terms, 'the peace of mind offered by the organisation' and to reduce levels of manufactured uncertainty does not require abject surrender to the formal restrictions or beliefs of the total institution, but will require the same types of tacit collaboration and 'tactful' behaviour that Goffman saw as necessary to the continuation of the performance of the organisation in process.

Human resources – strategy into surveillance

In a wider sense, manufactured uncertainty could be said to be representative of the overall effect of the use of tests and other selection and appraisal techniques discussed in earlier chapters. They will not only (as indicated in Chapter 8) act to increase managerial certainty in decision-making but will also yield increased levels of self-monitoring and environmental scanning by individuals and groups. This may explain why psychological knowledge and technique continues to be an important operational element of strategy, regardless of the lack of success in generating intrinsic motivation and commitment. This role is mainly concerned with implementation rather than with formulation, but even so the role of psychological discourse here could be said to be in opening up operational possibilities for the systematic application of problem-solving and change strategies. Psychological knowledges, then, provide both theoretical legitimacy and technical assistance to projects aimed at the control and utilisation of the 'human resource' in a rational-efficient manner. If you like, the 'real' psychology here is simply in the name, once you internalise the discourse which constructs people as human resources, the rest is just window-dressing.

According to Rose (N. Rose, 1989) the psychological sciences have, over time, 'provided the means for the translation of human subjectivity into terms of the new languages of government of schools, prisons, factories, the labour market and the economy', constituting the domain of subjectivity as 'a possible domain for rational management' (p. 121). Following Foucault, Rose claims that the way to understand the 'mental sciences' is as, 'techniques for the disciplining of human difference: for individualising humans through classifying them, calibrating their capacities and conducts, inscribing and recording their attributes and deficiencies, managing and utilising their individuality and variability' (p. 123). A good example of this is in the 'panoptic power' of surveillance provided by modern information technology. Zuboff discusses the 'psychology of visibility' (1988: 342–55) and examines the methods of resistance to and coping with surveillance and 'panoptic power' within systems designed to control behaviour and increase managerial certainty. For example, 'cheating' on performance appraisal was rife at one site studied, often with the collaboration of foremen, who would release their access codes to allow operatives to maintain efficiency ratings by changing the time 'pricing' of tasks. At the same time, though, information systems could be manipulated to report on how often prices changed in order to provide new measures of performance. The normative power of technologically based transparency of information is enormous because it can engender 'shame' based on 'anticipatory visibility' (1988: 345) and this is only countered by the ingenuity of operatives in manipulating the system and in the possible collectivism engendered by the realisation that everyone is explicitly monitoring everyone else – though this in itself can be a source of normative power where access to information is restricted.

Deetz (1992: 40–3) gives an account of how Foucault's concept of disciplinary power is enacted in overt and self-surveillance in the modern corporation. With the 'battery of psychological (and chemical) tests – experts in attitudes, culture and bodily fluids, the corporation assesses the purity of one's mind and soul' (1992: 40–1), but possibly more importantly the forms of social negotiation and impression management identified by Goffman in the 1960s have been incorporated, so that the 'hopes, dreams and personal commitments' of most employees are brought 'under prior assessment by their own private public eye' (p. 41). The implication for some, according to Deetz, is that the workplace becomes a game, not necessarily for pleasure or even profit, not life or death, but of work or non-work, advancement or stagnation and slippage. The distancing this produces reinforces the necessity to be seen to play within the hierarchically defined rules, whilst making the social and interpersonal relations of the workplace ever more instrumental. This harks back to Kunda's comments that 'life as theatre becomes an all encompassing reality; and the ability to establish a life and a self-independent of the corporation's influence is diminished' (1992: 225).

Another interpretation of accounts such as those of Rose or Deetz is that the role of the psychological sciences in human resource strategies is simply a stage, and not the final stage, in a process that has been going on for over a century – the main departure in more recent developments being that the link is more explicit, in that strategy itself has moved to espouse openly the individualisation of the employment relationship and actively to incorporate peoples' reactions to control systems which in the past tended to utilise psychological knowledge in an indirect, or often covert, manner.

The most easily accessible account of the history of this process is probably given by Hollway (1991), who refers to Rose (ch. 4: 58–61) in charting the dependence on the use of new concepts in statistics which could link individual differences comparatively to population distributions based on the 'normal curve'. Again the give-away is in the terminology: what fits is normal and can be managed, and what does not fit is deviant and can be controlled out. Progress here is in the production of finer techniques of discrimination, once more based on statistical advances. The development of 'non-parametric' statistics, to deal with relationships not fitting normal curves, gave great impetus to the development of social psychology and through this to the 'science' of Organisational Behaviour. The possibilities opened up here are of the incorporation of the full range of human behaviour into organisational repertoires, as opposed to the previously more prescribed gatekeeping functions. In these fine distinctions of difference lies the genesis of the 'developmental' approach to management, which at the same time individualises the relation to the organisation and offers up even a lack of talent or skill as a method of regulation and appropriation of commitment. In this sense, probably the most influential technique to come out of current organisational psychology is that of goal-setting (Locke) discussed above, which in essence delineates the parameters of acceptable performance standards, but which is still essentially a manipulative rather than a participative technique on the basis that the range of goal-related behaviours allowable requires the exertion of self-monitoring of their linkage to organisational mission.

The range and scope of psychology's contribution is demonstrated very well by Hartley and Stephenson (1992: 10–11), who cover areas beyond the focus on job analysis and selection that Hollway takes. Socialisation, meaning, reward, commitment, control, conflict, bargaining, group dynamics are all seen to be influenced by psychological discourse – though it is socialisation, conceptions of work and meaning that are most emphasised. Evidence on how exposure to Human Resource Strategies is intended to relate to psychological functioning is given for example by O'Brien (1992: 57–8) who refers to Kohn and Schooler (1983) on the effects of work on personality to point out that many jobs are low in what is termed 'occupational self-direction', which is 'a function of substantive complexity, the closeness of supervision and routinization' (O'Brien, 1992: 58). Where people lack occupational self-direction this has adverse consequences for both their desire to seek work which exercises their autonomy and skills and for their overall job performance (1992: 58). This is the challenge for HRS: competition in terms of costs, markets and resources in the modern environment does not admit to 'going through the motions' or 'muddling through'. The dawn of the appraisal systems and PRP move us back from the positive reinforcement paradigm of Human Relations to the active punishment of non-goal-directed behaviour. The punishment is in not receiving rewards or in being held back in a career path, along with the recognition of an inability or unwillingness to 'pull with the team'. What this may in the end lead to, though, is large-scale 'satisficing', a form of *bounded rationality* where people do not seek optimal choices or decisions, but only those that satisfy limited constraints – that is, those set by current strategies.

Where there have been increases in overall cost efficiency in the workplace, these have not in the main tended to come from the movements like QWL and Job Redesign which attempted to address directly the factors which mediate occupational self-direction, but have been more likely to stem from factors such as the replacement of labour, decreases in the necessity for supervision and work intensification. Though no matter whether the social relations of work have been structured around automated technologies, cell-based production techniques or around low wages and a pool of unemployed, all can act to encourage self-monitoring and regulation of behaviour to normative standards. The crucial factor here is who sets the standards – the work-group or occupational community or the policy-setting levels of organisational management.

Thus overall importance of psychology to HRS lies in that 'managerial control strategies can never be anything more than variable, contradictory and incomplete: hence control has to be continuously constructed and reconstructed (Keenoy, in Hartley and Stephenson, 1992: 107): a reconstruction that is dependant both on operational technologies which can retrofit human behaviour into current strategy and legitimating discourse. The classic model of HRM from Guest (Hartley and Stephenson, 1992: 129) is a good indication of the extent to which psychology both drives and is driven by Human Resource Strategy. Rather than being a strategy which links people and policy through superordinate goals, this can be seen as an essentially pragmatic process. Policies are driven simply by what can be achieved out of the desired organisational outcomes considering the state of current knowledge. These policies are then bartered to the workforce, under the banner of achievable Human Resource outcomes and the ideological legitimations of leadership, culture and strategy. It is, however, not too difficult to imagine the fate of policies or HRM outcomes which become counter-productive to overall organisational outcomes or allow self-direction based on communities of interest antithetical to those outcomes.

Probably the best illustrations of the links between psychology and HRM strategies are given by Steffy and Grimes (1992), who do actually make distinctions between the more eclectic and client-orientated personnel/occupational psychology and the more theoretical/critical organisational psychology (sometimes nowadays described as 'work psychology'). They argue that the self-regulating discourse of personnel/organisational psychology (POP) not only shapes the 'policies and practices that regulate human resource activities' (1992: 182), but that it can 'systematically restrict workplace democracy and participation'. The notion is that the activities of POP regulate the 'internal labour markets' of organisations, claiming legitimacy through rigorous control of methods, factors, variables and practices. This is essentially sympathetic magic for the 1990s, if your strategy doesn't work, then you aren't performing the rituals properly!

Steffy and Grimes underwrite their argument with the assertion that surveillance and documentation coerce human behaviour both spatially and temporally (1992: 192). Experience is contoured by positioning both in structural/hierarchical terms and in 'queues' produced by selection and appraisal systems. Such queuing systems promote individual competitiveness and can hinder organisational democracy and productivity, especially where work requires 'team effort and collective responsibility' (p. 193). In addition, the encouragement of Type A behaviour, 'trying to accomplish more in shorter periods of time', 'produces conflict between work and self . . . forcing the self to adjust to work, and not vice versa' (p. 193). On these bases, at least, the actuality of control and influence systems outweigh the rhetoric of mission and integrative and harmonising goals.

Conclusion

Bowles and Coates (1993: 18) claim that 'the evidence is that technologies of regulation are being deployed more extensively by employers', in terms of more systematic testing, appraisal and review procedures. At the same time, they recognise that in their own area of concern, performance appraisal (PA) techniques, distrust of both their validity and utility is rife amongst both managers and employees. There is still often an idealised view of the benefits of PA to the organisation, but the practical difficulties, lack of relevant skills in practitioners and appraisees and the awareness of the 'top-down' control aspects of PA by employees, make PA a more troublesome proposition in reality than in rhetoric.

As a counter point to the view that technologies of regulation are becoming more pervasive, Johns (1993), in reviewing the adoption of industrial/ organisational (I/O) psychology-based personnel practices in the USA, concludes that such techniques are actually taken up less frequently than might be expected on the basis of their 'scientific' merit. In the areas covered – recruiting, training, performance appraisal and compensation systems – the tendency appeared to be that where I/O practices were taken up their implementation was often of a casual nature and frequently violated what was acknowledged to be currently valid I/O prescriptions for their use. Johns recognises that the introduction of I/O practices is linked to OD concerns with resistance to change, and that if such change is desirable, the adoption of 'less than optimal human resource practices' (1993: 571) needs to be understood.

The question arising from these arguments appears to be 'if managers want to achieve systematic regulation of behaviour and control of psycho-social factors, why don't they do it properly?'. If we return to the comments made in Chapter 5 on Deetz and others concerning power and Foucauldian anaysis we need to remember that it is the fact of resistance to control and the existence of personal and group agendas and identities that produces the requirement to regulate and discipline. In our current 'sub-total' institutions it is the rhetorical and ideological systems of control that appear to be given the serious treatment and support rather than the technical and behavioural systems. This smacks of a degree of 'self-evangelism' by and from managers, who seem to be the ones who need convincing that commitment can be mobilised, resulting in an endless striving to mobilise their own commitment to the changes they espouse.

In the next chapter, we shall move on to examine how the construction and maintenance of identities is implicated in the production of control and self-control in employees and managers alike and the contrivances through which such *identity work* is achieved. This dialectic between the shaping of identities and the forms of resistance and coping which arise out of that domination is for many of us, *the* experience of being organised.

CHAPTER 11

Identity work

Social organization is both means and bar to control. The concrete physical and biological settings in which actions occur are crucial. It is thus the outcomes and contentions among identities which is what cumulates into social organisation. (Harrison, 1992: 16)

Explanations of identity

As argued in Chapter 8, the mainstream agenda in OB can be shown to refer to common and basic processes through which individuals develop identities. Through these processes, notably learning, perception and socialisation, the individual is seen to develop a distinctive personality and patterns of motivation. There are many useful things to learn from examining that journey, but as an account of the development of subjectivity and identity within an organisational context, it has distinct limitations. It fails adequately to understand individual identity as a social reality through which we transact with our environment. Hence we deal with objective reality through a subjective construction which interprets and shapes our whole world in terms of what we value about ourselves. Our focus on subjective identity lies in this process, because as individuals we guide our actions according to what will in our view best defend, enhance or substantiate our identities. As Knights and Willmott (1985) argued, each of us is effectively engaged in securing for ourselves identities which provide both a sense of personal stability and a basis for directing our activity. Identity in this light is a tool which we use to present ourselves in – and possibly transform ourselves into – images appropriate to our social, cultural and work context.

Unless one takes personality and identity as being entirely a genetically determined phenomenon, there can be little doubt that an individual's identity is to a great extent determined by social contexts and pressures. In researching differential socio-emotional development in male and female children, Lewis found that as early as biological influences can be distinguished, there are parallel differences in the treatment of the two sexes by adults and other children (M. Lewis, 1975). Thus though biological influences undoubtedly have some effects on personality in the same way that they have an influence on hair colour and general bodily characteristics, these effects cannot be easily differentiated from social or environmental influences.

According to Weigert et al. (1986: 31) 'identity is a definition that transforms a mere biological individual into a human person. It is a definition that emerges from and is sustained by the cultural meanings of social relationships activated in interaction.' To extend the above example, if someone dyes or changes their hairstyle, they have taken steps to place a self-directed social construction on the body they were born with. They are taking for themselves an identity produced out of what they select as attractive or appropriate out of the social values, expectations and fashions of their time. The tradition of sociological social psychology represented by Weigert and other writers tries to avoid the contradictions which have existed between notions of personal and social identity. They take the view that identity is a social product which is both bestowed on individuals by others and appropriated by individuals for themselves. It takes the form of a *typified self*, in that it is any of a number of self-produced categorisations out of what is available to the individual within the various situations in which they participate.

If the focus is shifted from personal to social identity, it is possible to see that we are constantly representing our subjective selves to the others in our social environment. In the way we dress, speak and behave we present a changing image of who we are to those with whom we interact: our identity is, in this sense, a negotiated construction. Depending on whom we are dealing with at the time, we can present an image which is intended both to appear appropriate to the situation and to appear consistent with the expectations of the other. Using a Symbolic Interactionist framework, Erving Goffman (1971) explored this conception of self within a dramaturgical metaphor: representation of social identity being a performance analogous to that of an actor. The image presented is not necessarily the 'real' self of the person, but is a situationally appropriate image sustained both by the 'actor' and by those observing and/or interacting with the performer. The others involved collaborate with the actor to enable him or her to present a consistent performance and hence a social identity consistent within the situation. The students in a lecture theatre, for example, collaborate with the lecturer to maintain an image of authority for the latter and of subordination for themselves, even though they may in no way consider themselves socially or intellectually inferior to the lecturer. They simply exercise *tact* in order to continue participating in the production of a performance which fits the perceived rules of the situation.

The interface between social and personal identity lies in this act of interpersonal negotiation. A social identity does not simply spring fully formed from the demands of the situation, but requires effort and practice from the individual and appropriate feedback from others. Thus the contexts from which we are able to construct a unique subjective identity for ourselves consist mainly of 'rationalised' performances, and we construct our personal identity out of the strategies and responses we devise to deal with the situations we encounter. The problems which many people find in discovering their 'own' identity may in part arise from the consequences of trying to be consistent over time and from the wide range of images they have had to present to survive in a complex and changing social environment.

The idea that we each possess a core identity which relates to what we value about ourselves is examined in the social learning conception of identity (Miller, 1963). As a source of meaning, identity links us to others in the social structure through perceived similarities and processes of identification. As definition identity sets us apart from others, it is the basis of social comparison in that it shows us the things and people with whom our particular set of personal meanings debar us from identifying. Personal, subjective identity consists of the meanings and images we have found accurately to represent us in the past. Social identity, where it is different to the former, consists of the negotiated position between our personal identity and the meanings and images demanded of us in our current social context.

This leads us to a final aspect of identity as a linking concept between differing levels of explanation. We gain identities through interaction and association with others, but the major source of these interactions and associations is not other individuals in themselves but the social and cultural groupings to which we belong. These groups provide us with points of reference and comparison out of which we can define ourselves. Social groupings are in turn defined in terms of the social structure within which they exist. Through this route identity is directly moulded by social structure. For this reason, Miller (1963) saw identity as the foundation of the links between social structure and personality and fundamental as such to the explanation of socialisation, motivation and psychological conflict. Our personal transactions with social structures are conducted for the most part through the organisations we belong to, work for and with which we have to deal. Organisations attempt to socialise people into their particular workplace cultures. Management attempts to influence individual motivation to its advantage. The amelioration of the psychological, interpersonal and group conflicts engendered by these activities is a major rationale for the involvement of social and behavioural scientists in organisations.

Redefining the agenda

To understand more adequately the individual's development towards becoming a participant in organisations who is active, yet acted upon, we also need further to redefine some of the issues and agenda. For example, because so much of OB takes the structures, workings and goals of organisational life for granted, it underestimates the degree to which the environment restricts sources of meaning for secure identities and imposes costs on individuals. The resources which an individual can bring to an *identity project* will depend on their *situational power* in the organisation. Admittedly, this situational power does not depend simply on a person's place in an organisational hierarchy. An individual's perception of their own situational power, whether at an interpersonal, group or organisational level, will also condition how secure they feel. Thus a shopfloor worker can construct an identity just as, or even more, secure as that of someone with more position power. These identities are also not necessarily situation specific: they can provide meaning and support outside the context within which they were constructed, though there are of course limits. The 'organisation man', secure in his or her identification with organisational goals and objectives, may generalise associated attitudes and behaviours to situations where such an identity may be inappropriate.

Nevertheless, the attitudes, behaviours, and abilities through which our identities are externally communicated will reflect the constraints placed on us at work and the standards and values of the dominant organisational cultures with which we are in contact. The individual and group identities we eventually secure will be favourable, neutral or antagonistic to organisations on the basis of the climate and context in which they are constructed in, mediated by our experiential base and the standards of comparison this gives us.

The treatment of identity in mainstream psychology also tends to neglect contextual issues because it treats identity in the same fashion as we tend to do in everyday life, as inherent in the person. Breakwell (1987: 95) argues that psychologists 'tend to treat identity as the origin of action', and use it as a 'motivational variable'. In contrast, we have to see identity as the outcome of interaction within particular material contexts which act as constraints on available sources of meaning and on the process of identity construction.

The central limiting factor on available sources of meaning is the context of *fragmented* and *commodified* work. Labour is reduced to abstract capacities which serve the ends of production rather than those of the person; as in the appropriation by work organisations of the *use-time* available to individuals for developing and pursuing their own capacities, abilities and interests (Seve, 1978). Subjectively, this reduction of the relations between people and things to their value in a system of exchange both increase feelings of powerlessness and decreases feelings of personal responsibility. In an externally controlled environment, the most individuals can often hope for is to maintain or increase their situational power and material resources. Our relationships with, and our attribution of motives to, others are reduced to their instrumental function in the process of, 'accumulation without regard to need' (Wexler, 1983: 122). Socio-psychological models of motivation continually reflect this, as in the rational calculations of personal advantage we are assumed to make in exchange and equity theory or the assessments of personal power in Lee and Lawrence's 'political model' of motivation (see Chapter 8).

The instrumentality of relationships also extends into the definition of gender identities in the workplace. Hearn and Parkin (1987) identify the *desexualised* nature of work organisations as reinforcing patriarchy and sexism. Instrumentality in the continuing forms of fragmented, Taylorised work relations defines masculinity and reproduces organisational work as a male concern:

> The workman is, potentially at least, nothing more than the doer of the task, without feelings and emotions. The ideal workman would appear to almost lose physical presence, or be a mere disembodied bearer of role, in effect part of a machine system. (Hearn and Parkin, 1987: 19)

Women workers are in general separated from the dominantly male culture of organisations and feminine gender identity is suppressed or at best marginalised. Women managers especially are often required to exhibit what is almost a male gender identity in work and are often viewed as exceptions to women in general. Hearn and Parkin (1987: 108) cite as an example the lack of appropriate female role models in management on which to base standards and the subsequent development of the 'image' or clothing consultant to advise women in particular on what is termed 'executive' or 'power' dressing. Likewise domestic labour is not viewed as 'real' work in the fashion that paid work is, the identity construct of 'worker' being reserved for the latter. Women's labour in organisations can often be an extension of domestic labour, as in the example of bosses' secretaries who act as, 'office wives, protecting their charges from unnecessary interference and strain, making tea, buying presents, even cleaning their bosses' false teeth', (1987: 92).

Sexual, and racial, discrimination in labour markets is reinforced by stereotypical categorisations of women and black workers which portrays them as 'naturally' inferior in various abilities or only suited to certain types of work. Notions such as women being better suited than men to boring, repetitive tasks serve to legitimise restricted access to labour markets. Black workers in particular can be discriminated against in the recruitment and selection process on the basis of a stereotyped lack of acceptability in white workplace cultures. Jenkins (R. Jenkins, 1986) notes that the causes of racism are often attributed to those who are discriminated against; 'managers do, in the main, see black workers as posing problems for their organisations. These problems were typically seen to be created by black workers, not by white racism' (1986: 114).

Predominantly white, male management, whose workplace identities would be expected to be closely aligned with organisational goals, would not be expected to view problems as created by their own racism or by racism institutionalised into workplace cultures. Rather, they would be seen to reside in those who demonstrably deviate from the cultural standards they have come to see as 'natural'. White workers are viewed as individuals, whereas black workers are perceived as groups characterised by often contradictory stereotypes: 'if you've got a problem with one of them, you've got a problem with all of them, whereas with the whites, you're just dealing with an individual' (R. Jenkins, 1986: 99). Of course, the fact that people tend to fall back on the resources of group identity in the face of discrimination and consequent situational powerlessness, is wholly understandable. The unfortunate effect is that it simply acts to reinforce stereotypes. Falling back on group identity is also a perceived problem with white workers, especially when that identity is crystallised in trade union activity. But this type of resistance is at least seen as acceptable in the sense that its source is a competing power structure, which is also likely to be seen as part of the same socio-cultural framework, and thus their actions are legitimised, though disapproved of.

It is important to recognise that any form of organisational domination does not only or primarily occur through overt coercion such as threats to job security. Consent has to be mobilised because domination by coercion is often 'inefficient': it requires constant reinforcement of coercive pressures and extensive monitoring of reactions to them. Domination of the individual through self-limitation and constraint is far more effective. This is engendered through individual assimilation of, and accommodation to, dominant workplace cultures and ideologies, as discussed in Chapters 7 and 10. At its most visible level, this process can be seen in the internalisation of the norms and accepted standards of behaviour in work-groups which occurs in organisational socialisation and in the construction of the 'concertive controls' proposed by J.R. Barker (see Chapter 10). If consent is not present, the pressures to shape ourselves in appropriate images may not be perceived as legitimate and may actively promote resistance. In Westwood's (1984) account of the lives of women at 'Stitchco' the women participated in a patriarchal labour process which from the management view was 'harmonious' in its appeals to both common progressive goals and paternalistic values. The women, however, had a 'clear understanding that there were sides in industry and that these sides maintained an uneasy truce which was easily broken' (1984: 25). Westwood argues that the, 'deprivation, pain and waste that black and white working-class women live with on a daily basis', can be, 'a spur to action rather than defeat'. As such, domination becomes the source of an identity project which empowers their creativity and resourcefulness, sisterhood being the focus of a resistance which does more than enable their survival in a hostile environment.

When we attempt to construct an identity that offers us a degree of protection from uncertainty (Knights and Willmott, 1985) we often find ourselves in competition with others for sources of meaning. This may take the form of access to and 'possession' of material resources for living and the symbols on which we place value. In order to maintain an identity we attempt to control our environment and those in it and to resist those pressures which act to define our identities for us. The sense of individual meaning we gain from identity gives us a basis to resist external manipulation, but at the same time places us in competition with those in a similar position to ourselves who could aid us in our resistance. Thus we could both resist the attempts to shape our identities made by groups in organisations, and yet use our positional or situational power in those groups to enhance our identities at the expense of others. The separation that this achieves acts to blind us to the fact that an organisation is a structure of *interdependence* and the success of systems of control depends upon our compliance with managerial demands. By neglecting the context in which we compete for sources of meaning we can become estranged from one of the major sources available to us, the collective identity and power of those with similar interests.

We have already recognised that, in terms of identity construction, the contextual issues raised above are not necessarily simply sources of constraint. They may for some individuals be the very factors which allow them to secure identity. The worker with worries over job security may find meaning in defining themselves in line with nationalist or traditionalist sentiments which can give expression to their fears through hostility to 'immigrant' workers or women who should remain at home. Similarly hostility and resistance to organisational goals and practices may arise out of the conditions of exploitation, domination and alienation which renders others submissive. It would appear that identities are constructed out of whatever meanings are readily available and are constrained only by the individual's ability to sustain them. Thus the construction of identity is a continuous process which has to be understood in the context of the workplace, where it is maintained and reproduced on a daily basis.

Organisations and identities

If our society is characterised by the involvement of individuals in organisational structures, then organisations are characterised by their attempts to *control the performance and behaviour* of the individuals of whom they consist. It is this rule-bound control of individual behaviour which distinguishes organisational behaviour from other forms of social organisation. Home and family life, for example, are undoubtedly organised, and controls and sanctions are placed on the behaviour of family members. But this control is in no sense as systematic as that existing in even a small commercial organisation. On this basis, for work organisations of any type to maintain their present forms of authority, hierarchy and control it becomes necessary to produce some kind of change in the types of regulation to which employees will consent – this was the main theme of Chapter 10. There is, of course, a great amount of prior socialisation for work contained in our experience of schooling and this is presently being extended in the kinds of job training discussed in Chapter 3 to 'fit' youth better for work. This, however, merely serves to illustrate that organisations depend on being able to mould people into the kind of workers they need.

However, organisations do not simply transform individual identities at work by some form of brainwashing; nor do they simply depend on individuals recognition of economic necessity to ensure their consent to the control of their performance in their work. The concept of 'economic man' is not adequate to the explanation of how a worker's consent to change and rationalise his or her working practices can be obtained. The rules and procedures used to control work-related behaviour will often conflict with the individual's attempt to secure a stable and favourable identity. Unless, that is, people can manage to construct for themselves a workable identity out of the very rules which constrain them. Alternatives can include becoming an 'organisation man'; setting themselves up in opposition to their employers; or distancing themselves from the whole affair and concentrating their lives on external interests. Whatever the tactics employed by individuals as mechanisms for survival and coping, they may in time transform themselves into an image that functions in a way that is useful to the organisation for which they work. Even the deviant or militant worker is useful in this sense in terms of providing an image of what the 'good ' employee should not be, and in providing a focus for the attribution of blame.

Identity becomes not only the basis of individual involvement in organisations but also the basis for manipulation by them. This is achieved through a negotiated transaction between organisational strategies of control and individual strategies for securing identity. The consequences of this negotiation are not always positive for the organisations concerned. We all to some extent cope in a creative fashion with the constraints of work or unemployment. Strategies used to survive can become powerful tools for extending our own abilities and capacities. Those who try to manipulate our behaviour must face the fact that they are attempting to interfere with the self-perceptions and judgements that actually make us what we are. If manipulation is perceived as going too far, it may do no more than to encourage employee identities more resistant to organisational control.

Identity work and situational power

Subjective experience in organisations consists of lived relationships bounded by social, organisational and work-group cultures in the context of structural and ideological constraints. These form the three basic contexts within which individual identity is continually reproduced. Lived relationships are the subjective arena of identity construction. Even though our subjective 'now' is informed by our past experience and moulded by the pressures brought to bear on us, we still act as if we are independent and self-directed entities. Thus our everyday existence can continue as if it largely bypasses the influence of cultural and structural constraints on our behaviour.

Social, organisational and work-group cultures are the arenas in which 'fitting behaviour' is moulded and regulated and in which we perform 'identity work' (Goffman, 1971; Cohen and Taylor, 1978). Just as our perceptions of the world are simplified by the use of stereotypical categories, the activities we carry out in the workplace are simplified by the use of stereotyped categories of behaviour. This process of constructing and enacting scripts we shall refer to as *'scenariotyping'*. These various cultural contexts also represent the medium of communication and translation of structural contexts to everyday existence. These are the limiting factors on identity construction in work and social life. They act to define possible sources of meaning and activity in hierarchical organisations and also provide the contextual limitations on what is acceptable practice for those who study, design and intervene in organisations.

Individual and group concerns with job security, status, promotion, conflict and satisfaction, can be characterised under a number of related categories. Included are the prediction and control of reality; coping with uncertainty; retaining autonomy and discretion; and maintaining or enhancing individual assessments of situational power. For the individual these represent the tensions created by trying to maintain and monitor the *strategies* through which we enact behaviours. A secure identity, or at least an identity which is not too severely threatened, forms both a bulwark against threats and provides personal standards for social comparison and action. The ability to control the various categories of individual and group concerns can also represent sources and reflections of organisational or situational power. The strategies utilised by individuals and groups to secure or appropriate identity will seek to control sources of power and meaning. As a consequence, identity construction may threaten the organisation of work (Weigert, 1986, Knights and Willmott, 1985, Breakwell, 1987).

Organisations, in trying to reduce uncertainty (see Chapter 10), are willing to allow room for the maintenance of worker identities in so far as they make the control of behaviour and production processes more effective. In implementing the introduction of CNC, machine tools firms such as Westland

Helicopters have allowed an element of manual input from operators on the basis that human intervention is necessary in automated processes because they are not absolutely error-free (Corbett, 1985a). Such decisions allow operators to exert some levels of skill and discretion within labour processes with increasing tendencies towards deskilling. Thus alongside gains in the reduction of uncertainty in the production process there may also be benefits to the organisation in reducing the level of threat to skilled identities implied by automation.

The greater the effort put into attempts to define employee's work life, the greater the use of undefined areas by workers to develop 'informal work-group cultures'. Cultures of this type can provide workers with a degree of autonomy and a basis for active resistance. By the same token, membership of subcultural groups in organisations may provide the benefits to threatened identities which they do for subcultures in wider society: 'the threatened can regain self-esteem, generate positive distinctiveness and promote continuity', (Breakwell, 1986: 141). Although Breakwell argues that societal subcultures have virtually no impact on power structures, they are, she maintains, the focus of possible social concerns and the associated 'moral panics' (Cohen, 1973) which identify them as being 'scheduled for control'.

This is not to say, of course, that managers never recognise this tendency and take steps to short-circuit the development of informal groups which may, in time, become hostile to organisational goals. Drago and McDonough (1984: 67) quote a management planning document from the General Food's Topeka plant where they were initiating a controlled participation experiment; 'No power groups will exist within the organisation that create an anti-management posture'. In trying to predict and control reality, for most of us it is our subjective concepts and values that are most amenable to change, as we cannot on our own hope to change the structural framework that surrounds us in the organisations within which we work. Even for those with the power to change the form of, and processes within, organisations there is still no absolute security of position or certainty that their actions will produce results fully in line with their goals. Thus, in coping with the uncertainties of organisational life, most individuals are forced either into a strategy of accommodation which necessitates a gradual redefinition of self and subjective reality, or a strategy of assimilation which requires these to be subjected to the superordinate goals of the group.

Putting the pressure on

All people working in organisations face pressures to mould their identities to fit normative expectations. According to Kunda (1992: 11), 'under normative control, membership is founded not only on the behavioural or economic transaction . . . but, more crucially, on an experiential transaction'. Although the expectations which arise originate within the interactions, goals, strategies or policies of the various individuals and groups in an organisation, in subjective terms they can also appear to originate in the organisation itself. In the OB literature expectations are mainly dealt with through the notion of *role*: the roles we wish to play ourselves, the roles others wish or expect us to play and the roles demanded of us from our relations with work organisations. The total number of *role expectations* which impinge on any individual is referred to as a *role-set*, and can comprise of contradictory demands from workmates, supervisors, management, customers or clients and from home or social life. The role expectations are not separate and neutral consequences of status, position or skill. Rather, they are specific and interdependent products of a social organisation of work which itself depends for effective production on the internalisation of role demands. The divisions of labour which result in fragmented work are likewise dependant on *role specialisation* being perceived as a natural social order.

Role control

Salaman (1979: 133–6) raises the possibility that variations in role discretion and role expectations may be linked to strategic decisions on the forms of control exercised over different categories of workers. Professional employees face contradictory expectations arising from their peers, their external professional associations and from the organisation itself. These have to be handled by the individual and managed by the organisation. Direct control by managers over professionals, involving rule-bound job definitions and tightly regulated behaviour, may conflict with the latters' values and socialisation. A more effective form of control can be achieved through a focus on their role as a professional, performing their organisational duties to the satisfaction and benefit of their masters or clients.

In contrast to the forms of control appropriate to professionals, 'Role type control is less commonly employed with workers because senior members of organisations (and, possibly, the workers themselves) see the workers as being in conflict with the goals and reward system of the enterprise' (Salaman, 1979: 136). The moulding of worker's attitudes and behaviour can be identified with, 'adjusting one's perspectives on what one will be able to achieve' (Frese, 1982: 210). Since such 'adjustments' necessitate at least some internalisation and legitimation of structures of regulation, it may be expected that role-type control would be possible at most levels of organisations. But of course not everyone in an organisation 'knows their place' or is resigned to power-lessness and helplessness. The informal socialisation of workers, or 'learning the ropes', will consist largely of learning the shortcuts around, and resistance to, organisational controls. Such knowledge and its associated activities confer at least some small sense of personal autonomy, meaning and hence identity to workers. Consequently direct controls, combined with elements of technical and bureaucratic control where possible or appropriate, are more often employed by management at lower levels of organisations.

Socialisation within work is not necessarily directed at the technical aspects for other grades. When examining the socialisation of skilled manual workers into their workplace identities, Penn argues that such socialisation is more directed at: 'instruction into the appropriate actions of the trade' (1986: 4). Such instruction and the identities it produces are aimed at generating scripts for interaction in the workplace. They deal with: 'Norms and procedures held to be appropriate for dealing with three groupings found in the workplace: fellow workers, other workers and management' (1986: 4).

This process builds on *anticipatory socialisation* into work in the home and at school, in that apprentices require a commitment to deferred gratification and continued learning after the end of formal schooling. Hence there is a form of pre-selection for skilled manual work in that those who have previously internalised appropriate forms of meaning are preferred: 'a certain degree of seriousness and moral uprightness is required by a sponsor who already works in a firm' (1986: 4). In contrast, 'tearaways' who define their identities as inimical to authority and those who seek immediate extrinsic gratification in work are not wanted (Willis, 1977). Organisations, then, try to get the right kind of material to mould into the images they require.

The types of assessment techniques used in recruitment and selection procedures also reflect differential concerns; this time with the personality dimension of identity. The study by Hollway (1984) cited in the section on personality in Chapter 8, shows that the assessment of managers, and hence the forms of control used over them, are related to the 'fit' of their personalities into dominant organisational cultures. When reviewing organisational recruitment procedures in the British Army and Ford UK, Salaman (1979) also notes that this 'fit' is shown by the candidates' willingness to demonstrate an 'appropriate' range of attitudes.

In this sense, roles are scenariotyped scripts which are themselves as essential to the labour process as the working practices, labour and machinery through which they are played out. Attempts to increase worker 'participation' can thus be seen not only as efforts to place individual goals more in line with organisational goals, but as attempts to produce role-based control of workers. The aim is to produce workers who will themselves initiate the enactment of the correct scripts, rather than having to be directed to do so. This produces savings for the organisation in terms of the amounts of direct supervision necessary and in terms of the number of supervisors needed. There is currently a parallel emphasis on the operational skills 'content' seen as necessary to make management education more responsive to the 'needs' of business. The management trainee is assumed to have the necessary role commitment and motivation to consent to organisational control structures. Thus 'education' becomes a process of exposing the trainee to the 'skills', techniques and attitudes which will be required of them and then teaching them how to recognise the appropriate contingencies in which particular scripts should be enacted.

Role stress

The psychological pressures on individuals have been well-documented, not in terms of pressures to mould identity, but in terms of the intrapsychic conflicts they can produce. Interpersonal conflicts and conflicts between role expectations are seen as causative factors in producing anxiety and stress. An example of the conflicts which fulfilling a role may induce is seen in Hochschild's (1983) notion of *emotional labour*. Hochschild characterises emotional labour as, 'a covert resource, like money or knowledge, or physical labour, which companies need to make the job done' (1993: xii). This was originally identified in occupations where individuals have to manage their emotions in order to serve the commercial purposes of the enterprise. Recent writings on emotional labour (see Fineman, 1993) have extended such notions to the full range of behaviour in work organisations. Using flight attendants and bill collectors, Hochschild (1983) showed how people are constrained to maintain emotions in their work – friendliness for the stewardess; suspension of trust and sympathy for the debt-collector – which relate only to the requirements of the job. This requirement extends beyond individuals and includes collective emotional labour:

> It is not simply individuals who manage their feelings in order to do a job; whole organisations have entered the game. The emotion management that keeps the smile on Delta Airlines competes with the emotion management that keeps the same smile on United and TWA. (Hochschild, 1983: 185–6).

In such situations, where management attempts to mould the social identities of individuals and groups into images consonant with commercial demands, people often become estranged from their own feelings. As an interdependent process, emotional labour requires both the collaboration of the client and the adjustment of personal feelings to accommodate the client's demands. For the emotional labourer identification with the job itself can lead to difficulties in making constant adjustments to situations and considerable socio-emotional costs may be incurred. Work in the 'caring' professions requires that people identify closely with their work and that they exercise self-control over their role-based work. The responses people make when they cannot take the demands that their work places on them are examined in the section below on individual responses to pressures on identity.

The problem with role-based stress as an explanatory concept is that it has the effect of portraying the process as natural and individually-based, instead of as a product of the historically produced conditions of work. In his study of responses to the pressure of work in 'Powerco', Sturdy (1987) notes that management are aware of the negative effects that such pressures have on employee morale and yet would not want to completely remove backlogs of work as it would portray their sections as overstaffed and on occasion would leave people with little or nothing to do.

The anxieties and pressures of work at Powerco led to the practice of 'shifting' in the employees, where people, even in conditions where motivation and commitment might not be expected, indulged in 'unceasing effort beyond what would be expected from even the most committed worker' (1987: 35). Their compulsion to keep ahead of the work and not let backlogs build up, to relieve pressure by getting work 'shifted', extended to refusing breaks and feeling frustrated rather than relieved when interruptions such as computer breakdowns stopped the work. Though partially based in the desire to increase security in work, shifting, according to Sturdy acts, for the individual not only as a relief for the helplessness they feel, but as a mechanism which obscures the experience of subordination itself. By using shifting to cope with the pressure of work, the individual co-operates with the structures of workplace control to produce a sense of identity which offers some level of autonomy and responsibility. At the same time, shifting paradoxically increases the pressures employees feel as both management and themselves come to depend on the gains stemming from their increased productivity. Identities can, then, be reactively moulded as a response to situational stress factors and in directions which reproduce the experience of subordination and domination in work.

Stress control?

The role of the organisation in producing unhealthy systems and conditions of work is in danger of being ignored. In its place we get systems of stress 'management' reinforcing the self-attribution of stress and anxiety as personal problems to be coped with rather than structural issues to be contested.

In order for such programmes to succeed, they have to change both attitudes and cultural factors in the workplace and become part of managerial strategies for moulding the identities of workers. The Control Data Corporation (see Chapter 9) places great emphasis on group sessions where, 'eventually group members learn to help one another to sustain the changes in their behaviour, and they practice various techniques and strategies to avoid failure'

(McKenna, 1987: 402). The feeling that a person can cope with adverse situations can both be a source of meaning and danger to them in, for example, working in difficult and dangerous occupations, such as construction or agricultural work. The result would be to divorce a person's view of their working conditions from their desire for personal safety to the extent that they take unnecessary risks or adhere to dangerous practices.

The ability to deal with and to some extent actually relish a high-pressure working environment is seen as a valued characteristic in managers. The person who is able to cope with the conflicting demands of a managerial position is encouraged to view this capacity as a personality trait which indicates their suitability as a leader. Through such a process it is no surprise that organisational élites come to view themselves as those most fit to lead and survive in the given environment. Such legitimations, though active in the securing of managerial identities, are not necessarily part of any conscious conspiracy of control or domination. They may simply be the habitual response managers have learned in order to cope with various situations where their identities are threatened. Domination and control would thus be outcomes of the scripts managers use in their daily activities, these outcomes requiring from managers, some level of self-justification which ideologies can supply.

It does appear that material on the moulding of identities in organisations tends to focus on professional, skilled and managerial workers. However, such concepts as emotional labour and the utility of 'wellness programmes' would indicate that organisations may routinely attempt to mould the identities of all levels of employees. Aichholzer and Schienstock (1985) examine opportunities for maintaining identities in the face of the intensification of control surrounding the introduction of new technologies. Such intensification is seen in 'tighter binding of human actions with machine processes, an increasing transparency of the labour process as a whole, a rising vertical integration and extension of technological control to white collar work' (1985: 20). They also note a number of apparent 'counter-tendencies' to increased control. These include the reintegration of fragmented work-roles, the revaluing of 'marginal' human functions in work and an emphasis on problemsolving activities. Aichholzer and Schienstock argue that these counter-tendencies in effect pressurise workers to internalise controls in order to soften the new problems of control raised by new forms of technology and work organisation and that this questions the 'maintenance of individual and collective identities in the modern labour process' (1985: 81).

It is, however, possible to identify aspects of the analysis of the shaping of work around technologies which do offer redefinition of psychological pressures and stresses in directions which integrate notions of psychological well-being and growth into the design of work. In particular, the identification of dimensions (see Figure 10.3) through which the degree of flexibility and discretion available to employees can be analysed offers insights into how

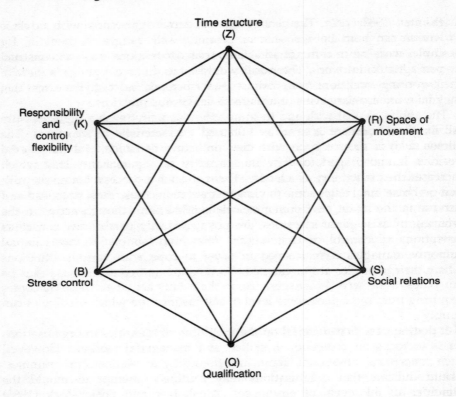

Source: F. Rauner, R. Rasmussen and J. M. Corbett, 'The Social Shaping of Technology and Work: Human Centred CIM Systems', *Artificial Intelligence and Society*, vol. 2 (1980) 56.

FIGURE 10.3   The interrelation of dimensions of experiencing and shaping of work

workers can have inputs to the process of shaping their work-related behaviours, objectives and environment (Rauner *et al.*, 1988: 55–7).

- *Time structure* – time pressures imposed and possibility of individual or group planning use of time themselves.
- *Space for movement* – degree of formalisation versus choice governing movement of workers within and between job functions.
- *Social relations* – degree of formalisation versus informal possibilities in workplace interactions and organisational communications.

- *Responsibility and control flexibility* – scope and degree of responsibility available to workers and possibilities for self-management and control.
- *Qualification* – range of functional abilities related to task and work processes, and possibilities of learning and personality development.
- *Stress control* – degree of control over physical and psychological pressures resulting from work organisation and human-machine interactions.

All six dimensions are to be viewed through their relations to the others. This allows analysis of, in the first instance, the extent to which a labour process permits 'humane' work, and in the second of the dimensions along which increased flexibility and discretion would most benefit psychological well-being. These six interrelated dimensions should enable both more precise determinations of the restrictiveness inherent in a labour process and a focus which emphasises the necessity of designs which enable subjective as well as operational flexibility, thus allowing room for the constructive use of subjective variables in analysing individual experience.

Responses to pressures on identity

The production of scenariotyped behaviours and the ideological formulations which justify them enables people, collectively or individually, to enact their own situational power and resist controls. This does not, however, explain why individuals and groups try to resist organisational controls. Resistance is in itself both a source of meaning and a pressure on identity. This is founded on the perception by individuals of contradictions between the goals, ideologies, approved identities and required behaviours which are exhibited in organisational settings. Leonard (1984: 116–18) identifies four sources of pressures leading to resistance, avoidance and dissent; which provide a useful framework for discussion and reaction.

- *Contradictory consciousness* This arises from competing ideologies based on the material interests of groups and classes. Because dominant ideologies partly clash with people's actual experiences of everyday life, they can never have more than an imperfect influence on identities. Leonard cites class, gender and ethnic struggles as examples of the conflicts which produce psychological disturbances in individuals and can produce acts of deviance, but at the same time still result in a general submission to the demands of the dominant order. These acts of deviance may be directed towards material gains, individual protest or to fulfil particular values not acceptable to the social order. There may be important consequences for organisations in the form of theft, industrial sabotage, or other 'destructive' actions.

- *Unconscious resistance* Leonard represents this partly in Freudian terms as the struggle of id against ego and superego. The individual attempts not to repress or bury those impulses which 'are unacceptable or inconvenient to dominant social forces' (1984: 117). However, impulses to act against the social order may be renounced and buried in the unconscious because the obstacles to action are too great or perceived situational power is too little. Anxiety and frustration are the likely results of everyday unconscious resistance, though at its extreme, internal conflicts could result in forms of mental disorder. Leonard identifies tendencies to neurotic and psychotic illness with social class position. In organisational terms neurotic reactions could be characterised as consistent with the frustrations caused by conflicts around the role-based control and supervisory responsibilities of professional and managerial classes (Kets De Vries and Miller, 1984, have noted neurotic syndromes in managers of failing firms). Psychotic reactions, characterised as escapes into alternative realities, are associated with the working classes. In a parallel concept, the Hungarian psychologist, Laszlo Garai (see Eros, 1974), refers to individuals having recourse to 'fictive satisfactions', when the specifically human 'need' for self-realisation and non-alienated activity is blocked. These can take the form of destructive impulses, cynicism or the ritual affirmation of helplessness, all of which are likely to be perceived as unmotivated or individually deviant.

- *The development of individual capacities* This arises from the attempt to avoid the dehumanising effects of alienated labour. It may lead to the development of personal activities either within work or outside it, which are directed at benefits for the individual rather than the organisation. Outside work they may develop artistic, literary, craft or sporting skills (these also being fictive satisfactions) which 're-humanise' their lives; making active and identity-enhancing use of their time, rather than merely recuperating from work. Within the workplace people can develop capacities from the exploration and development of their skills which extends beyond what is demanded by wage labour. Wilkinson (1983b) provides an example of CNC machine tool operators, some of whom effectively redefined the technology which had deskilled them and brought some interest back into their work by teaching themselves to programme the computers and to edit computer tapes.

    However, just as is the world of fashion or popular music, where people's creative and autonomous control over their own image and expression are eventually incorporated into commercial products, the smart company will incorporate the efforts of individuals to indulge in non-alienated activity into the organisation of the labour process. In the world of the work organisation the 'revolt into style' may be transformed into the instrumental rewards of the suggestion box.

- *Participation in collective action* This 'contains contradictions between hope and despair, optimism and depression, depending on the balance of political forces at any given time' (Leonard, 1984: 118). Capacities are further developed through joining informal coalitions to pursue some more or less specified goal, or becoming formally involved in unions, professional and other associations. The immediate benefit is in an enhancement of situational power through collective strength. Leonard sees benefits in collective resistance, in that it counters individualistic impulses and moves towards altruistic activity which attempts to transform social relations into forms beneficial to the individual and group. It also raises consciousness about forms of change that are available, associated with a redefinition of self that can counter subordination.

These forms are neither exhaustive, nor mutually exclusive. Nor does it necessarily follow that resistance is inevitable, even though it may be structured into the forms and processes of organisations. Where there are no overt conflicts, it is possibly easier for individuals to accept managerial definitions of reality, to become 'organisation people' and to gain meaning from their appointed role. For the purpose of clarity, our further examination of responses to pressures, and threats to identity, is divided into responses at individual and group levels. It must be remembered, however, that these responses are interdependent processes, which can be conceptually separated, but which are all part of the cycle of organisational control and resistance.

Individual responses

In securing and maintaining a stable and meaningful identity, an individual is faced with the difficulty of presenting consistent images to the other people with whom must deal. The pressure engendered by the necessity to perform both organisationally and interpersonally derived roles involves a continuous process of identity management to maintain situational fit or appropriateness. As long as this does not threaten core identity, people can follow the scripts they learn from others in order to fulfil their various role expectations. When threat does arise, they are left with the choice to submit or resist: both involve possibly substantial redefinitions of the identities they have secured.

The management of identities has been explored in work such as that of Goffman (1961) on *impression management*. The individual, like an actor on stage, attempts to maintain a consistent and believable performance for their audience – those who have a significant influence over the role they play. When used in this sense, identity is malleable and instrumentally defined. However active and manipulative such identities are, they are still dependant on the collaboration of others not to interfere with the performance. We know that the performance of an actor is not real. But, according to Goffman, we exercise 'tact' to allow the performance to proceed, as in the case of a management 'pep-talk'.

The management of impressions is one example of the process of identity work referred to earlier. Kunda's study of 'Tech' (1992, ch. 5) provides numerous and excellent examples of forms of identity work (also see Van Maanen, 1992 on the linkage of identity work to discourses of masculinity). These include routine *identity displays* of behaviours which either embrace or distance the worker from organisational roles, and *artifactual displays*, for example, of signs and posters, in personal workspaces which supply the image of 'a strong individual surviving in a hard, competitive, often irrational world' (p. 196). Both types of display are seen as dramatic performances which balance the display of the successful organisational self with an image of ability to organisational concerns giving oneself some space for manoeuvre. But such performance may break down in the context of threats and constraints in the work environment, and we may be forced to respond with impressions and performance which are 'out of character' for the expected role. Kunda characterises these as *enlargement dramas*, where in formal or informal circumstances the routine order of role-playing is allowed to break down temporarily and the individual is allowed to enlarge upon the self she generally presents, exhibiting attitudes or capabilities beyond her required role. Such dramas are often associated with temporary or marginal members of organisations. Similarly, individuals may experience difficulty in coping with situations where their projected images are not adequate to achieving some measure of control or meaning. For example, Hochschild, in examining the supervision of emotional labour, cites the reaction of a flight attendant whose, paycheque had been mishandled, 'I can't take this all day and then come back here and take it from you! You know I get paid to take it from the passengers, but I don't get paid to take it from you' (1983: 18).

The scenariotyped behaviours demanded of those Hochschild examines can, like those demanded of people in the caring professions, conflict with the levels of commitment involved in their work. Such constrained responses can have serious consequences for mental health and social relationships. In order to respond to conflicts between commitment and capacity to act, people may *burnout*. Storlie (1979) argues that this occurs where the individual confronts an intractable reality which cannot be changed, so that the only effective response is to change themselves: the end result being that they continue to 'go through the motions', but remove any emotional or identity investment they had in their work. This acts as a defence mechanism against the stresses that may result from the conflicts between their own tendencies and their role demands. Emotional labour can thus lead the individual into a removal of emotion, labour being reduced to mere activity. This may have some benefits to the employer, but for the employee such numbing of emotional response leads to a loss of a central source of meaning for them, (see Kunda, 1992: 198–204, for an extended discussion).

The identity work we perform depends to a great deal on our ability to utilise and manage the scripts available to us. Conversely, we need to break free of the habituated scripts we use to '*make out*' when the conditions under which we employ them become untenable. Opportunities to secure new or enhanced meanings, symbols, capacities and goods are as much pressures on our identities as are threats to them. The types of opportunity we will respond to will depend upon the current identities and strategies we employ, our perceived power and ability to take them and our expectations concerning what benefits we can hope to obtain. Breaking free from established patterns of identity work can therefore be difficult, as Sloan's (1987) study of sales work illustrates. The salesmen had invested a great deal in a conception of professional identity which could legitimate the arduous work and their manipulative relations with customers. Professionals did not need unions. There was also a gendered dimension whereby masculinity was central to the identity; 'A little alcohol and a lot of imagination reproduced a culture in which reps were not only professional salesmen, but were also professional lovers' (1987: 31); the 'heroic' males of Insco are apparently not alone!

All of the above are responses to the identity concerns of individuals. It is difficult to locate them in a framework which is solely based on different categories of resistance or dissent. The relatively unconscious coping strategies identified by Roy (see Chapter 8) can be seen as responses to identity concerns, but are essentially strategies of accommodation rather than resistance. Typical forms of individual response to pressure contain a combination of coping strategies, instrumentally derived tactics and accommodation to the dominant culture, as well as different types of resistance. As far as the individual is concerned, they are making-out in the best fashion possible in the given circumstances, the form of response being determined in subjective terms by what appears to work. As long as there are available scripts which satisfy goals and identity concerns, there are no real bars to an individual fitting into whatever forms of work and survival they have access to.

Such strategies or responses could in one sense be said never entirely to fail. With the capacity to redefine meanings and manage impressions, human beings are capable of creating their own self-fulfilling prophecies, shifting the ground on which they stand to justify both success and failure. We not only manage the impressions we give to others, but those we produce of ourselves. Central to this are self-attributed judgements which justify our actions in terms of our current identity concerns and environmental influences.

In counterpoint to strategies which lead to extremely negative consequences for the individual, there are forms of making-out which can lead more unambiguously to social recognition, approval and self-justified identities. Recognition as a leader in an organisation is one such form. Pressure to define identity in line with the assumed leadership qualities would in turn lead to behaviours and self-perceptions supportive in subjective terms. The failure of others to recognise an individual as a leader, or attempts to undermine their leadership, might lead to perceived contradictions with their self-justified role. These could be handled by more autocratic attempts at control, justified by attributions of deviant characteristics to those causing the disturbance. Conversely, if strategies to cope with the situation fail and put the identity of the ostensible leader at risk, he could distance himself from the role on the basis that dealing with such people was impossible or not worth the effort.

The strategies suggested in the example above are two of those that Knights and Willmott (1985) identify as being used by individuals secure identities and reduce anxiety. These are described as *domination* and *distancing*. In organisations, a strategy of domination would involve those with power over the distribution and possession of scarce resources using it to give themselves the illusion of independence and security. It is partially an illusion, because such reliance acts to obscure the interdependence of social relations. Managers or others can then ignore the fact that their power is dependant on the compliance of their subordinates.

Compliance in this sense is related to Rotter's (1972) notion of internal and external *loci of control*. People who feel that they are externally controlled may also put themselves into a state of *'learned helplessness'* where the tendency to comply becomes part of the way they define themselves (Seligman, 1975). To subordinates, however, compliance may simply be their way of making-out and avoiding 'identity damaging disciplinary controls' (Knights and Willmott, 1985: 25). Strategies which employ the, 'cynical distancing of self from the activities and social relations within which individuals are immediately involved' (1985: 27) reinforce individualism and subordination.

Distancing is also one of the main forms of identity work identified by Cohen and Taylor (1978). Unlike Knights and Willmott, their focus is not on power and interdependence, but rather on 'escape attempts' from, or resistance to, the mundanity and unpleasantness of everyday life – in other words, on subjectively making-out. However, the strategies they see as employed in identity work can still have relevance to the understanding of how making-out is incorporated into the social relations of production. Cohen and Taylor start out at the level of the 'regularities which we happily accept as part of life' (1978: 26). These regularities are not necessarily tedious behavioural repetition, but are scripts to which we unreflexively accommodate as a method of managing the 'paramount reality' of our objective world. Scripts in this sense are more than the 'mindless' behaviour posited by Langer or the 'sensorimotor' activity posited by Hacker and Volpert (see Chapter 8).

The habitual dependence on scripts referred to by Cohen and Taylor can be a defence against uncertainty and provide meaning through its very regularity. However, our capacity for self-reflection allows us to create a 'zone for self' or 'identity domain' (1978: 32), which enables us to distance ourselves from those who appear to be committed to the scripts which they live by. The capacity to be self-reflexive can effectively remove the need actually to do anything about the conditions of our existence, because we critically separate ourselves from them in our thoughts. At the same time, we often deprecate those we see as not having our own level of critical self-awareness, defining them as something less than ourselves. The paradox here is the likelihood that our fellow workers are having the same thoughts as and about ourselves. But they do not see our thoughts, only our regulated actions and routine behavioural displays.

A concomitant capacity which self-reflexiveness endows us with is the release of the *escape into fantasy*, where we can alter the conditions of our life to our own satisfaction. This form of escape is akin to the strategy of unconscious resistance identified by Leonard. Leonard's identification of these escapes with position in the organisational hierarchy can now be understood, in that fantasy is free. Cohen and Taylor also note socially institutionalised routes of escape which are seen as legitimate self-expression, and where 'assertions of meaninglessness of the activity are virtually taboo' (1978: 95). These *activity enclaves* give us free areas in our lives, where, in the terminology of Seve and Leonard, we can develop 'personal concrete capacities'. Such socially approved escapes from work or the lack of it include hobbies, games, sports, holidays, and the attractions of mass culture.

On the other hand, there are less socially approved activity enclaves which more resemble Garai's fictive satisfactions, in that they are often socially viewed as self-obsessive or destructive. 'Preoccupations' with sex, gambling, drugs and even dependence on therapy are examples of this form of escape. They are, however, only different from other forms in terms of the social, legal and historical contexts in which they are carried out. Again, self-reflexiveness carries its own internal contradictions. Distancing ourselves from the roles we play is, in the end, another limited and passive strategy which tends to confirm existing organisational structures and separates the individual from the possibilities inherent in social relations.

Finally, to escape from this vicious spiral of making-out through reconstruction of identity concerns, Cohen and Taylor identify the strategy of *self-conscious reinvestment*. The individual becomes recommitted to aspects of the very regularities – language, rituals, clothes – from which they are escaping. Within work organisations this represents the return to the fold, making something of one's life or the rescue of career. All of these means of psychic escape can be utilised to further managerial control, either by employee's dependence on the financial and social supports necessary to pursue them or, in the case of reinvestment, the cleaving back to the very structures of control themselves. For those who run organisations, the problem is to monitor the identity work of employees to ensure that they do not overstep the bounds of the acceptable. For the employee, the problem is to discover the appropriate mode of escape, enjoyment and making-out for the subjective and objective conditions pertaining at the time.

Group responses

Individuals use groups actively to transform their personal and social identities. For example, the reflexiveness involved in the raising of consciousness of disadvantage in social groups can be the spur for responses to pressures which direct the use of groups as technologies of action. Thus interest groups can actively promote not only the material interests of members but also their development of positive identities as mechanisms for making-out. The patriarchal nature of power relations in organisations is currently being contested throughout industry, commerce and the professions by women's groups which rely on their own systems of *networking* to counter the male cliques who generally control their destinies. Such networks provide both a forum for ideas and information and work to heighten awareness of the position of women in organisations. Their capacity for social transformation will be dependant not only on the extent and nature of the contacts they can build up but also on the extent to which they can empower women to develop strong individual and group identities. On this basis they are often more than promotional or defensive interest groups, in that they act to foster the recognition and self-development of the capacities of all women. 'Our purpose is to help women to develop their potential – not to foster élitism' (North-West Women into Management, 1987). The use of networking by managers in the social construction of leadership, negotiation and teamworking is discussed in some depth by Hosking and Morley (1991: Part 3).

The recognition of group identity by members and those outside group boundaries, will be a major determinant of the kinds of responses groups will make to threats to their identity. The better defined the identity of a group, the greater the value of the group to its members as a source of social support, comparison and evaluation. The more effective these processes are, the greater the range of external pressures which can be perceived as affecting the group; and thus the more likely that some kind of collective response will be demanded. Likewise, the stronger the identity of a particular group, the more the likelihood of other competing groups perceiving them and their actions as sources of threat, and thus the more likely that competitors will take action which once more demands some form of response.

An important factor is the extent to which group identity is constructed around a coherent set of values, common instrumental strategies for maximising extrinsic rewards or the needs and desires of group members for affiliation and interaction. This is most visible in the contestation over control of the labour process between management and workers. But that conflict is also manifested within intergroup relations. Thompson and Bannon (1985) show that the instrumental and anti-authoritarian attitudes of the better paid 'high-flying' groups caused friction not only with management, but with lowly rewarded and traditional craft work-groups. Each group identity was strengthened by the conflict and the prime target of resentment was more often other work-groups, rather than management. Individual identities can, of course, suffer in intergroup struggles, but this is a measure of the extent to which group membership provides powerful means of resisting pressures from outside. The pressure to conform can outweigh the pressure to secure oneself against uncertainty and damage. Brown confirms the above example, arguing that intergroup conflict acts to strengthen group and intra-group identities and when groups do resist management: 'the psychological satisfactions an individual may gain from his group membership may be more potent than the rewards (or threats) the management can hold out' (H. Brown, 1980: 167). For management the problem of how to disrupt, short-circuit or redirect group identities is central for securing organisation goals, mobilising consent, exerting influence and promoting 'motivation' and organisationally directed goals. The types of response made are examined in the next section.

Even when there is only a tacit, unacknowledged sense of group identity, the stereotyped judgements of power-holders about particular groups may lead them to form sub-cultural units. They are likely to be based around resistance to managerial activities rather than in a coherent ideology of their own. Individual cohesion within such a group may be low and resistance may not be co-ordinated in any sense. It may not even be visible as such, but manifested in jokes at the expense of superiors, general stubbornness and lack of co-operation (Nichols and Beynon, 1977). At this level, pressure on individual identity may be no more than disapproval at not joining in or, at worst, definition as being somehow different. Over time, the benefits – in terms of access to sources of meaning – of belonging to such a group may coalesce it into a true subculture with the ability to protect members against threats to identity.

Much of the informal organisational processes, including subcultural groupings, are generated within the free areas which groups and their members carve out for themselves within labour processes. Whether formally or informally constituted, such groups have to in some fashion reduce the possible internal tensions which might develop out of any contradictory goals and identity concerns of their members. The internal dynamics of groups have been seen largely to consist of role-based mechanisms and processes directed at the maintenance of the group. According to Breakwell, 'group dynamics are the most frequent sources of threats to identity. These threats need not be personalised: they are directed at the individual as a group member, a cipher in a social category, not as a personality' (1986: 128). The detailed operation of such processes will be group-specific; but, like the actions of individuals, it will be orientated towards identity securing strategies. Just as the construction of individual identities depends in part on competition with others for sources of meaning, the production of group identities depends on gaining access to symbols and resources or behaviour patterns which serve to distinguish the group from others.

At the extremes of group response to pressures on identity are traditional forms of industrial action and attempts at 'self-management'. The first could be seen in accounts by skilled workers involved in the 1987 British Telecom strike. A persistent theme was that the background to the action was as much in a 'gut reaction' to the way in which management attitudes and behaviour represented an attack on their self-perceptions and identities as skilled workers; as it was about pay and conditions. Pressure of this sort on individual identities can be the triggering factor which alerts workers to the possibilities and benefits which Leonard identifies in collective action. In this sense, the rhetorical focus on empowerment through the self-management of personal development in current HRM strategies and organisational learning initiatives (see Chapter 10) will always run the risk of actually engendering resistance.

Self-management as a strategy for making-out ranges from the individual setting up in business to 'be your own boss', to large-scale worker co-operatives. The use of group and intergroup self-management as a strategy could be seen as evidence of Garai's hypothesised need for non-alienated activity to motivate people towards transformations of work in the direction of self-control. Such efforts would act initially to reinforce the interdependence of productive relations and reinforce the security of previously constructed workplace identities, such as the craft pride of workers in the Triumph Meriden co-operative in the 1970s. However, attempts to secure autonomy and self-direction may simply be part of strategies to defend existing work against movements of capital, no matter how alienating. Unless the financial and management processes under which co-operatives operate are constructed differently from conventional businesses, the only extra source of meaning available in such work may be a collective identity and a set of common goals.

Self-management, though, is not restricted to the total direction of a business with which a sole trader or co-operative must contend. It can just as readily be a tactic within overall struggles to achieve control of the portions of the labour process. In attempting to control the speed of a production line or the throughput of work in a particular department, a group is actively trying to manage its environment. Parallel for professional groups are the 'collective mobility projects' (Armstrong, 1984) discussed in Chapter 4. Claims on access to decision-making power by professional groups such as accountants, engineers and personnel specialists rest in part on their ability to restrict sources of meaning to members, and to use specialised knowledge to downgrade the competence of other groups.

In the above sense, any form of resistance to external control, by groups or individuals, is a type of strategy for increasing the scope of self-management. It could thus be seen as a basic response, at different levels of the organisation, to constraints embodied in the work situation. Describing such action as resistance runs the risk of being a purely ideological judgement based on the damage done to existing structures of power and reward. But dominant groups do have their own needs for autonomy, discretion and non-alienated activity. It is therefore probable that they will define other people's self-management as a threat to their identities and produce regulatory responses.

The activities of managerial groups in this area are the focus of the next section.

Management: from response to regulation

The form and content of control processes are influenced by the responses of managerial groups to pressures on the identities produced in their role as agents of capital. Mobilising their consent to expose themselves to the threats and pressures of management roles has its own particular place in the labour process. It also underpins the mobilisation of consent of production workers to comply with that supervision. Resistance and contestation by other individuals and groups are threats to managerial identities which are only somewhat ameliorated by the situational power they wield. As we discussed in Chapter 4, managers have been reported often to feel frustrated and ineffectual in their workplace roles and that they have little control over the strategic policies which determine their activities. This will depend of course on the position and situational power of the managers involved, but does point to the fact that managerial work has its own levels of alienation and partialisation. If this is so, then dominant organisational groups will also expend effort and devise strategies to secure and defend their identities. Hochschild (1993: xi), for example, notes that managers are involved in emotional labour in regulating not only their own feelings but those of others.

Effective managerial identity work can utilise worker resistance and associated damage to productivity and profitability as an ideological justification for managers' own strategies to enhance identity. By being perceived by peers and superiors as being capable leaders who are able to contain, regulate or negate disturbances to the efficient flow of work, managers are able to secure sources of meaning which in turn reinforce their ideological supports.

The fashion for reorganising production processes into semi-autonomous work-groups provided examples of the way in which interventions by management act both to secure managerial identities and short-circuit potential worker resistance. As we saw in Chapter 5, such work-groups give employees some latitude of decision-making over operational matters and integrate different levels of production-related skills into more flexible working on more 'natural' units of work, turning production-line assembly into a semblance of unit or small-batch production. Wall *et al.* (1986), in a long-term study of autonomous work-groups, identified the justifications underlying their implementation as being in their assumed effects in increasing intrinsic motivation to work, enhancing employee satisfaction, improving group performance and reducing labour turnover; as well as suggested increases in organisational commitment and improvements in mental health.

The results of this study indicated that 'employees clearly appreciated the autonomous work system. On balance managers did too, though clearly there were costs in terms of personal stress arising from the difficulties involved in managing and maintaining the system' (1986: 298). Of the assumed effects, only intrinsic job satisfaction and productivity were significantly increased, along with reported perceptions of increased autonomy. Labour turnover actually increased through increased dismissals of those who could not or would not fit in with the new systems. The increased productivity was not due to employees working any harder. If anything, their individual productivity was lower in comparison to those working on more traditional lines. Improvements largely flowed from reduced indirect labour costs, due to decreases in the need for direct supervision of the work-groups. This organisational benefit can be seen as a gain at the expense of increased managerial effort, with greater responsibilities being generated in monitoring and managing the new system.

Although suffering increased stress, the fact that managers thought the effort worthwhile indicates that associated productivity benefits provide enough possibilities for enhanced situational meaning to offset personal costs. When such a system becomes established, it is also possible that managers may also gain from new sources of meaning. As they are directly responsible for co-ordinating teams of workers who are more satisfied in their work, it is likely to enhance self-perceptions of managerial effectiveness; though this potential is limited by possible conflicts with existing managerial ideologies, as we shall point out below. Increased intrinsic worker satisfaction is also a potential source of meaning to managers, because greater intrinsic satisfaction may reduce the scope for contradictory consciousness arising in workers. If this leads to short-circuiting of potential resistance in employees, then managerial identities are further secured.

However, in one of the most widely studied implementations of autonomous working, conflicts with ideological conceptions of managerial control were seen to interfere with the factors which made such systems of work more effective. In a case study based on this material, the experimental assembly of trucks within an autonomous work-group system in the Volvo company between 1974 and 1976, Blackler and Shimmin (1984: 117–19) note that workers finishing their daily quota of work were allowed some relaxation around their work station. Senior managers, however, saw this relaxation as 'slack' which could be taken up and controlled by increasing work quotas. This obviously produced demoralisation in the workforce. Allowing slack time is contrary to the managerial conception of how productivity is to be maximised, even though it may be one of the major factors which produces the sense of autonomy for workers which allows the system to succeed. An enhanced source of workplace meaning for one group appears in this case to be an unacceptable threat to the processes of control which supply meaning to another group. This example illustrates the point that the ideological underpinnings which control systems provide for managerial identities may, in some circumstances, be more central to them than the control outcomes in increased profit. In this sense, strategies of control, regulation and discipline become part of the instrumental transformations of social reality which managerial groups set as the goals of their own identity work.

Strategic choices about organisational design can, however, be reinforced by a level of indoctrination into the dominant organisational goals. Such indoctrination may be a primary level of response to the attempts of members to secure a measure of autonomy and discretion within their work and to create free areas where they can develop their own identities and capacities. Lynn (1966) argues that the behaviours of even 'democratic leaders' can approximate to the principles of 'brainwashing'. Prescriptions to maintain warm and friendly relations with subordinates go hand-in-hand with maintaining a social distance between themselves and the group.

> We see here the dual role of the brainwasher: the aloofness corresponds to the threatener role, the friendliness to the protector role. The authoritarian leader is only playing the threatener role and misses out on the friendliness. Vice versa with the *laissez-faire* leader. It is the brainwashing, democratic leader who plays both roles who is the most effective. (1966: 270)

Such indoctrination can take place within both formal and informal socialisation, and function to reinforce self-control, rather than self-management. The study of bakery salesmen by Ditton (1974) showed how the salesmen were trained to cheat their customers in order not to lose out themselves when they ended up short in their takings. Supervisors both tacitly and overtly encouraged this activity as it short-circuited possible conflicts with workers, such as those that could be caused by the firm trying to recoup losses from the drivers' pay. The socialisation process also worked to weed out salesmen who would not or could not collaborate in theft and to legitimise it to others as the only real means for making-out in the job. Hence there was no objection to them making a little for themselves on top of balancing their books. Comments from a sales manager, such as 'They're not real salesmen if they can't make a bob or two on the side, are they?' (1974: 36), indicate that the ability to steal was linked to job competence, the same manager being noted for encouraging valued salesmen to, 'use fiddled cash personally'.

This socialisation into theft was of course only sanctioned by management to the extent that salesmen did not begin to steal from their employers as well as their customers. Mars (1983) has claimed that fiddling can increase job satisfaction, and raise work rates and productivity by making the process of work more interesting and binding those involved together. It can be used by management as a reward, as in Ditton's example, as long as they 'turn a blind eye', or can still be used as a method of 'cracking the whip'.

The final irony for management is that they lose control of the fiddle that they themselves have started. The workforce then seize it, and use its unofficial and unsanctioned ability to increase their wages (especially in times of national restraint) as a basic condition of employment. (Ditton, 1974: 36)

The strategies and identity work of managerial groups are likewise incorporated into organisational processes through the ideological legitimations which supply positive self-attributions. Organisational ideologies play a crucial role in underpinning identities, particularly those of management. Salaman (1979: 199–212) locates five. *Structuralism* presents organisational processes as outcomes of politically neutral principles of management and achievement based on merit, with, 'managers operating as referees of a variety of competing demands and pressures' (p. 199). Markets complement internal hierarchies as functionally necessary principles. The ideology of achievement within structuralism links it to the approach of *psychologism*, where organisational performance is the responsibility and outcome of individual behaviour. People are resources, and where their qualities, abilities and goals are not in line with neutral structures, they must be moulded to fit. Conflicts of interest are avoided through the rational application of objective and neutral procedures for assessment and feedback. *Consensualism* presents the specialised division of labour and differentiated rewards as a necessary precondition of the achievement of overall organisational goals benefiting all members. The organisation survives by virtue of consensus, whilst conflict is due to the pathological personalities and behaviours of individuals or to inadequate communications. *Welfareism* focuses on integrating the commitment of employees through concern for their well-being and happiness. The emphasis is on 'personal relations at work, on less onerous and oppressive forms of control, on more relaxed supervisory methods, on some changes even in the organisation of work' (p. 209). *Legalism* presents the social relations of production as being determined by the binding contractual agreements between the parties involved in the enterprise. Conflict is handled through negotiation and appeals to the obligations, rights and duties of participants. The contract implies consent to direction of effort by those who are assigned 'the right to manage'.

Whether or not such ideologies in practice act as coherent guiding principles of organisations, they do present some common themes – notably the neutrality of managerial practices, the rational and consensus-based form of organisations and the emphasis on individual responsibility for exhibiting appropriate behaviours and identities. If internalised by employees, they have the effect of reducing uncertainty for dominant groupings and thus to increase their situational power in securing strategic identities. They risk failure in the light of the contradictory consciousness raised by perceived conflicts between espoused values and actual practice. Knights and Collinson give the example of a US-owned firm in Britain that directed its communicative efforts through a house magazine that:

> simply exacerbated the 'them and us' attitudes since the harmonious and efficient image of Slavs depicted by it conflicted dramatically with the experience of shop floor workers. The shop floor was insulted by what it saw as the deceptive 'propaganda' in the magazine. (1987: 9)

Ideologies of this sort survive in part because dominant groupings have the power to shape cultural meanings on the workplace; and also because they can call on the expertise of their peers and outside professionals to justify them or supply the technologies of regulation to make them applicable to changing circumstances.

Organisational Development is a good example of the importance of managerial identity to strategic interventions in the organisation of work. 'Technologies' employed in OD interventions include team reviews, sensitivity training, performance counselling and the redesign of jobs. They largely depend on *social facilitation* effects for their operation – in other words, on pressures brought to bear on individuals through the effects of social comparison processes, group norms and the perceptions of expected rewards. An important aim is the achievement of a 'best fit' between the policy goals of the organisation and the workplace identities of both employees and those which manage them. The latter is important successful in that interventions have to convince the managerial client that they have bought the right strategy (Evden, 1986). Any doubts, or sophisticated ideas such as failure being a valuable learning experience, undermines the positive identities such interventions can reinforce.

The utility of managerial education outside – though sponsored by – organisations, could also be said to be based on reinforcing the ideological identity work required of managers. A secure cultural identity is an important factor in reducing employee uncertainty and thus organisational cohesiveness. The content of managerial education is effectively directed at making concrete the notion that systematic control over complex and variable processes is possible. The reduction of uncertainty provided by the ideas themselves, backed up by the demonstration of techniques which purport to provide reliable diagnostic and control procedures, acts as a powerful enabling factor in the maintenance of ideological structures. The expected payoffs for the employee in both financial terms and in terms of career mobility are thus bought through a process of personal identity work. This increases the employee's self-perceived competence at handling the contingent uncertainties of organisational life with the concomitant organisational gains of increased effort and commitment in overcoming goal barriers.

Conclusion

Identity work is conscious and unconscious, individual and collective, competitive and collaborative. It is the vehicle of our self-expression and enactment and at the same time binds us to systems of ideological self-legitimation through which we accede to systems of control, both internal and external. The networks we access and the roles we are expected to take on in the workplace provide the scripts, our interactions and negotiations with others the arena in which we act them out. It appears that what we strive towards in producing consistent role performances and in maintaining a secure identity is a situation where we do not have to negotiate who and what we are with others, where our concerns, actions and status are automatically legitimate. In this sense, identity work is the medium through which we express power over ourselves, others and situations.

We buy into systems of control in order to increase our situational power and at the same time we resist pressures to make us completely controlled by our role and the demands of others. In many ways identity work is the primary work of organising, if not of organisations themselves. As such, it must also be the primary work of those who structure the processes of organising towards corporate ends. The appeal of management, beyond the extrinsic rewards, must be that to some extent just being a manager automatically affirms and protects identity. This would of course be at the expense of diminishing the manager's capacity to resist the role demands the position confers. Manager as communicators of role demands have in effect committed themselves to controlling the identity work of others, which in turn commits them to one or another form of response to such pressures, which in turn. . .

It is through identity work that the condition of being a subject and of being subject gains substance for managers and workers alike and the negotiation and pursuit of identity concerns and projects are the drama of everyday organisational experience. As we have seen, the psychological processes which underwrite that drama cannot give an adequate account of it in purely mechanistic terms, but neither can interpretative or structural accounts afford to ignore the influence those processes have on us in our journey to becoming fully-fledged participants in the modern work organisation.

PART 3

CHAPTER 12

Theorising organisations

The story so far

In reviewing new writing on organisation theory at the beginning of the decade, Reed (1991: 120) commented that it was in a 'state of intellectual flux and uncertainty'. We hope in previous chapters to have captured some of the ebb and flow of such debate. But as this is an introductory text, we could not let the shadow of grand theory fall too heavily across the pages. This final chapter pulls in the other direction, though nothing too ambitious is attempted. We do not try to develop any new classificatory schema and steer clear of complex epistemological or methodological questions. Instead, the emphasis is put on examining more of the theoretical resources that underpin organisational research and analysis, reflecting back on some of the substantive issues we have dealt with elsewhere.

In those chapters, we have, of course, discussed theory, whether that be Weber's account of bureaucracy, a labour process analysis of control, or population ecology explanations of organisation–environment relations. So what's different here? Many of the theories we have looked at are specific to particular issues, such as the resource dependency theory of power. Others, such as institutional theories of convergence and diversity, have broader application but are still specific to the organisational sphere. The purpose of this chapter is to dig a little deeper and look at the resources provided by more general social science theories, sometimes labelled *paradigms*, an approach pioneered by Burrell and Morgan (1979). A paradigm is a conceptual map that draws on basic differences in the philosophy of science and social theory to enable us to see the world (and the place of organisations within it) in a distinctive way.

The world has moved on since Burrell and Morgan, whose schema never closely fitted organisational analysis (Ackroyd, 1992). But many of the underlying issues remain. For example, the most basic dividing line is how *structure* and *action* are theorised. When Marx wrote that, 'men make history, but in circumstances not of their own choosing', he was trying to express a sense of both change and constraint. Unfortunately, much of organisation theory fails to match that requirement. There is considerable determinism in which organisations and managers adapt to environments, and employees carry out goals or roles.

In the past two decades, a growing number of writers have tried to move away from this way of thinking, drawing from frameworks such as Gidden's (1984) concept of *structuration*. Structures are sets of formal and informal rules which generate common expectations and sanctions, and resources consisting of material goods and services which affect life chances. But these are not conceived of as 'external' forces, but things that people draw on in their social interactions. Structures become both the medium and outcome of that interaction. Action is conceived more precisely as *agency*. Agents deploy a range of causal powers, sometimes on behalf of others who command greater resources, sometimes to bend and break rules, but always purposeful and reflexive.

In trying to explain organisational phenomena, we cannot help drawing on an understanding of these issues, and in this book there has been an implicit approach to *theorising*. For example, trying to understand the reciprocal interaction of structure and agency informed how we view management. There is a tendency in mainstream literature, particularly of the popular variety, to see managers as free-floating individuals, always able to shape the destiny of their organisation. To conceive of managers as an agency of others, as a set of activities locked into structural constraints, goes against the grain. Yet that is the nature of the relations between ownership and control in a capitalist economy. This view, taken in the book, is often caricatured. Weir refers to 'the vulgar Marxist rhetoric of the inevitable polarisation of organisation between the two fundamental classes of bourgeoisie and proletariat. The managers are simply a muddle in the middle according to this way of thinking' (1993: 16). Or try Watson talking about the managers at ZTC, 'They were indeed interested in control, but it was control over their own circumstances. . . Managers were not seeking control on behalf of other groups' (T. Watson, 1994: 85). But such an explanation is all agency and no structure. Yes, managers are individuals with their own identities and values, struggling to make sense of their world and fight their corner within it. That makes a difference, but what they may seek and what they can do are often two different things, as his own fascinating case makes clear. Managers are an agency of control, but the interesting questions start there, because that has to be achieved in the messy reality of particular firms with particular employees, in particular economies, governed by particular parties. A sense of management as agency is not about any simple functional necessities, but, as Armstrong's recent work demonstrates, about the struggles of different professional or occupational groups to become the key core group in the workings of the enterprise. Any account of contemporary organisation must be at least *capable of* illuminating all levels, from the broader institutional constraints, through the sectional conflicts and down to real flesh and blood individuals.

In this sense, concepts such as structuration do not end debates. There has been substantial and salient criticism (Layder, 1987). It also has to be applied (Whittington, 1991b). Which structures, which agencies and in what circumstances? Nor is it the only useful principle of theorising: in Chapter 1 we outlined others which have guided our efforts in this book, including the need to be reflexive in not taking organisational processes for granted, to locate theory and practice in their historical and comparative contexts, and for explanations to be multidimensional. We have tried to utilise an approach which can explain the embeddedness of organisational action. Throughout the book we have been highly resistant to any variety of deterministic, 'one best way', or single, over-arching explanations for complex processes. Yet clearly action is not random. The reciprocal interaction of different structures and agencies still produces specific patterns. When these patterns take on a durable, systematic form, we have referred to 'organising logics' with their own modes of rationality. Some of these are institutionally framed at national level, others have a systemic or sectoral character. None are self-contained: all are shaped by wider processes such as gender divisions and ideologies.

Social theories also have their own logic, some of which is compatible with our implicit approach, some of which is not. It is time to spell that out in greater detail than we have been able to so far.

Resources for orthodoxy

Organisation analysis has a unique relationship with a practitioner community, providing theoretical resources which range from standard academic research to simple 'how to do it' manuals. If we were to take a narrower version of management theory, it would be accurate to say that practice has unevenly drawn on two basic traditions: a rational, mechanistic one that came to the fore with Taylor and Scientific Management; and a stream of more normative, organic thinking that is particularly associated with Human Relations (Barley and Kunda, 1992). But management thinking, on the surface at least, draws lightly on theory. What are the deeper roots and means of explanation?

Weber, bureaucracy and rationality

We outlined Weber's views in some detail in Chapter 2 and his writings on bureaucracy reappear in a variety of contexts. Yet his intellectual legacy is, as we shall see, not straightforward, for it is claimed by both mainstream and critical traditions. The basis of the former claim is not difficult to identify. The current high priest of orthodoxy states that: 'Much of Organisation Theory derives from Weber's (1968) work on authority and bureaucracy' (1985: 6). If as one of its advocates asserts, mainstream theory, 'has as its central problematic the design of efficient organisations' (Hinings, 1988: 2), Weber's model of bureaucracy remains the template. Its characteristics of functional specialisation, hierarchy, depersonalisation, formal rules and the like are projected as general laws, with the arguments concerning the key contemporary and determinant variable – size, technology or any other factor.

Weber also provides orthodoxy with the theoretical sinew of rationality. Rationalisation was a theory of the transition from traditional to modern societies. For Weber, social stability was established through acceptance of authority as a form of control which people regarded as legitimate. Previous societies had been dominated by limited forms of authority based on charisma (personal qualities of leaders), or tradition (established rights and customs of dominant groups). Weber's theory went beyond economic life. Rationalisation was held to encompass processes as diverse as law, politics, religion and scientific method itself. All were becoming governed by impersonal objectives, procedures and knowledge; embodied in structures and processes which 'confronts individuals as something external to them' (Brubaker, 1984: 9). All provided a framework for coping with uncertainty. In this sense, mainstream theory draws on the idea that rational calculation makes the world more purposeful and manageable (Clegg, 1990: 32–3).

More specifically we saw in Chapter 2 that Weber believed that the rational organisation of labour required its disciplined subordination to management and organisational goals. In this: Taylor was a resource Weber saw in his schemas for the potentially 'scientific' character of management, echoes of the themes of rationality and formal control. Paralleling his own work, Taylor saw management by 'scientific' methods as a move away from traditional authority, where owners and managers attempted to control by inefficient, personal means. Orthodoxy also sustains its conservatism through Weber's emphasis on the market embodying rationality, because it was the classic example of a disenchanted, impersonal realm dominated by the calculation of advantage, without intrusion of moral considerations (Holton and Turner, 1989: 179). Alternatives were dismissed: 'More and more the material fate of the masses depends upon the steady and correct functioning of the increasingly bureaucratic organisations of private capitalism. The idea of eliminating these organisations becomes more and more utopian' (Weber, 1984: 36).

However, Donaldson and other mainstream writers fail to acknowledge that for Weber rationalisation was a a morally and politically problematic development. Weber makes an important distinction between *formal* and *substantive* rationality. The former refers only to the calculability of techniques and procedures: 'What makes modern capitalism rational is not its ends but the unprecedented extent to which actions of its economic agents are calculated' (Sayer, 1991: 96). In contrast, the latter emphasises the values concerned with the desired ends of action. The key point is that while formal techniques are of a specific type, such values and ends inevitably differ. Thus space is opened up for recognition of contested rationalities between groups and individuals. Indeed, Weber acknowledged that the formal and substantive were always potentially in conflict, frequently making pessimistic comments about human needs being subordinated to the former. The formally rational such as the pursuit of profit by merging and 'asset stripping' companies may be substantively irrational in terms of its social consequences. In this sense, Weber does make some separation of rationality and efficiency, as there could in principle be different views of what constitutes either category. For example, workers' co-operatives and private ownership could both be regarded as efficient on the basis of different value criteria.

These kind of points form part of the basis of a defence of Weber by some writers (for example, Albrow, 1970) against the normal way his ideas are used in mainstream theory. But though this has some validity, it is not clear how significant it is. Aside from the fact that Weber is not always clear about the separation and its consequences (see Storey, 1983: 26–34), from the viewpoint of evaluating mainstream perspectives as a whole, most theorists influenced by Weber have acted as if rationality and efficiency are the same thing. As a result, they have tended to be rather uncritical of existing organisations. Reed notes, 'The causal link which he is thought to have identified between rational bureaucracy and technical efficiency provided a substantive focus and theoretical bone of contention from which a general theory of organisations, based on a systems frame of reference, could be constructed in the course of the 1950s' (1985: 17).

Weber's model of bureaucracy has of course been endlessly refined and renewed. As we saw in Chapters 3 and 6, some *neo-Weberians* have sought to offset its simplicities by developing alternative designs within bureaucracy, such as those influenced by contingency models (Fischer and Sirriani, 1984: 9). Others have built from the distinction between formal and substantive rationality in order to uncover the neglected aspects of the functioning of bureaucratic organisations, their empirical research revealing two key processes. First, the inefficiencies arising from the following of impersonal rules, such as the displacement of the original goals by obsession with narrow interest and ritual by the office-holder. Second, the dependence of bureaucratic organisations on informal, innovative behaviour and consensual human relations. These writers, such as Blau and Gouldner, have greater affinities with social action theory, which we shall examine later.

Durkheim, human relations and social needs

The other 'founding father' of sociology to have a significant impact on organisational analysis has been Durkheim, though there is a marked contrast to Weber. Durkheim's contribution to understanding the transition to modernity centres around the significance of the *division of labour* in sustaining the social solidarity necessary for the survival of the 'organism' of society or enterprise. Writing in the late nineteenth century, he observed that the more complex division of labour in industrial, urban society was undermining traditional values and social order of a 'mechanical' kind held together by faith in a common morality. But at the same time it was laying the basis for a more effective integration of individuals in society, which was labelled 'organic solidarity'. This advanced industrial, technological division of labour was inevitably based on specialisation, hierarchy, and functional interdependence between tasks and occupations. Durkheim recognised that the new arrangements and formal structures contained sources of social disorganisation, conflict and harmful individualism; summed up in the term *anomie*. Any effective division of labour could therefore only take root and bind people together when it was sustained by new social values, by moral communities such as professional or occupational groups; and when workers had an understanding of their place within the overall scheme of production.

This kind of formulation was later interpreted through mainstream theory in terms of the permanent tension between the technical and formal needs of the organisation and the social needs of those who worked in it. It was therefore management's role not just to organise the former, but to carry out running repairs on the latter. This necessitated paying specific attention to the *informal* side of the organisation, particularly to the primary groups that people belonged to, such as work-groups. In the 1920s and 1930s this theme was taken up and popularised by Elton Mayo, who had identified problems arising from the breakdown of traditional skills and values associated with the rise of mass production. Researchers could help management to re-integrate the worker by identifying social needs and relating them to common values which led to identification with the company. Human relations analysis also drew from a Durkheimean framework . . . when it 'defined the anomic consequences of capitalism as abnormal, as a deviation from the ideal circumstances of organic solidarity' (Hamilton, 1980: 70).

Barnard (1938) extended the analysis with emphasis on how large-scale organisations could become 'co-operative social systems', based on specialised competencies and common goals. He more clearly defined the role of the executive and the specialised managerial function in terms of defining and communicating goals, and securing workforce effort. A key feature of the human relations approach is the social engineering role given to management through maintaining equilibrium and integrating the parts of the organisation.

The vehicle is not formal structures of co-ordination and command, but values, informal practices and the 'logic of sentiment'. Though a subordinate aspect of organisational analysis for considerable periods, as we saw in Chapter 7, it has recently reappeared within a new socio-economic context and new management writings on corporate culture such as Peters and Waterman's *In Search of Excellence*. Attention is being focused once again on employee's social needs, the human side of the enterprise, and to creating and sustaining unity through common cultures.

Interestingly, the emphasis on *corporate* culture clashes with some central features of Durkheim's perspective which depended on the existence of professions and other intermediary groups to generate moral communities. For Durkheim, the modern individual must be equipped to question moral systems, not just to need to identify with the collective or its symbols (Dahler-Larsen, 1994: 10). In addition, Durkheim provided a critique of market rationality, which tends to foster excessive egoism and acquisitive individualism. This is just one example of a growing trend in social theory to see a different, more critical legacy from Durkheim's work (Pearce, 1989; Starkey, 1992). But, even more so than Weber, it remains the case that this is not how Durkheim has been used as a resource.

Systems theory

Mainstream organisational analysis has increasingly presented itself as divorced from broader theory. One of Donaldsons's (1985) central arguments is that organisations can be studied as an independent realm. If the outside world comes into it, it is as the 'environment', a backcloth against which it is possible specify relationships between contingencies, structure and performance. As Willmott observes, this various factors in this environment, 'must be registered and controlled if strategic adjustments are to be successfully achieved. There is minimal consideration of the relevance of social theory . . . for the study of organisations' (1990: 45). Nevertheless, Donaldson is happy to describe orthodoxy in terms of a 'functionalist-positivist' approach.

While the latter refers to the continual search for valid cause and effect knowledge, the former helps to helps sustain the orthodox focus on organisations as purposeful, interdependent systems. In doing so, the approach draws from the basic organic analogy used by Durkheim and others, in which all social systems have to adapt to the environment to survive. In such biological analogies, system parts (or sub-systems) are interconnected and each are functional to the viability of the organisation – for example, by generating binding social values. This became a theme of *functionalist* social theory (Parsons, 1951) which regards social systems as self-regulating bodies, tending towards a state of equilibrium and order. Donaldson (1985: 29) argues that there *is* movement within equilibrium, but it is a process of internal adjustment between the sub-systems, normally triggered by external change such as those in technologies or markets. Nevertheless any breakdown of order tends to be treated as pathological and the non-rational elements confined to the informal organisation.

The classical theories, including Scientific Management and Human Relations, can be conceived as *closed system* perspectives, previously discussed in Chapter 3. By treating the organisation as a structure of manipulable parts that could be internally regulated, it appeared as if a rational means–ends relationship could be optimised. It was a question of re-balancing the human and technical, or formal and informal components, when one changed more rapidly than the other (R. Brown, 1992: 45). The focus on manipulating the parts, as we know, shifted to an *open systems* approach – organisations coping with uncertainty through exchange and transaction; with *contingency theory*, with its emphasis on 'designing organisations rationally so that their internal coherence and external match to their environments are both maximised' (Tsoukas, 1994c: 4), the most popular variant.

Woodward, one of the most noted contingency theorists, sums up the intellectual confidence felt by those pursuing this approach from the 1950s onwards:

> Even more important from the point of view of ultimate theory building is the fact that various schools of thought are beginning to see themselves as concerned with the study of systems . . . the starting point is the identification of a system and the subsequent questions asked are very much the same: what are the objectives and strategic parts of the system under review and how are these parts interrelated and interdependent? One result is that those concerned with the study of organisation are beginning to develop a common language, on whatever discipline their work is based. (quoted in Eldridge and Crombie, 1974: 93)

Barley and Kunda link the dominant organisational theory during this period under the heading 'systems rationalism'. Although not all its components could be described in terms of systems theory, operations research, decision-making theory and process theories of motivation shared the emphasis on controlling organisations though managing the boundaries between sub-units and the interface between inputs and outputs. In this wave of theorising 'employees were largely absent' (1992: 380), which is another way of saying that agency had been squeezed out of the picture. Individual behaviour is seen as 'determined by and reacting to structural constraints that provide organisational life with an overall stability and control' (Astley and Van de Ven, quoted in Mills and Murgatroyd, 1991: 5). The next wave was set to react against these images of orderly entities and passive people.

Critical alternatives

Social action theory

The most significant sign of a major alternative to mainstream perspectives emerged with an attack on the dominant systems theory by Silverman (1970). He brought together elements of an approach described as the *action frame of reference* or social action theory. It was not new, drawing on the phenomenological writings of Schutz (1967) and Berger and Luckman (1967). In fact its methods can partly be traced back to Weber's conception of a social science, rather than his writings on bureaucracy. For Weber, such a science begins from interpreting social action, and the subjective meanings and purposes attached to it. This rests on a distinction between the natural and social worlds, but retains an attempt to situate individual action within material structures. Donaldson recognises another, 'interpretative' Weber and remarks that the approach works by 'gaining insights into the subjective world of actors and constructing a model of motivated actions of the typical actor in a particular social setting' (1985: 107). His complaint is merely that those who take this up ignore the 'structural', deterministic Weber.

In renewing an action perspective, Berger and Luckman popularised the concept of *social construction of reality*. Rather than conceiving of people as products of systems and institutions, they are 'actors' who create these patterns through their own meaningful activity. However, it was accepted that the products of their action – for example, organisational structures – appear to them as 'things' with an independent existence. Social construction was one of the aspects of a dialectical approach discussed earlier, and it puts a necessary stress on the possibility of change through purposeful reflection and action.

Silverman was able to apply these kind of ideas more specifically to organisations, considering them as social constructs produced and reproduced through their members' activities. This was largely neglected in systems theory, which regards organisations as part of the 'natural' world governed by 'laws' concerning their structures and effects on behaviour. Hence, as we have argued, systems theory has reified organisations and taken their basic features for granted. Silverman did not ignore structure, recognising that *roles*, as systematic patterns of expectations, were developed in the interplay between organisations and their environments. His study was largely theoretical, but others were of a more empirical nature, utilising the concept of organisations as *negotiated orders* (see Day and Day, 1977). By the early 1960s Strauss *et al.* (1963) had been analysing the negotiated order in hospitals, while other notable studies included those concerned with police and legal practices (Bittner, 1967; Cicourel, 1968), and welfare agencies (Zimmerman, 1971). A recurring theme was that controls exercised through rules in formal organisations were inevitably incomplete and unsuccessful. Any degree of effective co-ordination and co-operation is dependent on constant reworking of rules and goals, and formal and informal negotiation processes involving all participants. The subsequent customs and practices in any workplace act as a constraint on management.

The critique developed through action theory challenged the consensual and objective images of organisations that were often based on 'favoured' managerial definitions. By focusing on the realities of multiple goals and competing groups, dimensions of organisational life, such as work patterns and practices could be demystified. It shed light on why organisations do not operate as they are supposed to. As we saw in Chapter 6, this latter emphasis tied into empirical work by *neo-Weberians*, who were also concerned with the bending of bureaucratic rules through the value-systems of employees (Blau, 1955; Gouldner, 1955). Indeed, Silverman utilises some of these studies extensively. He notes, for example, how Gouldner shows that industrial relations in a gypsum mine had been based on an 'indulgency pattern': implicit rules rooted in give and take rather than formal codes. When management attempted to introduce changes which clashed with the established values and practices and reasserted formal rules, it generated grievances and strike activity.

In organisation theory as such, the action perspective made its impact through John Child's (1972) concept of strategic choice, which was directed against the environmental determinism of contingency theory and discussed in detail in Chapter 3. The theoretical significance is drawn out by Brown: 'This criticism emphasises "agency" as against "structure", that is the role of actors – managers, workers, or whoever – in choosing to pursue certain goals and/or follow certain lines of action albeit within constraints set by the actions of others and the context within which they are placed' (1992: 36).

Meanwhile, during the 1970s Silverman and other writers shifted the action approach in the more 'radical' direction of *ethnomethodology*. Though 'translated' as people-centred, it is actually only concerned with the production of a common-sense world and eschews any attempt at analysis of causation which would impose external categories. Nor is it concerned with the relation between ideas and interests or social and organisational structures present in the Weberian tradition. It restricts itself to accounting for the processes through which members construct their everyday life. Structures tend to be viewed at best as temporary patterns created by interpersonal action and based on available stocks of knowledge. Though some useful material on the 'organisational work' of reinterpreting these stocks of knowledge and routine practices was generated (Silverman and Jones, 1976), it soon became difficult to locate any notion of *organisation* in the traditional sense. Phenomena such as power or control, which are expressed through relatively durable structures beyond specific situations and face-to-face interactions and meanings, are simply outside its frame of reference.

Though taken to extremes in ethnomethodology, these weaknesses were inherent in action theory. In Silverman's earlier work he argued that technological and market structures were meaningful only in terms of the understandings and attachments of participants. Though structures require the involvement of actors in their reproduction, something like a product or labour market does have a structural existence partly independent from how particular individuals think or act – as anyone who has lost their job, or a fortune on the stock exchange, will testify. Concepts such as role which were used to link subjective action and structure are useful, but not substantial enough to carry the burden of explaining organisational behaviour. The more disconnected action theory became from wider concerns, the more it became 'buried in an obsessive concern for the minutiae of "everyday life" as exemplified in the intricacies of organisational routines' (Reed, 1985: 48). This is linked to a further problem limiting its capacity to act as a critical resource. Despite the emphasis on empirical studies – as we raised earlier and as Silverman has admitted – the approach is aimed at providing a *method* of analysis, rather than a theory of organisations. Nevertheless, Silverman and social action theory continues to be a focus for discussion (Hassard and Parker, 1994) and influence (Tsoukas, 1994c).

Radical structuralism

To escape the limits of an action approach, theory must move beyond how organisations and their environments are subjectively constituted to some kind of structural explanation of the dynamics of organisational development within capitalist societies. This section examines some of the resources that can be found for that purpose by reworking and extending the concepts provided by Marx and Weber. We use the common heading of 'radical structuralism' to signify that such theorising begins from an account of the structural framework of organisational behaviour, but is directed towards a critical explanation of the processes of regulation and change.

Marx and labour process theory

Marx had little to say about issues of administrative or even political organisation, and even less about the specific question of bureaucracy. When he made observations about bureaucracy, they were very Weberian, with references to systematic division of labour, hierarchies of knowledge and mechanisms of formal behaviour (Sayer, 1991: 78). Nevertheless, as Goldman and Van Houten note, 'Systematic study of the sociology of organisations is almost absent in the classical and modern Marxist traditions' (1977: 110). Those wishing to generate a discussion from Marx have had to rely on fragments of a critique of the Prussian bureaucracy and writings on the Paris Commune of 1871 as a model of the possibility of elimination of bureaucracy through a fully democratic administrative system (Marx, 1984). Marxist theory has tended to focus on the dynamics and contradictions of capitalism as a whole and issues concerning the distribution of the surplus product, neglecting changes in productive processes, organisational forms and occupational structures. Some Marxist concepts have been influential, if often misunderstood – notably his account of the alienation of labour. But they have remained unconnected to any systematic organisational analysis.

However, during the last twenty years Marxist-influenced theory and research has had a profound effect on all of the disciplines concerned with work organisation. This trend worries Donaldson (1985: 127), who argues that, 'Marxism is a theory of society therefore it cannot be a theory of organisation'. Clegg (1988: 10) makes the apposite response that applying the same criteria to Weber would place his work on bureaucracy outside the level appropriate to organisation theory. But there is a different point to be made. It is not the full apparatus of Marxist theory of history and society that has been influential, but a narrower set of ideas, though still central to his account of the working of capitalist production. That vehicle has been *labour process theory*, set in motion by Braverman's (1974) reworking of Marx's analysis of capitalist production (for a full account of labour process debates see P. Thompson, 1983). We discussed this mainly in Chapter 4 as the framework for an explanation of control. Here we examine the deeper theoretical context.

Though more obviously influential in industrial sociology, labour process theory has provided conceptual tools observable in a wide range of critical organisation writers such as Clegg, Dunkerley, Salaman, Storey and Burrell. Clegg and Dunkerley begin *Organisations, Class and Control* by defining the theoretical object of organisational analysis: 'For this volume we have proposed as such an object the concept of organisation as control of the labour process' (1980: 1). What enables such an argument to be made? Marx may not have been interested in an understanding of organisations *per se*, but he was centrally concerned with issues of work organisation and organisation of work. By this we mean a combined emphasis on work organisations as the site of key economic processes and contradictions, and the meeting place of capital and labour; as well as organisation of work in terms of questions including the division of labour, relations of authority and control, and the distribution of rewards.

Donaldson also rightly observed that: 'To qualify as distinctly neo-Marxian one would need to show the connection between work life in the organisation and change at the societal level' (1985). That is exactly the strength of labour process theory, which Donaldson misses because the 'Marxism' he attacks is an earlier, much more general and less successful application to the sphere of work organisation. Marx defined the form of a society and economy in a manner strongly conditioned by an understanding of work relationships. Each mode of production gives rise to class relations, which, under capitalism, are based on the sale and purchase of labour power. The partial antagonism between capital and labour as collective classes arises from the exploitation and appropriation of the surplus labour by capital based on its ownership and control of production. This is a far cry from the notion of fair exchange implied in mainstream theory. Work relations therefore cannot be analysed in general, but only as they are shaped by the demands of a specific system of production. As we explained in Chapter 4, the central characteristic of this process is the nature of labour as an active and indeterminate commodity. In other words, when it is purchased by capital, the outcomes remain mere potential. The goal of profitable production may be thwarted by workers asserting their own needs and self-organisation. In many ways this is a more sophisticated account of what industrial relations and other disciplines call the *wage-effort bargain*, the exchange of effort for reward, which has at its core of the employment relationship (Edwards and Scullion, 1982).

The above processes cannot be understood within the confines of one organisational unit. Competition between enterprises and the conflict within the employment relationship creates an accumulation process which compels capital constantly to reorganise production. Certain general features of work organisation and organisation of work tend to follow.

1. Employers need to exercise control over labour, both at the level of general directive powers and over working conditions and tasks. At the same time, it is necessary to motivate employees and gain some level of consent and co-operation. Meeting these diverse and sometimes contradictory needs is the function of management systems and agents.
2. There are constant pressures to cheapen the costs of production, notably labour. This may take place through deskilling, relocation of plant, work intensification or some other means; though subject to constraints, including worker resistance and market variations.
3. A division of labour must be structured around the above objectives, involving the design of work and division of tasks and people to give the most effective control and profitability. This is sustained by hierarchical structures and the shaping of appropriate forms of science and technology.

Let us restate this and spell out the consequences with more specific reference to organisations.

- Work organisations are distinct from other organisations and can only be properly understood within a theory of capital accumulation and labour processes. This 'political economy' must take in relationships to institutional environments at regional, national and international level.

- 'Organisations are structures of control' (Salaman, 1981: 143). This involves more than control over uncertainty, monitoring objectives or means of getting work done. They are administrative apparatuses concerned with control over productive activity in order to maximise the surplus. Managerial agency, though inherently variable and multi-layered, develops in this context.

- In advanced capitalist societies large-scale organisations are strategic units acting as mechanisms which integrate economic, political, administrative and ideological structures (Burrell, 1980a: 99).

- Organisational structures and processes – including management and worker organisation, control and reward systems, and job design – therefore involve political issues, decisions and choices.

- Organisations do not embody any universal rationality, but rather contested rationalities arising from the partly antagonistic relation of capital and labour. Organisational change will reflect the subsequent dialectic of control and resistance.

This is not merely a question of the 'seamy side' of otherwise excellent organisations, as Gareth Morgan appears to believe (1986: 316–17). Relations of exploitation and domination are integral to capitalist and other class-divided forms of work organisation. Nevertheless, the underlying principles of the relations between organisations and capitalist society are at a very general level. They involve no laws or functional imperatives concerning *specific* forms of control, organisational structures, management strategies or job designs. Nor does reference to class necessarily incorporate particular models of consciousness or social change. All these and other matters are empirical questions to be determined by research and the unfolding of real events. The renewal of Marxist and labour process theory has generated or influenced a tremendous amount of historical and contemporary research at a more 'micro' level. As we have shown in other chapters, this is particularly true in areas such as managerial strategies and control (Friedman, 1977; R. Edwards, 1979, Edwards and Scullion, 1982); technology, skill and work design (Wilkinson, 1983a; Child, 1985; Thompson and Bannon, 1985; Gabriel, 1988); and the sexual division of labour (Pollert, 1981; Cavendish, 1982; Westwood, 1984).

The selective and qualified use of Marx suggested here and by other theorists has inevitably led to accusations that labour process theory is no longer Marxist (Cohen, 1987). Authentic affinity with Marxism is only of concern to those who zealously guard orthodoxy and the sacred text. Even more importantly, even if the resource provided by labour process theory is valuable, there are still many gaps in explanations of key organisational processes. Some of this can no doubt be remedied by further research, but it is important to recognise the limits inherent in the perspective. It sets organisations specifically in the context of *capitalist production*, which is both its strength and weakness.

- Though the labour process is the core of productive activity, it does not encompass all aspects. Any theory of the role of organisations in capitalist society must deal with the *full circuit of capital* (Kelly, 1985; Nichols, 1986); including its realisation through the sale of commodities on the market, financial issues and the prior purchase of labour (see Chapter 4 for full discussion). It would be very misleading for any critical theory to proceed on the assumption that organisational processes and managerial activities were based solely on the control of labour; neglecting factors such as sales and marketing, financial controls, supply of components and product quality. Even the employment relationship, though intimately connected to the labour process, is constituted on a far wider basis (Littler, 1982). Institutions such as the state and the family, plus different cultural values and patterns in a given society, shape the distinctive character of employment relationships as can be seen by observing examples from Japan or farm work. Labour process theory is thus only a partial contribution to such analyses, though paradoxically it is in some ways ideally suited to organisation studies given that the dominant managerial theories are also overwhelmingly concerned with 'the labour problem'.
- Not all work organisations are based on commodity production, or are capitalist in character. Those in health, education or other parts of the public sector, are, at least for the moment, concerned with services for use not profit. It is possible to construct a Marxist-oriented analysis which shows the links between the various types of public and private sector within the totality of capitalist society, (Heydebrand, 1977; T. Johnson, 1972). But it remains the case that not all organisational processes or forms of work activity can be understood solely through a theory whose categories are geared to explaining capitalist production – despite distorted attempts to do so, such as Bellaby and Orribor's (1977) analysis of the health service.
- Non-profit making organisations in capitalist societies and forms of administration and enterprise in 'socialist' ones such as those in China and the former Soviet bloc countries also show evidence of bureaucracy, power hierarchies and work fragmentation: 'contemporary socialist societies appear to be at least as bureaucratic and with as much of a self-perpetuating bureaucracy as capitalist ones' (Dunkerley and Salaman, 1986: 87). This suggests that the dynamic of bureaucratisation is partly independent of capital–labour relations, and that critical theory requires concepts that enable us to focus on that problem.

This is where Weber comes in, for he has the wider account of bureaucratic rationalisation which is a necessary part of explaining these processes. For example, he perceptively predicted that state socialist systems would be *more* bureaucratic than capitalism because of the absence of countervailing power structures between the state and markets. In a command economy, the power of bureaucratised management would increase, as would the dictatorship of the official (Sayer, 1991: 145–6).

Radical Weberianism

Though defenders of orthodoxy such as Donaldson recognise a radical Weber, many critical theorists, particularly those of a Marxist persuasion, have been hostile to the Weberian tradition (Marcuse, 1971; Johnson, 1980). Their objections relate to many of the points raised earlier in the chapter. This includes the tendency to argue that there is a bureaucratic imperative obliterating organisational differences within and between societies; that there is an inherent rationality of technique; and the identification of rationality with capitalism and the market. Also, there are genuine limits to Weber's own categories – for example, the emphasis on the bureaucratic hierarchy of offices has far less relevance to shop floor employees. Nevertheless there are radical Weberian perspectives, and critical writers who aim at some kind of synthesis of key aspects of Marx and Weber's analysis of work organisations (Salaman, 1979, 1981; Littler, 1982).

They rightly point to common concerns with control and domination by management and bureaucratic élites: 'For both Marx and Weber the major elements of the structure of modern large-scale organisations stem for the efforts of those who own, manage and design the organisation, to achieve control over the members' (Salaman, 1979: 20–1). Weber recognised that control rested on the 'complete appropriation' of all the material means of production by owners. In addition, both made an attempt to explain organisational dynamics within wider social and political structures rather than as independent, isolated phenomena, subject to their own 'laws'; though clearly the analysis of structural contexts differed. Marx's account of alienated labour and Weber's emphasis on the 'iron cage of industrial labour' share a concern for the fragmented and dehumanised nature of work. Weber saw that maximum formal rationality favoured economically powerful groups and their ability to use superior resources to dictate terms and conditions in what may appear as a freely made contract or legal equality (Brubaker, 1984: 42–3). Social tensions and sectional conflicts between different interest groups was therefore inevitable.

Overlaps are less surprising than they appear. Both theorists shared a similar view of the necessity for modernity to sweep away the traditional social relations based on conceptions of natural order, personalised power and patriarchy. Capitalism was a flawed, but dynamic system compelled constantly to revolutionise production and all social spheres. The difference, as Sayer observes, was that for Marx, 'what makes modernity modern is, first and foremost, capitalism itself' (1991: 12). In contrast, for Weber, 'capitalism is but one theatre among others were the drama of rationality is played out' (1991: 134). Weber was surely right in this, but wrong in some of the ways he understood this relationship.

The central dividing line of radical Weberians from orthodox interpretations is a rejection of Weber's *fatalism* about the relations between bureaucracy and industrial societies. They do not believe that bureaucracy is necessarily universal or inevitable; but rather that it is a pervasive tendency which takes specific forms and therefore can and must be countered. Like some contemporary labour process theorists, there is more emphasis on bureaucratic control as a *management strategy* (Burawoy, 1979; Edwards, 1979; Clawson, 1980). Though not unique to any system of production, bureaucracy has to be explained through its relations with that wider formation. It's capitalist social relations that dictate the need to appropriate the means of production from workers, not some law of bureaucratic rationalisation.

However, in these discussions of syntheses and overlaps between critical perspectives, we should not lose sight of some of the more distinctive Weberian contributions. Modern states and enterprises involve complex functions, management of competing interests, and performance of problematic tasks according to observable rules and norms. Some of these processes are created by and reflect specific relations of production, as in layers of supervision whose sole function is labour control and discipline. Certain functions may be artificially expanded and new ones absorbed by bureaucrats themselves as a form of self-preservation. But, as Polan notes, bureaucratic forms are a necessary object of analysis in their own right: 'Only as a result of conceding to the bureaucracy its genuine, legitimate and distinct functions can one begin to determine the boundaries of its powers and construct political control procedures that may successfully police those boundaries' (1984: 71).

Weber's insights allow us to focus on a number of key areas. Power is frequently constructed and legitimised through 'rationalisation', particularly through the expertise associated with science and technology, and what Weber described as 'control based on knowledge'. Whereas Marx provides insights from an analysis of the consequences of the private ownership of the means of production, Weber identified the problem of concentration of power through the *means of administration*:

> The bureaucratic structure goes hand in hand with the concentration of the material means of management in the hands of the master. This concentration occurs, for instance, in a well known and typical fashion, in the development of big capitalist enterprises, which find their essential characteristics in this process. A corresponding process occurs in public organisations. (1984: 33)

Finally, work organisations operate on different levels, and in some of these, formal control procedures are important. As Littler (1982) points out, Weberian categories are especially important in understanding the employment relationship and the career structure of officials in particular. More generally, bureaucratic procedures and rules are relevant to the analysis of processes such as recruitment, reward and promotion. As we argued in

Chapter 7, there is a strong case that a modified and updated Weberian analysis of bureaucracy and rationalisation remains indispensable for an understanding of contemporary work organisation. With the relevant elements derived from a Marxist tradition, they emphasise the continuity in social relations in and beyond large-scale organisations in a capitalist society. It is precisely this notion of continuity which has been under attack in the last decade.

The post-modern challenge to rationality

Post-modernism is the least cohesive of the general social theories we have examined, the term being loosely applied to an overlapping set of ideas about society and knowledge deriving from French social theorists such as Baudrillard, Lyotard and Derrida which have become increasingly influential in organisation theory in recent years (Clegg, 1990; Parker, 1992; P. Thompson, 1993; Hassard and Parker, 1993). It lays claim to be the most radical break from orthodoxy, but the orthodoxy is different from the systems and related ideas we have talked about so far. Anything with 'post' automatically specifies its opposite, so the orthodoxy must be *modernism*. This may appear puzzling – after all, existing social theories have not traditionally been defined by that label. But as we indicated in Chapter 6, for Clegg (1990: 2), organisation theory is a 'creature' of modernity, while Gergen (1992: 211–12) includes almost the full range of organisational and behavioural theories in the modernist camp.

So, what is modernity? In some usages, it designates a a type of society or *epoch* (the ontological dimension); at its simplest, industrialism in which the dominant feature is the large-scale, hierarchical bureaucracy concerned with rationality and planning throughout social and economic life. Willmott sums up the argument thus: 'Its ideal is the expertly designed, perfectly ordered and controlled world in which all ambivalence and indeterminacy are attenuated, if not wholly eliminated' (1992: 70). But within such conceptions we see the seeds of another designation, modernism as a way of thinking, a way of representing knowledge about society and organisations (the epistemological dimension). Above all, it is held to be characterised by a concern for developing the 'grand narrative', a coherent story about the development of the social and natural world, revealed through the application of reason and science (Cooper and Burrell, 1988).

Post-modernists develop a dual challenge in both these dimensions of what society is and how we should look at it. We have already outlined the basis of the former in Chapter 6. Rapid social change, the shift from a society based on production to one based on information, the emergence of segmented markets dominated by more discerning consumers, and turbulent environments are said to be demanding diversity and flexibility in work organisations which are released from their bureaucratic iron cage. Though it is not their exclusive property, post-modernists concerned with the workplace embrace the notion of the post-bureaucratic organisation in which the old specialised division of labour and centralised control no longer holds sway. In turn, social theorists with a broader societal remit use this tenuous evidence of 'debureaucratisation' and reprofessionalisation' to sustain a broader vision of post-modernisation (Crook *et al.*, 1992).

In the sphere of knowledge and *epistemology*, post-modernists reject the tradition of grand narrative. The search for the coherent story (Braverman's theory of the degradation of the labour process in the twentieth century), or the total picture (Weber's account of the interrelated processes of rationalisation) is both pointless, because of the fragmentation of economic and cultural life; and dangerous, because it submerges diverse voices and the multiplicity of 'local' phenomena. Difference, incoherence and fluidity are preferable and more realistic because meaning cannot be fixed; it is what we make it through language which constructs rather than reflects reality. At its most extreme, this kind of thinking is seen in Baudrillard and his concept of *hyperreality*. In a media-saturated world that thrives on spectacle and encourages politicians to employ 'spin doctors' to put a twist on events as, before and after they happen, it becomes impossible to distinguish between the real and fictive. We cannot refer to distortion of reality, because there are too many realities for it to be measured against. For example, Baudrillard claimed that during the Gulf conflict it was impossible to know whether any events had taken place. This was literally a war of words in which all our information was second-hand, simulated and structured through media manipulation (for a critique see Norris, 1992).

Most post-modernists in organisation theory would not go this far, but many do embrace the view that 'truth' is a product of language games. We have Derrida's 'nothing exists outside the text', taken as the interplay of different discourses (Hassard, 1994: 9). In this context, the task of the social theorist is not to construct the authentic explanation, but to *deconstruct* texts in order to reveal the contradictions, origins, instabilities and gaps. For example, this process of re-reading may uncover the silences on gender issues in the classics of 'malestream' organisation theory (Calás and Smircich, 1992). Though such treatment is 'exposed' to public gaze, it may be regarded as inevitable, for discourse always bears the imprint of the social identity of its producers. This 'perspectivism' adds a further layer to the conception of multiple viewpoints and realities.

In our previous discussions in this book, an emphasis on the primacy of language and discourse emerged most strongly in Chapter 5, through an examination of the ideas of Foucault and post-structuralism on power. Here, power is not a thing possessed by sovereign agents, but operates through discourses which produce knowledge and disciplinary practices that define and constrain the identities of workers, consumers and citizens. The danger is that any subject of action is lost in the interplay of discourses (Newton, 1994). But perhaps the most famous illustration in organisation theory of the abandonment of the search for the truth lying beneath the surface of social relations, is Morgan's *Images of Organisation*. Morgan does not just analyse organisational life in terms of series of metaphors – the machine, the psychic prison, the tool of domination – those images are treated as of equal validity. Despite representing contradictory 'claims', they are all 'true' in their own terms, their 'cognitive power and empirical veracity can only be assessed in terms of the purposes for which they are constructed and used . . . reality is what you make of it' (Reed, 1990b: 36). Also influential in applications of post-modern and post-structural epistemology is the shift of concern from analyses of control and rules to the construction of organisational life through cultural and symbolic resources, as we saw in Chapter 7.

There is a tension between post-modernism as epoch and epistemology. Logically, an approach which rejects narrative and totalising pictures should be hostile to or uninterested in an alternative conception of society. Indeed, there is a major gap between those theorists such as Clegg who are quite happy to use conventional tools of rational enquiry to develop accounts of post-modernity, and those who prefer the discursive 'production of organisation' to the 'organisation of production'. But the distinction is not so clear cut. Continuities and commonalities arise in at least three ways. In both dimensions there is a shared language of fragmentation and fracturing of the theoretical and practical order (Reed, 1991: 125). This imagery is taken from the origins of post-modernism as a perspective in art and culture, where eclecticism, stylistic promiscuity, paradox, and mixing of modes replaces hierarchical judgements of value and distinctions between high art and popular culture (Featherstone, 1988).

They are also linked by a rejection of the 'false promises' of rational design, the idea that knowledge should offer methodologies for defining the most rational means of controlling complex, large-scale organisations (Hassard, 1994: 4). Finally, and most importantly, there is the inconvenient and much observed fact that post-modernism is itself a meta-narrative (Boyne and Rattansi, 1990: 39–40). The need to create pictures of reality is inescapable in the illustrative and conceptual acts of theorising and there is ample evidence that writers such as Lyotard, Morgan and Baudrillard draw on post-industrialism, information society and other models that take as their starting point some kind of epochal break (P. Thompson, 1993).

In practice, then, the post-bureaucratic organisation located in the post-modern epoch is a rival narrative to those traditions deriving from Marx and Weber. As we saw in Chapter 6, the evidence for any substantial presence for such a mode of organising is either absent of misunderstood. And, though discussion of wider theoretical models such as post-industrialism is beyond our scope, there are equally sceptical critiques on offer (for example,

Callinicos, 1989). Organisations may not be the 'tightly-coupled' rational machines beloved of systems theory, but when Hassard argues that, 'Above all, we should seek to explode the myth of robust structural relations through establishing the fragile character of organisational life' (1994: 16), this is merely standing orthodoxy on its head, rather then a realistic picture of the modern firm.

Just as there is considerable continuity in capitalist relations of production and in rationalisation processes, large-scale organisations are considerably more durable and able to marshal powerful resources than post-modernists allow. Power converts ambiguity into order, though the latter is not synonymous with the equilibrium of systems theory, because it is always contested and disrupted. New forms of theorising are in danger of moving so far away from rationality that they are unable to conceptualise *organisation* at all. This is not just a question of the nature of contemporary structure and agency, but the equally flawed alternative ways of seeing. As Reed comments:

> The theoretical glue once provided by an assumed epistemological commitment to rational analysis of 'organised rationality' has given way under the pressure exerted by a cacophony of voices which celebrate the reality of multiple and contested organisational rationalities which cannot be assessed or evaluated in any coherent way. (1993: 181)

It is true, as we have continually stressed in the book, that there are conflicting ends and means pursued by rival organisational actors and the diversity of organising logics and institutional settings. But contested practical rationalities need to be understood on rational grounds. How can we debate the *character* of organisational life if we cannot compare and evaluate theoretical claims or even Morgan's 'images' on rational grounds? If these remain self-contained, self-referential discourses, as Reed notes elsewhere (1991: 38), organisation theory just becomes a supermarket where metaphors or other means of representation are purchased according to preference and power.

There is an increasing and dangerous tendency in organisation theory to treat management strategy, corporate culture, Taylorism, Fordism and so on, only as discourses. Presented to us as texts, the subsequent deconstructions and re-readings are sometimes illuminating, but at the cost of being confinement to the world of inter-textuality, or parasitic dependence on other people's empirical work. The interplay of agency and structures has a real material existence. In his critique of post-modernism, Tsoukas persuasively illustrates the point:

> It is because actions are not taken and voices not uttered, in a vacuum that *not* all accounts are equally valid. No matter how much I shout at my bank manager he is not likely to lend me money if I am unemployed. This is not a figment of my imagination. Others also tell me they have had similar experience. (1992: 644)

It is because we need to understand these similarities of experience and their institutional underpinnings that some form of theoretical narrative is necessary. What we know is inherently incomplete, but we require a capacity to generate generalisable knowledge and to identify trends, if not laws; and empirical work that can help distinguish between rhetorics of the powerful and the realities of power.

There is a final challenge to rationality when post-modernism is combined with some perspectives within feminism, that argue that the dominant Weberian conceptualisation of rationality is a male one. Explanations have overlapping emphases. Some (Martin, 1990; Bologh, 1990; Putnam and Mumby, 1993) refer to the stress on instrumentalism, logic and calculability in the public realm and the exclusion of emotionality, intuitive experiences and the private realm. Others lean towards a kind of perspectivism in which masculinity is the driving force. For example, Hearn (1992) argues that it is mostly men who manage the introduction of rational method and men and masculinities that will be affected by it; while Bologh (1990: xv) addresses the ghost of Weber thus: 'Your vision, extensive and expansive as it is, is the vision from your body inscribed with your gender, your place, your time'. She shows that he had a patriarchal perspective based on ideas of mastery, control and impersonality.

The result is often projected as a distinction between male and female types of social action or rationality; the former embodied in authoritarian methods of control or hierarchical ways of decision-making, the latter in ways of organising dependent on emotional connection, nurturance, intimacy and co-operation (Ferguson, 1984; Grimshaw, 1986; Bologh, 1990). Though distinguished from any biological determination, it is still a dangerous formulation, which, as Witz and Savage (1992: 20) and Due Billing point out with reference to the work of Ferguson, is not established on any secure analytical basis. Due Billing observes that, 'There is a tendency in Ferguson's text to operate with an ideal (essentialistic) notion of "woman" and to equate femaleness with an ideology about female values' (1994: 177). The production of knowledge is a social process and an undoubtedly gendered one. Connections between masculinity, male privilege and the reproduction of organisation in the public sphere has been (Hearn, 1992) and still is (Roper, 1994) strong.

As a man of his times, Weber may well have been guilty of 'masculinism', though the stereotype of his lack of interest in the emotional may be more complicated (Albrow, 1992). More importantly, concepts and practice are distinguishable from context. Ideas of an essentially male rationality are static and deterministic, given that the overlay of rationality with masculinity is itself historically and socially produced. The fact that men have dominated women or had systematic advantages within the division of labour within bureaucracies, does not make bureaucracies male. As we saw in Chapter 6, women as well as men can and do benefit from bureaucracy, and can pursue successful struggles within rule-governed, instrumental processes. Bureaucracy cannot just be set aside as alien practical and conceptual territory, because it is not just a discourse. Rationalisation was and is a fundamental principle of life in industrial societies and does not 'belong' to men. For example, calculable rules, whether applied to feelings, job specifications of financial reporting systems, can be initiated and operated by women as employers and managers, and experienced at the receiving end by men and women. The task of organisation theory, is surely, as Ramsay and Parker (1992) argue, to plot the *intersection* between patriarchy, rationality and bureaucracy, not to collapse each into the other.

A further 'intersection' that has been a central theme of this book is that between the sociological/structural and psychological dimensions of action. Our view has been that different modes of analysis are needed to deal with the complexities and levels of human behaviour. People are constituted as individual subjects at the level of their identities, emotions and self-directed actions. But that process is informed by the same 'structural' phenomena that shape managerial strategies or job design, such as the social relations of production between capital, labour or gender. The next section examines some of the theoretical resources we have engaged with, in a similar manner to the previous discussion.

Critical social psychologies

Mainstream theory has long included a psychological component, but has tended treat people in organisations as 'psychologically determined entities' with abstractedly and individually defined needs. In addition, the 'sciences' of organisational behaviour have managed to produce better ways of manipulating the identities and behaviour of employees, but have not succeeded in addressing the problems that make such manipulation necessary. A redefinition of the traditional agenda of organisational psychology requires that individual, group and organisational behaviour be placed in a wider context, particularly the social relations of production, and gender relations. Specifically, this would account for subjective experience, while avoiding the overutilisation of rational-cognitive explanations that focus on the individual determinants and constraints of purposive activity. Instead, we seek to maintain a focus on how subjectivity is constructed within social and organisational structures.

Given these requirements and the limitations of existing perspectives, it is understandable that we have seen the development of a variety of critical social psychologies. This label covers a multiplicity of radical viewpoints which have utilised concepts from mainstream Western social psychology, Marxist and humanist perspectives and Freudian theory. The attempts to formulate 'Marxist psychologies' (Schneider, 1975; Seve, 1978; Leonard, 1984) are of particular interest to us, because the explanation of social behaviour is located specifically in an understanding of work organisations. This production of subjectivity and consciousness in the wider social world is also explored by Henriques *et al.* (1984) through an articulation with psychoanalysis and discourse theory that attempts to move beyond both individual and social determinisms.

Social psychology has historically encompassed a wide variety of critical traditions differing mainly in their concerns for internal critique of methodology and content as opposed to critique of the sociocultural relations of the knowledge they produce (Wexler, 1983). From work such as that of Moscovici (1972), Gergen (1973) and Rosnow (1981), we gain a focus on the methodological limitations of social psychology and its lack of relevance to social issues. These are essentially calls for reform which, in their understanding of human social relations in terms of relatively fixed characteristics and roles, follow the liberal tradition of social emancipation through individual transformation. Alternatively, we have the vein of critique characterised by Armistead (1974), Archibald (1978) and Larsen (1980), which focuses on examining radical alternatives within social psychology. Although not always consistent with each other, these critiques do maintain a perspective on the often repressive nature of socially organised relationships. Appealing to both humanist and Marxist theory, they are concerned with social transformations leading towards human emancipation and, like the more conventional methodological critique, they also appeal to internal procedural reform. Being essentially theoretical critiques, their focus is outside the specific contradictions of social existence, tending to enshrine critique as a principle in itself.

The tradition of the Frankfurt School – for example, in the work of Horkheimer, Adorno, Marcuse and latterly Habermas – examines the role of ideologies in the production of our knowledge of the social contexts in which we exist. This provides a self-reflexive critique of how social psychology operates both to uphold the current social order and to work against the possibility of a socially transforming discipline. The image produced is of an instrumentalised culture where psychology, in servicing and refining control procedures, acts to blind individuals to their capacities and lock them into dependence on commodity relations by presenting these as the inevitable 'natural order'. According to Van Strien, the conceptual framework developed by the Frankfurt School is of importance in moves towards an emancipatory social science, as it: 'puts science directly at the service of Man's consciousness of his own possibilities, interests and values' (1982: 18). However, as critique based on radical alternatives, it does have a tendency to be, 'broadcast without a specific audience at the receiving end' (p. 18). Criticism is again elevated as an emancipatory practice in itself, without linking it to the everyday experience of those whom it was assumed to benefit.

Such problems continue to be reproduced within the tradition, for example in Steffy and Grimes' critique of personnel/organisational psychology introduced in Chapter 10. This is itself essentially based on analysis of validation procedures through the Critical Theory of Foucault and Habermas. They claim that the *technical rationality* constructed by procedures validating theory and practice produce ideologically distorted perceptions and communications that are: 'sponsored by dominant groups to stabilise and legitimise their control and domination' (1992: 195). Their answer is to introduce new emphases on validity practices that are not bounded by technical rationality. Claims to valid action need to be sustained by social consensus and undistorted communications, on the basis that rational debate can undermine purely technical reasoning.

The problem is that the prescriptions they put forward do not differ greatly from those already used in conventional personnel and occupational psychology. At one point they recommend MBO, the precursor of goal-setting, as a 'participatory technique' (p.192). The necessary corollary to the new validation procedures, that the training of both 'social scientists and management students be multi-disciplinary, perhaps at the expense of specialisation' (p. 197) though laudable, is perhaps none too realistic at present. On this basis it would appear that however desirable and probably necessary, a psychology based on this tradition of Critical Theory will probably not provide a great deal of competition to current practices in terms of their influence on and role in HRM strategies.

Social action

As in our previous discussion, social action theory is also a resource, in this case because of the stress on the intersubjective nature of social behaviour as a form of negotiated order. The useful contribution of social action theories is first in the methodological emphasis that they maintain in rooting their work in accounts of subjective experience; and secondly, in the linking of accounts of how subjectivity is constructed to structures of control, culture and ideology in organisations. In relation to organisational psychology they represent that part of the domain of analysis characterised by subjective, partly rational action processes based on phenomenological, social constructionist models. They provide a link to the ethnomethodological tradition in sociology and to symbolic interactionism, which has been influential in both sociology and social psychology.

Symbolic interactionism, following from Mead (1934), has long been the area where an interface between sociological and socio-psychological conceptions of identity has existed. The construction of identity and the social milieu within which individual identity exists is, in this model, dependent on interaction with others and through others with the self. Subjectivity, then, is mainly a product of intersubjective processes and is constructed through the negotiation of social rules and conventions. The social production of subjectivity, though acknowledged, is addressed through an understanding of how the formal and informal processes of culture and ideology impinge upon individual functioning. This phenomenological emphasis on situated meaning in the construction of subjectivity is a necessary methodological focus in providing a reflexive account of organisational behaviour and informs much of our account of the securing and reproduction of identity in Chapter 11. What it lacks is the framework for understanding the social order which conditions action inside the organisation. Indeed, neither critical social psychologies nor social action theories present consistent theories of either subjectivity or its structural location. To expand on this theme, we turn to consider further the relations between Marxism and psychology.

Marxism, psychology and beyond

As we said earlier, Marxist contributions to psychology have been underdeveloped. In a broad sense, their understandings of subjectivity at work, whether described as psychologies or not, begin with the concept of alienation: the estrangement of creative capacities that means that 'work is external to the worker, that it is not part of his nature, and that, consequently, he does not fulfil himself in his work but denies himself' (Marx, 1963: 124–5). The reference to a 'human nature' is not to an eternal set of values or behaviours such as aggression or jealousy beloved of reactionary thinkers, but rather to certain characteristics which distinguish man's species-being, such as the capacity for purposeful and reflective action.

Utilising a Marxist framework, we can grasp that alienation is given specific and concrete form by its location in the capitalist labour process. When the worker no longer owns or controls the products of labour, individual needs and capacities are subordinated to the requirements of capital accumulation, with the psychological consequence that the worker feels a stranger in his or her work. Alienated labour deepens with the further development of capitalism, as new forms of science, technology and management are used to incorporate skills and knowledge. This ties in with the analysis of Braverman (1974), particularly the emphasis on the separation of conception and execution. Volpert, Hacker and other German organisational psychologists have produced some useful specific concepts in this area, particularly those of action regulation and the partialisation of action (Resch *et al.*, 1984). These integrate models of the cognitive structuring and regulation of work with the context-bound restriction of labour in fragmented and alienated activities. However, we should remember the qualifications made in earlier chapters. Management still need to engage the subjectivity and tacit skills of the workforce at some level to ensure profitable production; for example, through quality circles. But as a tendency running through management's structuring of work, alienation is a valuable point which confirms Marx's general analysis. Linked to the concept of alienation is that of *commodity fetishism*. The socially constructed relations between labour and capital embodied in the organisation of production and exchange, are experienced as an alien power and as the natural order of things. This is then reinforced by the dominant ideologies which proclaim, for example, that the operation of the market is determined by laws of supply and demand that are beyond human planning and control.

The problem with constructing a critical psychology from Marxism, however, is that there are no adequate tools for understanding how alienated social relations are subjectively experienced and acted on by the individual. Marxism tends to deal with individuals only as bearers of economic categories such as labour and capital, and many social scientists influenced by Marxism have explicitly rejected any psychological explanation, as we showed with reference to Clegg and Dunkerley's earlier work (1980). It is certainly necessary to have an account of the material structures which shape our experiences and personalities. But this does not mean that people are simply 'bearers' or that attitudes and behaviour can be 'read-off' from material circumstances (Leonard, 1984: 25). A purely structural analysis, even where it allows for human action and resistance, fails to get sufficiently inside those routine everyday experiences in which people react, adapt, modify and consent to work relations.

In their analysis of the Insco case, Knights and Collinson recognise that Marxist and labour process literature tend to produce critiques of social structures and institutions which take as given the behavioural practices which reproduce our concerns with identity. Such structures are both consequences of and give rise to the behavioural routines through which we generate secure identities for ourselves. Without accounts of identity, then, analysis of how structures and the power relations and strategies through which they are maintained will always be incomplete.

The absence of this social psychology from labour process theory means that it is unable to recognise how individuals, such as the men and women in our case study, seek security through controlling and/or subordinating themselves to others. (Knights and Collinson, 1986: 171). The absence of such tools of analysis helps explain why Marxists have had a tendency to try a forced marriage with Freudianism in order to borrow ideas, such as that of the unconscious and the dynamic model of personality (Schneider, 1975; Deleuze and Guattari, 1977); which was for some an attempt to reconcile the irreconcilable (O'Neill, 1985). Furthermore, if individuals do not recognise their common class interests within these categories, they are deemed to be suffering false consciousness. This concept denies the validity of what people think or feel merely because it does not correspond to a set of imputed interests they are supposed to have.

The only modes of reaction allowed are habituation to the demands of capitalist production or collectively to resist and seek to transform society (Leonard, 1984: 164, 206). Although we do not doubt either the existence or desirability of various forms of worker resistance, there are a far greater number of responses to alienated work. As Willmott (1989) observes, wage labour does not always destroy or deny the subjectivity of employees. The worker has an identity as labour, and indeed other identities such as gender and ethnicity. He or she may become attached to and seek to develop the valued aspects, such as the skilled image of the craft worker or the service to the community of the nurse. These processes are not unambiguously positive. Attachment to routines can diminish creative capacities. A popular story at Ford Halewood was of the man who left Ford to work at a sweet factory where he had to divide up the reds and blues, but left because he could not stand the decision-making (Beynon, 1975: 109). Identity projects can also be dominated by anxieties and constrained within the range of known possibilities, such as the aggressive salesman or feminine secretary. The search for a secure identity or sense of solid self can be self-defeating, either because the individual occupies a range of range of positions which pulls identity in different directions (Henriques *et al.*, 1984), or because the identity, like commodities, becomes fetishised (Willmott, 1989); treated as a thing to which there is no alternative. This may lead individuals to a self-defeating project of continual re-investment in the search for security, which in turn reproduces the very institutions which constrained their experiences in the first place. But, at the same time, such perspectives can over-state trends of this kind. Employee's pursuit of identity, whether occupational, class or gender, has always been tied to formal and informal self-organisation in the labour process. Not only does this generate positive meaning and attachments, the 'misbehaviour' is a continual problem for management (Thompson and Ackroyd, 1995).

New thoughts?

While the mainstream agenda in OB continues with its traditional concerns, labour process theory and critical organisational psychology have grasped the nettle of subjectivity with some enthusiasm. This has been boosted by the previously-discussed rise of the post-modern challenge and its meta-spirals of reflexive discourse. As Burrell (1994: 2) argues, we are moving from 'old thinking' in OB (and organisation theory in general) with its mechanistic emphasis on social engineering, to 'new thinking' characterised by *reflective action* and themes of 'openness, ambiguity, meaning and interpretation, narrative understanding, self-reflection, enactment and self-organisation'. These themes are not ubiquitously present, nor are they necessarily treated in a consistent manner, but this is entirely in tune with the post-modern predilection in art, literature, music and architecture, that has quite justly raised appropriation to the status of creativity. We shall not repeat earlier critical comments on the mode of analysis, but reflect on a more practical aspect. The humanistic sentiments of such work (see, for example, Vargish, 1994) echo Van Strien's argument that to develop emancipatory projects, mainstream social science can be, 'ransacked for their practical experience and theories of practice' (1982: 24). In this sense, such new thinking parallels our own attempt to tie together some of the common themes in OB through situating the concept of identity within structures of organisational domination and exploitation. The difference lies perhaps in the appeal of the new thinking to achieve change through the self-transformation of managers into a more humane and self-reflexive species. New thinking explores the theatre, values and projects of organisational life but with a focus on the experiences of professionals, managers and executives.

These developments seem to reflect the genesis of a critically informed social action theory of management – one that does not trade in the prescription of the mainstream agenda, but rather in narratives of practice, cautionary tales of where managers can go wrong. The question to be answered is whether managers will or even can transform themselves through such reflexiveness, at present there being no real signs that humanistic values are impinging on bottom-line definitions of organisational effectiveness, the ongoing rhetoric of empowerment not excepted.

This is not to say that the values inherent in 'new thinking' are not welcome, and indeed they provide a crucial route for the incorporation of issues of subjectivity into OB. Other routes are developing the themes of subjectivity and identity, albeit with the more prosaic aims of reforming the discipline rather than the subject or the client, as exemplified in Hosking and Morley's (1991) cognitive/political psychology of organising and Hollway's (1991) proposals on a movement towards a work psychology reflexive of the relations of knowledge, power and practice. The focus on management found almost everywhere today produces an appearance that the workforce is steadily becoming unreachable as a subject of study, except perhaps in case studies of organisational 'success'. This is especially true of attempts to research what Corbett (1994: 5) calls the 'dark side' of OB in issues such as, 'drug use, unethical behaviour, the secret workings of organisational cabals and violent behaviour'. Corporate discourses envision these as irrational and irrelevant to the construction of corporate harmony, regardless of their role in the everyday experience and identity work of organisational participants. It remains the role of critical organisation theory to get beneath these surface appearances of organisational life.

In using identity as a linking concept, we are in no way claiming that it is the complete answer to understanding issues connected to the 'subjective factor'; rather, that it is one means of taking our understanding further. Nor do we claim that it is possible at this stage to use identity or any other means to produce an integrated critical social psychology. Unfortunately, in redefining the agenda, there is no new and improved magical ingredient which will wash away all the contradictions between these perspectives and provide us with a realistic, emancipatory paradigm with which to proceed. What we have tried to do in Part Two of this book is to use the discussion of identity and subjectivity to address issues that arise in and across mainstream and critical theories and research, reassessing and integrating material within some consistent focus. The approach taken, though focusing mainly on the experiential level, is, we believe, compatible with the structural framework deriving from the perspectives informed by labour process and Weberian concepts in Part One.

Theory, knowledge and practice

Paradigm diversity or closure?

In this chapter we have tried to set out the main general resources available for theorising about work organisations. Our own prime resources have been labour process theory, radical Weberianism and elements of critical social psychology. It would be difficult to argue that these and other components of a critical approach could, or even should, be synthesised into a coherent explanation of work organisations. However, despite differences and some-times flatly opposed explanations, they can be drawn on as a resource for understanding the complexity of issues involved. In part, this is because there is some common ground. Referring to action theory and the more radical structuralist perspectives, Dunkerley and Salaman observe: 'Both seek to undermine the notion of inevitability in organisational structure; both seek to insert active human beings and groups and their values and interests into the complex processes which give rise to organisational structures' (1986: 93). Complementarity is often more feasible than synthesis – for example in that the labour process and Weberian analyses illuminate power and control through the discussion of means of production, and of administration.

This rather pragmatic view of theorising will be opposed by those who believe that theories can and must operate from within hermetically sealed boxes. For one of the assumptions made by Burrell and Morgan (1979) about the paradigms with which we began this chapter is that they were incommensurable. In other words, their basic differences about knowledge and the world were so basic that theory could only be developed within each framework, which would then do battle with the others. As paradigms frame and define relevant interpretation, 'any observations that do not seem to fit in particular approach belong in some other paradigm' (Ackroyd, 1994: 278). Ackroyd is rightly sceptical about the origins and consequences of the mentality of paradigm closure. Yet it is difficult for paradigms to 'speak' to one another, when they not only make different 'reality assumptions', but develop highly distinctive 'languages' of their own. It is, in fact, one of life's little ironies that many of those who believe most strongly in the constitutive power of language cannot write a sentence that can be understood without a dictionary, a gin and tonic and a great deal of patience! The problem of theoretical communication is compounded by the very different national traditions in organisation theory, as accounts of the past and present in North America (Aldrich, 1992) and Francophone analysis (Chanlat, 1994) reveal.

In some ways, intellectual fashion has moved on from closure. If anything, in these post-modern times, paradigm diversity is the (dis)order of the day. Gareth Morgan has certainly shifted his stance in this way, and now talks about the need to 'harness the possibilities which they offer' (1990: 27). A more concrete version of the same thing is offered by Hassard (1991) who re-interprets the same empirical data through the paradigmatic 'eyes' of each of Burrell and Morgan's original quartet. This is certainly an interesting exercise, but as Parker and McHugh (1991) observed of this effort, the ability to hop between languages is not the same as demonstrating its analytical usefulness. Proclaiming the value of multiple paradigms is really closure by any other name, for each speaks from behind its own walls. The post-modern relativist twist that everything is of equal value merely adds to the problem and is open to the same objections that were raised by Reed to Morgan's use of metaphors: that we end up with taking products down from the shelf instead of rigorous debate and research.

For it is, nevertheless, essential for theories and theorists to engage one another. This may not be as difficult as it appears. As Ackroyd (1992, 1994) reminds us, a lot of the best research is not led by a commitment to paradigms, or is stimulated by 'boundary exchanges' between them. It is possible to have reservations about the strategic exchange theory of Watson (1994) or the discourse analysis of Pringle (1989) but still find exciting and revealing accounts of managerial and secretarial work. Sometimes it is necessary to get behind the different languages and explore whether writers are saying substantively similar things. Other differences can be put down to level of analysis. It is perfectly legitimate to have a more structural or a more micro emphasis of management or some other aspect of organisational life. The key is not to close off analytically the possibilities of 'seeing' the other dimension.

Of course, sharp theoretical disagreements will remain, not so much because of different paradigms, but because rival claims are being made about organisations and society. Ultimately the key problem is not paradigm, but reality incommensurability. Organisations cannot be at the same becoming more and less bureaucratic. Theorising must always remain dynamic and open enough to recognise changes. The 'theoretical' tensions between agency and structure, in part, reflect permanent tensions in practice between co-operativeness and individualism, or normative and economic controls. That is why good theorising is dependent on good research. It will never by enough for theory to be triggered by texts. This seems a useful point to move towards a broader consideration of the uses of knowledge.

Management and theory

If we examine the interaction between theories and practices described in previous chapters, no mechanical and few direct relationships can be found. As with the approach to theorising by academics, organisational theories are a *resource* for practitioners, mostly, of course, for employers and managers. Taylor and Mayo, for example, were great synthesisers of ideas and practices in a way that management found useful, not just as a guide to action but as a way of clarifying and legitimating their role. Yet theorists, and Taylor was a prime case, frequently rail against companies that do not swallow their whole package but rather apply them selectively. As Chandler (1977: 277) observes, 'No factory owner . . . adopted the system without modifying it'. This should come as no surprise. Employers and managers are pragmatists and, with some exceptions such as the Quaker-owned companies in the UK, seldom show any intrinsic interest in ideas in themselves but rather for their 'use value'; or, as one senior manager is quoted in Gowler and Legge (1983: 213): 'There's no good ideas until there's cash in the till'.

This is one of the main reasons why, as Watson (1986: 2) correctly notes, there will never be a full and generally acceptable organisational or management theory. But it is not merely a case of a plurality of competing perspectives. The *partiality* of such theories is inherent in their use in control and legitimation processes. It is in the nature of theories of and for management that they give incomplete pictures. The perspectives and accompanying prescriptions only address aspects of the basic contradictions in capitalist work organisation. Therefore, at one level both theorists and practitioners respond within a continuum that has Taylor's minimum interaction model at one end and varieties of human relations at the other. Employers, of course, would like it both ways. Bendix gives an example of a management journal in 1910 calling for 'absolute authority as well as the willing co-operation of the workers' (1956: 272).

To some extent, they can do this by *combining* theories and practices within the continuum. So we saw in Chapter 2 that human relations did not challenge

Taylorism on its own terrain of job design and structures, but rather sought to deal with its negative effects and blind spots. That story of combination to deal with different dimensions of organisational experience is repeated through every period and sector. It is, of course, the case that management is not only trying to deal with the contradictory aspects of utilising human labour. Variations in strategy and practice reflect broader problems, such as harmonising different functions and sites of decision-making. But the resultant difficulties in managing the contradictions are similar – different routes to partial success and failure, as Hyman noted (see Chapter 4).

It would be wrong to give the impression that the choice and use of theories is solely an internal matter. This would reinforce the erroneous view that organisational theories as an historical sequence of 'models of man', the new naturally replacing the old as grateful managers learn to recognise the more sophisticated account of human needs and behaviour. Selectivity is also conditioned by *circumstances*, involving a number of key 'macro' and 'micro' dimensions. At the broadest level, organisational theories interact with the political economy of broad phases of capital accumulation. Taylorism and classical management perspectives emerged at a time when the scale and complexity of organisations and of markets were undergoing a fundamental change. The globalisation of markets and intensified competition, particularly from Japan, has stimulated major shifts in management thinking in the more recent period.

Yet there were so many misconceptions surrounding 'Japanisation' that it is difficult to disagree with the view that it is a bad abstraction (Dicken and Savage, 1987: 2), which conflates unrelated and non-essential factors behind an inappropriate racial tag. As Marchington and Parker comment, 'there must be some doubt as to whether there is anything inherently Japanese about the practices employed' (1987: 28). They point to the kind of British companies discussed in Chapter 7 that have a history of consensual, paternalistic management and encouragement of enterprise unionism. But we would put it another way. Japanisation, like other sets of management ideas and practices, is a resource which is drawn on selectively. So the Japanese experience can be seen either as confirmation of the need to retain managerial prerogatives or for the expansion of worker participation, or indeed as both (Streek, 1987: 295). Even unions can draw on those aspects which are perceived as egalitarian, such as single-status conditions. Interestingly, Wickens is bitingly critical of faddist managers, who 'have only an idealised, often out-of-date, sanitised version of Japanese-style management based on constantly recycled versions of the human resource and other management techniques of some of Japan's larger companies' (1987: 37).

To return to more general themes, ideological conditions are also influential, as evidenced by the spillover of entrepreneurial values from the political to the managerial sphere. At a micro-level, the choices made by particular companies reflect even more complex factors. In particular, the *sector*, with its specific product market and labour market, technological framework and political context, is a vital consideration. Each country, too, has its own unique configuration of intellectual, social and economic conditions mediating the form and content of organisational change. But just as there are global markets for products, so there are increasingly for ideas. This process is enhanced by the spread of pop-management and 'airport lounge' books, as the success of the excellence genre is testament to. Unfortunately, it reinforces the tendency for academics to form alliances with sections of management around particular perspectives or techniques as solve-all solutions. So much ideological investment is made in the process that the chosen vehicle can seldom meet the burden placed on it. Hence burn-out, cynicism and later fortunate loss of memory – until, that is, a new solution comes along! But why do managers so often become locked in this fatal embrace? This is an underdeveloped area (Huczynski, 1993; Thompson and O'Connell Davidson, 1994), but part of the explanation is that, as an interest group, management requires a means of defining and expanding its activities. Referring to the recent spread of interest in corporate culture, Thackray comments, 'Culture is particularly seductive because it appears to open up a new frontier of managerial activism' (1986: 86). This option is particularly attractive to the personnel or human resource teams of large corporations, reminding us that the adoption of theories and practices is also likely to be affected by the internal fissures within the managerial labour process. With the demise of the great practitioner-theorists such as Taylor and Fayol, and the growth of more specialised academic production, management is also in a more *dependent* position.

But the attraction is also a reflection of the fact that the meaning of management is inseparable from the management of meaning (Gowler and Legge, 1983). Organisational theories become part of a language and a sub-culture through which management tries to understand itself and legitimate its activities to others, even when those ideological resources are used in a contradictory and rhetorical way. The essence of these points is that regardless of the social influences, organisational and management theory has a level of autonomy and its own rhythm of development. Regardless of the cycles of interest in ideas and imitations of the fashion cycle, they have their own very real effects. And as they are grappling with genuine problems, it is possible to draw positive lessons, even for those of us who want to take the process of organisational change much further.

Learning from past and present

There is a danger in any book that focuses on critique of theoretical and practical orthodoxy, of simply knocking everything down. To paraphrase

Gouldner's comment for other purposes, critical social scientists have too often been morticians who bury people's hopes, and this has been further added to by the post-modern abandonment of belief in the possibilities of progress through any type of rational design. We believe that it is important for critical theory not just to proclaim the limits of existing organisational forms and practices. Those constraints arising from dominant relations of wealth, power and control are real enough, as observation of the very partial progress of QWL programmes or employee participation illustrates. But solely 'negative learning' implies an *essence* to work organisation under capitalism which denies it any significance. For instance, the *Work Relations Group* led by the noted American radical scholar Jeremy Brecher (1978: 20) argues that the history of such research 'exposes the shallow conceptions of "job enrichment", "workers' control" and the like as window dressing which leaves untouched the essential tyranny of the capitalist labour process'. Certainly many aspects of work reorganisation have been and still are based on increasing the intensity of labour, tightening controls and marginalising sections of the workforce. But when Marx wrote that the logic of competition between companies compels them constantly to revolutionise the means of production, he was recognising that by its very nature capitalism is a dynamic system.

The search for profitability involves innovations in technology, co-ordination of resources and utilisation of people's skills and knowledge that offer positive lessons relevant to any more democratic and egalitarian social order at work. This is not the same as the orthodox Marxist view, expressed by the founders of the Soviet Union, that a socialist society simply 'adds on' the techniques of capitalist work organisation to new property relations. Those techniques rather have to be added to, rethought and resituated in a new context of a fully democratic economy. For job enrichment or teamworking, however flawed, are also indicators of the great potential of human labour to create more efficient and satisfying forms of work. To argue that all this is mere superficial window dressing is to fly in the face of the reality that we all find some work situations more creative and rewarding than others. Furthermore, there appears in some spheres to be a lot more to learn about innovative forms of work organisation from capitalism than from existing and past state socialist societies.

A further reason for not regarding the worlds of today and tomorrow as wholly sealed off from one another is that there is much to learn from the existing practices of employees. As Brecher rightly says, there is a massive 'hidden history of the workplace' which needs to be recognised and uncovered. That history is based on the self-organisation of workers trying to resist and transform work relations. Admittedly that was easier to see when craft labour was dominant and many workers genuinely felt that they could run the factories better than their bosses. Old-style movements for workers' control are no longer feasible in a world of transnationals, global production and semi-skilled labour. But there remains a wealth of untapped experience and knowledge in employees' informal job-controls and patterns of organisation.

Though measures such as TQM are back-handed compliments from employers, little is learnt because workers' self-activity is seldom given institutional form. Discussions of alternative forms of organisation often depend on examples such as producer co-operatives. Such initiatives have grown rapidly in recent years, partly as a response to the economic recession and restructuring. As collectivist and democratic forms of management and ownership, co-operatives constitute an important experience, despite their critics from left to right who predict inevitable degeneration into traditional structures (Cornforth, 1988). But the fact remains that they are relatively marginal in the economy. With a few well-known exceptions such as the large-scale Mondragon movement in Spain, most are small, labour-intensive and self-financed and they flourish in areas of the market where there is little competition from mainstream organisations (Rothschild and Allen Whitt, 1986). Alternatives within the mainstream economy are few indeed and those that have taken place, such as the UK Lucas workers' alternative plan, have had to bear a heavy burden as exemplar and hope for the future (Collective Design Project, 1986). This initiative arose as a strategic means of local trade union organisation to provide a positive alternative to dependence on making armaments, based on production that was both socially useful and economically viable, and technology that was human-centred. Predictably, though highly praised by all and sundry, it did not get very far with management. But the emphasis on alternative technologies has perhaps had a more lasting impact and is tied into further design work done by the Control Systems Centre at UMIST (Corbett, 1985b). Such initiatives illustrate one of our central points, that positive connections can be made between the kind of theoretical critiques of technological determinism and deskilling made by labour-process and other writers, and practical initiatives in new forms of work design

We would also do well not to forget that the mainstream world of large-scale organisations includes the public sector. Such services in the UK, notably those in local government, have been given a rough ride in recent years, both with respect to their funding and sharp attacks on their efficiency. Some of the criticisms have been well deserved. Much local authority service provision has been characterised by over-centralisation, a lack of flexibility in meeting diverse consumer demands and poor managerial direction in setting and attaining goals. But the innovative organisational response, mainly from Labour local authorities, has been neglected (Goss and Parston, 1989). All these examples illustrate the need and potential for organisational theorists to broaden their conception of practitioners and extend contacts and collaboration to broader groups of clients, including those in the voluntary and public sectors, and to trade union and other employee organisations. Nevertheless, practice without theory is blind and such activity has to be underwritten by more extensive analytical work directed towards developing new thinking on renewing existing and extending alternative organisational forms. Rationality, for all its flaws, is not dead.

A guide to key reading

No matter how detailed or comprehensive its descriptions of the literature, no textbook is an island. It cannot and should not stand alone, and one if its functions is to stimulate those who use it to read further. The literature on work organisations is a large and diverse one. With over 500 references in the bibliography we are somewhat spoiled for choice, and the range of material published since the first edition indicates that organisation studies has been growing rapidly as an academic area. The books and articles listed below are not necessarily things we agree with, but ones we found to be useful, occasionally essential and sometimes stimulating. We have tried to stick to sources that are reasonably accessed and accessible, but that is not always possible. For reasons internal to academia, more material of importance is published in journals and some of this is reflected in our choice, though generally our advice is still for students to read journals such as *Work, Employment and Society, Organisation Studies, Journal of Management Studies, Organisation and Gender* and *Work and Organisation* for themselves.

General texts and theory

The previous paucity of texts going beyond the mainstream and standard US-influenced OB model is no longer the case. Within the more conventional format, McKenna (1994) and Arnold, Robertson and Cooper (1991) have better treatments of psychological theories and their applications than found in most OB texts. Watson (1986 and forthcoming new edition) provides a text which usefully overlaps into personnel and industrial relation's issues; while in another new edition, Sandra Dawson (1986; 2nd edn, 1993), though aimed mainly at service courses, has lively discussions in neglected areas such as power and technology as a social product. Perrow's (1979) *Complex*

Organisations is still one of the most readable and provocative commentaries, particularly on the American debates. As an examination of popular management writing, Huczynski's (1993) *Management Gurus* is a useful overview and a lot better than its title. From Donaldson (1985) we get an aggressive reaffirmation of the virtues of orthodoxy in *In Defence of Organisation Theory*. As this only came out in hardback, readers might try the symposium on the book in *Organisation Studies* (1988: vol. 9, no. 1). Though billed as examining 'theoretical perspectives in industrial sociology' and not always up-to-date in research terms, Richard Brown's *Understanding Industrial Organisations* (1992) is a thorough and very fair exposition of the systems, interpretative and labour process theories.

In recent years, textbooks have begun to reflect a radical agenda much more extensively. A shorter and less comprehensive book than our own, but sharing a similar orientation, is Glenn Morgan's (1990) *Organisations in Society*. It is particularly good on the international dimension and on the organisation–environment literature. The term 'radical', however, can have more than one meaning. Post-modernism has captured the attention of or influenced many academics unhappy with existing orthodoxies. Clegg's (1990) *Modern Organisations* and Gareth Morgan's (1986) *Images of Organisation* have been the most influential, though the heavier debates and expositions have been carried in journals, especially *Organisation Studies*. Look out for articles by Cooper and Burrell (1988), Parker (1992) and Hassard (1994), though these are all sympathetic. Other debates are carried out in 'readers' based on conference papers. As most papers are written to impress peer groups, a lot of this stuff is not easy, a problem exacerbated by the post-modern love of impenetrable jargon. Hassard and Parker's *Post-modernism and Organisations (1993)* is the place to start, particularly for the critical contributions from Reed and Paul Thompson.

Teachers and students often learn more from 'histories' of theory and practice, than from texts, and this ties in with one of our main themes of the necessity to see theories in their practical and historical context. We have found a number of books essential for that task. One of the oldest, but still a superb source of information on managerial ideologies, is *Work and Authority in Industry* from Bendix (1956). Two radical writers deserve mention for their historical accounts. On similar territory, it is still possible to learn much from John Child's (1969) *British Management Thought*. Clawson's (1980) study is marred by a rather crude Marxism, but its focus on the genesis of industrial bureaucracy up to and beyond the turn of the century is still valuable. Good quality business history, notably Chandler's work (1962, 1977, 1991) is also excellent source material on the evolution of management, corporate structure and strategy.

Moving the emphasis to the UK and further into the 1920s and later is Geoff Brown's *Sabotage* (1977). This could win a prize for the title least representative of the content of a book. But it is an important source of information on management and shop floor practices in areas such as the implementation of Taylorism and human relations. Richard Edwards (1979) and Friedman (1977) also contains a lot of valuable material of the contested terrain of the shop floor, as well being noted contributions to labour process theory in its own right.

Specific issues

On organisations and their environments, the older debates are still best found in Perrow again and the second edition of John Child's (1984) *Organisation: a Guide to Problems and Practice*, as are many of the readings collected together by Salaman and Thompson (1973). Wood's article (1979) provides one of the best critiques, mainly of contingency theory. On the population ecology perspective, Hannan and Freeman's (1977) article gives a lucid exposition and Aldrich (1992) puts it in a broader, comparative framework. Short journal introductions of institutional theories of environment-organisation relations are represented in Meyer and Rowan (1977) and Di Maggio and Powell (1983). These are American systems-orientated approaches. For a more European version of institutionalism see the edited collection by Whitley (1992b), or the journal piece by Maurice *et al.* (1980). The key 'environmental' issue now is globalisation and previously dominant debates on Japanisation have been largely subsumed within this framework. The current argument in favour of adoption of the latest form of Japanese methods, 'lean production', can be found in Womack *et al.*'s *The Machine the Changed the World* (1990) and in a more scholarly form in the journal article by Florida and Kenney (1991). More critical accounts can be found in the excellent collection *Global Japanisation?* by Elger and Smith (1994). On the broader globalisation front, Hirst and Thompson (1992) provide a fair, if critical summary, and Henderson (1989) is a very good sector study.

Recommending things in the sphere of the political environment is difficult, as much of the writing consists of highly specialised theories of the state. The best connections between the state and the public sector as workplace are Cousins (1987) and Farnham and Horton (1993) The former is particularly useful, as her readable book is very good on wider theoretical debates about bureaucracy, the labour process and gender.

In the area of management and managerial work, an excellent summary and evaluation of the literature is in the journal article, What do Managers Do? by Hales (1986), or his new book (1993) *Managing Through Organisation*. Willmott's two articles (1984, 1987) on similar issues are also valuable. Some of these articles can be found in a special issue of the *Journal of Management Studies* (vol. 21, no. 3). *Controversies in Management* by Berkeley Thomas (1993) is more mainstream, but a useful overview. The second edition of M. Rose's (1988) *Industrial Behaviour* remains idiosyncratic, but usefully updates his commentary on managerial thinkers to include labour process analyses of management. Watson's (1994) account of his participant observation research as a manager in a large manufacturing company is an invaluable reflection on theory and practice.

On management control strategies, the most interesting material continues to be carried in journals, notably *Work, Employment and Society*, including two definitive pieces by Hyman (1987) and Streek (1987). That journal has also carried a number of articles by Armstrong (1984, 1987b, 1989) which constitute an important body of work on management and the organisational professions. The empirical work on control and resistance by Edwards and Scullion (1982) is indispensable. A survey of labour process debates on management strategies of control can be found in P. Thompson (1983; 1989 2nd edn); while some of the well-known empirical work is collected together in readers edited by Knights and Willmott (1986a and b) and Wilkinson and Willmott (1994). There is now some useful material around taking a deeper and analytical look at HRM. Readers should start with Legge's (1995) new text, and the readers by Storey (1992) and Blyton and Turnbull (1992) are also useful.

Power is no longer a neglected issue. Useful accounts of mainstream writing on power, on internal politics and decisionmaking can be found in Lee and Lawrence (1985), and Pfeffer (1992). Clegg's (1992) text on power is a major contribution to in this area, though it is very difficult in parts. A lot of the newer debates connect power with gender and sexuality in organisations. Knights and Willmott's (1986a) collection on gender and the labour process has been followed by more explicit material such as Mills and Tancred's (1992) *Gendering Organisational Analysis* and Savage and Witz's (1992) *Gender and Bureaucracy*. Hearn and Parkin's (1987) initially unique account of the interrelationships between sexuality and organisational life has led to the reader by Hearn *et al.* (1989). Empirically and theoretically lively material traversing both these areas include classics such as the studies of women factory workers by Pollert (1981) and Westwood (1984), Hochschild's (1983) *The Managed Heart*, Cockburn's (1983) *Brothers*, as well as the more recent *Secretaries Talk* (1989) by Pringle. Of related interest is the recent volume on *Organisations and Emotion* edited by Fineman (1993). A new book by Wilson (1995) takes in all the aspects of gender and organisations and promises to be the most comprehensive account of issues and literature.

Moving to issues raised in our 'Beyond Bureaucracy? chapter, Mintzberg's (1983) *Structures in Fives: Designing Effective Organizations* represents the advanced guard of mainstream thinking. Again, John Child (1984) gives a comprehensive and practical account of wide range of issues and research. Essential readings for the newer debates on flexible working are Atkinson (1985) for the model of the flexible firm, and Piore and Sabel (1984) for the theory of flexible specialisation. The collection edited by Clutterbuck (1985) is lightweight, but useful for an understanding of a section of management thinking. Excellent critiques are provided by K. Williams *et al.* (1987), Wood (1989) and Pollert (1988a and b), who also edited the comprehensive and critical (1991) volume *Farewell to Flexibility*. Ritzer's (1993) The *McDonaldisation of Society* is a marvellous antidote to the rhetoric of post-bureaucratic organisation.

Organisational culture may also have passed its peak as the 'hottest' topic of discussion in organisational and management writing, but it is still important. One place to start is *Corporate Cultures* by Deal and Kennedy (1988). The quality of evidence is often abysmal, but the flavour of the argument is there. Peters and Waterman's (1982) *In Search of Excellence* is more famous and is a bit more theoretical. More critical, though necessarily more demanding theoretical discussion can be found in journal articles by Smircich (1983), Ray (1986) and Willmott (1993a). There are lots of broader sociological accounts of workplace culture, but by far the best empirical account that connects into organisational debates is Kunda's (1992) *Engineering Culture*.

Critical psychologies

We have already given references for some of the key mainstream behavioural texts. What about the critical sources we have found useful? The first thing that must be said is that many of these are fairly difficult pieces, but nevertheless repay reading. One of the more accessible is Leonard's (1984) *Personality and Ideology*. Though we do not share its view that Marxism is a viable basis for a theory of the individual, it does a good job in situating psychological theories within a materialist account of the social order. From a different tradition – Foucault and discourse theory – *Changing the Subject* by Henriques *et al.* (1984) is heavy going in parts. But it has a useful emphasis on the production of subjectivity and psychological knowledge, with a wealth of material on applications to gender, work and other areas. Even heavier is Wexler's (1983) comprehensive and reflexive critique of social psychology in the tradition of the Frankfurt of Marxism. Articles by Seivers (1986) and Van Strien (1982) provide critical discussions of the issues of motivation and practical interventions by psychologists respectively.

On the question of identity, Weigert *et al.* (1986) provide a detailed treatment of the theories and applications of the concept from a sociological social psychology perspective. We used extensively the article by Knights and Willmott (1985) on Power and Identity in Theory and Practice. Two other, more empiricallybased contributions in this area are *Coping with Threatened Identities* by Breakwell (1986), which provides useful models of the process;

and Cohen and Taylor's (1978, and still preferable to its second edition!) witty and readable *Escape Attempts: the Theory and Practice of Resistance to Everyday Life*. For those wishing to go deeper into the debate, there is Shotter and Gergen's (1989) *Texts of Identity*, which provides a discourse-orientated approach. The impact of such themes on 'New Thinking' in OB can be followed up in books of readings such as Tsoukas (1994c). Fineman (1993) and Newton (1995) deal with related areas such as emotional labour and stress.

The themes of discipline, surveillance and impression management can be examined in case material in Zuboff (1988) and, again, Kunda (1992). An excellent range of general case material can be found in *Critical Cases in Organisational Behaviour* by Corbett (1994). Finally, to return to the more general texts, Hollway's (1991) *Work Psychology*, Hosking and Morley's *Social Psychology of Organising*, and Johnson and Gill's (1993) *Management Control and Organisational Behaviour* have been particularly helpful in producing this new edition.

Bibliography

ACAS (1988) *Labour Flexibility in Britain: The 1987 ACAS Survey*, London: ACAS Occasional Paper 41.

Acker, J. and D. R. Van Houten (1992) 'Differential Recruitment and Control: the Sex Structuring of organizations', in A. J. Mills and P. Tancred (eds) *Gendering Organizational Analysis*, London: Sage.

Acker, S. (1992) 'Gendering Organizational Theory', in A. J. Mills and P. Tancred (eds) *Gendering Organizational Analysis*, London: Sage.

Ackers, P. and J. Black (1991) 'Paternalist Capitalism: An Organization in Transition', in M. Cross and G. Payne (eds) *Work and the Enterprise Culture*, London: The Falmer Press.

Ackroyd, S. (1992) 'Paradigms Lost: Paradise Gained? Notes on the Discovery of Meta-Theory in Organizational Analysis', in M. Reed and M. Hughes (eds) *Rethinking Organization: New Directions in Organization and Analysis*, London: Sage.

Ackroyd, S. (1994) 'Recreating Common Ground: Elements for Post-Paradigmatic Theories of Organization, in J. Hassard and M. Parker (eds) *Towards a New Theory of Organizations*, London: Routledge.

Ackroyd, S. and P. A. Crowdy (1990) 'Can Culture be Managed? Working with "Raw" Material: The Case of English Slaughtermen', *Personnel Review*, vol. 19, no. 5: 12–13.

Ackroyd, S., G. Burrell, S. Hughes and A. Whitaker (1987) 'The Japanisation of British Industry', paper presented at Conference on: *Japanisation of British Industry*, UWIST, also in *Industrial Relations Journal*, Spring 1988, vol. 9, no. 1.

Adair, J. (1979) *Action-Centred Leadership*, Aldershot: Gower.

Adams, J. S. (1965) 'Injustice in Social Exchange', in L. Berkovitz (1965) *Advances in Experimental Social Psychology*, vol. 2.

Adkins, L. (1992) 'Sexual Work and the Employment of Women in the Service Industries', in A. Witz, and M. Savage (eds) *Gender and Bureaucracy*, Oxford: Blackwell.

Adler, P. S. (1993) 'Time-and-Motion Regained', *Harvard Business Review*, Jan.–Feb.: 97–107.

Aglietta, M. (1979) *A Theory of Capitalist Regulation*, London: New Left Books.

Aichholzer, G. and G. Schienstock (1985) 'Labour in Conflict: Between Capital Interests and the Maintenance of Identity', paper for *20th Annual Meeting of the Canadian Sociology and Anthropology Association*, University of Montreal.

Ajzen, I. (1988) *Attitudes, Personality and Behaviour*, Milton Keynes: Open University Press.

Ajzen, I. and M. Fishbein (1980) *Understanding Attitudes and Predicting Social Behaviour*, New Jersey: Prentice-Hall.

Albrow, M. (1970) *Bureaucracy*, London: Pall Mall.

Albrow, M. (1973) 'The Study of Organizations – Objectivity or Bias?' in G. Salaman and K. Thompson (eds) *People and Organizations*, Harlow: Longman.

Albrow, M. (1992) 'Sine Ira et Studio – or Do Organizations Have Feelings?' *Organization Studies*, vol. 13, no. 3: 313–29.

Alderfer, C.P. and K.K Smith (1982) 'Studying intergroup relations embedded in organizations', *Administrative Science Quarterly*, 27: 35–65.

Aldrich, H.E. (1979) *Organizations and Environments*, Englewood Cliffs, NJ: Prentice-Hall.

Aldrich, H.E. (1992) 'Incommensurable Paradigms? Vital Signs from Three Perspectives', in M. Reed and M. Hughes (eds) *Rethinking Organization: New Directions in Organization and Analysis*, London: Sage.

Aldrich, H.E. and J. Pfeffer (1976) 'Environments and Organizations', in G. Inkeles *et al.* (eds) *Annual Review of Sociology*, vol. 2.

Aldrich, H.E. and U. Stabler (1987) Organizational Transformation and Trends in US Employment Relations, paper at ASTON-UMIT Labour Process Conference.

Allen, J. and N. Henry (1994) 'Fragments of Industry and Employment: Contract Service Work and the Shift Towards Precarious Employment', paper to Conference: *Work, Employment and Society in the 1990s*, Sep., University of Kent.

Allen, S. and Workowtiz, C. (1987) *Homeworking: Myths and Realities*, London: Macmillan.

Alvesson, M. (1988) 'Management, Corporate Culture and Labour Process in a Professional Service Company', paper presented at Conference on the Labour Process, ASTON-UMIST.

Alvesson, M. (1991) 'Corporate Culture and Corporatism at the Company Level: A Case Study', Economic and Industrial Democracy, vol. 12: 347–67.

Alvesson, M. and Y. Due Billing (1992) 'Gender and Organisations: Towards a Differentiated Understanding', *Organisation Studies*, vol. 13, no. 12: 73–102.

Amin, A. (1989) 'A Model of the Small Firm in Italy', in E. Goodman *et al.* (eds) *Small Firms and Industrial Districts in Italy*, New York: Routledge.

Amin, A. (1991) 'Flexible Specialisation and Small Firms in Italy: Myths and Realities', in A. Pollert (ed.) *Farewell to Flexibility*, Oxford: Blackwell.

Amsden, A.H. (1992) *Asia's Next Giant: South Korea and Late Industrialisation*, Oxford: Oxford University Press.

Andreff, W. (1984) 'The International Centralisation of Capital and the Reordering of Work Capitalism', *Capital and Class*, 22: 58–80.

Anthony, P.D. (1990) 'The Paradox of the Management of Culture or "He Who Leads is Lost"', *Personnel Review*, vol. 19, no. 4: 3–8.

Archibald, W.P. (1978) *Social Psychology as Political Economy*, Toronto: McGraw-Hill Ryerson.

Argyle, M. (1974) *The Social Psychology of Work*, Harmondsworth: Penguin.

Argyris, A. (1967) 'Today's Problems with Tomorrow's Organizations', *Journal of Management Studies*, vol. 4, no. 1: 31–55.

Argyris, C. and D.A. Schön (1978) *Organisational Learning: A Theory of Action Perspective*, Reading, Mass: Addison-Wesley.

Arias, M.E. (1993) 'MNCs, Organizational Models, and Local Firms in Developing Countries: the case of the Pharmaceutical Industry in Ecuador', paper presented at the *11th EGOS Colloquium*, Paris.

Armistead, N. (1974) *Reconstructing Social Psychology*, Baltimore: Penguin.

Armstrong, P. (1984) 'Competition between the Organizational Professions and the Evolution of Management Control Strategies', in K. Thompson (ed.) *Work, Employment and Unemployment*, Milton Keynes: Open University Press.

Armstrong, P. (1986) 'Management Control Strategies and InterProfessional Competition: the Cases of Accountancy and Personnel Management', in D. Knights and H. Willmott (eds) *Managing the Labour Process*, Aldershot: Gower.

Armstrong, P. (1987a) The Divorce of Productive and Unproductive Management, paper to 5th International Labour Process Conference, Aston.

Armstrong, P. (1987b) 'Engineers, Management and Trust', Work, Employment and Society, vol. 1, no. 4: 421–40.

Armstrong, P. (1988) 'The Personnel Profession in the Age of Management Accountancy', Personnel Review, vol. 17, no. 1: 25–31.

Armstrong, P. (1989) Management, Labour Process and Agency', *Work, Employment and Society*, vol. 3, no. 3: 307–22.

Armstrong, P. (1991) 'The Influence of Michel Foucault on Historical Research in Accounting: An Assessment', paper presented at the *Academy of Accounting Historians Research Methodology Conference*, University of Mississippi, Dec.

Armstrong, P., P. Marginson, P. Edwards and J. Purcell (1994) 'Divisionalisation, Trade Unionism and Corporate Control: Findings from the Second Company-Level Industrial Relations Survey', paper to 12th Annual International Labour Process Conference, Aston.

Arnold, J., I. T. Robertson and C. Cooper (1991) *Work Psychology: Understanding Human Behaviour in the Workplace*, London: Pitman.

Aronoff, J. and J.P. Wilson (1985) *Personality in the Social Process*, New Jersey: LEA.

Asch, S. E., H. Block and M. Hertzmann (1938) 'Studies in the Principles of Judgements of Attitudes: I. Two Basic Principles of Judgement', *Journal of Psychology*, 5: 219–51.

Atkinson, J. (1984) 'Manpower Strategies for Flexible Organizations', *Personnel Management*, Aug.

Atkinson, J. (1985) *IMS Report no. 89*, Falmer, Sussex: IMS.

Atkinson, J. and D. Gregory (1986) A Flexible Future: Britain's Dual Labour Force, *Marxism Today*, Apr.

Bacharach, S.B. and E.J. Lawler (1980) *Power and Politics in Organizations*, London: Josey-Bass.

Bachrach, P. and M.S. Baratz (1962) 'Two Faces of Power', *American Political Science Review* 56: 947–52.

Baldamus, W. (1961) *Efficiency and Effort: An Analysis of Industrial Administration*, London: Tavistock.

Bales, R. F. (1950) *Interaction Process Analysis: A Method for the Study of Small Groups*, Mass: Addison-Wesley.

Bandura, A. (1977) *Social Learning Theory*, Englewood Cliffs, NJ: Prentice-Hall.

Bandura, A. (1986) *Social Foundations of Thought and Action: A Social Cognitive Theory*, Englewood Cliffs, NJ: Prentice-Hall.

Bandura, A. and R. H. Walters (1963) *Social Learning and Personality Development*, New York: Holt, Rinehart & Winston.

Banton, R., P. Clifford, S. Frosh, J. Lousada and J. Rosenthall (1985) *The Politics of Mental Health*, London: Macmillan.

Barham, K. and C. Rassam (eds) (1989) *Shaping the Corporate Future: Leading Executives Share their Vision and Strategies*, London: Unwin Hyman.

Barker, J.R. (1993) 'Tightening the Iron Cage: Concertive Control in Self-Managing Teams', *Administrative Science Quarterly*, 38: 408–37.

Barker, R. and H. Roberts (1993) 'The Uses of the Concept of Power', in D. Morgan and L. Stanley (eds) *Debates in Sociology*, Manchester: Manchester University Press.

Barley, S.R. and G. Kunda (1992) 'Design and Devotion: Surges of Rational and Normative Ideologies of Control in Managerial Discourse', *Administrative Science Quarterly*, vol. 37: 363–99.

Barnard, C. (1938) *The Functions of the Executive*, Cambridge, Mass: Harvard University Press.

Bartitz, L. (1960) *The Servants of Power*, Middletown: Wesleyan University Press.

Bartlett, C. and S. Goshal (1990) 'The Multinational Corporation as an International Network', *Academy of Management Review*, 4.

Bartlett, C. and S. Goshal (1992) 'What is a Global Manager?', *Harvard Business Review*, Sep.–Oct.: 124–32.

Bass, B. M. (1985) Leadership and Performance Beyond Expectations, New York: Free Press.

Basset, P. (1989) 'All Together Now', *Marxism Today*, Jun.

Batstone, E., A. Ferner and M. Terry (1984) *Consent and Efficiency*, Oxford: Basil Blackwell.

Bavelas, A. (1950) 'Communication Patterns in Task-Oriented Groups', *Journal of the Acoustical Society of America*, 22: 725–30.

Beck, U. (1992) *The Risk Society: Towards a New Modernity*, London: Sage.

Becker, H. S. *et al.* (1963) *Boys in White*, Chicago: University of Chicago Press.

Beech, H. R., L. E. Burns and B. F. Sheffield (1982) *A Behavioural Approach to the Management of Stress: A Practical Guide to Techniques*, Chichester: John Wiley.

Beer, M., B. Spector, P. Lawrence, D. Quinn Mills and R. Walton (1985) *Human Resource Management: A General Manager's Perspective*, Glencoe, Ill: Free Press.

Bell, D. (1960) *The End of Ideology*, New York: Collier Macmillan.

Bellaby, P. and P. Orribor (1977) 'The Growth of Trade Union Consciousness Among General Hospital Nurses', *Sociological Review*, vol. 25.

Bendix, R. (1956) *Work and Authority in Industry*, New York: Harper & Row.

Benne, K. D. and P. Sheats (1948) 'Functional Roles of Group Members', *The Journal of Social Science*, Spring: 41–9.

Bennis. W. (1966) *Changing Organizations*, New York: McGraw-Hill.

Benson, J. K. (1977) 'Innovation and Crisis in Organizational Analysis', in J. K. Benson (ed.) *Organizational Analysis: Critique and Innovation*, London: Sage.

Benson, J. K. (ed.) (1977) *Organizational Analysis: Critique and Innovation*, London: Sage, Contemporary Social Science Issues, 37.

Berg, M. (1985) *The Age of Manufactures*, London: Fontana.

Berger, P. L. and T. Luckman (1967) *The Social Construction of Reality*, London: Allen Lane.

Berggren, C. (1993) Lean Production – the End of History? *Work, Employment and Society*, vol. 7, no. 2: 163–88.

Berkeley Thomas, A. (1993) *Controversies in Management*, London: Routledge.

Berle, A. A. and G. C. Means (1935) *The Modern Corporation and Private Property*, New York: Macmillan.

Best, M. (1990) *The New Competition: Institutions of Industrial Restructuring*, Harvard, Mass: Harvard University Press.

Beynon, H. (1975) *Working for Ford*, Wakefield: E.P. Publishing.

Biddle, B. J. (1979) *Role Theory: expectations, Identities and Behaviours*, London: Academic Press.

Biggart, N. W. (1989) *Charismatic Capitalism: Direct Selling Organizations in America*, London: University of Chicago Press.

Bittner, E. (1967) 'The Police on Skid Row: A Study of Peace Keeping', *American Sociological Review*, vol. 32, no. 5: 699–715.

Bittner, E. (1973) 'The Concept of Organization', in G. Salaman and K. Thompson (eds) *People and Organizations*, Harlow: Longman.

Blackler, F. (1982) 'Organizational Psychology', in S. Canter and D. Canter (eds) *Psychology in Practice: Perspectives in Professional Psychology*, Chichester: John Wiley.

Blackler, F. and S. Shimmin (1984) *Applying Psychology in Organizations*, London: Methuen.

Blau, G., F. Linnehan, A. Brooks and D. K. Hoover (1993) 'Vocational behaviour 1990–1992: Personnel Practices, Organisational Behaviour, Workplace Behaviour and Industrial/Organisational, Measurement Issues', *Journal of Vocational Behaviour*, 43: 133–97.

Blau, P. M. (1955) *The Dynamics of Bureaucracy*, Chicago: University of Chicago Press.

Blau, P. M. (1964) *Exchange and Power in Social Life*, New York: Wiley.

Blau, P. M. (1970) 'A Formal Theory of Differentiation in Organizations', *American Sociological Review*, 35: 201–18.

Blau, P. M. and R. A. Schoenherr (1971) *The Structure of Organizations*, New York: Basic Books.

Blau, P. M. and W. Scott (1963) *Formal Organizations: a Comparative Approach*, London: Routledge and Kegan Paul.

Blauner, R. (1964) *Alienation and Freedom*, University of Chicago Press.

Blyton, P. and P. Turnbull (1992) *Reassessing Human Resource Management*, London: Sage.

Boddy, D. and D. Buchanan (1992) *Take the Lead: Interpersonal Skills for Project Managers*, London: Prentice-Hall.

Bologh, R. (1990) *Love or Greatness: Max Weber and Masculine Thinking – A Feminist Inquiry*, London: Unwin Hyman.

Boreham, P. (1980) 'The Dialectic of Theory and Control: Capitalist Crisis and the Organization of Labour', in D. Dunkerely and G. Salaman (eds) *The International Yearbook of Organization Studies 1980*, London: Routledge & Kegan Paul.

Boreham, P. (1992) 'The Myth of Post-Fordist Management: Work Organization and Employee Discretion in Seven Countries', *Employee Relations*, vol. 14, no. 2: 13–24.

Bowles, M. L. and G. Coates (1993) 'Image and Substance: The Management of Performance as Rhetoric or Reality?', *Personnel Review*: 3–21.

Boyne, R. and A. Rattansi (eds) (1990) *Postmodernism and Society*, London: Macmillan.

Bradley, H. (1986) 'Work, Home and the Restructuring of Jobs', in K. Purcell *et al.* (eds) *The Changing Experience of Employment, Restructuring and Recession*, London: Macmillan.

Bramble, T. (1988) 'The Flexibility Debate: Industrial Relations and the New Management Production Practices', *Labour and Industry*, vol. 1, no. 2.

Brannen, P. (1983) *Authority and Participation in Industry*, London: Batsford.

Braverman, H. (1974) *Labor and Monopoly Capital: The Degradation of Work in the Twentieth Century*, New York: Monthly Review Press.

Brazier, M., J. Lovercy, M. Moran and M. Potton (1993) 'Falling From a Tightrope: Doctors and Lawyers between the Market and the State', *Political Studies*, vol. XCLI: 197–213.

Breakwell, G. M. (1986) *Coping with Threatened Identities*, London: Methuen.

Breakwell, G. M. (1987) 'Identity', in, H. Beloff and A. M. Colman (1987) *Psychology Survey 1987*, Leicester: British Psychological Society.

Brecher, J. (1978) 'Uncovering the Hidden History of the American Workplace', *Review of Radical Political Economics*, vol. 10, no. 4, Winter.

Brewis, J. and D. Kerfoot (1994) 'Selling Our "Selves"? Sexual Harassment and the Intimate Violations of the Workplace', paper presented to the BSA Conference: *Sexualities in their Social Context*, University of Central Lancashire, Mar.

Briggs, P. (1987) 'The Japanese at Work: Illusions of the Ideal', paper presented at Conference on: *Japanisation of British Industry*, UWIST. Also in *Industrial Relations Journal*, Spring 1988, vol. 19, no. 1.

Broad, G. (1987) 'Beyond Quality Circles: A Critical Review of Employee Participation in Japanese Industry', paper presented at Conference on: *Japanisation of British Industry*, UWIST.

Brown, G. (1977) *Sabotage*, Nottingham: Spokesman.

Brown, H. (1980) 'Work Groups', in G. Salaman and K. Thompson, (eds) *People and Organizations*, Harlow: Longman.

Brown, R. (1965) *Social Psychology*, London: Coller-Macmillan.

Brown, R. (1992) *Understanding Organizations: Theoretical Perspectives in Industrial Sociology*, London: Routledge.

Bryman, A. (1984) 'Organization Studies and the Concept of Rationality', *Journal of Management Studies*, vol. 21: 394–404.

Bryman, A. (1993) 'The Nature of Organization Structure: Constraint and Choice', in D. Morgan and L. Stanley (eds) *Debates in Sociology*, Manchester: Manchester University Press.

Buchanan, D. (1986) 'Management Objectives in Technical Change', in D. Knights and H. Willmott (eds) *Managing the Labour Process*, Aldershot: Gower.

Buchanan, D. and A. Huczynski (1985) *Organizational Behaviour: An Introductory Text*, London: Prentice-Hall International.

Buford, B. (1991) *Among the Thugs*, London: Secker.

Burawoy, M. (1979) *Manufacturing Consent: Changes in the Labour Process Under Monopoly Capitalism*, Chicago: University of Chicago Press.

Burawoy, M. (1985) *The Politics of Production*, London: Verso.

Burchell, S., C. Clubb and A. Hopwood (1985) 'Accounting in its Social Context: Towards a History of Value-Added in the United Kingdom', *Accounting, Organizations and Society*, vol. 10, no. 4: 381–413.

Burgoyne, J. G. (1993) 'The Competence Movement: Issues, Stakeholders and Prospects', *Personnel Review*, vol. 22, no. 6: 6–13.

Burnham, J. (1945) *The Managerial Revolution*, Harmondsworth: Penguin.

Burns, J. M. (1978) *Leadership*, New York: Harper & Row.

Burns, T. (1982) *A Comparative Study of Administrative Structure and Organizational Processes in Selected Areas of the National Health Service* (SSRC Report, HRP 6725) London: Social Science Research Council.

Burns, T. and G. M. Stalker (1961) *The Management of Innovation*, London: Tavistock.

Burrell, G. (1980a) 'Radical Organization Theory', in D. Dunkerley and G. Salaman (eds) *The International Yearbook of Organization Studies 1979*, London: Routledge & Kegan Paul.

Burrell, G. (1988) 'Modernism, Post Modernism and Organizational Analysis: The Contribution of Michel Foucault', *Organization Studies*, vol. 9, no. 2: 221–35.

Burrell, G. (1992) 'Sex and Organizations', in A. J. Mills and P. Tancred (eds) *Gendering Organizational Analysis*, London: Sage.

Burrell, G. (1994) Foreword to H. Tsoukas (ed.) (1994d) *New Thinking in Organizational Behaviour*, London: Butterworth & Heinemann.

Burrell, G. and G. Morgan (1979) *Sociological Paradigms and Organizational Analysis*, London: Heinemann.

Business Week (1983) 'A Work Revolution in US Industry', 16 May.

CAITS (1986) *Flexibility, Who Needs It?* London.

Calás M. and L. Smircich (1992) 'Rewriting Gender into Organization Theorising: Directions from Feminist Perspectives', in M. Reed and M. Hughes (eds) *Rethinking Organization: New Directions in Organization Analysis*, London: Sage.

Callan Hunt, G. (1992), 'Men and Women in Nontraditional Jobs: An Exploratory Study of Men in the Pink Ghetto', *Association of Management*, Aug.

Callinicos, A. (1989) *Against Postmodernism: A Marxist Critique*, Cambridge: Polity.

Campbell, A. and B. Currie (1987) 'Skills and Strategies in Design Engineering', paper presented to 5th International Labour Process, UMIST.

Campbell, G. (1994) 'The Languages of Workplace Reform, paper to 12th International Labour Process Conference, Aston.

Carchedi, G. (1977) *On the Economic Identification of the Middle Classes*, London: Routledge & Kegan Paul.

Carey, A. (1967) 'The Hawthorne Studies: A Radical Criticism', *American Sociological Review*, 32: 403–16.

Carr Mill Consultants (1973) Report on the Herzberg Seminar, Blackpool.

Carter, P. and P. Jeffs (1992) 'The Hidden Curriculum: Sexuality in Professional Education', in P. Carter, T. Jeffs and M. Smith (eds) *Changing Social Work and Welfare*, Buckingham: Open University Press.

Carter, R. (1985) *Capitalism, Class Conflict and the New Middle Class*, London: Routledge & Kegan Paul.

Casey, B. (1991) 'Survey Evidence on Trends in "Non-Standard" Employment', in A. Pollert (ed.) *Farewell to Flexibility*, Oxford: Blackwell.

Cattell, J. M., Eber and Matsuoka (1970) *Handbook for the 16PF*, Colombia: IPAT.

Cavendish, R. (1982) *Women on the Line*, London: Routledge & Kegan Paul.

Chandler, A. (1962) *Strategy and Structure: Chapters in the History of the Industrial Enterprise*, Cambridge, Mass.: MIT Press.

Chandler, A. D. (1977) *The Visible Hand*, Cambridge Mass.: Harvard University Press.

Chandler, A. D. (1990) *Scale and Scope: the Dynamics of Industrial Capitalism*, Cambridge, Mass.: Harvard University Press.

Chanlat, J–F. (1994) 'Francophone Organizational Analysis (1950–1990): An Overview', *Organization Studies*, vol. 15, no. 1: 47–80.

Cherrington, D. J. (1989) *Organizational Behaviour: The Management of Individual and Organizational Performance*, Boston: Allyn & Bacon.

Cherry, L. (1978) 'On the Real Benefits of Eustress', *Psychology Today*, Mar.: 60–70.

Child, J. (1969) *British Management Thought*, London: Allen & Unwin.

Child, J. (1972) 'Organization Structure, Environment and Performance: the Role of Strategic Choice', *Sociology*, vol. 6, no. 1: 1–22.

Child, J. (1973) (ed.) *Man and Organization*, London: Allen & Unwin.

Child, J. (1982) 'Professionals in the Corporate World', in D. Dunkerley and G. Salaman (eds) *The International Yearbook of Organisation Studies 1981*, London: Routledge & Kegan Paul.

Child, J. (1984) *Organization: A Guide to Problems and Practice*, 2nd edn., London: Harper & Row.

Child, J. (1985) 'Managerial Strategies, New Technology and the Labour Process', in D. Knights, H. Wilmott and D. Collinson (eds) *Job Redesign: Critical Perspectives on the Labour Process*, London: Gower.

Child, J. (1987) 'Organizational Design for Advanced Manufacturing Technology', in T. D. Wall, C. W. Clegg and N. J. Kempt (eds) *The Human Side of Advanced Manufacturing Technology*, Chichester: John Wiley.

Child, J. and C. Smith (1987) 'The Context and Process of Organizational Transformations – Cadbury Limited in its Sector', *Journal of Management Studies*, vol. 24, no. 6: 565–93.

Child, J. and S. Rodrigues (1993) 'The Role of Social Identity in the International Transfer of Knowledge through Business Ventures', paper for the *11th EGOS Colloquium*, Paris, Jul.

Child, J. et al. (1983) 'Professionalism and Work Organization: a Reply to Kevin McCormack', *Sociology*, vol. 20, no. 4: 607–14.

Chorover, S. L. (1979) *From Genesis to Genocide: Meaning of Human Nature and the Power of Behaviour Control*, Cambridge, Mass.: MIT Press.

Cialdini, R. B. (1988) *Influence: Science and Practice* (2nd edn), London: Harper Collins.

Cicourel, A. V. (1968) *The Social Organization of Social Justice*, New York: Free Press.

Clairmonte, F. and J. Cavanagh (1981) *The World in Their Web: the Dynamics of Textile Multinationals*, London: Zed Press.

Clark, D. D. and R. Hoyle (1988) 'A Theoretical Solution to the Problem of Personality-Situational Interaction', *Personality and Individual Differences*, 9: 133–8.

Clawson, D. (1980) *Bureaucracy and the Labour Process: The Transformation of US Industry, 1860–1920*, New York: Monthly Review Press.

Clegg, S. (1977) 'Power, Organization Theory, Marx and Critique', in S. Clegg and D. Dunkerley (eds) *Critical Issues in Organizations*, London: Routledge & Kegan Paul.

Clegg, S. (1988) 'The Good, the Bad and the Ugly', *Organisation Studies*, vol. 9, no. 1: 7–13.

Clegg, S. (1989) *Frameworks of Power*, London: Sage.

Clegg, S. (1990) *Modern Organizations: Organization Studies in the Postmodern World*, London: Sage.

Clegg, S. and D. Dunkerley (1980) *Organization, Class and Control*, London: Routledge & Kegan Paul.

Clegg, S. and D. Dunkerley (eds) (1977) *Critical Issues in Organizations*, London: Routledge & Kegan Paul.

Clegg, S. and G. Higgins (1987) 'Against the Current: Organizational Sociology and Socialism', *Organization Studies*, vol. 8, no. 3: 201–21.

Clegg, S., P. Boreham and G. Dow (1987) *Class, Politics and the Economy*, London: Routledge & Kegan Paul.

Clutterbuck, D. (ed.) (1985) *New Patterns of Work*, Aldershot: Gower.

Cochrane, A. and R. Dicker (1979) 'The Regeneration of British Industry: Jobs and the Inner City', in Community Development Project, *The State and the Local Economy*, Newcastle.

Cockburn, C. (1983) *Brothers: Male Dominance and Technological Change*, London: Pluto Press.

Cockburn, C. (1990) 'Men's Power in Organizations: "Equal Opportunities" Intervenes', in D. Morgan (ed.), *Man, Masculinities and Social Theory*, London: Unwin Hyman.

Cockburn, C. (1991) *In the Way of Women: Men's Resistance to Sex Equality in Organizations*, London: Macmillan.

Cohen, Sheila (1987) 'A Labour Process to Nowhere?' *New Left Review*, 107: 34–50.

Cohen, Stanley (1973) *Folk Devils and Moral Panics*, London: Paladin.

Cohen, Stanley and L. Taylor (1978) *Escape Attempts: The Theory and Practice of Resistance to Everyday Life*, Harmondsworth: Pelican.

Collective Design Project (eds) (1986) *Very Nice Work if You Can Get It: The Socially Useful Production Debate*, Nottingham: Spokesman.

Collins, R. (1986) *Weberian Sociological Theory*, Cambridge University Press.

Collinson, D. (1992) *Managing the Shopfloor: Subjectivity, Masculinity and Workplace Culture*, Berlin: De Gruyter.

Collinson, D. (1994) 'Strategies of Resistance: Power, Knowledge and Subjectivity in the Workplace', in J. Jermier, W. Nord and D. Knights (eds) *Resistance and Power in the Workplace*, London: Routledge & Kegan Paul.

Collinson, D. and J. Hearn (1994) 'Naming Men as Men: Implications for Work, Organization and Management', *Gender, Work and Organizations*, vol. 1, no. 1: 2–22.

Collinson, D. and M. Collinson (1989) 'Sexuality in the Workplace: The Domination of Men's Sexuality', in J. Hearn, D. L. Sheppard, P. Tancred-Sheriff and G. Burrell (eds) *The Sexuality of Organization*, London: Sage.

Control Data Corporation (1985) 'Telecommuting', in D. Clutterbuck (ed.) *New Patterns of Work*, Aldershot: Gower.

Cooper, C. L. (1984) 'What's New In . . . Stress', *Personnel Management*, Jun.: 40–4.

Cooper, C. L. and M. J. Smith (1985) *Job Stress and Blue Collar Work*, Chichester: Wiley.

Cooper, D. (1994) 'Productive, Relational and Everywhere? Conceptualising Power and Resistance Within Foucauldian Feminism', *Sociology*, vol. 28, no. 2: 435–54.

Cooper, R. and G. Burrell (1988) 'Modernism, Postmodernism and Organizational Analysis: An Introduction', *Organization Studies*, vol. 9, no. 2: 91–112.

Coopey, J. and J. Hartley (1991) 'Reconsidering the Case for Organizational Commitment', *Human Resource Management Journal*, vol. 1, no. 3: 18–32.

Corbett, J. M. (1985a) 'The Design of MachineTool Technology and Work: Technical Science and Technical Choice', unpublished draft, Sheffield, MRC/ESRC Social and Applied Psychology Unit.

Corbett, J. M. (1985b) 'Prospective Work Design of a Human-Centred CNC Lathe', *Behaviour and Information Technology*, vol. 14, no. 1: 201–14.

Corbett, J. M. (1994) *Critical Cases in Organisational Behaviour*, London: Macmillan.

Coriat, B. (1980) 'The Restructuring of the Assembly Line: a New Economy of Time and Control', *Capital and Class*, 11: 34–43.

Cornforth, C. (1988) 'Patterns of Cooperative Management: Revising the Degeneration Thesis', paper to a Conference on: *New Forms of Ownership and Management*, Cardiff Business School.

Cousins, C. (1987) Controlling Social Welfare: a Sociology of State Welfare Work and Organization, Brighton: Wheatsheaf.

Coventry, Liverpool, Newcastle and N.Tyneside Trades Councils (1980) *State Intervention in Industry: a Workers' Inquiry*, Newcastle.

Cressey, P, and C. Cousins (1986) 'The Labour Process in the State Welfare Sector', in D. Knights and H. Willmott (eds) *Managing the Labour Process*, Aldershot: Gower.

Cressey, P. and B. Jones (1991) 'A New Convergence?', *Work, Employment and Society*, vol. 5, no. 1: 493–5.

Cressey, P. and J. MacInnes (1980) 'Voting for Ford: Industrial Democracy and the Control of Labour', *Capital and Class*, no. 11: 5–37.

Crompton, R. and G. Jones (1984) *White Collar Proletariat*, London: Macmillan.

Crook, S., J. Paluski and M. Waters (1992) *Postmodernization*, London: Sage.

Cross, M. (1985) 'Flexible Manning', in D. Clutterbuck (ed.) *New Patterns of Work*, Aldershot: Gower.

Crouch, C. (ed.) *State and Economy in Contemporary Capitalism*, London: Croom Helm.

Crowther, S. and P. Garrahan (1987) 'Invitation to Sunderland: Corporate Power and the Local Economy', paper presented at Conference on: *Japanisation of British Industry*, UWIST, also in *Industrial Relations Journal*, Special Issue, Spring 1988.

Crozier, M. (1964) *The Bureaucratic Phenomenon*, London: Tavistock.

Cummings, T. and C. L Cooper (1979 'A Cybernetic Framework for the Study of Occupational Stress', *Human Relations*, 32: 395–419.

Cummings, T. and M. Blumberg (1987) 'Advanced Manufacturing Technology and Work Design', in T. D. Wall, C. W. Clegg and N. J. Kemp (eds) *The Human Side of Advanced Manufacturing Technology*, Chichester: John Wiley.

Cutler, T. (1992) 'Numbers in a Time of Dearth: The Use of Performance Indicators to "Manage" Higher Education', paper to 10th International Labour Process Conference, Aston.

Cyert, R. M. and J. G. March (1963) *A Behavioural Theory of the Firm*, Englewood Cliffs, NJ: Prentice-Hall.

Dahl, R. (1957) 'The Concept of Power', *Behavioural Science*, 2: 201–15.

Dahl, R. (1958) 'A Critique of the Ruling Elite Model', *American Political Science Review*, vol. 52.

Dahl, R. (1978) 'Pluralism Revisited', *Comparative Politics*, 10: 191–204.

Dahler-Larsen, P. (1994) 'Corporate Culture and Morality: Durkheim-Inspired Reflections on the Limits of Corporate Culture', *Journal of Management Studies*, vol. 31, no. 1: 1–18.

Dahrendorf, R. (1959) *Class and Class Conflict in Industrial Society*, London: Routledge & Kegan Paul.

Daily Telegraph (1987) 'Workers Quit as Low Morale Hits Nissan Car Plant', 6 May.

Dandeker, C. (1990) *Surveillance, Power and Modernity: Bureaucracy and Discipline from 1700 to the Present Day*, Cambridge: Polity Press.

Daniel, W. W. and N. McIntosh (1972) *The Right to Manage?* London: Macdonald.

Daniel, W. W. and N. Millward (1983) *Workplace Industrial Relations in Britain*, London: Heinemann.

Davidson, M. and C. Cooper (1992) *Shattering the Glass Ceiling*, London: Paul Chapman.

Davis, K. (1991) 'Critical Sociology and Gender Relations', in K. Davis, M. Leijenaar, and J. Oldersma, J. (eds)

Davis, K., M. Leijenaar and J. Oldersma (1991) *The Gender of Power*, London: Sage.

Dawson, P. and J. Webb (1989) 'New Production Arrangements: The Totally Flexible Cage?' *Work, Employment and Society*, vol. 3, no. 2: 221–38.

Dawson, S. (1992) *Analysing Organizations*, London: Macmillan, 2nd edn (1st edn 1986).

Day, R. A. and J. V. Day (1977) 'A Review of the Current State of Negotiated Order Theory: An Appreciation and a Critique', *Sociological Quarterly*, 18 (Winter), 126–42.

De Vroey, M. (1975) 'The Separation of Ownership and Control in Large Corporations', *Review of Radical Political Economics*, vol. 7, no. 2: 1–10.

Deal, T. and A. Kennedy (1988) *Corporate Cultures: the Rites and Rituals of Corporate Life*, Harmondsworth: Penguin.

Deaux, K. and T. Emswiller (1974) 'Explanations of Successful Performance on SexLinked Tasks: What is Skill for the Male is Luck for the Female', *Journal of Personality and Social Psychology*, 24: 30–85.

Deetz, S. (1992) 'Disciplinary Power in the Modern Corporation', in M. Alvesson and H. Willmott (eds) *Critical Management Studies*, London: Sage.

Delamarter, R. T. (1988) *Big Blue: IBM's Use and Abuse of Power*, London: Pan Books.

Delbridge, R., P. Turnbull and B. Wilkinson (1992) 'Pushing Back the Frontiers: Management Control and Work Intensification Under JIT/TQM Regimes', *New Technology, Work and Employment*, vol. 7: 97–106.

Deleuze, G. and F. Guattari (1977) *AntiOedipus: Capitalism and Schizophrenia*, New York: Viking.

Dent, M. (1993) 'Professionalism, Educated Labour and the State: Hospital Medicine and the New Managerialism', *Sociological Review*, vol. 41, no. 2: 244–73.

Deutsch, M. and H. B. Gerard (1955) 'A Study of Normative and Informational Social Influences upon Individual Judgement', *Journal of Abnormal and Social Psychology*, 51: 629–36.

Dews, P. (1987) *Logics of Disintegration*, London: Verso.

Dex, S. (1985) *The Sexual Division of Work*, Brighton: Wheatsheaf.

Di Maggio, P. and W. Powell (1983) 'The Iron Cage Revisited: Institutional Isomorphism and Collective Rationality in Organizations, *American Sociological Review*, vol. 48: 147–60.

Di Tomaso, N. (1989) 'Sexuality in the Workplace: Discrimination and Harassment', in J. Hearn, D. L. Sheppard, P. Tancred-Sheriff and G. Burrell (eds) *The Sexuality of Organization*, London: Sage.

Dicken, P. (1992) *Global Shift*, London: Paul Chapman Publishing.

Dicken, P. and M. Savage (1987) 'The Japanisation of British Industry?: Instances from a High Growth Area', *Industrial Relations Journal*, Spring 1988, vol. 19, no. 1.

Dill, W. R. (1962) 'The Impact of Environment on Organization Development', in S. Mailick and E. H. Van Ness (eds) *Concepts and Issues in Administrative Behaviour*, Englewood Cliffs, NJ: Prentice-Hall.

Ditton, J. (1974) 'The Fiddling Salesman: Connivance at Corruption', *New Society*, 28 Nov.

Donaldson, L. (1985) *In Defence of Organization Theory: A Reply to the Critics*, Cambridge: Cambridge University Press.

Donovan, Lord (Chairman) (1968) *Report on the Royal Commission on Trade Unions and Employers' Associations*, London: HMSO.

Doray, B. (1988) *A Rational Madness: From Taylorism to Fordism*, London: Free Association Books.

Drago, R. and T. McDonough (1984) 'Capitalist Shopfloor Initiatives, Restructuring and Organising in the '80s', *Review of Radical Political Economics*, vol. 716, no. 4: 52–77.

Drake, R. I. and P. J. Smith (1973) *Behavioural Science in Industry*, London: McGraw-Hill.

Drucker, P. (1955) *The Practice of Management*, New York: Harper & Row.

Drucker, P. (1977) *People and Performance*, London: Heinemann.

Drucker, P. (1979) *Management*, London: Pan.

Drucker, P. (1992) 'The New Society of Organizations', *Harvard Business Review*, Sep.–Oct.: 95–104.

Du Gay, P. (1991a) 'The Cult[ure] of the Customer', *Journal of Management Studies*, vol. 29, no. 5, 615–33.

Du Gay, P. (1991b) ''Enterprise Culture and the Ideology of Excellence', *New Formations*, vol. 13: 45–61.

Due Billing, Y. (1994) 'Gender and Bureaucracies – A Critique of Ferguson's ''The Feminist Case Against Bureaucracy', vol. 1, no. 4: 173–93.

Duenas, G. (1993) 'The Importance of Intercultural Learning in the International Transfer of Managerial and Organizational Knowledge', paper for the *11th EGOS Colloquium*, Paris, July.

Dumaine, B. (1990) 'Who Needs a Boss? *Fortune*, 7 May: 40–7.

Dunford, R. and P. McGraw (1987) 'Quality Circles or Quality Circus? Labour Process Theory and the Operation of Quality Circle Programmes', paper 5th International Conference Labour Process, UMIST.

Dunkerley, D. and G. Salaman (1986) 'Organizations and Bureaucracy', in M. Haralambos (ed.) *Developments in Sociology*, vol. 2, Ormskirk: Causeway Press.

Dunkerley, D. and G. Salaman (eds) (1980a) *The International Yearbook of Organization Studies 1979*, London: Routledge & Kegan Paul.

Dunkerley, D. and G. Salaman (eds) (1980b) *The International Yearbook of Organization Studies 1980*, London: Routledge & Kegan Paul.

Dunkerley, D. and G. Salaman (eds) (1982) *The International Yearbook of Organization Studies 1981*, London: Routledge & Kegan Paul.

Dunning, J. H. (1986) *Japanese Participation in British Industry*, London: Croom Helm.

Easterby-Smith, M. (1992), 'Creating a Learning Organisation', *Personnel Review*, vol. 19, no. 5: 24–8, MCB University Press, Manchester.

Easterby-Smith, M., R. Thorpe and A. Lowe (1991) *Management Research: An Introduction*, London: Sage.

Eccles, R. G. and N. Nohria (1992) *Beyond the Hype: Rediscovering the Essence of Management*, Boston, Mass.: Harvard Business School Press.

Economic Progress Report (1986) 'A More Flexible Labour Market', no. 182, HM Treasury.

Edquist, C. and S. Jacobsson (1988) *Flexible Automation: The Global Diffusion of New Technology in the Engineering Industry*, Berkeley, CA: University of California Press.

Edwardes, M. (1978) *The Dark Side of History: Magic in the Making of Man*, St. Albans: Granada.

Edwards, P. K and H. Scullion (1982) *The Social Organization of Industrial Conflict: Control and Resistance in the Workplace*, Oxford, Basil Blackwell.

Edwards, P. K. (1990) 'Understanding Conflict in the Labour Process: The Logic and Autonomy of Struggle', in D. Knights and H. Willmott (1989) *Labour Process Theory*, London: Macmillan.

Edwards, R. (1979) *Contested Terrain: The Transformation of the Workplace in the Twentieth Century*, London: Heinemann.

Edwards, R., M. Reich and D. M. Gordon (1975) *Labour Market Segmentation*, Lexington, Mass.: D.C. Heath.

Ehrenreich, B. and J. Ehrenreich (1979) 'The Professional–Managerial Class', in P. Walker (ed.), *Between Labour and Capital*, Brighton, Harvester.

Eiser, J. R. (1986) *Social Psychology: Attitudes, Cognition and Social Behaviour*, Cambridge: Cambridge University Press.

Elbaum, B. and W. Lazonick (eds) (1986) *The Decline of the British Economy*, Oxford: Clarendon.

Eldridge, J. E. T. and A. D. Crombie (1974) *A Sociology of Organizations*, London: Allen & Unwin.

Elger, T. (1987) 'Flexible Futures? New Technology and the Contemporary Transformation of Work', *Work, Employment and Society*, vol. 1, no. 4: 528–40.

Elger, T. (1990) 'Technical Innovation and Work Reorganization in British Manufacturing in the 1980s', *Work, Employment and Society* Special Issue, May: 67–101.

Elger, T. (1991) 'Task Flexibility and Intensification of Labour in UK Manufacturing in the 1980s', in A. Pollert (ed.), *Farewell to Flexibiltiy*.

Elger, T. and C. Smith (1994) 'Global Japanisation? Convergence and Competition in the Organization of the Labour Process', in T. Elger and C. Smith (eds) *Global Japanisation*, London: Routledge.

Elliot, D. (1980) 'The Organization as a System', in G. Salaman and K. Thompson (eds) *Control and Ideology in Organizations*, Milton Keynes: Open University Press.

Elliot, K. and P. Lawrence (eds) (1985) *Introducing Management*, Harmondsworth: Penguin.

Emery, F. E. and E. L Trist (1965) 'The Causal Texture of Organizations', *Human Relations*, vol. 18, no. 1: 21–32.

Eros, F. (1974) 'Review of L. Garai's Personality Dynamics and Social Existence', *European Journal of Social Psychology*, vol. 4, no. 3: 369–79.

Esland, G. (1980) 'Professions and Professionalism', in G. Esland and G. Salaman (eds) *The Politics of Work and Occupations*, Milton Keynes: Open University Press.

Etzioni, A. (1961) *A Comparative Analysis of Complex Organizations*, New York: Free Press.

Etzioni, A. (1988), *The Moral Dimension: Towards a New Economics*, New York: Plenum Press.

Evden, D. (1986) 'OD and SelfFulfilling Prophecy: Boosting Productivity by Raising Expectations', *Journal of Applied Behavioural Science*, vol. 22, no. 1: 1–13.

Eysenck, H. J. (1947) *Dimensions of Personality*, London: Routledge & Kegan Paul.

Eysenck, H. J. and G. Wilson (1975) *Know Your Own Personality*, Harmondsworth: Penguin.

Farnham, D. and S. Horton (1993) 'The New Public Service Managerialism: An Assessment', in D. Farnham and S. Horton (eds) *Managing the New Public Services*, London: Macmillan.

Featherstone, M. (1988) 'In Pursuit of the Postmodern: An Introduction', in *Theory, Culture and Society*, vol. 5: 195–215.

Felstead, A. (1994) *Corporate Paradox: Power and Control in Business Franchise*, London: Routledge.

Ferguson, K. (1984) *The Feminist Case Against Bureaucracy*, Philadelphia: Temple University Press.

Festinger, L. (1957) *A Theory of Cognitive Dissonance*, California: Stanford University Press.

Fevre, R. (1986) 'Contract Work in the Recession', in J. Purcell, S. Wood, A. Watson and S. Allen (eds) *The Changing Experience of Employment, Restructuring and Recession*, London: Macmillan.

Fiedler, F. E. (1967) *A Theory of Leadership Effectiveness*, New York: McGraw-Hill.

Fiedler, F. E. (1976) 'Situational Control: A Dynamic Theory of Leadership', in, B. King, S. Steufert and F. Fiedler (1978) *Managerial Control and Organizational Democracy*, Washington: Winston and Wiley.

Filby, M. (1992) 'The Figures, The Personality and The Bums: Service Work and Sexuality', *Work, Employment and Society*, vol. 6, no. 1, 23–42.

Fineman, S. (ed.) (1993) *Emotion in Organizations*, London: Sage.

Finlay, P. (1985) 'Control', in K. Elliot and P. Lawrence (eds) *Introducing Management*, Harmondsworth: Penguin.

Finn. D. (1986) *Training Without Jobs*, London: Macmillan.

Fischer, F. and C. Sirriani (1984) *Critical Studies in Organization and Bureaucracy*, Philadelphia: Temple University Press.

Fisher, D. (1993) *Communication in Organizations*, 2nd edn, St Paul, Minnesota, West Publishing Co.

Fisher, S. (1986) *Stress and Strategy*, London: Lawrence Erlbaum Associates.

Fligstein, N. (1990) *The Transformation of Corporate Control*, Cambridge, Mass.: Harvard University Press.

Florida, R. and M. Kenney (1991) 'Organization vs. Culture: Japanese Automotive Transplants in the US', *Industrial Relations Journal*, vol. 2, no. 2: 181–96.

Fontana, D. (1985) 'Learning and Teaching', in C. L. Cooper and P. Makin, *Psychology and Managers*, London: BPS and Macmillan.

Fores, M. and I. Glover (1976) 'The Real Work of Executives', *Management Today*, Sep.

Fores, M., I. Glover and P. Lawrence (1992) 'Management Thought, the American Legacy and the Future of European Labour Processes in 1992', paper to 10th International Labour Process Conference, Aston.

Forsgren, M. (1990) *Managing the Internationalisation Process: The Swedish Case*, London: Routledge.

Foucault, M. (1972) *The Archaeology of Knowledge*, London: Tavistock.

Foucault, M. (1977) *Discipline and Punish: The Birth of the Prison*, Harmondsworth: Penguin.

Foucault, M. (1984) *The History of Sexuality: An Introduction*, Harmondsworth: Peregrine.

Fowler, A. (1985) 'Getting into Organizational Restructuring', *Personnel Management*, vol. 17, no. 2: 24–7.

Fox, A. (1974) *Beyond Contract: Work, Power and Trust relations*, London: Faber & Faber.

Fox, A. (1980) 'The Meaning of Work', in G. Esland and G. Salaman (eds) *The Politics of Work and Occupations*, Milton Keynes: Open University Press.

Francis, A. (1986) *New Technology at Work*, Oxford, Clarendon: OUP.

Fraser, N. (1989) *Unruly Practices: Power, Discourse and Gender in Contemporary Social Theory*, Cambridge: Polity Press.

Freedman, M. (1984) 'The Search for Shelters', in K. Thompson (ed.), *work, Employment and Unemployment*, Milton Keynes: Open University Press.

French, J. R. P. and B. H. Raven (1959) 'The Social Bases of Power', in D. Cartwright (ed.) Studies in Social Power, Ann Arbor Mich.: University of Michigan Press.

Frese, M. (1982) 'Occupational Socialisation and Psychological Development: An Underdeveloped Research Perspective in Industrial Psychology', *Journal of Occupational Psychology*, 55: 209–24.

Fridenson, P. (1978) 'Corporate Policy, Rationalisation and the Labour Force-French Experiences in International Comparison, 1900–29', paper presented at Nuffield Deskilling Conference.

Friedman, A. (1977) *Industry and Labour: Class Struggle at Work Monopoly Capitalism*, London: Macmillan.

Friedman, A. (1987) 'The Means of Management Control and Labour Process Theory: A Critical Note on Storey', *Sociology*, vol. 21, no. 2: 287–94.

Friedman, A. (1990) 'Managerial Strategies and the Labour Process', in D. Knights and H. Willmott (eds) *Labour Process Theory*, London: Macmillan.

Frost, P. J., L. F. Moore, M. R. louis, C. C. Lundberg and J. Martin (eds) (1985) *Organizational Culture*, Beverley Hills, CA.: Sage.

Fuller, A. and M. Saunders (1990) 'The Paradox of Open Learning at Work', *Personnel Review*, vol. 19, no. 5: 29–33.

Fuller, L. and V. Smith (1991) Consumers' Reports: Management by Customers in a Changing Economy, *Work, Employment and Society*, vol. 5, no. 1: 1–16.

Gabriel, Y. (1988) *Working Lives in Catering*, London: Routledge.

Galbraith, J. K. (1967) *The New Industrial State*, Harmondsworth: Penguin.

Galbraith, J. R. (1984) 'Organization Design: An Information Processing View', in R. Paton, *et al.*, *Organizations: Cases, Issues, Concepts*, London: Harper & Row.

Garnsey, E., J. Rubery and F. Wilkinson (1985) 'Labour Market Structure and Workforce Divisions', Unit 8 of Open University course *Work and Society*, Milton Keynes: Open University Press.

Garrahan, P. and P. Stewart (1992) *The Nissan Enigma: Flexibility at Work in a Local Economy*, London: Mansett.

Garrahan, P. and P. Stewart (1993) 'Working Leaner but Smarter, or Meaner and Harder?: New Management Practices and the Recomposition of Employee Attitudes – the Case of the Auto Industry in Britain', paper prepared for the American Sociological Association, 88th Annual Meeting, Miami Beach, Flordia.

Geary, R. (1985) *Policing Industrial Disputes: 1893–1985*, London: Methuen.

Gecas, V. (1986) 'The Motivational Significance of Self-Concept for Socialisation Theory', in *Advances in Group Processes*, vol. 3, E. J. Lawler (ed.): 131–56.

George, M. and H. Levie (1984) *Japanese Competition and the British Workplace*, London: CAITS.

Gergen, K. (1992) Organization Theory in the Postmodern Era', in M. Reed and M. Hughes (eds) *Rethinking Organization: Mew Directions in Organization and Analysis*, London: Sage.

Gergen, K. J. (1973) 'Social Psychology as History', *Journal of Personality and Psychologyt*, vol. 26, no. 2: 309–20.

Gibson, J. W. and R. M. Hodgetts (1986) *Organisational Communication: A Managerial Perspective*, Orlando: Academic press.

Giddens, A. (1982) 'From Marx to Nietzche? Neo Conservatism, Foucault and Problems in Contemporary Political Theory', in A. Giddens, *Profiles and Critiques in Social Theory*, London: Macmillan.

Giddens, A. (1984) *The Constitution of Society*, Cambridge: Polity Press.

Giles, E. and K. Starkey (1987) 'From Fordism to Japanisation: Organizational Change at Ford, Rank Xerox and Fuji Xerox', paper presented at Conference on: *Japanisation of British Industry*, UWIST.

Gill, C. (1985) *Work, Unemployment and the New Technology*, Cambridge: Polity Press.

Gill, J. and P. Johnson (1991) *Research Methods for Managers*, London: Paul Chapman.

Giordano, L. (1985) 'Beyond Taylorism: Computerisation and QWL Programs in the Production Process', paper presented at Conference on *The Labour Process*, ASTON–UMIST. Also published in D. Knights and H. Willmott (eds) (1988) *New Technology and the Labour Process*, London: Macmillan.

Glenn, E. K. and R. L. Feldberg (1979) 'Proletarianising Office Work', in A. Zimbalist (ed.) *Case Studies on the Labour Process*, New York: Monthly Review Press.

Glover, I., M. Kelly and R. Roslander (1986) 'The Coming Proletarianisation of the British Accountant?', paper to 4th International Labour Process Conference, Aston.

Glucksman, M. (1990) *Women Assemble: Women Workers and the New Industries in Inter-War Britain*, London: Routledge.

Goffman, E. (1961) *Asylums*, New York: Doubleday.

Goffman, E. (1971) *The Presentation of Self in Everyday Life*, Harmondsworth: Pelican.

Goldman, P. and D. R. Van Houten (1977)'Managerial Strategies and the Worker: A Marxist Analysis of Bureaucracy', in J. K. Benson (ed.) *Organizational Analysis: Critique and Innovation*, London: Sage.

Goldman, P. and D. R. Van Houten (1980) 'Uncertainty, Conflict and Labor Relations in the Modern Firm 1: Productivity and Capitalism's Human Face', *Economic and Industrial Democracy*, vol. 1: 63–98.

Goldsmith, W. and D. Clutterbuck (1985) *The Winning Streak*, Harmondsworth: Penguin.

Gordon, D. M. (1988) 'The Global Economy: New Edifice or Crumbling Foundations?' *New Left Review*, 168 (Mar.–Apr.): 24–65.

Gordon, D. M., R. Edwards and M. Reich (1982) *Segmented Work, Divided Workers*, Cambridge: Cambridge University Press.

Goss, S. and G. Parston (1989) *Public Management for New Times*, London: Labour Co-ordinating Committee.

Gouldner, A. (1955) *Wildcat Strike*, London: Routledge & Kegan Paul.

Gouldner, A. W. (1954) *Patterns of Industrial Bureaucracy*, New York: Free Press.

Gowler, D. and K. Legge (1983) 'The Meaning of Management and the Management of Meaning: A View From Social Anthropology', in M. J. Earl (ed.) *Perspectives on Management: A Multidisciplinary Analysis*, Oxford: Oxford University Press.

Granovetter, M. (1985) 'Economic Action and Social Structure: the Problem of Embeddedness', *American Journal of Sociology*, vol. 91, no. 3: 481–510.

Grant, W. (1983) 'Representing Capital', in R. King (ed.) *Capital and Politics*, London: Routledge & Kegan Paul.

Green, E. and C. Cassell (1994) 'Women Managers, Gendered Cultural Processes and Organizational Change', paper to 12th Annual International Labour Process Conference, Aston.

Grenier, G. J. (1988) *Inhuman Relations: Quality Circles and Anti-Unionism in American Industry*, Philadelphi: Temple University Press.

Grey, C. (1994) 'Organisational Calvinism: Insecurity and Power in a Professional Labour Process', paper to 12th Annual International Labour Process Conference, Aston.

Grieco, M. and R. Whipp (1985) 'Women and Control in the Workplace: Gender and Control in the Workplace', in D. Knights and H. Willmott (eds) *Job Redesign: Critical Perspectives on the Labour Process*, Aldershot: Gower.

Grimshaw, J. (1986) *Feminist Philosophers*, Brighton: Wheatsheaf.

Grossman, R. (1979) 'Women's Place in the Integrated Circuit', *Radical America*, vol. 14, no. 1: 29–48.

Guest, D. E. (1987) 'Human Resource Management and Industrial Relations', *Journal of Management Studies*, vol. 24, no. 5: 503–21.

Guest, D. E. (1989) 'Personnel and HRM: Can You Tell the Difference?' *Personnel Management*, Jan.: 48–51.

Guest, D. E. (1990) 'Human Resource Management and the American Dream', *Journal of Management Studies*, vol. 27, no. 4: 377–97.

Guest, D. E. (1992) 'Right Enough to be Dangerously Wrong: An Analysis of the In Search of Excellence Phenomenon', in G. Salaman (ed.) *Human Resource Strategies*, London: Sage.

Gummeson, E. (1991) *Qualitative Methods in Management Research*, London: Sage.

Gutek, B. (1985) *Sex and the Workplace*, London: Josey-Bass.

Habermas, J. (1971) *Toward a Rational Society*, London: Heinemann.

Habermas, J. (1987) The Philosophical Discourses of Modernity, Cambridge: Polity Press.

Hacker, W., W. Volpert and M. Von Cranach (eds) (1982) *Cognitive and Motivational Aspects of Action*, Amsterdam: North Holland Publishing Company.

Hackman, J. R. and G. R. Oldman (1980) *Work Redesign*, Reading, Mass.: Addison-Wesley.

Hain, P. (1986) *Political Strikes*, Harmondsworth: Viking.

Hakim, C. (1990) 'Core and Periphery in Employees' Workforce Strategies: Evidence from the 1987 ELUS Survey', *Work, Employment and Society*, vol. 4, no. 2: 157–88.

Hales, C. P. (1986) 'What do Managers Do? A Critical Review of the Evidence', *Journal of Management Studies*, vol. 23, no. 1: 88–115.

Hales, C. P. (1988) 'Management Processes, Management Divisions of Labour and Managerial Work: Towards a Synthesis', paper presented to 6th International Labour Process Conference, Aston.

Hales, C. P. (1993) *Managing Through Organisation*, London: Routledge.

Hall, P. A. (1986) 'The State and Economic Decline', in B. Elbaum and W. Lazonick (eds) *The Decline of the British Economy*, Oxford: Clarendon.

Hall, R. H. (1973) 'Professionalisation and Bureaucratisation', in G. Salaman and K. Thompson (eds) *People and Organizations*, Harlow: Longman.

Hall, R. H. (1977) *Organizations: Structure and Process*, 2nd edn, Englewood Cliffs, NJ.: Prentice-Hall.

Hallet, S. (1988) 'Privatisation and the Restructuring of a Public Utility: A Case Study of BT's Corporate Strategy and Structure', paper to *Conference on New Forms of Ownership and Management*, Cardiff Business School.

Hamilton, G. G. and N. W. Biggart (1988) 'Market, Culture and Authority: A Comparative Analysis of Management and Organisation in the Far East,', in C. Winship and S. Rosen (eds), 'Organizations and Institutions', *American Journal of Sociology*, 94, supplement, Chicago: University of Chicago Press.

Hamilton, P. (1980) 'Social Theory and the Problematic Concept of Work', in G. Esland and G. Salaman (eds) *The Politics of Work and Occupations*, Milton Keynes: Open University Press.

Hammond, V. and K. Barham (1987) *Management for the Future: Report on the Literature Search*, Ashridge Management College.

Handy, C. (1st edn. 1976; 2nd edn. 1980) *Understanding Organizations*, Harmondsworth: Penguin.

Handy, C. (1984) *The Future of Work*, London: Basil Blackwell.

Handy, C. (1989) *The Age of Unreason*, London: Business Books.

Handy, C. (1994) *The Empty Raincoat*, London: Hutchinson.

Hannan, M.T. and J.H. Freeman (1977) 'The Population Ecology of Organizations', *American Journal of Sociology*, 82: 929–64.

Harris, R. (1987) *Power and Powerlessness in Industry: An Analysis of the Social Relations of Production*, London: Tavistock.

Harrison, E. and M. Marchington (1992) 'Corporate Culture and Management Control: Understanding Customer Care', *Paper to Employment Research Unit Annual Conference*, Cardiff Business School, Sep.

Harrison, R.G. (1984) 'Reasserting the Radical Potential of OD', *Personnel Review*, vol. 13, no. 2.

Hartley, J.F. and G.M. Stephenson (eds) (1992) *Employment Relations*, Oxford: Blackwell.

Hassard, J. (1991) 'Multiple Paradigms and Organizational Analysis: A Case Study', *Organization Studies*, vol. 12, no. 2: 275–99.

Hassard, J. (1994) 'Postmodern Organizational Analysis: Towards a Conceptual Framework', *Journal of Management Studies*, vol. 31, no. 3: 1–22.

Hassard, J. and D. Pym (eds) (1990) *The Theory and Philosophy of Organizations*, London: Routledge.

Hassard, J. and M. Parker (1993) *Postmodernism and Organizations*, London: Sage.

Hassard, J. and M. Parker (eds) (1994) *Towards a New Theory of Organizations*, London: Routledge.

Hawkins, K. (1978) *The Management of Industrial Relations*, Harmondsworth: Penguin.

Hearn, J. (1992) *Men in the Public Eye*, London: Routledge.

Hearn, J. and W. Parkin (1987) *Sex at Work: the Power and Paradox of Organization Sexuality*, Brighton: Wheatsheaf.

Hearn, J. and W. Parkin (1992) 'Gender and Organizations: A Selective Review and a Critique of a Neglected Area', in A.J. Mills and P. Tancred (eds) *Gendering Organizational Analysis*, London: Sage.

Hearn, J., D.L. Sheppard, P. Tancred-Sheriff and G. Burrell (1989) (eds) *The Sexuality of Organization*, London: Sage.

Heckscher, C. and A. Donnellon (eds) (1994) *The Post-Bureaucratic Organization*, London: Sage.

Heider, F. (1946) 'Attitudes and cognitive organisation', *Journal of Psychology*, 21: 107–12.

Heider, F. (1958) *The Psychology of Interpersonal Relations*, New York: John Wiley.

Held, D. (1984) 'Central Perspectives on the Modern State', in D. Held *et al.* (eds) *States and Societies*, Oxford: Martin Robertson.

Hellriegel, P., J.W. Slocum Jr and R. Woodman (1992) *Organizational Behavior*, 6th edn, St Paul, West Publishing Company.

Henderson, J. (1989) *The Globalisation of High Technology Production*, London: Routledge.

Henderson, J. (1992) 'Global Economic Integration, Business Systems and States in East Asian European Development', paper presented at the *First European Conference of Sociology*, Vienna, Aug.

Henderson, J. (1993) 'Industrial Policy for Britain: Lessons from the East', *Renewal*, vol. 1, no. 2: 32–42.

Hendry, C., A. Pettigrew and P. Sparrow (1988) 'Changing Patterns Of Human Resource Management', *Personnel Management*, Nov.

Henriques, J. *et al.* (1984) *Changing the Subject: Psychology, Social Regulation and Subjectivity*, London: Methuen.

Hershey, R. (1993) 'A Practitioner's View of "Motivation"', *Journal of Managerial Psychology*, vol. 8, no. 3: 10–13.

Herzberg, F. (1968) 'One More Time, How Do You Motivate Employees?', in S.J., Carroll, F.T. Paine and J.B. Miner (1977) *The Management Process*, 2nd edn, New York: Macmillan.

Herzberg, F. *et al.* (eds) (1959) *The Motivation to Work*, New York: John Wiley.

Heydebrand, W. (1977) 'Organisational Contradictions in Public Bureaucracies: Toward a Marxian Theory of Organisations', in J.K. Benson (ed.) *Organisational Analysis: Critique and Innovation*, London: Sage Contemporary Social Science Issues 37.

Hickson, D.J. (1971) 'A Strategic Contingencies Theory of Interorganizational Power', *Administrative Science Quarterly*, 16: 216–29.

Hickson, D.J. (1973) 'A Convergence in Organization Theory', in G. Salaman and K. Thompson (eds) *People and Organizations*, Harlow: Longman.

Hickson, D.J. and A.F. McCullough (1980) 'Power in Organizations', in G. Salaman and K. Thompson (eds) *People and Organizations*, Harlow: Longman.

Hickson, D.J., C.R. Lee, R.E. Schneck and J.M. Pennings (1973) 'A Strategic Contingencies Theory of Intraorganizational Power', in G. Salaman and K. Thompson (eds) *People and Organizations*, Harlow: Longman.

Hill, S. (1991) 'Why Quality Circles Failed but Total Quality Management Might Succeed', *British Journal of Industrial Relations*, vol. 29, no. 4: 541–68.

Hindess, B. (1982) 'Power, Interests and the Outcome of Struggles', *Sociology*, 23: 535–58.

Hinings, B. (1988) 'Defending Organization Theory: A British View from North America', *Organization Studies*, vol. 9, no. 1: 2–7.

Hirschorn, L. and T. Gilmore (1992) 'The New Boundaries of the "Boundaryless Company"', *Harvard Business Review*, May–Jun.: 104–15.

Hirst, P. and G. Thompson (1992) 'The Problem of Globalisation: International Economic Relations, National Economic Management and the Formation of Trading Blocs', *Economy and Society*, vol. 21, no. 4: 359–395.

Hirst, P. and J. Zeitlin (1991) 'Flexible Specialisation versus Post-Fordism: Theory, Evidence and Policy Implications', *Economy and Society*, vol. 20, no. 1: 1–56.

Hitt, M.A. *et al.* (1986) *Management Concepts and Effective Practice*, St. Paul, Minn.: West Publishing.

Hobsbawm, E.J. (1975) *The Age of Capital: 1845–1875*, London: Weidenfeld & Nicholson.

Hochschild, A.R. (1983) *The Managed Heart: Commercialisation of Human Feeling*, London: University of California Press.

Hochschild, A.R. (1993) Preface to: Fineman, S. (ed.) *Emotion in Organizations*, London: Sage.

Hofstede, G. (1977)' Humanisation of Work: the Role of Values in a Third Industrial Revolution', working paper, Brussels: EIASM.

Hofstede, G. (1980) *Culture's Consequences: International Differences in Work Related Values*, Beverley Hills CA.: Sage.

Hofstede, G. (1986) 'Review of E.H. Schein, Organizational Culture and Leadership: a Dynamic View', *Organization Studies*, vol. 7, no. 2.

Holland, S. (1975) *The Socialist Challenge*, London: Quartet.

Hollander, E.P. (1964) *Leaders, Groups and Influence*, New York: Oxford University Press.

Holloway, J. (1987) 'The Red Rose of Nissan', *Capital and Class*, no. 32: 142–64.

Hollway, W. (1984) 'Fitting Work: Psychological Assessment in Organizations', in J. Henriques *et al.*, *Changing the Subject: Psychology, Social Regulation and Subjectivity*, Londo : Methuen.

Hollway, W. (1991) *Work Psychology and Organisational Behaviour: Managing the Individual at Work*, London: Sage.

Holton, R. J. and B. S. Turner (1989) *Max Weber on Economy and Society*, London: Routledge.

Honey, P. and A. Mumford (1982) *Manual of Learning Styles*, Honey.

Höpfl, H. (1992) 'The Challenge of Change: The Theory and Practice of Organizational Transformations', paper to *Employment Research Unit Annual Conference*, Cardiff Business School, Sep.

Höpfl, H., S. Smith and S. Spencer (1992) 'Values and Variations: The Conflicts Between Culture Change and Job Cuts', *Personnel Review*, vol. 21, no. 1. 24–38.

Hopper, T., D. Cooper, T. Lowe, T. Capps and J. Mouritsen (1986) 'Management Control and Worker Resistance in the National Coal Board: Financial Controls in the Labour Process', in D. Knights and H. Willmott (eds) *Managing the Labour Process*, Aldershot: Gower.

Hopwood, A. (1974) *Accounting and Human Behaviour*, London: Prentice-Hall.

Horne, J. H. and T. Lupton (1965) 'The Work Activities of Middle Managers', *Journal of Management Studies*, vol. 2, no. 1: 14–33.

Hosking, D. and I. Morley (1991) *A Social Psychology of Organising: People, processes and Contexts*, Hemel Hempstead: Harvester Wheatsheaf.

House, R. J. and T. R. Mitchell (1974) 'A Path-Goal Theory of Leadership', *Journal of Contemporary Business*, Autumn: 81–98.

Howard, S. (1985) 'Big Blue's Big Family', *International Labour Reports*, Mar.–Apr.

Huczynski, A. A. (1993) *Management Gurus*, London: Routledge.

Hunter, L. and J. MacInnes (1992) 'Employers and Labour Flexibility: Evidence from the Case Studies', *Employment Gazette*, Jun.: 307–15.

Hyman, R. (1980b) 'Whatever Happened to Industrial Sociology?', in D. Dunkerley and G. Salaman (eds) *The International Yearbook of Organisation Studies 1980*, London: Routledge & Kegan Paul.

Hyman, R. (1986) 'Trade Unions and the Law: Papering Over the Cracks?', *Capital and Class*, no. 31: 93–114.

Hyman, R. (1987) 'Strategy or Structure: Capital, Labour and Control', *Work, Employment and Society*, vol. 1, no. 1: 25–55.

Hyman, R. (1988) 'Flexible Specialisation: Miracle or Myth?' in R. Hyman and W. Streek (eds) *Trade Unions, Technology and Industrial Democracy*, Oxford: Basil Blackwell.

Hyman, R. (1991) 'Plus ça change? The Theory of Production and the Production of Theory', in A. Pollert (ed.) *Farewell to Flexibility*, Oxford: Blackwell.

IPM Digest (1986) 'Flexibility: In Search of a Definition', no. 253, Aug.

Israel, J. and H. Tajfel (eds) (1972) *The Context of Social Psychology: A Critical Assessment*, London: Academic Press.

Itoh, M. (1984) 'Labour Control in Small Groups', *Radical America*, vol. 18, no. 2/3.

Jackson, T. (1994) *Organisational Behaviour in International Management*, Oxford: Butterworth–Heinemann.

James, K., C. Lovato and G. Khoo (1994) 'Social Identity Correlates of Minority Worker's Health', *Academy of Management Journal*, vol. 37, no. 2: 383–96.

Janis, I. (1972) *Victims of Groupthink*, Boston, Mass.: Houghton Mifflin.

Jeffreys, S. (1990) *Anticlimax*, London: The Women's Press.

Jenkins, C. D. (1979) 'Psychosocial modifiers of response to stress', *Journal of Human Stress*, vol. 5, no. 4: 3–15.

Jenkins, D. (1973) *Job Power: Blue and White Collar Democracy*, Welwyn Garden City: Doubleday.

Jenkins, R. (1982) 'Management, Recruitment Procedures and Black Workers', working papers Ethnic Relations, no. 18, Birmingham Research Unit on Ethnic Relations.

Jenkins, R. (1984) 'Divisions Over the International Division of Labour', *Capital and Class*, vol. 34: 28–57.

Jenkins, R. (1986) *Racism and Recruitment: Managers, Organisations and Equal Opportunties in the Labour market*, Cambridge: Cambridge University Press.

Jessop, B. (1982) *The Capitalist State*, Oxford: Martin Robertson.

Jessop, B. (1992) "Towards the Schumpetarian Welfare State: Global Capitalism and Structural Competitveness', unpublished paper.

Johns, G. (1993) 'Constraints on the Adoption of Psychology-Based Personnel Practices: Lessons from Organizational Innovation, *Personnel Psychology*, 46: 569–92.

Johnson, A. and K. Moore (1986) *The Tapestry Makers: Life and Work at Lee's Tapestry Works*, Birkenhead: Merseyside Docklands Community Project.

Johnson, P. and J. Gill (1993) *Management Control and Organizational Behaviour*, London: Paul Chapman.

Johnson, T. (1972) *Professions and Power*, London: Macmillan.

Johnson, T. (1980) 'Work and Power;, in G. Esland and G. Salaman (eds) *The Politics of Work and Occupations*, Milton Keynes: Open University Press.

Johnston, L. (1986) *Marxism, Class Analysis and Socialist Pluralism*, London: Allen & Unwin.

Jones, A. M. and C. Hendry (1994) 'The Learning Organisation: Adult Learning and Organisational Transformation', *British Journal of Management*, vol. 5, no. 2: 153–62.

Jones, A. N. and C. L. Cooper (1980) *Combating Managerial Obsolescence*, Philip Allan.

Jones, G. (1978) 'Ideological Responses to Deskilling of Managerial Work', paper presented at *Conference on Deskilling*, Nuffield.

Jones, O. (1994) 'Professionalism and Work Study: An Alternative Perspective on Subjectivity and the Labour Process', paper to 12th International Labour Process Conference, Aston.

Joyce, P. (1980) *Work, Society and Politics*, London: Methuen.

Kahle, L. R. (1984) *Attitudes and Social Adaptation*, Oxford: Pergamon.

Kamata, S. (1982) *Japan in the Passing Lane*, London: Pantheon.

Kamin, L. (1979) *The Science and Politics of IQ*, Harmondsworth: Penguin.

Kanter, R. M. (1968) 'Commitment and Social Organisation: A Study of Commitment in Utopian communities', *American Sociological Review*, vol. 33, no. 4: 499–517.

Kanter, R. M. (1984) *The Change Masters*, London: Unwin.

Kanter, R. M. (1993) *Men and Women of the Corporation*, 2nd edn, New York: Basic Books.

Karasek, R. and T. Theorell (1990) *Healthy Work: Stress, Productivity and the Reconstruction of Working Life*, New York: Basic Books.

Karmel, B. (ed.) (1980) *Point and Counterpoint in Organizations,?* Illinois: Dryden.

Katz, D. and R. Kahn (1970) 'Open Systems Theory', in O. Grusky and G. A. Miller (eds) *The Sociology of Organizations: Basic Studies*, New York: Free Press.

Katz, D. and R. L. Kahn (1966, 2nd edn 1978) *The Social Psychology of Organisations*, New York: John Wiley.

Katz, G. (1982) 'Previous Conformity, Status, and the Rejection of the Deviant', *Small Group Behaviour*, 13: 402–14.

Keenoy, T. (1992) 'Constructing Control', in J. Hartley and G. M. Stephenson (eds) *Employment Relations*, Oxford: Blackwell.

Keith, B. and D. Collinson (1994) 'Policing Gender: Barriers to Change in the Police', paper to 12th Annual International Labour Process Conference, Aston.

Kelley, H. (1971), 'The Warm–Cold Variable in First Impressions of Persons', *Journal of Personality*, 18: 431–9.

Kelly, A. and T. Brannick (1987) 'Personnel Practices and Strong Organizational Cultures in Ireland', paper presented at Conference on: *Japanisation of British Industry*, UMIST.

Kelly, J. E. (1985) 'Management's Redesign of Work', in D. Knights, H. Willmott and D. Collinson (eds) *Job Redesign: Critical Perspectives on the Labour Process*, Aldershot: Gower.

Kelly, K. (1994) *Out of Control: The Rise of Neo-Biological Civilisation*, Reading, Mass.: Addison-Wesley.

Kelman, H. (1961) 'The Processes of Opinion Change', *Public Opinion*, 25: 57–78.

Keltner, J. W. (1973) *Elements of Interpersonal Communication*, Calif: Wadsworth.

Kerfoot, D. and D. Knights (1994) 'Empowering the "Quality Worker": The Seduction and Contradiction of the Total Quality Phenomenon', in A. Wilkinson and H. Willmott (eds) *Making Quality Critical*, London: Routledge & Kegan Paul.

Kern, H. and M. Schumman (1984) *Das Ende der Arbeitesteilung? Rationalising in der Industriellen Produktion*, Munchen: C. H. Beck.

Kerr, C., J. J. Dunlop, F. H. Harbison and C. A. Mayers (1960) *Industrialism and Industrial Man*, Cambridge, Mass.: Harvard University Press.

Kets de Vries, M. R. F. and D. Miller (1984) *The Neurotic Organisation: Diagnosing and Changing Counterproductive Styles of Management*, San Francisco: Jossey-Bass.

Khandwalla, P. N. (1973) 'Viable and Effective Organizational Design of Firms', *Academy of Management Journal*, vol. 16, no. 3: 481–95.

Kitschelt, H. (1992) 'Industrial Governance Structures, Innovation Strategies, and the Case of Japan: Sectoral or Cross-National Comparative Analysis?' *International Organization*, vol. 45, no. 4: 163–88

Klein, H. J. (1989) 'An Integrated Control Theory Model of Work Motivation', *Academy of Management Journal*, vol. 14, no. 2: 150–72.

Knights, D. and D. Collinson (1987) 'Shop Floor Culture and the Problem of Managerial Control', in J. McGoldrick (ed.) *Business Case File in Behavioural Science*, London: Van Nostrand.

Knights, D. and G. Morgan (1990) 'The Concept of Strategy in Sociology: a Note of Dissent', *Sociology*, vol. 24: 475–83.

Knights, D. and H. Willmott (1985) 'Power and Identity in Theory and Practice', *Sociological Review*, vol. 33, no. 1: 22–46.

Knights, D. and H. Willmott (1989) 'Power and Subjectivity at Work: From Degradation to Subjugation in Social Relations', *Sociology*, vol. 23, no. 4: 535–58.

Knights, D. and H. Willmott (eds) (1986a) *Gender and the Labour Process*, Aldershot: Gower.

Knights, D. and H. Willmott (eds) (1986b) *Managing the Labour Process*, Aldershot: Gower.

Knights, D. and H. Willmott (eds) (1988) *New Technology and the Labour Process*, London: Macmillan.

Knights, D. and H. Willmott (eds) (1990) *Labour Process Theory*, London: Macmillan.

Knights, D., H. Willmott and D. Collinson (eds) (1985) *Job Redesign: Critical Perspectives on the Labour Process*, London: Gower.

Knoke, D. (1990) *Political Networks: The Structural Perspective*, New York: Cambridge University Press.

Kohn, M. L. and C. Schooler (1983) *Work and Personality: an Inquiry into the Effects of Social Stratification*, New Jersey: Ablex.

Kolb, D. A. (1976) *The Learning Style Inventory: Technical Manual*, Boston, Mass.: MacBer & Co.

Komter, A. (1991) 'Gender, Power and Feminist Theory', in K. Davis, M. Leijenaar, and J. Oldersma, J. (eds) *The Gender of Power*, London: Sage.

Kotter, J. (1982) *The General Manager*, New York: Free Press.

Kouzmin, A. (1980) 'Control in Organizational Analysis: the Lost Politics', in D. Dunkerley, and G. Salaman (eds) *The International Yearbook of Organization Studies 1979*, London: Routledge & Kegan Paul.

Kraft, P. and S. Dubnoff (1986) 'Job Characteristics in Computer Software', *Industrial Relations*, (USA), vol. 25, no. 2: 179–95.

Kram, K. E. (1983) 'Phases of the Mentor Relationship', *Academy of Management Journal*, 26: 608–35.

Kreiger, J. (1983) *Undermining Capitalism*, London: Pluto.

Kunda, G. (1992) *Engineering Culture: Control and Commitment in a High Tech Corporation*, Philadelphia: Temple University Press.

Labour Research Department (1986a) 'Flexibility Examined', Bargaining Report, London: LRD.

Labour Research Department (1986b) 'Franchising – Who Really Benefits?' Aug., London: LRD.

Labour Research Department (1988) 'Stress at Work: The Trade Union Response', London: LRD.

Landes, D. S. (1969) *The Unbound Prometheus*, Cambridge: Cambridge University Press.

Landry, C. *et al.* (1985) *What a Way to Run a Railroad: An Analysis of Radical Failure*, London: Comedia.

Lane, C. (1991) 'Industrial Reogranisation in Europe', *Work, Employment and Society*, vol. 5, no. 4: 515–39.

Lane, T. and K. Roberts (1971) *Strike at Pilkingtons*, Glasgow: Fontana.

Langer, E. J. (1981) 'Rethinking the Role Of Thought in Social Interaction', in J. H. Harvey, W. Ickes and R. F. Kidd, *New Directions in Attribution Research*, vol. 2, New York: Erlbaum.

Larsen, K. S. (1980) *Social Psychology: Crisis or Failure?*, Monmouth, Oregon: Institute for Theoretical History.

Lasch, C. (1985) *The Minimal Self: Psychic Survival in Troubled Times*, London: Picador.

Lash, S. and J. Urry (1987) *The End of Organized Capitalism*, Cambridge: Polity Press.

Lawlor, E. E. (1976) 'Control Systems in Organizations', in H. D. Dunnette (ed.) *Handbook of Industrial and Organizational Psychology*, Chicago: Rand McNally Publishing.

Lawrence, P. R. and J. W. Lorsch (1967) *Organization and Environment*, Cambridge, Mass.: Harvard University Press.

Layder, D. (1987) 'Key Issues in Structuration Theory: Some Critical Remarks', *Current Perspectives in Social Theory*, vol. 8: 25–46.

Layton, E. T. (1969) 'Science, Business and the American Engineer', in R. Perruci and J. E. Gersth (eds) *The Engineer and the Social System*, New York: John Wiley.

Lazarus, R. S. (1966) *Psychological Stress and the Coping Process*, New York: McGraw-Hill.

Leavitt, H. J. (1951) 'Some Effects of Certain Communication Patterns on Group Performance', *Journal of Abnormal and Social Psychology*, 46: 38–50.

Leavitt, H. J. (1978, 4th edn) *Managerial psychology*, Chicago: University of Chicago Press.

Lee, B. (1985) 'Internal Politics', in K. Elliot and P. Lawrence (eds) *Introducing Management*, Harmondsworth: Penguin.

Lee, R. and P. Lawrence (1985) *Organizational Behaviour: Psychology at Work*, London: Hutchinson.

Legge, K. (1978) *Power, Innovation and Problem-solving in Management*, London: McGraw-Hill.

Legge, K. (1989) 'Human Resource Management – a Critical Analysis', in J. Storey (ed.) *New Perspectives in Human Resource Management*, London: Routledge.

Legge, K. (1995) *Human Resource Management: Rhetorics and Realities*, London: Macmillan.

Lehman, C. and T. Tinker (1985) 'The Not-So-Great Society: the Role of Business Literature on Reshuffling Johnson's New Deal', paper to 3rd International Labour Conference, UMIST.

Leonard, P. (1984) *Personality and Ideology: Towards a Materialist Understanding of the Individual*, London: Macmillan.

Lessem, R. (1985) 'The Enabling Company', in D. Clutterbuck (ed.) *New Patterns of Work*, Aldershot: Gower.

Lessem, R. (1986) *The Roots of Excellence*, London: Fontana.

Lewin, K. (1947) 'Frontiers in Group Dynamics', *Human Relations*, 1: 5–41.

Lewin, K., R. Lippitt and R. K. White (1939) 'Patterns of aggressive behaviour in experimentally created social climates', *Journal of Social Psychology*, 10: 271–301.

Lewis, M. (1975) 'Early Sex Differences in the Human: Studies of Socioemotional Development', *Archives of Sexual Behaviour*, vol. 4, no. 4: 329–35.

Lewis, R. (1984) (ed.) *Open Learning in Action: Case Studies, Open Learning Guide 1*, London: Council for Educational Technology.

Lindblom, C. E. (1959) 'The Science of Muddling Through', *Public Administration Review*, vol. 19: 79–88.

Linstead, S. and R. G. Grafton Small (1992) 'On Reading Organization Culture', *Organization Studies*, vol. 13, no. 3: 331–45.

Lipietz, A. (1982) 'Towards Global Fordism?', *New Left Review*, vol. 132: 33–47.

Lippman, W. (1922) *Social Opinion*, New York: Harcourt Brace.

Littler, C. R. (1980) 'Internal Contract and the Transition to Modern Work Systems', in D. Dunkerley and G. Salaman (eds) *The International Yearbook of Organization Studies 1979*, London: Routledge & Kegan Paul.

Littler, C. R. (1982) *The Development of the Labour Process in Capitalist Societies*, London: Heinemann.

Littler, C. R. and G. Salaman (1982) 'Bravermania and Beyond', *Sociology*, vol. 16, no. 2: 25–69.

Lloyd, M. (1993) 'The (F)utility of a Feminist Turn to Foucault', *Economy and Society*, vol. 22, no. 4: 437–60.

Locke, E. and G. P. Latham (1984) *Goal Setting: A Motivational Technique that Works!* London: Prentice-Hall.

Lodge, D. (1990) *Nice Work*, Harmondsworth: Penguin.

Loveridge, R. (1982) 'Business Strategy and Community Culture', in D. Dunkerley and G. Salaman (eds) *The International Yearbook of Organization Studies 1981*, London: Routledge & Kegan Paul.

Lucas, M. (1986) *How to Survive the 9–5*, Thames: Methuen.

Lukes, S. (1974) *Power: A Radical View*, London: Macmillan.

Lukes, S. (1982) *Power: A Radical View*, London: Macmillan.

Lupton, T. and D. Gowler (1969) *Selecting a Wage Payment System*, London: Kogan Page.

Luthans, F. (1981) *Organization Behaviour*, 3rd edn, New York: McGraw-Hill.

Lynn, R. (1966) 'Brainwashing Techniques in Leadership and Childrearing', *British Journal of Social and Clinical Psychology*, 5: 270–3.

MacInnes, J. (1987) *Thatcherism at Work*, Milton Keynes: Open University Press.

Maddock, S. and D. Parkin (1993) *Gender Cultures, Women's Choices and Strategies at Work, Women in Management Review*, vol. 8, no. 2: 3–9.

Maguire, M. (1986) 'Recruitment as a Means of Control', in K. Purcell, S. Wood, A. Watson and S. Allen (eds) *The Changing Experience of Employment, Restructuring and Recession*, London: Macmillan.

Mangum, G. L and S. L. Mangum (1986) 'Temporary Work: the Flip Side of Job Security', *International Journal of Manpower*, vol. 7, no. 1: 12–20.

Manz, C. C. and H. P. Sims (1989) *SuperLeadership: Leading Others to Lead Themselves*, Calif., Prentice-Hall.

March J. G. and H. A. Simon (1958) *Organizations*, New York: John Wiley.

Marchington, M. (1982) *Managing Industrial Relations*, London: McGraw-Hill.

Marchington, M. and P. Parker (1987) 'Japanisation: a Lack of Chemical Reaction?' paper presented at Conference on: *Japanisation of British Industry*, UWIST.

Marchington, M., M. Wilkinson, P. Ackers and J. Goodman (1993) 'The Influence of Managerial Relations on Waves of Employee Involvement', *British Journal of Industrial Relations*, vol. 31, no. 4: 553–76.

Marcuse, H. (1971) 'Industrialisation and Capitalism', in O. Stammer (ed.), *Max Weber and Sociology Today*, Oxford: Blackwell.

Marginson, P. (1991) 'Change and Continuity in the Employment Structures of Large Companies', in A. Pollert (ed.) *Farewell to Flexibility*, Oxford: Blackwell.

Marglin, S. A. (1974) 'What do Bosses Do? The Origins and Functions of Hierarchy in Capitalist Production', *Review of Radical Political Economics*, 6: 60–102.

Mars, G. (1983) *Cheats at Work: An Anthology of Workplace Crime*, London: Unwin.

Marsden, R. (1993) 'The Politics of Organizational Analysis', *Organization Studies*, vol. 14, no. 1: 93–124.

Martin, J. (1990) 'Deconstructing Organisational Taboos: The Suppression of Gender Conflict in Organisations', *Organisational Science*, vol. 1: 1–21.

Martin, J. and C. Siehl (1983) 'Organizational Culture and Counterculture: An Uneasy Symbiosis', Organizational Dynamics, Autumn: 52–64.

Martin, P. and D. Nicholls (1987) *Creating a Committed Workforce*, London: Institute of Personnel Management.

Martinez Lucio, M. and S. Weston (1992) 'Human Resource Management and Trade Union Responses: Bringing the Politics of the Workplace Back into the Debate', in P. Blyton and P. Turnbull (eds) *Reassessing Human Resource Management*, London: Sage.

Marx, K. (1963) *Early Writings*, trans. T. B. Bottomore, London: Penguin.

Marx, K. (1984) 'The Spirit of Bureaucracy and Beyond Bureaucracy: The Paris Commune', in F. Fischer and C. Sirriani (eds) *Critical Studies in Organization and Bureaucracy*, Philadelphia: Temple University Press.

Maslow, A. H. (1954) *Motivation and Human Personality*, New York: Harper & Row.

Mather, C. (1987) 'Disposable Workers', *New Internationalist*, Jul.

Mathews, J. (1993) 'Organizational Innovation: Competing Models of Productive Efficiency', paper to *5th APROS International Colloquium*, Honolulu, Hawaii.

Maurice, M., A. Sorge and M. Warner (1980) 'Societal Differences in Organising Manufacturing Units', *Organization Studies*, vol. 1, no. 1: 63–91.

Mayo, E. (1946) *Humon Problems of an Industrial Civilisation*, New York: Macmillan.

McArdle, L., S. J. Proctor, M. Rawlinson, J. Hassard and P. Forrester (1994) 'Total Quality Management and Participation: Employee Involvement or the Enhancement of Exploitation?' in A. Wilkinson and H. Willmott (eds) *Making Quality Critical*, London: Routledge.

McClelland, D. (1961) *The Achieving Society*, New Jersey: Van Nostrand.

McCullough, A. and M. Shannon (1977) 'Organisation and Protection', in S. Clegg and D. Dunkerley (eds) *Critical Issues in Organizations*, London: Routledge & Kegan Paul.

McGregor, D. (1960) *The Human Side of the Enterprise*, New York: Harper & Row.

McHugh, D., D. Groves, A. Alker ' "Cultural Heuristics" and Behavioural Change: What do we Learn from a Learning Organisation', paper presented at conference on: *The Strategic Direction of HRM*, Nottingham-Trent University, Dec.

McKenna, E. (1987) *Psychology in Business: Theory and Applications*, London: Lawrence Erlbaum Associates.

McKenna, E. (1994) *Business Psychology and Organisational Behaviour: A Student's Handbook*, Hove: Lawrence Erlbaum Associates.

McKinlay, A. and P. Taylor (1994) Power, Surveillance and Resistance: Inside the 'Factory of the Future', paper to 13th International Labour Process Conference, Aston.

McKinnon, C. A. (1979) *Sexual Harassment of Working Women*, New Haven, Conn.: Yale University Press.

Mead, G. H. (1934) *Mind, Self and Society*, Chicago: Chicago University Press.

Mechanic, D. (1962) 'Sources of Power of Lower Participants in Complex Organizations', *Administrative Science Quarterly*, 7: 349–64.

Meek V. L. (1988) "Organizational Culture: Origins and Weaknesses', *Organization Studies*, vol. 9., no. 4: 453–73.

Melling, J. (1982) 'Men in the Middle or Men on the Margin?' in D. Dunkerley and G. Salaman (eds) *The International Yearbook of Organisation Studies 1981*, London: Routledge & Kegan Paul.

Merton, R. K. (1949) *Social Theory and Social Structure*, Glencoe, Ill: Free Press.

Meyer, J. W. and B. Rowan (1977) 'Institutionalised Organizations: Formal Structure and as Myth and Ceremony', *American Journal of Sociology*, vol. 83, no. 2: 340–63.

Meyer, M., W. Stevenson and S. Webster (1985) *Limits to Bureaucratic Growth*, New York: Walter De Gruyter.

Meyer, P. B. (1986) 'General Motors' Saturn Plant: a Quantum Leap in Technology and its Implications for Labour and Community Organizations', *Capital and Class* 30: 73–96.

Miliband, R. (1969) *The State in Capitalist Society*, London: Weidenfeld & Nicolson.

Miller, D. R. (1963) 'The Study of Social Relationships: Situations, Identities and Social Interaction', in S. Koch (ed.) *Psychology: a Study of a Science*, vol. 5, New York: McGraw-Hill.

Miller, E. J. and A. K. Rice (1967) *Systems of Organization: the Control of Task and Sentient Boundaries*, London: Tavistock.

Miller, G. A., E. Galanter and K. H. Pribram (1960) *Plans and the Structure of Behaviour*, London: Holt.

Miller, H. G. and J. R. Verduin (1979) *The Adult Educator: A Handbook for Staff Development*, Houston, Tex.: Gulf.

Miller, N. E. and J. Dollard (1953) *Social Learning and Imitation*, New Haven, Conn.: Yale University Press.

Miller, P. M. (1989) 'Strategic HRM: What it Is and What it Isn't', *Personnel Management*, Feb.

Miller, P.and T. O'Leary (1987) The Entrepreneurial Order, paper presented to 5th International Labour Process Conference, UMIST.

Mills, A. J. (1991) 'Organizational Discourse and the Gendering of Identity', paper to Conference: *Towards a New Theory of Organisations*, University of Keele.

Mills, A. J. and P. Tancred (eds) (1992) *Gendering Organizational Analysis*, London: Sage.

Mills, C. W. (1959) *The Power Elite*, New York: Oxford University Press.

Mills, A. J. and S. J. Murgatroyd (1991) *Organizational Rules,: a Framework for Understanding Organizations*, Milton Keynes: Open University Press.

Millward, T., M. Stevens, D. Smart and W. R. Hawkes (1992) *Workplace Industrial Relations in Transition, The ED/ESRC/PS1/ACAS Surveys*, Aldershot: Dartmouth.

Mintzberg, H. (1973) *The Nature of Managerial Work*, New York: Harper & Row.

Mintzberg, H. (1983) *Structure in Fives: Designing Effective Organizations*, Englewood Cliffs, NJ.: Prentice-Hall.

Mischel, W. (1973) 'Towards a Cognitive Social Learning Reconception of Personality', *Psychological Review*, 80: 200–13.

Mitter, S. (1986) *Common Fate, Common Bond: Women in the Global Economy*, London: Pluto.

Mitter, S. (1988) 'Flexible Casualties', *Interlink*, no. 5.

Montgomery, D. (1976) 'Workers' Control of Machine Production in the Nineteenth Century', *Labor History*, vol. 17, no. 4: 486–509.

Morgan, D. and L. Stanley (eds) (1993) *Debates in Sociology*, Manchester: Manchester University Press.

Morgan, G. and D. Hooper (1987) 'Corporate Strategy, Ownership and Control', *Sociology*, vol. 21, no. 4: 609–27.

Morgan, Gareth (1986) *Images of Organisation*, London: Sage.

Morgan, Gareth (1990) 'Paradigm Diversity in Organizational Research', in J. Hassard and D. Pym (eds) *The Theory and Philosophy of Organizations*, London: Routledge.

Morgan, Glenn (1990) *Organizations in Society*, London: Sage.

Morgan, K. and A. Sayer (1984) 'A "Modern" Industry in a "Mature" Region: the Remaking of Management–Labour Relations', working paper, Urban and Regional Studies, University of Sussex.

Morris, J. (1987) 'The Who, Why, and Where of Japanese Manufacturing Investment in the UK', paper presented at conference on: *Japanisation of British Industry*, UWIST.

Moscovici, S. (1972) 'Society and Theory in Social Psychology', in J. Israel and H. Tajfel (eds).

Moscovici, S. and M. Zavalloni (1969) 'The Group as a Polarizer of Attitudes', *Journal of Personality and Social Psychology*, 12: 125–35.

Mueller, F. (1994) 'Teams Between Hierarchy and Commitment: Change Strategies and the "Internal Environment" ', *Journal of Management Studies*, vol. 31, no. 3: 383–403.

Mueller, F. (1994a) 'Societal Effect, Organizational Effect Globalisation', *Organization Studies*, vol. 15, no. 3: 407–28.

Mullins, L. (1993) *Management and Organization Behaviour*, London: Pitman, 3rd edn (1st edn 1985).

Munro, R. (1994) 'Governing the New Province of Quality: Autonomy, Accounting and the Dissemination of Accountability', in A. Wilkinson and H. Willmott (eds) *Making Qaulity Critical*, London: Routledge & Kegan Paul.

Murakami, T. (1994) 'Teamwork and Trade Union Workplace Representation in the German and British Car Industry', paper to 12th International Labour Process Conference, Aston.

Murphy, L. R. and S. Sorenson (1988) 'Employee behaviours before and after stress management', *Journal of Organisational Behaviour*, vol. 9: 173–82.

Murray, F. (1983) 'The Decentralisation of Production and the Decline of the Mass Collective Worker', *Capital and Class* 19: 74–9.

Murray, F. (1987) 'Flexible Specialisation and the Third Italy', *Capital and Class*, no. 33: 84–95.

Murray, P. and J. Wickham(1985) 'Women Workers and Bureaucratic Control in Irish Electronic Factories', in H. Newby, (ed.) *Restructuring Capital, Reorganisation in Industrial Society*, London: Macmillan.

Myers, C. S. (1926) *Industrial Psychology in Great Britain*, London: Jonathan Cape.

Myers, M. T. and G. E. Myers (1982) *Managing by Communication: An Organisational Approach*, New York: McGraw-Hill.

Nadworthy, M. (1955) *Scientific Managment and the Unions*, Cambridge: Mass.: Harvard University Press.

Naisbitt, J. and P. Aburdene (1985) *Reinventing the Corporation*, London: Macdonald.

NEDO (1986) *Changing Working Patterns*, report prepared by the Institute for Manpower Studies for the National Economic Development Office in Association with the Department of Employment, London: NEDO.

Neimark, M. and T. Tinker (1986) 'On Rediscovering Marx: Dissolving Agency Structure in Dialectical Unity', paper to 4th International Labour Process Conference, Aston.

Nelson, D. (1975) *Managers and Workers: Origins of the New Factory System in the United States 1880–1920*, Madison: University of Wisconsin Press.

Newman, R. and J. Newman (1986) 'Information Work, the New Divorce', *British Journal of Sociology*, vol. 36.

Newton, T. (1994) 'Resocialising the Subject? A Re-Reading of Grey's "Career as a Project of the Self"', *Sociology*, 28.2, Working Paper Series, Department of Business Studies, University of Edinburgh.

Newton, T., with J. Handy and S. Fineman (1995) *'Managing' Stress: Power and Emotion at Work*, London: Sage.

Nichols, T. (1986) *The British Worker Question*, London: Routledge & Kegan Paul.

Nichols, T. and Beynon, H. (1977) *Living With Capitalism*, London: Routledge & Kegan Paul.

Noble, D. (1979) 'Social Choice in Machine Design', in A. Zimbalist (ed.) *Case Studies in the Labour Process*, London: Monthly Review Press.

Nohria, N. (1992) 'Is a Network Perspective a Useful Way of Studying Organizations?' in N. Nohria and R.G. Eccles (eds) *Networks and Organizations*, Boston, Mass.: Harvard Business School Press.

Norris, C. (1992) *Uncritical Theory: Postmodernism, Intellectuals and the Gulf War*, London: Lawrence & Wishart.

North-West Women Into Management (1987) Newletter, Manchester, Jun.

Nyland, C. (1988) 'Scientific Management and Planning', *Capital and Class*, no. 33: 55–83.

O'Brien, G.E. (1992) 'Changing Meanings of Work', in J.F. Hartley and G.M. Stephenson (eds) *Employment Relations*, Oxford: Blackwell, 44–66.

O'Connell Davidson, J. (1993) *Privatisation and Employment Relations: The Case of the Water Industry*, London: Mansell.

O'Connell Davidson, J. (1994a) 'On Power, Prostitution and Pilchards: The Self-Employed Prostitute and Her Clients', paper presented to 12th Annual International Labour Process Conference, Aston.

O'Connell Davidson, J. (1994b) 'What Do Franchisers Do? Control and Commercialisation in Milk Distribution', *Work, Employment and Society*, vol. 8, no. 1: 23–44.

O'Neill, J. (1986) 'The Disciplinary Society: From Weber to Foucault', *British Journal of Sociology*, vol. xxxvii, no. 1: 42–60.

O'Neill, N. (1985) 'Marxism and Psychology', in M. Shaw (ed.) *Marxist Sociology Revisited*, London: Macmillan.

O'Reilly, J. (1992) 'Where Do You Draw the Line? Functional Flexibility, Training and Skill in Britain and France', *Work, Employment and Society*, vol. 6, no. 3: 369–96.

OECD (1977) *The Development of Industrial Relations Systems: Some Implications of the Japanese Experience*, London: OECD.

Offe, C. (1984) *Contradictions of the Welfare State*, London: Hutchinson.

Ogbonna, E. (1992a) 'Managing Organizational Culture: Fantasy or Reality?', *Human Resource Management*, vol. 3, no. 2.

Ogbonna, E. (1992b) 'Organization Culture and Human Resource Management: Dilemmas and Contradictions', in P. Blyton and P. Turnbull (eds) *Reassessing Human Resource Management*, London: Sage.

Ogbonna, E. and B. Wilkinson (1988) 'Corporate Strategy and Corporate Culture: the View from the Checkout', *Personnel Review*, vol. 19, no. 4.

Oldersma, J. and K. Davis (1991) 'Introduction', in K. Davis, M. Leijenaar and J. Oldersma (eds) *The Gender of Power*, London: Sage.

Oliver, J. (1993) 'A Degree of Uncertainty', *Management Today*, Jun.

Ouchi. W. G. (1981) *Theory Z*, Reading, Mass.: Addison-Wesley.

Ouchi, W. G. and J. B. Johnson (1978) 'Types of Organizational Control and Their Relationship to Emotional Well Being', *Administrative Science Quarterly*, vol. 23, Jun.: 293–317.

Palmer, B. (1975) 'Class Conception and Conflict', *Review of Radical Political Economics*, vol. 17, no. 2: 31–49.

Parker, M. (1985) *Inside the Circle: A Union Guide to QWL*, Boston: Labor Notes.

Parker, M. (1992) 'Post-Modern Organizations or Post-Modern Organization Theory?' *Organisation Studies*, vol. 13, no. 1: 1–17.

Parker, M. and D. Jary (1994) 'Academic Subjectivity and the New Managerialism', paper to 12th International Labour Process Conference, Aston.

Parker, M. and G. McHugh (1991) 'Five Texts in Search of An Author: A Response to John Hassard's "Multiple Paradigms and Organizational Analysis: A Case Study"', *Organization Studies*, vol. 12, no. 3: 451–6.

Parker, M. and J. Slaughter (1988) *Choosing Sides: Unions and the Team Concept*, Labor Notes, Boston: South End Press.

Parsons, T. (1951) *The Social System*, New York: Collier Macmillan.

Pascale, R. T. (1990) *Managing on the Edge*, Harmondsworth: Penguin.

Pascale, R. T. and A. G. Athos (1982) *The Art of Japanese Management*, Harmondsworth: Penguin.

Pearce, F. (1989) *The Radical Durkheim*, London: Unwin Hyman.

Pearson, R. (1986) 'Female Workers in the First and Third Worlds: the "Greening" of Women's Labour', in J. Purcell, S. Wood, A. Watson and S. Allen (eds) *The Changing Experience of Employment, Restructuring and Recession*, London: Macmillan.

Penn, R. (1985) *Skilled Workers in the Class Structure*, Cambridge: Cambridge University Press.

Penn, R. (1986) 'Socialisation into Skilled Identities: an Analysis of a Neglected Phenomenon', paper to 4th International Labour Process Conference, Aston.

Perloff, R. M. (1993) *The Dynamics of Persuasion*, New Jersey: Lawrence Erlbaum Associates.

Perrow, C. (1979) *Complex Organizations: A Critical Essay*, Illinois: Scott Foreman.

Perrow, C. (1992) 'Small Firm Networks', in N. Nohria and R. G. Eccles (eds) *Networks and Organizations*, Boston, Mass.: Harvard Business School Press.

Peters, T. J. (1987) 'There Are No Excellent Companies', *Fortune*, 27 April.

Peters, T. (1989) *Thriving on Chaos*, London: Pan.

Peters, T. (1992) *Liberation Management: Necessary Disorganisation for the Nanosecond Nineties*, New York: Alfred Knopf.

Peters, T. J. and N. Austin (1985) *A Passion for Excellence*, New York: Random House.

Peters, T. J. and R. H. Waterman (1982) *In Search of Excellence: Lessons from America's Best-Run Companies*, New York: Harper & Row.

Pettigrew, A. (1973) *The Politics of Organizational Decisionmaking*, London: Tavistock.

Pettigrew, A. and R. Whipp (1991) *Managing Change for Competitive Success*, Oxford: Blackwell.

Petty, R. E. and J. T. Cacioppo (1981) *Attitudes and Persuasion: Classic and Contemporary Approaches*, Iowa: Wm. C. Brown Co.

Pfeffer, J. (1981a) *Power in Organizations*, London: Pitman.

Pfeffer, J. (1981b) 'Management as Symbolic Action', *Research in Organisational Behaviour*, 3: 1–52.

Pfeffer, J. (1992) *Managing with Power: Politics and Influence in Organizations*, Boston, Mass.: Harvard Business School Press.

Pheysey, D. (1993) *Organizational Cultures: Types and Transformations*, London: Routledge.

Phizacklea, A. (1987) 'Minority Women and Economic Restructuring: The Case of Britain and the Federal Republic of Germany', *Work, Employment and Society*, vol. 1, no. 3: 309–25.

Pierson, C. (1984) 'New Theories of State and Civil Society', *Sociology*, vol. 18, no. 4: 563–71.

Pinchot, G. (1985) *Intrapreneuring*, New York: Harper & Row.

Piore, M. J. (1986) 'Perspectives on Labour Market Flexibility', *Industrial Relations*, vol. 25, no. 2: 146–66.

Piore, M. J. and C. F. Sabel (1984) *The Second Industrial Divide: Possibilities for Prosperity*, New York: Basic Books.

Pitelis, C. (1993) 'Transnationals, International Organisation and Deindustrialisation', *Organisation Studies*, vol. 14, no. 4: 527–48.

Polan, A. J. (1984) *Lenin and the End of Politics*, London: Methuen.

Pollard, S. (1965) *The Genesis of Modern Management*, London: Edward Arnold.

Pollert, A. (1981) *Girls, Wives, Factory Lives*, London: Macmillan.

Pollert, A. (1988a) 'Dismantling Flexibility', *Capital and Class*, no. 34, (Spring): 42–75.

Pollert, A. (1988b) 'The Flexible Firm: Fixation or Fact?' *Work, Employment and Society*, vol. 2, no. 3: 281–316.

Pollert, A. (ed.) (1991) *Farewell to Flexibility?* Oxford, Blackwell.

Pollert, A. (1991) 'The Orthodoxy of Flexibility', in A. Pollert (ed.), *Farewell to Flexibility*, Oxford: Blackwell.

Poole, M. and R. Mansfield (1992) 'Managers' Attitudes to Human Resource Management', in P. Blyton and P. Turnbull (eds) *Reassessing Human Resource Management*, London: Sage.

Porter, M. E. (1990) *The Competitive Advantage of Nations*, London: Macmillan.

Poulantzas, N. (1975) *Classes in Contemporary Capitalism*, London: New Left Books.

Prethus, R. (1962) *The Organizational Society*, London: Macmillan.

Pringle, R. (1989) *Secretaries Talk: Sexuality, Power and Work*, London: Verso.

Proctor, A. J., M. Rowlinson, L. McArdle, J. Hassard and P. Forrester (1994) 'Flexibility, Politics and Strategy: In Defence of the Model of the Flexible Firm', *Work, Employment and Society*, vol. 8, no. 2: 221–42.

Pugh, D. S. (ed.) (1971) *Organization Theory*, Harmondsworth: Penguin.

Pugh, D. S., D. J. Hickson, C. R. Hinings, K. M. MacDonald, C. Turner and T. Lapton (1963) 'A Conceptual Scheme for Organizational Analysis', *Administrative Science Quarterly* vol. 16.

Pugh, D. S., D. J. Hickson, and C. R. Hinings (1968) 'Dimensions of Organization Structure', *Administrative Science Quarterly*, vol. 13: 65–103.

Pugh, D. S., D. J. Hickson, and C. R. Hinings (1969) 'An Empirical Taxonomy of Structures of Work Organizations', *Administrative Science Quarterly*, vol. 14.

Pugh, D. S. and D. J. Hickson (1973) 'The Comparative Study of Organizations', in G. Salaman and K. Thompson (eds) *People and Organisations*, Harlow: Longman.

Pugh, D. S. and Hickson, D. J. (1976) *Organization Structure in its Context: the Aston Programme 1*, London: Saxon House.

Purcell, J. and K. Sissons (1983) 'A Strategy for Management Control in Industrial Relations', in J. Purcell and R. Smith (eds) *The Control of Work*, London: Macmillan.

Purcell, J.m S. Wood, A. Watson and S. Allen (eds) (1986) *The Changing Experience of Employment, Restructuring and Recession*, London: Macmillan.

Putnam, L. L. and D. K. Mumby (1993) 'Organizations, Emotion and the Myth of Rationality', in S. Fineman (ed.) *Emotion in Organisations*, London: Sage.

Quinn Mills, D. (1993) *Rebirth of the Corporation*, New York: John Wiley.

Rainbird, H. (1991) 'The Self-Employed: Small Entrepreneurs or Disguised Wage Labourers?' in A. Pollert (ed.) *Farewell to Flexibility?* Oxford: Blackwell

Rainnie, A. (1988) *Employment Relations in the Small Firm*, London: Routledge & Kegan Paul.

Ramazanoglu, C. (1987) 'Sex and Violence in Academic Life or You Can't Keep a Good Man Down', in J. Hammer and M. Maynard (eds) *Women, Violence and Social Control, Explorations in Sociology*, no. 23, London: Macmillan.

Ramsay, H. (1983) 'Evolution or Cycle? Worker Participation in the 1980s', in C. Crouch and F. Heller, *Organizational Democracy and Political Processes*, London: Pitman.

Ramsay, H. (1985) 'What is Participation For: A Critical Evaluation of "Labour Process" Analyses of Job Reform,' in D. Knights, H. Willmott and D. Collinson (eds) *Job Redesign: Critical Perspectives on the Labour Process*, London: Gower.

Ramsay, H. (1991) 'Reinventing the Wheel? A Review of the Development and Performance of Employee Involvement' *Human Resource Management Journal*, vol. 1, no. 4: 1–22.

Ramsay, K. and M. Parker (1992) 'Gender, Bureaucracy and Organizational Culture', in A. Witz and M. Savage (eds) *Gender and Bureaucracy*, Oxford: Blackwell.

Randle, K. and A. Rainnie (1994) 'Control, Contradiction and Complexity in a Pharmaceutical Research Company', paper to 12th International Labour Process Conference, Aston.

Rauner, F., L. Rasmussen and M. Corbett (1988) 'The Social Shaping of Technology and Work: Human Centred CIM Systems,' *Artificial Intelligence and Society*, vol. 2: 47–61.

Ray, C. A. (1986) 'Corporate Culture: the Last Frontier of Control'? *Journal of Management Studies*, vol. 23, no. 3: 287–97.

Reed, M. (1984) 'Management as a Social Practice', *Journal of Management Studies*, vol. 21, no. 3: 273–85.

Reed, M. (1986) *Redirections in Organizational Analysis*, Tavistock: London.

Reed, M. (1990a) 'The Labour Process Perspective on Management Organization: A Critique and Reformulation', in J. Hassard and D. Pym (eds) *The Theory and Philosophy of Organizations*, London: Routledge.

Reed, M. (1990b) 'From Paradigm to Images: The Paradigm Warrior Turns Post-Modernist Guru', *Personnel Review*, vol. 19, no. 3: 35–40.

Reed, M (1991) 'Scripting Scenarios for a New Organization Theory and Practice', *Work, Employment and Society*, vol. 5.no. 1: 119–32.

Reed, M. (1992a) 'Experts, Professions and Organizations in Late Modernity', paper to Employment Research Unit Conference, Cardiff Business School.

Reed, M. (1992b) The Sociology of Organisations, London: Harvester.

Reed, M. (1993) 'Organizations and Modernity: Continuity and Discontinuity in Organization Theory', in J. Hassard and M. Parker (eds) *Postmodernism and Organizations*, London: Sage.

Reed, M. and M. Hughes (eds) (1992) *Rethinking Organization: New Directions in Organization and Analysis*, London: Sage.

Rees, T. (1992) *Women and the Labour Market*, London: Routledge.

Resch, M., W. Hacker, K. Leitner and T. Krogoll (1984) 'Regulation Requirements and Regulation Barriers: Two Aspects of Industrial Work', in M. Thomas (ed.) *Design of Work in Automated Manufacturing Systems*, Oxford: Pergamon.

Rhinesmith, S. (1991) 'Going Global From the Inside Out', *Training and Development*, vol. 45: 42–7.

Ritzer, G. (1993) *The McDonaldization of Society*, London: Pine Forge Press.

Roeber, J. (1975) *Social Change at Work*, London: Duckworth.

Roethlisberger, F. G., and W. J. Dickson (1964; 2nd edn) Management and the Worker, New York: John Wiley.

Roper, M. (1994) *Masculinity and the British Organization Man Since 1945*, Oxford: Oxford University Press.

Rose, G. (1978) *The Melancholy Science: An Introduction to the Thought of Theodore W. Adorno*, London: Macmillan.

Rose, M. (1975; 2nd edn 1986) *Industrial Behaviour*, Harmondsworth: Penguin.

Rose, M. and B. Jones (1985) 'Managerial Strategy and Trade Union Responses in Work Reorganization Schemes at Establishment Level', in D. Knights, H. Willmott, D. Collinson (eds) *Job Redesign: Critical Perspectives on the Labour Process*, London: Gower.

Rose, N. (1989) 'Individualising Psychology', in J. Shotter and K. J. Gergen (eds) Texts of Identity, London: Sage.

Rosenman, R. H., M. Friedman and R. Strauss (1964) 'A Predictive Study of CHD', *Journal of the American Medical Association*, 189: 15–22.

Rosnow, R. L. (1981) Paradigms in Transition: The Methodology of Social Enquiry, New York, Oxford University Press.

Rothschild, J. and J. Allen Whitt (1986) *The Co-operative Workplace: Potentials and Dilemmas or Organizational Democracy and Participation*, Cambridge: Cambridge University Press.

Rothwell, W. J. and H. C. Kazanas (1986) 'The Attitude Survey As an Approach to Human Resource Strategic planning', *Journal of Managerial Psychology*, 2: 15–18.

Rotter, J. B. (1972) 'Generalised Expectancies for Internal versus External Control of Reinforcement', in J. B. Rotter *et al.* (ed) *Applications of a Social Learning Theory of Personality*, New York: Holt, Rinehart & Winston.

Roy, D. F. (1973) 'Banana Time, Job Satisfaction and Informal Interaction' in G. Salaman and K. Thompson (eds) *People and Organizations*, Harlow: Longman.

RSA Inquiry (1994) *Tomorrow's Company: The Role of Business in a Changing World*, London: Royal Society of Arts.

Rueschemeyer, D. (1986) *Power and the Division of Labour*, London: Polity Press.

Sabel, C. F. (1982) *Work and Politics and the Division of Labour in Industry*, Cambridge University Press.

Sabel, C. F. (1991) 'Mobius Strip Organizations and Open Labour Markets: Some Consequences of the Reintegration of Conception and Execution in a Volatile Economy', in J. Coleman and P. Bourdieu (eds) *Social Theory for a Changing Society*, Boulder, Colo.: Westview Press.

Salaman, G. (1979) *Work Organizations: Resistance and Control*, London: Longman.

Salaman, G. (1981) *Class and the Corporation*, London: Fontana.

Salaman, G. (1986) *Working*, London: Tavistock.

Salaman, G. and K. Thompson (eds) (1980) *Control and Ideology in Organizations*, Milton Keynes: Open University Press.

Salaman, G. and K. Thompson (eds) (1973) *People and Organizations*, Harlow: Longman.

Salancik, G. R. and J. Pfeffer (1978) 'A Social Information Processing Approach to Job Attitudes and Task Design', *Administrative Science Quarterly*, 23: 224–53.

Sandberg, A. (1993) 'Volvo Human-Centred Work Organization – the End of the Road?', *New Technology, Work and Employment*, vol. 8, no. 2.

Sandelands, L. E. and V. Srivatsan (1993) 'The Problem of Experience in the Study of Organizations', *Organization Studies*, vol. 14, no. 1: 1–22.

Sargent, A. G. (1983) *The Androgynous Manager*, New York: AMACOM.

Saunders, C.S. (1981) 'Management Information Systems, Communication and Departmental Power: An Integrative Model', *Academy of Management Review*, 6: 431–42.

Sayer, A. (1986) 'New Developments in Manufacturing: the Just-in-Time System'. *Capital and Class*, no. 30: 43–72.

Sayer, D. (1991) *Capitalism and Modernity: An Excursus on Marx and Weber*, London: Routledge.

Sayles, C.R. (1958) *Behaviour of Industrial Work Groups*, New York: Wiley.

Schein, E.H. (1965) *Organizational Psychology*, 1st edn, Englewood Cliffs, NJ: Prentice-Hall (also 1980, 3rd. edn).

Schein, E.H. (1985) *Organizational Culture and Leadership: A Dynamic View*, San Francisco: Jossey-Bass.

Schneider, M. (1975) *Neurosis and Civilisation: A Marxist/Freudian Synthesis*, New York: Seabury.

Schutz, A. (1967) *The Phenomenology of the Social World*, Evanston: North Western University Press.

Schwartz, H.S. (1983) 'A Theory of Denotic Work Motivation', *Journal of Applied Behavioural Science*, 14: 204–14.

Scott, J. (1985) 'Ownership, Management and Strategic Control', in K. Elliot and P. Lawrence (eds) *Introducing Management*, Harmondsworth: Penguin.

Scott, W.R. (1978) 'Theoretical Perspectives', in M.W. Meyer *et al.* (eds) *Environments and Organizations*, San Francisco: Jossey-Bass.

Seivers, B. (1986) 'Beyond the Surrogate of Motivation', *Organization Studies*, vol. 7, no. 4.

Seligman, M.E.P. (1975) *Helplessness*, San Francisco: Freeman.

Selznick, P. (1949) *TVA and the Grass Roots*, Berkeley, Calif.: University of California Press.

Selznick, P. (1957) *Leadership in Administration*, Evanston: Row Peterson.

Senge, P.M., (1992) 'Building Learning Organisations: The Real Message of the Quality Movement', *Journal for Quality and Participation*, Mar.

Seve, L. (1978) *Man in Marxist Theory and the Psychology of Personality*, Sussex: Harvester Press.

Sewell, G. and B. Wilkinson (1992) '"Someone to Watch Over Me": Surveillance, Discipline and the Just-in-Time Labour Process', *Sociology*, vol. 26, no. 2: 271–89.

Shaiken, H. *et al.* (1986) 'The Work Process under More Flexible Production', *Industrial Relations*, vol. 125, no. 2: 167–83.

Shamir, B. (1991) 'Meaning, Self and Motivation in Organisations', *Organisation Studies*, 12/3: 405–24.

Shaw, M. (1990) 'Strategy and Social Process: Military Context and Sociological Analysis', *Sociology*, vol. 24, no. 3: 465–73.

Sheppard, D. (1989) 'Organizations, Power and Sexuality: The Image and Self-image of Women Managers' in J. Hearn D.L. Sheppard, P. Tancred-Sheriff and G. Burrell (eds) *The Sexuality of Organisation*, London: Sage.

Shotter, J. and K.J. Gergen (1989) *Texts of Identity*, London: Sage.

Shrivastava, P. (1983) 'A Typology of Organizational Learning Systems', *Journal of Management Studies*, 20, 1, 7–28.

Shutt, J. (1985) 'Tory Enterprise Zones and the Labour Movement', *Capital and Class*, no. 23: 19–44.

Silver, J. (1987) 'The Ideology of Excellence: Management and NeoConservatism', *Studies in Political Economy*, 24, Autumn, 105–29.

Silverman, D. (1970) *The Theory of Organizations*, London: Heinemann.

Silverman, D. and J. Jones (1976) *Organizational Work: The Language of Grading and the Grading of Language*, London: Macmillan.

Simon, H. A. (1960) *Administrative Behaviour*, New York: Macmillan.

Sims, D., S. Fineman and Y. Gabriel (1993) *Organising and Organisations: An Introduction*, London: Sage.

Sirriani, C. (1984) 'Participation, Equality and Opportunity: Towards a Pluralist Organizational Model', in F. Fischer and C. Sirriani (eds) *Critical Studies in Organization and Bureaucracy*, Philadelphia: Temple University Press.

Sisson, J. (1990) 'Introducing the Human Resource Management Journal', *Human Resource Management Journal*, vol. 1, no. 1: 1–11.

Skinner, B. F. (1971) *Beyond Freedom and Dignity*, New York: Knopf.

Skocpol, T. (1979) *States and Social Revolutions*, Cambridge: Cambridge University Press.

Slaughter, J. (1987) 'The Team Concept in the US Auto Industry: Implications for Unions', paper presented at *Conference on Japanisation of British Industry*, UWIST.

Sloan, M. (1987) 'Culture and Control at Salesco: a Participant Observation Study', unpublished BA Dissertation, Lancashire Polytechnic.

Smart, B. (1985) *Michel Foucault*, London: Tavistock.

Smircich, L. (1983) 'Concepts of Culture and Organizational Analysis', *Administrative Science Quarterly*, 28: 339–58.

Smith, C. (1987) 'Flexible Specialisation and Earlier Critiques of Mass Production', paper to 5th International Labour Process Conference, UMIST.

Smith, C. (1991) 'From 1960s' Automation to Flexible Specialisation: a déjà vu of Technological Panaceas', in A. Pollert (ed.) *Farewell to Flexibility*.

Smith, C. and T. Elger (eds) (1994) *Global Japanisation? The Transnational Transformation of the Labour Process*, London: Routledge.

Smith, C. and P. Meiskens (1995) 'System, Society and Dominance in Cross-National Organizational Analysis', *Work Employment and Society*, forthcoming.

Smith, C. and P. Thompson (1992) *Labour in Transition: the Labour Process in Eastern Europe and China*, London: Routledge.

Smith, D. (1987) 'The Japanese Example in South West Birmingham', paper presented at *Conference on Japanisation of British Industry*, UWIST.

Smith, V. (1990) *Managing in the Corporate Interest: Control and Resistance in an American Bank*, Berkeley, Calif.: University of California Press.

Snyder, M. and S. Gangestad (1986) 'On the Nature of Self-Monitoring: Matters of Assessment, Matters of Validity', *Journal of Personality and Social Psychology*, 51: 123–39.

Sorge, A. *et al.* (1983) *Microelectronics and Manpower in Manufacturing*, Aldershot: Gower.

Staber, U. and H. Aldrich (1987) 'Organizational Transformation and Trends in US Employment Relations', paper presented to the 5th Intenational Labour Process Conference, UMIST.

Standing, G. (1986) *Unemployment and Labour Market Flexibility: the United Kingdom*, International Labour Office: Geneva.

Stanko, E. (1988) 'Keeping Women in and Out of Line: Sexual Harassment and Occupational Segregation', in S. Walby (ed.) *Gender Segregation at Work*, Milton Keynes: Open University Press.

Starkey, K. (1992) 'Durkheim and Organizational Analysis: Two Legacies', *Organization Studies*, vol. 13, no. 4: 627–42.

Steers, R. M. and L. W. Porter (1987) *Motivation and Work Behaviour*, New York: McGraw-Hill.

Steffy, B. D. and A. J. Grimes (1992) 'Personnel/Organization Psychology: A Critique of the Discipline', in M. Alvesson and H. Willmott (eds) *Critical Management Studies*, London: Sage.

Steiner, T. and B. Miner (1978) *Management Policy and Strategy*, West Drayton: Collier-Macmillan.

Stewart, E. (1967) *The Reality of Management*, London: Pan.

Stewart, E. (1970) *The Reality of Organizations*, London: Macmillan.

Stewart, E. (1976) *Contrasts in Management*, Maidenhead: McGraw-Hill.

Stodgill, R. M. (1974) *Handbook of Leadership*, New York: Free Press.

Stone, K. (1973) 'The Origins of Job Structures in the Steel Industry', *Radical America*, vol. 7, no. 6.

Storey, J. (1983) *Managerial Prerogative and the Question of Control*, London: Routledge & Kegan Paul.

Storey, J. (1985) 'The Means of Management Control', *Sociology*, vol. 19, no. 2: 193–211.

Storey, J. (ed.) (1989) *New Perspectives on Human Resource Management*, London: Routledge.

Storey, J. (1992) *Developments in the Management of Human Resources*, Oxford: Blackwell.

Storlie, F. J. (1979) 'Burnout: The Elaboration of a Concept', *American Journal of Nursing*, Dec.: 2108–111.

Strauss, A., L. Schatzman, D. Ehrlich, R. Bucher and M. Sabshim (1963) 'The Hospital and its Negotiated Order', in E. Friedson (ed.) *The Hospital in Modern Society*, New York: Macmillan.

Streek, W. (1987) 'The Uncertainties of Management in the Management of Uncertainty: Employers, Labour Relations and Industrial Adjustment in the 1980s', *Work, Employment and Society*, vol. 1, no. 3: 281–308.

Stringer, P.(ed.) (1982) *Confronting Social Issues: Applications of Social Psychology*, Vol 2, London: Academic Press.

Stryker, S. (1980) *Symbolic interactionism: A social structural version*, Menlo Park, Calif.: Benjamin/ Cummings.

Sturdy, A. (1987) 'Coping with the Pressure of Work', paper presented to 5th International Labour Process Conference, UMIST.

Supple, B. (1991) 'Scale and Scope: Alfred Chandler and the Dynamics of Industrial Capitalism', *Economic History Review*, vol. XLIV, no. 3: 500–14.

Sussman, L. (1991) 'Managers: On the Defensive', *Business Horizons*, Jan.–Feb.: 83.

Sweiger, D.M., W.R. Sandburg and J.W. Ragan (1986) 'Group Approaches for Improving Strategic Decision Making: A Comparative Analysis of Dialectical Inquiry, Devil's Advocacy and Consensus', *Academy of Management Journal*, 29: 149–59.

Swieringa, J. and A. Wierdsma (1992) *Becoming a Learning Organisation*, Wokingham: Addison-Wesley.

Taber, T.D. (1991) 'Triangulating Job Attitudes with Interpretative and Positivist Measurement Methods', *Personnel Psychology*: 577–600.

Tailby, S. and P. Turnbull (1987) 'Learning to Manage Just-in-Time', *Personnel Management*, Jan.

Taylor, F.W. (1947) *Scientific Management*, New York: Harper & Row.

Taylor, W. (1991) 'The Logic of Global Business: An Interview with ABB's Percy Barnevik', *Harvard Business Review*, Mar.–Apr.: 91–105.

Tedeschi, J.T., B.R. Schlenker and T.V. Bonoma (1971) 'Cognitive Dissonance: Private Ratiocination or Public Spectacle?', *American Psychologist*: 685–95.

Teulings, A. (1986) 'Managerial Labour Processes in Organised Capitalism; the Power of Corporate Management and the Powerlessness of the Manager', in D. Knights and H. Willmott (eds) *Managing the Labour Process*, Aldershot: Gower.

Thackray, J. (1986) 'The Corporate Culture Rage', *Management Today*, Feb.: 67–70.

Thackray, J. (1988) 'Flattening the White Collar', *Personnel Management*, August.

Thackray, J. (1993) 'Fads, Fixes and Fictions', *Management Today*, June.

Thompson, E. P. (1967) 'Time, Work Discipline and Industrial Capitalism', *Past and Present*, 38: 55–97.

Thompson, J. D. (1967) *Organizations in Action*, New York: McGraw-Hill.

Thompson, P. (1989) *The Nature of Work: An Introduction to Debates on the Labour Process*, London: Macmillan.

Thompson, P. (1984) 'The New Vocationalism: the Trojan Horse of the MSC', *Social Science Teacher*, vol. 13, no. 2.

Thompson, P. (1993) 'Postmodernism: Fatal Distraction', in J. Hassard and M. Parker (eds) *Postmodernism and Organisations*, London: Sage

Thompson, P. (1994) 'Corporate Culture: Myths and Realities, West and East', paper for Conference: *Convergence versus Divergence: the Case of Corporate Culture*, Dunaújváros, Hungary.

Thompson, P. and S. Ackroyd (1994) 'Ain't Misbehavin': Power and Consent in Organizational Sexuality', paper presented to the BSA Conference: *Sexualities in their Social Context*, University of Central Lancashire, Mar.

Thompson, P. and S. Ackroyd (1995) 'All Quiet on the Workplace Front: A Critique of Recent Trends in British Industrial Sociology', forthcoming.

Thompson, P. and E. Bannon (1985) *Working the System: The Shop Floor and New Technology*, London: Pluto.

Thompson, P., J. Flecker and T. Wallace (1995) 'Back to Convergence? Globalisation and Societal Effects on Work Organization', in T. Boje (ed.) *The Welfare State and the Labour Market in a Changing Europe*, M. E. Sharpe, New York.

Thompson, P., C. Jones, D. Nickson, T. Wallace and B. Kewell (1993) 'Transnationals, Globalisation and Transfer of Knowledge', paper for the *11th EGOS Colloquium*, Paris, Jul.

Thompson, P. and J. O'Connell Davidson (1994) 'The Continuity of Discontinuity: Management Rhetoric in Turbulent Times', *Personnel Review*, August.

Thompson, P., T. Wallace and J. Flecker (1992) 'The Urge to Merge: Organizational Change in the Merger and Acquisition Process', *International Journal of Human Resource Management*, vol. 3, no. 2: 285–306.

Thompson, P., T. Wallace, J. Flecker and R. Ahlstrand (1994) 'It Ain't What You do It's the Way that You Do It', paper to 12th Annual International Labour Process Conference, Aston, to be published in *Work, Employment and Society*, March 1996.

Thurley, K. and S. Wood (1983) *Industrial Relations and Management Strategy*, Cambridge: Cambridge University Press.

Tichy, N., C. Fombrun and M. A. Devanna (1982) 'Strategic Human Resource Management', *Sloan Management Review*, 47–61.

Tichy, N. and Devanna, M. A. (1986) *Transformational Leadership*, London: John Wiley.

Toffler, A. (1970) *Future Shock*, New York: Bantam Books.

Tomlinson, J. (1982) *The Unequal Struggle? British Socialism and the Capitalist Enterprise*, London: Methuen.

Tompkins, P. K. and G. Cheney (1985) 'Communication and unobtrusive control in contemporary organisations', in R. D. McPhee and P. K. Tompkins (eds) *Organisational Communication: Traditional Themes and New Directions*, Calif.: Sage.

Torrington, D. (1989) 'Human Resource Management and the Personnel Function', in J. Storey, (ed.) *New Perspectives on Human Resource Management*, London: Routledge.

Towers, B. (1987) 'Managing Labour Flexibility', *Industrial Relations Journal*, vol. 18, no. 2: 79–83.

Townley, B. (1990) 'Foucault, Power/Knowledge and its Relevance for HRM', paper presented at *Employment Research Unit Annual Conference*, Cardiff Business School, Sep.

Townley, B. (1993) 'Performance Appraisal and the Emergence of Management', *Journal of Management Studies*, vol. 30, no. 2: 27–44.

Transnationals Information Centre (1987) *Working for Big Mac*, pamphlet, London: TICL.

Trist, E. L., G. W. Higgin, H. Murray and A. B. Pollock (1963) *Organizational Choice*, London: Tavistock.

Trist, E. L. and K. W. Bamforth (1951) 'Some Social and Psychological Consequences of the Longwall Method of CoalGetting', *Human Relations*, vol. 4, no. 1: 3–38.

Tsoukas, H. (1992) 'Postmodernism, Reflexive Rationalism and Organizational Studies: A Reply to Martin Parker', *Organization Studies*, vol. 13, no. 4, 643–49.

Tsoukas, H. (1994a) 'Socio-Economic Systems and Organizational Management: An Institutional Perspective on the Socialist Firm', *Organization Studies*, vol. 15, no. 1: 21–45.

Tsoukas, H. (1994b) 'What is Management? An Outline of a Metatheory', *British Journal of Management*, vol. 5, 289–301.

Tsoukas, H. (1994c) 'From Social Engineering to Reflective Action in Organizational Behaviour', in H. Tsoukas (ed.) *New Thinking in Organizational Behaviour*, London: Butterworth & Heinemann.

Tsoukas, H. (ed.) (1994d) *New Thinking in Organizational Behaviour*, London: Butterworth & Heinemann.

Tuckman, A. (1994) 'Ideology, Quality and TQM', in A. Wilkinson and H. Willmott (eds) *Making Quality Critical*, London: Routledge & Kegan Paul.

Tuckman, B. W. (1965) 'Developmental sequences in small groups', *Psychological Bulletin*, 63: 384–399.

Turnbull, P. J. (1986) 'The Japanisation of British Industrial Relations at Lucas', *Industrial Relations Journal*, vol. 17, no. 3: 193–206.

Turnbull, P. J. (1987) 'The Limits to Japanisation: Just-in-Time, Labour Relations and the UK Automotive Industry', paper presented at *Conference on Japanisation of British Industry*, UWIST.

Van Maanen, J. (1992) 'Drinking our Troubles Away', in D. M. Kolb and J. M. Bartunek (eds) *Hidden Conflict in Organisations: Uncovering Behind the Scenes Disputes*, London: Sage.

Van Strien, P. J. (1982) 'In Search of an Emancipatory Social Psychology' in P. Stringer, (ed.) *Confronting Social Issues: Applications of Social Psychology*, vol. 2, London: Academic Press..

Vargish, T. (1994) 'The Value of Humanities in Executive Development', in H. Tsoukas, (ed.) *New Thinking in Organizational Behaviour*, London: Butterworth & Heinemann.

Vroom, V. H. (1964) *Work and Motivation*, New York: John Wiley.

Vroom, V. and F. C. Mann (1960) 'Leader Authoritarianism and Employee Attitudes', *Personnel Psychology*, 13, 125–40.

Vroom, V. H. and P. W. Yetton (1973) *Leadership and Decision Making*, Pittsburgh, University of Pittsburgh Press.

Wainwright, H. (1987) 'The Friendly Mask of "Flexibility"', *New Statesman*, 11 Dec.

Walby, S. (1986) *Patriarchy at Work*, Cambridge: Polity.

Walker, C. R. and R. H. Guest (1952) *Man on the Assembly Line*, Cambridge, Mass.: Harvard University Press.

Wall, T. D., C. W. Clegg and N. J. Kemp (eds) (1987) *The Human Side of Advanced Manufacturing Technology*, Chichester: John Wiley.

Wall, T. D.,,N. J. Kemp, P. R. Jackson and C. W. Clegg (1986) 'Outcomes of Autonomous Workgroups: A Long-Term Field Experiment', *Academy of Management Journal*.

Wallace, C. (1993) 'Reflections on the Concept of "Strategy"', in D. Morgan and L. Stanley (eds) *Debates in Sociology*, Manchester: Manchester University Press.

Walzer, M. (1985) 'The Politics of Michel Foucault', in Couzens Hey (ed.) *Foucault: A Critical Reader*, Oxford: Blackwell.

Wardell, M. (1986) 'Labor and the Labor Process', paper at ASTON–UMIST Labour Process Conference.

Watson, J. B. (1930) *Behaviourism*, Norton.

Watson, T. (1980) 'Understanding Organizations: The Practicalities of Sociological Theory', in D. Dunkerley and G. Salaman (eds) (1980) *The International Yearbook of Organization Studies 1980*, London: Routledge & Kegan Paul.

Watson, T. (1986) *Management, Organization and Employment Strategy: New Directions in Theory and Practice*, London: Routledge & Kegan Paul.

Watson, T. (1994) *In Search of Management: Culture, Chaos and Control in Managerial Work*, London: Routledge.

Webber, A. (1993) 'What's So New About the New Economy?' *Harvard Business Review*, Jan.–Feb., 24–42.

Weber, M. (1968) *Economy and Society*, New York: Bedminster Press.

Weber, M. (1984) 'Bureaucracy', in F. Fischer and C. Sirriani (eds) *Critical Studies in Organization and Bureaucracy*, Philadelphia: Temple University Press.

Webster, F. and K. Robins (1993) 'I'll be Watching You: Comment on Sewell and Wilkinson', *Sociology*, vol. 27, no. 2: 243–52.

Weick, K. (1987) 'Organizational Culture as a Source of High Reliability', *California Management Review*, vol. xxix, no. 2: 112–27.

Weigert, A. J., J. Smith Teitge and D. W. Teitge (1986) *Society and Identity: Towards a Sociological Psychology*, New York: Cambridge University Press.

Weir, D. (1993) 'Why Isn't There any Good Management Research?' *British Academy of Management Newsletter*, no. 15, June.

Weitz, S. (1977) *Sex Roles: Biological, Psychological and Social Foundations*, New York: Oxford University Press.

Wellin, M. (1984) *Behaviour Technology: a New Approach to Managing People at Work*, Aldershot: Gower.

West, P. (1994) 'The Concept of the Learning Organisation', *Journal of European Industrial Training*, 18, 1: 15–21, MCB University Press.

Westwood, S. (1984) *All Day, Every Day: Factory and Family in the Making of Women's Lives*, London: Pluto.

Wexler, P. (1983) *Critical Social Psychology*, Boston: Routledge & Kegan Paul.

Wheeler, S. and D. Lyon (1992) 'Employee Benefits for the Employer's Benefit: How Companies Respond to Stress, *Personnel Review*, vol. 21, no. 7: 47–65.

Whitaker, A. (1986) 'Managerial Strategy and Industrial Relations: a Case Study of Plant Relocation', *Journal of Management Studies*, vol. 23, no. 6: 657–78.

White, H. C. (1992) *Identity and Control*, New Jersey: Princeton University Press.

Whitehead, T. N. (1936) *Leadership in a Free Society*, Cambridge, Mass.: Harvard University Press.

Whitehead, T. N. (1938) *The Industrial Worker*, London: Oxford University Press.

Whitley, R. (1984) 'The Fragmented State of Management Studies', *Journal of Management Studies* vol. 21, no. 3: 331–48.

Whitley, R. (1987) 'Taking Firms Seriously as Economic Actors: Towards a Sociology of Firm Behaviour', *Organization Studies*, vol. 8, no. 2: 125–47.

Whitley, R. (ed.) (1992a) *Business Systems in East Asia*, London: Sage.

Whitley, R. (ed.) (1992b) *European Business Systems: Firms and Markets in Their National Contexts*, London: Sage.

Whitley, R. (1994) 'The Internationalisation of Firms and Markets', *Organization*, vol. 1, no. 1: 101–24.

Whittington, R. (1988) 'Environmental Structure and Theories of Strategic Choice', *Journal of Management Studies*, vol. 25, no. 6: 521–36.

Whittington, R. (1991a) 'The Fragmentation of Industrial R&D', in A. Pollert (ed.) *Farewell to Flexibility*, Oxford: Blackwell.

Whittington, R. (1991b) 'Putting Giddens into Action: Evolving Accounts of Managerial Agency', paper for *Conference: Towards a New Theory of Organizations*, University of Keele.

Whyte, W. H. (1956) *The Organization Man*, New York: Simon & Shuster.

Whyte, W. H. (1957) *The Organization Man*, London: Jonathon Cape.

Wickens, P. D. (1987) *The Road to Nissan*, London: Macmillan.

Wickens, P. D. (1992) 'Lean Production and Beyond: The System, its Critics and the Future', *Human Resource Management Journal*, vol. 3, no. 4: 75–89.

Wiener, N (1948) *Cybernetics: Control and Communication in the Animal and the Machine*, Cambridge, Mass.: MIT Press.

Wilkinson, A. (1992) 'The Other Side of Quality: Soft Issues and the Human Resource Dimension', *Total Quality Management*, vol. 3, no. 3: 323–9.

Wilkinson, A., M. Marchington and J. Goodman (1992) 'Total Quality Management and Employee Involvement', *Human Resource Management Journal*, vol. 2, no. 4: 1–20.

Wilkinson, A. and H. Willmott (1994) 'Introduction', in A. Wilkinson and H. Willmott (eds) Making Quality Critical

Wilkinson, B. (1983a) *The Shopfloor Politics of New Technology*, London: Heinemann.

Wilkinson, B. (1983b) 'Technical Change and Work Organization', *Industrial Relations Journal*, vol. 14, no. 2: Summer.

Wilkinson, B. (1986) 'Human Resources in Singapore's Second Industrial Revolution', *Industrial Relations Journal*, vol. 17, no. 2: 99–114.

Williams, K., T. Cutler, J. Williams and C. Haslam (1987) 'The End of Mass Production?' *Economy and Society*, vol. 16, no. 3: 405–39.

Williams, K., C. Haslam, J. Williams, T. Cutler with A. Adcroft, and S. Juhal, (1992a) 'Against Lean Production', *Economy and Society*, vol. 21, no. 3: 321–54.

Williams, K., C. Haslam, J. Williams and T. Cutler (1992b) Ford-v-"Fordism": The Beginning of Mass Production', *Work, Employment and Society*, vol. 6, no. 1: 517–48.

Williams, R. (1988) 'The Development of Models of Technology and Work Organization with Information and Communication Technologies', paper presented to 6th International Labour Process Conference, Aston.

Williamson, O. (1975) *Markets and Hierarchies*, New York: Free Press.

Williamson, O. (1981) 'The Economics of Organization', *American Journal of Sociology*, vol. 87: 548–77.

Willis, P. (1977) *Learning to Labour*, Farnborough: Saxon House.

Willmott, H. (1984) 'Images and Ideals of Managerial Work', *Journal of Management Studies*, vol. 21, no. 3: 349–68.

Willmott, H. (1987) 'Studying Managerial Work: A Critique and a Proposal', *Journal of Management Studies*, vol. 24, no. 3: 249–70.

Willmott, H. (1989) 'Subjectivity and the Dialectics of Praxis: Opening up the Core of Labour Process Analysis', in D. Knights and H. Willmott (eds) *Labour Process Theory*, London: Macmillan.

Willmott, H. (1990) 'Beyond Paradigmatic Closure in Organizational Enquiry', in J. Hassard and D. Pym (eds) *The Theory and Philosophy of Organizations*, London: Routledge.

Willmott, H. (1992) 'Postmodernism and Excellence: The De-differentiation of Economy and Culture', *Journal of Organizational Change*, vol. 5, no. 1: 69–79.

Willmott, H. (1993a) 'Strength is Ignorance; Slavery is Freedom: Managing Culture in Modern Organization', *Journal of Management Studies*, vol. 30, no. 5: 515–52.

Willmott, H. (1993b) 'Managing the Academics: Commodification and Control in the Development of University Education in the UK', unpublished paper.

Willmott, H. (1994) 'Theorising Agency: Power and Subjectivity in Organization Studies', in J. Hassard and M. Parker (eds) *Towards a New Theory of Organizations*, London: Routledge.

Wilson, F. M. (1995) *Organizational Behaviour and Gender*, London: McGraw-Hill.

Winfield, I. J. and M. Kerrin (1994) 'Catalyst for Organisational Learning: The Case of Toyota Motor Manufacturing UK Ltd', *The Learning Organization*, vol. 16, no. 3, 4–9, MCB University Press.

Winstanley, D. (1986) 'Recruitment Strategies as a Means of Control of Technological Labour', paper at ASTON–UMIST Labour Process Conference.

Wise, S. and L. Stanley (1990) 'Sexual Harassment, Sexual Conduct and Gender in Social Work Settings', in *Social Work and Social Welfare Handbook*, Buckingham: Open University Press.

Witz, A. (1986) 'Patriarchy and the Labour Market: Occupational Controls and the Medical Division of Labour', in D. Knights and H. Willmott (eds)

Witz, A. and M. Savage (1992) 'The Gender of Organizations', in A. Witz and M. Savage (eds) *Gender and Bureaucracy*, Oxford: Blackwell.

Witz, A., S. Halford and M. Savage (1994) 'Organized Bodies: Gender, Sexuality, Bodies and Organizational Culture', paper presented to *BSA Conference: Sexualities in their Social Context*, University of Central Lancashire, Mar.

Womack, J., D. Jones and D. Roos (1990) *The Machine that Changed the World*, New York: Macmillan.

Wood, S. (1979) 'A Reappraisal of the Contingency Approach to Organization', *Journal of Management Studies*, vol. 16, no. 3: 334–54.

Wood, S. (ed.) (1982) *The Degradation of Work: Skill, Deskilling and the Labour Process*, London: Hutchinson.

Wood, S. (1986) 'The Co-operative Labour Strategy in the US Auto Industry', *Economic and Industrial Democracy*, vol. 7, no. 4: 415–48.

Wood, S. (ed.) (1989a) *The Transformation of Work?* London: Hutchinson.

Wood. S. (1989b) 'The Japanese Management Model', unpublished paper.

Woodward, J. (1958) *Management and Technology*, London: HMSO.

Woodward, J. (1965) *Industrial Organization: Theory and Practice*, London: Oxford University Press.

Woolf, J. (1977) 'Women in Organisations', in S. Clegg and D. Dunkerley (eds) *Critical Issues in Organisations*, London: Routledge & Kegan Paul.

Wray, D. (1994) 'Paternalism and its Discontents: A Case Study', paper to 12th International Labour Process Conference, Aston.

Wright, E. O. (1976) 'Contradictory Class Locations', *New Left Review*, no. 98.

Wright, S. (1994) 'Culture in Anthropology and Organizational Studies', in S. Wright (ed.) *Anthropology of Organizations*, London: Routledge.

Yates, D. (1986) 'Is Dual Labour Market Theory Dead? The Changing Organization of Work: the Employer's Perspective', paper presented at *Conference on the Labour Process*, ASTON–UMIST.

Zeitlin, M. (1974) 'Corporate Ownership and Control: the Large Corporation and the Capitalist Class, *American Journal of Sociology*, vol. 79, no. 5: 1073–119.

Zimbalist, A. (ed.) (1979) *Case Studies on the Labour Process*, New York: Monthly Review Press.

Zimbardo, P. G., E. B. Ebbesen and C. Maslach (1977) *Influencing Attitudes and Changing Behaviour*, 2nd edn, Reading, Mass.: Addison-Wesley.

Zimmerman, D. (1971) 'The Practicalities of Rule Use', in J. Douglas (ed.) *Understanding Everyday Life*, London: Routledge & Kegan Paul.

Zuboff, S. (1988) *In the Age of the Smart Machine; The Future of Work and Power*, Oxford: Heinemann.

Name index

Subject index